Personnel

**THE MANAGEMENT OF
PEOPLE AT WORK**

Personnel

THE MANAGEMENT OF PEOPLE AT WORK

Dale S. Beach

Professor, School of Management
Rensselaer Polytechnic Institute

4th EDITION

Macmillan Publishing Co., Inc.
NEW YORK

Collier Macmillan Publishers
LONDON

Earlier editions
copyright © 1965, 1970 and 1975
by Dale S. Beach

A preliminary edition of this book was copyrighted
© 1963 by Dale S. Beach

Macmillan Publishing Co., Inc.
866 Third Avenue, New York, New York 10022

Collier Macmillan Canada, Ltd.

Library of Congress Cataloging in Publication Data

Beach, Dale S
  Personnel: the management of people at work.

  Includes bibliographies and indexes.
  1. Personnel management.   I. Title.
HF5549.B32   1980   658.3   79-14409
ISBN 0-02-307040-4 (Hardcover Edition)
ISBN 0-02-978490-5 (International Edition)

Printing: 5 6 7 8   Year: 2 3 4 5 6

ISBN   0-02-307040-4

To Shirley, Jeffrey, Eric, and my mother, Octavia E. Beach

Preface

Personnel management, also called human resource management, continues to evolve and grow both as an academic discipline and as a field of application in work organizations throughout the country. This, the fourth edition of *Personnel*, incorporates the new developments that are important and relevant to the field of personnel management.

This book has been designed for use in courses in personnel management, human resource management, management-employee relations, and related courses, dealing with the management of a work force in college and university programs in business administration, management, industrial relations, and public administration. It is also suitable for use in management development programs and as a reference for executives, personnel administrators, and supervisors in both private and public sector work organizations.

The management of people is an integral part of the process of management. It is really the heart of management—not something that can be delegated solely to the personnel department. Getting out production and managing people are inseparable. There must be a partnership between the managers and specialists in the personnel department and operating managers throughout the organization. Not only do those pursuing careers in personnel work require education and skills in human resource management but so also do those pursuing careers in the various functional areas of management (production, finance, marketing, engineering administration, and the like) and in general management.

In the years since the publication of the first edition of this book in 1965 greater emphasis has been given to the management of people in the work establishments of this country. Several forces have operated to cause this increasing significance of human resources management. A principal factor has been the enactment of many protective labor laws in the areas of equal employment opportunity, worker health and safety, and pension reform. Other moving forces have been changing societal values, higher employee expectations regarding the quality of work-life, new knowledge in the behavioral sciences, and the development of new approaches and methodologies for personnel management.

The personnel function itself has acquired greater stature in business firms throughout the land. Personnel executives possess more influence in helping to shape organization-wide policies and programs than they did just a few years ago. Top corporate executives have learned that effective personnel programs and processes are essential to the attainment of enterprise objectives.

This edition of *Personnel* contains four new chapters: Human Resource Planning, Equal Employment Opportunity, Career Development, and Quality of Working Life. Every chapter throughout the book has been updated. Additionally, chapters devoted to the following topics have been substantially revised: leadership and supervision (now combined and expanded to also include management systems), participative management, organization development, health and safety, and benefits and services.

Federal labor legislation has exerted a truly powerful impact upon human resource management. This fact is brought out in many places throughout the book. Other topics added to the book include the expectancy model of motivation, transactional analysis, behaviorally anchored rating scales for performance appraisal, the occupational disease crisis, alternative work schedules, new developments in employee benefits, pension reform, compensation systems for professionals and managers, and functional job analysis.

Eight new case studies and two experiential exercises have been added. Cases appear at the ends of most chapters.

Managing People at Work: Readings in Personnel, Third Edition, has been designed to be a companion volume to this textbook. It contains timely articles by recognized authorities on all the major topics in personnel management. Included in this work are articles that summarize and synthesize research findings, analyze trends, point new ways and challenge old ways, and offer a richness of thought and a variety of perspectives.

The author wishes to express his sincere appreciation to those whose constructive suggestions and cooperation have aided in the development of this work. Professor Clifford E. Smith of Iowa State University reviewed the manuscript for the fourth edition and provided many helpful ideas. Professors Herbert Oestreich of San Jose State University and William M. Timmins of Brigham Young University have given many constructive suggestions. I wish also to thank all those who have used the third edition in the classroom and who have provided questionnaire critiques.

The following persons supplied many helpful ideas that contributed to the development of earlier editions and for this I am grateful. These individuals are Professors Orlando Behling, Earl Brooks, Raymond L. Hilgert, Roy V. Kirk, George H. Labovitz, Clifford E. Smith, Rodney E. Wyse, and Dr. Edwin A. Fleishman.

Dean Joseph A. Steger of Rensselaer Polytechnic Institute has provided substantial cooperation throughout the course of work on this book. I wish to thank Mrs. Ruth Ashley for her especially competent work in typing and preparation of the manuscript for the fourth edition. She has been very helpful.

Dale S. Beach

Contents

part III
Organization and jobs

part IV
Employment and development of people

part V
Understanding and managing people

part VIII
Perspectives

Personnel

**THE MANAGEMENT OF
PEOPLE AT WORK**

I

MANAGEMENT AND THE PERSONNEL FIELD

1

Management, employees, and the personnel field

This book is about the management of people at work. Although humans have for centuries collected into groups to form durable organizations for the purpose of accomplishing mutual goals, it is only in recent years that an organized body of knowledge has developed encompassing the theory and practice of personnel management—also called human resource management. This is partly because scientific and systematic inquiry into most branches of science has occurred primarily within the past hundred years. Work in the physical and life sciences occurred somewhat earlier and at a more rapid rate than in the social sciences. Personnel management, which is an applied, professional field of work as well as an academic discipline, derives much of its foundations from the social sciences, which have really emerged in the main since 1900. The principal social sciences which have contributed to the development of personnel management are psychology, industrial sociology, labor economics, political science, and cultural anthropology. The professional disciplines of management and public administration have also made their contributions. To the foregoing must be added the important accomplishments made by personnel management practitioners in industry, governmental organizations, and consulting firms.

Now it is certainly true that men engage in many endeavors long before the scientists come along to provide the theoretical explanations. To a certain extent this has been so in the field of personnel management. Frederick W. Taylor and his disciples were designing and installing wage incentive plans long before the modern sociologists and social psychologists developed theories to explain the complex motivational and social factors involved. Workers have been hired and fired for centuries without benefit of formal theory to guide those in charge. Even today a great deal that comprises the field of personnel management is based upon the accumulated trial-and-error experiences of countless employers. But the research studies of scientific investigators are gradually adding to the fund of knowledge available to the management practitioner. He is entering firmer ground when he makes decisions in regard to organization, hiring, training, compensation, discipline, and supervision. The management of people at work is partly an art and partly a science. Undoubtedly for many generations to come, the successful manager will still have to rely upon a good deal of judgment, intuition, and trial-and-error in directing his work force. But more and more the manager can come to decide on actions and predict consequences as a result of applying scientific knowledge.

So far we have related the recent emergence of personnel management as a distinct field of endeavor and as an academic discipline concurrent with the recent development of the social sciences. But there are other and quite different reasons as well. The farmer who manages his own family farm with the help of his wife and children has little need for the knowledge and skills of personnel management. The master craftsman who runs his own shop in town with the help of one or two people to make wagons, shoe horses, print newspapers, or to make clothes has little need to employ sophisticated personnel management techniques. Until the latter part of the nineteenth century the economic activity of the United States was primarily centered upon agriculture and the handicrafts and trading of the country village. The financial tycoons were just beginning to put together their industrial empires in the late nineteenth century. The technology of mass production did not arrive until the early twentieth century. The point being made here is that personnel management problems did not really become pressing until we had large aggregations of people working together in one organization, and the American economy did not reach the point of widespread large-scale organizations until the twentieth century.

In the small establishments of yesteryear employee relations problems were handled largely on an informal basis between the owner and the individual employee. Elaborate organization structures did not exist. Personnel policies were rarely reduced to writing. Rather they evolved through practice and custom. Hiring arrangements were very simple. Psychological tests did not exist. The new employee learned by watching his fellow workers. Accident prevention programs and safety engineering were practically nonexistent. Because management was not recognized as a distinct field of endeavor or as a profession, management training was also nonexistent.

Terminology—Work Organization

Issues, problems, and principles involved in the management of people at work are common to all kinds of organizations: factories, offices, retail stores, hospitals, government agencies, and educational institutions. To emphasize this universality the term *work organization* will be used frequently throughout this book. It is a general term selected to apply to all kinds of establishments or organizations whether they be private business enterprises, governmental organizations, or nonprofit private bodies. It excludes social and religious bodies. In order to provide for a variety of language the terms *company, corporation, enterprise*, and *establishment* will be used from time to time.

MANAGEMENT

To a considerable extent the manager of today has achieved his position because of his knowledge, skill, and ability and not because the control of financial assets has entitled him to a seat in management. Although there are thousands of family-owned businesses in this country, these are predominantly small in size. The vast majority of medium- and large-sized enterprises are directed by hired professional managers. The corporate form of business enterprise coupled with the diffusion of stock ownership, such that a single individual rarely has a controlling interest, has led to a separation of ownership from management. The board of directors then seeks to hire competent managers. Our industrial technology has become extremely complex. The managerial skills required to guide the modern corporation are likewise complex. These and other factors have resulted in the development of a professionalization of management. Although managers are actually hired employees, as a class they tend to identify their interests closely with those of the owners of the business. Top management considers the welfare of the corporation and its own welfare as identical on most issues.

In the field of public administration, as a consequence of the merit or civil service system, the vast majority of the administrative personnel are selected on the basis of well-defined standards of competence. This system is most advanced at the federal level and least at the municipal level. In contrast to the private business system the policy-making positions at or near the top are filled by either popular election or by political appointment.

Thus far we have spoken of management as a group or class of people. Management also connotes a distinct kind of activity or process. *Management is the process of utilizing material and human resources to accomplish designated objectives. It involves the organization, direction, coordination, and evaluation of people to achieve these goals.*

In analyzing the work of management, Newman and Summer state that the total task of management can be divided into organizing, planning, leading, measuring, and controlling.[1] Koontz and O'Donnell view the functions of management as planning, organizing, staffing, directing, and controlling.[2] Harbison and Myers have attempted to include the frames of reference of both economists and industrial management writers by listing the functions of management as (1)

---

[1] William H. Newman, Charles E. Summer, and E. Kirby Warren, *The Process of Management* (Englewood Cliffs, N.J.: Prentice-Hall, Inc., 1972), pp. 11–14.

[2] Harold Koontz and Cyril O'Donnell, *Principles of Management: An Analysis of Management Functions*, 5th ed. (New York: McGraw-Hill Book Company, 1972), pp. 46–49.

the undertaking of risk and the handling of uncertainty; (2) planning and innovation; (3) coordination, administration, and control; and (4) routine supervision.[3] Although in the very small firm all of these functions may be performed by the owner, in a company of any reasonable size these tasks are dispersed among various members of the entire management team.

If one studies the day-to-day activities of a manager, it will be found that he devotes a high percentage of his time to interacting with other people. In preparing plans he must consult his colleagues and subordinates. In organizing he must work closely with his subordinates to define and guide the relationships among them. The manager accomplishes results *through* and with others. He leads, persuades, and influences. At times he conducts and at other times he participates as a member in decision-making conferences. The practicing manager must be skilled in the art of human relations. He spends a great deal of his time communicating with others, mostly through face-to-face contact.

Management involves the act of accomplishing results through other people. The skilled space technology manager does not design a spacecraft himself. The manufacturing executive does not build automobiles himself. The university president does not teach. The role of the manager is to assemble the best work team he can obtain and then to provide a supportive motivational environment to guide that team to accomplish agreed-upon objectives.

The essence of management is the activity of working with people to accomplish results. It involves organizing, motivating, leading, training, communicating with, and coordinating others. Lawrence A. Appley, President of the American Management Association for many years, has written that management is the development of people and not the direction of things. He maintains that management and personnel administration are one and the same.[4]

Now the reader should not jump to the conclusion that the successful manager need only possess knowledge and skills in the fields of personnel management and human resources. This person must also be trained in other fields, such as the technology of his particular industry, management science and administration, and personal communication skills. In addition, the modern-day executive must have knowledge of the economic, social, and political environment in which he or she lives and works. The degree of competence a manager must have in these areas is determined primarily by the particular circumstances of job, company, level in the organization, and geographical location. Notwithstanding these other areas of competence demanded of the manager, his "world" is primarily one of human interaction.

A LOOK AT PERSONNEL MANAGEMENT

Personnel (or human resource) management is challenging and often exciting work. It comprises an amazing variety of activities. To introduce the reader to the field of personnel management we shall here give several samples of activities involved in the "management of people at work." The samples given below

[3] Frederick Harbison and Charles A. Myers, *Management in the Industrial World: An International Analysis* (New York: McGraw-Hill Book Company, 1959), p. 8.
[4] Lawrence A. Appley, "Management the Simple Way," *Personnel*, Vol. 19, No. 4 (January 1943), pp. 595–603.

are not meant to be all-inclusive of the personnel field. They are given to provide the "flavor" of the human resource activities that occur in work organizations. Later chapters of this book will contain in-depth treatments of the topics suggested in the items to follow.

- A supervisor meets with a group of three new employees to welcome them to his department, to introduce them to fellow employees, to show them the layout and facilities, and to generally orient them to their new situation.
- A middle-level manager conducts management-by-objectives meetings with each of the supervisors working in his department. In these private meetings the manager and the subordinate discuss job objectives, performance measures, and work accomplishments in a mutual problem-solving manner.
- The personnel director receives many pieces of information, directly and indirectly from the employees, which reveal serious discontents and frustrations. The employees claim that the front-line supervisors practice favoritism and discrimination. Many employees have been discharged arbitrarily. There is some evidence that employees are reacting to this situation with a high rate of absenteeism, outspoken complaining on the job, and some talk of inviting a union to organize the employees. In cooperation with other top-level executives the personnel director makes plans to systematically assess the state of morale by means of an attitude survey. He contemplates establishing a comprehensive organization development effort to improve understanding among management and the employees and to generally enhance organizational effectiveness.
- A supervisor and his employees are convened to receive official recognition and an award from the president of the company for achieving new production goals.
- Management wishes to do a better job of identifying those persons within the organization who have high potential for success in managerial positions. With assistance from a consultant, the personnel department creates an assessment center for selecting managers.
- The company and the union have just finished bargaining their first labor agreement. A permanent labor–management committee, composed of an equal number of representatives from the union and the company, has been established to meet monthly to discuss and resolve employee relations problems. Both parties have high hopes that this committee will become an effective instrument for problem solving.
- The supervisor of benefits and services (a member of the personnel department) makes a comprehensive study of the current employee benefits (health insurance, pension, life insurance, dental insurance, paid leaves and so on). Management wishes to ascertain whether the current schedule of benefits is adequate to meet employee needs and if it is competitive with that provided by other firms.
- A production supervisor devotes special attention to an employee whose performance has seriously declined over the past several weeks. He holds private meetings with the individual to determine the cause of the decline and to work out a corrective program of action.
- The supervisor of health and safety (a member of the personnel department) participates with members of the engineering department in planning the in-

stallation of new production equipment to insure that it meets health and safety standards.

- Representatives of the personnel and the industrial engineering departments and of various operating departments hold a series of meetings to plan the redesign of various production jobs. The goal is to enrich these jobs to enhance both productivity and employee satisfaction.

The foregoing activities which comprise but a part of the whole of human resource management, demonstrate that personnel work is carried on by both the members of the personnel department and by the other members of management throughout the enterprise.

The responsibility of the personnel department is to formulate personnel policies in cooperation with other members of top management, to plan and develop personnel programs, to carry out certain personnel service activities (such as analyzing jobs, interviewing and testing job applicants), and to insure that the entire range of personnel activities are performed effectively throughout the entire organization.

The responsibility of the other supervisors and managers in all the departments and divisions of the organization is to manage their own work forces to achieve performance goals and to maintain employee well-being. These managers play a key role in performing such human resource responsibilities as employee orientation and training, performance appraisal, communications, leadership, discipline, grievance handling, and maintenance of workplace health and safety.

Constructive and sound management of an enterprise's human resources is crucial to effective organizational performance. If management neglects this responsibility the enterprise may founder.

THE LABOR FORCE IN AMERICA

The United States has experienced great economic progress over the past one hundred or so years. This has occurred through the process of industrialization which converted a largely agricultural nation in the nineteenth century into a very complex, advanced industrialized society in the twentieth century. Important features of our industrialized economy have been vast capital investment in plant and equipment, mass production and continuous production processes, sophisticated managerial and organizational methodologies, and rapid technological advances.

How has the American worker fared during this process of industrialization and economic growth? What changes have occurred in the nature and composition of the labor force?

The labor force includes the noninstitutional population, sixteen years of age and over, who are employed plus all those who are unemployed but who are actually seeking work.

Rising Status of Labor

The average working man or woman in the United States has risen to unprecedented heights in terms of his standard of living, educational attainment, freedom of opportunity, and voice in affairs affecting him. Let us briefly examine some of these matters.

Standard of Living. The best measure of improvement in the level of living of working people is the change in "real wages" between two periods. "Real wages" show the relative purchasing power of wages in terms of a base period when changes in the price level have been canceled out. Bloom and Northrup have tabulated hourly and weekly earnings of production workers in manufacturing from 1914 through 1975 in terms of 1967 dollars. Real weekly earnings went from $36.27 in 1914 to $114.88 in 1975. Thus, 1975 earnings were 3.17 times as much as 1914 earnings.

However, this optimistic view must be cautioned by the scant growth in real wages since the mid-1960's. Real wages in the 1965–1967 period ranged from $113.79 to $115.58 per week. Real wages in 1974 were $119.16 and in 1975 were $114.88.[5]

Shorter Work Time. In 1850 the average work week for all industries was 70 hours. By 1970 it had declined to 39.6 hours. The greatest reductions occurred between 1900 and 1947.[6] In 1976 the average work week in the private sector of the economy for production or nonsupervisory workers stood at 36.2 hours.[7]

Prior to 1940 paid vacations for hourly paid workers were rare. Sometimes they received a week off in the summer but without pay. Salaried employees, however, often got a paid vacation. By the 1970's nearly all classifications of workers (except those in agriculture and construction) received paid vacations. Vacation policies for hourly paid and salaried employees have become nearly identical. Typically an employee receives a two-week paid vacation after one year of service, three weeks after ten years, and four weeks after twenty years.

Before World War II major national holidays were frequently observed in private industry but without pay. As of the late 1970's, the prevailing practice as to grant about nine paid holidays per year.

Thus, we can see that on the average the American worker devotes fewer hours per week and fewer days per year to his job. This does not necessarily mean that he sits idle during his remaining waking hours. He may consume them in a variety of ways, such as engaging in more recreational pursuits, working around his house, commuting longer distances to work, or holding an additional part-time job. But there can be no doubt that this added time off the job has given the American worker greater freedom in determining what he does with his life.

More Education. There has been a long-term trend toward increased education for the population. In March 1977 72.7 percent of the civilian labor force had graduated from high school and 16.9 percent had graduated from college.[8]

---

[5] Gordon F. Bloom and Herbert R. Northrup, *Economics of Labor Relations*, 8th ed. (Homewood, Ill.: Richard D. Irwin, Inc., 1977), p. 399.

[6] *Monthly Labor Review*, Vol. 81, No. 1 (January 1958), p. 24; *Monthly Labor Review*, Vol. 94, No. 2 (February 1971), p. 5.

[7] U.S. Department of Labor, Bureau of Labor Statistics, *Handbook of Labor Statistics 1977*, Table 68.

[8] Kopp Michelotti, "Educational Attainment of Workers, March 1977," *Monthly Labor Review*, Vol. 100, No. 12 (December 1977), pp. 53–57.

This higher educational attainment has contributed to better jobs and higher income for the people involved.

Expectations and Demands. Aside from those changes that can be clearly documented with statistical data, it seems clear also that modern workers as a group or force in society have greater expectations and greater wants than did their forefathers of a few generations ago. They want better homes, cars, food, and clothing than could be obtained years ago. Many things considered luxuries years ago are now held to be necessities. Parents expect their children to finish high school and even obtain some college or technical institute education. They expect to spend more and more on services and recreation. This continual drive for more and more can be explained in terms of the psychological theories of motivation. As more basic needs for the necessities of life are satisfied, man strives to satisfy his higher social and egoistic drives. The fulfillment of these cannot be directly measured. Generally in these psychological and social areas man's wants are never satisfied—he always wants more.

Today employees expect to have a greater voice in their own destiny at their place of employment. A considerable share of the labor force has found union membership to be an avenue for this expression. Through the collective bargaining process, workers make greater demands upon management not only for such material things as higher wages and more fringe benefits but also for fair treatment, freedom from discrimination, and a say-so in matters affecting them. To a considerable extent the ideals of political democracy, which are so much a part of the American culture, have seeped into the workplace. Management in recent years has come to be interested in and to pay attention to the ideas of its employees. The techniques for providing for employee participation have been many. Among these are collective bargaining, consultative supervision, democratic leadership, labor-management cooperation, productivity bargaining, and suggestion systems.

Changing Composition of the Labor Force

Over the years a great many changes have occurred in the way people earn a living. In the mid-nineteenth century four out of five persons who worked for a living worked for themselves. Most were farmers, shopkeepers, and craftsmen. By the last quarter of the twentieth century, nine tenths of the labor force worked for someone else. Thus, we are a nation made up primarily of wage- and salary-earners. Whereas self-employed persons largely determine their own employment conditions, these are set by management for wage and salary workers.

There has been a long-term trend of increases in white-collar employment, both in absolute numbers and in percentage of the labor force. This effect has been especially pronounced since World War II. By 1956 white-collar workers had outnumbered blue-collar workers. In 1946 white-collar workers comprised 33.4 percent of all employed persons; in 1972 this had grown to 47.7 percent. In 1946 blue-collar workers comprised 40.9 percent of all employed persons; by 1972 the figure had declined to 35.0 percent. During this same period, service workers increased from 10.7 percent to 13.5 percent and farm workers declined from 15 percent to 3.8 percent.[9]

Within the foregoing broad occupational groups, the occupations showing the most striking rate of growth are those in the professional and technical category. In 1946 they constituted 6.6 percent of total employment[10] and thirty years later the figure had increased to 14.7 percent.[11] There has been an especially rapid increase in the number of scientists, engineers, and technicians employed in industry. Professional employees have increased rapidly. Professionals like doctors and lawyers who are self-employed did not increase so much.

Another long-term trend has been the decline in employment of unskilled labor. More and more tasks formerly performed by unskilled laborers have been taken over by machines. One implication of this fact is that dropouts from high school can usually qualify for nothing but unskilled jobs and these opportunities are disappearing.

In 1890 the total labor force in the United States consisted of 83 percent males and 17 percent females.[12] A woman would be working for a living only if she were unmarried or widowed. Few jobs were open to women in those days. Those who worked would commonly hold jobs as domestic servants, as needle trades workers, or as clerks in stores. By contrast in 1975, 40 percent of the labor force was made up of women.[13] Several forces have operated to increase both the number and percentage of women in the labor force in recent years. Among these are a steady decline in the fertility rate since the late 1950's, fewer children born and expected by women, increasing availability of household labor-saving appliances, equal employment opportunity actions by the Federal government, and the women's liberation movement. Once-sharp distinctions between men's occupations and women's occupations are disappearing. Women now hold jobs as jockeys, telephone linewomen, sailors on U.S. Navy ships, engineers, executives, and university professors. The annual income of women, however, is still less than that of men. In 1974 the median weekly earnings of full-time women workers, ages 25–54, in the economy as a whole were only 60 percent of the earnings of men workers in the same age grouping.[14] To some extent, women are concentrated in lower-paying occupations. However, discrimination by employers has been the cause of a considerable amount of the differential. The Equal Pay Act of 1963 and the Civil Rights Act of 1964 outlaw discrimination

---

[9] Paul M. Ryscavage, "Changes in Occupational Employment over the Past Decade," *Monthly Labor Review*, Vol. 90, No. 8 (August 1967), pp. 27–30; *Monthly Labor Review*, Vol. 96, No. 11 (November 1973), p. 89.

White-collar workers, according to government statisticians, include professional, technical, and kindred workers; managers, officials and proprietors; clerical workers; and sales workers. Blue-collar workers include craftsmen, foremen, and kindred workers; operatives; and laborers. Service workers include private household workers and others such as policemen, firemen, and barbers. Farm workers include farmers, farm managers, and farm laborers.

[10] Ibid. p. 28.

[11] *Handbook of Labor Statistics 1977*, op. cit. Table 6.

[12] Gertrude Bancroft, *The American Labor Force: Its Growth and Changing Composition* (New York: John Wiley & Sons, Inc., 1958), p. 34.

[13] Andrew M. Sum, "Female Labor Force Participation: Why Projections Have Been Too Low," *Monthly Labor Review*, Vol. 100, No. 7 (July 1977), pp. 18–24.

[14] Deborah P. Klein, "Women in the Labor Force: The Middle Years," *Monthly Labor Review*, Vol. 98, No. 11 (November 1975), pp. 10–16.

on the basis of sex. We can expect the gap in annual earnings and job opportunities to close as these laws are effectively enforced and as public attitudes change.

EVOLUTION OF THEORY AND PRACTICE OF PERSONNEL MANAGEMENT

One of the best ways to understand the present is to examine the past. The past is our prologue. We shall trace the various managerial theories and practices relating to the treatment and direction of employees from the early 1800's to the present. In studying these developments, it is important for the reader to keep in mind that at any one period there existed a variety of ideologies and practices. The diverse movements do not fit into a neat package of unified philosophies and practices commencing at one point in history and ending clearly at another.

The people contributing to the development of the personnel management field have had varied backgrounds and professions. An important group have been the university scholars, writers, and researchers who have pushed back the frontiers of knowledge. A large amount of soundly based experimentation and research has been conducted by these people in areas such as small-group theory, organization theory, motivation, morale, productivity, leadership, personnel testing, fatigue, accidents, and personnel evaluation.

Another significant group of contributors have been the management practitioners themselves: industrial executives, personnel specialists, and consultants. These have been active in such fields as work measurement, wage incentives, job evaluation, organization design, industrial training, executive development, and union–management relations.

A third group have been government legislators and administrators who have shaped and administered public policy in the areas of wages, hours, collective bargaining, workmen's compensation, unemployment, and equal employment opportunity. These programs have had a decided impact upon the management of people at work in private business.

A fourth and final group of influential people have been the leaders of organized labor: Samuel Gompers, John L. Lewis, Philip Murray, Walter Reuther, George Meany, and their followers. In a large measure, their influence in the personnel field has been felt through labor legislation advocated by organized labor and through management policies and programs adopted in response (and sometimes in opposition) to union initiative.

Early Philosophies

The United States followed somewhat after England in becoming an industrialized nation. It was not until 1880 that less than 50 percent of the American labor force was engaged in agriculture. Being culturally close to the British, American entrepreneurs tended to adopt many of the British attitudes toward workers.

One of the pioneer industrialists was Robert Owen (1771–1858), a Scottish textile manufacturer, who in 1813 wrote a book entitled *A New View of Society*. If Owen were alive today he would be called a paternalistic employer. He built model worker villages by his cotton mills at New Lanark, Scotland. He built decent health and sanitation facilities in his factories and established schools for children and workers. Eventually he abolished child labor in his mills. Owen's views and practices contrasted sharply with those of the majority of employers in that period, for he took a genuine interest in the welfare of his people. He advised other manufacturers to devote as much attention to their "vital machines" (that is, workers) as they did to their inanimate machines.

Andrew Ure, in his *Philosophy of Manufacturers,* published in London in 1835, praised the factory system over the coexisting cottage or putting-out system of home production. He defended the widespread use of child labor in the textile industry against the then current public criticism. He was a spokesman for the prevailing belief of members of the entrepreneurial class that workers left to themselves were lazy and ignorant. But factory employment improved their morals and health and gave them higher wages than could be obtained in agriculture or cottage production. He denounced any combination of workers (that is, unionization) as a product of agitators who caused violence and crime.

Others whose works have a bearing on early managerial thought were Adam Smith, who wrote the *Wealth of Nations* in 1776, and Charles Babbage, who wrote *On the Economy of Machinery and Manufactures* in 1832. Smith emphasized that if each individual worked for his own economic self-interest, the greatest good would accrue to society. Babbage subscribed to Smith's ideas. In addition, he concentrated upon developing such principles of manufacturing as the division of labor. Babbage emphasized mutuality of interests between employer and workers. Hard work and high productivity were a source of good wages for the worker and high profits for the employer. In this book he advocated the adoption of such motivational techniques as wage incentives, profit sharing, and plans of employee participation in the establishment of shop rules. Babbage like Ure, however, was opposed to unions of workingmen.

Scientific Management

Frederick W. Taylor was the real father and driving force behind the scientific management movement.[15] He and his followers Frank and Lillian Gilbreth, Henry L. Gantt, Morris L. Cook, and Harrington Emerson exerted a profound effect upon management thought and practice not only in the United States but throughout the world.

Although Taylor created a number of important shop management techniques, such as time study, methods study, functional foremanship, standardization of tools, a differential piece-rate system, instruction cards for workmen, and a cost control system, he proclaimed that scientific management was primarily a mental revolution on the part of workingmen and management alike and not simply a set of efficiency devices.

Taylor preached cooperation between labor and management but in a different

---

[15] A full explanation of Taylor's contributions and impact would be beyond the scope of this book. The interested reader may wish to consult the following works: Frederick W. Taylor, *Principles of Scientific Management* (New York: Harper and Row, 1919); Robert F. Hoxie, *Scientific Management and Labor* (New York: Appleton-Century-Crofts, 1915); George Filipetti, *Industrial Management in Transition,* rev. ed. (Homewood, Ill.: Richard D. Erwin, Inc., 1953), chs. 2 and 3.

way than that of most modern writers. He believed that by scientific measurement of work (that is, time study), specification of the best method, selection and placement of the right worker in the right job, and establishment of an appropriate wage, the source of most of the conflict between management and labor would be removed. The increased output, higher wages through wage incentives, and higher profits for the employer would cause harmony to prevail.

Implicit in Taylor's consulting activities and writings was a full acceptance of the "economic man" concept that dominated management thinking for such a long time, both before and after his time. This is the notion that man is primarily motivated to maximize his economic gain. The concept further holds that each person is individualistic in nature. It ignores the social and psychological drives of man.

In his book entitled the *Principles of Scientific Management,* Taylor asserted that no single element of his system constituted scientific management, but rather it was the entire program and philosophy that was its hallmark. He summarized this as (1) science, not rule of thumb; (2) harmony, not discord; (3) cooperation, not individualism; and (4) maximum output, in place of restricted output.[16]

The scientific management movement has had a great impact upon management–employment relationships and upon management in general. It contributed greatly to the professionalization of management. It elevated management by plan, system, and design while causing management by hunch and intuition to decline. It brought the engineer into a more active role in designing man–machine systems and even entire factory production systems. The work measurement and wage incentive systems introduced by the scientific management pioneers have become accepted practice (with improvements, of course) throughout a large segment of industry. Not only have these contributed to higher productivity, lower unit costs, and higher take-home pay, but they have "muddied the waters" of labor–management relations and caused innumerable disputes. The emphasis upon differences in worker abilities and a scientific selection of employees laid the groundwork for the widespread acceptance of the industrial psychologist and his selection testing programs.

Welfare Movement

In the early 1900's the welfare movement became fairly widespread in American industry. This movement aimed to uplift the physical, hygienic, social, and educational conditions of working-class people for their own benefit and to make them better employees. Many factors contributed to the interest of employers in welfare programs. As corporations grew, top management became more distant from the workers and there occurred a decline in the tenor of relationships. Social reformers and writers had for some time awakened the general public to certain exploitive and sweatshop conditions of the factory system. Many towns that grew up around a single local industry lacked essential housing and decent community facilities. Thus, corporate executives perceived a need and an opportunity to improve the well-being of their people as a positive value in itself and

[16] Taylor, op. cit., p. 140.

as a way of generating greater employee loyalty and possibly greater productivity.

These early welfare programs included health facilities; wash-up and locker facilities; lunchrooms; recreation facilities for employees and their families; libraries, schools, and classes in English for immigrants; disability and group insurance, and pension programs; and savings and legal aid programs.

By the 1920's welfare work in industry had declined and become somewhat discredited. Some companies operated their programs in a highly paternalistic manner and continued them only as long as the workers evidenced genuine appreciation. Other employers offered these benefits to their employees to placate them into accepting long hours, low wages, and bad working conditions. In short, opportunism and expediency were the motives of some businessmen. Executives became disillusioned when baseball and horseshoe-pitching leagues, company picnics, reading rooms, savings associations, and company housing did not increase productive efficiency. Employees became disillusioned when they sensed that employer interest in them was not always genuine.

Employment Management

Prior to the 1911–1920 decade, the hiring of workers was performed principally by line supervision. In effect the foreman did his own hiring and firing. At about this time a number of forces began to operate that demonstrated to top management in American corporations the need for establishing a specialized department to handle employment management.

Frederick W. Taylor had emphasized the need for proper selection and placement of workers on jobs for which they could become superior producers. A number of researchers had demonstrated the very considerable costs associated with high labor turnover. World War I created a demand for the hiring of many thousands for work in defense production factories. War production alone caused the creation of a great number of employment departments in industry. About this time a feeling developed among top managements that foremen were overburdened with problems of production, training, maintenance, and other supervisory duties and that they should be relieved of the responsibility for hiring and firing. There was considerable criticism in the management literature of that period of the "rough and ready" manner in which foremen had performed the employment function.

Thus employment management departments sprang up throughout industry around the time of World War I. In 1912, the first employment managers' association was formed in Boston. In 1915 the Amos Tuck School of Dartmouth College offered the first training program for employment managers. The employment departments performed the functions of recruiting, selection, job placement, and record keeping. In some concerns their responsibilities also included training, grievance handling, welfare program administration, and final decision making on discharges for hourly workers. These early employment departments were the forerunners of the modern personnel or industrial relations department.[17]

[17] A detailed explanation of the development of the employment management activity in industry is contained in Henry Eilbirt, "The Development of Personnel Management in the United States," *Business History Review*, Vol. 33, No. 3 (Autumn 1959), pp. 345–364.

Industrial Psychology

Industrial psychology had its beginnings in 1913 when Hugo Munsterberg (the father of industrial psychology) published his *Psychology and Industrial Efficiency*.[18] Major contributions to the professional practice of personnel have been made by industrial psychology in personnel testing, interviewing, attitude measurement, learning theory and training, fatigue and monotony studies, safety, job analysis, and human engineering (now commonly called human factors analysis). Of all these areas, the major application of the knowledge and techniques of industrial psychology has been in testing for employment, job placement, promotion, and training. Psychologists have made a major contribution, over the years, by their adherence to careful experimentation, rigorous research designs, and use of sophisticated statistical methods.

As a rule, even today, only the very large corporations employ professionally trained psychologists on a full-time basis. But the knowledge, findings, and skills of industrial psychology have been applied rather extensively through education, publication, and consultation services.

Health and Safety

The passage of workmen's compensation laws by most of the states occurred in the 1910–1920 period. These laws hold the employer financially responsible for all injuries occurring to workers while on the job. Employers since that time have been required to carry workmen's compensation insurance to compensate injured workers for medical expenses, loss of weekly earnings while off the job, and for loss of earning power due to permanent physical damage. Because premium rates are adjusted upward or downward to reflect the accident experience of a company, this has served as an incentive for the employer to eliminate the causes of accidents in his plant.

The passage of these laws was a prime force causing employers to take positive steps to reduce and prevent work injuries and to organize company health programs. Thus, we saw the creation of such positions as safety engineer, safety director, company physician, industrial nurse, and medical director. In more recent years the position of industrial hygienist has been added by many large companies.

In 1913 the most influential nationwide organization devoted to the promotion of occupational safety was formed. This is the National Safety Council, a nonprofit organization devoted to research, education, technical service, and publication in the field of safety. It is a membership organization composed largely of manufacturing, public utility, and transportation companies, as well as insurance companies in the liability and workmen's compensation fields.

The fields of industrial hygiene and industrial medicine have grown up during the same era as the accident prevention movement. Both the American Industrial Hygiene Association and the Industrial Medical Association have worked to improve conditions of health at the workplace.

Concerned about a significant nationwide increase in work injury frequency that took place between 1960 and 1970 and about the prevalence of occupational

[18] (Boston: Houghton Mifflin Company, 1913).

diseases, Congress enacted the Occupational Safety and Health Act (OSHA) in 1970. It provides for Federal safety and health standards, government inspections of workplaces, and a system of citations and penalties.

Unionism and Management Reactions

Efforts by American workers to form trade unions to represent their interests in dealings with employers became very widespread and intense commencing in the mid-1880's. In this era, and indeed for many years thereafter, the principal efforts of the unions were directed toward getting the employers to recognize them and to bargain over wages, hours, and other employment conditions.

All through the years, and even up to the present time, employers generally have not taken kindly to unionization of their workers. Basically entrepreneurs and managers opposed unionism for their workers because such action constituted a serious challenge to their authority. With the enhanced bargaining power derived from unified action and the ever-present threat of a strike, a union was in a position to demand a voice in wage-rate determination; job assignments; promotion, transfer, and layoff policies; work schedules; working conditions, work loads, and many other vital factors. When a union entered the picture, the authority of the employer was no longer supreme. In addition, union demands exerted a strong impact upon the cost of doing business.

During the 1920's managements in American industry, acting both individually and in concert through their various associations, launched a great ideological campaign against unions. This took the form of open-shop campaigns, company-established unions and welfare capitalism (paternalism). The main features were education, training, indoctrination, and welfare programs.

Then came the Great Depression, the formation of the CIO, intensified union-organizing activity, and the passage of the National Labor Relations Act (Wagner Act) in 1935. The Wagner Act signified positive encouragement of collective bargaining as public policy. Peaceful means via National Labor Relations Board elections were instituted to settle the violence-fomenting issue of union recognition.

Not until the late 1930's and the 1940's did American management begin to develop a sophistication and maturity in the field of labor relations. Faced with the near inevitability of dealing with unions on a permanent basis, corporations established such positions as vice-president of labor relations and industrial relations director. Commencing in the 1940's, a number of major universities established industrial relations centers or schools that engaged in the triple functions of research, adult education extension activities, and on-campus undergraduate and graduate instruction. As people have become trained in the disciplines of labor economics, industrial relations, and human resources, and have taken responsible positions in industry, the field has become professionalized to a large extent.

In the 1960's unionization of government employees at the federal, state, and local level spread rapidly. This was initially fostered by President Kennedy's Executive Order 10988 of 1962, which required Federal government agencies to recognize as exclusive bargaining agents unions that, by a secret ballot, have been shown to represent a majority of the unit.

Unionism has had a number of tangible influences upon the management of personnel. Among these have been the adoption of sound employee grievance handling systems, almost universal acceptance of arbitration to resolve conflicts of rights, due process discipline practices, expansion of employee benefit programs, liberalization of holiday and vacation time-off, clear definition of job duties, and job rights via seniority. Also union pressures have forced management to install rational, defensible wage structures. Decision making in these and related areas has tended more and more to become a joint consultative process between management and union.

Labor Laws

Commencing with the enactment of workmen's compensation laws in most of the states by 1920, government legislation has increasingly become an instrument for improving the conditions of working men and women. Labor laws have exerted a profound effect upon the way human resources have been managed within work organizations. Below is a chronological listing of the principal Federal labor laws which regulate labor-management relations and personnel practices.

a. National Labor Relations Act, as amended (Wagner Act—1935 and Taft–Hartley Act—1947): Guarantees to employees the right to form unions of their own choosing; requires employers to bargain with unions certified as bargaining agent by the National Labor Relations Board.

b. Fair Labor Standards Act—1938 (amended many times): Establishes a minimum wage and premium pay for hours worked in excess of 40 in a week.

c. Labor–Management Reporting and Disclosure Act—1959: Regulates the internal governance of labor unions and provides certain member rights.

d. Equal Pay Act of 1963: It is illegal to pay women less than men (or men less than women) where they are doing work that requires equal skill, effort, and responsibility.

e. Title VII—Equal Employment Opportunity (of Civil Rights Act of 1964) as amended by Equal Employment Opportunity Act of 1972; Executive Order 11246—1965 as amended: Both of these laws and the executive order prohibit discrimination in employment on basis of race, color, religion, sex, or national origin. They apply to hiring, testing, upgrading, pay, benefits, training, and other conditions of employment.

f. Age Discrimination in Employment Act of 1967, as amended: Prohibits discrimination against employees, 40 through 69 years of age, in regard to hiring, discharge, retirement, pay, and conditions of employment.

g. Occupational Safety and Health Act—1970: establishes specific health and safety standards in the workplace and provides for Federal (or in some cases state) enforcement.

h. Rehabilitation Act of 1973: Requires private employers having Federal government contracts to take affirmative action to hire and advance qualified handicapped persons.

i. Employee Retirement Income Security Act of 1974: Establishes standards for the operation of pension plans and protects employee rights to their pensions.

Rational Wage and Salary Administration

Years ago wages were set for individuals in a very haphazard manner. A person's pay frequently depended upon the strength of his personal ties to his boss, whether he had been hired during a period of business prosperity or recession, and a crude guess by management of the going rates in the local area. Increases in pay after a man had worked for a period of time were often based upon whim and expediency. Although this untenable situation still exists in some companies, the trend for the past thirty-five years has been toward rational, systematic pay administration.

Two major driving forces behind this movement have been the pressures generated by unions and the War Labor Board of World War II. Although the systems of logic of unions and those of management are often opposed in relation to wage determination, it has been clear that union pressures both at the bargaining table and through the grievance procedure have induced management to adopt a well-thought-out, defensible compensation program. In certain industries, such as steel, the union and managements have cooperated jointly to administer a job evaluation program. When it was called upon to resolve labor disputes and later when it was called upon to administer the wage stabilization program, the War Labor Board formulated a number of sound principles that were used in arriving at wage decisions in companies. In many cases the Board directed that companies establish formal wage structures, job evaluation programs, and reasonable pay administration policies.

Today industry has pretty well accepted the principles of basing internal wage differentials upon differences in job content, having a formal job-grade structure, and surveying the labor market area to ascertain going rates for jobs of equivalent content.

Education

Employee Training. Although the apprenticeship system of training workers has existed for centuries, it provided formalized training only for the small minority of workers who were in the skilled trades. Widespread training of production workers, and to some extent of foremen, began during World War II, with the Training Within Industry program. This program was designed to develop employee skills in manufacturing industries for the war effort. Many thousands received training in the three principal TWI programs of Job Instruction Training (JIT), Job Methods Training (JMT), and Job Relations Training (JRT). The principles and techniques developed in the Training Within Industry program have had a great impact upon industrial training in the years since. Industrial executives have learned that employees do not learn new jobs and new skills simply by watching others and by trial and error. The time required of the average man to reach acceptable performance can be significantly shortened by placing him in a proper training environment.

Management Development. Since the early 1950's American industry has devoted a great deal of time and money to formal management development programs. This has been owing to several factors. There has been a growing recognition that management is an emerging profession that depends upon a distinctive body of knowledge and teachable skills. Years ago businessmen assumed that by working long years as an individual contributor, whether as a craftsman, clerk, or engineer, a man would develop the necessary abilities to function as a supervisor or executive. Such an assumption proved to be false. Prospective managers must be placed in the proper environment involving both on-the-job and classroom learning experiences if they are to develop managerial skills.

Management development activities have taken many forms. They have included personnel assessment, performance appraisal, counseling, job rotation, and special assignments. They have included a large variety of in-service training courses, university programs, and conferences and seminars run by professional associations, consultants, and industry associations. A great many schools of management and schools of business at universities have been conducting special, nondegree, management education programs for middle and upper levels of management. Both the American Management Association and The Conference Board give a variety of management education short courses and seminars.

Organization Development

In the 1960's a new field of activity, namely organization development, was created. Objectives of organization development are to facilitate problem solving on the job and to improve the quality of decisions, to accomplish change more effectively, to reduce destructive conflict and make it more productive, to increase commitment to organization objectives, and to foster collaboration among individuals and groups. Organization development is often guided by an outside consultant having training in applied behavioral science. Among the methods he may use are sensitivity training (laboratory training), managerial grid workshops, team building, confrontation meetings, survey feedback, change in organization structure, job enrichment, and process consultation.

Organization development is related to management development. However, management development focuses mainly upon improving the performance of managers as individuals, whereas organization development seeks to improve the overall performance of entire groups, departments, and the organization as a whole.

Human Relations and Behavioral Science

Management's interest in human relations commenced, for the most part, in the 1940's, especially after World War II. Many factors operated to cause this development at that time. The rapid expansion of unionism in the late 1930's and early 1940's caused management everywhere to be more sensitive to the problems and needs of its work force. Management could not ignore festering human problems and employee complaints because the union would not let these issues go unnoticed. Some managements saw the rise of unionism as a challenge to provide so sound a personnel program and so enlightened a leadership that their employees would find no need for a union.

Another factor causing management interest has been the rising educational attainment of the labor force. Educated employees demand better leadership. Industry and government have been employing more engineers, scientists, and technicians and fewer unskilled workers. The gulf separating managers from employees has narrowed. Educated employees want to contribute their ideas in the managerial decision-making processes.

Starting in the 1940's, academics in our universities produced a great body of published material dealing with human relations in industry. Much of this was based upon a growing body of research evidence.

The research experiments of Elton Mayo and his Harvard University colleagues at the Hawthorne Works of the Western Electric Company in Chicago from 1927 to 1932 created the theoretical and intellectual foundations of what we call the human relations movement. Human relations advocates in both the universities and industry advanced a number of propositions. They showed that the enterprise was a social system. The informal work group developed its own norms and standards and was a source of worker control. Human behavior has both its rational and nonrational components. Feelings and values are legitimate and important concerns of the manager. Human relations principles were turned into practice by means of supervisory training programs which emphasized concern for the worker, the need to be supportive and friendly, and the desirability of consulting employees on matters affecting them.

By the early 1960's the term "human relations" faded in popularity and the modern term "behavioral science" replaced it. Behavioral science is much more than a new label for a set of older concepts. Behavioral science is a branch of the social sciences. It consists of the disciplines of cultural anthropology, psychology, and sociology. *Behavioral science is essentially the scientific study of human behavior.* Modern behavioral science tends to emphasize sophisticated research and experimental designs. Educated managers in industry have shown a keen interest in trying to apply many of the important findings and prescriptions that have emanated from behavioral research and theorizing.

Modern behavioral science has tended to be normative and value oriented. It is also humanistic and exhibits an optimisitic view of the nature of people and their potentials. It tends to emphasize genuine employee participation in decisionmaking, group methods of supervision, and concern for the development of interpersonal skills.

Significant contributors to behavioral science applied to work organizations have been Douglas McGregor, Frederick Herzberg, Rensis Likert, Abraham Maslow, Chris Argyris, Robert R. Blake, and Jane S. Mouton.[19] These people could be called the modern pioneers. They are now being followed by a second generation of important contributors.

CONTEMPORARY TRENDS AND DEVELOPMENTS

Let us point out some of the principal issues that have engaged the attention of human resource specialists and policy-makers in recent years.

[19] Douglas McGregor, *The Human Side of Enterprise* (New York: McGraw-Hill Book Company, 1960); Frederick Herzberg, *Work and the Nature of Man* (Cleveland: World Publishing Company, 1966); Rensis Likert, *The Human Organization* (New York: McGraw-Hill Book Company, 1967); Abraham Maslow, *Eupsychian Management: A Journal* (Homewood, Ill.: Richard D. Irwin, 1965); Robert R. Blake and Jane S. Mouton, *The Managerial Grid* (Houston, Texas: Gulf Publishing Co., 1964); Chris Argyris, *Integrating the Individual and the Organization* (New York: John Wiley & Sons, Inc., 1964).

Great advances have been made in recent years in providing increased employment opportunities for blacks and other minorities and for women at all levels of work. This has been caused by pressure from minority groups, women's liberation organizations, Federal government enforcement of the Civil Rights Act of 1964, and enforcement of the various state equal-employment opportunity statutes.

Job discontent and alienation on the part of blue-collar and lower-level white-collar employees, especially in the large mass production industries, has caused business executives to rethink the traditional approach that has been taken toward the organization of work, supervision, and employee development. This spreading employee discontent has been related to the generally higher educational levels possessed by the work force and to rising expectations. Young workers especially are less willing to put up with drudgery and monotony on the job. Such conditions in the past were accepted by workers. Many progressive companies have established ongoing programs to improve the quality of working life of their employees.

In recent years there has been increased emphasis upon individual job rights, appeal mechanisms, and due-process procedures. Arbitrariness in the treatment of people—in their job assignments, in transfers, in layoffs, in discharges, and in pay—has been resisted more and more by employees. Progressive managements have recognized these problems and taken steps to insure just treatment of their people.

More attention is being given to involving people in the process of making decisions about matters that affect them and about matters where they can make a contribution. This is commonly carried out through consultation, committees, meetings, joint union–management committees, and the like.

Managers, economists, accountants, and human resource experts have joined together in recent years to work on human resource valuation and accounting. Among the questions they are jointly asking in regard to an individual company are these: How much money does the company spend on recruitment and selection of people? How much is spent on training and development? What is the return on investment in training? How much human capital is lost due to turnover? Is the value of the company's human assets increasing or decreasing? Should money spent on recruitment, selection, training, and development be treated as a current expense (as is done conventionally) or as a capital investment? The work in this area is still in its early stages but wide recognition has been given to the fact that conventional accounting practice in preparing financial statements ignores the value of a firm's human resources.[20]

Managers especially have been forced to devote more attention to social responsibilities and the environment. There is widespread acceptance that a corporation has multiple goals and multiple clients. The pure profit motive no longer stands alone as the unitary focus of the business. Issues such as consumer satisfaction, pollution caused by the firm, minority group job opportunities, the

---

[20] See Eric Flamholtz, "Should Your Organization Attempt to Value Its Human Resources?" *California Management Review,7 Vol. XIV, No. 2 (Winter 1971), pp. 40–45; R. Lee Brummet, W. C. Pyle, and Eric Flamholtz, "Human Resource Accounting in Industry," *Personnel Administration* (July–August 1969).

impact of the organization upon the community, ethics, and morality are pressing to the forefront.

In its early days, personnel management focused upon the hourly paid worker. This concern is still important. But with the great expansion of employment in the clerical, professional, technical, and managerial areas, personnel activities have been more and more concerned with these groups.

Collective bargaining and unionization of groups in federal, state, and local government have expanded very rapidly since the mid-1960's. Public school teachers are predominantly unionized at the present time. Unions now exist for professors at several hundred college campuses.

Many organizations, especially those experiencing growth and change and those employing large complements of high talent personnel (managerial and professional employees), have established ongoing programs of human resource planning so that they can effectively meet their future staffing needs.

GENERAL OBSERVATIONS

This chapter has explained the relatively recent emergence of personnel management as a distinct field of endeavor. We have examined the nature of management, both as a field of activity and as a group or class of people. It was shown that management involves working with and through others to accomplish organizational objectives. A manager himself does not operate a machine, design products, or wait on customers (except in an emergency). He creates the environment in which employees can work effectively to accomplish the goals of the enterprise and at the same time obtain substantial satisfaction of their needs.

We have provided an introduction to the management of people at work (or human resource management) by giving several examples of personnel management activities that illustrate the rich variety and challenge it entails.

An analysis of the changes that have occurred in the American labor force over the past several decades gives us a better picture of the situation encountered by the modern executive who must establish realistic policies for managing his work force. Perhaps most notable of these developments have been the rising standard of living enjoyed by the American worker and his greater educational attainment. The modern work group is in a position both to expect more from the employer and to make substantially greater contributions to the running of the business than was his counterpart of two and three generations ago.

We have traced the developments in theory and practice of managing people in work organizations. Management has gained, over the years, a more realistic appreciation of the great worth and potentialities of its work force both in terms of individuals and the group as a whole. Because people are truly the most precious resource of any company, management has evolved rather elaborate programs for developing, maintaining, motivating, and caring for its work team.

Finally, we have described some of the more prominent contemporary developments in the field of human resource management. Among these are equal employment opportunity, employee rights, participation in decision making, human asset valuation, and quality of working life.

Questions for review and discussion

1. Explain the reasons for the relatively recent emergence of personnel management as a specialized, professional area of management and as an academic discipline.
2. Define the term *management*. What are the functions of management?
3. Based upon your knowledge of personnel management to this point, what kinds of knowledge, skills, and training are necessary for successful performance in this field of work?
4. Why do you think such a large number of Federal labor laws such as the National Labor Relations Act, equal employment opportunity laws, and the Occupational Health and Safety Act have been enacted? Do you think such laws are necessary or would a system of "Voluntarism" work just as well?
5. What effect has the higher educational attainment of the labor force had upon management–employee relationships?
6. Why has there been a long-term decline in the percentage of unskilled in the labor force, whereas the number of white-collar workers has increased greatly?
7. Describe prevailing philosophies of entrepreneurs and economists during the nineteenth century as they relate to management, work, and workers.
8. What was the "scientific management movement"? What has been its effect upon the field of personnel management?
9. Describe the relationship of the following to personnel management theory and practice:
   a. The growth of unions
   b. Human relations and behavioral science
   c. Rational wage determination
   d. Industrial psychology
10. Identify principal contemporary issues in the management of people at work. What is the significance of each?

Suggestions for further reading

AMERICAN SOCIETY OF MECHANICAL ENGINEERS. *Fifty Years Progress in Management*. New York: The Society, 1960.

BENDIX, REINHARD. *Work and Authority in Industry*. New York: John Wiley & Sons, Inc., 1965, ch. 5.

EILBIRT, HENRY. "The Development of Personnel Management in the United States," *Business History Review*, Vol. 33, No. 3 (Autumn 1959), pp. 345–364.

EITINGTON, JULIUS E. "Pioneers of Management," *Advanced Management–Office Executive*, Vol. 2, No. 1 (January 1963), pp. 16–19.

GEORGE, CLAUDE S., JR. *The History of Management Thought*, 2nd ed. Englewood Cliffs, N.J.: Prentice-Hall, Inc., 1972.

KERR, CLARK, JOHN T. DUNLOP, FREDERICK HARBISON, AND CHARLES A. MYERS. *Industrialism and Industrial Man*. Cambridge Mass.: Harvard University Press, 1960.

LING, CYRIL C. *The Management of Personnel Relations: History and Origins.* Homewood, Ill.: Richard D. Irwin, Inc., 1965.

MERRILL, HARWOOD F., Ed. *Classics in Management,* Rev. ed. New York: American Management Association, Inc., 1974.

MILLS, TED. "Human Resources—Why the New Concern?" *Harvard Business Review,* Vol. 53, No. 2 (March–April 1975), pp. 120–134.

RUSH, HAROLD M. F. *Behavioral Science: Concepts and Management Application.* Personnel Policy Study No. 216, New York: National Industrial Conference Board, Inc., 1969.

SPATES, THOMAS. *Human Values Where People Work.* New York: Harper and Row Publishers, 1960.

URWICK, LYNDALL, ed. *The Golden Book of Management.* London: Newman Neame, Ltd., 1956.

WALKER, CHARLES R. *Modern Technology and Civilization.* New York: McGraw-Hill Book Company, 1962.

Philosophy, principles, and policies

The pattern of beliefs, attitudes, and values of those who establish and manage an organization sets the tone for that enterprise in all of its relations with its customers, employees, shareholders, suppliers, and the public at large.

Executives, especially businessmen, sometimes hold that they are practical men who handle each problem on the basis of its merits and of the situation. If asked to express their philosophy of management, many would be hard pressed to articulate a unified, consistent set of guiding principles. Yet whether they express their philosophies or not and whether they are always fully aware of it or not, those who manage the work organizations of our society usually possess some fundamental beliefs about the nature of man and his behavior in an organizational context. To a considerable extent each enterprise possesses a distinctive personality or character. Often this business character is a reflection of the person who founded the firm, as is the case of Thomas Watson and the International Business Machines corporation or of George Eastman and the Eastman Kodak Company. In other cases the corporate character seems to transcend the personality of any one man, as with the Bell Telephone System (American Telephone and Telegraph Company). But in any event a particular image or character comes to one's mind at the mention of any of these companies.

In this chapter we shall examine the role of philosophy and ethics in shaping the character of an organization, with particular reference to the management of people. The basic beliefs and assumptions that managers hold regarding the nature of man and the behavior of people in organized group activity determine the methods and procedures they employ to accomplish organizational objectives. We shall examine also the important issue of organizational objectives, especially with reference to a business enterprise. In guiding the affairs of a company, executives apply a certain philosophy or set of guiding principles to achieve the goals of the organization. If the goals are unclear or contradictory the business may founder. Likewise if the philosophy or creed of those in charge is confused or in conflict with prevailing standards of morality in the society of which it is a part, then again the enterprise is likely to fail.

Finally we shall examine the subject of personnel principles and policies. We shall discuss the necessity for creating a set of sound personnel policies and for communicating and applying these throughout the organization.

Ethics and Managerial Philosophy

Ethics, which are a set of moral principles, should play a very significant role in guiding the conduct of managers and employees in the operation of any enterprise. Although there are those who would say that any action that optimizes profit and that conforms to the established laws of the land is justified, such a standard is clearly insufficient. The traditional "ethics of the market place" are no longer adequate behavior in our society, if indeed they ever were.

Ethics is concerned with what is right and what is wrong in human behavior. It is normative and prescriptive, not neutral. It addresses the question of what ought to be. Ethics refers both to the body of moral principles governing a particular society or group and to the personal moral precepts of an individual.

From what source do people derive their moral principles? One major source has been the doctrines—primarily religious and political—that have been promulgated over the years since the beginning of recorded history. Significant among these have been the Mosaic Ten Commandments, the Athenian principles of democracy and individual excellence, the British conception of individual justice under the law, the U.S. Declaration of Independence, the Bill of Rights of the U.S. Constitution, and the United Nations Declaration of Universal Human Rights. Another source is the values and norms of a given society. These are related to religious teachings, custom, and tradition, and vary from society to society. Among mankind in Western Europe and North America the principles of human dignity, personal freedom, and the rights of private property ownership have been highly valued. A further guide to ethical conduct is the codes and standards formulated by particular organizations, professions, fraternal groups, and business groups. Thus such diverse organizations as the American Medical Association, Rotary International, The National Electrical Manufacturers Association, The Association of Consulting Management Engineers, and a great many corporations have drawn up formal statements of ethical standards to guide the conduct of their members.

Some people subscribe to a utilitarian reference in determining what is right and what is wrong. They hold that a proposed course of action be judged from the standpoint of the greatest good for the greatest number of people. From this point of view there are few absolute standards and each issue must be judged by studying its impact upon all affected parties.

Simple moralistic and religious precepts such as the "golden rule," while desirable as a foundation, are seldom sufficient to guide human decisions that often require an evaluation of several competing interests. Should salary increases be based upon merit or seniority? In order to provide jobs for racial minorities, should an employer reject qualified nonminority individuals who are competing for the same limited job openings?

We must recognize that generally accepted values change over time. Child labor in industry was wisely accepted in the United States until the middle 1930's. Today it is not only illegal but it is so widely rejected as to be scarcely a subject for conversation. Countless occupations were closed to women and blacks on a de facto basis until the mid-1960's. Prior to this time employers justified discrimination in their own minds. But since the 1960's there has been a pronounced shift in public sentiments toward equal employment opportunity.

Because the business community exercises such a pervasive influence upon the economic, political, and social life of the American society, the general public has a right to expect high standards of moral conduct not only from business executives as individuals but also from the corporation itself as an entity. A chief executive officer cannot absolve his corporation from accountability for the acts of major executives who behave in a grossly improper fashion simply by saying that they violated company policy.

There are countless situations arising every day in the big corporation that put individuals to the test of ethical conduct. These are but a few:

1. Although management has a legal right to discharge a long-service employee who violated a certain company rule, should it do so in the instant case?
2. Are the advertising claims for a particular consumer product likely to mislead the public?
3. Is it proper for a top executive of a corporation to own a controlling interest in a principal supplier?
4. Does a large corporation that is the principal source of employment in a town have any moral duty to consider carefully the impact of its planned factory shutdown upon the town's economy and the lives of the population?
5. Is it ethical to seek actively to destroy the local union with which the employees have cast their lot because it interferes with the unrestrained operation of the business?

Public concern with ethical (and unethical) conduct in business and government is high. Transgressions by persons occupying high office tend to generate waves of public indignation, and well they should. Following the price-fixing conspiracy by major corporations in the electrical industry, Luther Hodges, Secretary of Commerce in President Kennedy's administration, convened a Business Ethics Advisory Council in 1961 to formulate a code of business ethics. Scandals—major and minor—do occur throughout each year. The fraudulent activities of the Equity Funding Corporation of America, which operated in mutual funds and insurance, were brought to light in 1973. Hundreds of millions of dollars were involved in illicit transactions. The uncovering of illegal corporate political contributions to president Richard Nixon's re-election campaign in 1972 (this information emerged from the Watergate investigations), opened up further investigations by the U.S. Department of Justice and the Securities and Exchange Commission. The general public learned for the first time that many of America's most respected and powerful corporations had, for a number of years, made illegal campaign contributions to candidates for United States public offices and had engaged in widespread foreign bribery to obtain business contracts from governments throughout the world.

More and more we see discussion of ethical issues in articles in management journals. One wonders whether the general level of morality and ethical behavior is rising or declining among personnel in our organizations—public and private. Measurement is difficult in this area but qualitative evaluations have been offered by various observers. Clarence Walton offers the view that personal morality in America is declining yet the level of moral performance of institutions is rising. He attributes the improvement in organizational morality to the internally enforced standards and controls of the formal organization upon the individual members. In other words the bureaucracy has been a positive force for righteous conduct.[1]

ORGANIZATION OBJECTIVES

The objectives of an organization are the results it wants to achieve. In place of the term *objectives*, executives sometimes speak of the terms *goals* or *purposes*. These three words are essentially synonymous when used in this context.

It is important that the leaders of an organization clearly establish its objectives and that the members of that organization agree upon these as desirable ends to be achieved. In democratically oriented organizations the members are expected to help shape the objectives.

Why is it important that the objectives of an organization be clearly established and agreed upon? There are many reasons for this.

1. Human beings are goal-directed. People must have a purpose. They must have something to work for. Announced organizational goals provide meaning to work.
2. Objectives serve as standards against which to measure performance.
3. If the participants in the organization have been sufficiently educated so that they believe in the objectives, then there is less need for close control of their behavior. Such education promotes voluntary cooperation and coordination. Self-regulated behavior is achieved.
4. Objectives stand out as guidelines for organizational performance. They help set the tone for action by participants. They also help establish the "character" of the organization.

Objectives of the Business Enterprise

In our discussion of organizational objectives, we shall concentrate upon the business enterprise because it stands as the cornerstone of productive activity in our society.

[1] Clarence C. Walton, *Ethos and the Executive* (Englewood Cliffs, N.J.: Prentice-Hall Inc., 1969), pp. 107–109.

Fallacy of Profit As Sole Objective.   Oftentimes we will hear an employer or business executive assert that the only justification for the existence of his company is to make a profit. This is lauded as the noblest of business objectives and is held to be consistent with the statement of Adam Smith, who described capitalism as a system in which every individual must have freedom to pursue his own economic self-interest and that in so acting, the natural forces of competition would take hold to achieve the best interests for society as a whole. In talking in this vein the businessman may concede that his company has certain responsibilities it must meet, but these are all viewed as distinctly subsidiary to the primary goal of profit.

If a man starts his own business concern and if he is the sole proprietor, his goal very likely may be to make as good a living for himself and his family as possible. In deciding whether he is making a good living, he would undoubtedly lump together the salary he draws from the business with the profit. Our sole proprietor may have subsidiary motives, such as engaging in a kind of business he enjoys and achieving respect from his employees and from the general public, but all in all, economic gain is still probably his most important goal.

Now if a business becomes incorporated and a number of shareholders acquire interests in the firm, then there is a tendency for the executives in charge to assume that the primary objective of operating the corporation is to make profits for these owners. This condition often prevails when the members of one family are major stockholders and are also active in the management.

But when a corporation grows substantially in size, when the ownership becomes diffused among many stockholders, none of whom possesses a controlling interest, and when the direction of its affairs is entrusted to a group of hired professional managers, we can say that the situation has changed substantially. The situation is especially changed when we are talking about a medium- or large-sized corporation that represents a concentration of great economic, social, and political power. Such a corporation may be the principal source of jobs, the major payer of property taxes, and, through its purchasing function, a major consumer in the area. As a group the managers may occupy positions of leadership in such organizations as the school boards of education, community chest, service clubs, charitable institutions, and religious bodies. Thus, the corporation may directly and indirectly exert vast power in a community, a region, or even the nation. The national influence is especially apparent in the case of large corporations that have plants throughout the country and in the case of large corporations that do a substantial portion of their business with the Federal government.

Proper Role of Profits.   For the modern corporation profits are not an end in themselves. Profit is no more the only goal of a corporation than is eating the only goal of man. Profits, like food, are necessary for the continued existence of a business in a free enterprise economy. It must make profits to attract investment capital. Profit should be looked upon (1) as an incentive to produce goods or to perform services and (2) as one important guide for measuring the success of a firm.

However, profit and related monetary measures, such as costs and sales, should not be used as the sole measures of performance in an organization. Rensis Likert has presented some convincing arguments for using other mea-

sures in addition to these. He maintains that management can show a very favorable record in the short run by using pressure-oriented supervision and close
controls when measured by conventional performance figures of output, costs,
and profits. But the good record may be achieved at the expense of a depletion
of human resources so that in the long run the whole organization may suffer. In
addition to employing the usual measures of profits, costs, product quality, and
technical efficiency, Likert argues in favor of evaluating the performance of an
organization in terms of such factors as extent of member loyalty, extent to which
the organization's objectives are compatible with members' own goals, level of
members' motivation, amount of anxiety felt by people in the organization, character of the decision-making process, and adequacy of the communication process.[2]

Goals of a Modern Publicly Owned Corporation

Whereas the tendency formerly was to view the objectives of the corporation
solely from the standpoint of its owners, now scholars and business executives
conceive of the matter in much broader terms. A business enterprise has multiple goals and multiple interest groups who are intimately involved and who
have legitimate rights and interests. The stockholders want a good return on
their investment, the employees want job security and adequate wages, the customers want a product or service of specified quality, delivered on time and at a
fair price. Suppliers want the firm to treat them fairly and pay prices that permit
them to exist, and the community expects the modern company to be a good corporate "citizen" and to use its power in a way that advances the interests of the
general public. The professional managers who direct the affairs of the enterprise
are expected to balance the interests of all parties to the best advantage of all. A
survey by the *Harvard Business Review* of approximately 3,500 corporate executives (primarily middle- and top-level managers in a wide variety of industries)
revealed that a substantial majority believe that a corporation's duty is to serve as
fairly and equitably as it can the interests of four sometimes competing groups—
owners, employees, customers, and the public.[3]

It is pretty widely recognized that a business corporation really has multiple
objectives. These may be viewed in the framework presented in the preceding
paragraph, in which it is held that the corporation seeks to serve the wants and
needs of the various interest groups that are vitally affected by it. Eells and Walton have expressed the objectives of the corporation as (1) profit making; (2) service; (3) social responsibility; and (4) survival.[4]

In *The New Industrial State* John Kenneth Galbraith devotes his attention to
the very large American corporations and their interaction with our economic
system. He has coined the term "technostructure" to designate that complex
whole of managers, staff experts, professionals (engineers and scientists), and administrators who really make the key decisions and control the affairs of the cor-

---

[2] Rensis Likert, *New Patterns of Management* (New York: McGraw-Hill Book Company, 1961), chs.
5 and 13.
[3] David W. Ewing, "Who Wants Corporate Democracy?" *Harvard Business Review*, Vol. 49, No. 5
(September–October 1971), pp. 146–147.
[4] Richard Eells and Clarence Walton, *Conceptual Foundations of Business*, rev. ed. (Homewood,
Ill.: Richard D. Irwin, Inc., 1969), pp. 534–537.

poration. From the standpoint of the technostructure, the goals of the corporation in rank order priority are (1) survival and a secure level of earnings; (2) greatest possible rate of growth as measured in sales; (3) technological virtuosity that creates new products, jobs, and customers; and (4) social goals such as building a better community, schools, public health, and the like.[5]

Social Responsibilities. Increasingly in recent years spokesmen for business and for the public have emphasized that business firms must bear substantial social responsibilities. We live in a very interdependent world. Urban crises, air and water pollution, strikes, plant shutdowns, and expansions of employment all have significant impacts upon both business and the general public. Few would now deny that private industry has a real stake in the welfare of the people and the nation. The enthusiasm with which big businessmen across the country contributed to the National Alliance of Businessmen, which was launched in 1968 to help solve the problem of the hard-core unemployed, attests to this recognition of their real social responsibilities.

The Committee for Economic Development is a private organization of corporate presidents and board chairmen and university presidents that prepares policy recommendations based upon research and informed discussion. Its report dealing with corporate social responsibilities generally endorses business activities that help improve our society. It lists ten major areas in which companies in the aggregate are performing in the public and social area. These are economic growth and efficiency, education, employment and training, civil rights and equal opportunity, urban renewal and development, pollution abatement, conservation and recreation, culture and arts, medical care, and government. Under the heading of employment and training the report lists (1) active recruitment of the disadvantaged; (2) functional training and remedial education; (3) provision of day-care centers for children of working mothers; (4) improvement of work/career opportunities; and (5) retraining of workers affected by automation or other causes of joblessness.[6] Of course, not every corporation can provide substantial efforts in all of the ten major areas.

The Xerox Corporation grants paid leaves of absence to limited numbers of its employees to devote up to a year's time to social welfare projects ranging from aiding the mentally retarded to assisting ex-convicts to resume life in their communities.

Schools of business and of management at a large number of universities now offer courses variously titled Management and Society or Business and Its Environment. These explore the interrelationships of private business and the public. Among the issues they cover are business and government, business values and ideology, ethics and social responsibility, social power and responsibility, consumerism, minority and female job rights, and ecology.

Because of increased concern with social action programs by private business

---

[5] John Kenneth Galbraith, *The New Industrial State* (Boston: Houghton Mifflin Company, 1967). Galbraith asserts that profit maximization is not a goal of the technostructure because it does not benefit this group once a level of earnings has been achieved that is sufficient to placate the stockholders. For the technostructure, growth is all important because it benefits this group with more jobs, more promotions, and more pay.

[6] *Social Responsibilities of Business Corporations* (New York: Committee for Economic Development, 1971).

concerns, some leaders in the field have begun to undertake a systematic assessment of these activities. This work is just beginning. Mostly the top managements of individual companies have been asking such questions as What are we doing now? What should we be doing? How much does it cost? What results have we achieved? It is very difficult for a company really to measure what impact it has had in certain social areas. Thus, it may be hard to prove that a company's efforts to improve the quality of health care or of education in a community have had any demonstrable success. But an inventory of what a firm is actually doing and a frequent monitoring of this work ought to provide some qualitative gauges. And with time, top management, the employees, and the public can gain an appreciation of what is being done and where it is leading.[7]

Public and Non-profit Organizations

When we think of public and non-profit organizations we refer to such entities as government, the military, schools and colleges, hospitals, and charitable and philanthropic foundations. The profit motive does not exist in such institutions. Generally the motive of service to the organization's constituents is paramount. Other goals may be survival, stability, economy of operation, efficiency, and growth. But just as with the corporation, the goals are multiple, not unitary.

MANAGING PEOPLE AT WORK

The way managers treat and deal with their subordinates in order to accomplish the multiple objectives of the organization is determined primarily by management's system of beliefs about the nature of man and about the determinants of cooperation in an organized endeavor. The fundamental assumptions that leaders hold condition their actions. How will they go about seeking performance from others? Will they trust people? exert tight control? centralize decision making? Or will they create the conditions by which people can create, achieve, and assume responsibility?

We shall portray two dissimilar frames of reference. One will be called the "traditional" or "authoritarian" philosophy. Certain principal components of this philosophy have also been referred to as "Theory X," the pessimistic view of man, and the bureaucratic approach to organization and management. The other school of thought we shall designate as the "modern" or "human resource" philosophy of management. This has also been given such appellations as "theory Y," supportive management, management by integration and self-control, System 4 management, and the optimistic view of man. It should be clear upon reading these two descriptions that they represent wholly contrasting systems of belief. In actual practice the attitudes and behavior of business executives can be scaled along a continuum. Undoubtedly some clearly belong to the traditional camp, whereas others are entirely in the modern camp; but probably many managers also hold beliefs derived from both schools of thought. Some are also on the middle ground in their attitudes and day-to-day behavior.

[7] For ideas on conducting a social audit of a company see Raymond A. Bauer and Dan H. Fenn Jr., "What Is a Corporate Social Audit?" *Harvard Business Review*, Vol. 51, No. 1 (January–February 1973), pp. 37–48.

Traditional (Authoritarian) Philosophy

An early and rather widespread view of man is that he is selfish, rebellious, and uncooperative. Left to his own devices he tends to act in a mean and base manner. Therefore, the leader must be ruthless and strict in the way he controls his men, even to the point of harshness. The classic spokesman for this type of reasoning was the Florentine nobleman and political philosopher Niccolò Machiavelli. He stated that the "end justifies the means." A prince or ruler must put aside such questions as integrity, morality, and honor. He should follow any tactics that will maintain himself in power and preserve the state or the army. Machiavelli asserted that it was desirable for the ruler to *appear* to be straightforward, humane, clement, and trustworthy but that he should always be ready to follow the path of evil if the occasion should arise. He should have a spirit to adapt to the varying winds of fortune.[8]

Thomas Hobbes in his *Leviathan* (1651) asserted that men are acquisitive, and seek power and prestige. They want what their neighbor possesses. Therefore, man must submit to the authority and law of a ruler and the state to regulate and constrain these avaricious and selfish tendencies.[9]

Another underlying theme has been "social Darwinism" or survival of the fittest. During the nineteenth century Herbert Spencer, the British philosopher, derived social implications from Charles Darwin's biological theory. He preached the doctrines of individualism, liberty of action, and surival of the fittest. He claimed that the weak, the infirm, and the intemperate must fall by the wayside. Ultimately only superior human beings would survive. This process would evolve toward a superior type of society.

The ideas Adam Smith propounded in his *Wealth of Nations* in 1776 have served for two hundred years as the basis of our capitalistic system. He argued that the wealth of a nation was best served when everyone pursued his own self-interest in the utilization of his energy and capital. Government should not interfere in the economic system. Each man may seek as much private gain as possible, but the forces of competition in a free market will serve as a self-regulating mechanism. According to Adam Smith, the "invisible hand" of the marketplace, that is supply and demand and the price mechanism, provided a just allocation of scarce resources. Like Spencer, Smith glorified individualism and the pursuit of one's self-interest. Unrestrained competition and profit maximization ultimately resulted in the public good even though the individual entrepreneur sought only his own private gain.

In the field of employment relationships there are many who maintain that the company is in business to make a profit. The strongest and best-run firms survive; the inefficient ones fail. Likewise, among employees, individualistic competition is emphasized. The rewards go to the best producers, who are retained and promoted; those who are less efficient are demoted, laid off, or discharged.

In a capitalistic society in the Western world, the basic moral values to be derived from hard work, self-denial, saving, and pursuit of monetary gain have been preached, directly or indirectly, over the years. Max Weber has written a

---

[8] Niccolò Machiavelli, *The Prince*, Thomas G. Bergin, trans. (New York: Appleton-Century-Crofts, Inc., 1947). Machiavelli wrote this work in the year 1513.

[9] Thomas Hobbes, *Leviathan* (Indianapolis: The Bobbs-Merrill Company, Inc., 1958).

classic study in tracing the blending of the ideas of capitalism and those of Protestantism. In certain regions of Europe and in the United States this synthesis has resulted in the practice of the aforementioned behavior. It has been considered a necessary virtue.

During the late nineteenth and early twentieth centuries, a great deal of both fiction and nonfiction was written publicizing the assertion that those who rose to the top in industry did so because of hard work, perseverance, superior innate abilities, and greater energy. It was felt that abundant opportunity existed in America for anyone to achieve personal and economic success if he tried hard enough. If a man did not succeed in the business world, if he forever remained a laborer or a clerk, it was because he was lazy, noncompetitive, and unimaginative.

People in the Organization.   According to Douglas McGregor, the traditional managerial view regarding people in a work organization is that the average worker has an inherent dislike of work, avoids responsibility, lacks ambition, and wants to be closely directed. Faced with this fundamental "fact" the only course open to management is to exercise close control and to coerce and threaten workers in order to get them to exert sufficient effort to attain organizational objectives. McGregor has labeled this managerial philosophy "Theory X." [10] In fact, if managers continually treat their subordinates as if these assumptions are actually true, this pattern of management can be self-validating. In one deals with his subordinates as if they are indolent shirkers who cannot be trusted to behave responsibly, then they will tend to act that way, especially in an authoritarian environment.

A basic tenet of the traditional point of view is that the authority of the employer is supreme, the authority is synonymous with power, and that authority comes from the top and is transmitted down through the organization structure. Authority and controls are the basic integrating force. Control is exercised through command. The power and right to make decisions must be centralized at the top.

In such a system the front-line supervisor is viewed as an agent of higher management. His job is to obtain obedience to orders received from his own boss. He tells his subordinates what to do and how to do it. He is expected to exercise close supervision over their activities. He tends to be highly production centered, not people oriented. The supervisor is expected to meet production goals, control costs, and maintain proper product quality.

Efficiency is enhanced when the organization is carefully defined and when job duties and responsibilities are clearly specified. Employees are expected to assume neither fewer nor more responsibilities than contained in their job descriptions. Maximum efficiency is achieved when policies, procedures, rules, and methods are clearly spelled out. The emphasis is upon fitting the man to the job rather than adapting the job to the man. Standardized, predictable performance is the goal. This is the essence of the bureaucratic model of organization.

The motives of man that are tapped are primarily the lower-order needs: physical and economic security. In practice people are induced to produce through

[10] Douglas McGregor, *The Human Side of Enterprise* (New York: McGraw-Hill Book Company, 1960), ch. 3.

"the carrot and the stick." This means monetary incentives on the one hand and threats, fear, and the specter of discharge on the other hand. The response of the employees to such leadership can be either hostility or docile compliance. Actually those who rebel against authoritarian leadership tend to drift away from the organization; those who remain respond in a conforming sort of manner. They learn to accept it and gain certain economic and security satisfactions. They occupy a dependency relationship to their superiors and to the employer generally.

Authoritarian or Theory X management is very widespread and pervasive. It is standard in all military forces and is very common in private business, industry, and in government bureaucracy. It often is effective in achieving performance up to a certain level. It frequently achieves satisfactory results especially in the short run. But it seldom elicits real enthusiastic response from the organization members. High achievement, creativity, and a feeling of self-responsibility are sacrificed in favor of a moderate level of predictable and regimented performance.

Paternalism.   A fairly common variant of traditional, autocratic management is paternalism. This is basically benevolent autocracy. Management treats its employees well by providing job security, decent working conditions, and adequate pay. In return the employees are expected to be cooperative, loyal, and productive. A dependency relationship is created. The organization members are expected to be docile and do what they are told. As long as they stay in their place, they will be taken care of adequately. But the people are not expected to stand on their own two feet and make decisions for themselves. There is little delegation of authority and responsibility in a paternalistic enterprise. As in the bureaucratic autocracy, decision making and influence are tightly held at the top. In the paternalistic enterprise people are taught to expect that the organization will take care of them in time of trouble if they themselves have been loyal to the organization.

Role of the Union.   Traditionalists in management generally do not accord a real place for a union in their thinking. They tend to feel that the authority of management should be supreme and that if a union represents the employees, it will try to restrict management's freedom of action. If a union has won bargaining rights and certification as a result of a National Labor Relations Board election, then management will certainly recognize the union and bargain over wages, hours, and other conditions of employment as required by law, but there will be no attempt by management to open up to bilateral determination any subjects that are not absolutely required by law. In effect the union will be confined to as small a role in the affairs of the business as possible.

Modern (Human Resource) Philosophy

The modern philosophy of management is based upon an optimistic view of the nature of man. He is considered to be potentially creative, trustworthy, and cooperative. He is not inherently predatory. Man is not predisposed by inheritance or instinct to be either mean or good. Rather his behavior reflects the character of his life experiences as he matures. Man has potential for growth, achievement, and constructive action with others. It is the job of management to nurture and tap man's productive drives.

The writings of such behavioral scientists as Douglas McGregor,[11] Rensis Likert,[12] Chris Argyris,[13] Frederick Herzberg,[14] and Blake and Mouton[15] are richly illustrative of this modern school of management thought. This philosophy is somewhat ahead of actual practice in industry, although executives in the more progressive organizations are generally familiar with these ideas on the intellectual level and some have applied them in their day-to-day activities. As indicated previously, this pattern of management has been variously called "Theory Y," supportive management, and management by integration and self-control. Rensis Likert calls it "System 4" management.

Advocates of this school of thought hold that people possess innate capacity for exercising initiative, accepting responsibility, and making worthwhile contributions. They do not inherently dislike work. Work can be a meaningful, satisfying experience. Employees will actively work for the goals of the organization when such behavior is compatible with their own goals. This demands an integration of the goals of the organization with those of the individual. Commitment to organizational objectives is a function of the rewards associated with their accomplishment. Although external controls may be available, it is felt that the best control of employee behavior is self-control. Management should share information and objectives with subordinates. It is also advised to establish a climate where employees may contribute toward decisions affecting the business in those areas where they possess competence.

What is the role of the front-line supervisor under supportive, or Theory Y, type of leadership? He is expected to build a team that has a strong sense of responsibility for getting work done. He also is expected to represent his group to higher management as well as represent organizational needs to his people. He goes to bat for his employees when warranted. He has trust in them and they trust him. He tries to understand their problems. He is both people- and production-centered.

Whereas traditional management depends primarily upon economic motivation and "the carrot and the stick," Theory Y holds that all motives—economic, social, egoistic—must be activated. The employee is most highly motivated to work when the motivation is intrinsic—that is the person derives satisfaction from doing the work itself. Emphasis is placed upon activating the higher motives of responsibility, recognition, achievement, and innovation. People are taught to accept responsibility and exercise self-control. External discipline and control are minimized when employees and supervisors control their own behavior. They evidence a high degree of commitment to the company and its programs.

---

[11] Ibid.

[12] Likert, op. cit.; *The Human Organization: Its Management and Value* (New York: McGraw-Hill Book Company, 1967).

[13] Chris Argyris, *Personality and Organization* (New York: Harper and Row, 1957); and *Integrating the Individual and the Organization* (New York: John Wiley & Sons, Inc., 1964).

[14] Frederick Herzberg, *Work and the Nature of Man* (Cleveland: The World Publishing Company, 1966).

[15] Robert R. Blake and Jane Mouton, *The Managerial Grid: Key Orientations for Achieving Production Through People* (Houston: Gulf Publishing Company, 1964).

Some critics have mistakenly asserted that the style of management we have been describing is soft or ineffective. They say that management relinquishes its responsibility to run the business. Manifestly this charge is not true. Modern supportive management seeks to enlist the full creative energies of all organization members. It is more of an open system. Information is widely not narrowly shared. Under authoritarian leadership the planning and controlling are done by top management and the doing is carried out by the employees. But the more modern approach involves a wider spectrum of members in the planning, doing, and controlling processes. Nevertheless, management still bears full and final responsibility for guiding the enterprise and achieveing results.

How widely have the concepts we have been discussing become accepted by management practitioners? An interesting research project bearing on this subject has been conducted by Haire, Ghiselli, and Porter, all of the University of California. By means of a questionnaire they surveyed the attitudes of 3,000 managers in fourteen different countries throughout the world. They probed four areas of the manager's belief system: (1) belief in the individual's innate capacity for initative, individual action, and leadership; (2) belief in the value of sharing information and objectives; (3) belief in participative management; and (4) the belief that individual control should be by self-control rather than control by supervisors. The results of their survey revealed a paradoxical condition. Rather generally the managers surveyed believed in shared objectives, participation, and individual control; yet they tended to have serious doubts about the capacity of people to demonstrate initiative, individual action and leadership. The situation is paradoxical because the first premise above is a precondition for applying concepts 2, 3, and 4. The researchers conclude that their findings reveal a basic lack of confidence in the abilities of other people and that democratic leadership cannot succeed unless executives come to believe that lower-level personnel are capable of making worthwhile contributions at the decision-making level.[16]

Authority in the organization is viewed in a less absolute manner. The traditionalist maintains that authority is a fixed body of legitimate rights and powers that reside in the board of directors and the president of the organization. These are delegated down through the chain of command as required. The behavioral view is that authority and power become effective only when people accept them. A manager's influence and ability to get results are highly dependent upon the kind of relationships he builds up with his subordinates, peers, and superiors. Three managers may appear in the same level in the organization chart and yet each may effectively possess quite different amounts of authority and influence.

One practical manifestation of the human resource or modern approach to management is "management by objectives." Management by objectives is a system of management in which there is genuine collaboration between managers and their subordinates in developing performance goals and performance measures, and in evaluation of performance on an on-going basis.[17]

---

[16] Mason Haire, Edwin E. Ghiselli, and Lyman W. Porter, "An International Study of Management Attitudes and Democratic Leadership," Symposium Paper A9a, *International Management Congress*, CIOS XIII, 1963.

[17] The concept of management by objectives was originally formulated by Peter Drucker in *The Practice of Management* (New York: Harper and Row, 1954), ch. 11.

Role of the Union. Although not all writers of the modern school discuss unionism, a few do. The newer view accords a more significant role for the union than does the traditional philosophy of management. The union is not looked upon as the "enemy" or as a force that exists to make management's job more difficult. Rather it is recognized that for many sound reasons the union plays a very vital part in representing the interests of the employees. The process of managing the work force in an organization is probably the most important of all management functions. The holding of discussions with elected union leaders to make mutually satisfactory decisions on such issues as wage rates, work loads, transfers, safety, and employee suggestions is viewed as a legitimate way of managing the work force.

Traditional vs. Modern—Which Approach?

It is perhaps safe to say that the vast majority of executives in work organizations throughout the world lean closer to the traditional philosophy of management than to the modern view. This is evidenced by both their beliefs and their practices. Actually, it is somewhat more true of their practices than their beliefs. Many profess to believe in self-discipline, self-control, participation, group methods of leadership, management by objectives, development of subordinates' abilities, and the like, yet they continue to deny their people true opportunities for assuming responsibilities and for growing in the organization. Philosophically they hold that they would like to trust people more and grant more discretion to their subordinates; yet they continue to hoard company information and centralize decision making.

It seems reasonable to assume, however, that as the level of education of people in work organizations continues to rise and as more highly talented people enter industry, executives will come to grant greater autonomy and discretion to their people. Also as younger generations of managers rise in the business world, they will gradually apply more of these concepts of modern management, which they absorbed while in college and from participation in management education programs.

Tannenbaum and Davis do see a trend toward acceptance of Theory Y (McGregor) or System 4 (Likert) as a philosophy and style of management. They assert that growing evidence suggests that humanistic values not only resonate with an increasing number of people, but also are highly consistent with the effective functioning of organizations built on the newer organic model. Among the specific value changes that they believe are occurring are the following: (1) away from negative evaluation of individuals toward confirming them as human beings, (2) away from fearing differences among people toward accepting and utilizing them, (3) away from maskmanship and game playing toward authentic behavior, (4) away from distrusting people toward trusting them, and (5) away from primary emphasis upon interpersonal competition toward a much greater emphasis upon collaboration.[18]

[18] Robert Tannenbaum and Sheldon A. Davis, "Values, Man and Organizations," *Industrial Management Review*, Vol. 10, No. 2 (Winter 1969), pp. 67–86.

PERSONNEL POLICIES

A policy is a plan of action. It is a statement of intention committing management to a general course of action. When management drafts a policy statement to cover some feature of its personnel program, that statement may often contain an expression of philosophy and principle as well. Although it is perfectly legitimate for an organization to include philosophy, principles, and policy in one policy expression, it is well for the thoughtful student of personnel management to be able to separate the expression of principle from the policy statement.

The following is a statement of principle or objective in regard to the health and safety of company personnel:

> It is the intention of the company to provide a safe plant and a healthful working environment.

It can readily be seen that such a statement is quite general. A policy statement on the other hand is more specific. It commits management to a rather definite course of action, as shown in the following statement:

> Our policy is to institute every practical method for engineering safety into our processes and equipment, to provide protective clothing where necessary, to train employees in safe operating procedures, and to vigorously enforce established safety rules. Our policy is to provide a healthful plant by giving adequate attention to cleanliness, temperature, ventilation, light, and sanitation.

A policy does not spell out the detailed procedures by which it is to be implemented. That is the role of a *procedure*. A procedure is really a method for carrying out a policy. A policy should be stated in terms broad enough for it to be applicable to varying situations. Lower-level managers who apply policy must be allowed some discretion in carrying out the policy. The circumstances in Department A may differ from those in Department B; hence a rigid, excessively detailed, policy statement might cause an injustice if supervision were not granted some latitude.

Why Adopt Definite Policies?

Many organizations of all types have never created a set of personnel policies. Top management has never been sufficiently aware of the hazards of operating without them nor of the advantages to be gained from establishing a sound group of policies. Why should an organization have clearly established policies?

1. The work involved in formulating personnel policies requires that management give deep thought to the basic needs of both the organization and the employees. Management must examine its basic convictions as well as give full consideration to prevailing practice in other organizations.
2. Established policies assure consistent treatment of all personnel throughout the organization. Favoritism and discrimination are thereby minimized.
3. Continuity of action is assured even though top management personnel change. The president of a company may possess a very sound personnel

management philosophy, he may carry the policies of the organization in his head, and he may apply them in an entirely fair manner. But what happens when he retires or resigns? The tenure of office of any manager is finite. But the organization continues. Policies promote stability.

4. Policies serve as a standard of performance. Actual results can be compared with the policy to determine how well the members of the organization are living up to professed intentions.

5. Sound policies help to build employee enthusiasm and loyalty. This is especially true where the policies reflect established principles of fair play and justice and where they help people grow within the organization.

Policies Should Be in Writing

Although this proposition may seem self-evident, countless companies have never bothered to reduce their practices, customs, and traditions to writing. In fact many executives actually are opposed to writing the personnel policies on paper and disseminating them to all concerned. They contend that such action would tie their hands and limit their freedom of action. Now if these executives mean that it would prevent the continued application of expediency and inequitable treatment, the answer is yes, it would. But if they reject management by expediency and intend to abide by reasonable principles, then the answer is no. Written policies do not so tie the hands of management that it cannot use some discretion and flexibility in handling particular cases. Policies are stated in broad terms. They are designed to aid the operation of the business, not impede it.

Written policies let everyone know just what kind of treatment he can expect to receive from management. They let him know where he stands. Only when policies are reduced to writing can they be communicated to all employees.

In large organizations containing many dispersed plants, written policies are almost a necessity. They insure reasonably consistent treatment throughout the company on such matters as pay, promotion, transfer, layoff, pension rights, insurance benefits, training opportunities, and grievance handling.

Formulating Personnel Policies

If the chief executive officer of a company should decide that the time has come to prepare a comprehensive statement of personnel policies, what should the content be? How does management decide what its wage policy or its hiring policy should be? Policies are not created in a vacuum. There are five principal sources for determining the content and meaning of policies. These are (1) past practice in the organization; (2) prevailing practice among other companies in the community and throughout the nation in the same industry; (3) the attitudes and philosophy of the board of directors and top management; (4) the attitudes and philosophy of middle and lower management; and (5) the knowledge and experience gained from handling countless personnel problems on a day-to-day basis.

Because people are free to resign from their jobs and take employment elsewhere and because any company must make its employment opportunities attractive enough to recruit new people into the business, management must so design its personnel policies that they reflect current good practice. If all other companies grant two weeks of paid vacation after a year's employment, then it would be unsound for a firm to grant no paid vacation. Likewise, if prevailing practice is to pay a 10 percent premium to those who work the evening and midnight shifts, then a company has hopes to attract and retain qualified people must do something similar.

The actual work of formulating the written expressions of company personnel policy generally will be done by the personnel director. He will study existing documents, survey industry and community practices, and interview other executives with the organization to collect appropriate information. The actual and final decisions on the substantive content will, in most instances, be made by the president and the board of directors. Although the entire statement of personnel policy could be prepared by a very small group at the top of the structure or even by the president alone, there is considerable merit to the practice of bringing members of middle management (or even lower management in very small organizations) into the deliberations. These people can make particularly valuable contributions when it comes to evaluating the advantages and disadvantages of existing practices. And, of course, if these members of the management team are consulted, they will tend to support the fruits of their efforts when it comes to applying the policies.

Communicating Policies

The statement of the personnel policies does little good if it is locked in the company president's desk. It must be communicated throughout the organization.

All members of management, including shop foremen and office supervisors, are vitally concerned because they must interpret and apply the policies. Not

Figure 2-1
A Manager Discussing, with Two of His Supervisors, Personnel Policy Documents in Managers' Handbook.

only must the policies be communicated to all management personnel, but also a real education program should be set up to teach them how to handle various personnel problems in the light of the newly enunciated policy. A policy is worthwhile only when it is carried out on a day-to-day basis.

Many organizations publish and disseminate their personnel policies to all supervisors and managers by means of policy handbooks. These handbooks are often in looseleaf form to facilitate the insertion of new and changed policies. Often these books contain information on implementation of policies as well. Figure 2-1 shows a manager discussing policy information contained in a managers' handbook with two of his supervisors.

The most common way of informing nonsupervisory employees is by means of the employee handbook. But to achieve real understanding this should be followed up with an oral explanation and interpretation generally by first-line supervision.

Questions for review and discussion

1. What role should ethics play in the management of a business corporation?
2. Discuss possible ethical and policy implications of the following:
   a. Choosing individuals for promotion when there are whites, minorites, and females to select from
   b. Possible actions by managers when their subordinates challenge the propriety of certain orders or directives given to them
   c. The contemplated closing down of a plant due to declining profit margins where the plant is the principal employer in a community
   d. Determining the size of pay increases to be granted to salaried employees in a department
3. Why is it desirable for management to clearly establish the objectives of the organization?
4. Discuss the role of profit in the context of corporation objectives.
5. How do the goals of the family-owned company typically differ from those of the large, professionally managed, publicly owned corporation?
6. How might top management of a corporation translate a concern for social problems in the community into action?
7. Describe the "traditional" concepts of the nature of man and the ways of managing people in a work organization.
8. Describe the "modern" philosophy of the management of people.
9. What is "management by objectives"?
10. Why should an organization establish a definite set of personnel policies? Why should they be in writing?
11. Do policy statements "tie the hands" of management?

Case problem

Miss Carson, having just finished her junior year in college, obtained a summer job as a teller in the branch office of the Central City Commercial Bank. She was majoring in social science in college. This was her second summer with the bank; however, she was new to this particular branch.

This branch office was located in a declining commerical-residential section of the city. Much of the housing was substandard and a substantial number of the residents were either retired and subsisting on their monthly Social Security checks or else they were living on meager incomes or on welfare.

The first month on the job was uneventful as Miss Carson became adjusted to the routines of cashing checks, processing deposits, counting money, and reconciling the day's figures. Her relations with bank customers, fellow employees, and her supervisor were cordial.

One of the many services provided by this bank was that of a collection agent for the Mid-State Gas and Electric Company so that residents could conveniently pay their monthly bills. Miss Carson observed that invariably power company customers paid their bills about the second week of each month and that they were required to pay a 5 percent penalty. The power company bills stipulated this penalty on all accounts paid after the first of the month. When she advised a number of individuals that they could save this penalty charge by paying before the first day of the month, they explained that they could not afford to pay their electric bills until they had received their welfare or Social Security checks. These usually arrived on the third or fourth day of each month. Miss Carson felt that these unfortunate people were not in a position to readily pay the 5 percent penalty and that they were caught up in a huge impersonal system.

Having a social conscience and a desire to help these poor customers in some small way, Miss Carson decided to write a letter to the Mid-State Gas and Electric Company. She wrote the letter on her own time at home one evening and addressed it simply to the "President" of the power firm. In the letter she pointed out that a great many of the persons paying their bills at this particular bank were impoverished and were subsisting on either Social Security or welfare checks that arrived on the third or fourth day of the month. It would be very desirable if his company could change the date before which bills must be paid, without incurring a 5 percent penalty, from the first to the tenth day of the month. Miss Carson closed her letter by saying that this slight adjustment in the due date would probably cause little difficulty to the Gas and Electric Company but that it could give company officials a real sense of satisfaction by knowing that they had helped many unfortunate people in the community.

Miss Carson never received a direct reply from the Mid-State Company. Instead, about ten days later, she was summoned to see Mr. Webster, the personnel director, at the main office of the Central City Commercial Bank. It was Mr. Webster who had hired her both last summer and this one and Miss Carson had always considered him a warm, friendly person. She was unprepared for the harshness of his manner at this time.

Mr. Webster told her that the bank president had just received a letter from the president of the Mid-State Company threatening to remove its bill collection business (and possibly all its accounts) from the bank and to place it with a competitor bank because of the improper letter one of the bank's employees (Miss Carson) had sent to him. The Mid-State president had considered it impertinent for one of the bank's employees to tell it to change its business practices for the convenience of certain customers whose cause Miss Carson chose to champion. Mr. Webster told Miss Carson that this was a very grave matter and that she must immediately write a letter of apology to the Mid-State president. Failure to do so would make it necessary for him to discharge her.

After recovering from her initial shock at the storm that had been raised over her simple letter, she countered by stating that she thought large companies ought to be socially conscious and responsive to the problems of people in the community. Mr. Webster replied that a private business was not a social welfare agency. He further stated that it was inappropriate to discuss social issues at this time. The problem at hand was the threat to the bank's relations with an important account. Would she or would she not write the letter?

Miss Carson complied with this order and drafted a letter in Mr. Webster's office. His secretary immediately typed it for Miss Carson's signature.

Miss Carson went back to her job as a teller at the branch office and finished out the summer. Nothing more was said of the incident.

Questions

1. Was it improper for Miss Carson to send the letter to the president of the gas and electric company? Discuss.
2. Evaluate the reaction of the president of the gas and electric company to her letter. How would you have reacted?
3. Evaluate the response of the president of the Central City Commercial Bank and particularly that of Mr. Webster in this case.
4. Is a social conscience on the part of the management of a private business enterprise compatible with traditional business practices?

Suggestions for further reading

ANDREWS, KENNETH R. "Can the Best Corporations Be Made Moral?" *Harvard Business Review*, Vol. 51, No. 3 (May–June 1973), pp. 57–64.

BAUER, RAYMOND A., and DAN H. FENN, JR. "What Is a Corporate Social Audit?" *Harvard Business Review*, Vol. 51, No. 1 (January–February 1973), pp. 37–48.

BAUMHART, RAYMOND. *An Honest Profit*. New York: Holt, Rinehart & Winston, Inc., 1968.

DAVIS, KEITH and ROBERT L. BLOMSTROM. *Business and Society: Environment and Responsibility*, 3rd ed. New York: McGraw-Hill Book Company, 1976; Parts One and Two.

EELLS, RICHARD, and CLARENCE WALTON. *Conceptual Foundations of Business*, 3rd ed. Homewood, Ill.: Richard D. Irwin, Inc., 1974.

KNOWLES, HENRY P., and BORJE O. SAXBERG. "Human Relations and the Nature of Man," *Harvard Business Review*, Vol. 45, No. 2 (March–April 1967), pp. 22–24 ff.

LIKERT, RENSIS. *The Human Organization: Its Management and Value*. New York: McGraw-Hill Book Company, 1967.

————. *New Patterns of Management*. New York: McGraw-Hill Book Company, 1961.

McGREGOR, DOUGLAS. *The Human Side of Enterprise*. New York: McGraw-Hill Book Company, 1960.

————. *The Professional Manager*. New York: McGraw-Hill Book Company, 1967.

PURCELL, THEODORE V. "A Practical Guide to Ethics in Business." *Business and Society Review*, Vol. 13 (Spring 1975), pp. 43–50.

SEYBOLD, GENEVA. *Statements of Personnel Policy.* Studies in Personnel Policy, No. 169. New York: National Industrial Conference Board, 1959.

TANNENBAUM, ROBERT, and SHELDON A. DAVIS. "Values, Man and Organizations." *Industrial Management Review*, Vol. 10, No. 2 (Winter 1969), pp. 67–86.

WALTON, CLARENCE C. *Ethos and the Executitive.* Englewood Cliffs, N.J.: Prentice-Hall, Inc., 1969.

The personnel function

The work of personnel management pervades the entire organization. Personnel work must be carried on in the company too small to justify a separate personnel department. In larger establishments that do contain personnel departments, personnel management activities are performed by both operating managers and the staff personnel unit.

In this chapter we shall explore the terminology common to this field of endeavor, the personnel functions performed in organizations, the staff role of the personnel–industrial relations department, the division of authority and responsibility between line management and the staff personnel department in regard to the principal personnel functions, and organization of the personnel unit.

TERMINOLOGY

Over the years there has been some diversity in business practice in naming the function that is concerned with handling employment relationships. When specialized departments were first created in the 1920's and 1930's to handle the administration of the personnel program, they were usually called personnel departments. As a result of the rapid growth of unions in the 1930's and 1940's, many companies added the responsibilities of labor contract negotiations, contract administration, and grievance handling to the other activities of the personnel department. When this labor relations activity was combined with the personnel management work, many companies adopted the term *industrial relations* to apply to the new, enlarged function. This practice became especially prevalent in manufacturing companies, where the word *industrial* implied the concept of manufacturing and hence was deemed appropriate. In government, in hospitals and school, and in nonmanufacturing industries such as trade and finance the term personnel department is very commonly used. This term is employed even when the employees are represented by a union and the labor relations function is prominent.

Another frequently encountered term is *employee relations*. In current practice, then, the three terms—*personnel management, industrial relations,* and *employee relations*—are generally synonymous. If we wish to make fine distinctions, we can say that *industrial relations* is most often used in manufacturing firms, especially where the employees are heavily unionized and labor–management relations represent a substantial portion of the total function. The term *personnel department* or *personnel office* is used more commonly in nonmanufacturing organizations and in organizations where either the workers are nonunion or only a moderate portion are unionized. The term *employee relations* is often applied to both union and nonunion situations and to manufacturing and nonmanufacturing. In very recent years some corporations have used the term *human resources* to designate their personnel departments.

What is the content of this work? What functions are included under the designation *industrial relations* or *personnel management?* It encompasses the activities of recruitment and employment, human resource planning, employee training and management development, organization planning, organization development, wage and salary administration, health and safety, benefits and services, union–management relations, equal employment opportunity, and personnel research.

Looking at the matter from the standpoint of a field of knowledge or an academic discipline, we find that the terms *personnel management* or *personnel administration* have become widely accepted to designate that field concerned with all of the aforementioned topics plus applied human behavior areas such as supervision, motivation, work group behavior, communication, and managing change. In recent years schools of business administration and of management in universities have begun calling this academic area *human resources management* or *management of human resources.* The Academy of Management, which is a scholarly and professional society composed largely of university faculty members in schools of business and of management, changed the designation of its "manpower management" division to "personnel/human resources" division in 1975.

There are many departments, institutes, and schools of industrial relations (or industrial and labor relations) at colleges and universities throughout the country. These units carry on research, teaching, and extension programs in the whole broad areas of labor economics, organizational behavior, collective bargaining, labor law, income security, personnel administration, and labor union history and administration.

In order to be most accurate in describing this function or field of work in the business organization, it would perhaps be best to use the combined term *personnel management–industrial relations*. For the sake of conciseness, we shall use the term *personnel management* (or just *personnel*) and the term *industrial relations* interchangeably.

WHO DOES PERSONNEL WORK?

The very small company that employs, say, twenty-five or fifty people has no personnel department. Personnel policies and practices are generated by the president. Line management does the hiring, the training, the disciplining, and the firing. It establishes the rates of pay. Because the problems of production and sales usually seem more pressing to the employer, he generally does not develop a well-rounded, comprehensive personnel program. Decisions regarding employees are commonly made under the pressure of the situation without full regard for the long-run consequences.

In the larger organization it is not possible for the president and his line managers to handle adequately the many complex personnel management problems without specialized knowledge and help. Therefore, a personnel department must be established.

Now to the unsophisticated person it may seem that the creation of a separate staff personnel department is no different than the establishment of any other staff or service activity, such as engineering, purchasing, or advertising. If a company has grown to the point where functionalization becomes necessary, it can split off all product and equipment design work from line management and concentrate these duties in an engineering department. All relations with suppliers and the processing of purchase orders can be centralized in a purchasing department.

But personnel management is different from other staff specializations. Personnel management pervades the entire organization. Every individual who guides and directs the work of others, from the shop foreman all the way up to the corporation president, does personnel work. Now the nature of this work changes somewhat as one goes up the ladder of the organization structure. But regardless of level, every manager is truly a practicing personnel manager.

Consider for a moment the personnel management responsibilities of a first-line supervisor whether in factory or office. They are as follows:

Participate in the selection of new employees.
Orient new employees to their environment, organizational requirements, and their rights and privileges
Train employees.
Provide face-to-face leadership.
Appraise performance.
Coach and correct.
Counsel.
Recommend pay increases, promotions, transfers, layoffs, and discharges.
Enforce rules and maintain discipline.
Settle complaints and grievances.
Interpret and communicate management policies and directives to employees.

Interpret and communicate employee suggestions and criticisms to higher management.

Motivate subordinates and provide rewards for good performance and behavior.

Eliminate hazards and insure safe working practices.

It is not truly possible to separate the human relations and personnel functions of operating management from day-to-day problems such as getting out production, controlling costs, and meeting quality standards. Many personnel problems arise during the course of directing the work force and giving orders and instructions.

Staff Role of the Personnel Department

The personnel (or industrial relations) department operates in an auxiliary, advisory, or facilitative relationship to other departments in the organization. Any staff unit, whether it be personnel or otherwise, exists to help the line or operating departments do their work more effectively. It has been created in the first place to take advantage of specialized talent and knowledge.[1]

The personnel department generally performs the following roles:

1. Policy initiation and formulation.
2. Advice.
3. Service.
4. Control.

Let us examine each of these activities.

Policy Initiation and Formulation. The executive in charge of the personnel department (he may be called the personnel director, the industrial relations director, or the vice-president in charge of personnel) is the one individual most actively involved in policy creation. It is his responsibility to propose and draft new policies or policy revisions to cover recurring problems or to prevent anticipated problems. Ordinarily he proposes these to the president of the company, and it is upon the latter's authority that the policy is actually issued. When proposing a new or revised policy the personnel director must analyze problems that have occurred in the past, survey other companies to determine how they handle similar situations, discuss the matter with his colleagues and subordinates, and give due consideration to the prevailing philosophy in the organization. In effect he does all the necessary research and staff work, but in most cases the new policy is actually authorized by the president and/or the board of directors. On small policy matters the personnel director ordinarily may determine and institute policies himself.

---

[1] Line and staff concepts are discussed further in Chapter 6, "Organization." Line positions and departments are those without which the organization could not function even for a day. In a manufacturing company those who make the product and those who sell it are considered line. In a department store, buying and selling activities are considered line. In a college the faculty members are line, whereas such individuals as the dean of students, manager of purchasing, and the controller are staff.

Advice. A major portion of the activities of those engaged in staff personnel work is in the nature of counsel and advice to line managers. Countless examples can be given. A shop foreman may be confronted with a grievance over distribution of overtime. Another foreman may have a problem employee who he feels should be disciplined or even suspended. How should he go about doing this? At the time of the annual review of all salaried personnel for possible pay increases, the personnel manager plays a key role in advising operating managers on the administration of the program. An apparent concerted slowdown may occur in the assembly department. It may have been instituted by the union in retaliation for the cutting of piece rates the week before. How should production supervision handle this situation?

In all of the foregoing examples the personnel director and his staff are expected to be fully familiar with personnel policy, the labor agreement, past practice, and the needs and welfare of both the company and the employees in order to develop a sound solution. The successful personnel specialist must be people centered. He must be sensitive to the feelings, wants, and motives of other people. At the same time he must continually be cognizant of his obligation to preserve the structure and functioning of the organization. In fact, this really is the essence of personnel management. Management must seek to so direct and coordinate the efforts of the people that the goals of the organization are achieved while at the same time providing need satisfactions for the members of that organization.

In carrying out the advice-giving role, the members of the personnel department do much more than simply supply oral advice to other members of the organization. Advice also includes the preparation and communication of bulletins, reports, and procedural guidelines for the interpretation and implementation of policy. For example, the personnel department issues explanatory statements regarding the implementation of equal employment opportunity policy, compliance with the Occupational Safety and Health Act, and the application of a new union–company labor agreement.

Service. The service responsibilities of the personnel department are apparent when one examines such things as the employment, training, and benefits functions. The tasks of recruiting, interviewing, and testing job applicants are performed in the personnel office. Training programs are planned, organized, and often staffed through the personnel office. The personnel group must see that adequate instructional materials and facilities are available. Once pension and insurance programs have been set up, all claims must be processed through the personnel department. The maintenance of adequate employee records is a service function that permeates all functional specialties within the personnel field.

Control. The personnel department carries out important control functions. It monitors the performance of line departments and other staff departments to insure that they conform to established personnel policy, procedures, and practices. The control function of the personnel department is quite comparable to the activities of a quality control group that measures product variables to insure conformance to engineering specifications or to the activities of the auditing staff that inspects accounting records to ascertain conformance with prescribed standards.

What are some examples of the control functions of the personnel-industrial relations department? There are many. Company policy may declare that all salaried employees shall be appraised as to performance and potential at least once a year. If certain supervisors fail to transmit their performance appraisal reports to the personnel office when required, then a follow-up is clearly required. A control activity of particular contemporary importance is that of monitoring operating departments and divisions to insure their compliance with Federal and state nondiscrimination and affirmative action programs.

As part of a continuing program for bringing the safety message to production workers, foremen may be expected to conduct a brief weekly safety meeting for their men. If some foremen fail to do so, a member of the personnel department (usually the safety director) will certainly bring this matter to their attention. If discussion with the parties involved yields no direct improvement, then the safety director will generally bring the issue up with the foremen's immediate line superior.

A common form of staff control over line management personnel is *procedural control*. This means that managers and supervisors must follow established procedures in carrying out certain personnel management actions. For example, in order to discharge an employee who has allegedly committed a serious violation of a company rule, line supervision may have to follow a clearly defined procedure. Depending upon the particular circumstances, this may involve submitting written evidence, obtaining testimony of witnesses, notifying the union, and granting the man a full hearing.

To raise an employee's salary the supervisor generally must abide by certain procedures. This may involve submitting a performance rating form at the time of the request, keeping the size of the increase and the man's total salary within prescribed limits, and doing this at certain designated times of the year.

Many times the personnel unit will conduct continuing audits of the line departments. Examples are measures of accidents, grievances, absenteeism, voluntary quits, and disciplinary actions. Quite often the control activities of a staff unit, such as the personnel department, require that it exert pressure upon line managers and supervisors. If the control work is not done with proper regard for the need to build a cooperative, healthy relationship with line personnel, serious dissension can occur. The personnel manager and his staff should exert their principal efforts toward counseling and educating line supervisors regarding the need for following established policies, procedures, and practices. The errant supervisor should be permitted to correct his ways first. If all attempts at persuasion fail, then, of course, the problem must be discussed with higher management.

PERSONNEL AND INDUSTRIAL RELATIONS FUNCTIONS

Just what is the content of personnel and industrial relations activities? As stated before, personnel management activities are carried on both by the staff personnel department and by operating management in the course of directing the activities of the work force. Let us now examine the principal personnel functions and note the more common division of responsibilities between the staff personnel unit and operating, or line, management. It should, however, be borne in mind that variation from the pattern described may occur in particular companies because of special circumstances.

Employment

This function includes recruitment, selection, and induction into the organization. The initial decision to add someone to the payroll is made by line management. It is also its responsibility to determine the content of the job to be performed and the employee qualifications necessary to perform the job satisfactorily. Very commonly, statements of job content and employee qualifications have been previously worked out jointly between line management and the personnel unit. These are recorded in the form of job descriptions and job specifications. The personnel department must develop and maintain adequate sources of labor. It must also set up and operate the employee selection system, which may include interviews, selection tests, a medical examination, and reference checks. Quite commonly the role of the personnel group is one of screening with the final decision to hire or reject being made by the supervisor who requested the new employee. However, in the case of a large-scale hiring program of unskilled or semiskilled workers, the personnel department is commonly granted full and final authority to make the hiring decision.

The new employee's supervisor bears important responsibilities for introducing him to his new work environment. This is often called orientation or indoctrination.

Transfer, Promotion, Layoff

For these tasks the personnel department serves primarily in a coordinative capacity. When employees are moved from one department to another either because of the needs of the business or because of individual requests, the personnel records may be studied to ascertain that they possess the requisite skills. Layoffs typically are processed by the personnel department to insure that the proper order of preference is followed. This can become quite complicated if combinations of job, departmental, and plant-wide seniority rights must be observed. When a vacancy occurs in a position, it may be filled by promotion from within or by direct hiring from outside the company. This decision is often made jointly between the personnel director and the executive in charge of the department where the vacancy has occurred. Many companies have established policies to cover matters of this type. The actual final decision as to which candidate is chosen for the promotion is largely made by the executive in whose unit the vacancy has occurred.

Training and Development

On-the-job training and coaching are performed by the line supervisor or by a specially designated employee who acts in the role of an instructor. It is the responsibility of the personnel-industrial relations group to determine training needs in cooperation with line management. Once the needs are established, the personnel training specialists must design a program to accomplish the desired results. If the program takes the form of in-service classroom courses, it usually is administered by the personnel unit.

Coaching, performance appraisal, and postappraisal counseling, job rotation, understudies, and special broadening assignments are largely executed by operating managers but coordinated by a central personnel staff.

For those enterprises that are engaging in an organization development activity the personal manager or the personnel specialist serves in a consulting role to an operating department. He plans programs in cooperation with managers of operating departments, diagnoses "people" problems, conducts various workshop type programs, and provides feedback to the managers about ongoing problems.

Compensation Administration

The work of designing and installing a job evaluation program is handled, for the most part, by the personnel department with some consultation with line managers. The decision to adopt a particular pay structure with pay grades and fixed minima and maxima for the grades is a top management responsibility.

The day-to-day work of analyzing jobs, evaluating their dollar worth according to a formal job evaluation plan, and maintaining suitable records is a staff personnel function.

Periodic wage and salary surveys of the labor market area are conducted by the personnel specialists, but any firm decision to raise or change the entire pay schedule is practically always reserved for the chief executive officer of the organization.

Health and Safety

A significant part of an occupational health program is the identification and control of agents within the working environment that can cause occupational disease. Some agents can be gases, dusts, fumes, toxic chemicals or metals, noise, heat, radiation, biological substances, and stress. Industrial hygienists are employed to identify and control such hazards to health.

Other important elements of an employee health program are preemployment medical examinations, periodic examinations for those working on jobs having exposure to occupation disease-causing agents, rendering of first-aid, treatment of minor ailments such as colds and headaches, and providing health education information. Small companies typically hire physicians, nurses, and industrial hygienists only on a consulting or part-time basis. Large firms tend to be staffed with full-time personnel in these areas.

The safety program is directed toward the prevention of work injuries. The main elements are engineering, education, and enforcement. The safety director, who is usually a member of the personnel department, works closely with the plant engineering unit to have machines and equipment properly guarded. New production processes and machines must be so designed and constructed that the possibility of human injury is remote. Employee safety education is a cooperative program conducted by both the staff safety director and all foremen. The safety director must prepare safety displays, distribute safety leaflets, and develop safety instructional material. Every foreman must instruct his people how to perform their jobs safely. He may also be called upon to run a weekly safety meeting. Enforcement of safety rules is primarily a responsibility of every foreman.

Strong emphasis has been given to the health and safety function since the enactment of the Occupational Safety and Health Act in 1970. Of course, progressive companies recognized this to be an important area of management responsibility long before the adoption of this Act.

Discipline and Discharge

Discipline has two principal meanings. In the first sense it means "training that molds or corrects." This means the achieving and maintaining of orderly employee behavior because the people understand and believe in the established codes of conduct. The second meaning of the term *discipline* refers to punishment of wrongdoers.

The supervisor, whether in factory or office, must bear primary responsibility for training his people to abide by the rules of behavior and for initiating punishment for the few whose conduct deviates from the norm.

The personnel department commonly assumes the responsibility for formulating the list of necessary rules together with the range of penalties for each offense. Frequently this list of rules and penalties is discussed and cleared with high-level line management before it is issued and communicated throughout the organization.

Most commonly, actual approval by the personnel department has to be obtained before an employee may be discharged. The reason is that discharge is a very severe penalty and should be used only when a very clear case can be shown. In addition, it is especially vital to achieve companywide uniformity in the handling of such cases.

Labor Relations

When a union has been certified by the National Labor Relations Board, as the result of an election, as the sole and exclusive bargaining agency for the employees, then management must bargain with it in regard to wages, rates of pay, hours of work, and other conditions of employment. The principal tasks involved in handling labor relations are contract negotiation, contract interpretation and administration, and grievance handling.

The personnel–industrial relations staff plays a very significant role in labor–management relations. The director of industrial relations usually serves as a key member of the bargaining team, often acting as chief management spokesman. In operating on a day-to-day basis under the terms of the labor agreement, line supervision often finds frequent occasion to consult the personnel staff regarding such matters as allocation of overtime, handling of transfers and layoffs, and the application of contract work rules.

Although nearly all grievance procedures as spelled out in the labor contract specify that the front-line supervisor shall be the first to hear and act upon an employee grievance, in all but the most routine cases the supervisor typically consults the personnel office before giving an answer. The personnel department is very commonly listed as either the second or third management step in the grievance procedure. In effect the personnel department representative is given line authority to make a binding settlement.

The personnel–industrial relations staff is granted such great authority in grievance handling in order to insure due regard for precedent and plantwide consistency of action. In addition, many grievances have plantwide or even companywide implications. Mishandling of a case could cause grave consequences.

Benefits and Services

Included under this category are pensions, group life insurance, hospital and medical insurance, sickness leave pay plans, supplemental unemployment compensation, loan funds, credit unions, social programs, recreational programs, and college tuition refund plans.

The actual decision to establish or to expand these programs is nearly always made by top line management upon the advice and consultation of the personnel staff. The actual design of pension and insurance programs requires a great deal of technical knowledge. These programs are generally worked out in conjunction with insurance companies or insurance consultants. After these plans are installed, the day-to-day processing of claims is handled by the personnel department.

Organization Planning

Organization planning requires the development of a concept of a company as a structure or system. It may require the delineation of the concepts of centralization or decentralization in terms of executive behavior and the locus of decision-making authority. The organization planning staff must prepare organization charts and position guides. It must counsel the chief executive officer and line management on organization theory and practice and with respect to company reorganization and expansion.

Originally this activity was carried on primarily in the office of the corporation president. And the president still has final responsibility in this area. But the growing complexity of large-scale enterprises and the increasing sophistication of organization theory has caused organization planning to emerge as a specialty in itself. The personnel office gathers data, does research, prepares plans, and gives advice to the office of the president in his vital area.

Organization Development

A Conference Board survey conducted in 1975 revealed that organization development has emerged as a major personnel activity since an earlier investigation in 1965.[2] Organization development (often called, simply, OD) is a general approach for improving the effectiveness of an organization that utilizes a variety of applied behavioral science methodologies. Among the objectives of OD are to increase the level of trust and supportiveness among people in the organization, enhance interpersonal skills, make communication more open and direct, di-

[2] Allen R. Janger, *The Personnel Function: Changing Objectives and Organization*, Report No. 712 (New York: The Conference Board), 1977, p. 48.

rectly confront problems, and to tap the knowledge of all who can contribute to problem solutions wherever they may be in the organization.

Consultants are often involved in OD work. They work jointly with management to collect data, diagnose problems, and work out solutions. Typical kinds of OD activities or interventions are confrontation meetings, team building, survey feedback, conflict resolution, T-group or laboratory training, and managerial grid exercises and projects.

Human Resource Planning

Another new function that has emerged in recent years is human resource planning (also called manpower planning). Sometimes a specific person or office has this as its primary responsibility; more commonly the responsibilities are shared by several people within the corporate personal unit. Human resource planning is the process by which a firm insures that it has the right number of qualified persons available at the proper times, performing jobs that are useful to the organization, and which provide satisfaction for the individuals involved. The principal elements involved in human resource planning are as follows: (1) goals and plans of organization; (2) current human resource situation including skills inventory; (3) human resource forecast including comparison of projected future demand for employees with projected supply; (4) designing programs to implement the plans (recruitment, selection, performance appraisal, transfer, promotion, training, motivation, compensation); and (5) audit and adjustment.

Many companies confine their human resource planning activities to those kinds of skills that are more commonly in short supply and that require a long development time. These are personnel in the managerial, professional, technical, and skilled trades fields.

Information and research data generated by manpower planning specialists are made available to personnel officers and operating executives in the divisions and plants. The implementation of the plans is, of course, a collaborative activity among personnel officers and many operating managers throughout the organization.

Equal Employment Opportunity

Several Federal laws have caused both public and private employers to place great emphasis upon equal employment opportunity. Among these laws and regulations are Title VII of the Civil Rights Act of 1964 as amended, Executive Order 11246 (1965) as amended, Equal Pay Act of 1963, and Age Discrimination in Employment Act of 1967. Employers are not allowed to discriminate in regard to race, color, sex, national origin, religion, or age. Government regulations require companies having more than 100 employees, or more than 50 employees if the company holds a government contract or subcontract, to designate an official to be in charge of the equal employment opportunity function and to serve as a point of contact with the government compliance agency.[3]

Very commonly the chief personnel executive in a company (that is, the individual in charge of the entire personnel department) bears the major responsi-

[3] Ibid., p. 83.

bility for insuring that the organization complies with the various equal employment opportunity laws and regulations. He often delegates the day-to-day detailed administration to someone within the personnel department who either specializes in this field of work or who performs these duties along with others such as the employment function. Usually the chief executive officer (CEO) of a company, whether he be called the chairman of the board or the president, plays a key role in the formulation and implementation of equal employment policy.

In the Conference Board survey mentioned earlier, 97 percent of the companies surveyed stated that equal employment opportunity had emerged as a major personnel function since 1965.[4]

Personnel and Behavioral Research

Although most companies do not conduct research in the personnel and behavioral area, there are some pacesetting firms which have done so. Among these are General Electric, International Business Machines, General Motors, American Telephone and Telegraph, Procter and Gamble, and Texas Instruments. A major area of experimentation in recent years has focused on ways of simultaneously improving worker productivity and increasing the quality of working life. Other important areas for investigation are employee attitudes and motivation, predicting success in management, and organizational relationships.

Personnel Information Systems

Today, many organizations have staffs of people trained in mathematical analysis, computers, and management information systems. Some companies have applied these capabilities to personnel work. Among the applications have been human resource planning, skills inventories, employee benefits analysis, and productivity studies.

ORGANIZATION FOR THE PERSONNEL FUNCTION

The executive in charge of the personnel department must be a member of the top management team. With assistance from members of his department he must set up management development programs, develop compensation plans for executives, advise the chief executive officer on compliance with equal employment opportunity regulations, and establish a viable relationship with the union which represents the hourly-paid employees. These are but a partial list of the many major executive responsibilities of the chief personnel officer in an organization. Truly the personnel department serves the entire organization. The executive in charge must have sufficient stature in the organization to be a trusted advisor and member of top management and to design and implement a really effective personnel program.

The top personnel executive should report organizationally to either the chief executive officer or the chief operating officer. Commonly in business organizations these officials are called the chairman of the board of directors and the

---

[4] Ibid., p. 40.

president, respectively. Because the quality of the human resources determine the success of an enterprise, the executive in charge of personnel should be involved in top management meetings at which enterprise strategy, plans, and programs are formulated. In terms of job titles the top or senior executives in charge of personnel most commonly holds the title of vice-president. The term director (of personnel) is also frequently used.

Unfortunately, the presidents of some companies are ignorant of the proper role of a personnel department; hence they relegate it to a low level in the organization and staff it with unqualified people. This sometimes happens in small companies. Just because a supervisor gets along well with others and has accumulated many years of company experience, this does not mean that he is the ideal choice for personnel manager. Some company presidents have the erroneous notion that personnel work is primarily one of record keeping, keeping the workers happy, running the employment office, and arranging the annual Christmas party. With such an attitude, the company is bound to acquire a third-rate personnel program.

Personnel management and industrial relations are an emerging profession. A great many colleges and universities offer complete programs of study in this field. Some offer specialized degrees in industrial relations. The field contains a vast body of knowledge, much of which is derived from sound research, and a considerable body of literature. There are a number of professional societies throughout the country representing practicing personnel managers and specialists. When looking for someone to head the personnel–industrial relations program, a company president would be well advised to seek an individual who possesses a proper professional background in terms of education and work experience.

Organization for a Medium-size, Single-plant Company

Figure 3-1 shows the sections comprising a typical personnel department in a single plant company having employment in the range of, say, 2,000–5,000 persons. The principal functions carried out in each of these sections are shown on this organization chart. Each section would be headed by a manager or supervisor and would contain personnel specialists such as job analyst, employment interviewer, safety engineer, and training specialist as required. In this example, it is assumed that certain categories of the work force, such as all the production and maintenance employees, are represented by a union; hence a labor relations section is included on the chart.

How large a personnel staff is necessary to service an organization of, say, 3,000 employees? The answer to this depends to a considerable extent upon the attitude of top management, which really determines how comprehensive a personnel program is to be carries on. Some companies have no formal training for either their employees or their managers. They may have no job evaluation system and never conduct a real area wage survey. They may provide only marginal first-aid facilities and have an inadequate safety program. With such an approach to personnel management, a company may get by with a very small personnel department and thereby save considerably on salaries. But it would certainly suffer in terms of lowered efficiency, more work injuries, lower morale, and more human relations problems.

Figure 3-1
The Organization and Functions of a Personnel Department.

Surveys have shown the average number of professional and technical staff members employed in the personnel department for various types of industries. These studies have shown the number of persons engaged in personnel work to range from about .60 to .90 per 100 total employees in the company. The ratio, as it is called, tends to be closer to the .90 figure for smaller companies and closer to the .60 figure for the very large corporations.[5] Using .75 per 100 employees as an average, we would expect to find approximately 23 persons in the personnel department (exclusive of clerical workers) in a company having 3,000 employees.

Large Divisionalized Companies

Very large corporations generally have many establishments scattered throughout the United States and in foreign countries. Organizationally they typically contain three broad levels of management; (1) top corporate headquarters; (2) division management; and (3) plant management. They are often decentralized in the sense that each division and plant manager has profit-center accountability. He possesses general authority and responsibility over his unit in order to obtain the results desired. He has nearly all the staff services such as personnel, purchasing, engineering, and accounting under his jurisdiction in order to realize

[5] Roberta J. Nelson, G. W. England, and Dale Yoder, "Personnel Ratios and Costs, 1962," *Personnel,* Vol. 40, No. 1 (January–February, 1963), pp. 17–26.

the goals of his unit. Thus, these large firms have a personnel–industrial relations group at corporate headquarters and at each of the plants. They may also have units at the division level.

The personnel director at the plant level typically reports to the plant manager. He receives policy direction and technical guidance from the headquarters group. He is responsible for administering the personnel program in the plant. This personnel director holds a rank equivalent to that of other major executives in the plant, such as the chief engineer, controller, and the manager of manufacturing.

Questions for review and discussion

1. "The activities involved in personnel management pervade the entire organization. They are not performed solely by those in the personnel department." Explain the foregoing.
2. Explain the following four roles performed by a personnel–industrial relations department:
   a. Policy initiation and formulation.
   b. Advice.
   c. Service.
   d. Control.
   Give examples for each of these.
3. Name and give the content of the principal personnel–industrial relations functions.
4. Describe the staff role of the personnel department.
5. Explain the duties and responsibilities of the personnel department and of line supervision with respect to the following functions:
   a. Employment.
   b. Training and development.
   c. Safety.
6. At what level in the organization structure should the executive in charge of the personnel–industrial relations department be situated? Discuss.
7. In a multiplant company do you think it would be practical to have the personnel manager in each plant report directly to the corporate personnel vice-president? Discuss.

Case problems

PROBLEM 1

Recently 700 employees of a county nursing home and the county home for the aged (two public facilities located on the same plot of land) voted overwhelmingly to be represented by a union. The collective bargaining unit includes a great variety of employee groups from custodial and maintenance to professional nurses and social workers. Upon being interviewed after the union had won bargaining rights, the employees claimed that arbitrary and inconsistent treatment by the supervisors comprised the main reasons for their voting in the union. They charged flagrant favoritism and discriminatory treatment. They also charged that the supervisors made it a practice to discharge employees for inconsequential reasons or without adequate prior warnings. Employees were subject to frequent criticism by their supervisors in regard to their job performance. Even though many of the supervisors had been promoted from the "ranks," many of them seemed to abuse their authority in dealing with their subordinates.

Top managers in both "homes" were genuinely surprised when they first learned, during negotiations, about the serious and wide-spread employee discontent.

Question

1. Assuming that there is substantial truth to the employee complaints, what does this indicate about the quality of personnel management in the two institutions? Specifically what seems to be wrong? What should be done to correct the conditions?

PROBLEM 2

The Latham-Craft Company manufactures several lines of wood and metal products consisting of kitchen bowls, toys, croquet sets, and lawn furniture. The firm has been in business fifty years and is family owned, the president being a major stockholder. Its branded items are well established in the marketplace. The company has earned a profit (though usually modest) for all but one of the past ten years. It employs a total of 350 people, of whom fifty are in the white-collar and managerial group. The production and maintenance employees are represented by a union.

The executive organization consists of the president, to whom report the sales vice-president, chief engineer, office manager, purchasing manager, director of product research and quality control, treasurer, and the plant superintendent. Sixteen factory foremen and two production control coordinators report to the plant superintendent.

The company is beset with a number of problems in regard to the management of its work force. The rate of employee turnover is high. This is caused by a high rate of voluntary quits and of discharges because of disciplinary problems and absenteeism. The company pays its production and maintenance employees rates that are equal to the average for the wood products industry but considerably below the going rates in its community, which contains companies in the automobile, electrical and steel industries.

The hiring of new workers is handled jointly by the purchasing manager, who does the initial screening, and the production superintendent, who makes the final hiring decision. Both complain frequently about the caliber of help they are able to obtain. Most are young men with little training and experience who have failed to finish high school. The probationary period as spelled out in the union agreement is sixty days. The purchasing manager does little or no checking into the background of the new hires. His reasoning is that the company invests little in them during their first few weeks on the job, and if they should prove unsatisfactory, they can be discharged easily.

The accident rate in the plant has been very high for several years. Most of the injuries occur when the employees get their fingers or hands caught while operating or servicing the machines. The company president has become concerned about the rising cost for workmen's compensation insurance, because the premium is based upon the actual loss experience in his plant. The foremen complain that whenever they try to suspend a worker for a serious infraction of a safety rule the company management usually backs down and rescinds the action in the face of pressure from the union business agent.

All of the present group of foremen have been promoted from the ranks of hourly paid employees. They have never received any formal training in supervision. They view their role as one of primarily pushing the workers to get out production. Very few exercise initiative or assume responsibility for seeing that housekeeping is improved, maintenance work is done on time, or that improved methods are instituted in their departments. The formen are somewhat demoralized. They see few opportunities for advancement or even for salary increases. The company has no system for evaluating the performance of any of its managerial or clerical employees. There is no formal salary structure. If a man has been doing a good job, if he has received no increase in pay for a long time, and if he complains firmly enough to his boss, he may receive a token pay increase.

The company does have a hospital and medical insurance plan as well as a pension plan. Claims are handled by the office manager.

For many years the company made small interest-free loans to employees to help them purchase necessary household items, for extraordinary sickness expenses, and the like. This policy was finally abandoned because of the administrative burden and because of the ill will generated when management denied a loan it felt was not justified. Recently there has been a rash of garnishments of employees' pay initiated by local small loan companies because employees have failed to repay their loans.

Questions

1. What appears to be the central problem in this company?
2. What organizational change or addition might be made to help solve the problem?
3. What personnel programs would you recommend be adopted?

Suggestions for further reading

BURACK, ELMER H. and EDWIN L. MILLER. "The Personnel Function in Transition," *California Management Review*, Vol. XVIII, No. 3 (Spring 1976), pp. 32–38.

BUREAU OF NATIONAL AFFAIRS, INC. *Personnel Management*. Washington, D.C.: BNA, Inc., 1970.

FOULKES, FRED K. "The Expanding Role of the Personnel Function," *Harvard Business Review*, Vol. 53, No. 2 (March–April 1975), pp. 71–84.

————, and HENRY M. MORGAN. "Organizing and Staffing the Personnel Function," *Harvard Business Review*, Vol. 55, No. 3 (May–June 1977), pp. 142–154.

HOFFMAN, FRANK O. "Identity Crisis in the Personnel Function," *Personnel Journal*, Vol. 57 (March 1978), pp. 126–132+.

JANGER, ALLEN R. *The Personnel Function: Changing Objectives and Organization* (Report No. 712), New York: The Conference Board, 1977.

MEYER, HERBERT E. "Personnel Directors Are the New Corporate Heroes," *Fortune*, Vol. XCII, No. 2 (February 1976), pp. 84–88, 139.

RITZER, GEORGE and HARRISON TRICE. *An Occupation in Conflict: A Study of the Personnel Manager*. Ithaca, New York: New York State School of Industrial and Labor Relations, 1969.

STAATS, ELMER B. "Personnel Management: The Starting Place." *Public Personnel Management*, Vol. 5 (November–December 1976), pp. 434–441.

II

LABOR-MANAGEMENT RELATIONS

Unions
and
management

Organized labor exerts a strong influence upon the individual company and upon the economic, social, and political climate in the United States. When the employees of a company are represented by a union, policies and practices affecting the employment relationship that were formerly decided by management alone are now subject to joint determination. Wages, hours, and other conditions of employment are bargained between union and management. The decisions reached in contract negotiations on economic items often have an effect upon the pricing of company products and services. This in turn may influence the competitive position of the firm in the product market. When management contemplates taking certain personnel actions, it must give consideration to the attitude and position of the union on these matters. Many actions that had been conducted between management representatives and employees as individuals (before the entrance of the union) are now carried on through union stewards and other elected officers. This is particularly true in grievance handling. The attitudes of the union often shape the way such management techniques as job evaluation, time study, and wage incentive plans are applied.

In the broader social, economic, and political sphere, we find that organized labor plays a very significant role. Labor unions tend to adopt rather definite stands on social issues, such as racial discrimination, medical and hopsital care for the general population, and public housing. They try to influence the decisions of state legislatures and the United States Congress on unemployment insurance, workers' compensation, and social security legislation (as do employer organizations, such as the National Association of Manufacturers). Economically the wage (broadly defined to include fringe benefits) settlements reached in major industries through collective bargaining often affect the volume of employment and rate of introduction of technological improvements not only in individual companies but also in the whole industry.

Because of the very prominent role that unions play in many organizations and in our society as a whole, it is important to develop an adequate understanding of why employees join unions; why some persons reject unionization; union membership and rate of growth; union organization, objectives, and behavior of unions; the effect of the union upon management; and factors contributing to harmonious labor–management relations. These topics and their ramifications will be covered in this chapter. Chapter 5, "Collective Bargaining," will be concerned with labor relations law, structure for bargaining, negotiating the agreement, principal bargaining issues, and dispute settlement procedures.

MOTIVATION TO JOIN UNIONS

Why do employees join a union? Since human behavior is goal directed, what drives and wants can be fulfilled by membership in a union? Let us now examine the objectives that employees expect to satisfy through union membership.

Greater Bargaining Power

The individual worker possess very little bargaining power in comparison with that of his employer. Very few employees are indispensable. A company can generally get along without a particular worker. The employer is in a position to say to the individual employee "Take or leave the wage and conditions of work I offer you." A worker's bargaining strength lies in his ability to quit if he is not satisfied with his wage rate and other conditions of employment. However, he soon learns that he cannot continually resign from one job after another when he is dissatisfied. This imposes too great a financial and emotional burden upon him. Therefore, employees have found that although their bargaining power as individuals is very limited, they can frequently equal that of the employer by organizing a union and taking concerted action. The threat or actuality of a strike by the union represents the economic and social power that often causes the company to increase its wages to a point where they are acceptable to the union.

The only situation in which an individual employee possesses considerable bargaining power occurs when he has a rare and valuable skill or talent. Thus, we find that in artistic and athletic professions, certain exceptionally gifted stars are able to bargain on equal terms with their employers. Likewise, certain executive and professional people in industry are able to command very high salaries because they possess an exceptional talent. But the vast majority of the wage and salary earners are in no such fortunate position. They are replaceable and must take pretty much what is offered them.

Make Their Voices Heard

The desire for self-expression is a fundamental human drive for most people. They wish to communicate their aims, feelings, complaints, and ideas to others. Most employees wish to be more than cogs in a large machine. They want management to listen to them. The union provides a mechanism through which these feelings and thoughts can be transmitted to management.

The entry of a union into an organization brings with it the establishment of a formalized grievance procedure. This provides a means by which employee complaints and problems are brought to the attention of management. The union stewards and officers represent the interests of the employees in presenting these problems to supervision and to higher management.

Minimize Favoritism and Discrimination

Supervisors must make a great many decisions that affect the pay, status, position, and work of their subordinates. Many of these decisions are highly subjective in nature. They are influenced by the personal relationships existing between the supervisor and each of his employees. Sometimes when one man is granted a larger wage increase than others, they feel that favoritism may have had a part in the decision. Unions press for equality of treatment. For example, one of their maxims is "One job, one rate." This means that all persons doing the same kind of work should received the same wage rate. As an alternative to this, we may find that the union accepts the concept of a range of wages for each job, but that it insists that all in-grade wage increases be made strictly according to seniority. So it is with other personnel actions, such as promotions, transfers, layoffs, and vacation preference. Unions advocate that the major (but not necessarily the only) criterion for decision making be seniority. It may not always result in the best person getting the promotion or being retained during a layoff, but it is an objective way of making difficult decisions.

Social Factors

People are commonly influenced in their actions by the behavior of their associates. Many employees are persuaded to join a union by their fellow workers. Often the individual is motivated to go along with the crowd—to be one of the gang. He seeks group acceptance and a feeling of belonging. Sometimes social motivation takes the form of group pressure. The individual who refuses to join the union often has a very difficult time at work. He may be ostracized, his machine may break down, or his lunch bucket may get "lost."

Cultural factors also play a part in the disposition of people to join a union. For those who have been raised in a working-class neighborhood where one's father and indeed all of the men in the community belong to the union, acceptance of the union as a normal part of the employment situation seems natural. This condition in which union membership is simply accepted as a way of life is true in certain areas and certain industries in the United States (for example, in coal mining areas, and in the garment industry in New York City). However, this condition represents a minority of the situations when one looks at the union movement in general.

Outlet When Advancement Blocked

Many employees will have nothing to do with a union as long as they are doing well in their careers. If their expectations in terms of pay increases, better jobs as they gain more experience, promotions and greater status do actually materialize, then they may feel that there is no necessity to pay dues to a union. They may even feel that the union would impede their progress because of seniority rules and because the individual member cannot get ahead faster than the entire group. However, we often find that when a person senses that his progress up the organizational ladder is blocked, when he can no longer get ahead on his own initiative, then he experiences a period of readjustment. Initially he may be frustrated. But often he turns to the union as an outlet for his wants. Through collective action the union may obtain the economic benefits from the employer that the individual could not get on his own. If the person has aspirations for a position of responsibility and leadership, he may even achieve an elective union office.

Compulsion Via the Union Contract

Many agreements that are negotiated between employers and unions contain a "union shop" provision (or some variation of it) that requires that all employees must join the union and pay dues within a certain period of time after they have been hired. If they refuse to join they may be discharged. A "union shop" clause in a labor agreement is one form of union security. Other aspects of the union security issue will be discussed in Chapter 5.

MOTIVATION TO REJECT UNIONS

Since only one fourth of the labor force in the United States belongs to unions, it must be apparent that many workers either definitely oppose the prospect of unionization for themselves or at least are timid and reluctant to join. What influences operate to cause employees to reject the union?

Cultural Factors

Many people in American society distrust unions and what they stand for. They feel that unions stand for collectivism, socialism, and the welfare state. They feel that unions are somewhat un-American, that they stand in opposition to the traditional American concepts of free enterprise, indivdual freedom, and individual initiative. They feel that a man should stand on his own two feet and get ahead on his own merits. They read in the newspapers that a powerful union has shut down an essential service or industry and that the public must suffer. They resent the union, its method of action, and what it stands for. Sentiments such as the foregoing are much more common in certain segments of our society than others. Geographically, they are common in the South, in rural areas, and in small towns. Small businessmen and farmers often hold such views. Likewise many in white-collar, professional, and executive occupations believe this.

Social Status and Individualism

Professional employees in the private sector (such as engineers and accountants) and self-employed professionals (such as physicians) have tended not to form or join unions. Instead they have sought to advance the interests of themselves and their professions through membership in professional associations. Many professionals argue that unionization and collective bargaining are appropriate for hourly paid, blue-collar workers, but that professionals have higher status and higher education and do not need (or should not need) unions to promote their interests. Also many professionals are individualistic in orientation. They feel that their employers will recognize them for their performance on the job. They feel they can bargain for themselves.

The kind of professional associations that have been most effective in promoting the interests of their members are those that are composed of self-employed professionals such as the American Medical Association and the American Bar Association. These associations work to control entrance to the profession by rigorous educational qualifications, examinations, and state licensing. These devices keep the profession from being overcrowded and thus keep incomes high.

Certain kinds of professionals have embraced unionism and collective bargaining rather strongly in the past decade. Principal among these have been public school teachers and nurses. Employed in large numbers in organizations, treated more as workers than professionals, and paid more modestly than other professionals, teachers and nurses have sought protection through union participation.

Identification with Management

White-collar, technical, and professional employees tend to identify themselves with management. Since they work in close proximity to supervisors and executives, there is a tendency to acquire the management viewpoint toward unions. These groups also feel that they can advance into management. They are looking upward. They wish to impress favorably their immediate superiors in the organization. They often feel that membership in a union might even hinder their chances of promotion.

Fear of Reprisal

Many employees do not join unions because they fear that management will punish them if they do so. Although the right of employees to form and join unions, free of interference by employers, has been protected by the National Labor Relations Act since 1935, the power of management in the workplace is great and pervasive. Mangement can discriminate in many subtle ways against prounion sympathizers in a workforce. Overt discrimination, such as a discharge or a demotion, can be appealed to the National Labor Relations Board. However, adjudication typically takes months and sometimes even years.

UNION MEMBERSHIP AND GROWTH

Unions in America first appeared on the scene during the 1790's and early 1800's. They were composed of such skilled craftsmen as shoemakers, tailors, carpenters, printers, and the like. They were formed initially as protective organizations to resist wage cuts and maintain acceptable conditions of employment. The rise of merchant capitalists as employers tended to accentuate the separate interests of employers and employees in the wage bargain. Price competition in the product market caused employers to cut wages or at least resist wage increases. In seeking to protect and improve their lot, unions of craftsmen posted their prices (wage scales) and refused to work for less. They also tended to resist any influx of lesser trained workers who would undercut their wage scale. Throughout most of the nineteenth century, unions in the United States were small and rather weak. The American Federation of Labor, officially organized in 1886 as actually a confederation of rather autonomous craft unions, proved to be an enduring and successful organization. However, its growth and impact during the closing years of the nineteenth century were rather limited. In 1890, total union membership in the United States was less than 400,000. By 1910, it stood at about two million. During the World War I era when employment levels were high, membership increased significantly. By 1920 it was slightly over five million. But from then until the depth of the Great Depression in 1933, the union movement lost membership. During the prosperous 1920's, when conditions would ordinarily have been favorable for union growth, employer organizations launched a massive offensive against unions. This took the form of "open shop" drives, antiunion publicity, resistance to unionization at the plant gate, employer-initiated welfare programs, and quasi unions in the form of employee representation plans. A lack of vigor in the leadership of the American Federation of Labor also contributed to the decline. Of course, mass layoffs and plant closings caused by the economic depression of the early 1930's caused people to lose the ability to pay their dues to maintain membership in their unions.

Rapid Growth—1935 Through Early 1950's

The most spectacular rate of union growth occurred during the period from the mid-1930's through World War II until the early 1950's (See Figure 4-1 which is a graph showing total union and employee association membership as a percentage of the labor force and of nonagricultural employment for the period 1930 to 1976.) This growth had a number of causes. Perhaps foremost among these was the passage of the Wagner Act in 1935 (officially designated as the National Labor Relations Act). This law granted workers the right to form unions of their own choosing without fear of employer intimidation or coercion. Outlawed were blacklists, company-dominated unions, and discharges for worker participation in union activities. The act provided a peaceful and democratic means for employees to express their wishes for or against union representation by means of elections conducted by the federal government.

Another important cause for this rapid expansion of the organized labor movement was the formation of the Congress of Industrial Organizations in 1935–1936. Led by colorful and able men, such as John L. Lewis as its first president, the CIO and its constituent national and international unions scored spectacular successes in organizing the mass production industries of the country, such as automobile, steel, rubber, electrical, and aircraft. The time was ripe for union organization in these industries. There was a powerful, pent-up demand.

Still another factor contributing to rapid union growth during this period was

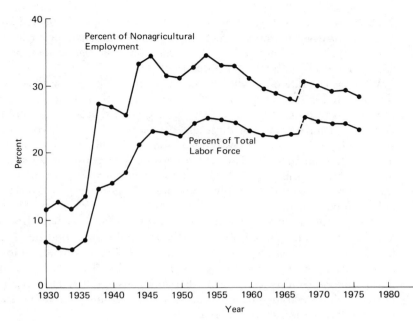

Figure 4-1
Membership of National Unions and Employee Associations as a Percent of Total Labor Force and of Employees in Nonagricultural Establishments, 1930–1976. (Exclusive of Canadian Membership.) The dotted lines in the curves 1967–1968 reflect the fact that employee associations that bargain collectively were first reported in 1968. *Source: U.S. Department of Labor, Bureau of Labor Statistics.*

the high level of employment and economic prosperity during World War II and for four years thereafter. During a period of booming business, companies are in a position to be conciliatory toward the demands of their workers and their unions. Wages can be increased and union security provisions bargained without serious immediate consequences to the employer.

An environmental factor that encouraged the growth and development of unions during this period was the generally sympathetic attitude toward unions and their aspirations held by the New Deal and Fair Deal administrations of President Roosevelt and Truman. The favorable political climate did not mean, however, that the administration in Washington always approved of organized labor's tactics. On more than one occasion during World War II and immediately thereafter, strikes by Lewis' coal miners imperiled the security of the nation. He had to be toned down by presidential action. On these occasions the Federal government seized mines to keep them operating.

Steady State in Private Sector Since Early 1950's

In 1950 total union membership stood at 14,267,000, whereas in 1976 it was 21,006,000. But if one takes into consideration the growth in the total labor force, we find that actually there has been little change in union membership over the years since 1950. In 1950 union membership represented 22.3 percent of the labor force, in 1960 it was 23.6 percent, in 1970 it was 22.6 percent, and in

1976 it was 20.1 percent. Since 1968 the U.S. Department of Labor has compiled statistics on membership of employee associations that engage in collective bargaining. If we include these, then union plus association membership equaled 23.2 percent of the total labor force in 1976.[1]

Why has the rate of growth slowed up so appreciably? There is no single factor responsible for this decline in rate of growth. Rather there are a multiplicity of causes. An important factor is that those groups that are still nonunion are difficult to organize. Many of these are concentrated in small companies of under 100 employees. It is very costly for unions to organize and administer contracts in these establishments. The South, primarily because of a cultural antipathy toward unions, remains a "tough nut to crack" for union organizers. Organizing campaigns in the textile and wearing apparel industries in the South have had only limited success.

Salaried and professional employees in private industry have been reluctant to join unions. While the number of unskilled and semiskilled blue-collar workers has decreased in many industries, the number of professional, technical, and administrative personnel has increased substantially. This change in the composition of the work force has meant that those groups that have traditionally supported unionism (blue-collar workers) are decreasing in relative size and those who resist unionization are increasing.

Public opinion, which was generally sympathetic to unions during the 1930's and 1940's has swung in the other direction to a certain extent. We live in a very interdependent society, and when essential goods and services are cut off during a strike, the public gets angry. Although it takes two parties to make a dispute, newspaper headlines usually indicate that it is the unions that have broken the peace and become the aggressors in a breakdown of negotiations. They are the ones who have gone on strike.

The exposure of corruption and racketeering in a few labor unions by the McClellan Committee of the U.S. Senate during hearings conducted from 1957 to 1959 added tarnish to the public image of the labor movement. Many people concluded from these hearings that a few labor leaders were using their positions of power to feather their own nests. That corruption did not end with these exposés is attested to by the murder of Joseph A. Yablonski and his wife and daughter in December 1969. Yablonski had opposed incumbent United Mine Workers President W. A. Boyle in an election contest for the union presidency in November 1969. Yablonski claimed the election was rigged in favor of Boyle. In March 1970 the U.S. Department of Labor took court action to set aside the election. Certain lower union officials were convicted of the murder in 1973. In April 1974 W. A. Boyle himself was convicted in a Pennsylvania court of planning and arranging for Joseph Yablonski's murder.

Anti-Union Pressures.   Faced with increasing difficulty in organizing nonunion employees throughout the country, the AFL-CIO strongly supported a "labor law reform" bill that was submitted to the 95th session of the U.S Congress in 1977. This bill was also supported by Jimmy Carter, the President of the United States. This proposed law would have made a number of changes in the National Labor Relations Act (discussed in the next chapter) that would have blunted the

---

[1] Data from U.S. Department of Labor, Bureau of Labor Statistics.

ability of antiunion employers to block the unionization of their employees. Although this bill was passed in the House of Representatives, it was stopped by a filibuster in the Senate. American business firms had put together a multi-million dollar lobbying campaign to prevent this measure from becoming law.

Since the mid-1970's there has been a thriving business in offering antiunion training seminars throughout the country. Management consultants and trade associations have learned that there is a large market for such programs among the business community. Even a few universities have gotten into the act. These seminars are billed with such titles as "How to Maintain Nonunion Status," "De-Unionizing," "The Process of Decertification," and "Managing Without Unions." These training courses teach managers how to operate their personnel programs so that employees will feel little need for unions. They also teach a whole host of techniques that can be used to frustrate a union organizing drive once it has begun and to get rid of a union after it has won bargaining rights through a National Labor Relations Board election. There is little doubt that managers of business firms are becoming more sophisticated at repulsing unions.[2]

Sometimes executives become so concerned with their own antiunion posture that they overlook the possibility that their employees may have a justifiable need for union representation in determining terms and conditions of employment. Lacking a union, the employees may feel helpless and voiceless in regard to improving their employment conditions.

Growth in Public Sector

Whereas union membership in the private sector has not grown as fast as the total labor force since the early 1950's, there has been a very rapid growth of unions and of collective bargaining in the public sector since the mid-1960's. This public sector growth has taken place at the Federal, state, and local government levels. Between 1966 and 1976, the American Federation of State, County, and Municipal Employees grew from 281,000 to 750,000 members. During the same time span the American Federation of Teachers increased its membership from 125,000 to 446,000.[3]

Commencing in the mid-1960's, many employee associations that had previously confined their economic activities to lobbying and informal negotiations with state and local units of government, turned full scale into straight collective bargaining. Among these are the National Education Association (teachers) and the New York State Civil Service Employees Association. In 1956 total union membership in Federal, state, and local governments stood at 915,000. By 1974 it had grown to 2,291,000. If one adds to this figure the membership of employee associations that engage in collective bargaining we find a total membership of 5,345,000 in the public sector.[4]

A major stimulus to growth of collective bargaining in the public sector was the issuance by President John F. Kennedy on January 17, 1962, of Executive

[2] See for example, "Firms Learn Art of Keeping Unions Out; Figures Indicate They're Passing Course," *Wall Street Journal*, (April 19, 1977), p. 48.
[3] "Labor Union and Employee Association Membership–1976," *News Release* (Washington, D.C.: Bureau of Labor Statistics, U.S. Department of Labor), Table 7.
[4] *Directory of National Unions and Employee Associations, 1975.* Bulletin 1937 (Bureau of Labor Statistics, U.S. Department of Labor, 1977, Washington, D.C.), Table 16.

Order 10988, entitled "Employee Management Cooperation in the Federal Service." This order required Federal agencies to recognize, as exclusive bargaining agents, unions that represented a majority of the employees as determined by a vote of those in the bargaining unit. This represented a major advance for the aspirations of government employees. The National Labor Relations Act of 1935 (Wagner Act), which granted collective bargaining rights to employees in private industry, specifically excluded public employees from its coverage. Executive Order 11491, "Labor-Management Relations in the Federal Service," issued by President Richard M. Nixon on October 29, 1969, replaced E. O. 10988 and substantially improved the mechanisms for conducting collective bargaining in the Federal service.

The Federal action encouraged many states to adopt laws that granted to state, municipal, and public-school employees the right to form unions, to have these recognized as bargaining agents, and to negotiate contracts and process grievances. The New York State law, for example, evolved as a result of a study committee appointed by Governor Nelson D. Rockefeller and headed by Professor George Taylor of the University of Pennsylvania. New York's Public Employees' Fair Employment Act, popularly called the Taylor Law, became effective on September 1, 1967. It established a Public Employment Relations Board to administer the act. State agencies and local governments (counties, municipalities, towns, and school boards) are required to bargain with those unions that have been granted recognition. As of 1977 26 states had enacted broad laws providing or allowing for collective bargaining by public employees.

Professionals

Concurrent with the growth of unionization in public employment has been the increase in collective bargaining by professionals. Traditionally professional employees, perhaps subconsciously thinking of the model of self-employed physicians and lawyers, rejected unionism as beneath their dignity. They believed that, through their professional associations, they could educate employers to adopt sound employment practices. Within this framework, they felt that individuals could bargain their own salaries and other conditions of employment.

However by the mid-1960's many professional groups realized that they were falling behind the gains made by trade unions. This was true not only in salaries and fringe benefits but also in regard to grievance processing and general job rights.

The National Education Association with 1,887,000 members as of 1976, mainly represents primary and secondary public school teachers. Through its state affiliates, it negotiates contracts with local school boards throughout the country.

The American Association of University Professors long opposed collective bargaining in colleges and universities. It worked vigorously for a system of "shared responsibility" in which both faculty and administration shared in the governance of a university. It still holds to the position of heavy faculty participation in university governance. However, since about 1970 it has followed a policy of endorsing collective bargaining as a major additional way of achieving its objectives. Both the National Education Association and the American Federation of Teachers have competed with the American Association of University

Professors for the right to represent college professors in collective bargaining. A 1978 study revealed that college and university faculty at over 500 institutions were organized for purposes of collective bargaining. This represented about 20 percent of all institutions and covered about 25–30 percent of all faculty and professional staff in institutions of higher education.[5]

The American Nurses Association now engages in widespread collective bargaining. Professional athletes in baseball, football, basketball, and hockey are represented by unions which negotiate contracts with their respective leagues.

Except for those professionals employed in governments that have had enabling legislation or executive orders, the spread of collective bargaining among professionals has not occurred without a struggle. Employers have usually resisted this movement. Oftentimes it was only after strikes, as in football and baseball, or extended court litigation that employers recognized the employee associations and engaged in collective bargaining.

Commentary on Union Viability

The lesson of history tells us that unions in the United States thrive and grow only when supported positively by legislation or other governmental encouragement. The unionization of the mass production industries in the late 1930's and early 1940's was dependent, in large part, upon the material support given to collective bargaining by the Wagner Act. Certain AFL trade unions were able to demonstrate modest success prior to the passage of this law primarily because they represented craftsmen—notably in the building and printing trades and on the railroads—who occupied strategic positions in their industries. They established a system of job control through union agreements that made their positions reasonably strong. But the laissez-faire economic and legal environment that predominated prior to the 1930's constituted a hostile climate for the collective bargaining aspirations of the masses of blue- and white-collar workers. In those days the employer could discharge union-minded workers with impunity. The courts of that day viewed the business and property rights of employers much more sympathetically than the job rights of workers.

Although few still claim that the Taft–Hartley Act was the principal cause for the decline in the rate of union growth that set in about 1947, it is clear that the many restrictions upon union power contained in the act have served to dampen the union advance to some extent.

Evidence in the field of public employment in the 1960's revealed that government employees have had a powerful desire to participate in decision making with respect to the terms and conditions of their employment. Following closely upon the issuance of Kennedy's Executive Order 10988 and the passage of favorable legislation in many states, they joined up by the hundreds of thousands. Without the pent-up demand, this would not have occurred. Likewise, without the sympathetic executive and legislative support, this could not have occurred. The governmental support for unionization in the mid-1930's and again in the mid-1960's (for the public sector) was initiated to meet a pressing and widespread problem.

[5] Joseph W. Garbarino and John Lawler, "Faculty Union Activity in Higher Education—1978," *Industrial Relations*, Vol. 18, No. 2 (Spring 1979), pp. 244–246.

Distribution of Union and Association Membership

Seventy-five percent and over of the total employees in the following industries belong to unions: ordnance, transportation, transportation equipment, and contract construction. Among the industries in which 50 to 70 percent of the employees are unionized are electrical machinery, food and kindred products, primary metals, telephone and telegraph, paper, petroleum, and tobacco manufacturers. At the other end of the scale, we find that the following industries have a very low percentage of organized employees: instruments, service, trade, agriculture and fishing, finance, and textile mill products.[6]

Figure 4-2 shows the distribution of membership of national unions and employee associations (combined) by states. Examination of this figure indicates that New York, Michigan, and West Virginia rank first, second, and third in the precentage of employees in nonagricultural establishments that belong to unions. The three states that rank lowest in percentage of employees belonging to unions are North Carolina, South Carolina, and Mississippi.

UNION ORGANIZATION AND FUNCTIONS

There are about 173 national and international unions in this country (many unions call themselves "international" because they have members in Canada as well as the United States). Examples of such unions are the Automobile, Aerospace and Agricultural Implement Workers of America, the International Association of Machinists, the United Steelworkers of America, and the International Ladies' Garment Workers Union. Each of these types of unions is composed of a national headquarters organization, intermediate bodies primarily set up for administrative purposes, and many local unions. Commonly in manufacturing, for example, each organized plant or establishment will have its own separate local union. There are about 78,000 local unions in the United States.

A simplified schematic organization chart of a union would look as shown in Figure 4-3.

Uniting the majority of national and international unions is the AFL-CIO, which was formed in 1955 through a merger of the American Federation of Labor and the Congress of Industrial Organizations. About 108 national and international unions belong to this loosely knit federation.

The Local Union

The local union is the basic, and a very important, unit of organization of a union. If it is a craft union, such as the carpenters', then a local may consist of all unionized carpenters in a particular town or city even though they may work for different employers; if it is an industrial union, then the local may consist of all union members in a particular factory.

Local unions are generally operated in a democratic fashion, with officers elected usually for a term of one year by the dues-paying members. Each member has one vote, and election rules ordinarily require advance notice of im-

---

[6] *Bureau of Labor Statistics*, op. cit., pp. 70–71.

State	Total Union and Association Membership (Thousands)	Total Membership as a Percent of Employees in Non-agricultural Establishments (Percent)	State	Total Union and Association Membership (Thousands)	Total Membership as a Percent of Employees in Non-agricultural Establishments (Percent)
All States	23,408	29.9	Missouri	595	33.4
Alabama	278	23.9	Montana	73	31.1
Alaska	45	37.2	Nebraska	99	17.8
Arizona	156	21.1	Nevada	81	31.4
Arkansas	116	18.1	New Hampshire	58	19.0
California	2,607	33.3	New Jersey	898	32.3
Colorado	220	23.0	New Mexico	63	17.6
Connecticut	382	30.3	New York	3,215	45.4
Delaware	55	23.5	North Carolina	201	9.8
Florida	416	14.7	North Dakota	38	19.7
Georgia	287	15.8	Ohio	1,522	36.4
Hawaii	129	38.7	Oklahoma	148	16.8
Idaho	54	20.6	Oregon	270	32.2
Illinois	1,684	37.1	Pennsylvania	1,849	40.9
Indiana	729	36.2	Rhode Island	111	30.3
Iowa	251	25.1	South Carolina	105	10.3
Kansas	137	17.5	South Dakota	31	15.1
Kentucky	309	28.9	Tennessee	328	20.9
Louisiana	211	17.7	Texas	620	14.2
Maine	83	22.8	Utah	94	21.5
Maryland-District of Columbia	545	25.5	Vermont	37	23.2
Massachusetts	632	26.6	Virginia	288	16.1
Michigan	1,388	42.4	Washington	485	40.6
Minnesota	421	28.3	West Virginia	239	41.9
Mississippi	93	13.3	Wisconsin	548	32.1
			Wyoming	33	24.3

Figure 4-2
Distribution of Membership of National Unions and Employee Associations by State, 1974. *Source: Directory of National Unions and Employee Associations, 1975, Bulletin 1937, U.S. Department of Labor, Bureau of Labor Statistics, Washington, D.C., 1977, Table 19.*

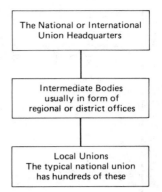

```
┌─────────────────────────┐
│  The National or International │
│     Union Headquarters       │
└─────────────────────────┘
            │
┌─────────────────────────┐
│    Intermediate Bodies       │
│    usually in form of        │
│  regional or district offices │
└─────────────────────────┘
            │
┌─────────────────────────┐
│       Local Unions           │
│  The typical national union  │
│    has hundreds of these     │
└─────────────────────────┘
```

Figure 4-3
Schematic Organization Chart of a Union.

pending elections, open nominations, and secret ballots. The elected officials usually consist of a president, secretary-treasurer, and an executive board. Some unions also have a business agent, trustees, a negotiating committee, and a grievance committee. Every local union also has a number of shop stewards who are elected by the employees in each department of the company.

The president of a local is most commonly a worker who has been elected by the membership to be its principal leader but who devotes only part of his work time to his union duties. It is only very large locals (consisting of several thousand members) that can afford to have a full-time, salaried president. In most instances the president has a regular job, is paid a wage by the employer, and attends to his union responsibilities during the work day (for which the company grants him time off) and on his own time such as evenings and on weekends. Many unions pay these part-time union presidents a few hundred dollars a year in salary plus their necessary expenses for attending international union conventions and for other items. The local president is sometimes the chief union spokesman in contract negotiations with company representatives. He becomes involved in major union grievances, leads the members in time of a strike, and in general tries to create and maintain teamwork and solidarity among the group. His job has many political overtones to it. He often is placed in the position where he must "deliver the goods" in dealings with the company or risk being defeated for re-election. The political nature of his job is emphasized when the union is divided into factional groups.

Certain unions, especially those in the construction, clothing, and metalworking industries, have a business agent. He is a full-time, salaried union official who is usually elected by the membership. He exercises a great deal of power and in many instances overshadows the local president in authority, influence, and prestige. His duties and responsibilities are manifold. He plays a key role in contract negotiations with the employer, is alert to see that the employer and his management representatives abide by the contract, helps settle grievances, and leads the union members when there is a strike. In addition, he may also have to administer the operation of the local's headquarters, direct clerical help, handle union publicity, and make arrangements for business meetings.

A shop steward is another important person in a local union organization. Although the term *steward* is the one most commonly used, in some unions he is called a departmental representative, a committeeman, or a grievance man. The shop steward appears at the same level in the union organization structure as does a foreman in the company structure. However, he does not have the authority over the workers that a foreman has. Technically speaking, he is not considered to be an "official" of the local, although his position is vital to union operations. He is usually elected for a term of one year to represent the employees in that department in the processing of their grievances to management. He represents the interests of the employees and goes to bat for them when he feels they have a justifiable grievance. He is on guard to insure that supervision lives up to the letter and spirit of the labor–management agreement. If there is no "union shop" provision in the labor agreement which requires employees to join the union, then he takes steps to increase the membership by persuading people to join. If there is no payroll checkoff of union dues, then he must also collect dues from the members.

The locals are the heart of any union. Although there is a trend in the direction of more and more contract negotiations being conducted at the national level of the union, what with multiemployer bargaining becoming more prevalent, it can be said accurately that the majority of all negotiations are still conducted at the local level. Even in those situations where the top management of a multiplant company bargains a labor–management agreement with national union officials, it is common practice for each local to bargain a supplementary agreement with local plant management over local issues, such as work standards, time study, rest periods, seniority rules, and so on. In addition to carrying on contract negotiations, other functions of the local are to obtain new members, handle grievances, administer the agreement with management, and conduct strikes when other choices fail to resolve disagreements. In addition, many locals carry on an active program of social activities for their members.

Intermediate Organizational Units

For purposes of coordinating the activities of a number of local unions in a given area and to act as an intermediate unit of union government, most national unions have established intermediate organizational bodies. Usually these are set up on a geographical basis. In garment workers unions all of the locals in a city in several crafts will be grouped together in a joint board. Ordinarily the joint board will have an office or building of its own that will serve as headquarters for all of the locals in that joint board. The chairman of the joint board will assist the business agents in contract negotiations, and in many instances he will actually conduct them. Other unions, such as the United Automobile Workers, are divided into regions, with each one being supervised by a director. The United Mine Workers and the United Steel Workers call their regions districts. In the railroad industry all of the locals of a single railroad company are grouped into a system federation.

National and International Unions

The top organizational entity of a union is called the national or international (if it contains branches and locals in Canada). For brevity the term *national* will be used here. A great deal of power, authority, and responsibility resides in the national. Let us look at the functions performed by the national.

First of all the national officers establish basic policies. For basic guidance in setting policy, the officers are bound by the constitution of the union. The national frequently sets the wage policy that locals must seek to accomplish. Uniformity of practice among all of the organized enterprises in a given area or industry not only on wage matters but also on seniority rules, group insurance practices, and others, is often a union goal. The national union provides a host of services to the locals. It may send out specialists to help the locals negotiate their contracts with management. It provides data to the locals on such matters as cost of living, comparable wages, and details of the contract settlements in other companies. Because the turnover of local union officers is rather high, many nationals find that they must continually train key personnel of the locals in such subjects as parliamentary procedure, grievance handling, labor law, and the administration of a local. National unions also build up strike funds in their treasuries with which to pay benefits to members when on strike and to take care of the many extra costs required during a strike.

Most nationals are continuously involved in efforts to expand their unions. This means that they are attempting to organize the unorganized or nonunion employees of certain industries. It also means that they may try to persuade the workers in a company who already belong to another union to give up their allegiance and switch membership to their own union. This activity is called "raiding" and is officially discouraged by the AFL-CIO. However, it still goes on to a considerable extent.

Elected officials of the national consist of a president, secretary-treasurer, and several vice-presidents, who usually represent regions and who constitute the executive board. This executive board is theoretically the top policymaking body in the interval between conventions.

In addition to the elective positions, there exist at the national level a considerable number of appointed staff specialists. These include lawyers, economists, statisticians, and public relations personnel. Most unions have a research director, who, along with his staff, is responsible for collecting, analyzing, and disseminating economic and other information that can be of great value to the union and its locals in collective bargaining. Another key appointive position is that of educational director. His job is to set up training programs for local union officers and stewards so that they can conduct the affairs of the union more effectively.

International representatives are a key group of appointive personnel. Their main responsibility is to aid the local unions both at contract negotiation time and in the day-to-day administration of the union. It is not uncommon to find the international representative acting in the role of chief union spokesman during contract bargaining. He may also have to show local officials how to set up and keep financial records, educate them as to their rights and responsibilities under the law, and perform a multitude of other services. Another prime duty of an international representative is to organize unorganized plants and establishments in his assigned jurisdiction.

THE AFL-CIO

AFL-CIO is the American Federation of Labor–Congress of Industrial Organizations. It is really a confederation of semiautonomous labor unions that was formed in 1955 by the merger of the American Federation of Labor and the Congress of Industrial Organizations.

The activities of the AFL-CIO are manifold. Two of its principal functions are the organization of unorganized employees and the securing of federal, state, and local legislation that is favorable to the organized labor movement and, more generally, of benefit to working men and women throughout the country. It carries on an active research program and publishes a great volume of information in the fields of economics, employment, collective bargaining, labor statistics, labor law, and so on. Through its many publications, the AFL-CIO seeks to get its message to the general public, its own union constituents, and to such special interest groups as businessmen, farmers, consumers, and elected government leaders. The AFL-CIO has many special staff groups and committees that function in such fields as civil rights, international affairs, economic policy, safety and health, education, and social security. The Federation has, as another of its important functions, the settling of jurisdictional disputes between its member unions. Its constitution contains a "code of ethical practices" that outlaws any corruption, racketeering, communism, or fascism in member unions. It is up to the Executive Council and the president to implement this code.

Organization Structure of AFL-CIO.

Figure 4-4 shows the organization structure of the AFL-CIO. It should be emphasized that this is a loose federation of independent national and international unions. The president of the AFL-CIO does not have the power to compel a member union to follow his directives. Most of the leadership of the president and the Executive Council is exercised through persuasion, influence, and appeals to the good sense of leaders of member unions. Appeals to public opinion also play a part. The only really significant sanction that can be applied is that of suspension or expulsion from membership in the organization. This action must be approved by the Convention.

The Convention is the legislative body of the organization. It meets once every two years. The delegates are composed primarily of officials of affiliated unions. The number of persons that each union is allowed to send is determined by its total membership.

The president supervises the affairs of the organization, appoints study committees that make recommendations to the Convention, presides at conventions, calls meetings of the Executive Council, appoints staff department heads and union organizers, and serves as the official spokesman for organized labor in the United States.

The Executive Council serves as a policy-making group. It roughly corresponds to the board of directors in a corporation. It is composed of the president, secretary-treasurer, and thirty-three vice-presidents (who in turn are presidents of their own national unions). It has the authority to direct the activities of the Federation and to make such decisions as are necessary to promote the best interests of the AFL-CIO. It keeps informed of legislative affairs affecting the labor force, makes rules that are consistent with its constitution, and can conduct investigations into the affairs of member unions that it suspects are under corrupt or totalitarian influences. The Council has the authority, upon a two-thirds vote of its members, to suspend a member union found guilty of internal corruption,

Figure 4-4
Structure of the AFL-CIO. *Source: U.S. Department of Labor, Bureau of Labor Statistics,* Directory of National Unions and Employee Associations, *1975. Bulletin 1937, Washington, D.C., 1977.*

racketeering, or communist or fascist influences. The Council also has the responsibility to oversee the extension of union organization and to charter new national unions.

The "Trade and Industrial Departments" of the AFL-CIO (Building Trades,

Food Trades, Industrial Union, Maritime Trades, Metal Trades, Public Employees, Railway Employees, and Union Label) are composed of the member national unions that operate in these particular industries. The purpose of these departments is to help coordinate collective bargaining activities among member unions and to settle jurisdictional work disputes. The Union Label Department promotes the sale of union-made goods by having unionized manufacturers attach "union-made" labels on items such as clothing, magazines, and books.

INDEPENDENT UNIONS

Of the 173 national unions in this country, 108 are affiliated with the AFL-CIO and 65 are unaffiliated. The two largest unions in the country—the Teamsters and the Automobile Workers—are outside the orbit of the AFL-CIO. The Teamsters Union was expelled from the AFL-CIO around 1960. The United Automobile Workers Union voluntarily disaffiliated in 1969 because of policy clashes between Walter Reuther, the late president of the UAW, and George Meany, President of the AFL-CIO. Other large independent unions are the International Longshoremen's and Warehousemen's Union and the United Mine Workers Union.

UNION OBJECTIVES AND BEHAVIOR

Unions basically seek to advance the interests of their members. In this sense they are no different from any other voluntary organization, such as the United States Chamber of Commerce, the Farm Bureau, or the American Legion. Unions work to achieve a better life for their membership. This means an ever-increasing standard of living, more leisure time, and financial protection against many of the risks of life—namely unemployment, injury on the job, sickness, and insufficient income in old age. Another, and a more specific, set of union goals consists of job security, job rights, and opportunity for advancement. Practically all unions have the foregoing as their goals. In addition to these, some segments of the labor movement have broader social goals. They advocate government legislation to affect improvements in educational opportunities, obtain better housing, and insure equal opportunities in employment, education, and housing regardless of race, color, or national origin. They are continually pushing for improvements in protective labor laws. Many have sought some form of federal government participation in health and medical insurance.

There exist two principal means by which unions seek to fulfill their goals. First and foremost is collective bargaining. This involves the union serving as a representative of the employees in the negotiating of a formal written agreement with management, which in turn represents the employer. Collective bargaining also includes within its compass the day-to-day administration of the agreement, the enforcement of the agreement, and the resort to collective action (such as a strike and picketing). The second principal way in which unions advance their aims is through efforts to influence government legislation. These take the form of grass-roots campaigns to elect the friends of labor to political office, lobbying, and the dissemination of mass information to mold public opinion.

We have talked so far about the objectives of unionism to advance the economic and social position of its constituents. This is its principal goal. But in addition, most unions have social and fraternal goals. They provide a feeling of belonging for the members. This gives members a sense of identification and purpose. Union meetings, picnics, banquets, and the feeling of solidarity evidenced on a picket line emphasize the social and fraternal aspects of unionism. For some persons, unionism is almost a way of life in the same sense that top executives in industry tend to integrate their lives wholly with the corporation. To be sure, this way-of-life attitude holds true for only a small proportion of union members—most of these are officials and stewards.

Although we have been discussing union goals in general, it should be pointed out that there exist some important differences in the specific objectives and behavior of craft unions as distinct from industrial unions.

Craft Union Objectives and Behavior [7]

Craft unions, as illustrated by those in the building trades (carpenters, bricklayers, electricians, ironworkers, and so on), the printing industry, and the artistic professions tend to be the epitome of business unionism. They concentrate on goals related to the employment relationship. Primarily they seek control over jobs and job rights. They have an underlying belief that job opportunities are scarce in both the short and long run. They seek to protect in every way possible not only the job rights of their members but also their skill rights. Primarily representing skilled craftsmen, the unions tend to oppose the technological advances that will reduce or water down the level of skill needed. They fear that a reduction in pay might follow.

By restricting the supply of labor, craft unions hope to keep the price (that is, wage) for that labor high. There is little doubt that many of them have been eminently successful. There are many devices by which these unions restrict the supply of labor. One is to control the number of apprentices in training at any one time. Another is to obtain licensing regulations in cities and towns so that only a licensed plumber or electrician will be permitted to do certain work. The closed shop is still a further means of keeping people out of a trade. Although outlawed by the Taft-Hartley Act, the closed shop does exist in a de facto sense in the building, maritime, and longshoring trades. The closed union (refusal to admit outsiders into union membership), high initiation fees, and the union hiring hall are other devices for restricting and controlling the supply of labor. It should be pointed out that the majority of craft unions do not have closed shops, they are not closed unions, and some do not operate hiring halls; however, a significant minority do attempt to limit entrance to the trade through one or more of these devices.

In addition to controlling the supply of labor, craft unions establish what they consider to be a fair work pace. The example of bricklayers being permitted to

---

[7] For a detailed analysis of craft union and industrial union objectives, strategy, and tactics see Edwin F. Beal and Edward D. Wickersham, *The Practice of Collective Bargaining*, 3rd ed. (Homewood, Ill.: Richard D. Irwin, Inc., 1967), pp. 9–14 and ch. 3.

---

lay only so many bricks per day is well known. Whereas in factories, management generally has the upper hand in establishing and enforcing work standards, in construction the union tends to be dominant. In part, this is a consequence of relative bargaining power. In many of the industries in which craft unions predominate, employers are small and the union is big.

Most craft unions are fortunate because of the fact that their membership is composed largely of skilled workers who are in short supply in the labor market and who are difficult to replace. Thus, when many craft unions call a strike, as, for example, in the building trades, they need post only token pickets who carry signs explaining the strike. The strike becomes a waiting game—a contest of economic holding power. The employer usually would be unable to hire any significant number of replacements because of the usual shortage of skilled workers. Added to this situation is the fact that any other unions that have been accustomed to dealing with the company will now refuse to cross a picket line. Thus the company is completely shut down until an agreement is reached with the union.

Industrial Union Objectives and Behavior

Whereas craft unions gain their strength by artificially restricting the number of workers in a trade—that is by keeping people out—industrial unions acquire power by doing just the opposite. An industrial union that has been recognized by a company as the bargaining agent for the employees seeks to encourage all of the workers—unskilled, semiskilled, skilled, and sometimes even white-collar—to join the union. The union hopes to develop a feeling of solidarity among all who work in that company and in that industry. In contrast to craft unions, the initiation fees and monthly dues of an industrial union are modest.

The strike behavior of an industrial union is usually quite different from that of a craft union. The factory union seeks total and simultaneous action by all of the workers. Because semiskilled workers predominate in most factories, replacements can rather easily be recruited by management if it decides to keep the plant in operation during the strike. To bring the union to terms during a strike, a company can follow either of two tactics. It may simply elect to shut down the plant and wait out the union. In this case, it counts upon the fact that its economic holding power is greater than that of the workers and the union. (Workers' savings are usually exhausted after a few weeks.) On the other hand, management may try aggressively to break the strike by hiring nonunion replacements and launching a back-to-work movement. Because a permanently replaced economic striker loses all claim to his former job, his situation and that of the union becomes desperate at this point. The union usually resorts to mass picketing at the plant gate to prevent scabs and strike-breakers from going to work. This usually leads to picket line violence. But mass picketing has been held to be illegal under the Taft–Hartley Act, and the local police usually prevent such picketing when they see it occurring. Thus, an industrial union often is faced with a dilemma. If the company hires nonunion workers to keep operating, the union can either resort to mass picketing in violation of the law, or it can risk losing the strike by posting only token pickets and allowing nonunion workers to walk through the picket line. This description of the strike behavior of an industrial union shows why it must have the support of the vast majority of the workers in order to win a strike. A concerted refusal to work must be, for all practical purposes, a 100 percent refusal.

The principal bargaining issues in a factory, in addition to the usual wages and hours, are union security, management security, job security, and control of work pace. The union seeks some form of compulsory unionism, such as the union shop, in order to maintain a secure position. By requiring all employees in the bargaining unit to belong after they have been employed at least thirty days (the union shop), the union is assured of financial security and 100 percent membership. Because the turnover in many factories is rather high, the unions feel that they would be continually faced with the problem of persuading new workers to join if they did not have a union shop provision in the contract.

Whereas workers in craft unions obtain their security and rights to a job primarily through the union, factory workers seek their security from their company. This explains why the union places such great emphasis upon handling job changes—promotions, transfers, layoffs—on the basis of seniority. This eliminates the possibility of any favoritism or discrimination. It is an objective method, and most workers tend to accept it as fair.

The amount of work that a worker must do in a day—the pace at which he must work—constitutes a frequent point of clash between workers and the union on the one hand and management on the other. This was evidenced by the famous strike at the General Motors Lordstown, Ohio, plant in 1972. To operate its plant efficiently and to control labor costs, management feels that it must have full control over the amount of work turned out by each employee. It may use time and motion studies and other industrial engineering techniques to set work standards. But unions often cry "Speed-up" or "Stretch-out." The speed of assembly lines and the amount of relief time are perennial bargaining issues in the automobile industry. Industrial unions push grievances over work standards, and they often become a hotly contested issue.

IMPACT OF THE UNION UPON MANAGEMENT

After a union has won bargaining rights for the employees in an organization, management finds that the way it handles employment relationships and its manner of dealing with employees is considerably altered. Let us now examine the effects of the union upon the management of people in the company.

Restriction upon Management's Freedom of Action

Unilateral action and individual dealings with workers over wage adjustments, hours, and the conditions of work are no longer possible. The first-line supervisor must be sure he does not violate the labor agreement in handling his employees. He is continuously aware of the presence of a shop steward who will go to bat for the workers in presenting their complaints and grievances. Basically the greatest change that occurs with the advent of the union on the scene is the restriction upon management's freedom of action. Its flexibility becomes limited.

Management is closely bound by the conditions set forth in the union–employer agreement. At times, this loss of managerial freedom to act may impair plant efficiency. It may not be able to shift workers from one job to another as easily as before. If a man is asked to perform certain tasks that are of a higher skill than he has been accustomed to previously, both he and the union will usually demand a higher job classification. If sales decline and management finds it necessary to reduce the size of the work force, it cannot lay off the least competent employees. Instead it must lay off those having the least seniority. If management wishes to install a profit-sharing or pension plan, it cannot do so without consulting the union and obtaining its consent. Thus we see that management has considerably less freedom to operate the business as it sees fit than before the union entered the picture.

Union Pressure for Uniformity of Treatment

Another effect of the union upon management is its insistence upon uniformity of treatment of all employees. For example, unions usually advocate that all employees who are assigned to the same job should receive exactly the same rate of pay or at least that in-grade increases in pay be based solely upon seniority. Management officials often claim that unions introduce a leveling effect upon the employees, so that individual initiative is discouraged. The psychology of individual differences tells us that among people there is great variation in aptitudes and skills. To be sure, those on the payroll of a given company will have a much smaller range of abilities than the general population, because the employee selection process has eliminated those of inferior abilities. One of the principal reasons unions press for uniformity of treatment of all employees and for the rule of seniority to be applied to most job changes is that they do not want to introduce cliques, factionalism, and "fair-haired" boys among the union membership. Because everyone pays the same dues, he is entitled to the same benefits.

Improved Personnel Policies and Practices

On the other hand, it is fair to state that the presence of the union encourages management to become fully conscious of employee wants and needs. Any omissions or faults in a company's labor policy and its manner of carrying out the policy will tend to be quickly noted by the local union officials. Thus, we find that many organizations have found it advantageous to institute supervisory and executive training programs that contain a strong emphasis upon sound personnel policies, labor relations, and human relations. Good leadership on the job tends to reduce the number and severity of problems about which the employees and union stewards may submit grievances. In fact, some companies have deliberately gone "all out" to provide for their employees' needs and wants, to exercise good leadership, to foster social groupings around company-sponsored recreational activities, and to maintain high morale. This is intended to blunt the union's "sword," so that the employees will feel little need for the union. Local union leadership may thereby be rendered impotent, because the employees are content and the company takes care of them.

One Spokesman for the Employees

In a sense the presence of the union simplifies management's problems in dealing with employees because it can look to the elected union leaders as spokesmen for the employees. How will the workers react to rotating instead of fixed shifts when the plant must operate around the clock? When business is slack, would the workers prefer a reduced work week (work sharing) to layoffs for a certain percentage of the work force? For these and other employee relations questions the local union leaders are generally in a good position to feel the pulse of the work force and fairly represent their attitudes to management. In those relationships that have developed to a stage of mutual respect and maturity, management often finds that it has much to gain by engaging in joint consultation with union officers on such subjects as working conditions, plant safety, suggestion system operation, and similar topics. Such action need not infringe upon management prerogatives, and many actually result in improved plant efficiency.

Centralization of Labor Relations' Decision Making

Because of the critical importance of many labor relations decisions, top executives have a tendency to take authority in labor matters away from lower ranks of supervision and centralize this in the industrial relations department. This is quite noticeable in grievance handling. Although in theory the first-level supervisor occupies the first step in the grievance procedure in all organizations, in actual practice he is often required to go to the industrial relations manager before he can give a definite answer. He then becomes a messenger boy. The power to discipline is sometimes taken away from the supervisor when there is a union. The reason for this state of affairs is that a union often does not accept the word of lower management if a decision does not meet with its approval. It goes directly to the top of the organization in many cases.

In the long run a company will develop better labor–management relations and better day-to-day leadership on the job by thoroughly training its supervisors in labor policy, personnel relations, and the elements of supervision. Top management should help foremen to do a better job instead of acquiescing in or encouraging their being bypassed.

UNION-MANAGEMENT CLIMATE

American labor history prior to the 1950's was turbulent. It was filled with such elements of strife as violent battles on the picket line, blacklisting of union sympathizers, sit-down and sympathy strikes, calling out of the state militia to maintain order, mass picketing, and importation of hired strikebreakers. The symbols of the struggle between management and labor stand out vividly on the pages of American labor history—the Homestead and Pullman strikes of the 1890's, textile strikes in Lawrence and Lowell, Massachusetts in 1912, the great steel strike of 1919, the open-shop drives in the 1920's launched by employers, the sit-down strikes in the automobile industry and the strikes against "Little Steel" during the 1930's—these and others are highlighted as one reviews the background of present-day labor relations. But, to a considerable extent, the relations between employers and unions have substantially improved in recent years. There is growing evidence that the managements of our business firms have come to accept the fact that unions are here to stay. Management has learned to live with unions. Unions have achieved a measure of security, for the most part they are respectable, and they have accepted the fact that higher wages and benefits for their members depend upon healthy businesses and increasing productivity.

When the management of an organization is faced with the prospect of dealing with a union as the bargaining agent for its employees, it basically has two choices: (1) opposition, or (2) acceptance.[8] Within each of these choices are a variety of approaches. Opposition may take the form of forceful action to weaken the union and to break off the bargaining relationship or it may involve subtle attempts to discredit the union in the eyes of the workers and to build up respect, loyalty, and pride in the company and complete trust in management. Patterns of acceptance vary along a continuum, from grudging acceptance with strong attempts at controlling the power of the union to accommodation, to labor–management cooperation, and occasionally even to collusion and the making of special deals between the top leaders of the union and those of management.

The majority of the relationships in the United States, as far as management's approach is concerned, can be classified into one or the other of two forms of acceptance. It may take the form either of reluctant acceptance of the union coupled with positive management action to contain the union within certain limits or else accommodation. In the former the employer zealously seeks to preserve the traditional management prerogatives and to use a wide range of strategies and tactics to keep the union from gaining the upper hand. It implies an acceptance of the union as a legitimate institution that possesses certain rights under the laws of the land. However, management feels that it must continuously press to keep the union from encroaching upon management's freedom to operate the business in a profitable manner. Accommodation as a characterization of a type of bargaining relationship is becoming increasingly common. It implies a rather complete acceptance of the union by management, and both union and management have considerable respect for each other. Collective bargaining is confined to the traditional areas of wages, hours, and other (well-accepted) conditions of employment. There are no excursions into labor–management consultation and cooperation on such topics as safety, cost reduction, productive efficiency, and employee suggestions. These latter joint activities are found in those bargaining relationships properly classified as labor–management cooperation. Under this setup, both the union and the management are working for the same goals. There is a maximum of joint dealings on ways to increase productivity, cut costs, eliminate waste, and improve working conditions. However, labor–management cooperation represents a very advanced stage of relationship and of working harmony and is not particularly common in the United States.

The negotiation of special deals and of collusive arrangements by management and union officials is not common, but it does occur. Sometimes employers and unions work together to keep other companies out of a particular product market. The McClellan Committee hearings of 1957–59 uncovered situations in

[8] For a well-known classification system of bargaining relationships see Benjamin M. Selekman, Stephen H. Fuller, Thomas Kennedy, and John M. Baitsell, *Problems in Labor Relations*, 3rd ed. (New York: McGraw-Hill Book Company, 1964), pp. 2–8.

which employers signed "sweetheart" contracts with union leaders at substandard wages. The union leaders sometimes took a direct money payoff in exchange for granting a low wage contract to the company.

Sound Labor Relations

When relations between management and union are sound, there is a substantial degree of peace between the parties. Strikes occur only infrequently. There is an acceptance by each party of the need of the other to exist as an institution. Also both management and the union believe they are getting a fair deal in their relationships with each other.

The attitudes and philosophies of the leaders in management and the union are powerful determinants of the character of the relationship. Research has shown that where harmonious relations occur, management fully accepts the union as an institution and understands its need to exist. It accepts collective bargaining as a desirable way of handling employment relationships. Management understands the political nature of the union leaders' position and their need to sometimes "play politics" to maintain rank and file members' support. Union leaders dealing with private companies accept the free enterprise system and the need of the firms to make a profit. They are concerned for the continued viability of the organization.

Both parties recognize that they have shared interests. They understand that they will continue to live and deal with each other for many years to come. A problem that is of serious concern to one party must, of necessity, be addressed by the other. It cannot be ignored. Differences and conflicts inevitably do occur between management and union leaders from time to time, but these are resolved through a rational process of problem solving and a reconciling of positions. Neither side tries to overwhelm the other by the use of power and force. Flexibility, give and take, and some compromises must occur from time to time.

Economic factors also significantly affect the probability that sound labor-management relations will exist. Harmonious relationships are more likely to exist where the employer is strong, financially viable, and where the demand for the employer's product or service is good. Competition is not cutthroat. Marginal firms struggling to survive tend to have poor labor management relations. They cannot afford to provide competitive wages and benefits. Employment conditions, generally, in such firms are mediocre or worse and such a state of affairs is bound to cause conflict between union and management.[9]

Questions for review and discussion

1. Why is it important for students and practitioners in management to have a sound understanding of labor union philosophy, objectives, and organization?

[9] A pioneering and significant research study into factors contributing to sound union–employer relationships is described in Clinton S. Golden and V. D. Parker, eds., *Causes of Industrial Peace Under Collective Bargaining* (New York: Harper and Row, 1955). For an analysis of the impact of economic conditions upon labor-management relations, see Herbert R. Northrup and Harvey A. Young, "The Causes of Industrial Peace Revisited," *Industrial and Labor Relations Review*, Vol. 22, No. 1 (October 1968), pp. 31–47.

2. How does personnel management in a unionized organization differ from that in a nonunion establishment?
3. What motivates employees to form and to join a union?
4. Compare the status, position, and rights of an individual factory worker before and after the entry of a union into the plant.
5. Compare the objectives, practices, and tactics of a craft union (such as the carpenters or electricians) with those of a professional society like the American Medical Association.
6. Why has the American labor movement failed to increase its total membership (expressed as a percentage of the labor force) significantly since the early 1950's?
7. Explain the reasons for the great growth in union representing government employees commencing in the mid 1960's.
8. "Prior to the 1940's, at a time when the typical industrial worker had few basic job rights and little defense against arbitrary treatment, unions were certainly necessary. However, in this day and age of enlightened management, which fully recognizes its social responsibilities, there is little real need for unions. Unions no longer have a vital role to play in employee-management relations." Defend or refute the foregoing statement.
9. Figure 4-2 shows that certain states such as North Carolina, South Carolina, Mississippi, and Texas have a very low percentage of employees in non-agricultural establishments who are members of unions. How do you explain this condition?
10. A national union for scientists and engineers is engaging in an active campaign to organize the engineers in a medium-sized electronics company (total of 4,000 employees; 500 engineers and scientific personnel). As an engineer in this company, what would be your attitude toward joining the union? As the president of the company, what would be your attitude? Would you as the president take any action in regard to the organizing campaign?
11. What attitudes and behavior on the part of management tend to build harmonious, constructive union-management relations? What union attitudes and behavior?
12. In recent years field organizers and office employees of several national unions have sought to organize their own unions to obtain bargaining rights with their employers (that is, the national unions). Their efforts have usually been opposed by the top union leadership. What would motivate these top officials to oppose unionization of their own employees?

Suggestions for further reading

BARBASH, JACK. "The Labor Movement After World War II," *Monthly Labor Review*, Vol. 99, No. 11 (November 1976), pp. 34–37.
BEAL, EDWIN, F., EDWARD D. WICKERSHAM, and PHILIP K. KIENAST. *The Practice of Collective Bargaining*, 5th ed. Homewood, Ill.; Richard D. Irwin, Inc., 1976.
CHAMOT, DENNIS. "Professional Employees Turn to Unions," *Harvard Business Review*, Vol. 54, No. 3 (May–June 1976), pp. 119–127.

ESTEY, MARTEN. *The Unions: Structure, Development and Management*, 2nd ed. New York: Harcourt Brace Jovanovich, Inc., 1976.

MILLS, DANIEL QUINN. *Labor-Management Relations*. New York: McGraw-Hill Book Company, 1978.

NASH, AL. *The Union Steward: Duties, Rights, and Status*. Ithaca, N.Y.: N.Y. State School of Industrial and Labor Relations, Cornell University, 1977.

REUTHER, VICTOR G. *The Brothers Reuther*. Boston: Houghton Mifflin, 1976.

SCOTT, RACHEL. *Muscle and Blood*. New York: E. P. Dutton & Co., Inc., 1974.

STEIBER, JACK. *Public Employee Unionism: Structure, Growth, Policy*. Washington: The Brookings Institution, 1973.

TAFT, PHILIP. *Rights of Union Members and the Government*. Westport, Conn.: Greenwood Press, 1975.

Collective bargaining

Collective bargaining is concerned with the relations between employers, acting through their management representatives, and organized labor. It is concerned not only with the negotiation of a formal labor agreement but also with the day-to-day dealings between management and the union. The nature and course of collective bargaining are heavily influenced by labor law. Especially in recent years the structure for bargaining, the manner of dealing, and the content of collective bargaining have become closely regulated by Federal (and to some extent state) labor law. Because the direction of people in so many organizations is so closely intertwined with union–employer relationships, it is essential that the student and the practitioner of management develop a sound knowledge of collective bargaining. This chapter will delve into the nature and characteristics of the collective bargaining process. It will explore the legal framework for bargaining, with particular emphasis upon the Taft–Hartley and Landrum–Griffin acts. The structure for bargaining, negotiating the agreement, the content of collective agreements, substantive issues, and dispute settlement methods are covered in this chapter.

THE NATURE OF COLLECTIVE BARGAINING

Collective bargaining has existed in the United States since the early 1800's. However, it did not develop into its present form until comparatively recently. In the very early days the general practice was for either the employer or the union, depending upon their relative economic strengths, to notify the other party of the wage rates and other conditions of employment that it intended to put into effect. There was very little negotiation and discussion between the parties. If one party refused to accept the terms imposed by the other, then either a strike or a lockout ensued.

In 1885 Samuel Gompers was called to testify at hearings into labor relations conducted by the Commissioner of Labor Statistics of the State of New York. In reporting to the state legislature on this investigation, the Commissioner used the term *arbitration* to designate the process by which employers and unions would negotiate with one another to settle their differences. In the hearings themselves Gompers used both the words *arbitration* and *conciliation* to cover the process by which unions and management bargained with one another. The modern term *collective bargaining* was actually first used by Sidney and Beatrice Webb, the well-known historians of the British labor movement, just prior to 1900.[1]

The nature, scope, and methodology of collective bargaining are continuing to evolve even today. Collective bargaining is dynamic. But in order that the reader obtain a concrete understanding of what is involved in modern-day collective bargaining, the following definition is given:

Collective bargaining is concerned with the relations between unions representing employees and employers (or their management representatives). It involves the process of union organization of employees; negotiation, administration, and interpretation of collective agreements covering wages, hours of work, and other conditions of employment; engaging in concerted economic action; and dispute settlement procedures.

The bargaining is collective in the sense that the chosen representative of the employees (that is, a union) acts as the bargaining agent for all the employees in carrying out negotiations and dealings with management. The process may also be considered collective in the case of the corporation in which the paid professional managers represent the interests of the stockholders and the board of directors in bargaining with union leaders. On the employer side, it is also collective in those common situations in which the companies have joined together in an employer association for purposes of bargaining with a union.

Characteristics of Collective Bargaining

Collective bargaining has been characterized as a form of industrial democracy and industrial government. The management and union representatives sit down at the bargaining table, where they deliberate, persuade, try to influence, argue, and haggle. Eventually they reach an agreement, which they record in the form

---

[1] For the evolution of concepts and terminology in this field see Vernon H. Jensen, "Notes on the Beginnings of Collective Bargaining," *Industrial and Labor Relations Review*, Vol. 9, No. 2 (January 1956), pp. 225–234.

of a labor–management contract. This is the legislative phase, in which the two parties create a type of company-wide set of laws and regulations. This "industrial law" sets forth the rights and responsibilities of the company, the union, and the employees. Ordinarily management takes on the authority and responsibility to administer and operate the agreement. Management initiates actions in conformance with the agreed-upon provisions. This corresponds to the executive function of government. When employees or the union feel they are being denied their rights under the contract, they may submit a grievance to management. This may, if conditions warrant, be eventually taken to an impartial arbitrator for a final decision. This is analogous to the judicial function of government.

Some who are not thoroughly familiar with the collective bargaining process have asserted that there is no essential difference between the negotiating of a commercial contract (for, say, the buying or selling of a commodity) and the bargaining of a labor agreement. But this point of view is somewhat naïve. The employment of human beings cannot be handled in the same manner as the purchase of physical goods. If one businessman contracts with another for the purchase of a load of lumber and the seller delivers inferior merchandise, the buyer can terminate the relationship at that point. But this cannot be done in the relations between management and labor. Generally speaking, the union and the management must learn to live with one another whether they like it or not. They must accommodate to each other. Under the labor law of the land, once bargaining relationships have been commenced, both sides must honestly seek an agreement. They must bargain in good faith. Dealings cannot arbitrarily be broken off.

Further, the negotiation of a labor agreement is quite different from the handling of a commercial contract because of the human relations and political aspects of labor–management relationships. A union is a political-economic organization. Union leaders, being elected, must represent the interests of their constituents. They are often placed in a position where they must cater to the pressures of a strong faction within the union. Union leaders are interested in being re-elected. They have to contend with dissident groups within the ranks. They cannot always negotiate a contract with management according to the cold logics of an issue. In short, the social aspects of collective bargaining set it apart from the negotiation of an ordinary business contract.

THE LEGAL FRAMEWORK OF COLLECTIVE BARGAINING

Labor–management relationships are heavily regulated by both Federal and state labor laws at the present time. This state of affairs commenced in the 1930's with the passage of the Norris–LaGuardia and Wagner acts. Prior to this time the policy of the federal government was to leave the two parties—unions and employers—alone and to exert a minimum of legislative interference. Although prior to the 1930's there existed only a minimum of statute law that dealt directly with collective bargaining, there were an abundance of court decisions that did, in effect, create a common law that provided a form of regulation for labor–management relations. Thus, we find that common law and the court interpretations played a major part in expressing government labor policy from 1800 through the early 1930's, whereas since then statute law has played the dominant role. Each of the major labor relations laws has been enacted in response to pressing needs of society in general as well as needs of the direct parties involved—employees, unions, and employers. An intelligent understanding of the management of people at work and of labor–management relations is not possible without a brief study of the law of collective bargaining.

Pre-Wagner Act Era—Labor and the Courts[2]

Prior to the passage of the Wagner Act in 1935, the basic struggle of unions was for existence and recognition. They sought to exist in an environment in which the economic and political power of the business organization were dominant. Employers were strongly antiunion in their sentiments and actions. Unions, if they successfully met the struggle to survive, then had to win recognition from the employer as the bargaining agent for his employees.

Employers, for their part, did not take the rise of unions complacently. They looked upon unions as a challenge to their basic rights to operate their businesses as they saw fit. They considered that unions threatened the property rights of ownership. It was felt that unions interfered with the relations between management and the workers.

During this era Federal and state courts tended to be sympathetic to the views of employers. As rational bases for their rulings, jurists used three principal common-law concepts: (1) the necessity for preserving free competition with a minimum of interference in the affairs of business organizations; (2) the sanctity of private property rights; and (3) the right to freedom of individual contract.

When unions sought to improve the conditions of employment for their members during the early part of the nineteenth century by calling strikes, they found their efforts frustrated by court orders that held strikes to be criminal conspiracies. It was not until 1842 that the legality of strikes per se was established. This arose as a result of a Massachusetts court decision. Henceforth, judges examined union motives and methods in strike actions to decide whether the strike should be ruled illegal or not.

In 1890 Congress passed the Sherman Act to outlaw business combinations and conspiracies in restraint of trade. Although there is real doubt as to whether Congress ever intended to include union activities within the coverage of this law, nevertheless for many years employers were successful in obtaining court orders to break union strikes under the guise that they constituted combinations and conspiracies in restraint of commerce among the states. It was not until the Apex Hosiery Company and the Hutcheson cases of 1940 and 1941 that the United States Supreme Court ruled that labor unions are not generally subject to antitrust prosecution under the Sherman Act. Later Supreme Court decisions have specified certain limited circumstances in which unions may be liable to antitrust prosecution.

For many years employers were quite successful in impeding union activities by obtaining court injunctions whenever unions called an organizational strike or a strike to improve economic conditions. An injunction is a legal device derived

---

[2] A comprehensive analysis of common and statute labor law and court opinions can be found in Charles O. Gregory, *Labor and the Law*, 2nd rev. ed. (New York: W. W. Norton & Co., Inc., 1958).

from English common law. It is a court order prohibiting a certain activity in order to prevent property damage when there is no other remedy at law. Courts in the United States went beyond the original English concept, because they granted injunctions to employers if there was impending or actual interference with their business even though there had been no damage to physical property. During the late nineteenth century and the first three decades of the twentieth century, the repeated and widespread use of the labor injunction served effectively to render unions impotent.

In 1932 Congress passed the Norris–LaGuardia Anti-Injunction Act, which effectively rendered the Federal judicary neutral in labor disputes. It defined permissible union activities in very broad terms and placed such tight restrictions upon the issuance of an injunction that for all practical purposes the private injunction has ceased to be used as a device to defeat strikes.

The Wagner Act—1935

Labor unrest was rampant during the 1930's. The Great Depression, which began in 1929 with the stock market crash, had caused approximately one fourth of the labor force to be unemployed by 1933. Wage cuts were widespread. Industrial workers in the mass production industries were ripe for unionism. Management during this era had not been sufficiently alert nor enlightened to adopt sound industrial relations policies in keeping with the needs of their employees.

In June 1935, the National Labor Relations Act—popularly known as the Wagner Act after its author and sponsor, Senator Robert Wagner of New York—became law. With the adoption of this far-reaching law, public policy became one of encouragement for collective bargaining as preferable to individual bargaining. The act, in effect, encouraged the unionization of employees and provided the mechanism of secret ballot elections to ascertain the free choice of workers. If the employees voted for union representation, employers were compelled to bargain with that union over wages, rates of pay, hours of work, and other conditions of employment.

The heart of the Wagner Act was contained in Section 7, which stated that "employees shall have the right to self-organization, to form, join, or assist labor organizations, to bargain collectively through representatives of their own choosing, and to engage in concerted activities for the purpose of collective bargaining or other mutual aid or protection."

Unfair Labor Practices of Employers.   To insure that employees could actually engage in collective bargaining activities without retaliation by their employers Section 8 of the Act listed five practices that employers were forbidden to undertake. The law stated that it shall be an unfair labor practice for an employer (1) "To interfere with, restrain, or coerce employees in the exercise of the rights guaranteed in Section 7." Examples of employer conduct prohibited by this provision are (a) threatening employees with loss of jobs or benefits if they should join a union, (b) threatening to close down the plant if a union should be organized in it, and (c) spying on union gatherings.

The second unfair labor practice made it illegal "to dominate or interfere with the formation or administration of any labor organization or contribute financial support to it." This provision of the law put an end to the company-dominated unions (generally called "employee representation plans") that flourished in the 1920's and early 1930's. The third unfair labor practice of employers made it illegal to discriminate in regard to hiring or tenure of employment or any term or condition of employment in order to encourage or discourage membership in a union. This provision prevented a company from demoting or discharging a worker because he was active in forming the union. It also made it illegal to refuse to hire a qualified job applicant because he belonged to a union. The fourth unfair labor practice prevented discharging or discriminating against an employee who filed charges or testified before the National Labor Relations Board, the agency charged with the administration of the law. The final unfair labor practice was refusal to bargain in good faith. Thus if management put into effect a unilateral wage increase without discussing it with the union, this constituted a violation of the law.

National Labor Relations Board.   In order to provide machinery for operating the Wagner Act, the National Labor Relations Board was established. The Board had (and still does have) two major functions. The first is to conduct representation elections to determine if the employees in a company wish to be represented by a union. An important part of this responsibility is the task of deciding which employees should be in the bargaining unit and which should be excluded. If a union wins a bargaining election, then the board certifies that it shall be the "sole and exclusive bargaining agent" for all of the employees in the unit. The second major function is that of adjudicating charges of employer unfair labor practices. If the Board decides that an unfair labor practice has occurred, it is empowered to order a cease and desist order, to order the reinstatement of a wrongfully discharged employee, or to order the payment of back wages.

Experience Under the Wagner Act.   This law played a significant part in fostering the growth of organized labor. In 1935, total union membership stood at about 3.9 million, whereas in 1947, when the Taft–Harley Act was passed, it had reached 15 million. Other factors, of course, contributed to this rapid expansion as well.

Representatives of American management expressed vigorous objection to the Wagner Act on the grounds that it was very one-sided and that it tied the hands of management while giving the unions free rein. It is true that the Act sought to encourage unionization and collective bargaining and imposed no restraints whatever on union behavior. There was great unrest, and many bitter struggles occurred between labor and management during the 1935–1947 period. Much of this could be attributed to the fact that unions and management were going through the difficult process of learning to live with one another. A record number of strikes occurred in 1946. The general public and Congress tended to blame unions for the wave of strikes that occurred during this period. A reaction set in against unions, and this culminated in the passage of the Taft–Hartley Act in June, 1947, over President Truman's veto.

Taft–Hartley Act—1947

Officially titled the Labor–Management Relations Act, the Taft–Hartley Act amended the Wagner Act to a considerable extent. In addition, it initiated a number of new provisions completely beyond the scope of the Wagner Act. The primary purposes of this new law were to regulate and restrict the activities of unions, to protect individual employees and employers against the power of unions, and to attempt to restore a balance of power in labor relations. The Taft–Hartley Act is a very complicated law; therefore we can cover only the highlights here.

The law basically retains all of the provisions of the original Wagner Act that were designed to guarantee to employees the right to form and join unions and to engage in collective bargaining free of any restraint or coercion by the employer. Section 7, dealing with rights of employees, contains the original wording of the Wagner Act plus the statement that employees shall also have the right to *refrain* from any or all of such activities related to union organization and collective bargaining.

The five unfair labor practices of employers contained in Section 8 were retained. However, Congress added six unfair labor practices of unions.

Unfair Labor Practices of Unions. The first unfair union practice consists of restraining or coercing employees in the exercise of rights guaranteed in Section 7 of the Act. The National Labor Relations Board and the courts have interpreted this to outlaw mass picketing, which bars nonstriking employees from entering the plant. Also outlawed are violence on the picket line in connection with strikes and threats to do bodily injury to nonstrikers.

The second unfair labor practice of unions involves causing or attempting to cause the employer to discriminate against an employee in order to encourage or discourage union membership. When the second unfair union practice is combined with the original third unfair employer practice as revised by the Taft–Hartley Act, the net result is to outlaw the closed shop. (The union shop that requires union membership on or after the thirtieth day of employment is legal under the act.)

The third practice consists of a union refusal to bargain in good faith. Examples of such union conduct are the insistence upon the inclusion of illegal provisions, such as a closed shop or a discriminatory hiring hall, in a contract and adamant refusal to make a written contract of reasonable duration.

The fourth unfair practice in reality consists of four separate activities as follows:

1. Requiring an employer or self-employed person to join a union.
2. Forcing an employer to cease handling the products of or doing business with any other person. This is the ban on secondary boycotts. What is a secondary boycott? Let us assume that a union has a dispute with Company A (the primary employer). The union is unsuccessful in taking direct action against Company A, so it pickets or otherwise takes action against Company B (a secondary employer) to induce B to cease buying from or selling goods to A. This action is one type of secondary boycott.
3. Forcing an employer to bargain with one union when another union is already the certified bargaining agent.
4. Forcing the employer to assign particular work to employees in one union rather than to employees in another union. This provision outlaws the jurisdictional strike. Jurisdictional disputes are prevalent when a number of craft

unions struggle for control of the same jobs. Each of the competing unions hopes to obtain employment for its own members.

The fifth unfair labor practice is that of charging excessive or discriminatory initiation fees. In judging whether a particular fee is excessive, the Board considers the practices and customs of other unions in the same industry and the wages currently paid to the employees affected.

The sixth unfair practice is that of causing or attempting to cause an employer to pay money or another thing of value for services that are not performed or not to be performed. This outlaws featherbedding. Unions tend to engage in this practice when employment opportunities for their members are declining. It is a common reaction to prevent displacement of workers due to technological advances.

As with unfair employer practices, the National Labor Relations Board has the power to issue cease and desist orders in connection with union unfair labor practices. It can order a union to reimburse an employee for any wages he may have lost as a result of union discrimination or coercion, and it can require the refund of dues and fees illegally collected. Charges of unfair employer or union practices can be filed at any of the board's regional offices by employers, unions, or individual employees.

Supervisors and Professionals.   The Taft–Hartley Act contains provisions that have an important effect upon certain groups of employees. Whereas foremen and supervisors had received some protection by the National Labor Relations Board if they sought to unionize during the years when the Wagner Act was in effect, the Taft–Hartley Act excluded supervisors from the definition of employees. They are now considered to be members of management and receive no protection under the act if they choose to form a union. Professional personnel, such as engineers and scientists, are considered to be employees and do receive the full protection of the law in regard to self-organization. However, the board is not allowed to include them in the same bargaining unit as all other (nonprofessional) employees, unless a majority of them vote for inclusion in the larger unit. This provision gives recognition to the fact that professional employees feel their problems and interests are quite distinct from those of production and maintenance workers.

Free Speech.   Under the Wagner Act management complained vigorously that it was not allowed to speak freely in connection with unions and their activities. To meet this situation the law states in Section 8c that "the expressing of any views, argument, or the dissemination thereof, whether in written, printed, graphic, or visual form, shall not constitute or be evidence of an unfair labor practice under any of the provisions of this Act, if such expression contains no threat of reprisal or force or promise of benefit." Employers now have considerable latitude to make antiunion speeches to their employees as long as they do not threaten workers or promise benefits. Unions also have the right of free speech.

National Emergency Disputes.   In order to provide a means of settling labor–management disputes and strikes that imperil the national health and safety, a systematic procedure has been established to deal with this serious problem. Whenever, in the opinion of the President of the United States, a threatened or actual strike or lockout will affect an entire industry or substantial part thereof such that the health and safety of the nation will be endangered, he is empowered to appoint a board of inquiry that will investigate the facts in the dispute and report back to the President. Upon receiving this report, the President may direct the Attorney General to petition a federal district court for an injunction to prevent or terminate the strike or lockout. Upon the issuance of this injunction the strike must terminate, and the two parties must make every effort to settle their differences with the help of the Federal Mediation and Conciliation Service. If the strike is not settled, then at the end of 60 days the board of inquiry must make a public report on the status of the dispute and the current position of the two sides. Within 15 more days, the National Labor Relations Board must conduct a secret ballot of the employees to ascertain whether they wish to accept the employer's last offer to the union. The results must be certified to the Attorney General within 5 days. The injunction must be discharged at the end of 80 days if the strike is still not settled. The President must make a full report to Congress, together with any recommendations he wishes to make. The union has a right to strike after the 80-day injunction is lifted if no agreement has been reached.

Between 1947 and 1977 the national emergency provisions of the Act were utilized 34 times. The industries most frequently involved have been maritime, shiploading and unloading (stevedoring), atomic energy, aerospace and coal mining. In the vast majority of those cases in which the dispute continued to the point of a last offer vote by the striking employees, they have voted to reject the employer's offer. Generally they feel that they have more to gain by supporting the position taken by their elected union leaders than by supporting the position of the employer.

Health Care Employees. In 1974 Congress amended the Taft–Hartley Act to bring under coverage of the act employees of nonprofit, private hospitals and nursing homes. Thus, these employees have all of the representational and collective bargaining rights that have been available to private-sector workers since 1935. Special dispute settlement procedures were created for the health care field. If there is a contract negotiation dispute, the Federal Mediation and Conciliation Service may invoke a 30-day no-strike, no-lockout period and set up a fact finding board to make a recommendation for settlement. During this time the Service continues its mediation efforts. At the end of the 30-day period, the union may give a 10-day strike notice to the health care facility and the Service. After the 10 days the union can legally strike.

Appraisal of the Act. The Taft–Hartley Act was passed primarily to control and restrain union activities. It has been partially successful in this respect. There has been a noticeable decline in secondary boycott and jurisdictional strikes. However, the ban on featherbedding has not been effective. The law has been a factor in retarding the organization of nonunion sectors in the South. Employers acquired a potent new device to weaken union organizing campaigns by use of the "free speech" provision. In addition, they can delay a representation election by charging the union with an unfair labor practice if any hint of coercion occurs during the campaign. The inclusion of union unfair labor practices has required unions to exercise the same degree of responsibility in collective bargaining as has been required of employers (via employer unfair labor practices) ever since the Wagner Act became law in 1935.

The Landrum–Griffin Act—1959

During the late 1950's dramatic exposés were made of racketeering, violence, lack of democratic procedures in unions, and collusion between unions and employers. A large share of these malpractices occurred in the Teamster's Union. The basic work of uncovering and publicizing these abuses was done by the Senate Select Committee on Improper Activities in the Labor or Management Field, which conducted investigations and public hearings from 1957 through 1959. This Senate committee was popularly known as the McClellan Committee, after its chairman, Senator McClellan of Arkansas. The law that was passed as a result of the work of this committee is known as The Labor–Management Reporting and Disclosure Act of 1959, commonly called the Landrum–Griffin Act (after its sponsors). This law does far more than merely require the reporting of certain information by unions and management as its name implies. It establishes very detailed federal regulation of the internal affairs of unions, regulates the conduct of union officers, and drastically curtails recognition and organizational picketing. In addition it has made certain amendments to the Taft–Harley Act, including prohibitions against hot-cargo agreements and other types of secondary boycotts. Because the Landrum–Griffin Act is very lengthy and complicated, it will be possible to mention only the highlights here.

The Act contains seven titles, each dealing with a major subject area. We shall discuss briefly all titles except title VI, which deals with miscellaneous provisions.

Bill of Rights of Union Members.   A considerable number of the provisions of the Landrum–Griffin Act are designed to insure that unions are run democratically with full protection for the rights of individual members. Title I of the law, entitled "Bill of Rights," contains some of these provisions. This title stipulates that members shall have the right (1) to attend, participate in, and vote at union meetings and elections; (2) to meet, assemble, and express views at union meetings; (3) to vote on increases in dues and fees; (4) to testify and bring suit when unions infringe the rights of members; and (5) to receive notice and a fair hearing before any union disciplinary action can be taken except for nonpayment of dues. Enforcement of these five "Bill of Rights" provisions is accomplished by employees themselves, who must bring a civil action in a federal district court.

Reporting Requirements.   Title II specifies those reports that unions, union officers, employers, and labor consultants must file with the Secretary of Labor. They become public information when they are filed.

Unions must file a copy of their constitutions and bylaws with the Secretary of Labor as well as a complete explanation of their administrative practices. They must also file a detailed financial report annually.

Union officers and employees must report on any financial interests or income from a company whose employees the union represents or actively seeks to represent. This is designed to uncover or eliminate "conflict of interest" transactions in which union leaders and appointive officials take loans, gifts, and under-the-table payments from management in return for special concessions. Bona fide wages for services as an employee and investments in securities that are traded on an exchange under the Securities Exchange Act are exempted from the reporting requirements. Employers must report any payment or loan to a union or union officer, except the wages paid to a union officer who is at the same time a regular employee. Employers must report payments to employees or a group of employees designed to get them to persuade other employees to exercise or not exercise their self-organizational rights.

Trusteeships.   When a national or international union takes over control of the operation of a local union, including control or seizure of its property and funds, this action is called a trusteeship. In effect, the national ejects the local officers, appoints new local leaders, and closely supervises the running of that union. The McClellan Committee found that though many trusteeships were established to eliminate dishonesty and corruption and to insure democratic processes in local unions, a great many were set up to strengthen the power of corrupt national union officials, to plunder the treasuries of the seized locals, and to thwart the growth of competing political factions.

Under the Act a national union must file a report with the Secretary of Labor for each trusteed local every six months. The report must contain a detailed explanation of why the trusteeship was established or why it has been continued. It is unlawful to count votes of national convention delegates from a trusteed local unless they were elected by secret ballot in an election where all members in good standing could vote. It is also illegal for the national to take any funds from the local except for normal per capita taxes and assessments that are paid also by other locals. A trusteeship will be presumed valid only for eighteen months and will be considered invalid after that period unless clear and convincing proof to the contrary is given.

Election of Union Officers.   Title IV of the Landrum–Griffin Act requires that elections of union officers in local unions be conducted at least once every three years, once every four years in intermediate bodies, and once every five years in a national or international union. At the local level the elections must be by secret ballot of members in good standing. For intermediate bodies and nationals it must be either a secret ballot of all members in good standing or by representatives who were chosen by a secret ballot.

To insure that democratic procedures are followed, the act stipulates that campaign literature must be distributed on equal terms for all candidates at their expense. Lists of members under union security agreements must be made available for inspection without discrimination, and any candidate has the right to have an observer at the polls and at the counting of the ballots. It is illegal for the union to use union dues and assessment funds to promote the candidacy of any person.

Fiduciary Responsibilities.   Title V restates the common law applicable to trust relations by declaring that union officers, agents, and shop stewards occupy positions of trust and that they must hold and use the funds and property of the organization solely for the benefit of the members and in accordance with the constitution and bylaws of the organization. The act makes it a Federal crime for an officer or union employee to embezzle, steal, or willfully misappropriate union assets. Violation of this provision carries with it a penalty of a fine of up to $10,000 and imprisonment up to five years.

Amendments to the Taft–Hartley Act. The Landrum–Griffin Act makes a number of important changes and additions to the Taft–Hartley Act. These are as follows:

1. Tight restrictions are placed upon organizational and recognition picketing. Such picketing is prohibited if another union has been lawfully recognized by the employer, a valid NLRB election has been conducted within the preceding 12 months, or if the picketing union has not filed an election petition within a reasonable time (not to exceed 30 days).
2. Economic strikers whose jobs have been taken by other workers are granted the right to vote in any new NLRB representation election up to 12 months after the strike has begun. This provision was added to prevent an antiunion employer from deliberately getting rid of a union by hiring new workers and then obtaining a new election.
3. It is an unfair labor practice for employers and unions to enter into "hot-cargo" agreements. During the 1947–1959 period the Teamsters Union, in particular, used such contracts as a way of getting around the ban on secondary boycotts contained in the original Taft–Hartley Act. Under a hot-cargo contract an employer agrees to refrain from handling or dealing in the products of any other company or to cease doing business with any other person with whom the union has a dispute.

General Observations of the Act. The Landrum–Griffin Act imposes quite detailed and sweeping controls upon the conduct of union affairs. It requires that they be operated in a democratic fashion. Although most of the general public will applaud this objective, the question may be asked whether it is right to single out only one type of organization in our own society and require that it be run democratically. Should the same principle be applied by law to farm organizations, corporations, and nonprofit institutions? A major objective of the law is to eliminate racketeering, corruption, and collusion between employers and union leaders wherever it exists. A major premise of Congress in passing the law was that union members, if given adequate control over their officers through democratic procedures, would see that their unions were run honestly and with due respect for the rights of the membership. This seems to be a sound generalization; however, there have been instances in the past where democratic unions were nevertheless corrupt.[3]

Practically all of the provisions of the act were put in for the purpose of correcting some specific abuse or evil in the labor–management field. Taken as a

---

[3] See Philip Taft, *Corruption and Racketeering in the Labor Movement*, New York State School of Industrial and Labor Relations, Cornell University, Ithaca, New York, Bulletin 38 (February 1958), pp. 26–28.

whole the act appears to be sound, although there may be some who would quarrel with the extremely close regulation it demands of internal union affairs.

STRUCTURE FOR COLLECTIVE BARGAINING

The listing below shows the various structures for conducting contract negotiations that exist in the United States.

A. Single-Employer Bargaining.
  1. Single-Plant.
  2. Multiple Plants.
B. Multiple-Employer Bargaining.
  1. Local Area (City or Labor Market).
  2. Region-wide.
  3. Industry-wide.

The majority of agreements throughout the country are bargained by a single company dealing with a single union. However, there has been a very pronounced trend for many years toward multiemployer bargaining. Usually when companies band together to bargain with one or more unions, they set up a formal organization with a paid, professional staff. This is called an employer association. On the other hand, sometimes companies cooperate with one another during contract negotiations in order to present a united front to the union, but they do not go so far as to set up a formal or enduring association. In various negotiations with the United Automobile Workers Union, General Motors, Ford, and Chrysler have cooperated in this fashion to reduce the possibility of the union "whipsawing" one firm against another in this very competitive business field.

In single-employer bargaining in the field of manufacturing, a company may have contracts with more than one union, but negotiations are usually conducted separately with each union. Many large multiplant companies, such as General Motors and United States Steel, have practically all of their plants organized by a single union. Each local union of the United Auto Workers from each plant of General Motors, for example, elects representatives to what is known as a conference board, which meets to prepare bargaining demands and bargaining strategy. The actual negotiations are handled by the General Motors Department of the union, which is a permanent organizational branch of the union located at national headquarters in Detroit. Quite often, the president of the national union takes part in negotiations, particularly when the going gets tough. A master agreement is signed to apply to all plants. Then each plant negotiates a supplementary agreement with its local union to cover issues that apply specifically to that unit.

Multiemployer Bargaining

This type of bargaining originated with craft unions at the city level for bargaining with a number of employers under a single contract. Thus a local of the carpenters union may sign an agreement with a number of construction firms in an area. The most common practice in the construction industry at present is for all of the unions (for example, carpenters, electricians, operating engineers, laborers, and bricklayers) to bargain jointly through their building trades council with an employer association composed of all unionized contractors in the area. The negotiation process is centralized and simultaneous for all crafts. When agreement is reached, separate contracts are signed between each local of each union and each employer.

Multiemployer bargaining is extremely common in the local area in construction, hotels and restaurants, laundries, dry cleaning, retail stores, dairy products, book and job printing, and local delivery trucking.

Regional multiemployer bargaining is common in the following industries: pulp and paper, lumbering, nonferrous metal mining, maritime and longshoring, trucking, and textile manufacturing.

Industry-wide bargaining is a term used to designate that type of bargaining that covers many companies in an industry that are distributed widely throughout the nation. Although there is much talk about it, with charges that it is monopolistic, true industry-wide bargaining occurs in only a very few industries. It has been going on in the railroad and bituminous coal industries for a number of years. Figure 5-1 shows a contract bargaining session between negotiators for the United Mine Workers union and the Bituminous Coal Operators Association. Several years ago the basic steel industry shifted from pattern bargaining to industry-wide bargaining. Under pattern bargaining, which persisted until the late 1950's, the United Steel Workers of America bargained a contract initially with "Big Steel," that is, the United States Steel Company. This settlement then became the pattern for agreement with all the other major steel producers. Commencing in the late 1950's, all of the large steel companies have participated jointly in negotiations with the union.

Figure 5-1
A Contract Bargaining Session between Negotiators for the United Mine Workers (on the left) and the Bituminous Coal Operators Association (on the right). (*Wide World Photos*)

Reasons for Multiemployer Bargaining

The basic reason for the development and spread of multiemployer bargaining is to take wages out of competition. From the viewpoint of businessmen, this means that other companies who are competing in the same product market cannot obtain a price and cost advantage by paying lower wage rates for the same classes of labor. One firm may indeed obtain a lower cost advantage over its competitors, but it will be achieved by better management, greater efficiency, and technological improvements and not by paying lower wage rates.

Unions have frequently been the initiators of the demand for multiemployer bargaining. They have long realized that they could not force wages up in one firm if that firm was faced with low wage competition from other companies. Therefore, unions tend to press for uniformity of wages and conditions of employment among all unionized companies in an industry within the area of market competition.

In those industries with many small employers, unions find that contract negotiations and contract enforcement are simplified and less costly when bargaining is carried on with an employer association.

Just as individual workmen organized unions many years ago to increase their bargaining power, so have companies found it advantageous to pool their resources when confronted with a strong union at the bargaining table. By presenting a united front, they can often obtain a more favorable settlement than they could by acting individually.

Disadvantages of Multiemployer Bargaining

The general public and the consumer often suffer as a result of multiemployer bargaining. A generous wage increase may be granted by the employers, and this may then be followed by a price increase by all the firms. The consumer is then given no choice. He cannot patronize one company that bargained more vigorously with the union to obtain a more favorable settlement, because all companies are covered by the same agreement.

When a strike occurs, the entire industry may be shut down. This can cause great inconvenience to the buying public.

The marginal employer who cannot afford to pay the wages or meet the working conditions agreed upon in association bargaining is often placed at a serious disadvantage.

NEGOTIATING THE AGREEMENT

Years ago union–employer labor agreements were generally for one year's duration. During the inflationary period just after World War II, many of these contracts could be reopened for wage negotiations at the end of only six months. This meant that both parties were involved in the ferment of preparation for and the actual conduct of contract negotiations nearly continuously. Since the early 1950's there has been a pronounced trend toward contracts of two and three years' duration. This provides greater security for both sides. It is evidence of greater faith in the grievance process and in day-to-day discussions to solve problems as they arise. It demonstrates increased maturity on the part of labor and management in their bargaining relationship.

Preparations for contract bargaining commence long before the actual negotiating sessions open. For the company the principal spade work is done by the industrial relations director. He and his staff must gather data on prevailing rates of pay and fringe benefit practices in the labor market area and in the industry. The company's financial situation must be analyzed carefully to determine what wage and fringe benefit improvements can be offered, if any. The experience of living with the present union agreement will undoubtedly have demonstrated a number of contract provisions that could be altered to management's benefit. The industrial relations director may hold discussions with plant supervision to collect views on troublesome problems that arose when administering the current agreement. Before entering the negotiations, management will have pretty well decided what its position will be regarding regarding expected union demands. It will have formulated its proposals and possible demands upon the union.

Assuming that the bargaining is being conducted by a local union, the union will normally elect a bargaining committee that includes the principal elective officials plus some shop stewards. The rank and file often participate in expressing their thoughts regarding bargaining demands at a general membership meeting. Many of these stem from unresolved worker complaints and grievances. The leaders cannot simply echo the often varied and conflicting wishes of the membership; but rather they must carefully weigh the merits of each issue and consider the hard realities of what is possible. Quite frequently the international union will help guide the preparatory process. It may insist upon certain uniform union-wide demands and a standard wording of contract clauses.

At the actual negotiating sessions the company may be represented by the chief executive officer, the industrial relations director, the treasurer or the controller, and the manager of manufacturing. The industrial relations director typically serves as chief spokesman. The chief spokesman for the union is usually either the international representative or the local union business agent. Other members of the team may include the local union president, secretary-treasurer, members of the executive board, and perhaps a few shop stewards.

Because the union demands practically always involve increased costs and sometimes restrictions on management's freedom of action, the company spokesmen generally resist or refuse to accede to these proposals. Management typically offers far less than the union demands. The union always asks for more than it really expects to get. A great many sessions may be required to reach agreement upon the issues and upon the specific contract language. The pressure on management is the threat of a strike with consequent loss of business. The union leadership will not call a strike lightly, because a lost strike can mean loss of jobs, a depleted union treasury, and a weakened union. Yet the elected union leaders are under considerable pressure from their constituents to show some gains, that is, to extract concessions from management.

Although strikes make exciting newspaper headlines, the vast majority of contracts are negotiated without a strike year after year. A strike usually occurs when one side (or both) miscalculates the other's limit.

SUBJECT MATTER OF COLLECTIVE BARGAINING

What are the issues about which management and labor negotiate when they meet at the bargaining table? Section 8(d) of the Taft–Hartley Act provides the underlying framework. It requires an employer and the representatives of his employees to meet at reasonable times, to confer in good faith about certain matters, and to put into writing any agreement reached if requested by either party. The parties must confer in good faith with respect to wages, hours, and other terms or conditions of employment, the negotiation of an agreement, or any question arising under an agreement.

Below is a list of topics commonly appearing in union–management agreements. This is a general list; any individual agreement would necessarily contain certain items particular to that situation. The order of topics varies from one agreement to another.

SUBJECT MATTER OF UNION–EMPLOYER AGREEMENTS

I. *Union Recognition and Scope of Bargaining Unit.*

II. *Management Rights (Management Security).*

III. *Union Security.*

IV. *Strikes and Lockouts*

V. *Union Activities and Responsibilities.*
>
> Check-off of dues.
> Union officers and stewards.
> Union bulletin boards.
> Wildcat strikes and slowdowns.

VI. *Wages.*
>
> General wage adjustments.
> Wage structure.
> Job evaluation.
> Wage incentives and time study.
> Reporting and call-in pay.
> Shift differentials.
> Bonuses.

VII. *Working Time and Time-Off Policies.*
>
> Regular hours of work.
> Holidays.
> Vacations.
> Overtime regulations.
> Leaves of absence.
> Rest periods.
> Meal periods.

VIII. *Job Rights and Seniority.*

> Seniority regulations.
> Transfers.
> Promotions.
> Layoffs and recalls.
> Job posting and bidding.

IX. *Discipline, Suspension, and Discharge.*

X. *Grievance Handling and Arbitration.*

XI. *Health and Safety.*

XII. *Insurance and Benefit Programs.*

> Group life insurance.
> Health insurance.
> Pension program.
> Supplemental unemployment benefits.

Substantive Issues

We shall now examine some of the principal substantive issues and note how union and management views tend to differ.

Union Security. The term *union security* refers to both the right of a union to exist as an organization and its right to continued existence in a particular company. The first right is guaranteed by the labor laws of the nation. It is the second right that has caused so much controversy between labor and management. It has been primarily because of long-standing employer opposition to unions that unions have pressed hard to get incorporated into the labor contract some provision that formally insures the union's continued presence in the company. Union security provisions may take any of the following forms:

1. *Union Shop.* All present employees are required to join the union. Newly hired employees must join within a specified number of days after being hired. (The Taft–Hartley Act says this period cannot be less than thirty days, except for the construction industry, where seven days are stipulated.)
2. *Modified Union Shop.* At the time the agreement is signed, present employees who do not belong to the union are not required to join. Those who already belong must continue their membership as a condition of employment, and all new hires must join within a specified number of days.
3. *Maintenance of Membership.* Popular during World War II, this type of union security has declined steadily since that time. Workers who do not belong to the union are not required to join; however, those who do join are required to stay in the union until a brief "escape period" (usually of ten to fifteen days) just prior to the contract termination date.
4. *Agency Shop.* Employees are not required to join the union but must pay a fee to the union for the bargaining services and benefits that the union provides for all in the bargaining unit.

About 80 percent of the employees covered by collective agreements in private industry work under some form of union security provisions.

As already indicated, unions nearly always demand contractual protection for their existence as the bargaining agent in a company. They usually seek the maximum form allowed by law, namely, the union shop. They feel that they need protection against management efforts to oust the union from the shop. Unions feel that all employees within a bargaining unit should pay to support the union, which, under the Taft–Hartley Act, bargains rates of pay and other conditions of employment for all workers regardless of whether they are union members of not. Unions are opposed to nonunion workers becoming "free riders" and enjoying benefits of union membership without supporting it financially. In an open shop the problem of maintaining union membership is extremely difficult in those organizations in which employee turnover is high.

Management views on union security (management tends to refer to it as compulsory unionism) are divided. Some companies encourage employee membership in the union because they do not want factional struggles between union and nonunion groups within the plant. Also they want all employees to belong and to participate in union affairs to that the union will faithfully represent the will of the majority of employees.

It is probably accurate to state, however, that the majority of employers oppose any form of compulsory unionism. Employer groups, such as the National Association of Manufacturers, have advocated state "right-to-work" laws that outlaw the closed shop, union shop, maintenance of membership, and all other forms of union security. As of 1976, twenty states have enacted such legislation. These are mostly Southern and Midwestern states, where antiunion sentiment is strong. The popular argument against compulsory unionism is that no person should have to join a union in order to obtain a job. Such a practice violates the allegedly inalienable right of citizens of the United States to obtain work free of such hampering restrictions. However, the primary reason why many employers and associations of employers oppose union security provisions is that they feel that the union shop grants the union too much economic power. They seek to blunt the power of unions and to discourage union growth by obtaining legislative bans at the state level on all forms of compulsory unionism. Thus, this is primarily a power struggle and not a matter of principle.

Management Rights. Professional business managers as a group and as a class have viewed with some alarm the extension of union influence into subject areas that had been traditionally considered to be exclusive management prerogatives. Management has argued that it has a right and even an obligation to make its own business decisions free from union interference. This concept stems from the property rights of ownership with management acting as the representative of the stockholders in the corporation. In collective bargaining relationships, management often seeks to obtain union agreement that certain specified subject areas, such as determination of products to be made, pricing the product, deciding production methods and processes, setting up accounting methods, direction of the work force, determination of job content, and so on, are sole and exclusive management rights. Basically the management rights issue is the counterpart of the union security problem. The former grants management security and a certain management sphere of influence. The latter provides security to the union as an institution.

Unions, in the United States, have not sought to share with management the authority and responsibility to operate the business. But they generally take the position that a fence should not be built around management prerogatives. They tend to believe that labor should have a voice in all those things that affect employees and employee relationships. They tend to adopt a pragmatic view. Although certain topics may not be of concern to the union today, conditions in the future may change in such a way that the union may become interested in negotiating over a particular subject. There are many subject areas over which management and unions differ sharply over the relative amount of union and management control. Examples are the setting of production standards, imposition of disciplinary penalties, assignment of duties to jobs, subcontracting of work outside the plant, scheduling of work, and the discontinuance of a kind of work.

Management rights clauses in labor agreements take one of two forms. The first takes the form of a broad statement that asserts that the control and operation of the business is vested exclusively in the company management except in so far as these matters may be limited by provisions in the agreement. The second type attempts to list all those management functions that are not subject to joint determination, such as methods of production, planning and scheduling production, job assignments, hiring, employee discipline, and formulation of plant rules.

Wages.   The topics that appear in the typical union contract under the heading of wages are many and varied. Among these are the general across-the-board wage adjustment, the pay grade structure, in-grade rate progression, special rates for learners and apprentices, job evaluation, time study, wage incentives, premium pay practice, reporting and call-in pay, cost of living or escalator clause, and productivity increments. Space does not permit an explanation and analysis of each of these items.[4]

When negotiating, management looks upon wages primarily as a labor cost. Fringe benefits are likewise translated into labor costs. A given union demand for x cents per hour increase in wages is expressed by management as a certain dollar increase in payroll for a month and a year. This affects the cost of goods sold.

In determining what its wage rates should be, management seeks (sometimes in only a general way) to pay rates equal to the average prevailing in its own labor market for each job classification. In deciding upon a wage policy, management also gives consideration to its own ability to pay (that is, profitability), future business expectations, productivity, and the relative supply of labor available in the local labor market.

Unions, for their part, seek to eliminate wages as a factor in competition among employers whom they have organized. They press for wage uniformity throughout an industry for the same class of work. Although this is the long

---

[4] For a discussion of wage issues under collective bargaining see Daniel Q. Mills, *Labor-Management Relations* (New York: McGraw-Hill Book Company, 1978), ch. 15; also, Gordon F. Bloom and Herbert R. Northrup, *Economics of Labor Relations*, 8th ed. (Homewood, Ill.: Richard D. Irwin, Inc., 1977), chs. 5, 11.

range union goal, unions frequently have to settle for something less. But certainly within each company they demand "equal pay for equal work." All employees on the same job should receive the same pay. Unions often demand a single rate for each job. Employers usually want a rate range for each job or for each labor grade in order to pay different wages to people according to variations in performance.

In making its wage bargaining demands upon management, a union typically gives consideration to the company's profit picture, the pattern of settlements in other companies in the same and allied industries, changes in the cost of living, and prevailing wage levels in the area and in the industry. It also keeps careful watch of the wage settlements obtained by rival unions to insure that it does as well.

Job Rights.   Unions try to furnish as much job security to their members as possible. In a craft union, in those common situations in which workers frequently change employers (for example, construction), the union members primarily look to their union for security. By maintaining their membership in the union they can usually obtain a job via the union hiring hall.

However, in the industrial union situation workers look to their employer for job security. This is why unions seek to have all job changes decided on the basis of company seniority. Unions feel that this is a fair and objective criterion for making transfers, promotions, and layoffs. They feel that it eliminates any likelihood of favoritism and discrimination influencing decisions on personnel changes of status.

Management typically desires the freedom to move people from one job to another and to lay off workers when business gets slack, unhampered by union-imposed restrictions. Management feels that the application of rigid seniority rules reduces efficiency and often causes unqualified workers to be assigned to jobs. There is no close correlation between ability and length of service.

The net result of these two opposing points of view is usually a compromise. In the vast majority of companies today, layoffs are handled on the baisis of seniority. This means that the most recent workers hired are the first to go in the event of a layoff. Management always retains full authority to promote a person out of the bargaining unit to an administrative or supervisory position. Criteria for promotion within the bargaining unit are frequently a combination of seniority and ability. Some contracts specify that when choosing from among several employees for a better job, seniority will be the deciding factor only when two or more candidates have equal qualifications. Other contracts state that the most senior man will receive the job, provided he has the minimum qualifications to do the work.

Grievance Handling.   The subject of grievances is dealt with extensively in Chapter 23, "Grievance Handling." However, there are certain collective bargaining aspects of grievance handling that must be mentioned at this point. Nonunion organizations usually do not have formal grievance procedures, although it is generally understood that employees have a right to discuss their dissatisfactions and problems with their immediate supervisors. But the entry of a union into an organization nearly always brings about the establishment of a grievance procedure. Ordinarily an employee who wishes to obtain satisfaction and settlement of a grievance will present it to his supervisor or to his shop steward, who will represent him in discussions with the supervisor. The supervisor as a representative of management will give an answer to the employee and the steward. If they are not satisfied with this action, they may appeal the decision to successively higher levels of management until a mutual agreement is reached. In processing the grievance up through the management hierarchy, higher officials in the union structure enter the picture at each step. Generally, officials of the union at each step occupy positions in the union hierarchy that roughly correspond to those in the management organization with whom the grievance is discussed.

Basically, in presenting grievances to management, the union is asserting that the company has not faithfully and properly administered the terms of the labor agreement. The contract establishes the *rights* of the company, the union, and the employees. The grievance procedure provides the means for adjudicating and interpreting the way in which the labor agreement is applied in practice.

Ninety-four percent of the agreements in force in the United States provide for arbitration as the final step in the grievance procedure. Most agreements provide that the union, if not satisfied with top management's answer to a grievance, can appeal it to an impartial arbitrator who will hold a hearing, listen to testimony from both sides, and examine briefs and documents that may be submitted by the parties. After hearing all of the facts he will render a decision (usually within thirty days) and submit a written statement of his award together with his reasons. In submitting an unresolved grievance to arbitration both parties usually agree that the arbitrator's decision will be final and binding.

PUBLIC SECTOR COLLECTIVE BARGAINING

To this point in this chapter we have talked about collective bargaining in the private business sector of the economy. Collective bargaining in government employment, at federal, state, and local levels, burst upon the scene in the early 1960's and has expanded rapidly since then.

Special Context of Public Collective Bargaining

Much of public sector collective bargaining is modeled after private sector bargaining because the latter emerged first and its laws and procedures are well established. However, there are unique aspects to collective bargaining by government which should be pointed out.

Sovereignty. Traditionally, public officials and writers in political science adopted the view that the government possesses sole authority that cannot be given to or shared with anyone. They held that government exercises its sovereign power in trust for the people. Thus, only the government can establish terms and conditions of employment. Often this view was convenient for government officials who wanted to continue the unilateral establishment of terms of employment. A more recent point of view is that government has, for a very long time, negotiated contracts for personal services with doctors and teachers and for products and services with private companies. Thus, it can just as well negotiate contracts with unions representing employees. In reality, the traditional view was a manifestation in the public sector of the opposition to unions and collective bargaining that held sway among private sector employers for many years.

Finances and the Market. In private business the employer is subject to the discipline of the product or service market. He cannot readily afford to give in to union demands for higher wages and fringe benefits because he may not be able to pass these higher costs on to the customer in the form of higher prices without cutting into the company's sales volume.

In place of market restraints, the public employer must contend with budget restrictions and taxation limitations. Although the American taxpayer has shown considerable tolerance for rising taxes, he has at times dug in and made a stand. The decade of the 1970's furnished abundant evidence of taxpayers voting down school budgets that tended to escalate year after year. This action probably did not indicate an anti-education bias. Rather, school budgets were the only ones that were put before the voters. Also from time to time, citizens do turn out of office elective leaders who have been too loose with the purse strings. The Proposition 13 referendum in California in 1978 is another manifestation of taxpayer resistance to high taxes.

Separation of Powers. In private industry unions negotiate with management, which has formal authority to make binding contracts. In the public sector unions negotiate with representatives of the executive branch of government. However, authority for appropriating money and approving budgets resides in the legislative body. In school systems in many jurisdictions, the voters must authorize the budget and the tax rate.

In some governmental units the distinction between the executive and legislative branches is blurred, for both may participate in labor negotiations.

Ban on Strikes. In both common and statute law, strikes by government employees have traditionally been illegal. Although the Taft–Hartley Act of 1947 deals primarily with private sector collective bargaining, it does contain a specific prohibition against strikes by employees of the United States government or any agency thereof.

In 1970 employees of the U.S. Postal Service struck in violation of the law. This was practically the first strike ever held against the federal government. Strikes at the state and local level do occur occasionally. Public employee strikes usually involve teachers, sanitation workers, clerical employees, policemen, and firemen at the local level. In 1979 several thousand correction officers (guards) in the prisons of New York State struck for more than two weeks.

Some labor relations experts argue that there ought to be a limited right to strike by public employees. They contend that the test ought to be whether the service is essential to the public welfare or not. In recent years the states of Alaska, Hawaii, Pennsylvania, Minnesota, Oregon and Vermont have legalized public employee strikes if no emergency or major inconveniences are involved.

Who Is Management? In the private sector all members of management from foremen on up are effectively excluded from unionization and collective bargaining. However, government practice, although varying widely from one jurisdiction to another, tends to permit lower- and middle-level administrators to union-ize and negotiate contracts with government.

Federal Government

President Kennedy's Executive Order 10988, issued in 1962, affirmed the right of federal employees to join or refrain from joining unions. It created procedures for bargaining unit determination and for union recognition. It required agency heads to bargain in good faith with those unions that had achieved exclusive rec-ognition rights.

President Nixon's Executive Order 11491 of 1969, which superseded E.O. 10988, reaffirmed its basic principles and made improvements in labor relations policy and procedure. It assigns to the Assistant Secretary of Labor authority to determine appropriate bargaining units and supervise recognition procedures. Formerly this was handled by the heads of the various agencies of the govern-ment. The order lists proscribed unfair labor practices of government agency management and of unions. These generally parallel the unfair labor practice provisions of the Taft–Hartley Act. It also specifies standards of conduct of labor organizations.

The order created the Federal Labor Relations Council, which has the respon-sibility of administering the order, handing appeals from decisions of the Assis-tant Secretary of Labor, deciding negotiability issues, determining exceptions to arbitration awards, and handling other matters to effectuate the purposes of the order. This council has responsibility comparable to, but broader than, that of the National Relations Board in the private sector.

The order also set up the Federal Service Impasse Panel, which has responsi-bility for prescribing procedures for negotiation disputes after the parties have been unable, on their own or with the help of the Federal Mediation and Concil-iation Service, to resolve their impasse.

The order also allows for arbitration of grievances. Exceptions to the award can be filed with the Federal Labor Relations Council for final adjudication.

State and Local Government

The extent to which the states have made provision for collective bargaining for public employees varies widely. Some 26 states have enacted broad coverage statutes that require public employers to bargain in good faith with represen-tatives of their employees. New York, Wisconsin, Michigan, and Massachusetts have well-staffed agencies and comprehensive procedures for administering their public employment collective bargaining laws. Some states require that public employers must "meet and confer" but not necessarily that they must negotiate contracts.

Prior to the advent of collective bargaining, personnel policies and practices were administered by state and municipal civil service commissions. These com-missions have had primary responsibility for handling job definitions, pay clas-sifications, hiring, promotions, transfers, and grievances. Labor negotiations have been superimposed upon these systems and some confusion and duplica-tion of authority have resulted. Unions have looked upon civil service commis-sioners as agents of the chief executive and have tried to establish terms and conditions of employment as well as grievance procedures that are separate from civil service control.

STRIKES AND DISPUTE SETTLEMENT

A *strike* is a concerted withholding of labor supply in order to bring economic pressure to bear upon the employer to cause him to grant the employees' and/or the union's demands. It is a test of economic strength and a contest of staying power. Generally in free societies (as contrasted with totalitarian regimes) the right to strike is considered a fundamental right of working people. This does not mean, however, that workers have an unrestricted right to strike under all circumstances. Under our labor law secondary boycott, jurisdictional, and sympathy strikes are illegal.

A *lockout* consists of a shutdown of a plant or place of business by management in the course of a labor dispute with his employees and their union for the purpose of forcing acceptance of his terms. Management ordinarily desires to keep a business in full operation, because work stoppages are costly; they stop production, interrupt sales, and may cause a company to lose its customers. Unions are usually initiators of work stoppages if progress at the bargaining table breaks down. However, we do find that management sometimes resorts to a lockout of the employees after a strike has begun. This is a way of retaliating against the union and is designed to bring the union to its knees. It has become increasingly common in recent years, where companies are organized into an employer association, for all to lock out their workers if the union should strike just one of the member companies.

Dispute Settlement Methods

When there are disagreements between labor and management, they ordinarily meet with one another to negotiate a settlement that will be acceptable to both parties over matters of *interest* (that is, the interests of the two sides in negotiating a new agreement) and over matters of *right* (that is, interpretation of the agreement as in grievance handling). However, there are times when an impasse is reached. The parties are at loggerheads, and resort to economic force sometimes ensues. At this point one of several dispute settlement methods may be brought into the picture.

Voluntary Arbitration. This procedure is most commonly used as the terminal step in a grievance procedure as previously described. Generally either side to the dispute may initiate action to take the unresolved grievance to arbitration. In disputes over matters of interest, as when labor and management are at odds over wages for a new contract, voluntary arbitration is only infrequently employed. This is because it is difficult for an outsider to perform a legislative function and impose a set of conditions upon the two disputants. The union and management are most intimately aware of all ramifications of the problem. The stronger party is rarely willing to let an outsider impose conditions upon it which its adversary could not win across the bargaining table.

Figure 5-2
Secretary of Labor, Ray Marshall, Mediating the Negotiations between the United Mine Workers Union and the Bituminous Coal Operators Association in Washington, D.C. during the 1977–78 Coal Strike.

Compulsory Arbitration.   Compulsory arbitration is arbitration imposed by the government as a last resort when the union and employer are unable to agree upon a settlement. It is compulsory in the sense that the parties must submit the dispute to arbitration and they must abide by the award of the arbitrator (or arbitration panel). Compulsory arbitration is unpopular with both labor and management, because it opens the way for a struggle at a higher level, namely at the political and governmental level. The responsibility for working out common problems is transferred to a government-appointed body. Compulsory arbitration is not currently used to settle contract negotiation disputes in the private sector in the United States. However, during World War II a form of compulsory arbitration was used by the War Labor Board to settle private sector disputes.

In the public sector several states have enacted statutes providing for compulsory arbitration for certain categories of public employees, most commonly police and firefighters. Thus in 1974, New York State provided for arbitration of police and firefighter impasses after mediation efforts had failed. A recent innovation in arbitration is "final offer" arbitration. This is used in some states as a final step to settle contract negotiation impasses in the public sector. The arbitrator or arbitration board must choose for its award either the final offer of the union or the final offer of the employer. Presumably such an arrangement tends to induce the parties to retreat from extreme positions at the bargaining table and make realistic final proposals.

Conciliation and Mediation. These terms are synonymous. They refer to the activity of a third party, often a government official, to help the disputants reach an agreement. The conciliator or mediator helps to keep the parties talking; he makes suggestions; and he tries to persuade and influence them to reach an agreement. He has no final power of decision making, however. The Federal Mediation and Conciliation Service has the authority to offer its services in cases of labor–management disputes. Also, a union or a company may request help from this agency. Many of the industrialized states, such as California, Connecticut, Massachusetts, New Jersey, New York, and Pennsylvania, have a state mediation agency whose staff mediators perform services in a manner similar to their federal counterparts.

From time to time, when a strike occurs in a major industry, high level government officials mediate the dispute. Figure 5-2 shows Secretary of Labor, Ray Marshall, mediating the negotiations between the United Mine Workers union and the Bituminous Coal Operators Association during the coal strike of 1977–78.

Fact-Finding. Although rare in the private sector, factfinding is commonly provided by state statutes as a dispute settlement method for negotiation impasses in the public sector. A fact-finder (sometimes a fact-finding panel of three persons) is appointed by the state labor relations agency after mediation efforts have failed. The fact-finder holds a hearing at which the union and the governmental body involved present their viewpoints and evidence regarding all unresolved issues. The fact-finder then studies the information and issues a report containing recommendations for settlement of the issues. However, his recommendations are not binding on the parties.

In the private sector the Taft–Hartley Act does provide for the use of a Board of Inquiry for helping to resolve national emergency impasses.

Questions for review and discussion

1. What is meant by the term *collective bargaining?* What are its characteristics?
2. In what way were labor union activities subject to antitrust prosecution prior to 1941?
3. What role did the court injunction play in labor-management relations during the early decades of the twentieth century?
4. In what ways did the National Labor Relations Act (Wagner Act) aid the expansion of unions?
5. In what way does the Landrum–Griffin Act seek to provide democratic rights for union members?
6. Some authorities and practitioners claim that strikes are a necessary part of collective bargaining. Without the possibility of a strike, true collective bargaining cannot occur between the union and management. Other authorities assert that the practice of collective bargaining in the United States has matured to the point that peaceful settlement of contract negotiation disputes is nearly always possible. Hence the strike is not a necessary con-

comitant of collective bargaining. Take a position on this issue and substantiate your views.

7. What factors have contributed to the growth of multiemployer bargaining in recent years?

8. As the president of your own company (that is, you are a principal stockholder) would you favor or oppose the granting of a union shop provision to the union with which you have been dealing for several years? Explain your position.

9. In what ways does the entry of a union into an organization restrict management's freedom of action?

10. Distinguish between disputes over matters of *interest* and those over matters of *right*.

11. Explain differences between the context of collective bargaining in the public and the private sectors.

12. In collective bargaining what factors may bolster the union's power vis-a-vis the employer? What factors may bolster the employer's power?

Case problems

Note: Case problems for Chapter 4, "Unions and Management," and Chapter 5, "Collective Bargaining," are placed here because these two chapters deal essentially with the single subject area of labor–management relations.

PROBLEM 1: A TALK BY A PERSONNEL MANAGER

The personnel manager of a local manufacturing company was invited to speak before a class of college seniors taking a course in industrial relations at the university. He was a man of about forty-five and had arrived at his present position via the financial and accounting departments of his company. He had been personnel manager for three years at the time of his talk. As the subject of his lecture he chose to concentrate upon the relations between his company and the local union, with particular emphasis devoted to the political nature of the union. His talk, in abbreviated form, was as follows.

"Our company prides itself on having recognized unions early in the game and on having sound labor–management relations. We granted recognition to our union over forty years ago without there being a strike. I am proud to say that we have never had a single stoppage due to a labor dispute in all the years since.

"The management of our company believes in dealing honestly and in a straightforward manner with the employees and the union. We believe that common sense, logic, and sound business judgment should be all that are necessary to arrive at satisfactory agreements between union and management.

"I am continually annoyed, however, by the fact that political expediency seems to be the guidepost for the behavior of union leaders. Now, the elected officials of our local union consist of the president, vice-president, secretary-treasurer, chairman of the shop committee, and fifteen departmental stewards. All of these fellows are regular company employees who take on these union jobs as extra assignments. The union pays their president about one thousand dollars a year extra for his services. Stewards get no pay from the union. I think those people seek union jobs to be important; to be big shots in front of the men. Getting elected to a union office is nothing but a personality contest. When union election time is getting near, the incumbent officers and stewards become the biggest bunch of back-slappers and hand-shakers that can be found anywhere. They want to get re-elected. They try to show the boys that they are going to bat for them. If problems don't exist, they deliberately create them. They try to give the impression that they aren't letting the company get away with anything. At union meetings you rarely find good solid citizens in attendance. It is always the troublemakers and malcontents who go.

"It is difficult for me to understand, sometimes, why the union officers are so politically oriented. Why don't they act more responsible? Even when the company institutes some new fringe benefits or service for the employees, like new coffee machines or better washroom facilities, the union bigwigs try to claim that they had to work hard to extract these benefits from management.

"Let's take the case of the increase in pay for a special setup man's job on which two men were employed. The skill requirements of the job had increased. We offered the union fifteen cents more per hour, and they accepted. However, when the chairman of the shop committee informed the workers of their fifteen-cent raise, they complained that they should have gotten twenty-five cents per hour. The committeeman lacked the courage to tell them the increase was proper and just. Instead he returned the complaint to management and asked for a higher rate.

"Before closing I will give you students one other illustration of the political way our union officers act. Joe has been employed as a laborer for three years. He works on the evening shift, which starts at 4 P.M. At 8 P.M., he was reported to be under the influence of liquor. I was called into the case, as I was working late that evening. The evening superintendent and I talked to Joe in the presence of two shop stewards. Joe reeked of alcohol. He could not stand straight even while hanging on to a chair. He became belligerent toward the superintendent and myself. One of the stewards agreed that Joe was very drunk. We told Joe to report to my office at 10 A.M. the next day. He came in accompanied by the chairman of the shop committee and one of the stewards from the previous evening. They claimed that he had been taking antihistamine pills for a cold and that he was doctoring with brandy to ease his cough. They even claimed that a friend of Joe's had passed away and this upset him. They clearly lied to save his job. They wanted to build themselves up in the eyes of the other workers to show how much they did for them. I recommended immediate discharge for Joe, but upon appeal by the union, top management overruled me. He was suspended for two weeks without pay and then returned to his job."

Questions

1. Do you agree that all that is required for successful labor–management dealings is "common sense, logic, and sound business judgment"?
2. Why do you feel the union officers and stewards acted in such a "political" fashion?

3. What conditions are necessary in order for union leaders to act in a truly responsible manner?
4. Do you think that politics can or should be divorced from the affairs of a local union?
5. Based upon his talk, what do you surmise regarding the experience and knowledge of labor relations possessed by the personnel manager?

PROBLEM 2: MEDIATION OF A UNION-EMPLOYER DISPUTE

Bill Smith, a staff mediator for the State Labor Relations Board, was assigned to mediate a contract negotiations impasse between the County of Clarendon and the Public Employees Union, Local 561. The county seat was located in a small city about 175 miles away from Bill's office.

Upon receiving this assignment, Bill contacted the advocates for both the county and the union. The advocate for the union was Edgar Donovan, a field representative who worked out of the union's central office. The advocate for the county was Frank Carrington, a professional labor relations consultant. In addition to setting a date for a mediation session, Bill learned what progress had been made to date in their negotiations (several issues had been settled) and the nature and seriousness of their impasse on the unresolved issues. In his telephone conversations with the two advocates, Bill Smith learned that the union and the county had thoroughly discussed all the unresolved issues across the table. It was mutually agreed that the mediator would work with the union and county negotiating teams in separate rooms when he arrived at the county office building on the agreed date.

Accordingly, at the outset of the mediation session Bill Smith met with each bargaining team in separate rooms. In addition to Frank Carrington, the county was represented by the county administrative affairs officer and three members of the board of legislators (one of whom was the chairman of the board). In addition to Edgar Donovan, the union negotiating committee was composed of the local union president plus representatives from each of the major employee groups in the county—public works (2 persons), county hospital (1), social service (1), mental health (1), custodial (1), and office (1).

Bill first met with the union negotiating committee. He made a brief explanation of the mediation process and how he would work. At this meeting Edgar Donovan, union field representative, explained each issue, as well as the union's and the county's position on the issues. For a salary increase the union's last position before mediation was 10 percent for each of two years. Donovan stated that all the open issues were important to the union. He further stated that the union had made several concessions during the course of negotiations (which had been going on over a period of two months) and that the county had made hardly any concessions.

Then Smith met privately with the county negotiating team. Frank Carrington, the county spokesman, explained the background of negotiations and discussed each of the open or unresolved issues. The county's last salary offer before mediation was 2.5 percent for each of two years and 4 percent for a third year. He pointed out that when the county and the union had reached a contract settlement a year ago, the union membership had voted against ratification. The county did not want a repeat of that situation. The county felt that the union leaders had not done a good job of selling the contract settlement to the membership.

The mediator moved back and forth between the rooms occupied by the union and the county teams. He transmitted proposals and counter-proposals. He suggested grouping the proposals into packages. For example, one union package dealt with five issues. In this package the union offered to drop one of its proposals, the county should drop one of its proposals, and the county should grant three of the union proposals (which represented slightly compromised positions from earlier union stances).

By the end of the first mediation session, which had lasted six hours, tentative agreement was reached on six of the twelve issues that were at impasse. However, Bill realized that these were of lesser importance and the really difficult issues were still to be settled. The next mediation session was scheduled for one week hence. Two days after the first session, Bill telephoned Edgar Donovan to find out what salary increase the union would accept. Donovan replied that the union wanted a 7 percent increase for each of two years as a very minimum.

At the start of the second mediation session, Bill Smith talked briefly with each group separately. Then he asked to speak privately with Edgar Donovan out in the hall. After the two had been conversing in the hall for perhaps two minutes, Alice Fellows, the president of the local union, came out into the hall. She asked to join the discussion. The mediator wanted to know if the union would accept compromises on its proposals and if it would drop any items. While the three of them were standing in the hall, two of the union committee members came out of their room and walked slowly down the hall to the drinking fountain. The mediator then took the two union leaders into an empty office and closed the door. The union leaders explained the union position on the six unresolved issues and what compromises it could make. They then said that there were 200 employees in the department of public works out of a total of 700 in the bargaining unit. These people were pushing hard to have vacancies filled by awarding open jobs to the most senior qualified employees within the department. They claimed that sometimes the better jobs were filled by direct hiring from the outside and that political patronage sometimes determined who was selected. Also certain employees in the social service and mental health departments must be "on-call" in the evenings and on weekends. Currently they were given one-half hour of compensatory time off at a later date for each hour of "on-call" time. The county wanted to eliminate this compensatory time off because it said the employees weren't actually working during "on-call" time. These employee groups did not want to be "on-call" if they didn't receive some compensatory time off. Further, the union wanted the county to set up a disability insurance program to provide payments to those employees who were ill and had exhausted their sick leave days of entitlement.

After talking with the two union leaders, the mediator talked with the county team. He explained the union positions and possible compromises. But he did not discuss salary at this time. The county was strongly opposed to filling vacancies on the basis of the most senior qualified employee who applied. Bill Smith asked if the county would be willing, at least, to interview the three top qualified employees who apply. The mediator asked if the county would be willing to grant compensatory time off at a rate of ⅓ hour for each hour "on-call." The county said it could not afford to set up a disability insurance plan. The mediator suggested that a sick leave bank might be adopted as a substitute for a disability insurance plan. The cost would be very small.[5]

The county wanted to caucus privately on these matters so the mediator waited in the hall. A few minutes later Frank Carrington joined Bill in the hall. Together they went into the empty office. Carrington suggested that the county would be willing to make a package offer on all open issues. Carrington asked what salary increase the union would accept? Bill asked if the county would offer 7 percent for each of two years. Frank Carrington said, "No." The county was willing to pay 5½ percent for each of two years and would offer 6 percent for a third year if the union would sign a three year agreement. They then discussed the general outline of a package that might be acceptable to both the union and the county. Frank Carrington returned to his county team while Bill Smith met with the union. Smith explained that a package offer on all six unresolved issues was being formulated by the county team. One of the union representatives quipped that he wondered earlier, when Smith went out of the room with Edgar Donovan, whether they were going to go into the county meeting room by themselves.

In a few minutes, Bill Smith went into the county room to learn of its package offer. This offer consisted of the following: 1) 5 percent, 5 percent, and 6 percent salary increase for each of three years; 2) interview top 3 candidates for vacancies; 3) sick leave bank; 4) ¼ hour compensatory time off for each hour of "on-call" duty; 5) no concessions on the other two union proposals.

The mediator then transmitted this package to the union group. They asked for time to caucus privately. The mediator waited in the hall.

In ten minutes Edgar Donovan and Alice Fellows came into the hall and all three went to the empty office. The union leaders said the package was partially acceptable but they insisted on more money than offered by the county. Also the union was opposed to a three year agreement. Furthermore the department of public works people wanted two job titles increased in pay by 20 cents per hour. (This matter hadn't been mentioned before.) The public works department was the largest in the entire bargaining unit and this group had been principally responsible for voting down the contract the first time a year ago. Also, the two public works representatives weren't fully satisfied with the county offer to simply interview three employees for job vacancies; however, the rest of the committee had urged them to accept this and they had reluctantly done so. Smith asked if the union would accept 6½ percent for each of two years. They said, "Yes."

The mediator then met with the entire county team and expressed the concerns of the union. He pointed out the special interests of the public works employees. It seemed that the two issues standing in the way of a settlement were salary and the special concerns of the public works employees. (Bill Smith felt privately that both bargaining teams genuinely wished to reach an agreement this evening.) The mediator suggested that a settlement with the union could be

---

[5] In a sick leave bank each employee donates, say, one day per year of his accumulated sick leave to a fund of days to be granted to employees who are ill and who have exhausted their sick leave days of entitlement.

reached with a salary offer by the county of 6½ percent plus some concession to the public works group. The county asked to caucus privately.

A few minutes later Frank Carrington asked Smith to meet again with the county team to obtain their "final offer." This offer was for a salary increase of 6 percent for the first year and 6½ percent for the second year of a two year contract. There would be no special concessions for the public works group except that the top three employee-candidates for vacancies would be interviewed. Tentative agreements on all the other issues were reviewed.

Carrington and Smith walked out into the hall together. Carrington suggested that if the union was agreeable to the terms discussed, it would be best for the union to make this package offer to the county. The county would then accept. The salary increase was slightly greater than the amount authorized by the full county legislature of seventeen members. But he was confident his committee could sell this amount to the full legislature.

Bill Smith then presented the full package to the union bargaining team. The team accepted the entire package without change. No further mention was made of the special concerns of the public works group.

Both negotiating teams then met to work out the final contract language on all the issues that had been at impasse. At 2 A.M. the mediation session was concluded and the participants all shook hands with one another.

Within two weeks both the union membership and the county legislature had ratified the agreement.

Questions

1. Why did the mediator deal with the union and county teams in separate rooms instead of together?
2. Why did the mediator hold several private meetings with the advocates?
3. What do you make of the union team's behavior when Mediator Smith invited Edgar Donovan into the hall?
4. Why did the county want the final package to be presented as an offer of settlement terms by the union?
5. How do you evaluate the special concerns of the public works group? Why weren't their concerns pressed further at the end?
6. Why was mediation needed to help resolve the impasse? Why couldn't or didn't the parties reach the same conclusion without the services of a mediator?

Suggestions for further reading

Basic Patterns in Union Contracts, 8th ed. Washington, D.C.: Bureau of National Affairs, 1975.

ELKOURI, FRANK and EDNA A. ELKOURI. *How Arbitration Works*, 3rd ed. Washington, D.C., 1973.

MARTIN, JAMES E. "Union–Management Relations in the Federal Government: An Exploratory Analysis," *Public Personnel Management*, Vol. 5, No. 5 (September–October 1976), pp. 353–362.

MILLS, DANIEL QUINN. *Labor–Management Relations*. New York: McGraw-Hill Book Co., 1978.

MYERS, A. HOWARD and DAVID P. TWOMEY. *Labor Law and Legislation*, 5th ed. Cincinnati: Southwestern Publishing Co., 1975.

REHMUS, CHARLES M., ed., *Public Employment Labor Relations: An Overview of Eleven Nations*. Ann Arbor, Mich.: The University of Michigan, Institute of Labor and Industrial Relations, 1975.

SIMKIN, WILLIAM E. *Mediation and the Dynamics of Collective Bargaining*. Washington, D.C.: Bureau of National Affairs, 1971.

SLICHTER, SUMNER H., JAMES J. HEALY, E. ROBERT LIVENASH. *The Impact of Collective Bargaining on Management*. Washington, D.C.: The Brookings Institution, 1960.

TAYLOR, BENJAMIN J. and FRED WITNEY. *Labor Relations Law*, 2nd ed. Englewood Cliffs, N.J.: Prentice-Hall, Inc., 1975.

ORGANIZATION
AND
JOBS

Organization

Organization and the management of people at work are intimately related. The genesis of organization occurs when two or more people unite to achieve a common goal. If, for example, four friends decide to build a camp in the mountains to be used as a base for hunting and fishing trips, they must organize into a smoothly functioning team. The foremost organizational steps that these four friends must take are as follows: (1) decide their specific objectives for a camp in terms of location, cost, size, and design; (2) allocate different tasks to the individual persons according to their interests and abilities; and (3) develop the pattern of relations among the four individuals. This will involve designation of the person who will be in charge of the project, communication, coordination of efforts, and group and individual decision making. If the people in this group know one another well and are compatible, the problem of creating a smooth working team that successfully gets the camp built may not be particularly difficult. However, if one switches his thinking to the level of the large-scale organizations that have tended to become increasingly dominant in our society, he may appreciate that more careful planning and more complex organizational arrangements are required to make them function properly. To initiate, operate, and regulate entities having thousands of members is no simple managerial problem. Consider the organizational problems involved in managing the military forces of the

United States with its millions of men and women in uniform: the United States government itself, with its countless departments, bureaus, agencies, and services; or the great business corporations, such as the American Telephone and Telegraph Company, General Motors, and International Business Machines Corporation.

In order to function effectively, a large organization must systematize its way of doing things into plans, policies, procedures, rules, departments, specific jobs, and so on. A definite hierarchy of officials, managers, and supervisors must be established. The flexibility and informality characteristics of the small organization do not exist in large systems. On the other hand, the large organization exhibits greater stability than the small one.

In this chapter we shall explore the principal approaches that have been developed for the study of organization. We shall examine the issues of organization structure, delegation, decentralization, line and staff, and bureaucratic and organic systems of organization.

Organization Defined

An organization is a system, having an established structure and conscious planning, in which people work and deal with one another in a coordinated and cooperative manner for the accomplishment of recognized goals.

When we speak of an organization as a system, we mean that it consists of many interdependent constituent parts and that there are subsystems within the whole system. When we speak of structure, we mean that there is a degree of formality involved and that the members have designated roles to play. Conscious planning implies rationality, direction, and choice. People work in organizations in a coordinated and cooperative manner. Their behavior is not undirected and random. The activities are purposeful and goal seeking. The goals may be determined by concensus of involved parties both within and outside the organization or they may be set by fiat by one or more authority figures. The foregoing features distinguish an organization from a temporary grouping of people, an informal group, a friendship group, a crowd, a tribe, or a clan.

The process of organizing involves dividing all the work that has to be accomplished and assigning it to individuals, groups, and departments. This includes division of activities by level of authority and responsibility and also division of work across the establishment into different kinds or types. It entails the utilization of mechanisms for coordinating the efforts of individuals and groups. The relationships among members must evolve and become productive. Authority, responsibility, delegation, consultation, decision making, communication, and conflict resolution are all part and parcel of organization.

Examining the definition of organization and its amplifying ideas, one will conclude that it has wide application to all fields of endeavor. It includes not only business enterprises, but also government, the military, colleges and schools, churches, and such community service organizations as the Boy Scouts, Rotary, Kiwanis, and YMCA.

APPROACHES TO THE STUDY OF ORGANIZATION

Let us trace the evolution of theories of organization as these have developed since the early years of the twentieth century.

Classical

The earlier works have been designated the classical or traditional theories of organization and management. They belong to three main categories: (1) scientific management; (2) administrative management; and (3) the bureaucratic model of organization. Let us examine each in turn.

Scientific Management.   The founder of this movement was an American engineer and management expert, Frederick W. Taylor (1856–1915).[1] He did not create a general theory of organization; rather he propounded a number of related techniques and philosophies derived from his extensive management and consulting experience. He was primarily concerned with manufacturing management and efficiency. He initiated and developed systematic job study, time study, standardization of the job, task specialization, setting of a measured quota of work, wage incentives to induce high output, and careful worker selection and training. He advocated maximum worker productivity rather than restriction of output. He proposed the use of science in managing the shop.

Taylor removed the work planning responsibility from the employee and assigned it to a management specialist. He proposed a system of factory management called functional foremanship. Although it never took hold, it served as a forerunner of the expansion of staff planning and control in the factory.

The scientific management movement spread throughout the United States and Europe. Industrial leaders saw it as a way to higher productivity, greater profits, lower costs, and better control of the man–machine system. Philosophically it was based upon the Protestant ethic, economic man, rational man, and the competitive view of man.

Administrative Management.   Whereas scientific management focused upon the organization from the level of shop management, the administrative management theorists looked at the organization from the top down. Among its leaders were Henri Fayol, a French industrialist; Luther Gulick, an academician and public administration specialist; Lyndall Urwick, a British consultant and theorist; and James D. Mooney and Alan C. Reiley, General Motors executives.[2]

The administrative management theorists promulgated universal principles of organization and management. Although they each expressed their universal principles somewhat differently, the following represents a synthesis of their main propositions:

---

[1] Taylor's views are given in his *Principles of Scientific Management* (New York: Harper and Row, 1919).

[2] Henri Fayol, *General and Industrial Administration*, trans. by Constance Storrs (London: Sir Isaac Pitman & Sons, Ltd., 1949); Luther Gulick and Lyndall F. Urwick, eds., *Papers on the Science of Administration* (New York: Institute of Public Administration, Columbia University, 1937); James D. Mooney and Alan C. Reiley, *Onward Industry* (New York: Harper and Row, 1931).

1. Specialization of function and division of labor are necessary for efficiency.
2. Coordination of functions and people is to be performed by the manager of each unit.
3. The responsibility and authority of each supervisor and manager must be clearly delineated. There must be a clear line of authority from the top to the bottom of the structure (chain of command). Authority emanates from the top and flows downward through the organization. Responsibility must equal authority. Each person shall have only one boss (unity of command).
4. Orders, information, and complaints should flow primarily along the lines of the chain of command and there should be no by-passing of an individual manager in the chain of command.
5. The number of direct subordinates that one person can effectively supervise is limited to five or six, although the number may vary according to circumstances (span of control). Later formulations by some writers of the classical orientation reject a specific number as a universal limit but do hold that there is a limit, with the exact number depending upon many underlying factors that affect the complexity of the manager's job.
6. First design the organization and the jobs and then find the people to fit these jobs. Do not shape the job to fit the abilities and interests of the individual.

Bureaucratic Model.   The concept of bureaucracy as a model of formal organization was originated by the great German sociologist Max Weber, who did most of his writing during the 1900–1920 period. In looking at the development of civilization through the broad sweep of history, Weber viewed the world, especially industrialized societies, as becoming progressively more rational and secular. In constructing and operating the institutions upon which man is dependent for the necessities of life, mankind tended to base its actions more and more upon knowledge, rational decision making, and technology and less and less upon mysticism and the occult. Weber's ideas concerning bureaucracy were but a part of his total social theory based upon the study of religion, capitalism, industry, and the political structure of society. He viewed bureaucracy as the most efficient instrument for operating large-scale enterprises, both public and private.[3]

The principal features of bureaucracy are (1) clear-cut division of labor and a high degree of specialization; (2) each lower office is under the control of a higher one (hierarchy); (3) a system of rules impersonally administered; (4) employment and assignment to positions based upon qualifications, not nepotism or favoritism; (5) job security for employees; and (6) extensive use of records, documents, and files.

Critique of the Classical View.   Undoubtedly the classical theories of organization contain much that is of merit. In propounding their theories, the classical writers were giving what they observed to be truths about well-run and successful enterprises. Many establishments, both public and private, have been operated generally according to the principles formulated by these writers.

Yet in recent years the classical concepts and propositions have been subjected

---

[3] Max Weber, *The Theory of Social and Economic Organization*, trans. by A. M. Henderson and Talcott Parsons (New York: The Free Press of Glencoe, 1964).

to attack by contemporary theorists, primarily those of the behavioral science school of thought.

One major criticism has been that classical theory represented a mechanistic view of man in the organization. He was expected to be pliant and submissive—to do what he was told. Job performance as to both quantity and quality was highly standardized. The scope of job responsibilities was to be narrow. Individuality in the work role was to be minimized. Motivation to work was based primarily upon money incentives and authoritarian leaders. Scant attention was given to attitudes, morale, and group relationships. Excessive emphasis was placed upon fitting the person to the job. They did not allow that individual to shape his job in accordance with his special skills and abilities.

Authority tended to be viewed as a quantifiable entity that could be measured out and assigned to managers. If a manager had authority, he was also presumed to have power equivalent to his authority. Generally ignored were the dynamic aspects of power and influence, and the political aspects of an executive's role. Implicit was the notion that officials were all-seeing and all-knowning just because they had been assigned formal authority.

Although classical writers discussed line and staff responsibilities at some length, they accorded staff a distinctly subordinate and auxiliary role. Perhaps they should not be faulted too seriously, though, for failing to foresee the ascendancy of staff in our modern, complex, high-technology enterprises. After all, the classical observers did depict the organizational world as it existed in their day.

Behavioral Science

The early contributors in this field, who did their work from the late 1920's through the early 1950's, have been called the human relationists. They were not called behavioral scientists in those days. They were primarily psychologists and industrial sociologists who belonged to university faculties. Private industry was their laboratory.

The research investigations of Elton Mayo and his Harvard University colleagues at the Hawthorne Works of the Western Electric Company in Chicago from 1927 to 1932 marked the beginning of the human relations movement. This series of studies demonstrated the key importance of group pressures, social relations, and attitudes toward supervision and the job as determinants of group productivity.

Whereas classical organization theorists focused upon task, structure, and authority, human relationists emphasized human dimensions. The enterprise was viewed as a social system as well as an economic-technical system. The informal work group was identified as a major source of worker control. Both the formal organization structure created by management and the informal organization that just evolved had to be taken into account in explaining how and why an enterprise functioned as it did.

While traditional writers viewed the authority of the boss and pay as prime motivators, the human relations school emphasized the importance of psychological and social factors in shaping employee behavior.

Many human relations theorists held that participation in management planning and decision making yielded positive effects in terms of both morale and productivity.

Managers were told that human behavior in the company had both its rational and nonrational components. Feelings, sentiments, and values were legitimate and necessary concerns of the manager.

The impact of the human relations school has been great. Countless management-training programs in both industry and government have contained a heavy component of material in human relations, that is, in motivation, morale, leadership, interpersonal communication, counseling and listening skills, and group dynamics. Managers have been sensitized to the importance of the human dimension.

However, the human relations movement has had its share of critics. Much of the criticism pertains to the way it has been operationalized in industry. The charge has been made that the human relationists were soft in their demands upon workers, that human relations emphasized manipulation of the worker, that it ignored the influence of unions, and that it overlooked the effects of technology and the economic environment upon the organizational system.

The modern contributors have rejected the human relations label for themselves. Instead, they call themselves behavioral scientists, organizational psychologists, organization theorists, and organization development specialists. Because of the large number of contributors to this growing field, we can refer to only a few of the leaders here. The works of Douglas McGregor, Rensis Likert, Frederick Herzberg, Warren Bennis, and Chris Argyris are significant and generally representative of this field.[4]

Although each of these leaders makes his own unique contributions, there are unifying and consistent themes among their works. They exhibit an optimistic view of the nature of man. They believe in his basic goodness. They believe that high performance can better be achieved by self-direction and control than by rigid bureaucratic regulation. Rather than fragmentation of work and narrow job definitions, they propose job enrichment. Positive motivation (not punitive), supportive leadership, and group methods of supervision are emphasized. They hold that the desirable organizational climate is one in which employees and managers can be more open, genuine, and trusting of others. Collaboration and teamwork are preferable to the all-too-common destructive interpersonal competition that we witness in business enterprises.

Systems View

General systems theory has become popular in the past twenty years because of its apparent ability to serve as a universal model of systems including diverse physical, biological, social, and behavioral phenomena. Systems theory is rather abstract. Theorists seek generalizations that help explain the functioning of various entities and processes.[5]

---

[4] Douglas McGregor, *The Human Side of Enterprise* (New York: McGraw-Hill Book Company, 1960), and *The Professional Manager* (New York: McGraw-Hill Book Company, 1967); Rensis Likert, *The Human Organization* (New York: McGraw-Hill Book Company, 1967); Frederick Herzberg, *Work and the Nature of Man* (Cleveland: World Publishing Company, 1966); Warren Bennis, *Changing Organizations* (New York: McGraw-Hill Book Company, 1966); and Chris Argyris, *Interpersonal Competence and Organizational Effectiveness* (Homewood, Ill.: Dorsey Press, 1962).

[5] For sources on general systems theory applied to organization and management, see Richard A. Johnson, Fremont E. Kast, and James E. Rosenzweig, *The Theory and Management of Systems*, 3rd

A system is an organized whole, consisting of interrelating and interdependent parts. Organization theorists treat organizations as systems. They examine the relationships among the elements of the organization, the systems and subsystems of the organization, and interaction with other systems in the environment.

There are several important systems concepts that apply to organizations. Human organizations are predominantly *open systems*. This means that they interact with various elements of their environment. A business corporation, for example, interacts with many external groups such as customers, suppliers, the public, and various levels of government. It is affected by economic, social, and political forces. The business firm, in turn, affects the external groups with which it interacts.

Organizations tend toward a *dynamic or moving equilibrium*. The members seek to maintain the organization and to have it survive. They react to changes and forces, both internal and external, in ways which often create a new state of equilibrium and balance. *Feedback* of information from a point of operation and from the environment to a control center or centers can provide the data necessary to initiate corrective measures to restore equilibrium.

Organizations and the world of which they are a part consist of a *hierarchy of systems*. Thus, a corporation is composed of divisions, departments, sections, and groups of individual employees. Also the corporation is part of larger systems such as all the firms in its industry, the firms in its metropolitan area, and perhaps an association of many firms from many industries such as the National Association of Manufacturers.

Interdependency is a key concept in systems theory. The elements of a system interact with one another and are interdependent. Generally a change in one part of an organization affects other parts of that organization. Sometimes the interdependencies are not fully appreciated when changes are made. A change in organization structure and work flow in one department may unexpectedly induce changes in departments that relate to the first department.

Systems theory contains the doctrine that the whole of a structure or entity is more than the sum of its parts. This is called *wholism*. The cooperative, synergistic working together of members of a department or team often yields a total product that exceeds the sum of their individual contributions.

Systems theory helps organize a large body of information that might otherwise make little sense. It has made major contributions to the study of organization and management in recent years. Systems theory aids in diagnosing the interactive relationships among task, technology, environment, and organization members. Practitioners have adopted the system's conceptualization in designing, building, and operating management information systems and automation processes. Systems concepts have been applied in project and matrix organization designs.

In contrast to the classical models of organization, the systems approach has shown that managers operate in fluid, dynamic, and often ambiguous situations. The manager generally is not in full control of these situations. He must learn to shape actions and to make progress toward goals but he knows that results are affected by many factors and forces.

---

ed. (New York: McGraw-Hill Book Company, 1973); *Academy of Management Journal,* Vol. 15, No. 4 (December, 1972), entire issue devoted to systems theory.

However, systems theory applied to organization has its limitations. It is in its early stages of development. It does not, at present, comprise a consistent, articulated, coherent theory. Much of it constitutes a high level of abstraction. To be really useful to the professional practice of management, its spokesmen and leaders must move down to a more concrete and operationally useful range.

ORGANIZATION STRUCTURE

Organization implies structure. The total work to be carried on must be grouped by kind or type into divisions, departments, sections, and units. Likewise the work must be grouped into different levels; that is, the managerial hierarchy must be set up and defined. Means must also be divised to provide for coordination and integration of people and their activities.

Grouping Activities by Kind

There are five basic ways of grouping work activities. They are by (1) function, (2) location or geographical area, (3) product, (4) customer or client, and (5) number of persons. Let us examine each of these.

Function. Grouping activities according to similar work, skills, knowledge, and orientation is the most widely used of all bases of departmentation. This is done with both "brain work" and manual work types of activities. Thus, companies group all the engineers together into an engineering department and all the personnel specialists into a personnel department. Electricians may be grouped together in the electrical section of the maintenance department. Departmentation by *process* is closely akin to functional grouping. Thus all electroplating, machining, and electronic data processing may be grouped into separate departments. Figure 6-1 shows a manufacturing firm organized by function and process specialization.

Advantages of functional grouping are that it gains the efficiency and expertise of occupational specialization, it facilitates training of personnel, and it promotes cooperation because people with similar interests and values are grouped together. Process specialization in production departments provides for the collection of special purpose equipment into departments and avoids the costly duplication of machinery that occurs in manufacturing concerns in which equipment and processes are grouped by product responsibilities.

However, there are definite disadvantages. Overspecialization and the development of an insular, narrow viewpoint can occur among the personnel. If productivity in the factory is low, the mechanical engineer tends to see it in terms of a need for better machinery and conveyors, the industrial engineer thinks that the major problem is lack of production standards and wage incentives, and the training director sees this as a problem to be solved by better employee training. With functional departmentation, the broad viewpoint and concern for the whole organization tend to occur only at the level of top management.

Location and Geographical Area. Sales forces are typically organized by this method. Thus, a company may have a sales office in San Francisco to cover the

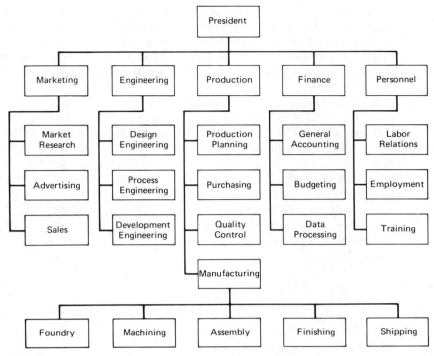

Figure 6-1
Chart Showing a Manufacturing Firm Organized by Function and Process.

western part of the country, one in St. Louis to cover the Midwest, and one in New York City to take care of the East. Automobile manufacturers locate assembly plants in different parts of the country and in foreign lands. Other examples are the U.S. Postal Service, Internal Revenue Service, and the Federal Reserve System. The usual reasons for organization by location are to get close to clients to obtain business and provide good service or to get close to sources of raw materials to minimize transportation costs.

Product. This method is very common in the manufacturing field. The General Electric Company, for example, has over one hundred separate product departments. Examples are the Clock and Timer Department, Power Transformer Department, Large Lamp Department, and the Silicone Products Department. Because GE also has a decentralized management structure, these product departments are self-contained in that they have their own engineering, sales, purchasing, accounting, and employee relations units as well as the production units.

In American industry there has been a strong trend toward product departmentation in recent years. Originally, many companies were organized functionally, but as they grew the problems of coordination and achieving a unified effort became so difficult that they set up product divisions with functional units within their divisions. While product departmentation gains unified accountability for performance of product lines, it does entail the possible disadvantage of duplication of effort by staff groups in each product department.

Customer or Client.   A sales force may be divided into those calling on government agencies, industry, and private individuals. The lending units of a bank may be specialized along the lines of a small installment department and a commercial department. This type of specialization may be advantageous if the personnel must cater to the special needs of particular classes of customers.

Number of Persons.   Oftentimes there are large numbers of employees who are doing the same thing, working in the same general location on the same products and for the same clients. Yet it is necessary for administrative control purposes to set up units, sections, and departments. Thus, in the Army, enlisted men are organized into squads, platoons, companies, battalions, and the like. In a large office one hundred clerks who are doing identical work may be grouped into four separate sections with a supervisor for each.

In considering all of the foregoing bases for grouping activities it ought to be noted that rarely does one enterprise adopt only one pure form. Rather, it uses a combination. And as technology and environmental influences dictate, it may change from one mode to another.

Project and Matrix Organization

The project form of organization is a combination of the functional and the product types of structures. It has been variously called *project management, program management, product management,* and *matrix organization.*[6] It came into prominence in the 1960's when the United States Department of Defense and the aerospace industry began using it extensively. For many years companies engaged in manufacturing and selling consumer goods have had product managers who pilot particular products from the initial development stage through manufacturing, market testing, and ultimate sales to the consuming public. A product manager's role is that of a planner, coordinator, initiator, expeditor, and persuader. He has substantial responsibility for the success of his product but normally possesses little formal authority.

The pure functional form of organization is often inadequate to meet the problem of obtaining synchronized effort on large complex projects and in situations in which product lines become diverse, market competition changes rapidly, and time schedules are tight. In such situations in which the functional departments are coordinated only at the level of top management, one finds that bottlenecks occur too often, there is confusion on priorities, project planning is inadequate, and too many problems get bucked upstairs to top management for resolution. To meet these difficulties, project and matrix forms of organization have been developed. Oftentimes projects have a finite duration. They are created, they live, and they terminate. One doesn't necessarily need the same people on a project throughout all phases of the work. By using project management, people can be shifted around as needed but they always retain their functional department home.

Project management can take a variety of forms. The three principal kinds are

---

[6] For sources on project management, see David I. Cleland and William R. King, *Systems Analysis and Project Management* (New York: McGraw-Hill Book Company, 1968); Jay R. Galbraith, "Matrix Organization Designs," *Business Horizons,* Vol. XIV, No. 1 (February 1971), pp. 29–40.

Figure 6-2
A Matrix Organization.

(1) staff project manager; (2) matrix; and (3) line project manager. Intermediate forms using task forces and committees are also used.

The staff project (or product) manager may be created when some general manager of a plant or division appoints an assistant to himself to coordinate one or more products that are designed, made, and marketed by the functional departments. This product manager would have staff coordinative and advisory responsibility but possess little formal authority over functional departments. For example, in a food products company he might be a product manager in charge of a line of new breakfast foods. He would have responsibility for coordinating and expediting product development, planning, food production, scheduling, cost control, test marketing, and advertising.

Matrix organization constitutes an overlay of horizontal authority and responsibility relationships on top of a functional structure. Figure 6-2 shows a matrix organization for a division of a corporation that has three major projects being carried on simultaneously. People remain in their functional departments of engineering, manufacturing, and marketing, but work on their respective projects. In fact, some of these functional specialists may devote parts of their time to all three projects. The project managers, in a sense, are competing with one another for the time and talents of the people in the functional departments. The project managers have responsibility for planning, funding and budget, scheduling, performance standards, completion dates, and customer relations. They must insure unified effort by all who work on their project. They resolve conflicts that may disrupt progress. Usually they have more responsibility than formal authority; hence they must get results by means of persuasion, informal influence, and appeals to cooperation. In many companies, they do have project budget money and this gives them a source of power. The managers of the regular functional departments, on the other hand, provide specialized personnel to work on the project. They must maintain a capability of personnel and systems in terms of the state of the art. They perform the personnel administration functions of selection, training, performance appraisal, salary administration, promotion, and the like.

Several large corporations have adopted the matrix form of organization in recent years. Among these are General Electric, Equitable Life Insurance, TRW Systems, Citicorp, Dow Corning, and Shell Oil.[7]

The third type of arrangement places the people necessary to complete a project under the full authority of a project manager for the duration of that project, which may be for six months or a year or more. This is line project management because the manager is directly in the formal line hierarchy. The manager has full authority and responsibility for project performance. Of course, he may still have to negotiate with other departments for the use of special services that are costly and must be shared by many departments.

Project and matrix forms of organization are quite advantageous for the kinds of situations we have described. However, there are problems with their use. The professionals and supervisors working in such an environment must accustom themselves to dual authority and a dual information and reporting system. This is particularly true in matrix organization. The process of forming and disbanding project teams can be unsettling to some people. A premium is placed upon collaboration and constructive conflict resolution. Opportunities for divergent pulls on the people abound. Thus, there exists a special challenge to the leadership skills of the managers.

Grouping Activities by Level

The grouping of work into different levels in the organization is another form of specialization. All manual work may constitute the bottom level in the organizational hierarchy. Supervision of this manual work makes up the foreman level; coordination and control of departmental operating and staff functions represent middle management; and policy making and overall direction of the business make up the top management level. Figure 6-3 shows a partial organization chart of a large manufacturing corporation. This chart shows typical functions, levels of management, and formal channels of authority. Including the board of directors, there are seven levels of management.

An important (but by no means exclusive) path for downward and upward communication is through the formal channel of authority. Orders, information, instructions, and requests for data flow down through the levels in the hierarchy. Information about work in progress, suggestions, questions, complaints, and grievances flow up the line. An important reason for not skipping intermediate supervisors when communicating is that they must know what is going on in their units. Their position, value, and status are strengthened if they serve as vital and essential links in the vertical channel of communication.

For an organization to work effectively there must be a great deal of lateral

---

[7] *Business Week,* (January 16, 1978), pp. 82–83.

Figure 6-3

Partial Organization Chart of a Large Manufacturing Corporation Showing Levels of Management and Formal Channels of Authority.

communication as well as vertical. If a worker has completed making certain items that are now ready for inspection, generally he need only notify the floor inspector that the work is complete. It would waste much time if he had to notify his foreman who would in turn pass the request up the structure until a single manager over both production and inspection was reached. This manager would then tell the supervisor of inspection to have an inspector examine the product. Such a procedure is, of course, too cumbersome. Indeed lateral communications and discussions should be encouraged. The settlement of many problems at subordinate levels reduces the burden on higher executives.

Levels of Management

If a very capable and promising first-line supervisor were promoted rather rapidly up the organization ladder, he would find that the nature of his activities would change. Although he would be a manager both as a first-line supervisor and later as a member of middle or top management, the emphasis given to the different segments of the management function would be materially altered. To be successful as he rises in the hierarchy, he must adjust his behavior, outlook, and general orientation. Front-line supervisors devote a high proportion of their time to immediate direction and interaction with their subordinates. Top management, on the other hand, spends a high percentage of its time on planning, policy development, forecasting, and participating in meetings. All levels perform the five management functions of planning, organizing, staffing, leading, and controlling; however, the emphasis given to each and the nature of the specific tasks within each major function are different.

If we look at a large manufacturing corporation, what generalizations can we make to describe the work and behavior of the principal levels?

Lower Management.   The term *lower management* includes assistant foremen, foremen, general foremen, and office supervisors. They instruct employees in the methods of performing their jobs, assign and reassign employees to specific jobs and tasks, and take prompt action to overcome delays and breakdowns in the production process. Definite production schedules of a short-term nature (daily and weekly) are assigned to them from higher authority. Their authority to make expenditures for capital improvements (tools, equipment, and so on) is extremely limited. As far as personnel actions are concerned, they have some limited say in selection of their subordinates, can assign minor disciplinary penalties, and have great authority in evaluating employees and obtaining in-grade wage increases for their people. They generally have full authority to take whatever steps are necessary to get production out on time. They can requisition materials and supplies, authorize overtime work, obtain maintenance and inspection services, and request technical assistance if necessary.

Middle Management.   In the multiplant corporation the term *middle management* includes supervisory and executive personnel in production, sales, engineering, accounting, and other functional fields both within the plants and at corporate headquarters. Titles such as manager of industrial engineering, plant controller, assistant plant manager, and district sales manager are typical. No sharp lines of demarcation exist between lower and middle management. The terms are relative. Middle managers transmit and sharpen up information and orders from top management. They help solve major difficulties when lower supervisors experience trouble. They operate within the policies and programs set by higher officials but shape them to fit the particular needs of their departments. They evaluate performance results in accordance with the program and standards established for them. They do not question, generally, the adequacy of the program itself. Considerable time tends to be spent in meetings with colleagues of similar rank.

Authority over such personnel matters as selection, training, changes of status and position, and settlement of grievance and disciplinary problems is considerable.

Top Management.   In the business corporation this includes the president, vice-presidents, and major executives. In the large organization it covers the top two levels and sometimes the third level below the board of directors. Top executives are concerned with corporate strategy and the formulation of both long- and intermediate-range plans and programs. The chief executive officer provides an integrating function for the entire organization. He gives it direction and purpose. He must balance the internal interests of the firm with its external environment. The top executive team must concern itself with the survival and growth of the organization. Group decision making through committees and meetings is common. Considerable time is devoted to deliberation and reading of reports. The world of the top manager involves a lot of contact with the public and outside groups, such as government officials, trade association personnel, and other business executives. Business travel tends to be rather frequent. Authority and responsibility in monetary and personnel matters are very great and actions are only checked by higher authority (for example, the board of directors) at relatively long intervals. There is a tendency to be insulated from the problems, needs, and views of rank-and-file employees and even of first-line supervisors.

Trusteeship Management.   The board of directors of an organization carries out a number of very important functions. For a business corporation, the board serves a trusteeship function by overseeing the direction of the business for the benefit of the stockholders, who are the owners. It decides upon the proper distribution of profits: for dividends, for retention in the business for expansion, and for paying off indebtedness. In both business and nonbusiness organizations, the board of directors also bears important trusteeship responsibilities for the employees, clients or customers, and the public. It must be remembered that it is at the discretion and indulgence of the public, operating through government, that private organizations exist.

Other vital functions of a board are the establishment of objectives, selection of the president and other top executives, approval of overall budgets, and auditing of results. The board must continuously review the operations of the organization and insure that it is viable and being run properly. If necessary it can replace the top executive team.

Boards of directors typically are composed of both insiders and outsiders. Insiders are major executives such as the president and key vice-presidents who have day-to-day operating responsibilities. Outside members do not work for the corporation. They may be major stockholders or people such as bankers, lawyers, and professionals who have an expertise that can be valuable to the firm. Although many boards are composed predominantly of insiders, management authorities generally hold that it is most desirable to have a substantial portion of outsiders on any board. They can act as an independent review of the performance of the management group.

DELEGATION AND DECENTRALIZATION

Because the single individual at the top of a pyramidal structure cannot do all the work of the organization himself, he delegates work to his immediate subordinates; they in turn redelegate part or all of this work to their subordinates and so on down to the nonsupervisory employees. There are three components of delegation.

1. Assignment of duties and functions to be performed.
2. Giving of authority to the subordinate sufficient to accomplish the results expected. Illustrations of the granting of authority are the right to purchase ma-

terials, the right to engage the services of an outside consultant, the right to hire employees and the right to speak for the company in public.

3. Holding the subordinate accountable or responsible for his actions. The superior expects the subordinate to carry out conscientiously the work assigned to him.

In every organization that has multiple levels of management, successive delegations must take place. The question is not whether it shall occur but rather to what degree it should occur. By and large, the successful manager is one who leans toward more delegation rather than less. Delegation has these advantages: (1) It unburdens the executive or supervisor from the details of his subordinates' jobs. This means that the superior has more time for planning and overall direction of his department and that his subordinates are encouraged to exercise broader decision-making responsibilities for their own work. (2) Because the subordinates exercise their own judgment and handle their activities on their own, they tend to generate greater commitment, enthusiasm, and pride in their work. (3) Delegation is a way of training subordinates to take on varied and larger projects and responsibilities. They learn to plan more effectively and evaluate their own work when they know that their immediate superior trusts them and is not going to make every decision for them.

In delegating work to those below him in the organization, the executive himself does not evade his own responsibility for the work. If the captain of a ship delegates the job of guiding the vessel through intricate waterways to a pilot and if that pilot runs it aground, the owners of the ship will hold the captain responsible. If the cashier of a commercial bank embezzles $100,000 from the bank, the bank president and board of directors are ultimately held accountable for this action. That fact that a superior is held accountable (within reason, of course) for the behavior of his employees is necessary for the orderly operation of the organization.

One of the problems occurring most frequently in connection with delegation is that executives are reluctant to delegate adequately to their subordinates. Delegation requires giving freedom to the employee to exercise some of his own initiative to get the job done. The superior must place confidence in his subordinates. He must recognize that they will not carry out each and every assignment precisely as he, the boss, would. In delegating, the boss should not then stand over his subordinates to control their every action.

One obstacle to effective delegation is the fear on the part of an executive of building up the abilities and prestige of his subordinates so that they can eventually overtake or unseat him. Management development and proper delegation go hand in hand. If an executive believes that his own position is insecure, he may hesitate to build up his subordinates to the point where they have as much know-how and outside recognition as he himself has.

Decentralization

Decentralization means placing the authority and decision-making power as close as possible to the level at which the work is done. As many functional specialties as are necessary to accomplish results are placed under the manager in charge of that organizational unit. Decentralization is really delegation on an organizationwide basis. Delegation involves superior-to-subordinate relations on a man-to-man basis; decentralization relates top management to lower-level organizational units. If an enterprise is centralized, most decisions, both major and minor, are made by the president and top management. On the other hand, in a decentralized approach division and departmental managers are granted considerable authority to run their own units as they see fit as long as they achieve the desired results.

A secondary meaning of the term decentralization relates to the physical or geographical dispersion of the units and facilities of a company. Thus, a company may have manufacturing plants and offices scattered throughout the country. The management control for a physically decentralized company could be either centralized or decentralized. When the term is used in literature without qualification the meaning is usually decision-making decentralization. This is its most important current usage and this is what we are concerned with.

What are the advantages of decentralization (relative to centralization)?

1. It permits quicker decision making. The managers who are closer to the work have the authority to take action.
2. Problems of coordination, communication, and red tape are reduced. If a product design problem comes up, it is not necessary to delay making a decision in order to contact a centralized engineering department.
3. Autonomy of subordinate units permits greater experimentation and flexibility to meet new conditions.
4. It encourages subordinates at every level in the structure to exercise greater initiative and ingenuity. Ideas do not have to be sold to top management before they can be tried.
5. It insures the development of more capable managers. They have had ample opportunity to "sink their teeth" into problems. Middle and lower managers are not messenger boys in the hierarchy. They have learned to stand or fall on their own decisions and actions.

Decentralization is not an unmixed blessing. Local units may fail to utilize the expert services that staff units at headquarters have to offer. There is a danger of duplication of effort by local units. For example, a marketing or personnel problem may be tackled from scratch in one plant, whereas another plant may have spent thousands of dollars to successfully solve the same problem. The problem of control is made more difficult under decentralization.

Factors Governing Decentralization or Centralization

Whether a particular enterprise should be managed on a centralized or a decentralized basis depends upon a number of factors. The absolute size of the firm in terms of dollar volume of sales, number of plants, and number of employees is an important factor. It is very difficult to coordinate day-to-day decision making in a huge corporation. Efficiency may be enhanced by making the subordinate units semiautonomous. Another important factor is the nature and history of the firm. If it has only one product line and has grown primarily from within, then the company is more likely to remain centralized. On the other hand, if a firm is engaged in the making of diverse and unrelated products and if it has grown by acquisitions and mergers, it is much more likely to be decentralized. It appears that speed and adequacy of decision making, flexibility, and efficiency are enhanced through decentralized operations for very large, multiproduct, diverse, and complex businesses.

It is very difficult to maintain centralized authority and control in a business that has branches and units scattered throughout the country and the world. This is particularly true if these units must deal directly with customers and the general public and must take prompt action on complex problems.

Some management functions are more amenable to decentralization than others. In the large multiplant company, such functions as purchasing, traffic, cost accounting, quality control, plant engineering, and personnel tend to be decentralized. Yet financial planning and resource allocation may be reserved for the very highest level of decision making and control. Marketing may or may not be decentralized depending upon the nature of the markets and the variety of products.

Human relations factors also are important. Talented division and departmental executives often are unwilling to accept close domination from their organizational superiors. They desire independence. They want to run their own show and to be rewarded for what they are able to accomplish in their own units. Innovation and adaptability are encouraged by decentralization. If every contemplated action must first be approved by the front office, frustration and hostility tend to be by-products. Decentralization can only succeed with competent well-trained managers. A company that is thin in talent below the top level would do well to hire and develop a strong management corps before launching into decentralization.

LINE AND STAFF

In very small organizations all the employees and supervisors are line personnel. But as organizations grow, it becomes necessary to employ specialists who give technical advice and provide services to line personnel. Thus, a personnel director can help a superintendent with his training, safety, and grievance-handling problems. A production engineer may design a fixture for a machine. In this case the factory supervisor might have neither the time nor the knowledge to design the item himself.

In organizations the following kinds of positions may exist. These are

A. *Line*

B. *Staff*
1. Specialized staff and service staff
2. "Assistant-to" staff
3. General staff

Line positions and personnel are directly involved in doing the work for which the organization was created. Generally the enterprise could not function, even for a day, without these activities. In a manufacturing concern, manufacturing and selling are considered line functions. Line personnel would be workers, foremen, superintendents, plant mangers, and the president. In a department store both buying and selling are line functions. In a university devoted to the discovery and dissemination of knowledge, the faculty is line.

Specialized staff and service staff are closely related in their roles and responsibilities. They are also the most widespread of the various staff types. Specialized staff departments provide planning, advice, and control functions for the entire organization. Industrial relations and personnel, engineering, research and development, legal counsel, and auditing are examples of specialized staff groups. Such units are usually composed of people who are technical experts in their fields. They frequently are professionals and technicians. In addition to providing advice and control functions for all departments of a company, specialized staff units located at the level of top management also bear heavy responsibilities for policy formulation. Thus the office of the vice-president of personnel would formulate policies in regard to executive compensation, recruitment, training, labor relations, organization development, manpower, and benefit programs.

Service staff aids the organization predominantly in a physical sense. Examples of service staff are purchasing, maintenance, inspection, a real estate department for property acquisition, and a stenographic pool. Like specialized staff, service staffs serve the organization as a whole.

In actuality a sharp distinction between specialized and service staffs is not possible nor really necessary. Many of the sections within a personnel department are engaged more in rendering services than they are in policy planning, advice, and control. This is true for the employment office and for the unit that administers pension and insurance benefits. Some service staff units give technical counsel and perform control functions. This is true for quality control and purchasing. In Figure 6-4 the personnel department is shown as having a dotted-line staff relationship with other line and staff departments within the company.

"Assistant-to" staff is depicted in this figure in the position of executive assistant to the president. The "assistant-to" position is created to relieve an executive of some of his burdens. It can be found at any level in the organization and there may be more than one assistant reporting to an executive. The President of the United States has several staff assistants: a press secretary, a military aide, assistant for Congressional relations, economic advisor, speech writers, and many others. The assistant to the president is apparently a growing phenomenon in American business. Assistants-to serve in the capacity that their bosses desire. Some are special purpose (for example, speech writers or public relations), but many are broad gauge. The broad-gauge ones often perform such assorted tasks as reviewing and commenting upon staff reports before they go to the chief, handling a multitude of administrative details, making special investigations, serving as a sounding board for the chief's ideas, and in general serving as one whom the executive can confide in.

It should be clear that an assistant-to is really a personal assistant. He performs as an extension of his superior. Of necessity, a close personal relationship must exist between this assistant and his boss.

There are certain dangers to the usage of this position. Some staff assistants may usurp their position and start to issue orders to those below their bosses in the structure. Generally speaking they have no authority to issue orders because such orders can cause dual lines of authority with attendant confusion. Although assistants-to have little formal hierarchical authority, they often exert tremen-

Figure 6-4

A Partial Organization Chart to Show Line and Staff Positions and Their Relationships.
The dotted lines from the personnel office to the various departments in the manufacturing division and to the foreman show the flow of specialized advice, aid, service, and
communication. The personnel office does not give direct orders to these individuals.

dous informal influence. When a subordinate wishes to see his boss, he may find
an assistant-to blocking his path. Although it may relieve the line executive of
worry, this screening out of subordinates' problems can be frustrating to the subordinate.

General staff, although seldom used in private business, is widely employed in
military forces throughout the world. It is also fairly common in government. It
is similar to assistant-to staff in its organization position. However, instead of
providing help to one executive, general staff consists of a group of experts who
operate an office. It is used primarily for planning. The Prussian general staff,
organized by Scharnhorst in the early nineteenth century, was a complete advisory service coordinated under a single head, the chief of staff. As a result of
inefficiencies during the Spanish-American War in 1898, Elihu Root, the Secretary of the Army under President Theodore Roosevelt, created the general staff
device for the United States Army.

Relations Between Line and Staff

Interactions between line and staff personnel contain the potential for conflict.[8]
The following are some typical examples of frictions between line and staff:

[8] In this discussion we should think not only of a staff group interacting with a line group or manager
but also of one staff group (say, personnel department) interacting with another staff group.

The foreman of the foundry department suspended a molder for two days without pay for insubordination. The industrial relations director then canceled the suspension on the grounds of insufficient cause.

After weeks of intensive analysis and study, a team of two young systems and procedures engineers submitted their comprehensive report, which revealed serious weaknesses in the handling of orders in the purchasing department. Their report was on the desk of the purchasing director for months. Then it was finally returned to them with the written comment "Deemed inadvisable to make changes in system at present time. Present system has been getting results. Installation of proposed plan is too costly." The two engineers felt that their efforts had been wasted.

What forces contribute to the problems that can exist in the relationships between line and staff? One potential source of trouble is the dual authority that may exist when staff individuals try to give orders to line personnel. A quality assurance engineer may tell a foreman to shut a machine down because it is making defective parts. Yet the foreman's boss may tell him to keep it running because the parts are very close to acceptable standards and a shutdown would hold up an entire assembly line.

The mission of many staff units is to initiate improvements and change. Line personnel, especially in operations and manufacturing, have a different orientation. They must turn out a product or perform a service on schedule. To them stability has a higher priority than change.

A staff person is usually a specialist. However, a line manager has to be a generalist. Different staff specialists who are called upon to help solve a problem in a manufacturing department may offer different diagnoses for the same ailment. If the accident record is poor, the plant engineer may recommend better machine guarding, whereas the personnel manager may recommend better, more intensified safety training. The line manager must help reconcile the differences and determine what is best for his situation.

Staff serves as an instrument for top management to control the performance of operating managers at lower levels. Staff collects data on performance, compares it with objectives and standards, and issues reports highlighting variances. Are payroll costs rising excessively? Is the absenteeism rate too high? What should be done about the labor troubles and work stoppages in plant A?

What measures can be taken to insure healthy staff–line relations? First, it ought to be pointed out that conflict in itself is not necessarily bad. Destructive conflict is bad. But the constructive interaction of conflicting points of view may yield a better solution than would result from a situation in which everybody emphasized harmony as the primary value.

If a staff specialist is called upon to enter a line department to solve a problem, he should work closely with the supervisor from the outset. The supervisor's ideas should be solicited. The diagnosis and recommendations should be worked out by the staff specialist on the basis of heavy inputs from the line supervisor. In certain instances both parties may share equal responsibility for the proposed solution. In this fashion, the line supervisor does not view the staff expert as a threat to his security. Rather, he looks upon him as one whom he can call on for assistance. There should be no contest to get credit in the eyes of higher management for the improvements. If profits, costs, efficiency, and morale are enhanced, *both* men should receive recognition.

In exercising its control function over line, staff can foster improved relations by discussing the performance with the line supervisors concerned before a written report goes to higher management. If the variance is negative, if performance is below standard, this gives line some advance warning and an opportunity to take corrective action.

Because staff gets results mainly on the basis of its technical competence and by the use of persuasion and influence rather than direct power and authority, it must have the full support of top line management. This means that the president must approve of the work and costs required for particular staff groups to be effective. If a line manager senses that the president is not really backing a personnel manager who is trying to launch a management development program, the likelihood of success is minimized.

BUREAUCRATIC AND ORGANIC SYSTEMS OF ORGANIZATION

The model of organization that has guided the thinking of managers for over fifty years has been the bureaucracy. This has been true even though they may not have knowingly adopted the bureaucratic design. The prescriptions of classical organization theory affected the thinking of managers through many sources: practical articles in trade journals and management handbooks, books on management policy and practice, attendance at seminars and conferences, and by copying older organization forms such as the military.

More recently another model of organization has come into prominence. This is the organic or the organic-adaptive pattern. It has particular relevance to complex, high-technology organizations operating in a changing environment.

Bureaucracy

The principal identifying features of a modern bureaucracy are the following:

1. *Formal authority.* Authority to command is formally assigned and regulated.
2. *Autocratic authority.* The authority system is essentially autocratic. Obedience to superiors is a condition of employment.
3. *Positional authority.* It resides in the office, not the person.
4. *Chain of command.* Orders, communications, and appeals flow vertically through the official hierarchy of offices.
5. *Job duties.* These are clearly defined.
6. *Employee qualifications.* These are clearly defined.
7. *Employee selection.* Based upon qualifications, not personal friendship or nepotism.
8. *Specialization of work.* Activities logically grouped by specialization of function. Narrow job jurisdictions.
9. *Education and training.* Occupations require specialized skills and training. Much training provided within the organization.
10. *Professionalization of management.* Administration handled by trained experts.
11. *Records and reports.* Extensive use of records, reports, documents, files.

12. *Procedures and rules*. Methods of work highly standardized. Rules of behavior are elaborate and impersonally administered.
13. *Job security*. Substantial job security in return for loyalty and subordination of individual goals to larger goals of the organization.
14. *Promotion from within*. Based upon qualifications and seniority. This is to recognize good performance, promote harmony, and enhance morale.
15. *Decision and planning aids*. Mathematical models, electronic computers, sophisticated accounting and financial techniques.

The bureaucracy is pervasive throughout our economic and political system. Most large-scale organizations—whether they be manufacturing concerns, banking firms, or governmental agencies—exhibit many or most of the characteristics of bureaucracy. The bureaucracy tends toward permanence. Its viability does not depend upon a single executive or group of executives. Executives and employees alike are replaceable.

In addition to being relatively permanent and stable, the large bureaucracy tends to build a reputation for consistency of action. The emblem of one of our largest insurance companies is a picture of the Rock of Gibraltar. This conveys integrity, stability, and permanence. The client can expect to receive uniform, consistent treatment. A meal in a Howard Johnson restaurant in Boston is essentially the same as in a Howard Johnson restaurant in Buffalo.

For the production of a standardized product or service on time, day-in and day-out, throughout the years, the bureaucratic form of organization cannot be surpassed. Its effectiveness for this kind of mission is high.

On the other hand, there are distinct disadvantages. There tends to be excessive sanctification of procedures and rules by the employees. They are taught to work in conformity with detailed procedures and regulations that are issued by higher authority. The purpose of these regulations is to insure uniformity in accomplishment of the objectives of the company. However, the intermediate and lower-level functionaries often look upon rule compliance as an end in itself. They do not realize that the rules are means to an end and not ends in themselves. When sanctification of the rules becomes excessive to the point of interfering with goal accomplishment and serving the needs of clients and employees, then we have the familiar case of "red tape." Red tape is the label applied to the routing of a client's case through excessively slow and cumbersome channels. The bureaucracy is inefficient for meeting the special problems that a client might have. It is inefficient in reacting to change.

The forces that maximize routine efficiency often mitigate against new methods and ideas. Foremost among these is the autocratic authority structure. Functionaries are rewarded for doing what they are told, not for suggesting changes in programs developed by their bosses. Most policies, programs, and plans are formulated from "on high" and lower-level personnel are indoctrinated to comply. Responsibility tends to be shifted upward. Problems that fall outside the narrow limits of one's jurisdiction are referred upward until they come to a manager who feels he has sufficient authority to render a decision.

Regimentation and monotony are other hallmarks of the bureaucracy. Narrow job roles, standardization of work, mass production techniques, and lack of employee responsibility for planning and control of his own job all contribute to the monotony.

A further criticism of bureaucracy, indeed of all large formal organizations, is that they enforce a condition of conformity, "group-think," and an "organization man" orientation upon the employees.

Organic System

A newer model of organization is the organic or organic-adaptive system.[9] Features of the organic system are

1. Job definitions are less rigid and narrow than in the bureaucracy. These can shift over time as conditions and job incumbents change. There is less emphasis upon enforced conformity to rules and regulations and more emphasis upon employee self-control through knowledge, information, and judgment.
2. Employees share a sense of commitment to the goals of the wider organization beyond their immediate job boundaries. There are shared beliefs about the values and goals of the organization.
3. Authority and power are delegated and dispersed. Specialized knowledge and experience are sources of influence and authority in addition to the authority of organizational position. The system is less autocratic than the bureaucratic system. Executives are *not* viewed as omniscient because they occupy a management position.
4. Communication is horizontal and diagonal (as well as vertical). Communication consists more of advice and information than of direct orders.
5. Collaboration and consultation are emphasized. There is a sharing of authority and responsibility.
6. In comparison with the bureaucracy there are often a wider span of control (more employees per supervisor) and fewer levels of management.
7. Organization members take on responsibilities for solving problems. This contrasts with the bureaucratic tendency to avoid individual responsibility and pass it on to the boss or someone else.

It ought to be recognized that the bureaucratic and organic conceptualizations given above are pure or polar types. Many enterprises contain some features of both and they are in between the two forms. Also, certain departments of a company, for example, production, may be operated according to the principles of a bureaucracy. Other departments, for example, research and development, may be operated according to the organic model.

Contingency Approach

The early view of organizational theorists was that there existed universal principles of organization and management. However, empirical research conducted during the past twenty years has shown that the optimal design of the organization depends upon many factors, both internal and external to the enterprise.[10]

[9] The organic system is depicted in Tom Burns and G. M. Stalker, *The Management of Innovation* (Chicago: Quadrangle Books, 1961). Warren Bennis uses the term organic-adaptive. See Warren Bennis, *Changing Organizations* (New York: McGraw-Hill Book Company, 1966).

[10] See, for example, Burns and Stalker, *Ibid.*; Joan Woodward, *Industrial Organization: Theory and Practice* (London: Oxford University Press, 1965).

Therefore contemporary thinking advocates the contingency approach to organizational design. This requires an evaluation of the many interacting forces when constructing and operating an organization.

Complex organizations, in which technology is advancing rapidly and market and social forces are also shifting, tend to have large and influential staff groups. Group decision making is common. There is a high ratio of administrative and technical personnel to production employees. Decision making is based more upon technical knowledge and less upon coercive power. Horizontal and diagonal relationships are just as important in work flow and decision making as vertical relationships. Project, matrix, and task force structures are more common here. There is more of a tendency to fit the job to the employee. Management by objectives is a fairly common management practice.

In contrast, those enterprises operating under standardized, stable conditions—such as the post office, steel industry, textiles, and wearing apparel—tend more toward the mechanistic or bureaucratic system. Thus, there is no *one* right pattern of organization and management. Practicing executives must be both enlightened and adaptable to shape their management systems to the situation and environment.

Questions for review and discussion

1. In what ways is a thorough understanding of organization essential to the practice of personnel management?
2. What are the principal characteristics of classical organization theory? Have you observed enterprises that are operated by these principles? Describe briefly.
3. Explain systems concepts as they apply to organization. How does systems theory aid in the understanding of organizational processes?
4. Explain project and matrix forms of organization and their applications.
5. Explain the processes of delegation and decentralization. Where might a centralized management be appropriate? Decentralized?
6. Describe the nature of the problems that often are encountered when staff and line personnel deal with one another. How can these be resolved?
7. Give the identifying features of a bureaucracy. Of an organic form of organization. Where is each most appropriately used?
8. Explain the principal levels of management, giving their characteristics and functions.

Case Problems

PROBLEM 1: THE ENGINEERING DEPARTMENT

The Engineering Department of the Schoharie Corporation contained several functional engineering sections. Each section was comprised of a manager, ten to fifteen engineers and technicians plus two or three draftspersons. These draftspersons prepared engineering drawings from oral instructions and sketches provided by the engineers within the section. The quality of the work performed by these draftspersons was generally considered to be very good by the engineers throughout the entire department. Each draftsperson had to possess considerable skill because he or she was generally assigned a variety of drawing projects ranging from simple to complex.

As part of its continuing responsibility to cut costs and improve efficiency throughout the company, the Methods and Systems Engineering (M&SE) section of the corporation made an analysis of all the drafting activities in the engineering department. It found out that some draftspersons were overloaded and others were idle for portions of the work day. The M&SE section prepared a plan to centralize all drafting services within a central service section of the engineering department. It successfully sold the proposal to the director of the engineering department and to the executive vice president of the corporation. The claimed advantages of the new plan were as follows: 1) Work loads among the draftspersons would be more uniform; 2) Idle time would be eliminated; 3) Greater specialization would be achieved by grouping draftspersons into four job classifications; 4) There would be closer control of each draftsperson's activities; 5) Training of new draftspersons would be more efficient in a central service section.

In accordance with the plan for reorganization, all of the 45 draftspersons were taken away from the functional engineering sections and placed in a newly created Drafting Services section within the engineering department. This new section, headed by a manager, had three coordinators who routed work to the individual draftspersons.

To obtain drafting service after the reorganization the following procedure was used: 1) Engineer filled out work order request which was signed by his group leader and the section manager; 2) Work order with engineering sketch was sent to drafting services section via interoffice mail (rush jobs hand carried); 3) Coordinator assigned work orders, in order received, to draftspersons according to his judgment of their skills and experience; 4) Completed drawings were sent by interoffice mail to section manager of section that requested them. He then gave them to group leader who in turn gave them to engineer who initiated original work order.

In operating under this new system the engineers soon learned that the drawings came back from the drafting services section with many errors. To get errors corrected required a repeat of the entire work order process with signatures, interoffice mail, etc. If the project was urgent, the engineer would make a personal trip to discuss the matter with the coordinator and draftsperson. Often the draftspersons were assigned drawing projects on which they had no previous experience. In these instances the draftsperson had to contact the initiating engineer via telephone or personally to obtain guidance and instructions.

To minimize mistakes and costly delays, the engineers began to prepare much more detailed sketches and written instructions than they formerly had done when the draftspersons worked in the same section with the engineer. The engineers found that sometimes their work orders were not signed by their own managers and sent to the Drafting Services section until several days after they had first initiated their orders. Sometimes sketches and drawings became temporarily lost in the process of passing through several offices and persons. The engineers felt that the productivity of the draftspersons was declining. Apparently, the draftspersons viewed each new drawing to be prepared as just another drawing in an unending series of drawings.

The engineers began to complain openly about the new system for obtaining engineering drawings. Their complaints were heard by the managers of the various engineering sections. These managers understood the problems and frustrations of the engineers but cautioned that more time should be allowed to work the defects out of the system.

Questions

1. Analyze this case from the standpoint of organization principles and human behavior concepts.
2. A work flow analysis and principles of technical efficiency initially indicated that the central drafting services system would be superior to the old organizational arrangement. What factors may have been overlooked in this technical analysis?
3. Analyze this case from the viewpoints of
   a. the engineers
   b. the draftspersons
4. Are problems such as those in this case endemic to all service pool arrangements (e.g. stenographic, maintenance, custodial)? Can pools work successfully?
5. How would you solve the problems brought out in this case?

PROBLEM 2: MANAGEMENT ASSOCIATES, INC.

Management Associates, Inc., is a management consulting firm that provides consultation services to business and industry on a wide variety of management problems. It deals in organization studies, attitude surveys, job evaluation, management development, efficiency studies, systems and procedures, selection testing, and management audits.

The organization consists of a president, an executive assistant to the president, two senior staff consultants, five staff consultants, and a number of secretaries and clerks. Offices are located in New York City.

The position of executive assistant to the President was created one year ago to relieve him of some of the administrative details of his job. The position is occupied by an ambitious man of thirty-four who started as a staff consultant four years ago. He has a bachelor of business administration from an Eastern college. His position involves answering correspondence from prospective clients, scheduling of work assignments, supervising the office clerks, screening visitors to see the president, and digesting reports and accounts of new developments for the president. When the president is pressed for time he often delegates to this assistant the responsibility of analyzing and reviewing the reports that the staff consultants have prepared for clients. This is prior to their submission to the clients.

The staff consultants have noticed that, in the year since the executive assistant has assumed his position, his influence and power in the organization have been on the rise. He has established a warm personal friendship with the president. The two frequently play golf together on Saturdays. They have noticed that he has developed the tendency of saying with increasing frequency phrases such as "The president would like you to fly to a new assignment in Chicago on Monday," or, "The president is too busy to see you now. I'll handle your problem," or, "Your report for this client needs complete revamping. I will not approve it this way."

In effect they have observed that he tends to "throw his weight around" and assume authority over their work that they do not think he possesses. This situation has been particularly disturbing to the five staff consultants, who are mostly in their late twenties and thirties and who have had experience with the firm ranging from three to ten years. The two senior consultants have a great deal of stature in their professional fields of competence, are older, and have generally had full and ready access to the president. They are rarely in the office and have tended to be aloof from the interpersonal office difficulties.

The tension between the executive assistant to the president and the five staff consultants has recently come to a head as a result of the very sharp criticism that two of them have received from the assistant in connection with their expense accounts. The president has a reputation for fair treatment of his subordinates; however, it is somewhat difficult to see him, because he is out of town frequently. When he is in the office his time is monopolized by visitors and the executive assistant. The men know that the president's judgment on salary increases for them is influenced by the executive assistant's attitude to a considerable extent.

Questions

1. What course of action, if any, should the staff consultants take? Should they act individually or as a group?
2. Would it be sound for the staff consultants to do nothing at the present time and wait to see how the situation develops?
3. What is the responsibility of the president in this problem?
4. Is a problem such as this inherent in the structural position of an "assistant-to"?

Suggestions for further reading

Academy of Management Journal, Vol. 15, No. 4 (December, 1972). Entire issue devoted to general systems theory.

BLAU, PETER M. *The Dynamics of Bureaucracy*, rev. ed. Chicago: University of Chicago Press, 1963.

CLELAND, DAVID I., and WILLIAM R. KING. *Systems Analysis and Project Management*. New York: McGraw-Hill Book Company, 1968.

DAVIS, STANLEY M. and PAUL R. LAWRENCE. "Problems of Matrix Organizations." *Harvard Business Review*, Vol. 56, No. 3 (May–June, 1978), pp. 131–142.

GALBRAITH, JAY R. "Matrix Organization Designs," *Business Horizons*, Vol. XIV, No. 1 (February 1971), pp. 29–40.

KAST, FREMONT E., and JAMES E. ROSENZWEIG. *Organization and Management: A Systems Approach*, 2nd ed. New York: McGraw-Hill Book Company, 1974.

KLEIN, LISL. *New Forms of Work Organization*. New York: Cambridge University Press, 1976.

KOONTZ, HAROLD, and CYRIL O'DONNELL. *Management: A Systems and Contingency Analysis of Managerial Functions*, 6th ed. New York: McGraw-Hill Book Company, 1976.

LAWRENCE, PAUL R., and JAY W. LORSCH. *Organization and Environment*. Boston: Harvard Business School, 1967.

MACE, MYLES L. "The President and the Board of Directors." *Harvard Business Review*, Vol. 50, No. 2 (March–April, 1972), pp. 37–49.

ROBBINS, STEPHEN P. *The Administrative Process*. Englewood Cliffs, New Jersey: Prentice-Hall, Inc., 1976.

Job
design
and
analysis

For a great many years the conventional practice has been for personnel managers to take the content of the jobs in an organization as a given factor. They would analyze these jobs to set proper rates of pay, and they would recruit, select, and train workers to fill these jobs. Engineers and production specialists were responsible for designing job content according to engineering principles and the needs of the production process. This is the way matters are still handled in a great many companies.

However, progressive managers have learned that designing jobs according to engineering and production needs is insufficient. Such a practice often yields jobs, groups of jobs, and work flow that make sense from a purely technical engineering standpoint but which produce poor performance and frustration from a human standpoint. Accordingly, the concepts and frame of reference of the behavioral sciences are now being blended with the engineering-production focus to develop jobs and work roles that are compatible with the technical-human-organizational matrix.

In this chapter we shall examine the changes in thinking that have occurred in regard to job design. Then we shall devote our attention to job analysis—the detailed and systematic study of jobs. Job analysis plays a role in manpower and organization planning, employee recruitment and selection, setting of proper rates of pay, work methods improvement, design of training programs, performance appraisal, accident prevention, and equal employment opportunity.

JOB DESIGN

The design of jobs—their content and structure—affects both productivity and employee motivation and morale. Historically, jobs in work organizations just evolved. It was the supervisor's job to assign workers to tasks and to group tasks into jobs. In the crafts—carpentry, iron working, electrical work, and machine shop work—the content of each trade evolved through tradition. Prior to the twentieth century, most jobs tended to encompass a variety of tasks and rather large units of accomplishment. A tailor made a complete suit, a baker performed all the operations required to make bread, cake, pies, and rolls.

Around the turn of the century two developments led to the fractionation of jobs into very narrow units. One was the scientific management movement, which utilized the technique of work measurement (time study) and the "scientific" analysis of jobs into their smallest units of accomplishment. The emphasis was upon high output (efficiency, it was called) through job study, methods improvement, job standarization, training, and wage incentives.

The second major development was the Detroit style of mass production introduced by Henry Ford in the automobile industry. The auto assembly line has been held to be the quintessence of minute division of labor, of machine pacing of the worker, and of repetitiveness. It has been considered to be highly efficient from an engineering sense. Other industries have adopted the assembly line and minute division of labor.

No longer was the determination of job content the responsibility of the production supervisor. Staff groups of production engineers designed and laid out the production processes. They specified the operations that were to be performed. Then came the industrial engineers, who related the worker to the production operations.

Engineering Approach to Job Design

Just what criteria have companies used to design jobs? Research by Davis, Canter, and Hoffman sheds light on this matter. In their investigation they found that the following criteria were considered important in designing jobs:

1. Break the job into the smallest components possible to reduce skill requirements.
2. Make the content of the job as repetitive as possible.
3. Minimize internal transportation and handling time.
4. Provide suitable working conditions.
5. Obtain greater specialization.
6. Stabilize production and reduce job shifts to a minimum.
7. Have engineering departments take an active part in assigning tasks and jobs.

These investigators learned that company managers believed that jobs should contain few tasks and be highly specialized. If more tasks should be assigned to an employee, this would increase the training time and lower the output. They believed that simple jobs not only yielded higher output but made workers happier. Excessive specialization may cause monotony but this can be overcome by the challenge of wage incentives.[1]

We might say then that the engineering approach to job design has focused upon tooling, equipment, machine controls, materials handling requirements, and the physiological configurations of the worker in relation to the work place. It has emphasized workloads and work pace and the assignment of workers who can match the demands of the job.

Doubts About Conventional Approach

Missing from the engineering framework has been an appreciation of the psychological nature of man and of the sociological and organizational environment in which man works. A time-study engineer may spend 30 minutes making a time study of a worker and then set a rate of say, 75 pieces per hour. However, this is the microscopic view. It ignores the abilities, attitudes, and aspirations of the individual and the effects upon the man's performance of the work group, supervision, and organizational practices.

As we have noted, primarily since the 1950's there has been a change in the nature of the work force. It is better educated and has higher expectations than that of a generation ago. Earlier generations of workers accepted drudgery and monotony because they had no alternative. Workers who have grown up in an era of affluence and of mass secondary school and college education expect more from work and have more to contribute. They are less submissive and seek more say-so about affairs in their place of employment.

A Different Orientation

Much of the recent innovative work in job design has been conducted by behavioral scientists, personnel researchers in industry, and enlightened industrial managers.

Although interest in job enlargement preceded his investigations by a few years, the work of Frederick Herzberg, a university psychologist, has been very significant in providing a theoretical formulation for job enrichment. Herzberg has conducted extensive research into work and has identified those factors that are motivators (achievement, recognition, work itself, responsibility, advancement, and growth) and those that are merely maintenance or hygienic factors (company policies, working conditions, interpersonal relations, pay, and job security). He asserts that work becomes more satisfying and the employee more productive as more motivators are introduced into the job content. He advocates enrichment of jobs. This means delegating to employees certain functions of supervision. The supervisor is expected to plan, organize, lead, and control the work of his subordinates. Traditionally the employee has been merely expected to *do* the productive tasks. *Job enrichment* means adding certain planning and

---

[1] Louis E. Davis, R. R. Canter, and J. Hoffman, "Current Job Design Criteria," *Journal of Industrial Engineering*, Vol. 6, No. 2 (1955), pp. 5–11.

controlling tasks to the doing. As noted earlier, this is often called vertical job loading or vertical job enlargement.

For example, a machine operator performing according to conventional engineering principles would load his machine, operate the controls, and remove the part from the machine. If his job were enriched, the operator would read the drawing of the part to be machined, obtain materials and hand tools, set up his machine, machine the parts, and inspect his own work. In terms of motivation theory, he would be activating his upper-level needs, such as achievement, responsibility, and intrinsic interest in the work itself.

Favorable results with job enrichment in terms of such measures as quality, quantity, attendance, costs, and morale have been found in such diverse applications as chemists and production workers in a chemicals company, janitors in an electronics firm, stockholder correspondents in a telephone company, and tax examiners in the Internal Revenue Service.[2]

Job Enlargement.   Job enlargement is a generic term that broadly means adding more and different tasks to a specialized job. It may widen the number of tasks the workers must do, that is, add variety. When additional simple tasks are added to a job that was initially simple in nature, this process is called horizontal job loading or horizontal job enlargement. This too presumably adds interest to the work and reduces monotony and boredom. Vertical job loading or enlargement is the same as job enrichment discussed above.

Job Rotation.   Having an employee on a routine, repetitive job move from one routine job to another every few hours or days is a form of job rotation that has been found in some instances to relieve boredom and monotony. Norman Maier has described an industrial application where job rotation improved employee response. There were two jobs, solderers and dusters in the central office of a telephone company. These were performed by women. The dusters had continuously to go over the equipment to keep it clean, and the solderers constantly looked for broken connections which they then repaired. Morale was low and turnover was serious. By permitting the women to exchange jobs every two hours, not only did morale improve, but productivity increased as well.[3]

Larger Units of Accomplishment.   To the inspector who visually examines objects as they come endlessly off the production line, his job can indeed be monotonous. However, by segregating the production units into batches or runs, he can achieve a greater sense of accomplishment when each batch is complete. Most of us have undertaken tasks that seemed endless. However, by establishing subgoals on the road to completion, we gain a sense of making real progress as we do our work. Examples occur in such activities as addressing Christmas

---

[2] For explanation of studies see Harold M. F. Rush, *Job Design for Motivation* (New York: The Conference Board, 1971); Frederick Herzberg, "One More Time: How Do You Motivate Employees?" *Harvard Business Review*, Vol. 46, No. 1 (January–February 1968), pp. 53–62; Robert N. Ford, *Motivation Through the Work Itself* (New York: American Management Association, 1969); and John R. Maher, ed., *New Perspectives in Job Enrichment* (New York: Van Nostrand Reinhold, 1971).

[3] Norman R. F. Maier, *Psychology in Industry*, 2nd ed. (Boston: Houghton Mifflin Company, 1955), p. 476.

cards, cutting the lawn, pulling weeds from the garden, and painting one's house.

Self-managed Work Teams.   Some firms have had success in using work teams of from, say, eight to fifteen members who collectively are given responsibility for certain planning, work flow, and control decisions. Individual team members are accountable to the group and the group as a whole is accountable to the manager. Examples are the General Foods Corporation in Kansas, Hunsfos Pulp and Paper Mill in Norway, Rade Koncar in Yugoslavia, and Syntex Corporation in Mexico and California.[4]

Perspective on Job Design

One important component of the modern effort to improve productivity and the quality of work life has been to emphasize job designs that contain some or all of the following features: a) autonomy, individual and group decision-making for planning and carrying out the work activities, b) opportunities for social interaction, c) whole units of work so the employee can experience a sense of accomplishment, d) utilization of a variety of skills and abilities, e) feedback on results achieved permitting self-evaluation of performance.

Although there have been many successful outcomes from work-redesign experiments in industry incorporating the foregoing principles, there have also been failures. There is no simple formula that can guarantee success to management in its job design efforts. A great many forces are interacting simultaneously in any job-employee-organization-management system. Job content and structure are only part of the system. Let us look at some of the factors that influence whether any particular design strategy will succeed.

People are different. Not every employee wants a challenging job with variety and decision-making responsibility. Some people are content to work on jobs of a simple, routine nature. People also vary in their needs for social interaction. Some prefer to work alone while others do better working as part of a group.

Sometimes management errs in its employee selection and placement process. It places people in jobs for which they are either underqualified or overqualified. The underqualified worker is frustrated because he lacks the skills to meet the job demands. The overqualified worker is also frustrated because he finds his job dull and boring. Because of the large influx of young people entering the labor force each year and because of rising educational levels, management often raises the hiring requirements for its jobs without realizing that placing overqualified employees in narrow, limited jobs can be self-defeating.

Sometimes changes in jobs and work flow can disrupt social and interpersonal relations that had been sound. Or changes may enhance previously poor relationships among employees, co-workers, and supervisors.

Mechanistic or bureaucratic organizational climates are more conducive to simple, standardized jobs having limited decisionmaking. On the other hand organic organization climates are supportive of enriched jobs and self-managed work teams.

---

[4] *Work in America, Report of a Special Task Force to the Secretary of Health, Education, and Welfare* (Cambridge, Mass.: MIT Press, 1973), pp. 188 ff.

Technology may inhibit the introduction of enriched jobs. For example, if there is an existing plant containing a high investment in machinery and equipment that was installed to be operated along scientific management and Detroit mechanization lines, then to redesign jobs and work flow would be very costly. On the other hand in planning a new manufacturing facility or in working with a service organization or with a salaried office group, there is considerable freedom to innovate.

In summary then, management must evaluate all the variables that interact with the job itself before proceeding with a program of work design or redesign.

JOB INFORMATION AND PERSONNEL MANAGEMENT

Accurate and up-to-date information is essential to the operation of a sound personnel program. An organization is composed of people who are grouped together into teams (designated as sections, departments, divisions, and so on) to do work in order to achieve agreed-upon goals. These basic elements, people and their assigned jobs—are organized into small units, which in turn are combined into larger units, such as divisions and plants, and these are finally related one to the other into companies, institutions, or governmental units.

Sound management practice requires that each of the entities above be defined and specified. The purpose and objectives of each organizational unit from the top on down to individual jobs should be determined, recorded, and communicated to appropriate parties involved. Likewise, the functions of each organizational unit and the relationship of one to the other must be established and agreed upon. This work is all part and parcel of good organization planning. The determination and recording of the specific content of each job and of the necessary employee skills and abilities to fill the jobs is likewise vital to successful administration. The method and procedure employed to determine the duties, responsibilities, working conditions, and working relationship of and between jobs and the human qualifications of employees are called job analysis.

What Is Job Analysis?

Job analysis is the process of determining, by observation and study, and reporting pertinent information about a specific job. It includes the identification of the tasks performed, the machines and equipment utilized, the materials, products or services involved, and the training, skills, knowledges, and personal traits required of the worker.

Modern-day usage of the term *job analysis* has tended to restrict it to the type of job study associated with various personnel programs, such as employee selection, job evaluation, wage surveys, training, accident prevention, and the like. However, the term is also sometimes applied to a detailed and quantitative study of jobs and job operations by industrial engineers in connection with time and motion study, methods improvement, and work measurement programs. The industrial engineering approach usually breaks down each job into detailed tasks and often specifies each hand and arm motion to be utilized by the worker. In other words, the work is subdivided into elements, and times are determined for each one. The goal is usually to establish a standard time for each type of opera-

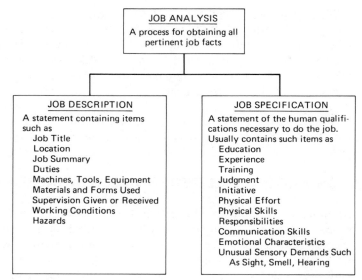

Figure 7-1
Job Description and Job Specification in Job Analysis.

tion performed by each worker. Work simplification and methods improvement are generally part and parcel of every analysis.

Because industrial engineering techniques, such as work simplification, methods engineering, time and motion study, and work measurement, are outside the scope of this book, our explanations in this chapter will be confined to job analysis from the personnel management viewpoint.

Simply stated, job analysis is a procedure for obtaining pertinent job information. This information is recorded, basically on two forms or pieces of paper, to make a permanent record. One is called a job description and the other is called a job specification. The relationship between these is shown in Figure 7-1.

The actual content and format of job descriptions and specifications varies greatly from one organization to another. Indeed there is even some confusion between the two terms in some circles. Some practitioners make no distinction between a job description and a specification. They use them interchangeably. However, the more common practice is to designate the objective listing of job title, summary, and duties as the description and to call the enumeration of employee qualifications the job specification. This latter term was originated by the United States Employment Service, and it seems very useful to distinguish between two quite different kinds of information. The determination of the human characteristics needed to fill a job calls for value judgments. The specification is actually derived from the description by translating the job activities and requirements into particular skills and abilities. But to a certain extent the level of ability demanded is dependent upon management policy and standards. For example, some organizations require that their secretaries have a post–high school business education (one to two years), whereas others accept simply a high school diploma and concentrate upon training from within.

Figure 7-2 shows a job description and specification for an experimental mechanic, a highly skilled hourly paid job. In this case the statement of job content

```
JOB DESCRIPTION AND SPECIFICATION

JOB ____Experimental Mechanic_____     JOB NO. __H 75_____

DATE EFFECTIVE_____August 21, 1978_____     GRADE ___12_____

JOB FUNCTION: Perform experimental and developmental work that requires
devising, machining, fabricating, assembling, and modifying components of new or
special equipment and machinery. Construct and run-in special purpose machinery
and equipment.
DUTIES: Working from rough sketches, machine drawings, and verbal instructions,
devise, construct, and modify, using various machine tools and assembly equipment,
components of generating equipment such as special trays, pumps, and heat ex-
changers as well as special machinery, equipment, and tools necessary for the man-
ufacture of company products. Analyze requirements of machinery and equip-
ment to be built, develop own work techniques, make alterations and tests as work
progresses in coordination with engineers and supervision. Follow through to in-
sure successful functioning of machinery or equipment.
     Set up and operate machine tools, solder parts, layout and perform bench
work as required.
          Read and interpret intricate machine and assembly drawings and sketches.
          May be required to machine parts to tolerances of .001 inch.
MACHINES, TOOLS, AND EQUIPMENT: Engine lathe, turret lathe, shaper,
planer, milling machine, boring mill, drill press, surface grinder, tool grinder, power
saw, hydro and mechanical presses, gages and precision measuring instruments,
soldering equipment, common hand tools.
DIRECTION OF OTHERS: Instruct others in the operation of machinery and
equipment he has developed and constructed. May supervise the activities of
helpers.
WORKING CONDITIONS: General shop and machine tool noise. Dirt, grease,
and coolants from operation of machine tools and assembly of machines and
equipment.
HAZARDS: Serious cuts, bruises, and burns may occur from operation of ma-
chine tools, soldering, and assembly activities.
EDUCATION: High school graduate or equivalent.
VOCATIONAL PREPARATION: Completion of machinist apprenticeship pro-
gram (4 years) or equivalent.
PREVIOUS EXPERIENCE: 3-4 years as journeyman machinist and mechanic
working on variety of machine tools and products.
IN- PLANT TRAINING: One year at company as machinist or mechanic, pref-
erably in experimental work.
MENTAL DEMAND: A high degree of ingenuity and judgment is required to plan
and build equipment when working from only rough sketches or verbal instructions.
Must exhibit considerable resourcefulness to experiment and make repeated trials
and adaptations of equipment where procedures are not well established.
PHYSICAL DEMAND: May lift and carry objects weighing up to 40 pounds occa-
sionally. Normal work position is standing or walking.

Analysis By _____     Approved By _____
```

Figure 7-2
Job Description and Specification: Experimental Mechanic.

(the job description) and the statement of employee qualifications (the job specification) are contained in one form.

Uses for Job Analysis and Job Information

A comprehensive job analysis program is an essential ingredient of sound personnel management. Job information derived from such a program has many important applications. These are as follows:

Organization and Manpower Planning. When it is determined that certain types and amounts of work must be done, this work must be divided into specific jobs at all levels in the organization, from unskilled laborer up through the chief executive officer. In establishing the organization structure, it is necessary to "package" the work to be done into meaningful units. Job analysis aids in determining the number and kinds of jobs and the qualifications needed to fill these jobs. Thus, it is an essential element of effective manpower planning. At managerial levels, accurate job descriptions and specifications are intimately related to the preparation of inventories of executive talent.

Recruitment, Selection, and Placement. To carry out an employment program, it is necessary to have clear statements of the work to be performed and of the skills and knowledge that must be possessed by the employees who will fill these jobs. Basically the goal is to match, as closely as possible, the job requirements with the worker's aptitudes, abilities, and interests. It is not possible to staff varied jobs accurately in an organization by having available job title data only. Full job information is necessary.

Equal Employment Opportunity. Equal employment opportunity laws, regulations, and court orders have made accurate job analysis of extreme importance. The burden of proof is upon the employer to justify an educational requirement, of say, a college degree for a specific job if that employer is charged with discrimination in hiring, placement, or promotion. Furthermore, if a company pays women less than men for performing jobs that on the surface appear the same, the burden of proof must be borne by management to show that in fact there are real differences in the duties and requirements of the work done by the men and women. If selection tests are to be validated by the *content validity* method (as opposed to *criterion related validity*), then very detailed and specific information on job tasks and worker skills must be obtained. And finally those employers covered by the Rehabilitation Act of 1973 (those holding government contracts) should study their jobs carefully to ascertain which ones could be performed adequately by persons with certain physical or mental handicaps.

Establishing Proper Rates of Pay. This involves a determination of the relative worth of jobs within the organization by means of the technique called job evaluation and a comparison of wages paid inside the organization with those paid for comparable jobs in other companies via a wage survey. The purpose of job evaluation is to insure internal pay equity of one job to another, whereas the purpose of surveying the going wages in a labor market is to insure that the level of wages within an organization is correct in relation to the community or the industry. For job evaluation purposes, job descriptions must be very complete; for conducting a wage survey, condensed descriptions are generally sufficient.

Redesign of the Job. Jobs may be studied in order to improve work methods, reduce errors, eliminate unnecessary handling of materials and duplication of effort, reduce fatigue, increase employee commitment and responsibility, and in general, to improve the performance of the employee–job unit. Quite often the optimum results in this work can be gained by combining the approaches of the industrial engineer, the human factors psychologist, and the organizational behaviorist.

Employee Training and Management Development.   Many firms provide new employees with copies of the descriptions and specifications for the jobs to which they have been assigned. This practice aids in orienting them and acquainting them with what they are expected to do. Job information is also very helpful to those who administer training and development programs. It helps them determine the content and subject matter needed in training courses. Selection of trainees is also facilitated by studying job information.

Performance Appraisal.   Job analysis data can be adapted to help establish clear-cut standards of performance for every job. Standards of performance are mostly qualitative (they may also contain some quantitative information) statements of what management expects of the employeesx assigned to each job. In evaluating the performance of each employee (for pay adjustments, employee development, and so on) the supervisor can compare the actual contribution of each man with the written standard. Performance appraisals can never become fully objective and impartial, but the usage of written standards helps make them more objective.

Safety and Health.   The process of conducting a detailed job analysis provides an excellent opportunity to uncover and identify hazardous conditions and unhealthy environmental factors (such as heat, noise, fumes, and dust), so that corrective measures can be taken to minimize and avoid the possibility of human injury.

Definitions of Terms

It is important that both the student and the practitioner acquire a clear understanding of the terminology involved in job analysis. Because this work is analytical in nature, it is perhaps especially important that clear-cut distinctions be made among the various job and occupational designations.

A *task* is the same as a duty. It is a component of a job. Whereas the methods and time-study engineer breaks a job down (for purposes of analysis) into very minute elements such as pick up part, place in machine, turn crank, and index fixture, the job analyst who is developing a job description uses larger units of work, which we call tasks. A task may be primarily physical, such as operating a drill press; primarily mental, such as analyzing data; or primarily interpersonal, such as consulting with someone else.

A *position* is a collection of tasks and responsibilities regularly assigned to one person. A *job* is a group of positions that involve essentially the same duties, skills, knowledge, and responsibilities. Thus, we can see that a position consists of the particular, and often unique, set of duties assigned to an individual. There may be ten people, all of whom are classified under the same job title, and yet each may perform slightly different work. Therefore, each would have a distinct position. An illustration of this would be the job of a secretary. All the secretaries in a business organization may have that as their job title. Yet the secretary to the treasurer may be a distinctly different position than the secretary to the plant manager, because the detailed requirements of the work will be different. In actual practice some people use the terms *job* and *position* interchangeably, and there probably is no great harm in doing so.

An *occupation* is a composite of many very closely related jobs found in many establishments. Basically, when we are within the four walls of an organization, we use the term *job*. But when we refer to that job as it may be set up in a number of companies, the variation is great enough that a more generalized description must be used to designate the work. We call this an occupational description. The *Dictionary of Occupational Titles*[5] is the standard reference work in the occupational information field. It contains the definitions of over 22,000 separate occupations, together with code numbers for each. It also gives worker trait requirements for principal kinds of occupations. The worker trait requirements are especially useful for vocational counseling and job placement. For each major occupation, the worker trait requirements specify educational development, specific vocational preparation, aptitudes required of the individual, vocational interests related to the job, worker temperaments required by the job, physical demands, and working conditions.

The terms *unskilled, semiskilled,* and *skilled* are commonly used to distinguish between skill levels among blue-collar or hourly paid workers. The lines of demarcation are not always sharp and distinct. Indeed the management of one plant may consider that certain jobs are skilled, whereas in another plant the same work may be relegated to the semiskilled category. Typically, the crafts or trades are considered to be skilled occupations, although even here technological advances over the years may reduce the level of training and experience required. A skilled job or occupation is one that requires comprehensive knowledge of work processes, independent judgment, and often considerable manual dexterity. Generally an apprenticeship or the equivalent is required to enter a skilled trade. Periods of apprenticeship in the United States vary in length from two to six years, with four years being the most common training period.

Semiskilled work constitutes the great bulk of jobs in our manufacturing industries. These jobs are often characterized by considerable manipulative ability confined to a definite work routine, alertness to avoid damage to products or equipment, and the exercise of judgment in the work situation. However, this judgment does not generally depend upon a wide or deep knowledge of the field of work. The learning period for semiskilled jobs commonly varies from several weeks to several months. A milling machine operator is an example of a semiskilled job. Whereas a machinist, who is a skilled worker, must be able to plan his work, set up, adjust, and operate not only a milling machine but all other machine tools as well, a person who can set up and operate only a single machine tool is considered to be semiskilled.

An unskilled job is one that requires an extremely short training period—generally from a few hours to one or two weeks. Common laboring work involving heavy physical effort to dig holes and ditches, carry materials and supplies, load and unload trucks, and so on, is an example of unskilled work. The percent-

[5] U.S. Department of Labor, *Dictionary of Occupational Titles*, 4th ed. (Washington, D.C.: U.S. Government Printing Office, 1977).

age of unskilled labor in the labor force of the country has steadily declined over the years because machinery has been replacing human muscle power.

A technician is one who possesses some formal education and training beyond the high school level, generally in a field of science and technology. A technician is a semiskilled professional or a subprofessional. Examples of technician-type occupations are electronics technician, layout draftsman, laboratory technician, and dental technician.

Swinging over to the white-collar occupations, we encounter the terms *executive, administrative,* and *professional.* In business and industry the term *executive* is often used rather loosely to designate anyone who holds a high-ranking management position, whether it be line or staff. Some would include only very high-ranking positions, such as president, vice-president, and general manager, and others include middle-management personnel within the scope of this term. Thus, in common parlance, the word *executive* has status connotations in addition to designating a kind of work. A more precise definition of an executive is that developed by the United States Department of Labor, Wage and Hour Division, for establishing overtime exemptions in connection with the Fair Labor Standards Act. In essence the department states that an *executive* is one whose primary duty consists of the management of an enterprise or a recognized department thereof. To be classified as an executive, a person must direct the work of two or more employees, have the authority to hire or fire or to effectively recommend hiring or firing of employees, and must customarily and regularly exercise discretionary powers. In addition he must not devote more than 20 percent of his time to activities of a nonsupervisory nature, and he must be paid a designated minimum salary per week to be exempt from the overtime requirements of the law. In effect these regulations include within the meaning of the term *executive* all those who exercise bona fide supervision, from a foreman all the way up to a corporation president.[6]

An *administrative* employee is one whose primary duty consists of office or nonmanual work directly related to management policies or general business operations. He exercises discretion and independent judgment. He directly assists a proprietor or a bona fide executive, or performs under only general supervision work along specialized or technical lines requiring special training, or he executes under only general supervision special assignments. He must be paid a designated minimum weekly salary and not devote more than 20 percent of his time to work other than that described above.[7] The terms *executive* and *administrative* both connote authority and status within the organization. However, an executive supervises other employees, whereas an administrative employee does not. He establishes, affects, or carries out policies but does not "boss" other people.

A *professional* employee is one whose work requires knowledge of an advanced type in a field of science or learning that is acquired by a prolonged course of specialized instruction and study. The work requires consistent exercise of discretion and judgment, and it is predominantly intellectual and varied in character. The output of professionals cannot be standardized in relation to a

---

[6] *Wage and Hour Division Regulations,* Part 541, Section 541.1.
[7] Ibid., Section 541.2.

given time period. Like executives and administrative employees, they must be paid a designated minimum weekly salary and cannot spend more than 20 percent of their time on nonexempt work.[8] Examples of professional employees are engineers, chemists, physicists, lawyers, and physicians.

ANALYZING JOBS—OBTAINING JOB INFORMATION

Methods of Analyzing Jobs

There are seven ways by which job information can be gathered: (1) observation, (2) questionnaire, (3) interview, (4) check list, (5) daily diary, (6) conference of experts, and (7) a combination of two or more of these.

It is generally not possible to use the observation method alone to gather enough information to prepare a job description and a specification. It is true that industrial engineers rely principally upon observation to conduct motion and time studies. However, they deal primarily with repetitive, short-cycle, unskilled, and semiskilled jobs. They do not have to develop a job specification that calls for value judgments on worker qualifications (best obtained by interviewing the supervisor). Actual observation is very desirable to acquaint the job analyst with the materials and equipment used, the working conditions and hazards, and to obtain a sharp, visual impression of just what is involved in the work.

The questionnaire method is popular with management engineering consultants who are hired to install a job evaluation plan and who feel they must accomplish a lot in a minimum of time. Usually, the procedure involves the preparation of a detailed questionnaire, which is then distributed to all employees, who fill it out on company time and who return it to their supervisors for verification. The supervisor is supposed to discuss any errors in the employee's response with him, make corrections, and then transmit it to the group responsible for conducting the job analysis program (generally the personnel department). Figure 7-3 shows an example of a questionnaire for collecting job analysis data directly from the employees themselves.

The questionnaire method requires somewhat less staff time than the interview method. In other words the cost of collecting the job data is lower with this technique. All the employees participate and answer questions about their jobs. With the interview method, only one or perhaps two individuals on a job are interviewed. However, the questionnaire approach has serious disadvantages. The accuracy of the information leaves much to be desired. Job analysis work requires specialized knowledge and training. The average employee, although he knows best just what his duties are, is not trained to identify the essential aspects of his work and often cannot express the information in a meaningful and clear fashion. Any questionnaire is open to varying interpretations. To depend exclusively upon questionnaires as the source of job information is bound to introduce some errors into the program.

Many organizations employ job analysts who interview the employee and/or his supervisor to obtain all the pertinent information. When the interview of both the supervisor and the employee is combined with a short observation at the job by a trained analyst, this procedure constitutes a very thorough and

[8] Ibid., Section 541.3.

INDIVIDUAL JOB ANALYSIS QUESTIONNAIRE

Name_____ Department _____

Payroll Title_____ Name, Immediate Supervisor_____

Instructions: Please read the entire form before making any entries. Answer each question as accurately and carefully as possible. When completed return this form to your supervisor. If you have any questions ask your supervisor.

Your Duties
What duties and tasks do you personally perform daily?

What duties do you perform only at stated intervals such as semi weekly, weekly or monthly? Indicate which period applies to each duty.

What duties do you perform only at irregular intervals?

Supervision of Others
How many employees are directly under your supervision? (List job titles and number of people assigned to each job.)

Do you have full discretionary authority to assign work; correct and discipline; recommend pay increases, transfers, promotions and discharge; and to answer grievances?

Do you only assign work, instruct, and coordinate the activities of your subordinates?

Materials, Tools, and Equipment
What are the principal materials and products that you handle?

List the names of the machines and equipment used in your work.

List the names of the principal hand tools and instruments used in your work.

What is the Source of Your Instructions? (e.g., oral, written, blueprints, specifications, etc.)

What Contacts Are You Required to Make with Persons Other Than Your Immediate Supervisor and Departmental Associates?

    a) Give the job titles and the department or organization of those with whom you deal.

    b) Describe the nature of these contacts.

Decisions
What decisions do you have to make without consulting your supervisor?

Responsibility
    a) Describe the nature of your responsibility for money, machinery, equipment, and reports.

    b) What monetary loss can occur through an honest error?

Figure 7-3
Employee Job Analysis Questionnaire.

Records and Reports
    a) What records and reports do you personally prepare?

    b) What is the source of the data?

Checking of Your Work
    a) How is your work inspected, checked, or verified?

    b) Who does this?

Physical Requirements
    a) What percentage of the time do you spend in the following working positions?

    Standing_____%,   Sitting_____%,   Walking about _____%?

    b) What weight in pounds must you personally lift and carry?_____pounds

    c) What percentage of the working day do you actually spend lifting and carrying this weight?_____%

    d) Are any special physical skills, eye-hand coordination, and manual dexterity skills required on your job?

Working Conditions
Describe any conditions present in the location and nature of your work, such as noise, heat, dust, fumes, etc., which you consider unfavorable or disagreeable.

Hazards
Describe the dangers or accident hazards present in your job.

THIS PORTION IS TO BE FILLED OUT BY YOUR SUPERVISOR.

Education Requirements
What is the lowest grade of grammar school, high school, or college required of a person starting in this job?

Previous Experience
    a) What kind of previous work experience is necessary for minimum satisfactory performance for a new employee on this job?

    b) Give the length of experience required.

Training
Assuming that a new employee on this job has the necessary education and experience to quality for the work, what training is necessary after the employee is on the job to achieve an acceptable performance level? (Specify training needed and period of time to acquire it.)

_____   _____
      Date   Signature of Supervisor

Figure 7-3 (Continued)

sound approach. It is the one most widely used. The analyst essentially asks the same kinds of questions that appear in Figure 7-3. However, the analyst knows how to differentiate between essential and nonessential information. He has a consistency of viewpoint and judgment. He can ask probing questions to uncover facts that might be overlooked if employees simply filled out a questionnaire. Because the analyst must compose and write the job description, he is in the best position to do so if he has actually seen the job being performed and if he has talked to the employee and his immediate superior. An important by-product of a job analysis program is that it often creates greater understanding and common agreement between the job holder and his boss on the precise requirements of his job. Often in actual practice, the analyst runs into cases in which the worker has stated that he performs a certain task, whereas the supervisor states that that task is really not a part of his job and belongs to someone else. The opposite is common also.

The check list method can be used in large organizations that have a large number of people assigned to the same or similar jobs. The staff group that prepares a check list for each of the various jobs in the enterprise or agency must first collect enough information to prepare a meaningful check list. Such information can be obtained by asking supervisors, methods engineers, and others familiar with the work to record the tasks comprising each job. When a check list has been prepared for a job, say a supply clerk in an Army depot, then it is sent to all supply clerks in all depots. The job holders are asked to check all listed tasks that they perform and to indicate by check mark the amount of time spent on each task as well as the training and experience required to be proficient in each task. They may also be asked to write in additional required tasks not contained on the prepared list. A typical job may contain 200 or 300 task statements. This technique is amenable to tabulation and recording on electronic data processing equipment. The check list method is rather costly and somewhat impractical for small organizations, however, because of the setup costs involved in developing check lists for every job.[9]

The daily diary method requires the job holders to record in detail their activities throughout each day. If done faithfully this technique is accurate and eliminates the error of memory recall of the questionnaire and check list devices. However, it adds considerably to the workload of each production employee and for this reason is seldom used in practice.

The conference of experts technique of collecting job information is quite useful for obtaining various viewpoints and an overall perspective of the jobs. However, supervisors, staff specialists, and technicians may be removed enough from the work itself that they lack intimate familiarity with its details and complexities. Thus accuracy suffers.

Content of Information Collected

As indicated previously, the nature of the information collected when analyzing jobs is determined by the use that will be made of the data. If a company simply

[9] A description of the check list method as applied by the United States Air Force is contained in Joseph E. Morsh, "Job Analysis in the United States Air Force," *Personnel Psychology*, Vol. 37 (1962), pp. 7–17.

wishes to prepare brief descriptions so that it can conduct a labor market wage survey, then the analyst will obtain only that information necessary to describe the significant duties and requirements of jobs with special emphasis upon those features that differentiate it from related jobs. Because the most common practice in business and industry is to prepare job descriptions and specifications for purposes of hiring, job evaluation, and for acquainting new people with the exact nature of their jobs and with what management expects of them, the content of information collected will be explained from this standpoint.

The items given below are the principal ones covered when analyzing jobs.

1. *Job Title and Location:* These designate the job and the organizational unit in which it is located. Some standardization of job titling is desirable.
2. *Job Summary:* This is included in most job descriptions to give the reader a quick capsule explanation of the job. It is usually one or two sentences in length.
3. *Job Duties:* A comprehensive listing of duties is included together with an indication of the frequency of occurrence or percentage of time devoted to each major duty. Always includes *what* the job holder does along with some indication of *how* he performs the tasks.
4. *Machines, Tools, and Equipment:* A listing of all the tooling and work aids used in the job.
5. *Materials, Products, Services:* Raw materials used and products made or services performed.
6. *Supervision Given:* For supervisory and group leader jobs, the number of persons supervised and their job titles are given.
7. *Relation to Other Jobs:* Identify jobs from which persons can be promoted into this job. Also state the jobs to which persons in this job can be promoted.
8. *Mental Skills:* Includes various mental skills such as ability to interpret complex data and ideas, resourcefulness, and ability to influence others.
9. *Physical Demand:* Kind and amount of physical exertion. Normal working position such as sitting or standing.
10. *Physical Skills:* Examples are manual dexterity and eye-hand-foot coordination.
11. *Responsibilities:* Examples are responsibility for product and equipment and responsibility for preventing monetary loss to organization.
12. *Working Conditions:* Environmental conditions such as cold, heat, dust, noise.
13. *Hazards:* Typical work hazards encountered (e.g. broken bones) and probability of occurrence.
14. *Education:* Identify specific kinds of reasoning, language, and mathematical skills required and amount of schooling needed to provide such skills.
15. *Vocational Preparation:* This includes vocational education, apprenticeship training, prior work experience, and in-plant job training.

FUNCTIONAL JOB ANALYSIS

Functional job analysis is a very detailed method for analyzing jobs and recording the job information collected. It was developed by the U.S. Training and Employment Service of the Department of Labor. The system is explained in the *Handbook for Analyzing Jobs* [10] and is used in the *Dictionary of Occupational Titles*, 4th ed. Functional job analysis is really a comprehensive system for collecting and classifying the various kinds of data which describe the work performed in jobs and the worker traits required to perform these jobs.

According to this approach the categories of information needed to properly analyze any job are as follows:

1. Work Performed
   a. Worker functions
   b. Work fields
   c. Materials, products, subject matter, and services
2. Worker Traits
   a. Training time
   b. Aptitudes
   c. Temperaments
   d. Interests
   e. Physical demands
   f. Environmental conditions

Worker Functions.   All job-worker situations involve a relationship of the employee to *data, people,* and *things.* The functional job analysis format gives a standard hierarchical classification of tasks under these three categories. There are six data handling tasks, "comparing" being the simplest and "synthesizing" the most complex. There are eight people tasks, "taking instructions-helping" being the simplest and "mentoring" the most complex. Of the seven thing tasks, "handling" is the simplest and "setting up" the most complex.

Work Fields.   All the jobs in the U.S. economy are classified under 100 different work fields. Some examples of work fields are welding, masoning, printing, writing, engineering, and teaching. In describing the content of each work field *methods verbs* are used. For example, for the surveying field methods verbs such as calculating, measuring, and plotting are used. Certain *machines, tools, equipment, and work aids* are used in the various work fields. In the surveying field, no machines are used but tools include drafting tools, levels, pencils, and pens. Equipment includes transits and geodometers. Work aids include blueprints, charts, maps, and rods.

Materials, Products, Subject Matter, and Services.   Jobs are characterized according to the items of these types that are involved. Materials mean raw materials being processed such as fabric, metal or wood. Products are final products made such as furniture, paper, or apparel. Subject matter includes such items as

---

[10] U.S. Department of Labor, *Handbook for Analyzing Jobs* (Washington, D.C.: Government Printing Office, 1972).

arts, biological sciences, natural sciences, and social science. Services include items such as transportation, communication, sanitation, and personal services.

Worker Traits.   The information here specifies the qualifications and temperaments required by the employee to adequately perform the job. It includes the following categories:

Training time. (a) general educational development and (b) specific vocational preparation.
Aptitudes. Eleven aptitudes such as intelligence, motor coordination, and manual dexterity.
Temperaments. These are personal traits required of the employee by the specific job-worker situation. There are ten factors such as adaptability to making generalizations and adaptability to performing under stress.
Interests. Five pairs of bi-polar vocational interest factors.
Physical demands. Six main categories such as strength, climbing, and seeing.
Environmental conditions. Seven factors such as heat, cold, noise, and hazards.

By using this detailed job analysis procedure, management can efficiently compare, compile, quantify, classify and summarize jobs and job information.

ADMINISTRATION OF THE JOB ANALYSIS PROGRAM

The responsibility for analyzing jobs and preparing descriptions and specifications is usually assigned to the personnel department. If the organization is very large, undoubtedly there will be a section within this department that does such work. This may be called the wage and salary section, employee compensation section, or the job analysis group. The reason for placing responsibility for job analysis within the personnel department is that it is intimately concerned with utilizing job information for so many of its other programs—that is, manpower planning, recruitment, selection, placement, training, job evaluation, area wage surveys, and safety.

Sometimes the industrial engineering department prepares the job descriptions and specifications, especially for production and maintenance type of jobs. Many feel this is logical because it is a natural outgrowth of the industrial engineer's activities in methods study and work measurement. Many practitioners feel that this work requires engineering talent, because it is analytical, precise, and detailed in nature.

Procedurally, it is advisable for those charged with the job analysis function to obtain full cooperation and participation from operating supervision. Many companies follow the practice of submitting the completed description and specification to the supervisor of the job involved for his approval. This is to insure that the job as described is accurately represented and that he agrees with the way it has been written up. Some firms also follow the practice of showing the job write-up to the job holder himself for his approval. This is particularly true for professional, executive, and administrative positions. The policy of obtaining approval from operating management reduces the possibility of later complaints and obstruction of the program.

If there is anything certain in our modern complex industrial system, it is the constancy of change. This applies well to jobs and positions. There are many circumstances that can cause changes in the nature, content, and worker requirements of jobs. New machinery and equipment may be introduced. Operating procedures may change. The company may be reorganized. If the firm grows and employment expands, jobs may become more specialized. Changing technology may add new skill requirements to some jobs and take them away from others. Therefore, a job analysis program must be kept up to date. Descriptions cannot be filed away and then forgotten. There are two ways of insuring that the information on file is an accurate representation of current conditions in the organization. One method places major reliance upon the operating supervisors. They must be trained to report any significant changes in the make-up of the jobs in their units. This responsibility is likely to rank quite low in their system of priorities because their superiors will generally emphasize production, costs, quality, and efficiency. The second approach is more positive, more thorough, and also more costly. It requires the job analysis group to conduct periodic audits (usually annually) of the jobs in every department in order to pick up and evaluate any noteworthy changes in the composition and nature of the jobs.

Questions for review and discussion

1. What factors have traditionally governed the design of jobs in industry? What problems have resulted from this approach?
2. What concepts have been applied to job design in more recent years? What considerations determine whether the traditional or the more modern approach will be successful in a given application?
3. Explain the meaning of the following occupational categories:
   a) Semiskilled labor.
   b) Skilled labor.
   c) Executive position.
   d) Administrative position.
   e) Professional position.
4. Explain how equal employment opportunity regulations have added special significance to sound job analysis.
5. What is "functional job analysis" as used by the U.S. Department of Labor?
6. What are the principal methods that can be used to analyze jobs? What method or methods would you use? Why?
7. Distinguish between a job description and a job specification. What information commonly appears on each?
8. If you were a job analyst in a company, would you describe jobs as they actually existed or as some supervisor or manager said they should exist? (Assume there is a difference between actual job content and requirements and proposed content and requirements).

Exercise

Make a thorough analysis of a job as it is currently being performed by interviewing an employee of your college or university (or in some other organization where you can obtain good cooperation). Concentrate upon interviewing the employee to obtain the information you desire. You may wish to supplement this with an interview with the person who supervises this employee plus a brief observation of the job and its work environment. Use the job analysis questionnaire in Figure 7-3 as your guide to the questions to ask. (This questionnaire can serve not only as a form for every employee himself to fill out but also as a schedule or guide to assist the job analyst in covering all the necessary points when interviewing an employee.)

After you have collected the necessary data, prepare a job description and a specification. Show these to the employee and/or his supervisor to determine whether they feel your write-up accurately describes the job and the human qualifications.

Suggestions for further reading

Davis, Louis E. and James C. Taylor, eds. *Design of Jobs*. Baltimore: Penguin Books, Inc. 1972.

Fine, Sidney A. and Wretha W. Wiley. *An Introduction to Functional Job Analysis*. Kalamazoo, Mich.: W. E. Upjohn Institute, 1971.

Hackman, J. Richard. "Work Design," Chapter 3 in Hackman, J. Richard and J. Lloyd Suttle. *Improving Life at Work*, eds. Santa Monica, Calif.: Goodyear Publishing Co., Inc., 1977.

Herzberg, Frederick. "The Wise Old Turk," *Harvard Business Review*, Vol. 52, No. 5 (September–October 1974), pp. 70–80.

McCormick, Ernest J. "Job and Task Analysis," In M. D. Dunnette, ed. *Handbook of Industrial and Organizational Psychology*. Chicago: Rand McNally, 1976.

U.S. Department of Labor. *Dictionary of Occupational Titles*, 4th ed. Washington, D.C.: Government Printing Office, 1977.

——. *Handbook for Analyzing Jobs*. Washington, D.C.: Government Printing Office, 1972.

IV

EMPLOYMENT AND DEVELOPMENT OF PEOPLE

Human resource planning

Why should management conduct human resource planning? Three hypothetical but very realistic examples will demonstrate the need.

The average age of the upper management personnel of the Longworth Corporation is high. Within six years three-fourths of all the managers at the levels of the president, vice presidents, and division heads will reach normal retirement age. The president and the director of personnel have recently met to discuss this situation. At this meeting the director of personnel agreed that he would prepare a plan for dealing with this problem of management succession.

In another company, the Glenmont Corporation, the director of research and development, with his immediate staff, is preparing a proposal for $1,000,000 to be submitted to the U.S. Department of the Energy for the development, design, construction, and testing of prototype solar energy cells. As a part of its proposal, Glenmont must provide a comprehensive description of the scientific, engineering, managerial, and technical support personnel who would be assigned to this project.

Our third company, The Exeter Company, has just signed a consent agreement with the Office of Federal Contract Compliance Programs of the U.S. Department of Labor and with the Equal Employment Opportunity Commission. In this agreement the company agrees to increase its employment of women and blacks and to upgrade women and blacks into skilled trades and supervisory positions. Within the next four years the company must increase its employment of these categories of personnel 25 percent above present levels. The Affirmative Action Coordinator in the personnel department must collect detailed work force data and classify employees by age, sex, race, job title, pay grade, department and the like in order to monitor progress toward meeting this goal.

Carefully constructed human resource plans, including skills inventories, forecasts of needs, and implementation programs are essential to meeting the needs described in the three foregoing examples.

Human resource planning is also sometimes called manpower planning. Other terms used to designate this function are personnel planning and employment planning. What is human resource planning? It is a *process for determining and assuring that the organization will have an adequate number of qualified persons, available at the proper times, performing jobs which meet the needs of the enterprise and which provide satisfaction for the individuals involved.* Let us examine this definition. Human resource planning is an ongoing process. It is not static. It involves many interrelated activities. The plan must be modified and updated as conditions require. It includes the planning and development of human resource programs, such as recruitment, performance appraisal, and training to assure that people's needs of the organization are met. Strictly speaking, we should call this function "human resource planning and action programming." But for conciseness of language, we shall simply say human resource planning and then know that this includes action programming. Furthermore, human resource planning requires detailed analysis of the present and the future to ensure that the organization has the right number of people available who possess the right kinds of skills to perform the jobs required by the enterprise when the work is needed. And finally, the definition acknowledges that the entire system should match the organization's needs for productive people with the needs of these people for personal career satisfaction.

REASONS FOR HUMAN RESOURCE PLANNING

The importance of systematic and comprehensive manpower planning has been recognized only in recent years. Traditionally, management assumed that it could always obtain the personnel it required whenever it needed them. For the most part, firms did not engage in formal human resource planning. A company may be able to get by with such a casual approach if it is small, changes little, and the skills it employs are relatively simple. But formal personnel planning is essential for the enterprise that is moderate to large in size, that experiences change in technology, products, markets, and internal organization, and that utilizes a lot of high talent personnel. In fact, it can be said that such planning is necessary for the viability of such organizations.

Let us now discuss reasons why organizations should carry on systematic human resource planning.

1. *Future Personnel Needs.* Planning is vital for determining personnel needs for the future.
2. *Cope with Change.* Human resource planning enables the enterprise to cope

with changes in competitive forces, markets, technology, products, and government regulations. Such changes often generate changes in job content, skill demands, number and type of personnel. Shortages of people may be induced in some areas while surpluses in other areas may occur.

3. *High Talent Personnel.* The mix of personnel employed in a great many organizations has shifted toward the high talent occupations—managerial and professional personnel. There is often a scarcity of high talent people. The lead time required to hire and develop such personnel is long. Much effort has to be devoted to long range career development, counseling, planned work assignments, and appropriate rewards. With many different, highly specialized, technical persons employed in the modern complex organization, and with these people performing functions that are highly interdependent, the organization becomes vulnerable if any shortage of talent occurs. Hence, planning is necessary to prevent shortages. Furthermore, technological change often upgrades some jobs and degrades others. For example, jobs that formerly required a bachelor of science in engineering degree may now require a masters degree. Or other jobs may have declined to the point where a technician can adequately perform the work. Such considerations must be included in the manpower plan.

    Another facet of the high talent personnel problem is the matter of management succession planning. Who will replace the retiring chief executive officer? From what pool of people will upper executives be selected and how will these individuals be groomed for their increased responsibilities?

4. *Strategic Planning.* The modern competitive enterprise engages in strategic planning. Top management evaluates the environment in which the organization operates, assesses the strengths and weaknesses of the enterprise, sets objectives, and determines programs for implementation. Human resource planning is an essential component of strategic planning.

5. *Equal Employment Opportunity.* The Federal government's equal employment opportunity and affirmative action regulations mandate that employers meet agreed goals for the employment and upgrading of protected categories of people in their work forces. Affirmative action programs must be implemented and monitored in regard to hiring, placement, training, compensation, and advancement.

6. *Government Contracts.* Thousands of companies and not-for-profit organizations sell products and services to the government. To bid for Federal government contracts, a firm must supply detailed information on its manpower resources. To be competitive, it must plan for and develop appropriate human resources.

7. *Foundation for Personnel Functions.* Personnel planning provides essential information for designing and implementing personnel functions such as recruitment, selection, personnel movement (transfers, promotions, layoffs), and training and personnel development.

THE PLANNING PROCESS

Planning for human resources should be tied-in with overall enterprise long range planning. Unfortunately, many enterprises do no formal long range or stra-

GOALS AND PLANS OF ORGANIZATION

Strategic planning: public policy, social trends, economic conditions, technology, market conditions, strengths and weaknesses of organization, projected outputs for planning periods.

CURRENT HUMAN RESOURCE SITUATION

Skills inventory: numbers of people grouped by job, department, organizational level, location, age, education, in-service training completed, performance.

HUMAN RESOURCE FORECAST

a. Present workforce: project retirements, layoffs, promotions, and quits for planning periods.
b. Demand for people: Translate plans and forecast for organization into demand for employees for planning periods.
c. Comparison of demand with supply: Net additions or subtractions found by comparing (a) with (b).

IMPLEMENTATION PROGRAMS

Recruitment, selection and placement; performance appraisal; career planning; transfer, promotion, layoff; training and development; motivation and compensation.

AUDIT AND ADJUSTMENT

Measure implementation progress, compare with plan, take corrective action. Change human resource plans if enterprise plans are altered. Periodically update skills inventory, forecast, and implementation programs.

Figure 8-1
Major Steps in the Human Resource Planning Process.

tegic planning. For many organizations, the creation and adoption of an annual budget constitutes the sole mechanism of planning for organization needs. Of course, if top management does not undertake strategic business planning and wishes to only go as far as the annual budgetary planning process, the personnel director can develop limited manpower plans and programs geared to the one year cycle. He can also campaign for more comprehensive and longer range planning as a means for strengthening the organization.

Many companies carry out systematic planning only for those categories of personnel which have been in short supply or for those types of skills which require a long development time within the organization. Basically both of these conditions generally apply to highly skilled and technical personnel and to managers. All organizations that conduct extensive yearly recruiting at the colleges and universities must carefully plan their needs and their utilization of management trainees, accountants, engineers, scientists, and sales personnel. Likewise, companies that employ large numbers of craftsmen must carefully plan the input to their apprentice training program as well as the placement of the graduates.

Because unskilled and semi-skilled hourly-paid personnel and routine clerical personnel are often abundantly available in most labor markets, many firms only plan for short term needs regarding these types of employees. However, such an informal approach may not be advisable even for these kinds of workers because some of these employees may eventually be upgraded to better jobs. A careful planning of needs, qualifications, utilization, training needs, and career paths would be worthwhile.

The major components of the human resource planning process are: (1) goals and plans of the organization, (2) current human resource situation, (3) human resource forecast, (4) implementation programs, and (5) audit and adjustment (see Figure 8-1). Organizations differ substantially in the degree of sophistication they exhibit in doing their manpower planning. Furthermore, this art is still developing, so that we have not yet reached the point at which there is a universally accepted set of procedures for carrying out the mechanics of the process. Although the degree of sophistication varies and the detailed mechanics vary, there is agreement upon the major processes and contents of manpower planning and this is what we shall describe.

Goals and Plans of Organization

Human resource planning is a part of the overall strategic planning for the entire enterprise. A personnel vice president and his staff cannot make useful plans for periods of let's say, one, three, and five years hence, unless they have data on possible corporate expansion, new products, new plants, new markets and so on. Important steps involved in overall planning for the enterprise are listed below:

1. Analyze and evaluate environmental influences.
   a. Political trends and legislation which will have an impact upon the business.
   b. Economic conditions such as competition, inflation, rate of change in gross national product, and unemployment level.
   c. Social trends in leisure time, consumer tastes, work values and retirement.
   d. Technological advances affecting the enterprise.
2. Identify the values and aspirations of the organization's directors and executives.
3. Identify and evaluate the internal strengths and weaknesses of the enterprise. Consider human, financial, and technical resources and existing facilities.
4. Develop a strategy which relates the strengths of the company and the aspirations of the executives with opportunities perceived in the environment.
5. Create specific enterprise objectives and plans for achieving these objectives.
6. Prepare plans for the functional areas of the business: production, finance, marketing, research and development, engineering, and personnel. Determine strengths, deficiencies and needs.
7. Communicate with members of the organization and involve them in the planning processes.

8. Evaluate progress toward implementation of plans and take corrective action where necessary.

The existing human resources within the organization constitute an important input into the development of the overall strategic plans for the enterprise. Furthermore, the output of the planning process described above provides data upon which the human resource plans and projections can be based. Is the corporation going to launch a major new product line? Must technical manpower be augmented in order to bid successfully for government R&D contracts? Shall an obsolete facility be closed down and a new one constructed? Are certain business functions going to be reorganized? All such activities as these impact heavily on manpower needs.

The Planning Period.   How far into the future shall we plan human resource needs? Of course, the human resource plan is derived from the overall enterprise strategic plan. Different kinds of businesses plan ahead for different numbers of years. Some businesses, such as electric utilities, oil companies, and telephone companies, plan ten to twenty years ahead. Such long range planning by businesses is the exception however. Most plan only for the fairly short run of say one to three years.

The extent and rapidity of change in the forces affecting the business determines the utility of forecasts into the future. Some establishments can tie their forecasts directly into population growth trends—public schools, postal service, public utilities—hence, longer range planning is feasible. In other lines of business—women's fashions for example—there is so much uncertainty about the future that planning and forecasting beyond one or two seasons is fraught with risk. Generally speaking however, manpower planning for up to one year is considered short range and is widely practiced. Planning for two to four years is considered intermediate range and planning for five years and beyond is called long range.

Current Human Resource Situation

The second phase of the planning process is the preparation of an inventory of personnel presently within the organization. This is often called a *skills inventory* or a manpower information system. A skills inventory consists of up-to-date information regarding the qualifications of selected categories of personnel. Normally, skills inventories are prepared only for certain categories of personnel such as all members of management, or all technical and professional personnel, or all craftsmen. A total manpower information system would include data on all employees within the organization. However, such a total information system is very rarely established because of the great cost of preparation and updating and because detailed information for many categories of personnel such as unskilled and semi-skilled would seldom be used.

The skills inventory has several important uses. When the human resource forecast is prepared later, one can compare the number, types, and skills specified by the forecast with the present baseline or current position given by the skills inventory to ascertain what skills must be developed from present personnel via training, upgrading and special development efforts or obtained from external manpower sources.

Another important use of a skills inventory is to find or identify talent within the organization for specific job openings. For example, which employees within the corporation meet the following job specification: masters degree in mechanical engineering, at least six years of responsible professional experience in internal combustion engine design, at least five years engineering supervisory experience, a proven record of innovation such as demonstrated by patents. Person to head a team of engineers engaged in the design and development of a new fuel efficient, non-polluting automotive engine. A skills inventory used in the talent search mode is available for screening a large number of people and for making a first rough cut at selection. It cannot, however, provide for a specific matching of interests, temperament, and ambitions with job parameters. Personalized selection is required after the pool of possible candidates is identified.

An up-to-date skills inventory is valuable for the preparation of rosters of qualified technical and managerial personnel to be submitted on project proposals for government contracts. Furthermore, an inventory can be used in conjunction with an affirmative action program to monitor progress toward meeting employment goals. And finally, the existence of skills inventory enhances the opportunities for employees to satisfy their career aspirations through development and promotion.

Practice varies as to just how much information is contained in a skills inventory. Some or all of the following may be included:

Personal Data: Name, date of birth, sex, marital status.
Education: Degree(s), colleges, dates, curricula. Special training courses.
Employment History: Company—present job, dates, pay grade. Previous employers—jobs, dates, pay.
Performance and Potential: Performance appraisal ratings, assessment center evaluations.
Career Goals: Personal preferences for special training, assignments, jobs, locations.

See Figure 8-2 for an illustrative human resource inventory card. The inventory data for each employee is obtained by having him fill out a personal history form. His supervisor should review and discuss this with him. If summary performance appraisal data is to be included, this can be obtained from the personnel folder in the personnel office. Such evaluative material must be treated with the utmost confidentiality. There is danger that some persons may view these performance evaluations as fixed and immutable. People could be unfairly labeled and damaged. A performance evaluation is someone's opinion about someone else. Performance can change—opinions differ. Therefore, this information must be used with great discretion.

An example of a comprehensive skills inventory system is that of the North American Rockwell Corporation (now called Rockwell International). Their skills index covers 34,000 technical, salaried employees in seven major aerospace and systems divisions. Each division has a highly trained personnel specialist who manages the index for his division. All skills index information is stored on com-

HUMAN RESOURCE DATA CARD

Saratoga-Acme Corporation

Name   Alton T. Farnam   Date of Birth 5/17/42   Hire Date   6/21/67

Sex   Male   Marital Status Married

Present Position   Director of Personnel   Dates   2/14/77–present

Prior Positions at Saratoga-Acme: Dates:

    Assistant Director of Personnel   4/11/74–2/13/77

    Employment & Training Manager   11/19/71–4/10/74

    Safety Director   6/21/67–11/18/71

Pre-Saratoga Experience: Dates:

    Production Supervisor, Raynor Corp.   6/2/65–6/20/67

    Management Trainee, Raynor Corp.   6/30/64–6/1/65

Education:

    Rensselaer Polytechnic Institute – B.S. in Management, 9/60–6/64

Special Courses:

    Advanced Management Program – Harvard Univ., 9/77–12/77

    Equal Employment Opportunity Seminar – AMA – Oct. 1976

Career Interests:

    Seeks promotion to senior executive position in general management

Performance in Current Position:

Unsatisfactory	Meets Minimum Requirements	Fully Satisfactory Performance	Consistently Exceeds Requirements	Outstanding
☐	☐	☐	☒	☐

Assessment Center Rating:

    Has potential for top executive position in general management. Needs exposure to other

    areas of management.

Development Needs:

    Transfer to general management position such as assistant manager or manager of operations.

Figure 8-2

A Sample Human Resource Inventory Card.

puter tapes. It is readily available for talent searches and for summary print-outs classified in various ways.[1]

[1] Robert H. Murphy, "A Personalized Skills Inventory: The North American Rockwell Story" in Elmer H. Burack and James W. Walker, eds., *Manpower Planning and Programming* (Boston: Allyn & Bacon, Inc., 1972).

Another corporation which has created a computerized human resource inventory system is the Xerox Corporation. The basic document is a personal history form made out by the individual. Together the individual and his manager discuss and record career goals and logical steps to attain the goals. Performance appraisal information is added to the document by the manager. Xerox has prepared lists of appropriate developmental experiences for candidates in various jobs which have a large population base. Xerox uses its system for career development and for manpower planning.[2]

Computerized System. Although the small organization can advantageously collect, store, and retrieve its manpower information manually by means of file folders, card files, and various proprietary filing systems, an electronic data processing or computerized system is practically a must for the larger organization that wishes to handle data for hundreds or even thousands of people. A computerized system is expensive. However, a computer offers great advantages in terms of tremendous data storage and retrieval capabilities. And the computer can supply print-outs of manpower information classified in many meaningful ways. If the personnel director and other members of top management are worried about a possible high concentration of upper level managers only a few years away from retirement and the problem of management succession, the computer can readily provide a print-out of the age distribution of all managers by level, job, and department. If the personnel director wishes to know precisely what progress the company is making toward its affirmative action goals, the computer can provide a print-out of the number and percentage of women and minority employees classified by pay grade, job title, and department. Walker reports that most large corporations have adopted, or are in the process of installing, computerized personnel information systems.[3]

Human Resource Forecast

The human resource forecast is a determination of the *demand* for people and of the appropriate types and skills for given time periods in the future such as one, three and five years hence. The forecast also requires the preparation of an estimate of the *supply* of people who will be available for the selected time periods. The supply is composed of two parts. The first part is an estimate of the numbers and types of employees presently on the payroll who still will be available by the ends of the chosen time periods. The second part of the supply is that portion which must be recruited externally. These figures for the planning periods are obtained by subtracting the internally available manpower from the projected demand. If the figures are positive, people will have to be hired; if negative, people may eventually have to be laid off.

The demand forecast is derived from the information generated in Step 1—Goals and Plans of the Organization of the human resource planning process, described earlier. Step 1 should provide the human resource planners with data on such factors as projected dollar volume of sales, units to be produced, number

[2] Douglas M. Reid, "Human Resource Planning: A Tool for People Development," *Personnel,* Vol. 54, No. 2 (March–April 1977), pp. 15–25.
[3] James W. Walker, "The New, More Substantive Approach to Manpower Planning," *Management Review,* Vol. 66, No. 7 (July 1977), pp. 29–30.

of clients to be serviced, new facilities to be constructed, new functional departments to be created and so on.

Generally, manpower planners must use a variety of techniques to project future personnel needs. The techniques available range from judgment to rather sophisticated quantitative models. We will describe four major categories of forecasting techniques. These are: (1) judgment and experience, (2) budgetary planning, (3) work standards data, and (4) key predictive factors.

Judgment and Experience. This category includes estimates made by people who are very familiar with the products, processes, and jobs in the business. It is appropriate for relatively short-run forecasts of, say, up to two years. Supervisors and managers of the various units of the business make estimates of future manpower needs by judgmentally converting information on short-term future business activity (units to be produced, clients to be served, projects to be completed) into numbers and types of people needed. *Rules of thumb and decision rules* are also subsets of this category. For example, the production manager may know from past experience that for every 1,000 unit increase in production output he must add a second shift of 15 more machine operators and one foreman.

The *Delphi* technique is a systematic way of obtaining and refining judgments by a group of experts. It was originally developed by the Rand Corporation as a way of doing technological forecasting but it can be applied to manpower planning and forecasting as well. A panel of persons very familiar with the problem at hand is formed. The experts work privately and not in an assembled group. This is to avoid concurrence and conformity induced by face-to-face peer group social pressure. Each expert is asked to make predictions of future events. A moderator or intermediary collects the predictions, summarizes them, and then distributes them to the panel members for another round of forecasts. Eventually, convergence of opinion takes place and an acceptable forecast is obtained.

Budgetary Planning. Most organizations, other than the very small single proprietorship, prepare annual budgets. A budget is a plan expressed in financial and numerical terms. It is both an instrument for planning and for managerial control. Most budgetary planning is done on an annual basis. Often the budget for the whole organization is built up from the individual departmental budgets. After the tentative departmental budgets are prepared, they must be combined and adjusted by upper level management to properly allocate resources among all units and to bring income and expenditures into balance. For many enterprises, the annual process of budget preparation and review constitutes the only formal planning that is done. In this case it can become the principal vehicle for planning of manpower needs. Individual departmental managers must translate activity levels (units to be produced, students to be enrolled, clients to be served, etc.) and projects (R&D development programs, new products to be introduced, etc.) into rather detailed needs for personnel, materials, expenses, equipment, and facilities. In creating the budget, the managers must itemize the various categories of personnel in detail and in aggregate. This process forces them to think through their plans and needs for the year and to justify these plans and needs to higher management.

Work Standards Data. By means of industrial engineering work measurement techniques, many companies have established rather comprehensive sets of data for man-hours or unit times to perform a great many tasks. These standards are most prevalent for direct production tasks but some companies have also prepared work standards for maintenance and clerical activities. The forecasting procedure involves the translation of overall enterprise volume of activity into production schedules for all production departments. The projected units of output for each department are converted into man-hours, man-days and number of employees by applying the established time standards.

The measured work standards technique generally cannot be used for determining professional, administrative, and executive personnel needs. Judgment, past experience, and managerial intent are the major determinants of how many and what kinds of personnel are needed. For example, the size of the corporate research laboratory is determined more by the attitudes of top management than it is by the volume of units produced by the company.

Key Predictive Factors. The essence of the "key predictive factors" technique is to find one (or a very limited number) of business factors or key indicators with which total manpower correlates highly. To identify such a factor, the human resource planning office must examine several business factors such as dollar sales volume, units produced, or number of clients served to find which factor or factors yields a good historical correlation between number of employees and changes in the business factor.

A considerable amount of quantitative analysis may be necessary to determine the relationships between changes in the various business indicators and changes in manpower. In some kinds of business the total number of employees is not directly proportional to product volume. For example, in a continuous process industry such as an oil refinery, it might require almost as many people to run a plant at 80 percent of capacity as at full capacity. Another consideration is that many enterprises make a variety of products (or services). Some of these may be quite labor intensive and others may not be. Therefore, the manpower analysis must be conducted separately for each of the product divisions. Charts and formulas can be created to show the aggregate figures for the corporation.

If manpower projections are being made for several years into the future, it is important to incorporate changes (hopefully improvements) in productivity into the calculations. For example, 10 years ago, a total hourly employment of 500 persons may have been necessary to produce 10,000 units of product per year. Five years ago, only 450 persons were needed to produce the same 10,000 units. Now our hypothetical company can produce 10,000 units with just 410 hourly employees. This is an improvement of roughly 2 percent per year. The future productivity improvement may be greater than or less than this 2 percent a year average. The manpower planners must investigate likely changes in technology, working hours, and manpower utilization in order to accurately estimate the probable efficiency improvement in the years to come.

Wikstrom describes the forecasting technique used by the Standard Oil Company (New Jersey), now called Exxon Corporation. For projecting total employment levels at refineries, the company uses "intensity adjusted capacity" as its key predictive factor. This factor is a composite of the size of the refinery in thousands of barrels of oil per day and the intensity of operations which measures the degree of use of more complex refining processes. The actual total employment for each of several past years is divided by intensity adjusted capacity in thousands of barrels per day to obtain a manpower coefficient of people per thousand barrels per day. This ratio has declined over the years due to technological improvements. To determine managerial and professional personnel needs, the company plots the historical ratio of such employees to total manpower for several years. Then it projects this same ratio into the future.[4]

Because a major strength of the Hewlett-Packard Company, a manufacturer of calculators and other precision instruments, lies in its professional personnel, it concentrates upon planning for these people. Working with historical data, year by year, the planners compute ratios of employees to sales dollars for the various functional departments. They also do this for the different grades or levels of employees. These ratios are then used to project future manpower requirements. The principal use of the forecast is for college recruiting.[5]

Statistical and operations research techniques constitute useful analytic tools for making manpower forecasts. Only in the last few years have organizations begun to systematically apply these techniques for human resource planning. Among the quantitative techniques available for use in this application are statistical correlation (linear, curvilinear, multiple regression), stochastic analysis incorporating probabilities, linear programming, network flow methods, and computer simulation.[6]

We have talked about ways of making estimates of human resource needs (demand analysis) for the future. While the planning group is making these projections it must also make a *supply* analysis. First it must determine the personnel presently available within the organization. The planning group must also forecast the probable losses from the current roster due to retirements, resignations, discharges, deaths, and disabilities. Figure 8-3 shows such an analysis for managerial and professional personnel in hypothetical Company A. In this figure, we see that at managerial level 5, there is one person (the president) who will reach retirement age before January 1, 1985. The company will have to find a replacement before that date. This chart only projects losses out of the present complement of personnel. Of course the staffing of an organization is dynamic. During the course of the five year analysis period, some people at lower levels will be promoted to higher ranks. Also new hires will be gradually added to replace the losses. And if Company A were a division of a very large corporation, some personnel would be expected to transfer out to other divisions and some people would transfer in from other divisions. Figure 8-3 shows that there will be 337 managerial and professional personnel available on January 1, 1985. By comparing this total with the projected demand for 1985, we can determine how many persons will have to be hired from outside the company. Of course, this is a prediction of what will happen over the course of the

---

[4] Walter S. Wikstrom, *Manpower Planning: Evolving Systems*, Report No. 521 (New York: The Conference Board, 1971).

[5] Ibid., pp. 32–33.

[6] For a description of both quantitative and judgmental techniques, see Don R. Bryant, Michael J. Maggard, and Robert P. Taylor, "Manpower Planning Models and Techniques," *Business Horizons*, Vol. XVI, No. 3 (April 1973), pp. 69–77.

	Current Personnel Jan. 1, 1980	Retirements	Other Losses*	Total Losses	Estimated Personnel Available Jan. 1, 1985
Managerial					
Level 5	1	1	0	1	0
" 4	6	1	0	1	5
" 3	34	6	1	7	27
" 2	97	15	6	21	76
" 1	185	20	34	54	131
Professional					
Level 4	17	2	1	3	14
" 3	27	4	4	8	19
" 2	46	1	9	10	36
" 1	39	0	10	10	29
Totals	452	50	65	115	337

*Other Losses include resignations, discharges, deaths, disabled, and early retirements.

Figure 8-3
Present Managerial and Professional Personnel Projected Five Years Ahead—Company A.

next five years. Conditions will change and some of the original assumption may have to be altered. Therefore, the forecast for both demand and supply should be updated annually or more often as conditions dictate.

Management Succession Planning. A special or particular type of human resource forecasting is management succession planning. This process is also called management progression forecast or management replacement planning.

Many companies follow a practice of filling most managerial vacancies by promotion from within. Some firms, especially for their middle and upper levels of managerial personnel, assign a rating to each individual indicating his or her potential for promotion. This rating is based upon the regular performance appraisal prepared by each person's immediate organizational superior. But in addition, for management succession purposes, each individual is evaluated in depth by a team of higher level managers. Assessment center data may also be utilized to develop the rating. These ratings are treated as highly confidential. Then, for each position, several individuals are identified as highly qualified to replace the incumbent should he leave the organization. By means of management succession planning, delays in filling vacancies can be avoided and people can be trained to take over the vacancies when they occur.

However, there is a real danger in designating certain people as the "crown princes" or "heir apparents." Giving particular managers an option or prior claim upon specific higher positions cuts all others off from a chance for these better jobs. It can destroy morale and give the masses of managers the notion that things have been "fixed" through political connections.

A better approach is to identify a pool of managers, all of whom have good potential for advancement. This pool of people can then be given special training and developmental assignments in accordance with their interests and organizational opportunities. None in the pool are given a claim upon a specific higher level job. But all are given opportunities to qualify for any of a number of jobs should they open up.

Implementation Programs

Implementation requires converting the human resource plan into action. For example, if a shortage of engineering personnel has been forecast and if the plans indicate both stepped up recruitment plus training and upgrading of present engineering talent, then both recruitment and development programs will have to be strengthened and expanded. We shall discuss principal implementation actions only briefly here because each of these matters are covered in depth in separate chapters, or major parts thereof, elsewhere in this book.

Recruitment, Selection, Placement. Often, the analysis of manpower needs reveals a shortage of specific critical skills such as certain specialized engineers, scientists, or middle level managers. In such cases the personnel executive must identify potentially good sources of supply and then efforts must be made to attract likely candidates to the company.

The selection program should be professionally designed and, among other considerations, special care should be taken to insure compliance with equal employment opportunity regulations in regard to such aspects as selection testing and the setting of qualification standards.

Usually, companies hire for specific job openings. However, some organizations hire a group of qualified individuals for the organization and not for specific jobs. Some examples are the employment of management interns in government and management trainees in private industry. In these cases, the group of trainees move through a variety of assignments over a one or two year period. Then the placement function is put into play. An effort is made to match individual job preferences and qualifications with organization needs.

Performance Appraisal. Performance appraisal has two fundamental uses. The first use is concerned with decisions in regard to pay increases, promotions, transfers, and discharges. The second use is concerned with employee development. This includes the identification of needs for self-improvement, training, and special broadening assignments. Management by objectives, which is a principal appraisal method as well as a system for managing, is a major technique used for individual (especially management) development.

Career Development. Formal, integrated career development in organizations is very new. However, certain components of what we now call career management have existed in some organizations for a long time. Some organizations have created channels or pathways of promotion. In the armed forces, for example, years of development have established various career paths for military officers. For unionized blue collar workers, some companies have set up occupational lines of progression. Often these have been built around the technology of manufacturing operations as in the making of steel or paper.

The contemporary concept of career development places much greater emphasis upon individual choice and self-analysis than formerly existed. In place of rather random movements, reassignments, opportunities and setbacks shaping the individual's occupational pathway through time, today progressive personnel departments are setting up career development systems that focus upon both individual career guidance and self-analysis plus planned opportunities and developmental activities.

Promotion, Transfer, Layoff, Retirement. Organizations are ever changing. Because of the needs of the business and the individuals, there is always some movement of people occurring. In implementing the human resource plans, some people may be promoted to jobs of higher responsibility and others may be transferred to different jobs either to fill definite vacancies or to perform assignments to develop the individual. Some units of the business may be forced to reduce the workforce via layoffs. Administering a layoff program can be quite complicated. The union–employer contract, for example, may spell out job, department, shift, or plant-wide seniority units or some combination thereof.

To effectuate certain parts of a manpower plan, some firms have offered inducements for early retirement for certain individuals or classes of personnel. Early retirement is supposed to be voluntary and not coerced; however, some managements place unwanted persons in meaningless or demeaning jobs to induce them to retire.

The 1978 amendments to the Age Discrimination in Employment Act of 1967 raised the protected age limit for employees in private industry and state and local government from 65 to 70, effective January 1, 1979. Thus, employers are no longer allowed to have a mandatory retirement age of 65, as has been traditional. Although the trend in recent years has been toward early retirement before age 65, this amendment has introduced a new dimension. There will be greater uncertainty in planning by management for replacement needs for retirees. Depending upon individual preferences and pension arrangements, people will be leaving organizations at ages spreading from about 60 up to 70.

Training and Development. As technology changes, as new products or services are introduced, as reorganizations occur, and as people are upgraded, there is a need for well designed and executed training and development programs. This includes formal classroom courses both in-house and at nearby colleges as well as on-the-job learning, coaching, and planned special assignments.

Motivation and Compensation. The entire system of motivation, leadership, compensation, and rewards serves to help accomplish the human resource plan. If the organization is not paying competitive rates, for example, for some of its key job classes, then it will have real trouble recruiting and retaining people. Or if the treatment of employees is perceived to be arbitrary and capricious (a leadership problem), then again the firm will have trouble meeting its manpower needs.

Audit and Adjustment

For any of various reasons, the programs for meeting the human resource targets may be falling short of objectives. A system for measuring progress should be set up. Many measures can be used depending upon the specific program being evaluated.

What percentage of the company's engineers have earned their professional engineer (P.E.) license (if the goal is to upgrade the engineering department personnel)? How many apprentices are being graduated each year from the machinist apprentice program (if the goal is to "grow from within" skilled tradesmen)? What percentages of first, second, third, and fourth level managerial positions are now occupied by women and blacks (if affirmative action goal accomplishment is being monitored)? Of course, if results fall short of targets, then changes must be made.

Another reason for reviewing progress is to ascertain if changes in the manpower plans are made necessary because of changed conditions or because some of the original planning assumptions have been proven wrong.

CONCLUSION

Just as general strategic planning, financial planning, and market planning are concomitants of the successful business organization, so too is formal human resource planning and development. Some firms drift along for several years without paying adequate attention to human resource programs, but long term organizational success cannot be achieved without a reasonable effort toward manpower planning and development.

We have discussed in some depth the five main components of human resource planning and implementation. These are: (1) goals and plans of the organization, (2) current human resource situation, (3) human resource forecast, (4) implementation programs, and (5) audit and adjustment. A major point made is that human resource planning should be closely linked to general institutional planning.

Effective personnel management is not the handling of a potpourri of various personnel functions such as hiring, training, compensation, and benefits. It is rather an integrated whole that is designed to enhance both organizational objectives and individual employee satisfactions. Sound human resource planning is a basic instrument for achieving this holistic view of personnel.

Questions for review and discussion ───────────────

1. Give reasons why it is desirable for complex organizations to carry out formal human resource planning.
2. Why should human resource planning be linked to the overall institutional or enterprise planning?
3. List and explain the key components of human resource planning.
4. What is a skills inventory? What does it contain? How is it prepared?
5. What methods can be used to make a forecast of human resource demand?
6. Show how human resource planning for a bank would differ from planning for a high technology firm that is heavily dependent upon obtaining large commercial and government contracts.
7. Using a club, campus or community organization with which you are familiar as a case example, prepare a three year human resource plan for officers and

committee chairmen. How would you insure that new officers and committee chairmen possess the skills and attributes needed to fulfill their responsibilities? How would you insure an adequate supply of people to staff the various positions?

Case problem ———————————————————————————————

THE REDMONT CORPORATION[7]

The Redmont Corporation is engaged in both manufacturing and research and development for civilian markets and for Federal government defense projects. Founded in 1947, the firm grew steadily and reached peak employment in 1974 of 2500 with annual sales of 100 million dollars. The years up to 1974 were the good years. Both management and the employees had been optimistic. The company had been successful in selling its products in civilian markets and government contracts had been coming in steadily. Wages and employee morale were good. Employment had increased gradually and rather steadily over the years.

But in 1974 business started turning sour. Late in 1974, the country began experiencing a general economic recession. Redmont started losing both government contracts and civilian business. Competition became intense. From peak employment of 2500 in 1974, the total workforce declined to 1500 by 1977. The production and maintenance employees were unionized; hence, these people were laid off according to seniority provisions of the union–company agreement. Sales and employment were stable in 1978. By 1979 business had improved somewhat and employment had increased to 1600.

The corporation has a machine shop, metal fabrication, and assembly operation employing about 600 people as of 1979. In the peak year of 1974 there were 1025 people employed in these three manufacturing departments. The Planning and Methods Section is a staff unit attached to the manufacturing division (comprising these three departments). The function of this section is to plan the flow of production job orders through all the manufacturing operations. The planner works from the engineering drawings to determine whether the shop has the capability of producing the parts and assemblies. Infrequently, work must be contracted out because of a lack of manufacturing capability.

If the product can be made within the shop, the planner must prepare a detailed planning sheet for each individual piece part and assembly to show all manufacturing operations and the sequence in which they are to be performed. This specialist must be able to read and understand complicated engineering drawings and specifications. The planner must possess a good knowledge of manufacturing methods, equipment, and processes. He must specify quality checks. After work orders are assigned to the shop, he must follow-up and devise solutions to manufacturing problems. Corrective action could involve revising the tooling, assigning to a different machine, selecting alternative manufacturing processes, changing sequence of operations, and revising the planning sheet instructions. The planner must be able to deal effectively with engineering, quality assurance, and production personnel.

[7] The author expresses his appreciation to Thomas Schoonmaker for the basic idea for this case.

In 1974 there were twenty planning and methods specialists in this section. By 1977, as a result of heavy layoffs throughout the company, this section had been cut back to only nine specialists. Although these people were not unionized, the company had generally cut back the salaried work force on the basis of seniority. Most of the eleven people lost by this section had been laid off, and the layoffs fell mostly upon the younger personnel. By 1979 eight of the nine planning and methods specialists were over 53 years of age.

The traditional source of planning and methods specialists had been the machine shop apprentice program. This four year program consisted of on-the-job training in a variety of machine tool processes and fabrication methods plus classroom work and theory at a local community college (tuition paid by the company). At the conclusion of the program, the graduates received a two year associate degree from the college plus their certificate as a journeyman machinist. The apprentice program was small with about seven or eight people graduating each year. Most took jobs as machinists while a very few went into salaried jobs in planning and methods, production control, and industrial engineering. After an apprentice graduate or a journeyman machinist had been assigned to the Planning and Methods Section, it took about a year and a half of guided on-the-job training and diversified assignments to develop him or her into a qualified planning specialist. In 1975 the company top management abolished the entire apprentice program because of the severe decline in business and of its forecast of continuing hard times in the future.

By 1979 company sales had improved somewhat from the depressed level of 1975–1978. The workload in Planning and Methods was getting heavier and with only nine people available—considerable overtime work was required.

The dilemma facing the Director of Personnel and top management was how to meet possible future manpower needs in the Planning and Methods Section. The traditional source of new personnel had disappeared with the abandonment of the apprentice program. With a somewhat uncertain business future, top management was very reluctant to make the financial and staffing investment needed to reactivate the program. Inasmuch as the section is staffed primarily with older personnel and the workload is increasing, how should manpower needs be met?

Some of the alternatives being considered are as follows:

a. Promote promising individuals from among current complement of machinists. However, the heavy layoffs of 1975–77 have depleted the ranks of younger machinists. The available personnel are mostly in their 50's.
b. Hire experienced persons from outside the company.
c. Recruit technical graduates from two-year community colleges. Set up an on-the-job training program within the Planning and Methods Section.
d. Do nothing. Wait and see if business continues to grow and the workload of this section requires continued overtime.

Question

Considering the various listed alternatives and other possibilities, choose a course of action for meeting the need for qualified planning and methods specialists now and for the future. What are the advantages and disadvantages of each alternative? Layout a specific course of action including techniques of implementation.

Suggestions for further reading

BRIGHT, WILLIAM E. "How One Company Manages Its Human Resources," *Harvard Business Review*, Vol. 54, No. 1 (January–February 1976), pp. 81–93.

BURACK, ELMER H. *Strategies for Manpower Planning and Programming*. Morristown, N.J.: General Learning Press, 1972.

—— and THOMAS G. GUTTERIDGE. "Institutional Manpower Planning: Rhetoric Versus Reality." *California Management Review*. Vol. XX, No. 3 (Spring 1978), pp. 13–22.

—— and JAMES W. WALKER, eds. *Manpower Planning and Programming*. Boston: Allyn & Bacon, Inc., 1972.

COLEMAN, BRUCE P. "An Integrated System for Manpower Planning." *Business Horizons*, Vol. XIII, No. 5 (October 1970), pp. 89–95.

FOLTMAN, FELICIAN F. *Manpower Information for Effective Management: Part 1: Collecting and Managing Employee Information*. Key Issues No. 10. Ithaca, N.Y.: N.Y. State School of Industrial and Labor Relations, Cornell University, 1973.

——. *Manpower Information for Effective Management: Part 2: Skills Inventories and Manpower Planning*. Key Issues No. 14. Ithaca, N.Y.: N.Y. State School of Industrial and Labor Relations, Cornell University, 1973.

PATTEN, THOMAS H. JR. *Manpower Planning and the Development of Human Resources*. New York: John Wiley & Sons, Inc., 1971.

VETTER, ERIC W. *Manpower Planning for High Talent Personnel*. Ann Arbor, Michigan: University of Michigan, Bureau of Industrial Relations, 1967.

WALKER, JAMES W. "Evaluating the Practical Effectiveness of Human Resource Planning Applications," *Human Resource Management*, Vol. 13, No. 1 (Spring 1974), pp. 19–27.

——. "Human Resource Planning: Managerial Concerns and Practices," *Business Horizons*, Vol. 19, No. 3 (June 1976), pp. 55–59.

Recruitment and selection

The human resources of most organizations are properly viewed as their most important asset. The successes and failures of the organization are largely determined by the caliber of its work force (starting with management) and by the efforts it exerts. Therefore, the policies and programs an enterprise adopts to meet its manpower needs are of vital significance.

The employment function of a personnel program encompasses the areas of human resource planning, recruitment, selection, placement and changes of employment status such as transfers, promotions, layoffs, and discharges.

In this chapter we shall be concerned with issues, policies, and techniques involved in the hiring of people to staff the organization. The chapter following this one is devoted to an in-depth look at two principal selection techniques—testing and interviewing.

The process of searching for a new employee is customarily initiated by a manager who decides that he needs to add to his staff or to replace someone who is leaving the organization. Commonly he makes a written request to the personnel department stating that he wishes to hire someone to fill a specific vacancy. The position to be filled is defined in terms of its job description and its job specification (human qualifications). The hiring activity should be integrated with the human resource plans of the company. These plans should forecast departments that are expected to grow and those that may decline. There should be a skills inventory so that present employees can be matched with job openings to provide for transfers and promotions. The employment manager must have a good understanding of the labor market and how it functions, sources of personnel, recruitment methods, and selection procedures.

Labor Market Considerations

A labor market is a geographic area within which employers recruit workers and workers seek employment. It is the place where the forces of supply and demand interact. It is usually thought to consist of a central city or cities and the surrounding territory in which persons can change their place of employment without changing their place of residence. When management decides to go into the labor market to obtain additional employees, it finds that it operates vastly different from product or financial markets. A labor market tends to be unstructured for the most part; it is unorganized. The procedures by which a company recruits workers and the methods by which workers go about obtaining jobs are highly variable. The process is not necessarily channeled through a public or a private employment agency. Laws and regulations governing the process are of a very minimal nature. In fact, if one looks at the process from the standpoint of workers seeking jobs, the whole procedure seems rather haphazard and catch-as-catch-can. Some job seekers obtain employment through friends and relatives, others through direct visits to the plant gate, others through their unions, and still others through employment agencies. Pure chance plays a large part in determining whether John Smith gets a job in plant A or in plant B.

A labor market is characterized by a great diversity of wage rates for the same occupations. If one were to examine occupational wage survey statistics compiled by the Bureau of Labor Statistics of the United States Department of Labor for any of a number of major cities in the country, he would find the highest wage paid for an occupation being in the nature of two to two and one half times that of the lowest. This variation in wages for the same kind of work is caused by many factors. Principal ones are differences among the employers in ability to pay, productivity, and management attitude toward wage levels. Certain non-wage factors, such as greater job security, may mean that a firm that pays only modest wages may still attract and hold the labor it requires. For in the labor market (except for very high-level talent) it is the buyer (employer) and not the seller (worker) who establishes the wage level.

Lack of labor mobility is still another characteristic of a labor market. An employee will not resign his job simply to take a job in another part of town because it pays 10 cents more per hour. Labor can be said to be "sticky." It tends to stick in one place. There are many reasons for this. One important reason is that the average working man possesses quite incomplete and inaccurate knowledge of job opportunities in his labor market. Wage rate data are not generally made public. If a job opening occurs in a company, it is often filled through informal contacts (you must know somebody to get the job) rather than being announced in the newspapers or listed with an employment agency. Besides a person can rarely determine in advance whether he would be really happy in another job just from the information he can gather in an interview. He must actually work on it a while to find out whether the supervisor treats him fairly, whether the other employees are congenial, and whether the opportunities for advancement reflect what he was told in the employment interview. From this it can be seen that many a worker is unlikely to quit his present job simply because the grass appears to be greener on the other side of the street. There are too many unknowns involved. An additional obstacle to labor mobility derives from the existence of seniority systems and added fringe benefits that accrue to long-service employees in a company. An employee who has built up a sizable pension fund in his account, gets four weeks vacation per year, and has acquired considerable job seniority will be quite reluctant to give up all these advantages to take a job with another company for only slightly more pay.

All the foregoing hindrances to labor mobility to not mean that people will not, at times, actively search for other employment. But they do serve to emphasize the point that the labor market and the process by which labor supply is allocated is quite disorganized.

Labor Supply to the Company

From the standpoint of an individual company, the considerations that determine the quantity and quality of labor that it can recruit are quite complex. The supply is influenced by the population in the labor market, the attractiveness of the jobs and the company (for example, wage rate, benefits and services, reputation of company for job security), amount of unemployment in the labor market, commuting patterns (location of the employer with respect to transportation lines), and the particular skills needed in relation to their availability in the local community. First to come to the attention of an organization seeking additional employees, quite logically, would be those who are presently unemployed. Those who are currently drawing state unemployment insurance benefits are registered with the local state employment service office. It has been the author's experience in working with unemployment statistics in industrial cities that those registered for unemployment benefits at any one time represent only 60 to 70 percent of the total number who are out of work. Many persons may have already exhausted their maximum number of weeks of benefits. Many people do not register if they are unemployed for only a very brief period.

The labor force is not fixed and unchanging in size. Annually, young people enter the labor force and older workers leave through retirements and disability. In any given community there may be a net in-migration or out-migration caused by a complex of factors. The principal factor is the availability of decent jobs. Also the pool of people who are available and looking for work expands and contracts over time. In times of high demand for labor, people who would not ordinarily seek employment, retired persons or certain housewives for example, may be drawn into the work force whereas in times of low demand, many people may withdraw from the labor force. Those who withdraw may include persons with very limited skills and those who suffer protracted unemployment and who have become discouraged about job prospects.

The personnel policies of an individual employer are a major determinant of its ability to obtain the labor that he requires. What kind of reputation as a place to work has an organization created for itself by its actions and treatment of present employees? Does the company arbitrarily cut itself off from such labor sources as particular racial or religious groups, persons over forty years of age, and the handicapped?

The experience of companies that have built new plants or facilities in towns or small cities where one would ordinarily expect they would find difficulty in obtaining sufficient labor has often revealed that a good reputation as a place to work (that is, good wages, steady employment, and so on) can exercise a powerful pull to draw people off the farms and from great distances to obtain employment. In-plant training programs for previously untrained people can frequently adequately supply the requirements for necessary skills.

RECRUITMENT AND SELECTION POLICY ISSUES

It almost goes without saying that the caliber of the work force of an organization largely determines its strength and its success as an enterprise. The employment policies of many companies are not formalized. They have just evolved as practices over the course of many years. They are changed and canceled as the immediate situation dictates. However, there is much to be gained from the adoption of carefully worked out, stable policies in the employment area.

Policies, being statements of intention and guides to action, can be positive instruments to shape the entire recruitment and selection program. They serve as necessary guides to the personnel department representatives and operating managers who must administer the hiring and placement program. They insure consistency of action throughout the entire organization. They let everyone knew where he stands and what he can expect in terms of treatment.

Fill Vacancies from Within or from Outside?

If an opening occurs for a business-machine operator or a buyer, should people be hired from the outside and assigned directly to these jobs? Most companies announce to their employees that they follow a policy of promotion from within as far as possible. There are several advantages to such a policy:

1. Most people expect to advance to positions of higher pay and status during their work careers. Therefore, this policy fosters high morale. One opening in a higher-level position may cause a succession of individual advancements as people each in turn move up.
2. Management can more accurately appraise the skills, knowledge, and personality characteristics of its present employees than it can job applicants who are interviewed in the employment office. Therefore, there is less risk of error in selection and placement.
3. The recruitment and selection problem is simplified because there are only a few entry jobs, and the formal education, skill, and knowledge requirements for these are relatively modest.

Although there are manifestly beneficial effects from following a policy of filling vacancies from within as much as possible, there are inherent problems and limitations also. In order for a company to fill its job openings from within, it must have in operation training programs by which people in lower-level jobs can learn new skills in order to qualify for upgrading to more demanding work. In a sense this is a strength and an advantage of the "fill vacancies from within" policy. However, small organizations often feel that they cannot afford the expense of comprehensive employee training programs. A policy of upgrading from within requires that the persons hired have aptitudes and potential for moving ahead. In some cases they may be overqualified for the entry jobs. If promotions do not actually materialize, these overqualified persons will be disappointed and frustrated at their lack of progress. An exclusive promotion-from-within policy prevents the infusion of new ideas and knowledge at the upper levels. This in effect might be called organizational inbreeding. Subordinates, having been taught and molded by their bosses, often know no other way of doing things. When promoted to positions of power and influence they tend to perpetuate outdated practices.

As a generalization, the most fruitful policy is probably that of filling the majority of vacancies from within but going to the outside when fully qualified talent is not available inside the organization. It is also probably wise to fill a moderate percentage of the higher-level managerial and professional positions by going to the outside labor market to inject new ideas into the organization.

Equal Employment Opportunity

Employers are required by law not to discriminate in regard to hiring, testing, pay, benefits and other conditions of employment on the basis of race, color, sex, national origin, or age. In practical terms this means that employers must provide job opportunities for blacks, Hispanic Americans, other minorities, women, and older persons (up to age 70). If the company holds Federal government contracts it must also create and implement an affirmative action plan to hire and promote members of the various protected groups (including handicapped persons who can perform the work).

It is striking to compare the assertions that many managers made twenty or thirty years ago with the actual experience of today. Formerly these managers stated that women or older persons or certain minority types couldn't possibly succeed in performing various kinds of jobs in their companies. But the actual experience of these same managers today shows that members of these protected groups are doing very well in their companies.

The topic of equal employment opportunity is covered at length in Chapter 11.

Disadvantaged Persons

It must be obvious that people are hired by a firm to do a job. Management will not hire someone unless it feels that that individual's productive contribution will exceed, or at least equal, the value of the wage paid to him. In classical economic terms, rational employers will hire workers (units of labor) up to the point at which their wage rate equals the marginal revenue product (the added sales revenue obtained from the output of an additional unit of labor). Should a company hire people who may not produce work whose value is as large as the wage paid them?

Commencing in the 1960's the Federal government during the administration of President Lyndon B. Johnson launched a major effort in cooperation with private business to provide jobs and job training for disadvantaged persons. Numerous categorical programs were created such as Manpower Development and Training Act programs, Job Opportunities in the Business Sector, and the Concentrated Employment Programs. Most of these categorical programs were abandoned with the enactment of the Comprehensive Employment and Training Act of 1973 (CETA). Under CETA the major responsibility for planning and operating manpower programs is handled by state and local governmental units which act as prime sponsors. Many non-profit consortia of business firms have been set-up around the country to work in cooperation with local government to provide jobs and skill training for the disadvantaged.

The National Alliance of Businessmen (NAB) was created in 1968. This comprises consortia of private business firms in the principal metropolitan areas of the country. Their purpose is to work with thousands of individual companies to encourage them to hire the disadvantaged. As of 1978 there were 120 NAB offices throughout the country.

Who are the disadvantaged? They are people who have great difficulty in finding useful jobs even in relatively good economic times. They possess one or more of the following characteristics:

a. undereducated, unskilled, or inexperienced;
b. considered by employers to be too young or too old;
c. subject to discrimination by employers;
d. lack basic work abilities and skills needed to hold a regular job;
e. chronically unemployed.

For a variety of reasons many companies have adopted a policy decision to employ some disadvantaged persons. They expect that with adequate orientation and training these workers will be able to become productive and fully competitive with employees possessing more traditional qualifications and backgrounds.[1]

Selection Standards—Credentials Barriers

Oftentimes companies adopt qualification requirements that lack a proven relationship to success or failure on the job.

Educational attainment is a principal selection hurdle used by most organizations. Thus some companies specify that a high school education is necessary for employment in unskilled and semiskilled factory jobs such as materials handler, laborer, and machine operator. A college degree is usually a prerequisite for admission into administrative and managerial positions. Some craftsmen and engineers are required to be licensed in order to perform certain tasks. As a screening device education possesses a considerable measure of merit. The process of going through elementary and high school and college is in itself a selection

[1] Sources on private sector initiatives and public–private sector cooperation in employing the disadvantaged are Committee for Economic Development, *Jobs for the Hard-to-Employ: New Directions for a Public-Private Partnership* (New York, 1978); Committee for Economic Development and Work in America Institute, *Training and Jobs Programs in Action* (New York, 1978).

screen. By and large those who possess the greatest perseverance and demonstrated ability to learn under the specified conditions of the educational system are the ones who successfully complete school. These are presumed to have the right talents and acquired skills, both technical and social. But heavy reliance upon a diploma or a college degree as a condition of employment yields some clear disadvantages.

It automatically eliminates from consideration those who have dropped out of school. By and large these are the poor, the underprivileged, and those who are poorly adapted to the discipline of the school system. Those who have not gone through the formal credentializing process are not necessarily unqualified. Sometimes the barriers are erected by a small elite group that is already in an occupation or profession and that wants to maintain its choice economic and social position by sharply restricting entrance to the field of work. Some craft unions, for example, achieve just such an end by artificially long periods of apprenticeship, high initiation fees, and contractual limits on the number of apprentices who can enter the trade. Certain professional associations act similarly by licensing rules and control of educational and internship programs. "Credentialitis" is another manifestation of the trend toward bureaucratization of modern organizational life. But this not only denies job opportunities to those who might do well if given a chance but it also artificially shrinks the pool of talent available to an industry, firm, or occupation. A number of brilliant men did poorly in school—Albert Einstein and Winston Churchill are two outstanding examples. The educational establishment tends to homogenize its students. The nonconformist is rejected or rejects himself.

If one grants the line of argument above to be true, what course of action should a personnel executive adopt for an employment policy? Clearly he should not ignore educational attainment as a selection guide. It does correlate with probability of occupational success in a generalized way when one is speaking of large numbers of persons. A realistic policy would be to set general educational qualifications for the various jobs in a company based upon a sound job analysis program. But deliberate emphasis can be given to hiring some people, say 5 to 15 percent of the total in a given category, who lack the formal education desired but who give promise of reasonable success by virtue of appropriate work experience, interest, motivation, and recommendation by qualified observers. Additional training can be obtained after hiring through participation in evening school and in-service corporate training programs.

The Lie Detector

Many organizations experience serious problems with employee theft and embezzlement. To combat this problem a large number of firms have hired polygraph operators to screen their people to identify potential and actual wrongdoers. Although theft and embezzlement constitute the prime problems inducing managements to use polygraph testing, other problem areas are employee lying, giving away trade secrets, drug abuse, and alcoholism.

In actuality there is no such instrument as a true lie detector. The polygraph is a surrogate for a lie detector. It is an instrument that is attached at various points on the subject's body. It measures rate of breathing, heart beat rate, changes in blood pressure, and skin current (galvanic skin response, associated with sweating of the palms of the hands). The theory behind the polygraph technique is that lying causes distinctive physiological reactions in a person who knows he is not telling the truth.

Accuracy rates in polygraph testing average about 75 percent.[2] Although the machine measures physiological states or changes fairly accurately, there is no simple correlation between these conditions and the truthfulness of the subject. There can be great individual differences in the reaction of people to various kinds of stress. Polygraph interpretations can be invalid when subjects show extreme nervousness; have high or low blood pressure, heart disease, and respiratory disorders; have pronounced neuroses or psychoses, or are pathological liars; and when they suffer from emotional and physical fatigue.

From a civil liberties standpoint, there are serious questions about the use of the polygraph. Among these are invasion of privacy, violation of the Fifth Amendment (of the U.S. Constitution) privilege against self-incrimination, the Constitutional presumption of innocence until proven guilty, and violation of the Fourth Amendment's protection against unreasonable searches.

Despite the serious doubts about the advisability of using the polygraph, it is very widely used in employment situations. Eighty-one percent of the firms responding to a survey conducted by the National Association of Chain Drug Stores reported that they used the polygraph. They used it for both preemployment screening and for checking on current employees.[3] Citing two university researchers, *Business Week* says one-fifth of the nations' largest companies in a wide range of business fields use lie detectors.[4]

Privacy of Employee Records

In direct opposition to the investigative philosophy of users of polygraphs has been the affirmative measures that several big companies such as Bank of America and International Business Machines Corporation have taken in recent years to protect the privacy of job applicants and employees.

For example, at IBM job applicants are not asked about the employment of their spouses, about possible relatives at IBM, about possible prior treatment for mental illness, or about arrest records (however, any convictions within past five years are asked about). IBM does not use polygraph or personality tests but it does use aptitude tests. Line or operating managers are allowed to see relevant information in the personnel files regarding employees' work performance and awards, however they cannot see information of a personal nature such as medical insurance claims, personal finances, or wage garnishments. Only personnel officials can see this information. Information is not given to outside creditors and attorneys without the employee's consent. Generally, employees have full access to their own personnel files.[5]

[2] Lykken, D., "The Right Way to Use a Lie Detector," *Psychology Today,* Vol. 8 (March 1975), p. 56.
[3] "Polygraph Usage in Chain Pharmacies," *Journal of the American Pharmaceutical Association*, Vol. NS16, No. 4 (April 1976), p. 182.
[4] *Business Week* (February 6, 1978), p. 100.
[5] "IBM's Guidelines to Employee Privacy," *Harvard Business Review*, Vol. 54, No. 5 (September–October 1976), pp. 82–90; "Private Files," *Wall Street Journal* (April 24, 1978).

SOURCES OF PEOPLE

Recruitment is the development and maintenance of adequate manpower sources. It involves the creation of a pool of available labor from which the organization can draw when it needs additional employees. Since the selection process involves a screening out or elimination of those not considered suitable for hiring, it is clear that any company must have on tap a larger supply of people than it will actually hire.

One convenient way of classifying the sources of supply is to divide the sources into the two categories: (1) inside sources and (2) outside sources. Thus if a particular job vacancy occurs, it can be filled by transferring or promoting another employee from within the company to that post. If there is to be a net addition to the size of the workforce then, of course, someone will have to be employed from the outside as well. In filling vacancies from within, it is still necessary to match job requirements with worker qualifications. The selection process must still be employed. But it means that present employees are given first chance for any better or more attractive jobs before outsiders are considered.

Inside Sources

The process of filling job openings by selecting from among the pool of present employees can be implemented by either of two methods. One involves a review of the personnel records and appraisal forms by the personnel director and members of operating management to find qualified candidates. Very frequently fresh performance ratings are prepared, a meeting of interested parties is convened, and a decision is made to give the job to one of the persons under review. With this procedure it is very common for the employees under consideration to be totally in the dark about the goings-on until the selection is formally announced. There is also the possibility that fully qualified potential candidates will be overlooked due to an oversight. Despite this weakness, this procedure is the one most generally followed in business and industry. Some organizations have formalized and systematized the process to the point where job vacancies are announced in writing to all appropriate members of supervision and management. They are requested to review all of their subordinates and submit nominations to the personnel office, which then coordinates the process of selection and placement.

Some companies have set up computerized data banks which contain qualifications and work history data on all their employees. A computerized skills inventory such as this can speed the process of searching for qualified candidates within the organization. It can also insure a wide scan throughout the entire organization instead of a purely localized search that might be carried out by informal methods.

Job Posting and Bidding. A more open approach to internal recruitment and selection is to announce all job vacancies on plant bulletin boards and to accept bids on these jobs from all interested employees. This procedure grants employees the same right to apply for a job that the employer would grant to outsiders who answer an advertisement in the newspaper. In unionized establishments the job posting and bidding procedure is normally spelled out in the labor agreement. Although unions nearly always seek to enhance promotional opportunities for their members through job posting and bidding procedures, it is true also that management in many nonunion companies has on its own initiative established a job posting policy. Such a policy helps accomplish the purposes of an equal employment opportunity program.

Outside Sources and Recruitment Methods

The particular sources and means by which workers are recruited vary greatly. It depends upon management policy, the type of jobs involved, the supply of labor relative to demand, and the nature of the existent labor market institutions, such as employment agencies, unions, and the like. Let us now examine the principal sources and methods for obtaining manpower.

Public Employment Agencies.   Every state in the United States has a state employment service, which operates branch offices in most cities of about 10,000 population or more throughout each state. The initiating force behind the establishment of these employment services was the Wagner–Peyser Act of 1933, which created the United States Employment Service and established a program of Federal-state cooperation. Federal funds are made available to the states on a matching basis for the support and administration of these state programs. In return for this Federal money the states must conform to standards and procedures prescribed by the United States government. Upon the passage of the Social Security Act in 1935 the state employment services were assigned the added responsibility of administering the unemployment compensation program. In order for an unemployed worker to be eligible for unemployment insurance benefits, he must register for employment and be ready and able to take a job if a suitable one is available. There has been a tendency over the years for the placements made by public employment offices to be concentrated heavily in certain occupational groups, such as domestic service, farm and construction labor, unskilled and semiskilled factory work, and retail store sales clerks. Professional, managerial, and white-collar groups tend to utilize other job-seeking methods.

Private Employment Agencies.   Privately operated employment companies are quite widespread throughout the United States. For a fee collected usually from the employee (after he is hired) but sometimes from the employer, they help to meet employer requests for people from their files of job seekers who have registered with them. In many jurisdictions the fees charged and the operations of these employment "brokers" are regulated by state law. Many agencies do a careful job of interviewing, testing, counseling, and screening to match the employer specifications and demands with the abilities and needs of the job applicant. A great many of these agencies concentrate upon white-collar office and retail sales personnel, because demand is generally high, and turnover is great. Thus, there is a continuous flow of business in these occupations.

Labor Unions.   It is primarily in occupations in which the employees are represented by craft unions that much of the hiring process is carried on through union hiring halls. Industries and occupations in which companies tend to obtain much of their labor force through union-controlled hiring halls are construction, longshoring, maritime, clothing, popular dance bands, and the like. Generally those union members who have been unemployed the longest are given the first opportunity to fill the job opening. The hiring hall system flourishes where there are many small employers and where employment is intermittent or casual. The union lends a degree of stability to the labor market situation and guarantees that unemployed workers will get jobs in their rightful turn.

Unsolicited Applicants at the Employment Office. For jobs requiring only routine abilities and skill, many employers are able to fill their labor needs largely by means of direct hiring at the gate. In a survey of 284 employers in the San Francisco Bay Area labor markets, it was found that for manual workers direct hiring at the gate was the second most commonly used source of workers. (Recruiting through labor unions was first.) For obtaining sales personnel, retail stores very commonly used this method also.[6] One of the most influential factors affecting the desirability of this method as a source is the image and reputation of the organization in the community. If a company, by its actions, has demonstrated that it treats its employees well, pays adequate wages, and has enlightened personnel practices, those seeking work will gravitate to that enterprise. Another important variable is the state of the labor market. In times of high unemployment even firms with a less glittering reputation will find a large volume of unsolicited applicants at the employment office.

Employee Recruiting. Some organizations announce to their own employees that they wish to hire additional people possessing such and such type of skills. The employees will then pass the word to their friends and relatives who may be seeking work. There are essentially two approaches to this type of employee recruiting. One is quite informal. In one steel company the personnel manager, working through production supervision and word of mouth, transmits the message that the company will start hiring production workers the next day. Generally speaking, this grapevine approach to recruitment produces a waiting line of applicants for unskilled and semiskilled jobs the next morning.

A more systematic approach is to organize the employee recruitment effort. Bulletin board announcements can inform employees of the specific qualifications candidates must possess to fill job openings. Periodic meetings can be held with selected employee groups to discuss the opportunities and needs for additional personnel. Special explanatory booklets can be prepared for distribution to employees. It is important, when conducting an employee recruitment program, that the sponsoring employee be apprised of the action taken on his candidate (that is, hired or rejected and why) and be given due credit when a person he recommended has been hired. The principal advantage of employee recruiting is that it is selective. Grossly unqualified persons will not be recommended by an employee, because he feels this would reflect adversely upon his own reputation.

Advertising. Advertising in newspapers, trade magazines, and professional society journals is a widely used method of recruiting. Although there are some

[6] F. T. Malm, "Recruiting Patterns and the Functioning of Labor Markets," *Industrial and Labor Relations Review*, Vol. 7, No. 4 (July 1954), pp. 507–525.

justifiable exceptions, employers who advertise for applicants should reveal their own identity rather than use a blind ad, in which the person must send a resume to a box number at the newspaper or magazine. Sound ethics suggests that the employer reveal his identity if he expects candidates to supply detailed autobiographical information. Likewise, this prevents the possibility of the employer's own employees (those who are dissatisfied and seeking to make a change) unknowingly applying for a job at their own company.

Schools and Colleges. At the secondary school level alert employment managers make it a practice to get acquainted with school principals and guidance counselors to inform them of job opportunities and employment practices in their companies. Even if a company is not hiring people for the present it often is sound to develop these channels and contacts in case of future needs.

At colleges and universities the recruitment of graduating seniors has been a large-scale operation for many years now. Nearly every institution of higher learning has a placement office containing rooms were employers can conduct interviews and give selection tests. This recruitment practice tends to be utilized primarily by the larger companies, which can afford to send teams of interviewers throughout the country and can afford to pay the travel expenses to the most promising students for visits to the plant where the final employment decision is usually made.

Special Problem of Professional and Managerial Personnel. Normally employers do not have difficulty in finding adequate employees for manual, clerical, sales, and general-run types of work. But they often do have a problem in obtaining the professional and managerial talent they require. The growing complexity and sophistication of technology has meant that increasing numbers of professionals and managers are needed to run our modern organizations. Examples of occupations for which demand in the economy as a whole is high and supply tends to be short are physicians, nurses, medical technicians, engineers, accountants, and capable executives and administrators.

The long-run solution to the shortage of personnel in these fields is for private organizations, government, and society in general to initiate programs that will channel more young men and women into these fields and to give more financial support to students and educational institutions.

In the short run the individual firm faced with a shortage of qualified talent must resort to an aggressive recruiting effort. Among the more prominent recruitment techniques are (1) advertising in newspapers; college papers, trade journals, and professional journals; (2) college recruitment and contacts with university professors; (3) management consulting firms; (4) executive recruiters and agencies; (5) professional association meetings.

Items 1 and 2 above have already been discussed in the context of general recruitment. A word about the other three methods is in order. Management consulting firms become intimately acquainted with the personnel of numerous client companies. Thus, they are often in a position to recommend an individual as a likely candidate for, say, a controller's or a marketing manager's position.

Executive recruitment firms must be distinguished from employment agencies that specialize in professional and executive talent. An executive recruitment firm works for the client company, which pays it a fee to find particular kinds of high-level talent. Oftentimes the recruiting firm seeks to entice executives to leave their present firm and go with the firm that has engaged the services of the recruiter. On the other hand, the employment agency charges a fee to the job seeker upon successful placement. The fees charged and general mode of operation are regulated by state laws. Quite often the company that hires the executive will pay his employment agency fee, so there is actually some blurring of the distinction between the two types of employment companies.

And, finally, the annual conferences that all professional associations hold almost always serve the added function of a marketplace where employers and job-seeking members of the association can meet and discuss job opportunities.

THE SELECTION PROCESS

Whereas the goal of recruitment is to create a large pool of persons who are available and willing to work for a particular company, the selection process has as its objective the sorting out or elimination of those judged unqualified to meet job and organization requirements. Thus, in a sense, recruitment tends to be positive in that it seeks to persuade people to apply for work at the company, whereas selection tends to be somewhat negative because it rejects a good portion of those who apply.

The most common approach to the selection problem is to choose individuals who possess the necessary skills, abilities, and personality to successfully fill specific jobs in the organization. Thus, the employment manager typically has in his possession an employment requisition initiated by some operating manager requesting, say, one design draftsman with five years drafting experience to start work on April 15 at a certain wage rate. This is essentially a problem of matching a person to the job. But what course of action should the employment manager follow when a bright young person, fresh out of technical school but with no practical experience, applies? The question being raised here is as follows. Does the employment policy of the company permit the hiring of a good candidate because he will be a valuable asset to the organization even if he does not meet the specific requirements of the present job opening? Let us now go one step further. What action should be taken if the company is not hiring anyone at present, but one or more very promising individuals applies for a job, and the employment manager has every reason to believe that hiring will be resumed within a few weeks or months? Should the good candidates be rejected, or should they be hired and placed in a reserve pool or training program in expectation of future needs? As implied earlier, the prevailing practice in industry is to reject all applicants in these hypothetical situations unless there is a specific job vacancy and the applicant meets the state qualifications.

But there is another approach to selection that admittedly is more feasible for a large than for a small organization. Under this system certain basic entrance standards are established, such as a minimum amount of education, minimum age, physical requirements, minimum score on a mental ability test, and so on. All those who meet or exceed these requirements of the organization are considered further for specific aptitudes, abilities, and vocational preferences that would fit them for one of a number of possible jobs. The military services, in effect, follow this policy of selecting first for the organization and then differentially placing men and women where they are best fitted.

Fundamentally, then, there can be certain very positive aspects to the selection process. Instead of concentrating simply upon the rejection of applicants, the employment manager can transform his thinking into the task of deciding where in the organization the applicant would best fit.

Employee selection is a two-way process. Those engaged in designing and implementing a hiring program must always remember that job candidates are making judgments to enable themselves to select the organization and the job just as managers are making judgments to select individuals. Hiring officials have a responsibility to provide job applicants with full and accurate information so that they can make reasonable responses throughout the entire recruitment and selection process.

Considerations in Making the Selection Decision

There are a number of important factors that must be taken into account when attempting to make a decision regarding an applicant or applicants.

Organizational and Social Environment. The selection process necessitates the matching of a person with the job in a particular organizational and social environment. Those charged with operating the hiring program must have available a complete set of job descriptions and specifications for all jobs in the organization so that they can have detailed knowledge of the duties and human qualifications necessary to fill these jobs. A prime objective of the selection process is to find out enough about the applicant's background, training, personality, aptitudes, skills, and interests so that this matching process can be done accurately. But there is more to it than this. Even if a person is eminently qualified to perform the work of, say, a bookkeeping machine operator or a quality control laboratory technician, he may fail because of the particular organizational and social environment in that company.

For example, in one company a very attractive and well-qualified young woman, age 21, was hired as a stenographer in an office containing several male engineers and two middle-aged, long-service female secretaries. Although the young woman performed her work well and the men liked her work, she was eventually frozen out and forced to resign because of the antagonism of the two older women, who were very jealous of her charms.

Many factors affect the success or failure of an employee besides his or her basic ability to do the job. Miller and Form have developed a rating scale method (analogous to a point rating plan of job evaluation) for evaluating the social skills required in the performance of jobs. They give consideration to seven social factors: scope of social contacts, status range of contacts, social demands off the job, social leadership, skill intensity, social participation, and direct and indirect personal responsibility for others.[7] In addition to these, many other environmental factors must be taken into account. Among these are social

[7] Delbert C. Miller and W. H. Form, *Industrial Sociology* (New York: Harper and Row, 1951), pp. 430–436.

cliques, degree of receptiveness of work group to newcomers, personality and idiosyncrasies of the boss, group standards and norms, and organizational pressures. In general, it is not actually possible to measure all these organizational and social influences. The best that can be done is for the employment manager to be perceptive and aware of these environmental factors so that he can judge whether a particular applicant will adapt himself successfully to the situation.[8]

Successive Hurdles or Multiple Correlation? The vast majority of employee selection programs are based upon the successive-hurdles technique. This means that to be hired, applicants must successfully pass each and every screening device (that is, application blank, interviews, tests, medical examination, and background check). Some candidates are rejected at each step or hurdle. For a person to go successfully from one hurdle to the next, he must meet or exceed the requirements for each hurdle. For example, the job seeker may be rejected as early as the application blank stage because the education and previous work experience that he has recorded may be insufficient to meet the established hiring standard. In designing a selection procedure according to the successive-hurdles method, the selection device that has the highest correlation with job success (validity) is placed first in the sequence, the one with the next highest relationship with on-the-job performance is placed second, and so forth. Those applicants who have little chance of succeeding on the job are eliminated at the first hurdle. Both the candidates' time and the company's time and expense are saved by not having to put grossly unqualified persons through the entire procedure before a decision is made.

The multiple-correlation approach, which is less commonly used, is based upon the assumption that a deficiency in one factor can be counterbalanced by an excess amount of another. For example the education of one candidate as shown on the application form may be below the job requirements, yet the interviewer may decide to carry the individual further along in the selection sequence because of his superior related work experience and apparent high motivation (as revealed during the interview). Also, if a battery of selection tests are used, the procedure may entail the compiling of a composite test score index. A low score on one test can then be counterbalanced by a high score on another. In the multiple-correlation technique a person is routed through all the selection steps before a decision is made. The decision criteria may be all reduced to numbers. Thus a scored application blank may be used, the interviewer may assign a numerical rating to the candidates, and of course all tests may be numerically graded. If the combined score on all selection criteria exceeds the level needed to qualify, then the job seeker is hired. If not, he is rejected.

Which selection method should be adopted? If an applicant is grossly unqualified to pass even the preliminary interview because he lacks essential abilities, there is no point in sending him through all the remaining hurdles. On the other hand, if a person looks reasonably good on the early hurdles, and is mediocre in one minor factor, there is some logic in giving him the full treatment before making the final decision.

---

[8] For additional thoughts on the subject of social and organizational environment see Milton M. Mandell, "The Effect of Organizational Environment" in M. J. Dooher and E. Marting, *Selection of Management Personnel* (New York: American Management Association, 1957), pp. 336–341.

Certain chance factors may cause a person to fail one hurdle (for example, the interviewer may dislike his looks, or the conditions under which a test is administered may be nonstandard); therefore, for borderline cases it makes sense to judge the *whole* person before rejecting anyone.

Avoid Gimmicks. Sometimes busy executives with pressing production problems seek easy gimmicks to evaluate human beings. Over the years there have been a host of pseudoscientific shortcuts to human appraisal. Some have claimed that it is possible to predict ability and personality according to the shape of one's head (physiognomy); according to body build (some types: mesomorphic, endomorphic, and ectomorphic); and a host of other oversimplified devices. The simple fact of the matter is that human beings are just too complex for simple gauges as these to be effective and accurate.

Selection Procedure

Selection procedures are most properly tailormade to meet the particular needs of the employing organization. The thoroughness of the procedure depends upon a number of factors. First, the consequences of faulty selection must be weighed. This is influenced by the length of the training period, money invested in the new employee, level and complexity of the job, and possible damage to the organization if the incumbent job holder fails.

A second factor influencing the thoroughness of the selection sequence is company policy and top-management attitude. Some organizations deliberately overhire and count upon weeding out poor performers after a few months on the payroll. This simply defers the selection decision until management has had a chance to observe the new employees' behavior closely. However, this procedure is costly for both the organization and the individuals involved. It wastes their time, because they might more profitably be employed elsewhere, where the employer does not overhire.

A third consideration governing the thoroughness of the hiring procedure is the length of the probationary period. A probationary period is an initial length of time a new employee has been on the payroll during which he has absolutely no job security rights. It is essentially a trial period, which usually varies in length from one employer to another from a minimum of thirty days to a maximum of one year. If the employees are represented by a union, the union usually seeks in negotiations to have a very short probationary period, whereas employers generally press for a long one. If the period is of short duration, the selection process must be quite accurate in its predictions, because a supervisor is hard pressed to be confident of his decision at the end of the period on whether to retain or discharge the new man. This problem is especially acute if the learning period on the job is much longer than the probationary period.

A Proposed Selection Procedure. Although it is true that the steps in the selection procedure should be varied to meet the special needs of the organization, the following is a model program that will work well in most cases. Adaptations can be made to suit individual situations. For example, the medical examination can be placed quite early in the procedure if physical stamina, agility, strength, and so on are critical to the work and if only a small portion of the general population can be expected to pass the examination. There are nine basic steps:

1. Reception in employment office.
2. Preliminary interview.
3. Application blank.
4. Selection tests.
5. Main employment office interview.
6. Investigation of applicant's background.
7. Final selection interview by manager or supervisor.
8. Medical examination.
9. Induction.

The decision to add persons to the payroll in particular departments of an organization is not made in the personnel department. This is a function of operating or line management, which then initiates an employment requisition that is sent to the personnel department.

In a large company processing a heavy stream of applicants at all times, the preliminary interview would be conducted by a special interviewer located in the employment office. But in most moderate or smaller-scale operations the preliminary interview and the main employment office interview would be conducted by one and the same person. Thus all candidates might be given a ten-minute screening interview, at which time the interviewer would inform applicants of the nature of the current job openings. He might then elicit data from the candidates pertaining to their education, experience, skills, job interests, and availability for accepting employment. If the requirements of the company and the interests and qualifications of the job seeker seem to match in this rough initial screening, the individual would be given a much more detailed and comprehensive interview.

Selection tests (often called psychological or personnel tests) should be administered prior to the main employment office interview so that the interviewer can have the test results before him when he evaluates the candidate.

It is now appropriate to examine in some detail each of the major selection devices.

Application Blank

The application blank is used to obtain information, in the applicant's own handwriting, sufficient to identify him properly (name, address, telephone number, sex, age, height, weight) and to make tentative inferences regarding his suitability for employment. Primarily the choice of questions on the blank should be such that they are valid predictors of employment success or failure. Superfluous questions should not appear. The application form should be complete enough to relieve the interviewer of the burden of recording considerable factual data that could better be written on the application by the job seeker. In addition, the questions must not by their wording or nature encourage dishonest answers, as do the following questions:

How often do you drink intoxicating beverages?
Do you have marital difficulties?
Have you ever broken the law?

There are two fundamental methods of evaluating a filled-in application form. One is the clinical method, and the other is the weighted or statistical method.

Clinical Evaluation. In the clinical method the interviewer carefully studies the answers to the questions to find meaningful patterns that can reveal important information regarding the individual's personality and make-up. Advocates of this method claim that a properly designed form can provide clues to a person's leadership ability, how he gets along with others, his industriousness, emotional stability, assertiveness, speaking ability, attitude toward his boss, and so on. It should be pointed out that the conclusions derived can be considered only tentative. They must be verified by further checking. Likewise an untrained and inexperienced interviewer would make some serious errors with this method. The evaluator should have a sound grounding in psychological and personnel management theory.

In explaining how to detect whether the applicant possesses energy and enthusiasm (necessary in selling work), G. J. Spencer has suggested the following as indicators: an unusual number and variety of activities, such as sports, extracurricular activities, types of jobs held, hobbies, and interests; past work experience in active type jobs; dislike of a previous job because it was too detailed and routine. Evidence of narcissism (love of oneself) can be found in the way the applicant writes his name, extracurricular school activities, hobbies, and plans for his future. Thus, if the applicant spells out his name in full as John Jonathan Jones and if he played the lead in two class plays, he is likely to have narcissistic tendencies.[9] William H. Whyte, Jr., has made a sharp criticism of this method of psychologically analyzing a job applicant in his book *The Organization Man.* Whyte's point of view is that in making these psychological predictions the analyst is projecting his own world, value judgments, and standards too heavily into the picture. He claims that even if interviewers and analysts are able to diagnose accurately an applicant's personality, personnel specialists are still not at all certain or in agreement upon what characteristics are essential for, say, a successful salesman or an executive.[10]

In perspective it seems safe to say that a well-trained interviewer is on solid ground if he makes only tentative inferences based upon a clinical study of the application blank and waits for much more conclusive evidence in interviews, tests, and background investigation.

Statistical Evaluation. An application blank can be designed so that there is an empirical relationship between subsequent job performance and the answers the applicants have given on the application form at the time of hiring. An application form that has been designed through statistical correlations is called a

[9] Gilmore J. Spencer, "The Application Form Revisited," *Personnel,* Vol. 36, No. 5 (September–October 1959), pp. 20–30.
[10] William H. Whyte, Jr., *The Organization Man* (New York: Simon & Schuster, Inc., 1956), ch. 15.

weighted application blank or a *biographical information questionnaire.* In order to use a weighted application form in selection, it is necessary to have a different form for each occupational group. Points are assigned to the various answers the applicant gives. A certain critical or passing score is necessary for the applicant to pass this hurdle.

In developing a weighted blank, it is necessary to identify those items of personal history of present employees that differentiate between groups of successful and unsuccessful employees. Thus, if it is found that an insurance company's successful life insurance salesmen tend to be married, have high living expenses, and belong to a large number of clubs and organizations, whereas their unsuccessful ones are single, have low living expenses, and belong to few organizations, these factors can be given a definite statistical scoring when evaluating a person's application. For picking store management trainees, a large retailing chain has found definite correlations with job performance and the following: location of last permanent residence, marital status, father's occupation, health, previous experience in retailing, rank in high-school or college class, and compensation of last previous job compared to starting salary of this job.

Reliance upon the statistical formula of a weighted application can result in false predictions in individual cases. However, it improves predictive probabilities. Or stated another way, it increases the employment office's batting average in the long run when hiring and rejecting large numbers of people.

Schneider reports that weighted application blanks have demonstrated greater predictive power (i.e. higher validity coefficients) than both intelligence and personality tests. He states that validity coefficients for biographical information are consistently superior to those obtained with other selection techniques when all techniques are developed with equal care. He says that biographical questionnaires work well because people's behavior over time is consistent and because people are more likely to succeed in environments where they have a previously established compatible response pattern.[11]

It ought to be noted, however, that the weighted application procedure may unjustly discriminate against people who have never had the opportunity to engage in the "right" personal history experiences that would give them a high score on the weighted application form.

Selection Tests

In recent years selection tests, which are usually constructed by industrial psychologists, have become a well-accepted part of the selection procedure for the majority of medium- and large-sized companies. They may not utilize them for all of the jobs for which they hire, but certainly for some. Widespread use of tests commenced with World War I, when the Army Alpha Test was used to aid in the selection and placement of soldiers. The testing movement picked up momentum between the two wars, and has certainly come into its own since the 1940's.

[11] Benjamin Schneider, *Staffing Organizations* (Pacific Palisades, Calif.: Goodyear Publishing Co., Inc., 1976), p. 203. For information on constructing weighted application forms see J. J. Asher, "The Biographical Item: Can It Be Improved?" *Personnel Psychology,* Vol. 25 (1972), pp. 251–269; George W. England, *Development and Use of Weighted Application Blanks* (Minneapolis: Industrial Relations Center, University of Minnesota, 1969).

The installation of a sound testing program in an organization is time consuming and costly. Just because a test has been found useful for selecting clerks in company A is no reason to assert that it will be useful for picking clerks in company B. Each test adopted must be proven out (validated) in one's own organization before reliance can be placed upon it. The proper way to look at tests is to ask this question. To what extent will a given test or test battery improve the accuracy of selection predictions over that obtained without tests? Will the organization obtain a higher percentage of successful employees through the use of tests? The theory and application of selection testing, because it is such a complex and important topic, will be treated at length in Chapter 10, "Selection Testing and Interviewing."

Interview

Despite the impressive development of the testing process as an aid to selection, the interview remains the single most important tool in the hiring program. The interviewer is in the unique position of being able to evaluate information obtained from the application blank, a preceding interview (such as the preliminary employment office interview), tests, and background investigation. He can integrate these data with his own impressions and observations to reach a decision regarding the suitability of the applicant for employment.

Interviewing is primarily an art, not a science. It is subjective. Untrained interviewers will make many erroneous judgments. They will often decide to accept or reject a person upon totally insufficient evidence. However, research studies have shown that adequately trained interviewers using sound procedures can and do achieve good results.

Interviewing, like selection testing, will be comprehensively treated in Chapter 10.

Medical Examination

The pre-employment medical (or physical) examination plays an important part in the screening process. It serves four major purposes:

1. To reject those whose physical qualifications are insufficient to meet the requirements of the work they are being considered for.
2. To obtain a record of the physical condition at the time of hiring in the event of a workmen's compensation claim for an injury that occurs later.
3. To prevent the employment of those with contagious diseases.
4. To place properly those who are otherwise employable but whose physically handicapped condition requires assignment to specified jobs only.

The first three purposes of the medical examination are generally well understood. The fourth is not. The examination should be used as a positive aid to selective placement and not as a device to eliminate all but the perfect physical specimen. Those with physical handicaps must live and seek to support themselves by gainful employment if at all possible. There is no need for their plight to be intensified by an arbitrary denial of employment opportunities. Fundamentally, physical standards should be geared to job requirements. They must be realistic and justified. The physical demands of all jobs are clearly not the same. Some require great physical stamina, others demand accurate color perception, and still others call for manual dexterity. The job analysis program should identify and record the specific physical demands of the various jobs and job families. Thus it can be determined to what jobs persons with specified physical handicaps may be safely assigned.

Large companies typically employ a staff physician or medical director. He is generally in charge of the entire medical program including the operation of a dispensary or infirmary. Organizationally he is usually a member of the personnel department. Small organizations, not requiring the full-time services of a physician, generally make arrangements with a panel of practicing doctors who will conduct pre-employment medical examinations on an individual fee or an annual retainer basis.

The principal content items of the normal physical examination are as follows: (1) medical history; (2) physical measurements such as height and weight; (3) general examination including skin, musculature, and joints; (4) vision and hearing; (5) clinical examination of eyes, ears, nose, throat, and teeth; (6) examination of chest and lungs; (7) blood pressure and heart; (8) urinalysis and blood tests; (9) chest X-ray. In special cases tests for drug addiction may be given. Also a neuropsychiatric examination may be given if medical history or physician's observation reveals an adjustment problem.

Background Investigation

An investigation into a promising candidate's background is too often overlooked by the employing organization. It requires a little time and money, but the trouble is generally well worth the effort. Previous employers and school officials can often provide valuable insights into the applicant's personality and behavior. Because—as stated previously—the best guide to what a person will do in the future is what he has done in the past, it behooves the careful employment manager to examine this past.

What are the sources for obtaining this background information? There exist four categories of sources. These are (1) school and college officials, (2) previous employers, (3) character references supplied by the applicant, and (4) other sources, such as neighbors of the applicant, the retail credit bureau, police records, and so on.

Category (3) is generally unreliable and can be eliminated for all practical purposes. It is a rare person who will list on his application persons who would supply anything but a most favorable recommendation. In addition, personal friends of the applicant have usually not been in a position actually to observe the work habits of the individual. They know him as a "nice guy," not necessarily as a worker in the work environment.

Previous employers are in a position to supply information regarding quantity and quality of work produced, cooperativeness, dependability, initiative, and relations with associates and supervisor. This is a good opportunity to verify the accuracy of information the applicant has given, such as jobs held, wage rate, wage increases, and reason for leaving. Previous employers can be asked if they would be willing to rehire the person and why.

If the person has graduated from high school within the last five to six years, it is advisable to contact the school principal or guidance counselor to obtain information on attendance record, grade point average, rank in graduating class, extracurricular activities, level of aspiration, motivation, emotional adjustment, and other impressions. Similar data can be elicited from college professors and department chairmen.

If the employment manager himself is doing the checking, his most fruitful approach is to do it by telephone or actual personal visit to the source of information. Previous employers and school officials will seldom be as frank and specific if they are called upon to write a formal reference letter. Conversation over the phone or in person permits a much deeper probing than can be obtained by letter.

Because other employers, supervisors, personnel men, and school officials have their biases, just like anyone else, it is very important to evaluate the source of each piece of information. Is a particularly negative appraisal due primarily to a clash of personalities between a former boss and the applicant? How well do the informants know the person?

Responsibilities of Line Management

Line or operating management plays a key role in an employee hiring program. Not only does the line manager or supervisor make the initial decision to add someone to the payroll, but he also conducts the final selection interview, at which point he can either accept or reject the candidate who has been sent to him from the personnel department.

Because personnel departments in industry were originally established many years ago to relieve operating managers of certain personnel responsibilities and to take advantage of specialized competence by means of centralization, the question may reasonably be asked as to why the line manager should be involved in the selection process. Could he not trust the personnel department to do a competent job? The answer is that organizationally the line or operating department manager is being held responsible for the successful and efficient operation of his unit. Accordingly, he must be given a say-so in the selection and placement of workers in his department. The caliber of his work force vitally affects the success of his efforts. The personnel department performs very valuable services for line management by recruiting, testing, and interviewing job applicants. Normally it will choose the individual it feels is best qualified to fit the particular work situation. He will then be sent to the department manager or supervisor for a final selection interview and decision. In most cases the line manager will concur with the choice of the personnel department. However, he should be granted the right of rejection.

There is still another reason for involving the prospective supervisor in this hiring process. Employment is a two-way street. Not only does the company have a right to reject the applicant, but also the candidate has the right to interview his future boss to decide whether he would like to work for that person.

Rejecting Applicants

Interviewers, being no different from most other people in this respect, frequently find it awkward to inform an applicant, directly to his face, that he does not measure up to the company's standards—that he is unsuitable. There is thus an urge to let the rejected applicant off lightly with such statements as "Perhaps at another time we will be able to hire you," or "We will keep your application on file and call you if we need you."

If those responsible for making the employment decision are sure in their own minds that the applicant should not be hired, there is no justification for holding out vague hopes to him. If he is a well-qualified individual but there are no openings at present for one of his talents but it is expected that there will be openings in the near future, then it makes sense to so inform him. But if he is definitely not suitable he should not be kept dangling.

The interviewer has the threefold objectives of maintaining the person's ego and self-concept, maintaining goodwill toward the organization, and definitely letting the applicant know that he is rejected. There are a number of ways of communicating to the person the fact that he is being rejected. If the applicant can clearly see that his vocational interests and aptitudes or his wage level needs are totally incompatible with the situation, he may reject himself by gracefully withdrawing. If the individual possesses certain skills and abilities that might be very appropriate in another job situation (other than that which is open in the company), he may be informed that while the pattern of his skills, interests, and abilities is good, they do not match the particular job for which the company is now hiring.

If the person possesses all the required technical abilities but is being rejected because of his personality, this presents a difficult challenge to the interviewer. Since personality traits cannot be measured objectively, there is danger of creating the feeling that he is being rejected capriciously or discriminated against if he is told his personality is unsuitable. This situation demands real skill on the part of the interviewer so that he can diplomatically convey the impression that the interviewee is being rejected. At times it is best to just imply that the company is going to pick just one or a very few out of a number of good candidates. The competitive situation will cause just the top few to be hired.

AUDITING THE RECRUITMENT AND SELECTION PROGRAM

In order to insure that the employment program is effective—that it accomplishes the results expected—and that it is carried on in the soundest way, it is desirable that a comprehensive periodic audit be made. To insure objectivity, it is advisable to have this audit performed by persons independent (organizationally) of the personnel department. Below is an outline that highlights the areas and questions to be covered in a systematic evaluation.

Audit of the Recruitment and Selection Program

I. *Analysis of the Program*

    A. Is the recruitment and selection program consistent with sound personnel management theory and practice?

        1. Have well-defined recruitment policies and procedures been developed?

2. Have well-defined selection policies and procedures been developed?
3. Are the employment policies consistent with public policy?
4. Do the wage levels, fringe benefits, and level of employee satisfaction within the organization have a beneficial effect upon the ability to attract and retain good employees?
5. Does the program adequately meet equal employment opportunity and affirmative action standards?

II. *How adequately are the program and its procedures communicated to all those involved in and affected by it?*

III. *How well is the program implemented?*
   A. Have those charged with carrying out the employment program been adequately trained?
   B. Does performance of the program match stated goals?
   C. Are policy and procedure manuals utilized?

IV. *Feedback*
   A. What image has been created in the minds of school officials, college placement officers, and public and private employment agencies by the actions of the company in conducting its hiring program?
   B. Have recently hired employees and rejected applicants been surveyed to gauge the type of treatment they have received in the selection process?
   C. How many persons have rejected the company as a poor place to work because of low wages, a poor reputation, and so on?

V. *Analysis of Results*
   A. Recruitment Program
      1. Is there a sufficient pool of applicants available from which to draw? How many persons apply for each job vacancy?
      2. Do those who apply possess the necessary skills? Is the recruitment effort selective?
   B. Selection Program
      1. How well do those hired perform on the job?
      2. What percentage of those who apply are hired?
      3. Of those hired what percentage are discharged during the probationary period? What percentage resign because the job and employment conditions were misrepresented to them?
      4. What portion of employee turnover can be attributed to faulty selection?
      5. What contribution does each of the selection tools (that is, tests, interview, medical examination, and so on) make to the program? How well do the predictions from each of the selection tools correlate with job success? Have these selection devices been properly validated?

The foregoing questions can serve as a broad guide to a very thorough and intensive analysis and evaluation of the employment program.

Questions for review and discussion

1. If you were president of your own company, what considerations would guide your judgment on the following employment issues:
   a. Hiring relatives of employees.
   b. Promotion from within as opposed to finding the best person available for the job, regardless of whether he is now a company employee or must be recruited from the outside.
   c. Hiring physically handicapped persons.
   d. Hiring college students for the summer.
   e. Hiring disadvantaged persons.
2. What procedure can an organization adopt to implement a promotion-from-within policy to insure that no qualified and interested employee is overlooked?
3. In what ways may the social and organizational environment affect the performance and adjustment of an otherwise fully qualified new employee?
4. Contrast the successive-hurdles approach to making a hiring decision with the multiple-correlation approach.
5. Explain ways in which a company's employment practices and procedures may change in accordance with changes in the supply-demand situation for labor.
6. An employment interviewer has decided that the applicant he is talking with is not suitable for hiring. Accordingly he informs the job seeker that he has nothing available at the present time but will keep his application on file and contact him if anything turns up. Evaluate this method of rejecting a job seeker.
7. Explain in some detail how you would go about analyzing and evaluating the effectiveness and efficiency of an employee selection program.
8. What is your opinion regarding the use of the polygraph (lie detector) to screen job applicants and present employees? Are there other methods to prevent or minimize employee theft and embezzlement?
9. Why does the properly developed weighted application blank have such high predictive power? Why do you think it isn't used more widely?

Suggestions for further reading

BUREAU OF NATIONAL AFFAIRS, INC. *Selection Procedures and Personnel Forms.* Rockville, Md.: Bureau of National Affairs, Inc. 1976.

CERULLO, THOMAS C. "The Polygraph and the Practicing Pharmacist," *Journal of the American Pharmaceutical Association*, Vol. NS16, No. 4 (April 1976), pp. 178–181.

FINKLE, ROBERT and WILLIAM JONES. *Assessing Corporate Talent: A Key to Managerial Manpower Planning.* New York: John Wiley & Sons, Inc., 1970.

HAWK, R. H., *The Recruitment Function.* New York: American Management Association, 1967.

KESSLER, CLEMM C. III, and GEORGE J. GIBBS. "Getting the Most from Appli-

cation Blanks and References," *Personnel*, Vol. 52, No. 1 (January–
February 1975), pp. 53–62.

MAYFIELD, EUGENE C. "Peer Nominations—A Neglected Selection Tool," *Personnel*, Vol. 48, No. 4 (July–August 1971), pp. 37–43.

SCHNEIDER, BENJAMIN. *Staffing Organizations*. Pacific Palisades, Calif.:
Goodyear Publishing Co., Inc., 1976.

YODER, DALE and HERBERT G. HENEMAN, JR. *Staffing Policies and Strategies*.
Rockville, Md.: Bureau of National Affairs, Inc., 1974.

Selection
testing
and
interviewing

The preceding chapter was concerned with recruitment and selection policies and procedures. The two employment techniques upon which greatest reliance is usually placed when making hiring decisions are selection testing and interviewing. The interview is the primary selection tool in nearly all employment programs. Testing programs have, in the past thirty years, achieved everincreasing significance in employee selection. In order to do full justice to these important hiring methods, this entire chapter is being devoted to the theory and application of testing and interviewing for selection.

Selection testing

In our society psychological tests are used for a variety of purposes. They are used in public and private schools and colleges for guidance and counseling students, for vocational guidance for adults seeking help in their careers, for assessment and counseling of patients in mental hospitals, for research into human behavior and personality, for choosing students for college admission, and for selection of employees in business and other organizations. We are interested, in our discussion, in the value and usage of tests in the employment process.

Not only are tests used as an aid for selecting new employees for the organization (their most common purpose in industry), but they are also used for differential placement or assignment to the most suitable job after a person has been hired. They are frequently used to select employees for promotion and transfer within the organization, to select candidates for assignment to a company training program, and to act as an aid for diagnosis when counseling individual problem employees.

A test (the term *psychological test* is commonly used because psychologists have done the most work in developing tests, and the field has tended to become their special province) has been defined in a number of ways. A broad definition is that given by Cronbach, who states that a test is a systematic procedure for observing a person's behavior and describing it with the aid of a numerical scale or a category-system.[1] Blum states that a test is a sample of an aspect of an individual's behavior, performance, or attitude.[2] We may define a psychological test as *a systematic procedure for sampling human behavior*. Usually, in employment situations a test is given under standardized and controlled conditions.

Tests are widely used in industry for employee selection. Practically all large corporations and a majority of middle-size firms use tests. A sample of 473 firms, having from 250 to over 5,000 employees, in a variety of manufacturing industries showed that tests were used by over 80 percent of the companies. Samples of firms in insurance, banking, utilities, retailing, and wholesaling showed that usage of testing ranged from 65 percent of the firms in retailing to 88 percent in insurance.[3] There are over 1,000 commercially available tests. The vast majority are distributed by a very few firms that specialize in psychological testing and test development.

Contributions of Tests to Selection

Most tests are objective. The score received by the person taking the test is not influenced by the opinions of those evaluating the test results. If tests are looked upon as a part of the total selection process (not as a substitute for other devices), they can add significantly to the accuracy of prediction of job success for applicants. In other words the utilization of valid tests can result in the hiring of better qualified employees. This in turn may mean less turnover of newly hired employees, lower training costs, and higher output and quality of work. It may also mean better adjustment to the job and working environment. Insofar as tests aid in the evaluation of people, fewer errors will be made in placement of employees on particular jobs. If a costly and lengthy training course is necessary for certain

[1] Lee J. Cronbach, *Essentials of Psychological Testing*, 3rd ed. (New York: Harper and Row, 1970), p. 26.
[2] Milton L. Blum, *Industrial Psychology and Its Social Foundations*, rev. ed. (New York: Harper and Row, 1956), p. 267.
[3] *Personnel Practices in Factory and Office: Manufacturing*, Studies in Personnel Policy, No. 194 (New York: National Industrial Conference Board, 1964), and *Office Personnel Practices: Nonmanufacturing*, Studies in Personnel Policy, No. 197 (New York: National Industrial Conference Board, 1965).

types of work, more accurate appraisal of candidates through testing would reduce the number of failures in the course.

FUNDAMENTAL GUIDES TO TESTING

Because the field of selection testing is an involved subject, it is important at the outset to examine some of the necessary requirements and conditions surrounding the use of tests.

1. Tests should be used only as a supplement to other selection devices, not as a substitute for them. Even a full battery of tests will provide only a small sample of a person's total pattern of behavior. Therefore, it is necessary to give credence to information derived from other procedures, such as interviews, application form, and background check to obtain a reasonably complete picture of the candidate.
2. Tests are more accurate at predicting failures than success. If we divide the characteristics that make for success on the job into the "can do" factors (skills, knowledge, general abilities) and the "will do" factors (personality and interest), we find that tests in their present stage of development are more accurate at measuring the "can do" characteristics. Therefore, if a man fails tests of capacity and ability, we can reasonably conclude that he is unable to perform the work satisfactorily. However, if he does pass these tests, he may still fail because of poor adjustment to his supervisor and work associates, lack of motivation, lack of interest in his work, family difficulties, and many other factors that are very difficult to predict at the time a person is hired.
3. Tests are most useful in picking a select group of people who are most likely to succeed on the job from among a much larger group. It is difficult for a testing program to reveal with certainty that a particular individual will succeed on the job. But such a program can predict rather well that a particular group, from among a much larger group who took the tests, will succeed on the job. Thus, as we noted in Chapter 9, tests can raise the batting average but will make errors on an individual case. By analogy a certain major league baseball player may have been a consistent .300 hitter for many seasons. However, for any particular game he may very well get no hits at all. Indeed he may strike out all four times at bat.
4. A test must be validated in one's own organization to be of any value. It is always necessary to test the test itself before any degree of confidence can be placed in its ability to predict successful performance on the job. This practice is a vital necessity, but it is often not done because of ignorance and the expense involved. A valid test is one that measures what it is supposed to measure. It will, with reasonable accuracy, predict success or failure on the job. The best way to validate a test (or a battery of tests) properly is to conduct a research study within the organization where it is to be used. Just because a certain aptitude test has been useful for picking assembly workers in company A, that is no reason to conclude that it will also be useful in company B. The job requirements and organizational environment in company B may be quite different from those in company A; therefore, different characteristics may be demanded of the workers.

5. Tests can make their greatest contribution in those situations where it has been difficult to obtain satisfactory employees by using other selection methods. Conversely, if it has been relatively easy to find good employees by other selection devices, there may be no need to resort to the expense of testing. Thus an employer picking common laborers probably has no need to test them, because there are many in the labor force who can do this work, and it requires few special abilities that cannot be identified by a physical examination and an interview.

   Taylor and Russell have constructed statistical tables by means of which an employment manager can determine the amount of improvement that can be obtained from using a test above the level or percentage of satisfactory employees hired without using a test. These tables will tell one the proportion of employees who will be satisfactory among all those hired for a given value of the proportion of present employees considered satisfactory (without using tests), the selection ratio (number hired compared to number tested), and a given value for validity of the test.[4]

6. Those who administer tests in an employment situation and then make decisions whether to hire or reject are cautioned not to consider the numerical score from the test to be a precise or exact measure of the characteristic being tested. If we are measuring the weight of all applicants, we can have confidence in the fact that if the scale shows one man to weigh 180 and another 178, then in fact there is a difference of two pounds between the candidates. But this is not so with test scores. Psychological tests are not so accurate that we can say that one man with a score of 92 is emphatically better qualified than another with a score of 90. Likewise, it is possible for an applicant to score a number of points below the passing score on a test and still be a successful employee.

7. If several applicants pass a selection test, those with the very highest test scores are not necessarily a better choice than those scoring lower. This is because the relationship between test score and job success is not always linear. For certain kinds of work it may be necessary to establish a maximum as well as a minimum score. For example, for certain types of routine repetitive work people with too high an intelligence may fail on the job owing to lack of interest, boredom, and monotony.

TESTING CONCEPTS

It is pertinent at this point in our discussion of selection testing to examine those significant testing concepts and methods that are essential to a sound understanding of how to use tests in a practical situation.

Reliability

The reliability of a test is the consistency with which it yields the same score throughout a series of measurements. If a test is to be of any value, the person

---

[4] H. C. Taylor and J. T. Russell, "The Relationship of Validity Coefficients to the Practical Effectiveness of Tests in Selection: Discussion and Tables," *Journal of Applied Psychology*, Vol. 23 (1939), pp. 565–578.

being tested should receive the same score (or nearly the same) or his relative standing in the group should show little change if he takes the test on April 15 or on May 12.

A considerable number of factors can cause a test to have low reliability. If the test is not administered under standardized conditions, the reliability will tend to be low. Thus, in a shorthand test for stenographers if the material is not dictated with the same degree of clarity and at the same speed every time, we cannot expect the test to be reliable. In addition people vary from time to time in their emotional state, their degree of attention, attitude, health, fatigue and so on. If a particular test has few test questions and is short, chance factors may determine whether an individual does or does not know a particular fact. Also luck in the selection of answers by guessing may introduce variance into the scores.

There exist four different ways in which the reliability of a test can be determined. More precisely there are four distinct types of test reliability. These are (1) equivalent- (alternate-) form; (2) test-retest; (3) split-half; and (4) odd-even item split.

The equivalent- or alternate-form type of reliability requires the creation of two essentially equivalent forms of the same test. These should be made up by a systematic selection of test items from the same universe or population of possible questions. The scores of a group of people on Form A of the test can then be compared statistically with their scores on Form B.

The test-retest method involves administering the test to a group of persons today and then having them take the same test at a later date. This is generally a good way of measuring reliability. However, the individuals may remember some of their answers from the first time and score slightly higher the second time, especially if it is a speed test.

The split-half form of reliability is found by dividing a test in half and relating scores obtained on the first half to scores on the second half of the same test.

The odd-even item split is simply another way of cutting a test in half. The scores on odd numbered test items and those on the even numbered items are correlated. Both the split-half and the odd-even methods are used to ascertain the internal consistency of a test.

The reliability can readily be determined by the test designer and is commonly reported in the manual that accompanies a test. Reliability is expressed by a coefficient of correlation, which will be explained on page 234. Generally the reliability coefficient should exceed .85.

Validity

The validity of a test is the degree to which it measures what it is intended to measure. Or expressed slightly differently, it shows the extent to which a test does the job for which it is used. In an employment situation a valid test is one that accurately predicts the criterion of job success. A criterion is a measurement of how satisfactory an employee is on the job or in the total employment situation. Actually there are five distinct kinds of validity:

1. Concurrent validity (present-employee method).
2. Predictive validity (follow-up method).
3. Content validity.

4. Construct validity.
5. Face validity.

Concurrent validity refers to the degree to which test scores relate to the performance of employees presently on the payroll. This is often referred to as the present-employee method of validating a test. The procedure involves giving the test to a group of present employees who are working on the job for which the selection test is to be used. Then the scores that they receive are correlated with some measure of their performance on the job. Commonly used gauges of job performance are quantity and quality of work, attendance, accident frequency, dollar volume of sales (for sales personnel), and supervisors' ratings. If those who receive high scores on the test are also the best workers, then the test is valid.

Predictive validity (follow-up method) is determined by giving the test in question to all who apply for the job. Since we are testing the test to see whether it is valid, acceptances or rejections are not made on the basis of test scores at this time. Rather the hiring decision is made on the basis of the other selection instruments, such as the application form and the interview. After those who have been hired have been on the job for a long enough time to obtain a true measure of their work performance (several months to a year or more), a statistical correlation is computed between the criterion of performance and test scores for the group of people involved. If those who made the highest scores at the time of hiring later turned out to be the most proficient workers and those who made the lowest scores turned out to be the poorest, then the test is valid.

In comparing the concurrent with the predictive method we find that the concurrent approach permits an immediate determination of the usefulness of a test. The predictive technique requires a long wait before one knows whether the test is going to be useful. Hence the concurrent validation is most commonly used in business and industry. However, this present-employee method possesses inherent weaknesses. With it we are dealing with a group of very select people, namely, those who have remained on the job for a period of time. They have passed their probationary period, and presumably most of the unsatisfactory employees either have been already discharged or have quit. Few supervisors will endure incompetent workers for an extended period of time. Thus, present employees are not a representative sample of future job applicants. If one is trying to validate an aptitude test he will find that the experience that present workers have had in that type of activity will cause them to score higher than untrained applicants. In addition, the validity coefficient obtained by using the narrow range of test scores and performance scores for this select group of people will tend to be lower than if the range of performance were very wide.

Content validity shows how well the subject matter or behaviors required in a test are representative of important aspects of performance on the job. Content validity is *not* measured by statistical correlation between test scores and job performance measures. Rather it is determined judgmentally and logically. The foundation for content validation is a thorough and detailed job analysis. Once the job analysis is completed, a test (or tests) is selected which includes significant portions of behavior actually required on the job. Content validity is most appropriate for achievement tests. Thus, a typing test for a typist would contain a representative sample of the kind of material that was actually required on the job. A skilled machinist must be able to read drawings of machine parts and assemblies. Thus, a test of this skill would logically contain mechanical drawing symbols, terminology, sketches, and conventional modes of representation.

Content validity is not appropriate for selection procedures which seek to measure intelligence, aptitudes, and personality. Generally, criterion related or statistical validity is preferred when trying to establish that a test is valid for selection purposes. However, content validity may be used in those situations where criterion-related validity is infeasible, as in the case of small organizations that hire too few persons to obtain a reasonable sample size.

Construct validity is a concept employed by psychologists to explain just what a particular test is measuring. Does the test measure and correlate with the theoretical construct or hypothesis? Thus, the concept of anxiety may be hypothesized to be measured by certain test items derived from the meaning and description of anxiety in its technical or scientific sense. Construct validity is most commonly used in clinical psychology, projective-personality techniques, and counseling with personality inventories. It is important in test development and research. The use of construct validity in the employment field is quite new. The effort involved in establishing construct validity involves much research including criterion related (statistical correlation) studies and possibly also content validity studies.

Face validity simply refers to whether the kind of test questions seem to relate to the job or subject in question. People are more willing to accept tests that seem logically valid. A test for hiring mechanics should, many people feel, contain questions relating to tools, gears, levers, cams, machinery, and so forth. However, face validity cannot be measured statistically. Also a test may appear logically valid on the surface, but a careful validation study may yield a very poor statistical correlation with the criterion.

In summary then, the most important types of validity for personnel management purposes are concurrent, predictive, and content.

Coefficient of Correlation

Correlation is a statistical concept that indicates the degree of closeness of relationship between two series of numbers. In selection testing it is applied to both reliability and to validity. However, it should be noted that a high degree of correlation between one factor and another does not necessarily mean that the first causes the second. All it means is that the first measure relates closely to the second. It may actually be that the first factor causes the second, or it may be that both factors are influenced by some other common factor that has not been determined.

A correlation coefficient can range from zero up to +1.00. A zero coefficient indicates absolutely no relationship between the two series of numbers, whereas a coefficient of +1.00 indicates a perfect positive relationship. Negative correlation is also possible. Thus a coefficient of −1.00 indicates a perfect inverse relationship between the two measures. For validation work it is impossible to obtain a correlation coefficient of +1.00. Commonly the validity coefficient for a useful single test ranges between .25 and .40. By using a number of tests and entering into a rather involved statistical process called multiple regression analysis, it is possible to develop a combined predictive equation from those several tests that often give a significantly higher validity coefficient.

If the correlation between test scores and job performance scores is .50, this means that the test is measuring or accounting for $(.50)^2 = .25$, or 25 percent of the variability. Other factors that are often unknown or at least not measurable account for the rest of the variation. Thus, tests generally cannot account for future problems that an employee may encounter, such as financial, health, or domestic difficulties, changes in the demands of the job, or unusual and unexpected job pressures.

There are a number of procedures for computing the coefficient of correlation. If there are only a few numbers involved, the rank-difference method can be effectively used. For a large number of individual cases the Pearsonian product-moment method is most appropriate. This technique requires that both test scores and criterion scores be quantitative and continuously distributed.

If it is not possible to obtain continuous data for job performance, as in certain cases in which supervisory ratings are employed, then the biserial correlation method may be appropriate. This is true if the data are divided into two groups, such as acceptable and unacceptable performance.[5]

DEVELOPING A TESTING PROGRAM

There are over one thousand tests on the market and literally scores of tests that purport to measure such attributes as intelligence or clerical aptitude. For a particular application one test is certainly not as good as another. It requires a great deal of planning, analysis, and experimenting to develop a useful battery of tests for a particular selection situation.

Because a great deal of technical knowledge is necessary to establish a new testing program, the services of a qualified person are required to guide the effort. Who is qualified to do this work? The individual in charge should be either a fully qualified industrial psychologist or else a personnel management specialist who has taken a number of college level courses in psychology, psychometrics, and statistics. For the administration of the ordinary testing program, the services of a professional psychologist are not required; however, the individual in charge must have had adequate training and experience in the theory and practice of testing and in statistics. If, on the other hand, a company wishes to conduct a full-scale testing program, including projective tests of personality, then only a professionally qualified psychologist who has had intensive graduate training in the psychology of personality can properly interpret such tests.

Steps to Install a Program

The steps that must be carried out to create a new testing program are as follows:

1. Decide objectives of testing program.
2. Analyze jobs to identify those characteristics that appear necessary for job success.

---

[5] Information on statistical analysis of tests and matters of test validation can be obtained from Marvin D. Dunnette, *Personnel Selection and Placement* (Belmont, Calif.: Wadsworth Publishing Company, Inc., 1966); Benjamin Schneider, *Staffing Organizations* (Pacific Palisades, Calif.: Goodyear Publishing Co., Inc., 1976).

3. Make a tentative choice of tests for a tryout.
4. Administer these tests to an experimental group of people.
5. Establish criteria of job success.
6. Analyze results and make decisions regarding test application.

Decide Program Objective.　A wide range of choices are available as far as testing objectives and policy are concerned. Shall tests be utilized only for hiring new employees, or shall they also be used for picking present employees for upgrading, transfer, and promotion? Shall all the present employees be tested (executives as well) in order to make a comprehensive assessment of present manpower capabilities? If the testing program is to be developed only for the selection of new employees, shall it be for all types of work in the organization or only for certain jobs? Initially should the testing effort be directed only toward improving the accuracy of selection for a particular group of jobs? If this last approach is adopted, it is logical to start with those jobs for which it has been difficult to find satisfactory employees in the past. Let us assume, in the discussion that follows, that a testing program is being set up for certain jobs. From this initial installation, it may be reasonable, then, to expand the program to cover all types of work in the organization.

Analyze Jobs　Although a great many companies have on file job descriptions and specifications that were prepared for job evaluation and recruitment and selection purposes, it is unlikely that the jobs were analyzed from the standpoint of identifying detailed human characteristics that may be revealed in selection tests. Job analysis of this type must be very specific and detailed. Generalities will not do, because they cover too wide a range of skills and aptitudes. Among the items the analyst will seek to uncover are the need for such things as motor habits, eye-hand coordination, finger and arm dexterity, perceptual and sensory abilities, and specific personality characteristics. One useful frame of reference for making this job analysis is to seek those attributes that differentiate good from poor workers.

Choose Tests for Tryout　Once the list of attributes deemed essential for success on the job has been uncovered, it is then possible to choose tests to measure these characteristics. Usually the test program designer will choose from among commercially available tests rather than undergo the time and expense of creating his own test to apply to this one job. This latter approach, though necessary at times, is quite costly. Generally the program designer will select an individual test to measure each of the essential job characteristics. Therefore he will, in essence, be constructing a trial test battery. In picking commercially available tests he will give weight to such factors as reliability, face validity, proper level of difficulty, ease of administration, and cost.

Administer Tests to an Experimental Group　It is now necessary to try out these tests by administering them to an experimental group. The best group upon whom to try out the tests consists of, as was discussed previously under the topic of *validity*, applicants for the job under consideration. It is absolutely essential none of these applicants be rejected on the basis of his test score during this trial period because it is not known as yet whether there is any relationship between test scores and future work performance. We are testing the test at this point. Because this follow-up method of ascertaining test validity is a very lengthy process, many organizations will find it advisable to administer the test battery to those presently on the job as well. There is no reason why concurrent and predictive (follow-up) validity cannot be computed in the same test tryout.

Establish Criteria of Employee Success   Establishing criteria of success is one of the more difficult parts of the test installation program. It is difficult, not because of a lack of criteria, but because it is extremely hard to find criteria that accurately, fully, and fairly measure job success. Most of the criteria available measure only one small aspect of the job. The one that is all inclusive—supervisor's ratings—is often inaccurate because it is so terribly personal and subjective. Where possible, it is most fruitful to obtain several measures of work behavior and performance and correlate test scores with each of these. The following is a list of commonly used criteria:

1. Quantity of output.
2. Quality of output.
3. Grades in training courses.
4. Accident frequency.
5. Attendance.
6. Rate of promotion in the organization.
7. Professional achievements, such as patents, published writings, and formal awards.
8. Performance ratings made by supervisor.

Analysis and Decision Making   Let us assume, for the present, that we are concerned with only one test and that we are relating scores on this test to a measure of job performance that is continuously distributed, such as units produced or dollar volume of sales. The most useful way of working with these data is to plot a graph of the criterion scores for the ordinate and the test scores for the abscissa. Figure 10-1 represents a hypothetical case of monthly dollar sales for thirty-one salesmen plotted against their test scores at the time of hiring. The product-moment coefficient of correlation between the criterion and test scores can be computed to find the validity coefficient.

Assuming that we have obtained a representative sample of the population of applicants in this validation study, it appears by inspection that this test will be a useful instrument for selecting salesmen. The dispersion of scores from the hypothetical trend line is not great. Those who score high on the test turn out to be good salesmen and vice versa.

The next question is where shall we place the passing or cutting score on the test? Before this can be done intelligently, it is necessary to establish the level of acceptable sales performance. Line Q-Q has been set at \$16,000. Now we can evaluate the alternatives related to placing the passing score far to the right (high) against placing it far to the left (low). The *selection ratio* is the number placed on the job or hired divided by the total number tested. If the cutting score (line A-A) is moved to the right, say to 80 or 90, we are almost certain not to have any failures. However, the supply of labor available to a particular organization may not permit it to be so "choosy." If the cutting score, line A-A, is

Figure 10-1
Scatter Diagram of Average Monthly Sales Versus Test Scores.

placed at 60, it is clear that some employees who passed the test sold less than $16,000 per month. These are called, "false acceptances." Likewise some who scored below 60 were successful, because they sold over $16,000. So a few future applicants scoring under 60 (false rejections) would be successful if they were not rejected at that figure. This is the risk inherent in all selection instruments that have a validity coefficient less than 1.00. They will always reject some potential successes and accept some future failures.

The decision of where to place the cutting score is determined by the level of acceptable performance expected, the supply of labor to the organization in relation to its needs for labor, the cost involved in screening many applicants just to hire a few, and the seriousness of hiring a failure (cost of training, and so on). Over a period of time some companies find it necessary to lower their standards if they cannot obtain people of the caliber they desire.

Combining Several Tests into a Battery. Because no single test can be expected to measure all the capacities and abilities necessary to perform a job satisfactorily, personnel specialists often find it advantageous to use a number of tests. A series of tests developed for a particular purpose is called a *battery*.

If, for example, a particular test has a validity coefficient with job performance of .29, it is often possible to utilize additional tests that measure different characteristics and thereby obtain a higher combined validity coefficient. The statistical procedure by which tests can be selected and combined in this fashion is called multiple correlation. Initially it is necessary to have a number of tests for which the validity coefficients are known. Presumably each test measures a different aptitude or ability. Those tests are used that have a high correlation with the criterion and a low correlation with each other. If they had a high correlation with each other, they would be measuring the same characteristic. The multiple correlation technique, which is explained in most standard statistics textbooks, se-

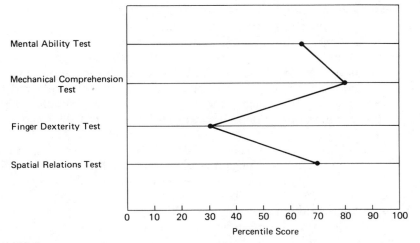

Figure 10-2
A Profile for Expressing Scores on a Number of Tests.

lects the most appropriate tests and develops weighting factors so that a prediction equation is constructed. With this prediction equation it is possible for a particular candidate to overcome a low score on one test with a high score on another and still obtain a passing composite score.

When a battery of tests is used, it is possible, instead of computing a composite score, to simply plot a profile of the scores that an applicant has obtained on the various tests, as shown in Figure 10-2. By means of this approach the profile can be compared with a normal or standard profile typical of successful workers in that occupation in the organization.

TYPES OF TESTS

Tests can be classified according to the type of human behavior measured as follows:

1. Aptitude.
   a. General mental ability or intelligence.
   b. Special aptitudes, such as mechanical aptitude, dexterity, manipulative capacity, clerical, sales, vision, and perception.
2. Achievement.
3. Vocational interest.
4. Situation.
5. Personality.

Aptitude tests measure the latent or potential ability to do something, provided the individual is given proper training. Achievement tests, also called proficiency tests, measure an acquired skill or acquired knowledge. Ordinarily this acquired skill is obtained as a result of a training program and on-the-job experience. With both aptitude and achievement tests, measures of maximum performance are ordinarily obtained, because it is expected that those being tested will exert their utmost while taking the tests.

If a company trains most of its employees for the work they have to do and if it hires inexperienced help and develops it within the organization, aptitude tests are most necessary to measure what new employees will ultimately be able to do. On the other hand if a company, as a matter of employment policy, hires only experienced stenographers and machinists, for example, then achievement tests are most appropriate for measuring the level of skills and abilities they already possess.

In addition to basic capacity to do a given kind of work, the success or failure of people at work is strongly determined by their personalities and how they interact with other people. Personality tests seek to evaluate such characteristics as emotional maturity, sociability, ascendancy, responsibility, conformity, nervous symptoms, and objectivity.

Situation tests are really combination tests representing elements of achievement, of aptitude, and of personality. Because they are quite different from standard objective, pencil and paper, tests they are properly classified as a distinct type of test.

General Mental-Ability Tests

Psychological testing really began with mental ability (also called intelligence) testing around 1900. More work has been done in creating, developing, experimenting, and refining general mental-ability tests than any other major type of test. The original work on mental-ability testing was done by Alfred Binet, a French physician, who created a test to classify school children according to their ability to learn and succeed at schoolwork.

Just what is meant by the term *intelligence?* Although a variety of sometimes conflicting definitions have been proposed, and thus there is no general agreement as to a precise definition, Thurstone has isolated the specific types of mental abilities that most of these tests measure. These are verbal comprehension, word fluency, memory, inductive reasoning, number facility, speed of perception, and spatial visualization.[6]

In reporting on the work of a great many investigators, Tiffin and McCormick state that significant positive correlations have been found between scores on general mental-ability tests and job success in a variety of clerical occupations, supervisory occupations, machine skills, utility plant work, and teletype work.[7]

Some of the more widely used tests for employee selection are the Otis Employment Tests,[8] Wesman Personnel Classification Tests,[9] Wonderlic Personnel Test,[10] and Adaptability Test.[11] Many of these brands of tests actually consist of

---

[6] L. L. Thurstone, *Primary Mental Abilities*, The Psychometric Laboratory, the University of Chicago, No. 50 (September 1948).

[7] Joseph Tiffin and Ernest J. McCormick, *Industrial Psychology*, 4th ed. (Englewood Cliffs, N.J.: Prentice-Hall, Inc., 1958), pp. 116–122.

[8] Published by Harcourt, Brace & World, Inc., also distributed by the Psychological Corporation.

[9] Published by the Psychological Corporation.

[10] Published by E. F. Wonderlic, also distributed by the Psychological Corporation.

[11] Published by Science Research Associates.

two or more tests designed for people of different educational attainments. Also some tests, such as the Wonderlic, have several forms that are intended to be equivalent to one another in difficulty level. This is to minimize the likelihood of a person obtaining a higher score than he normally would simply because he had recently taken the exact same test elsewhere.

Special Aptitude Tests

A great number and variety of tests have been created to measure capacity to learn a particular kind of work.

Mechanical aptitude tests, for example, measure the capacities of spatial visualization, perceptual speed, and knowledge of mechanical matter. They do not measure manual dexterity and manipulative skill. Mechanical aptitude tests have been found useful for selecting apprentices and other employees for the skilled mechanical trades as well as for certain technician jobs. Typical occupations for which such tests have proved useful are machinists, mechanics, maintenance workers, and mechanical technicians. Some widely used tests of this general type are the Bennett Test of Mechanical Comprehension, Revised Minnesota Paper Form Board Test,[12] Purdue Mechanical Adaptability Test,[13] and the Science Research Associates Mechanical Aptitudes Test. Figure 10-3 contains practice problems from the revised Minnesota Paper Form Board Test.

Psychomotor tests are those that measure such abilities as manual dexterity, motor ability, and eye–hand coordination. Tests of this type are primarily important for selecting workers to do semiskilled, repetitive operations, such as bench assembly work, packing, certain testing and inspection, watch assembly, and the like. Research has shown that rapid manipulative skill is relatively unimportant for the skilled mechanical and electrical trades. Understanding of the techniques and processes involved is more important for these occupations than is manual dexterity. Commonly used psychomotor tests are the Purdue Pegboard,[14] Minnesota Rate of Manipulation Test,[15] Mac Quarrie Test for Mechanical Ability,[16] the O'Connor Finger Dexterity Test,[17] and the Hand-Tool Dexterity Test shown in Figure 10-4.

Clerical aptitude tests have been created to measure specific capacities involved in office work. These typically have test items on spelling, computation, comparisons, copying, word meaning, and the like. Three examples of clerical tests are the SRA Clerical Aptitudes, the Minnesota Clerical Test, and the Short Employment Tests (SET).[18]

[12] Both the Bennett Test of Mechanical Comprehension and the Revised Minnesota Paper Form Board Test are published by the Psychological Corporation.
[13] Published by Occupational Research Center, Purdue University.
[14] This test and the SRA Clerical Aptitudes Tests listed below are published by Science Research Association.
[15] Published by Educational Test Bureau.
[16] Published by the California Test Bureau.
[17] Published by Stevens Institute of Technology and C. H. Stoelting Company.
[18] The Minnesota Clerical Test and the Short Employment Tests (SET) are both published by the Psychological Corporation.

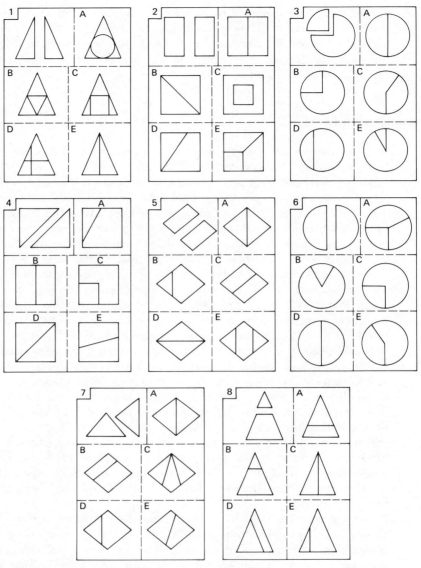

Figure 10-3
Practice Problems from the Revised Minnesota Paper Form Board Test, Series MA. (*Prepared by Rensis Likert and William H. Quasha. Reproduced by permission. Copyright 1941, renewed 1969, by The Psychological Corporation, New York, N.Y. All rights reserved.*)

Achievement Tests

If a company wishes to hire experienced employees who should already possess the requisite skills and knowledge, it would do well to investigate the value of specific achievement or proficiency tests to evaluate these candidates. Achievement tests can be classified into two categories. One measures job knowledge and may be either of the oral or the written type. The other category is a *work*

Manual of Directions

1965 REVISION

HAND-TOOL DEXTERITY TEST

George K. Bennett

Figure 10-4

The Hand-Tool Dexterity Test, 1965 Revision, by George K. Bennett. *Reproduced by permission. Copyright 1965 by The Psychological Corporation, New York, N.Y. All rights reserved.*

sample, in which a typical portion of the actual job is administered as a test. Thus, a stenographer may have to listen to a recording, take down the words in shorthand, transcribe these, and type them.

Quite logically many companies have developed their own achievement tests to select people for specific jobs. Because the work carried on in many organizations is peculiar to these businesses only, it is understandable that these tests are not distributed commercially. Many work sample tests have content validity only. Personnel specialists and operating supervisors have taken portions of real jobs and asked job candidates to do the work. If a man claims to have had experience as a truck driver or a milling-machine operator, there is probably no better way to find out if he can do the work than to try him out on it.

Vocational Interest Tests

Vocational interest tests are inventories of the likes and dislikes of people in relation to occupations, hobbies, and recreational activities. The basic assumption behind these tests is that there exists a definite pattern of interests for those who are successful in an occupation and that if one likes the same kind of things that practitioners in an occupation like, then the person being examined will like that kind of work.

One of the most widely used interest tests is the Strong Vocational Interest Blank, first published in 1927.[19] It contains 400 questions of the "like-indifferent-dislike" variety. The blank for men is scored for forty-seven occupations; the one for women is scored for twenty-seven occupations. Strong developed the scoring system for his test by administering it to successful members of each of the various occupations. If an examinee answers the 400 items in a pattern similar to the way in which, say, successful personnel managers have answered it, he is given a high score opposite the words *personnel manager* on the report form. In the late 1970's the Strong-Campbell Interest Inventory, which is a combined test for both men and women, was developed.

The Kuder Preference Record is another commonly used interest test.[20] It scores for ten broad interest areas or clusters. These are outdoor, mechanical, computational, scientific, persuasive, artistic, literary, musical, social service, and clerical. Profiles for a considerable number of occupations have been developed empirically in terms of these ten interest areas.

Because it is possible for a job-seeking person definitely to fake or slant his answers in a certain direction in order to be hired, interest tests are much more useful for individual vocational guidance than they are for employee selection.

Situational Tests

A situational test evaluates individuals in a real life-like situation by asking them to cope with or solve critical elements of a real job. An illustration of this type of test is the leaderless group discussion. In this test a group of candidates for a job (usually of a supervisory or executive type) are placed in a room, given a practical problem to discuss and solve, and are observed by others. No one is appointed leader. The observers note how they interact with one another. Who had the most useful ideas? Who emerged as a leader? Who conciliated opposing views? Who was most convincing in oral expression? These and many other qualities are

[19] Published by The Stanford University Press.
[20] Published by Science Research Associates.

noted by the observers. The group oral performance test makes it possible to evaluate effectiveness and skill in interpersonal relations.

Another type of situational test is the "in-basket" test. This simulates key aspects of the job of an administrator. It consists of realistic letters, telephone messages, memoranda, and reports that have supposedly collected in the "in-basket" on the desk of a manager. Each person taking this test is provided with adequate background information about the particular organization and its line of business. He is told that he is a new incumbent in his position and must take action on the various items in his in-basket. The candidate is asked to handle these materials in the most appropriate way. This may involve writing letters, notes, or self-reminders, delegating a matter to a subordinate, setting up a meeting with another person, deciding to make a phone call and the like. Scoring of the subjects' performance is carried out by a group of raters or assessors who consider both content and style of responses. The assessors may interview the candidates to learn their reasoning for each of their actions or nonactions on the items in the exercise. [21]

Both the leaderless group discussion and the in-basket test are widely used in industry to aid in the selection of managers, especially as components of assessment centers.

Personality Tests

There are two types of personality tests:

1. Objective, pencil and paper, tests (personality inventories).
2. Projective tests.

Because they are suitable for group testing and can be scored objectively, most personality tests are of the objective type. One well-known personality test is the Bernreuter Personality Inventory, which measures neurotic tendency, self-sufficiency, introversion-extroversion, dominance-submission, self-confidence, and sociability. Some other tests are the Humm-Wadsworth Temperament Scale, the Guilford-Martin Personnel Inventory, and the Minnesota Multiphasic Personality Inventory.

Personality tests of this type have the disadvantages of interest inventories. They can be faked by sophisticated candidates. There is a strong motivation always to give socially acceptable answers. In addition, self-report devices such as these reveal how a person thinks he would behave in a certain situation. This does not necessarily mean he would actually act that way in a real-life problem. In other words many persons do not really know themselves. Cronbach reports that personality inventories have had rather limited success in predicting employee performance on the job. [22] They are more useful for individual counseling.

[21] Further information on the in-basket test is contained in Norman Frederiksen, "Factors in In-Basket Performance," *Psychological Monographs: General and Applied*, Vol. 76 (1962), pp. 1–6; and Felix M. Lopez, Jr., *Evaluating Executive Decision Making: The In-Basket Technique* (New York: American Management Association, Research Study No. 75, 1966).

[22] Lee J. Cronbach, *Essentials of Psychological Testing*, 2nd ed. (New York: Harper and Row, 1960), p. 485.

A projective personality test is one in which the subject is asked to project his own interpretation into certain standard stimulus situations. The meaning he attaches to the stimulus depends upon his own values, motives, and personality. Theoretically the number of responses that various people can give to a single stimulus is infinite. Two well-known projective tests are the Rorschach and the Thematic Apperception Test.

The Rorschach test, developed in 1921 by Hermann Rorschach, consists of ten cards, each containing a different inkblot. These inkblots are of various colors. The person is asked to explain what he sees in each blot. His explanations provide clues to his personality. A full evaluation can be made only when the analyst knows about the subject's family background, education, past experiences, and has evaluations obtained from others who know the individual.

The Thematic Apperception Test, developed in 1938, consists of a series of twenty pictures, there being a different set for men and women. The person tested must interpret each picture by telling a story about it in terms of what he believes is happening and what will be the outcome.

All projective tests must be administered individually. Interpretation of the results is a job only for a qualified clinical psychologist or a psychiatrist. The interpretation is highly subjective and unstandardized. In a sense it is impressionistic. Quantitative scores are not developed.

Personality Testing in Perspective.   If one were to ask a representative sample of personnel managers the most common reason for employee failure on the job, they would undoubtedly say that temperament, personality, and adjustment to the job environment, not ability, are the main causes. Yet the measuring instruments now available—objective and projective tests—are not sufficiently advanced in their stage of development to obtain really accurate predictions of employee performance. In reviewing a number of validation studies in connection with employee selection in the British Civil Service, the Veterans Administration, the Air Force, and others, Cronbach concluded that evaluations made by those having psychological training were not necessarily superior to those obtained from peer ratings, that structured, group-performance, work-sample tests have good validity for jobs requiring group acceptance, and that the evaluators must have a clear knowledge of the psychological requirements of the tasks involved. In general Cronbach was critical of the value of impressionistic interpretations derived in much personality testing.[23]

Two psychologists, Guion and Gottier, have made a comprehensive analysis of published validation studies of both personality inventories and projective tests used for employee selection. The record is disappointing. Guion and Gottier state that it cannot be said that any of the conventional personality measures have demonstrated really general usefulness as selection tools in employment practice. In the conclusion of their study they assert:

> In brief, it is difficult in the face of this summary to advocate, with a clear conscience, the use of personality measures in most situations as a basis for making employment decisions about people.[24]

[23] Ibid., pp. 589–590.
[24] Robert M. Guion and Richard F. Gottier, "Validity of Personality Measures in Personnel Selection," *Personnel Psychology*, Vol. 18, No. 2 (Summer 1965), pp. 135–164. The authors investigated

Richard S. Barrett, another esteemed psychologist, has stated that a dismal history has been recorded by personality tests. The typical personality questionnaire, test, or inventory has not proved to be useful. Of the Rorschach inkblot test Dr. Barrett states that it has been studied very thoroughly but that it has accumulated a long record of failure as a selection device.[25]

A very scathing denunciation of personality testing has been made by William H. Whyte, Jr., in his book *The Organization Man.*[26] His criticisms are made in connection with the use of these tests for selecting and promoting executives in industry. Whyte claims that personality tests are being used to select only those who are conformists and hence "good" organization men. The testing process is not scientific, because the value judgments of the test designers determine the interpretations of an individual's personality to a large extent. Especially in interpreting a projective test, he claims that the analysis of a person is often more revealing of the personality of the psychologists than it is of the subject. Who can say that the values and standards of the test-makers and interpreters are right? Whyte further claims that the process by which personality tests are validated within an organization is erroneous and unscientific. It involves circular reasoning. In order to be hired the candidate must match the average profile of present company executives in terms of a pattern of traits. But how could different types of individuals ever be hired so that they themselves are included in a criterion group for a validation study if they had the wrong pattern of traits in the first place?

A number of thoughtful writers have pointed out that personality testing probes very deep into the individual's inner self, into his own private world. It is of utmost importance that the personnel specialists and psychologists not divulge this information to other organizations and persons in such a way as to injure the individual and damage his career. Gellerman has warned that the most potent danger to the privacy of the person is the fact that his test data are preserved but are not under his control. He advocates that the highest ethical and professional standards be followed in handling test results.[27]

Testing and Equal Employment Opportunity

Selection tests have the potential for inadvertently discriminating against racial and ethnic minorities, women, and older workers. If certain minority groups score lower on tests, does this mean they have less capability of adequately performing the jobs they are seeking than mainstream whites?

If the use of selection instruments such as tests results in an "adverse impact" upon protected groups, the burden of proof is placed upon the employer to show that the tests used are job related or predictive of performance on the job. This means the selection instruments must be validated. Standards and procedures for the proper use of selection instruments in the context of equal employment

---

95 different validation studies on 15 leading personality inventories, 11 validation studies on 6 projective tests, and 11 validation studies on 3 special inventories.

[25] Richard S. Barrett, "Guide to Using Psychological Tests," *Harvard Business Review*, Vol. 41, No. 5 (September–October 1963), pp. 138–146.

[26] William H. Whyte, Jr., *The Organization Man* (New York: Simon & Schuster, 1956), ch. 15.

[27] Saul W. Gellerman, "The Ethics of Personality Testing," *Personnel*, Vol. 35, No. 3 (November–December 1958), pp. 30–35.

opportunity have been developed by the Equal Employment Opportunity Commission in cooperation with other Federal agencies under authority granted to these agencies by Title VII-Equal Employment Opportunity (as amended) of the Civil Rights Act of 1964 and various other statutes. This topic is covered in depth in Chapter 11. "Equal Employment Opportunity."

SELECTION TESTING—A FINAL COMMENT

It was pointed out early in our discussion of testing that tests can be a valuable aid in improving the accuracy of personnel assessment. It was further explained that tests, before they are finally adopted for making employment decisions, must be validated in one's own organization. Selection tests are very appealing to managers who want to get the facts and make a definite assessment of people. In their eagerness some executives abandon their realism and sense to depend exclusively upon this crutch.

Ross Stagner has described an experiment in which a group of personnel managers themselves answered the questions on a published personality inventory. To determine whether they were gullible, all participants were given identical fake reports that contained statements taken from dream books and astrology charts. The person's name was written in red pencil at the top of each sheet. Thus, each personnel manager thought he was receiving his own personality score card. One half of the group of 68 managers considered their descriptions to be amazingly accurate, whereas an additional 40 percent felt them to be rather good![28] The point being made is that selection testing is a powerful tool. But it must be used only by those who have an adequate background in psychological theory and in personnel selection work.

The selection interview

The interview is the most universally used selection method. Although many employers do not use tests to aid in reaching an employment decision, there are hardly any who do not interview the applicant in order to help make a definite assessment. In fact, multiple interviews are commonly employed. In the proposed selection procedure outlined in Chapter 9, provision is made for three: the preliminary, the main employment office interview, and the final decision-making interview by the prospective supervisor. For high-level positions in many organizations, several operating executives interview the candidate and compare impressions before a definite decision is made.

The interviewer is in the unique position of being able to integrate all the information and impressions obtained about the applicant from all sources: application form, preliminary interviews, test scores, and background checks. The interviewer can assess the applicant on such attributes as personal appearance,

---

[28] Ross Stagner, "The Gullibility of Personnel Managers," *Personnel Psychology*, Vol. 11, No. 3 (Autumn 1958), pp. 347–352.

mannerisms, emotional stability, maturity, attitudes, motivation, and interests. He can gauge how well the candidate will adjust to the social situation in the organization. The interview permits deep probing into the person's home and family background, education, previous work experience, avocations, and other pertinent areas.

Interview Defined. *An interview is a conversation or verbal interaction, normally between two people, for a particular purpose.* The intention is to explore certain subject areas. Extraneous topics are ordinarily minimized. There are a great many types of interviews that occur in an organization, such as appraisal interview between supervisor and subordinate, a salesman dealing with a purchasing agent, a counseling interview, a grievance interview, a data-gathering interview in connection with a research project, and a job analysis interview. The basic principles of interviewing apply alike to all of these; however, the specific techniques employed will differ.

Objectives of the Selection Interview. The goals of a selection interview can be grouped into three broad categories. First, the interviewer seeks to obtain enough knowledge about the candidate to determine whether he is suitable for employment in the organization and for the particular job under consideration. Many will believe that this is the only purpose of an employment interview. But this is not so. Employment is a two-way proposition. Not only is the employer choosing an employee, but also the job seeker is choosing an employer. He may reject many as being unsuitable for his needs. Therefore, the interview has as a second purpose the giving of sufficient information about the organization, the job, and the people such that the applicant is able to make an intelligent decision on acceptance or rejection of the job if it should be offered to him. The third goal of an interviewing situation is to deal with the candidate in such a manner as to maintain and create good will toward the company and its management.

Limitations of the Interview. The author once met an industrial executive who claimed he could determine five minutes after a job seeker entered the office door whether he was suitable for hiring. Nonsense! Anyone planning to engage in employment interviewing must understand the inherent weaknesses of this technique. Fundamentally, the major defect of the interview is its subjectivity. The decisions made by the interviewer are based upon his opinion, and that opinion is subject to bias and prejudice. Two interviewers may interview the same candidate and come up with different evaluations.

The applicant, trying to create a favorable impression of himself in the eyes of the interviewer, may behave in an unnatural fashion. The behavior and responses of the applicant are considerably affected by the interviewer's own personality. Interviews are not standardized, and it is difficult to quantify the results.

Many attributes cannot be measured by an interview. Intelligence, motor abilities, manual skills, creativity, strength, health, and many other factors can be measured more appropriately by other devices.

However, numerous research studies have shown that when combined with other selection techniques, interviews that are conducted by properly trained personnel under the proper conditions do have a very positive and significant predictive value.

Some Research Findings.   In a comprehensive review of published research on the employment interview, starting with Walter D. Scott's pioneering investigations in 1915 through to the work of recent researchers, Eugene C. Mayfield has uncovered a number of important findings: (1) Interviewers are quite consistent in the way they rate the same interviewee. When re-interviewing the same person or listening to a tape recording of the original interview at a later date, they make about the same ratings as originally. (2) If different interviewers conduct an unstructured interview and have no prior information on the candidates, they generally come up with quite different ratings of the same interviewees. In other words, the interrater reliability is low. (3) Structured interviews, for instance, the patterned interview, yield fairly consistent ratings of the same persons by different interviewers. The interrater reliability tends to be high. However, if the interviewers used quite different structured forms, their ratings of the same candidates differed substantially. (4) Many investigators report rather low validity (predictions of job success) with the interview. However, very encouraging results are obtained when a team approach is used. The team method can be applied through the "board" technique in which three or four interviewers sit as a panel to interview applicants. The team method can also be used when applicants are interviewed separately by a number of persons who then compare judgments to arrive at a final group decision. (5) The attitudes and biases of interviewers heavily influence their ratings. (6) Interviewers tend to be influenced in their judgments more by unfavorable than by favorable information. They tend to search for negative data. Experiments have shown that it is easier to induce shifts in ratings toward rejection than toward acceptance. (7) Interviewers tend to arrive at their decisions to accept or reject fairly early in the course of an unstructured interview.[29]

Edwin E. Ghiselli, a psychologist, has reported on personal involvement in a situation where a moderate interviewer validity (coefficient of correlation of .35) was obtained for a group of 275 men hired as stockbrokers over a seventeen-year period. The interviewer had no prior information about the applicants. Each interview lasted about an hour.[30]

PSYCHOLOGICAL FOUNDATIONS FOR INTERVIEWS

A working knowledge of the psychological basis for interviewing is desirable for those who engage in this activity.[31]

[29] Eugene C. Mayfield, "The Selection Interview: A Re-evaluation of Published Research," *Personnel Psychology*, Vol. 17 (1964), pp. 239–260.

[30] Edwin E. Ghiselli, "The Validity of the Personnel Interview," *Personnel Psychology*, Vol. 19, No. 4 (Winter 1966), pp. 389–394. Other research studies on the employment interview are contained in W. V. Bingham, B. V. Moore, and J. W. Gustad, *How to Interview*, 4th ed. (New York: Harper and Row, 1959), ch. 1; Newell C. Kephart, *The Employment Interview in Industry* (New York: McGraw-Hill Book Company, 1952); Robert N. McMurry, "Validating the Patterned Interview," *Personnel*, Vol. 23, No. 4 (January 1947), pp. 263–272.

[31] Certain of the ideas presented here are derived from Robert L. Kahn, and Charles F. Cannell, *The Dynamics of Interviewing* (New York: John Wiley & Sons, Inc., 1957).

Motivation of Interviewee

The desire of the interviewee to explain himself fully and to reveal freely his experiences, goals, and attitudes is strongly influenced by the personality and behavior of the interviewer. The applicant is most likely to speak freely and honestly if he perceives that the interviewer understands him and accepts what he has to say. The interviewer must be empathic. He must understand the applicant's point of view and refrain from criticizing, directly or by implication, what he has said. The job seeker is most likely to be motivated to communicate freely and fully when he receives satisfaction from the interviewing process and when the personal relationship between himself and the interviewer is healthy and need-satisfying.

It is important to recognize that people are often unaware of the reasons for their own actions and attitudes. If called upon to explain why they behaved in a certain way, they may honestly not know their own motives.

Human beings exhibit both rational and nonrational or emotional behavior. An engineer may pride himself on being coldly objective and analytical in his work at the office, yet he may be guided almost entirely by his feelings and emotions in choosing a political party, buying a new suit, or choosing his friends. There is a great tendency for people to "think with their hearts" and not their minds. In an interviewing situation the interviewer should be perceptive when he seems to receive a very emotional response to such questions as "How did you get along with your boss?" or "Tell me about your childhood."

Barriers to Communication

If the person being interviewed feels there is a basic clash between his values and goals and those of the interviewer, he will tend to be inhibited. If he feels that the interviewer is not "with him," that he will reject, as being socially unacceptable, certain of his statements, then he will present only that information that will reveal himself favorably. Should the candidate feel that his statements and opinions might at any time be used to harm him, he will also be reluctant to speak freely. A vast gulf between the interviewer and the applicant in social status, language, and education can cause a breakdown in communication if the interviewer gives evidence of being snobbish, aloof, or indifferent toward the candidate.

Interviewer Bias

Countless research experiments have demonstrated that the opinions and biases of the interviewer have a powerful influence upon the decisions reached. An early and classic experiment in the field was conducted in 1914, when the New York Commissioner of Public Charities organized a study of the physical, mental, and social characteristics of 2,000 destitute men. Twelve men did the interviewing. One of the areas under investigation was the cause of the men's poverty. One of the interviewers, who happened to be a prohibitionist, attributed the men's destitution primarily to the excessive use of liquor, whereas another interviewer, who was a socialist, reported that their difficulty was due mainly to depressed economic conditions and factory layoffs. A more recent study by

Ferber and Wales, in connection with the public's attitude toward prefabricated housing, showed that the responses were definitely influenced by the interviewer's own bias toward such housing.[32]

In view of the foregoing, it is vital that each interviewer be made aware of the effects of bias upon evaluations. Each interviewer must seek to know fully himself and his own prejudices so that he can discount these biases when appraising people in the interview.

Past Is Clue to Future

The most accurate guide to how a person will perform in the future can be obtained by reviewing what he has done in the past. Most people's fundamental personalities, attitudes, and ways of behaving are developed early in life. In analyzing a person's background, it is necessary to explore his childhood environment, school and college experiences, previous job experience, social life and recreations, present family life, health, and financial picture. It is unsound for the interviewer to draw categorical and dogmatic conclusions from a single incident. If the applicant failed on one job, it does not necessarily follow that he will fail on all future jobs. If his grades in high school were only mediocre, it does not prove that the person has only a mediocre mentality. It is the whole pattern that counts. The interviewer must make tentative inferences from certain disclosures and then look for evidence in other facets of the person's life to substantiate the impression. If the inference cannot be verified by other facts, it should be rejected.

TYPES OF INTERVIEWS

Interviews can be classified according to the techniques and structure utilized. Such a method of categorizing interviews would be (1) planned, (2) patterned, (3) stress, and (4) panel.

The *planned* interview has also been referred to as the depth interview or the action interview. Basically, in this approach, the interviewer has outlined in advance the subject areas he wishes to explore. For the beginning interviewer this would be recorded in writing, although it would be unwise for him to refer to his notes frequently. The practiced interviewer knows from experience all the areas that must be explored. Subjects to be probed include home life, present domestic situation, education, previous work experience, social adjustment, attitudes, and recreational interests. The object is to get the individual to talk freely and expansively on these topics. The interviewer probes in depth for clues that would indicate potential success or failure on the job. In this interview it is also necessary to provide information about the organization, nature of the work, pay, opportunities for advancement, and demands made on the employee. The applicant must be given sufficient information to decide whether he would find the employment opportunity suitable to his needs and interests.

[32] Robert Ferber and Hugh Wales, "Detection and Correction of Interview Bias," *Public Opinion Quarterly*, Vol. 16 (1952), pp. 107–127.

The *patterned* interview, sometimes called the standardized interview, uses as its basis an extremely comprehensive questionnaire. It is therefore highly structured. Two of the best-known patterned interview procedures are the McMurry Patterned Interview Form[33] and the Diagnostic Interviewer's Guide developed by E. F. Wonderlic. McMurry has prepared different interview forms for office and factory jobs, for sales positions, and for executive positions. Since patterned interview forms ask so many detailed questions, no stone is left unturned in exploring the background, knowledge, attitudes, and motivation of the job seeker. In a survey of the interviewing practices of 273 companies, Mandell found that 72 (26 percent) used a patterned interview form.[34] Validation studies have revealed good results with this method. These favorable results are probably due as much to careful training of interviewers and sound selection procedures as they are to the form itself. Experienced interviewers generally do not like to be constrained by a rigid schedule of questions.

The *stress* interview was devised during World War II by the United States Government for selecting undercover agents for the Office of Strategic Services. In this type of interview the interviewer assumes a role of hostility toward the subject. He becomes an interrogator. He puts the man on the defensive and deliberately seeks to annoy, embarrass, and frustrate him. He seeks to cause the candidate to lose control of his emotions. Sometimes the candidate is assigned a problem of unusual difficulty and with considerable annoyances thrown into the situation. The object of the stress interview is to find those persons who are able to maintain control over their behavior when they are highly aroused emotionally. They must be able to act poised and well adjusted. They must be resourceful and have their wits about them in this situation.

The stress interview should be used only by a very well-trained person and only for those types of occupations in which action under stress is an essential ingredient of the job, for example, police work, spying, or secret agents. For the typical industrial or business situation this technique is generally inappropriate. It tends to inhibit open and complete response. When an interviewer deliberately adopts a hostile attitude toward the applicant, he finds that the latter, being on the defensive, will tend to guard his every response and give only socially acceptable answers.

In the *panel* interview there are three or more interviewers, often called an examining board, and a job candidate or interviewee. The panel technique is often used in various governmental jurisdictions (along with tests and other techniques) to select employees in professional and administrative classifications. It is alleged that the panel technique permits more comprehensive investigation of the applicant because there are several questioners and that the panel members, after the candidate has left the room, can discuss their individual interpretations of his performance. Presumably the impressions and biases of the interviewers can be brought out into the open and a consensus evaluation developed.

The panel technique has some serious disadvantages. The format is quite formal. It is harder to develop rapport with the candidate. He feels that he is under stress. Spontaneous responses are hard to get.

---

[33] Published by the Dartnell Corporation, Chicago.

[34] Milton M. Mandell, *The Employment Interview*, Research Study 47 (New York: American Management Association, 1961), p. 23.

PREPARING FOR THE INTERVIEW

A number of actions should be taken prior to the actual interview itself. Privacy is of utmost importance. The conversation between the interviewer and the interviewee must not be overheard. This is to insure unrestrained responses from the applicant.

Closely related to privacy is freedom from interruptions. Here is an illustration:

> The technical employment manager of one large company was repeatedly interrupted with telephone calls while he was talking to Bill Johnson. Whenever the phone rang, the manager asked Bill to leave the office until the call was completed.

Not only was this rude to Bill Johnson, but it also interrupted the channel of thought, so that it took several minutes to realign their thinking each time the interview was recommenced. Freedom from interruptions creates the impression in the individual that the interviewer considers him and what he has to say so important that he will devote undivided attention to the interview.

Enough time should be allowed to permit a complete exposition of all the facts necessary for a fair assessment of the job seeker. For a main employment office selection interview (not a preliminary interview), this would mean a time period of 25 to 30 minutes for candidates for unskilled and semiskilled work. On the other hand for higher-level jobs, such as technical, managerial, and sales, where personality and motivation are critically important, an allowance of one hour per interview is not excessive.

Immediately prior to the actual interview, the interviewer should study all available data pertaining to the applicant. This may include the application form, preliminary interviewer's comments, test scores, and so on. Certain facts may thus stand out and indicate the need for intensive investigation. Also, from past experience, the employment interviewer will know those areas that are critical to job success.

In order to insure that all of the vital areas have been explored, a guide sheet may be utilized. This is especially useful for beginning interviewers. The topics and items in Figure 10-5 can serve as a good check list.

CONDUCTING THE INTERVIEW

In commencing the interview, the employer representative must take the lead. His immediate objective is to establish a feeling of confidence and trust. He must develop a favorable emotional feeling or a feeling of harmony between the job-seeker and himself. This is called rapport. Generally this can be accomplished by showing that one is interested and going to be helpful and supportive in manner. The conversation should be opened with items that do not have sharp emotional overtones. Because the job-seeker is almost always under tension and apprehension, at least initially, the interviewer must create a relaxed atmosphere so that the individual will be able to express himself spontaneously.

Because a prime objective is to learn as much about the candidate as is necessary to make a reliable assessment, the interviewer must make skillful use of

Interviewer's Guide

A. *Appearance and Mannerisms*

Dress
Poise and bearing
Speech and voice
Facial expression
Neatness and cleanliness
Nervousness

B. *Early Home and Family Background*

Father's/Mother's occupation
Did parents live together or were
   they separated?
Numbers of brothers and sisters
Attitude toward father, mother,
   and siblings
Economic situation of family
Activities, hobbies, and interests
   when young
Social contacts, friends

C. *Education*

Did he actually graduate from high
   school, college?
Courses taken, major area of
   concentration
Reasons for choice of major course
   area
Rank in class
Courses liked best and least and
   reasons
Extracurricular activities
Method of financing higher
   education

Special recognition and honors
   achieved

D. *Work History*

Reasons for choice of jobs
Relations and attitude toward
   superiors on previous jobs
Reasons for changing jobs
Career goals
Type of work liked best
Method of obtaining previous jobs
Progress (salary increases, promotions,
   etc.) made

E. *Personality and Social Adjustment*

Marital status
Present interests and spare time
   activities
Spouse's interests and outlook
Financial responsibility
Emotional stability
Emotional maturity
His personal goals in life; level of
   aspiration
Attitudes toward work associates,
   toward authority
Sincerity
Initiative
Perseverance

F. *Health*

Past and present health problems
Observe physical limitations

Figure 10-5
Interviewer's Guide.

questions. He should use broad questions in order to encourage a thorough response. Thus, it is sound to say "Tell me about the duties, responsibilities and relationships of your last job." This is better than "Did you have to write reports? Did you take readings of the meters on the chemical equipment? How did you coordinate with other departments?" By opening up a general area for discussion in an interested but very broadly structured fashion, the interviewer will elicit those ideas that are most important in the applicant's mind. He will tend to speak about those things that are most critical to him. This will provide clues to his values and personality. If he wanders off the subject and wastes time the interviewer can gently channel the conversation by another question.

For the person who seems reluctant to speak, often a deliberate pause on the part of the interviewer can be stimulating. By looking at the individual in a warm but expectant manner, the interviewer can convey the idea that he is receptive and would like the man to amplify more fully.

Leading questions—those that signal a desired response—should be avoided because the applicant may then refrain from expressing his true feelings. Examples of leading questions are "Did you get along well with your supervisor?" "You would not object to shift work, would you?" Instead it would be better to say "Tell me about your last supervisor" or "How do you feel about shift work?"

By refraining from criticizing or acting shocked at the individual's responses, one thereby encourages him to reveal his true self. He will tend to talk about his failures as well as his successes if the interviewer does not show he is upset (by facial expression, voice, or nature of comments) by his revelations. The interviewer might indicate that others have had similar difficulties.

Immediately after the interview is completed and the candidate has left the room, the interviewer should record his impressions on a rating form. If several other interviews intervene, much will be forgotten. On the other hand it is generally unwise to engage in extensive note taking and impression recording during the course of the interview. Not knowing what is being recorded, in such a situation, the interviewee may become apprehensive. He may speak in a more guarded fashion henceforth. Occasional note taking of objective data is acceptable. However, recording of the subjective conclusions of the interviewer during the conversation should be avoided.

COMMON PITFALLS IN INTERVIEWING

It is pertinent to discuss some of the frequent errors made in selection interviewing. By being aware of these problems, a practicing interviewer can seek to minimize their occurrence in his work.

In judging people, probably all of us are, initially at least, prone to the condition called the halo effect. The halo effect is a situation in which a single prominent characteristic of the individual may dominate one's judgment of all his other traits. This can work in both a positive and negative fashion. Thus, if a person is neat, clean-cut, and alert, the interviewer might jump to the conclusion that he is also intelligent, ambitious, and dependable. Conversely if a person is sloppy and slovenly, the interviewer might conclude that he is also ignorant and lacking in essential skills and job knowledge. But these conclusions are not necessarily so. In rating an individual on each of a number of traits, the interviewer should have definite substantive evidence. If this has not been obtained, he must note that he cannot fairly judge certain attributes.

Previously, in discussing the psychological foundations of interviewing, the subject of interviewer bias was explained. Because man is not entirely a rational being, emotion, bias, and subjectivity cannot be eliminated. But it is essential that the interviewer be fully aware of his own attitudes and prejudices so that he can seek to discount them. Certain mannerisms or expressions of the applicant may evoke strong emotional overtones for the interviewer. These may be either positive or negative. But the key question is whether the matter has any real bearing on future job performance. Some interviewers subconsciously conclude that those who have interests and values similar to their own are therefore good prospects. In fact many organizations acquire a distinct "personality" because the employer tends to think that those who are just like himself are good people and those who have opposing attitudes, motivations, and values are not.

Finally, failure to listen is a common weakness, especially for untrained interviewers, who in their enthusiasm might tend to do most of the talking. But a talking interviewer can learn but little of the other fellow while he is vocalizing.

Questions for review and discussion

1. What is a selection test? What contribution can tests make to the employee selection process?
2. Because tests are objective and factual, could they be used in place of interviews for selection?
3. A personnel manager has stated that a certain test battery has been very accurate in predicting success for salesmen in his company. What reliance could we place in this same test battery for picking salesmen in another company?
4. Distinguish among the following kinds of validity.
   a. Content
   b. Concurrent
   c. Predictive
5. Distinguish between an aptitude and an achievement test.
6. Discuss the serious problems involved in the use of personality tests for selection purposes. Give and evaluate the various techniques that can be used to obtain information about a job applicant's personality and temperament.
7. What kinds of information about an applicant can be reasonably adequately obtained via the interview? What information cannot be adequately obtained and had better be gained by other methods?
8. Is there any way that the effect of interviewer bias can be minimized?
9. How can an interviewer obtain willing and full responses from an interviewee?
10. Of what value is a probing into the applicant's early home and family life?
11. Do you feel that there is a moral limit to how far a company should delve into a person's life by means of tests and interviews? Discuss.

Case problems

PROBLEM 1

The XYZ Company manufactures a wide diversity of industrial and consumer products. Each year it hires approximately twenty-five college graduates (engineering, business administration, and liberal arts graduates) by sending its college-relations manager to about fifteen college campuses to recruit graduating seniors. In a conversation with a college professor, the college-relations manager made the following statement:

"I have been doing nearly all of the college recruiting for my company for the past ten years. I have full authority to hire these new graduates. My company does not think it is necessary to invite the best prospects to the home plant for further interviews by other managers (as many other companies do). I allow one half hour for each interview. In that length of time I am able to make a pretty accurate evaluation of the prospect. Although I have full authority to hire on the spot, I generally wait until I return to my office. At that time I review my written notes on all the better persons whom I interviewed and then send out letters containing offers of employment. I have been quite happy with this method of hiring. My company has found it to be an economical and practical procedure."

Question

Evaluate this approach to the hiring of college graduates.

PROBLEM 2

The Ventnor Corporation is a growing firm that owns and operates three department stores in an urban area of 400,000 population in the East. It was established fifteen years ago by the current president.

The second person in the past year to hold the position of director of merchandising has just quit. In fact both of these individuals would have been asked to resign if they had not seen the handwriting on the wall and left voluntarily.

The occasion of the resignation of the second director of merchandising has prompted the president to call a meeting of the executive vice-president, the director of personnel, and himself to diagnose the problem of high turnover of managers hired from the outside and to come up with a course of corrective action. In the past two years nine middle- and top-level managers have either quit voluntarily or been asked to leave.

When the meeting convenes the director of personnel reviews the process of recruitment and selection. Candidates have been obtained both from a private employment agency and from responses to advertisements in newspapers and trade journals. Selection instruments consist of an application form, three tests (a mental ability test plus two personality tests), limited reference checking, and interviews with the executives concerned with the position involved.

The executive vice-president feels that they have made some errors of judgment in hiring certain individuals. Their resumes looked good and they talked as if they knew their work but a few weeks on the job often revealed their inability to get results. He says that the assistant store manager of the downtown store, hired last year, talked a good line but accomplished little on the job.

The president wonders if insufficient attention has been given to matching up the person with the job requirements. "At least on the surface it seemed that all those hired had a record of accomplishment in their careers but when dealing with other managers here they just didn't seem to fit into the organization. The controller hired in January lasted only five months. He came here and immediately started firing and demoting many persons on his staff. Some of these changes perhaps were necessary but he destroyed both morale and performance in the accounting department."

The director of personnel offers the view that they have placed too much emphasis on surface personality traits at the time of hiring and not enough on a proven record of performance in retail merchandising. Three out of the nine managers came from unrelated industries.

The executive vice-president points out that most of those hired had certain characteristics in common. They were all in their thirties and had moved around a great deal from job to job within a firm and from company to company. Many appeared to have moved up in terms of enlarged job responsibilities but some had simply made a number of lateral moves. All were ambitious and restless men. They tended to step on others in their drive to get ahead. Upon joining Ventnor most proved to be upsetting to the personnel with whom they had to work, especially so with their immediate subordinates.

In closing the meeting the president asks the director of personnel to investigate the desirability of engaging the services of a consulting industrial psychologist to review the managerial selection program and to help screen future candidates.

Questions

1. What is the problem here? Has the top management group decided what they want and how to achieve it?
2. Just how much risk is involved in hiring a major executive?
3. Offer possible reasons for the apparent failure of this management hiring program.
4. What responsibilities do the existing top management group have toward a newly hired manager? How can they influence his likelihood of success or failure?
5. What recommendations would you make to the president of this company?

Suggestions for further reading

BERGER, LANCE A. "Beneath the Tip of the Iceberg: How to Handle the Employee Selection Decision," *Personnel*, Vol. 54, No. 5 (September–October 1977), pp. 61–67.

CRONBACH, LEE J. *Essentials of Psychological Testing*, 3rd ed., New York: Harper and Row, Publishers, 1970.

DAPRA, RICHARD A. and WILLIAM C. BYHAM. "Applying the Assessment Center Method to Selection Interviewing," *Training and Development Journal*, Vol. 32, No. 4 (April 1978), pp. 44–49.

GUION, ROBERT M. "Content Validity: Three Years of Talk—What's the Action?" *Public Personnel Management*, Vol. 6, No. 6 (November–December 1977), pp. 407–414.

LEDVINKA, JAMES and SCHOENFELDT, LYLE F. "Legal Developments in Employment Testing: Albemarle and Beyond," *Personnel Psychology*, Vol. 31 (Spring 1978), pp. 1–13.

LOPEZ, FELIX M. *Personnel Interviewing: Theory and Practice*, 2nd ed., New York: McGraw-Hill Book Company, 1975.

McCormick, Ernest J. and Joseph Tiffin. *Industrial Psychology*, 6th ed., Englewood Cliffs, N.J.: Prentice-Hall, 1974.

Mahler, Walter R. *How Effective Executives Interview*. Homewood, Ill.: Dow Jones-Irwin, 1976.

Miner, Mary G. and John B. Miner. *Employee Selection Within the Law*. Washington, D.C.: Bureau of National Affairs, 1978.

Rogers, Jean L. and Walter L. Fortson. *Fair Employment Interviewing*. Reading, Mass.: Addison-Wesley Publishing Co., 1976.

11

Equal employment opportunity

This chapter deals with the special employment problems of nonwhites (predominantly blacks but also including some other groups)—Hispanic Americans, women, older workers, and handicapped persons.

Black Americans have experienced and do continue to experience lower earnings and much higher unemployment than whites. Although a few of the states had enacted laws in the 1940's banning discrimination on the basis of race, color, or national origin in regard to employment, housing, and places of public accommodation, it was the U.S. Supreme Court ruling in Brown v. the Board of Education, in 1954, that launched the great efforts throughout the nation in subsequent years to rectify decades of neglect and discrimination. While Brown v. the Board of Education dealt with public school segregation, it marked a great shift in the historic attitude of the Supreme Court and it also paved the way for a change in the public consciousness and for the civil rights legislation of the 1960's. Public demonstrations and civil rights campaigns in the 1960's, most notably those lead by Martin Luther King, Jr., awakened the nation to the plight of black Americans and spurred the institutions of government to take action to help them gain equality of treatment in employment as well as in education, housing, public accommodation, and in voting rights.

Although women were granted wage parity with men by the Equal Pay Act of 1963 and granted equal employment opportunity by Title VII of the Civil Rights Act of 1964, it was not until the 1970's that they began to make substantial advances in the labor force. Each succeeding decade in the twentieth century has seen increased labor force participation by women of working age; however, they have been confined by custom and the forces of discrimination to the lower paying occupations until very recently. Only in the 1970's have women moved into the better paying managerial, sales, and professional occupations in any substantial numbers. As in the case of blacks, laws on the books are insufficient to achieve economic progress and employment parity. People must help themselves and campaign for improvement in their condition. For females, the women's liberation movement has been the mechanism for focusing public attention upon the need for change.

Quite recently the special employment problems of older Americans have received greater national concern. Historically America has been a youth-oriented culture. With an increasing average of the population comprised of older people, and with the formation of more organizations to represent them, we now witness greater awareness of the problems confronting older citizens in the labor force. Among these problems are difficulty in obtaining jobs, forced retirements at an arbitrarily set age, and persistent employer preferences for hiring and promoting younger workers. Younger workers are presumed to be more vigorous, less rigid in their ways, and more physically attractive.

Traditionally physically and mentally handicapped persons who could adequately perform certain jobs have been largely confined to their homes, to state-run institutions, and to sheltered workshops. But the Rehabilitation Act of 1973 requires those firms holding federal government contracts to take affirmative action to employ qualified physically and mentally handicapped persons.

Under the American free enterprise system with its theoretically open and free labor markets, the employer was historically able to hire, promote, and fire whomever and whenever he wished. If the typical individualistic employer of say, 1935 or 1945, were to be transplanted to the 1980's, he would be surprised and even shocked to learn that racial and ethnic minorities, women, older workers, and handicapped persons have acquired substantial employment rights by law. Today even benign neglect of protected groups isn't allowed (passive discrimination is outlawed). Employers must take affirmative action to make job opportunities available.

A profound change has been occurring in the workplaces of America because of the pressures for equal employment opportunity and affirmative action. The actors in this ongoing drama are employers, unions, employees, Congress and the President, the courts, government regulatory agencies, organized minorities and women's groups and even the general public.

In this chapter we shall examine the special problems confronting nonwhites (especially blacks), Hispanics, and women in the labor force. We shall study the principal equal employment opportunity laws and the applications and interpretations that give meaning to them. The problems of older and handicapped workers will also be discussed along with the laws pertaining to them. Then we shall explore the impact of equal employment opportunity concepts and laws upon personnel programs in the areas of recruitment, selection, testing, training, promotion, layoff, and seniority systems. Finally, we shall discuss the concerns expressed by many people of possible reverse discrimination resulting from vigorous application of affirmative action mandates.

THE SITUATION OF NONWHITES AND HISPANIC AMERICANS

In population and employment statistics published by the government, the nonwhite category includes blacks, Asian Americans, and American Indians. Blacks comprise nine-tenths of this classification. To a considerable extent both the economic progress and the economic problems facing blacks have been derived from their massive migration from the rural South to the big cities of the North and West. This mass movement began during World War II with the opening up of thousands of jobs in defense industries. The migration continued from the 1940's through the 1960's. Lacking the education and skills necessary to qualify for good jobs in an industrialized economy, many blacks obtained only laboring jobs or else filled the ranks of the unemployed. Even though many northern states had enacted antidiscrimination laws in the late 1940's and early 1950's, the black in the North encountered pervasive discrimination in job and housing markets. Even if qualified, he was often denied a decent job. Even if financially able, he was denied housing in good neighborhoods. His home and life pattern were confined more and more to the big city slums.

For a good many years the unemployment rates for blacks have averaged about twice as high as those of whites. Figure 11-1 shows, for example, that in 1951 the white unemployment rate was 3.1 percent while the rate for blacks and other races was 5.3 percent. In 1976, a year of high unemployment generally, the rate was 7.0 percent for whites and 13.1 percent for blacks and other races.

Year	Race	
	White Percent	Black and Other Percent
1951	3.1	5.3
1956	3.6	8.3
1961	6.0	12.4
1966	3.3	7.3
1971	5.4	9.9
1976	7.0	13.1

Figure 11-1
Unemployment Rates of Black and Other Races Compared with Whites, 1951–1976.
(*Source: U.S. Department of Labor, et al,* Employment and Training Report of the President, *1977. Washington, D.C.: Government Printing Office, 1977, Table A-18, p. 166.*)

The annual incomes of nonwhite families have consistently been much lower than the incomes of white families. For example, in 1954 the nonwhite median family income expressed as a percentage of white median family income was 56 percent. In 1964 it stood at 56 percent again, and in 1974 it was 62 percent of white median income.[1]

[1] Source: United States Commission on Civil Rights, *Last Hired, First Fired: Layoffs and Civil Rights* (Washington, D.C.: Government Printing Office, 1977). Table 3A. Nonwhites include Blacks, American Indians, and Asian Americans.

In addition to having higher unemployment rates and lower family incomes, nonwhites are most heavily concentrated in low paying occupations and under-represented in high paying ones. Nonwhites in 1970 constituted 10.7 percent of the total labor force in the United States yet, for example, 26.5 percent of all nurses aides and 22.6 percent of all farm laborers were nonwhite. Conversely, among high paying occupations, only 2.8 percent of managers and administrators and 2.5 percent of bank officials and financial managers were nonwhite.[2]

Hispanic Americans. Hispanic Americans are persons of Mexican, Puerto Rican, Cuban, and Central or South American culture or origin, regardless of race. In 1975, there were 11.2 million Hispanics in the United States according to the U.S. Census Bureau. They are the fastest growing segment of the U.S. population. This is caused by a very high birth rate and large scale immigration from Latin America.[3] In 1968 the median family income of Hispanic Americans was only 65.3 percent of the median income of white families and 71.6 percent of white income in 1974.[4]

Living in Poverty

Poverty in America is not confined to any one race or ethnic group. However, in relation to their numbers in the population, blacks are more likely to be poor than whites. In 1975, for example, 29.3 percent of all blacks (and other races) had annual incomes below the officially designated poverty level, while only 9.7 percent of whites had such low incomes.[5] (See Figure 11-2.)

Careful observers of the poor (both white and black poor) in America have

	All Persons		Family Heads	
	White	Black & Other Races	White	Black & Other Races
	Percent Below Poverty Level			
1960	17.8	55.9	14.9	49.0
1965	13.3	47.1	11.1	39.7
1970	9.9	32.0	8.0	28.1
1975	9.7	29.3	7.7	25.3

Figure 11-2
Percentages of Persons below the Poverty Level by Race, All Persons and Family Heads. (*Source: U.S. Department of Labor et al,* Employment and Training Report of the president, *1975, Washington, D.C.: Government Printing Office, 1977, Table G-9, p. 291.*)

[2] *Changes in Occupational Characteristics: Planning Ahead for the 1980's,* Report No. 691 (New York: The Conference Board, 1976), Table 4-2, p. 38.
[3] The 11.2 million figure does not count 3.1 million U.S. citizens of Hispanic origin living in the Commonwealth of Puerto Rico. Source: U.S. Civil Service Commission, *EEO Information on Equal Employment Opportunity for State and Local Governments* (Washington, D.C.: Government Printing Office, 1977).
[4] United States Commission on Civil Rights, op. cit., Table 4A, p. 82.
[5] The poverty level as defined by the U.S. Department of Labor was $5,500 per year in 1975 for an urban family of four. This figure is annually revised to reflect upward movements in the Consumer Price Index.

identified a "culture of poverty" that seems to describe the life style of poor people and that also distinguishes them from other more fortunate groups. Culture means a way of life or a design for living. Many writers claim that the life style of the poor is a major cause of their very low level of income and that their way of life is transmitted from generation to generation. Oscar Lewis, an anthropologist who has studied poverty in many countries and among different ethnic groups, claims that there is a commonality in the characteristics and behavior of the poor in all societies—irrespective of race. He says they have strong feelings of marginality, helplessness, dependency, not belonging, and of inferiority.[6]

THE SITUATION OF WOMEN

Although not a minority group in society, women traditionally have received minority-like treatment in the labor market. But in recent years this undesirable condition has been changing for the better.

In the nineteenth century the majority of people lived on farms. Women in the family engaged not only in domestic activities—cooking, sewing, housecleaning, raising children—but also participated rather fully in numerous chores on the farm. Our agricultural society had become transformed into an industrialized society by 1900. Families flocked to the cities and women's roles changed.

The proper place for the housewife and mother was in the home. The role of the husband and father was to work away from home in shops and offices during the daytime. Young, single women typically obtained employment as seamstresses, domestic servants, clerks, stenographers, or, if educated, as schoolteachers. Gainful employment, for most young women, was viewed as a temporary interlude between school and marriage. Marriage was most preferred and it conferred a beneficial social position in the neighborhood. To be a single woman well into one's 30's was considered most unfortunate. The modern concept of a career woman, whether single or married, was unheard of.

The traditional, limited role of women in the economic life of our nation has been changing rapidly in recent decades. Women's labor force participation rate has been steadily increasing for many years.[7] In 1947 the female labor force participation rate was 31.8 percent. In 1976 it was 47.4 percent.[8] Forces that have brought about this greater tendency for women to be in the labor force are later age at marriage, declining birth rates, labor saving devices in the home, greater prevalence of divorce, and better educational opportunities. Another factor that has become significant since the late 1960's has been the persistence of inflation. Inflation has eroded the earnings of male family breadwinners and forced wives into the labor market to maintain family living standards.

Although nearly half of all women over the age of 16 are in the labor force, their annual earnings are decidedly inferior to those of men. In 1974 the median

[6] Oscar Lewis, "The Culture of Poverty," in Marc Pilisuk and Phyllis Pilisuk, eds., *Poor Americans: How the White Poor Live* (Chicago, Ill.: Aldine Publishing Co., 1971), pp. 21–28.
[7] The labor force participation rate is the percentage of persons of working age (16 years and over) in the noninstitutional population who are in the labor force, either employed or unemployed (but looking for work).
[8] *Employment and Training Report of the President,* 1977, op. cit., Table A-1, p. 136.

weekly earnings of full-time women workers, ages 25–54, in the economy as a whole were only 60 percent of the earnings of men workers for the same age grouping. When we examine specific broad occupational categories we find the situation comparable. The median weekly earnings of women clerical workers, age group 25–54, were 65 percent of those of men, women operatives earned 64 percent as much as men, and female sales workers earned only 42 percent of the male figure.[9] These large differentials in earnings between males and females are only partially explained by discriminatory practices. Women are concentrated in less skilled, lower paying occupations. This is due partly to guidance practices in family and school which have steered young women toward these lower paying occupations and partly to hiring and promotion policies of employers which have denied the better paying jobs to women. Labor market data also reveal that, on an average, women are part of the labor force for a fewer number of years than men. The average married woman spends about ten years out of the labor force while caring for children. Because of this many women do not participate in as much organizational job training and benefit from fewer years of merit and seniority wage increases.

Women have been making progress, however, by increasing their representation in the higher paying occupations. For example, in 1962 women constituted only 5.5 percent of total employed physicians. By 1974 their percentage had grown to 9.8 percent. Among lawyers and judges women comprised only 2.8 percent of the total employed in 1962 but they had increased to 7.0 percent by 1974. Likewise they increased from 19.2 percent of total employed college and university teachers in 1962 to 30.9 percent in 1974. Despite these specific instances of progress, women still are predominantly concentrated in the lower paying occupations. In 1974, women comprised 78 percent of all clerical workers, 75 percent of hucksters and peddlers, and 92 of all waiters or waitresses.[10]

EEO LAWS AND REGULATIONS

The first serious national effort to ban discrimination in employment was launched in 1941 when President Franklin D. Roosevelt by executive order created a Fair Employment Practices Committee, which was active throughout World War II. The executive order stated that employers and unions had a duty "to provide for the full and equitable participation of all workers in defense industries, without discrimination because of race, creed, color, or national origin." The committee lacked statutory authority to require compliance with its orders, but it did settle thousands of cases by conciliation. Since 1945 every president has had a similar committee whose jurisdiction was confined to establishments doing business with the Federal government. Under President Kennedy the committee was given the power to apply sanctions and to cancel government contracts.

With regard to legislation, the states preceded the Federal government by nearly twenty years. New York State pioneered by adopting a general an-

[9] Deborah P. Klein, "Women in the Labor Force: The Middle Years," *Monthly Labor Review*, Vol. 98, No. 11 (November 1975), pp. 10–16.
[10] Stuart H. Garfunkle, "Occupations of Women and Black Workers," *Monthly Labor Review*, Vol. 98, No. 11 (November 1975), pp. 25–35.

tidiscrimination law in 1945. By 1960 sixteen states had laws with positive enforcement powers. By 1967 the number had grown to thirty-two states. These included practically all the states excluding the South.

Beginning in 1963 and extending over the next ten years, Congress has enacted a number of significant laws that clearly demonstrate a national commitment to prohibit discrimination in employment. Concurrent with this legislative initiative has been activity by the President of the United States and the executive branch of the government to eliminate employment discrimination by organizations holding government contracts and to effectively enforce the antidiscrimination laws passed by Congress.

Chronologically in the order of their enactment are the following principal equal employment opportunity laws and orders:

1. Equal Pay Act of 1963.
2. Title VII—Equal Employment Opportunity of Civil Rights Act of 1964, as amended by Equal Employment Opportunity Act of 1972.
3. Executive Order 11246 (1965) as amended by Executive Order 11375 (1967).
4. Age Discrimination in Employment Act of 1967, as amended.
5. Rehabilitation Act of 1973.

The key features of these laws, except for the Equal Pay Act of 1963, are given in Figure 11-3.

The entire field of equal employment opportunity is very dynamic. It is not an area of settled law with hard and fast regulations and legal precedents. Rather as regulatory agency rulings and U.S. court decisions are issued, the area is evolving and changing. It is important that personnel executives, corporate officials, and their legal counsels keep abreast of changes in this evolving field of law and practice.

Equal Pay Act of 1963

The Equal Pay Act of 1963 was in the form of an amendment to the Fair Labor Standards Act. The law is administered by the Wage and Hour Division of the U.S. Department of Labor. It provides that it is illegal to pay women less than men for doing the same work on jobs requiring equivalent skill, effort, responsibility and under similar working conditions. Of course, the law makes it illegal to pay men less than women as well. But the purpose of the law was to eliminate the then rather widespread practice in industry of having separate men's and women's wage scales with women's being lower. Exceptions to the equal pay rule are permitted where a differential payment is based upon a seniority system, a merit system, or a piece rate system.

Title VII—Equal Employment Opportunity

Title VII of the Civil Rights Act of 1964 is labeled "Equal Employment Opportunity." Title VII was strengthened by the Equal Employment Opportunity Act of 1972. Before delving into this law, a quotation of the Supreme Court of the United States in its landmark Griggs v. Duke Power Company decision is in order because it describes so well the tone and purpose of Title VII.

Act or Order	Title VII of Civil Rights Act of 1964 as Amended by Equal Employment Opportunity Act of 1972	Executive Order 11246 (1965) as Amended by 11375 (1967)	Age Discrimination in Employment Act of 1967 as Amended	Rehabilitation Act of 1973
COVERAGE	All private employers of 15 or more persons, unions with 15 or more members, employment agencies, educational institutions, state and local governments.	All organizations with federal contracts or subcontracts over $10,000, federal government employment.	All private employers of 20 or more persons, unions with 25 or more members, employment agencies, state & local governments, federal government employment.	All private employers having federal contracts or subcontracts over $2500.
PRINCIPAL MANDATE OF ACT	Prohibits discrimination in employment, including hiring, testing, upgrading, pay, benefits, training, and other conditions of employment on the basis of race, color, religion, sex, or national origin.		Prohibits discrimination against employees 40 through 69 years of age in regard to hiring, discharge, retirement, pay, conditions and privileges of employment.	Employer must take affirmative action to employ and advance handicapped persons as defined in Act.
ADMINISTERED BY	Equal Employment Opportunity Commission	Office of Federal Contract Compliance Programs of U.S. Dept. of Labor, Civil Service Commission for federal employment.	Employment Standards Administration of U.S. Dept. of Labor.	Employment Standards Administration of U.S. Dept. of Labor.

EXEMPTIONS FROM COVERAGE	Private membership clubs that are exempt from taxation.	Organizations not holding federal contracts.	Organizations not holding federal contracts.	Organizations not holding federal contracts.
ENFORCEMENT AND SANCTIONS	First, EEOC attempts conciliation. If no settlement, EEOC may sue in U.S. District Court. Aggrieved individual may also file suit. Court may enjoin the unlawful employment practice and order appropriate affirmative action including reinstatement or hiring, back pay or other relief.	Federal government may revoke present contract or disqualify organization from future government contracts.	U.S. Labor Dept. tries conciliation, may file suit in U.S. District Court. Aggrieved individual may also file suit. Court may compel employment, reinstatement, promotion, back pay.	U.S. Labor Department tries conciliation, firm may be disqualified from government contracts. Labor Dept. may file suit in court.
AFFIRMATION ACTION PLAN REQUIREMENTS	Not specifically required by law but affirmative action may be required by court order.	Each contractor with 100 or more employees and holding a federal contract for more than $100,000 must maintain affirmative action plan. Goals and timetables required.	Affirmative action not required.	Each contractor with 100 or more employees and holding a federal contract for more than $100,000 must maintain affirmative action plan. Goals and timetables *not* required.

Figure 11-3
Principal Federal Laws and Orders Against Discrimination in Employment.

The objective of Congress in the enactment of Title VII is plain from the language of the statute. It is to achieve equality of employment opportunity and remove barriers that have operated in the past to favor an identifiable group of white employees over other employees. Under the Act, practices, procedures, or tests neutral on their face, or even neutral in terms of intent, cannot be maintained if they operate to 'freeze' the status quo of prior discriminatory practices.

. . . Congress did not intend by Title VII, however, to guarantee to every person a job regardless of qualifications. In short, the Act does not command that any person be hired simply because he was formerly the subject of discrimination, or because he is a member of a minority group. Discriminatory preference for any group, minority or majority, is precisely and only what Congress has proscribed. What is required by Congress is the removal of artificial, arbitrary, and unnecessary barriers to employment when the barriers operate invidiously to discriminate on the basis of racial or other impermissible classification.[11]

Title VII, as amended, covers all private employers of 15 or more persons, unions having 15 or more members, employment agencies, educational institutions both public and private, and state and local governments. This law prohibits discrimination because of race, color, religion, sex, or national origin in all employment practices including hiring, firing, promotion, compensation, and other privileges and conditions of employment.

Title VII is administered by the Equal Employment Opportunity Commission (EEOC) which is a five-member independent agency appointed by the President with the consent of the Senate.

An individual who feels he has been the victim of discrimination must file his complaint with the EEOC within 180 days of the date on which the claimed unlawful employment practice occurred. In those states having a state law against discrimination that has positive enforcement powers, the aggrieved person must first file a charge with the appropriate state agency. After allowing 60 days for the state to act, the individual may then file his charge with the EEOC and at this point the Commission may assume jurisdiction. The Commission makes agreements with state agencies whereby the latter will cooperate in carrying out the purposes of the federal law. Upon taking jurisdiction over a case the EEOC conducts an investigation and attempts to settle the matter by conciliation. If conciliation is not successful, the EEOC may bring a civil action in a U.S. District Court in order to obtain restitution for the claimed violation. Also, a complainant may, if he chooses, file his own complaint in a District Court to seek redress.

Executive Order 11246

Executive Order 11246 was issued by President Lyndon Johnson in 1965 and was amended in 1967 by Executive Order 11375. The Order as amended bans discrimination in employment because of race, color, religion, sex, or national origin for organizations holding federal government contracts. The Order also bans discrimination in Federal government employment but our discussion will concentrate upon the application of the Order to government contractors.

---

[11] From decision of Supreme Court of the United States, *Griggs v. Duke Power Co.*, 401 U.S. 424 (1971). Reported in *Employment Practices*, (Chicago: Commerce Clearing House, March 18, 1971).

The Order covers all organizations holding government contracts or subcontracts of $10,000 or more. Each organization with 100 or more employees and a prime contract or a subcontract for more than $100,000 is required to maintain a written affirmative action program for each of its establishments. The concept of a "written affirmative action program" was first articulated in 1968 by the Office of Federal Contract Compliance Programs (OFCCP) of the Department of Labor, which administers the Order. Subsequent orders issued by the Secretary of Labor and the OFCCP have explicitly spelled out the requirements of affirmative action programs. Each agency of the government which grants contracts to companies is responsible for obtaining compliance with the rules and regulations. A non-complying company may be denied a government contract initially or it may lose its contract.

The government has placed a great amount of force behind its efforts to get organizations to design and implement affirmative action programs. While such programs are mandated for government contractors (private companies, universities, indeed all organizations holding government contracts), other employers would do well to meet the overall standards because under Title VII of the Civil Rights Act an affirmative action program may be required as part of a conciliated settlement with the EEOC or it may be ordered by a federal court in settlement of a case.

The key features of an affirmative action program are as follows:

1. *Policy statement*
   The chief executive must issue a written statement declaring that the organization will not discriminate because of race, color, religion, national origin, sex, or physical handicap [12] in recruitment, hiring, training, compensation, and promotion.
2. *Communication of Policy*
   The commitment to EEO policy must be disseminated to recruitment sources, subcontractors, relevant unions, and all employees.
3. *Assignment of Responsibility*
   A major executive should be given responsibility to plan, coordinate, and evaluate the on-going program.
4. *Work-Force Analysis*
   Analyze the present work-force to determine the number of each minority type, women and handicapped in each job classification, pay grade, and department.
   Analyze the relevant labor market for the kinds of skills utilized in the company to determine possible underutilization of particular minorities, women or the handicapped.
5. *Goals and Timetables*
   This is a crucial part of an affirmative action plan and the feature that has caused controversy. For each major job classification, management must set a numerical goal for the employment of minority, women, and handicapped employees in reasonable relation to their representation in the relevant labor force. Dates for achieving these goals must be established.

---

[12] Affirmative action for the handicapped is required by the Rehabilitation Act of 1973.

6. *Implementation*

Actions must be carried out in the areas of recruitment, selection (qualifications requirements, applications, interviewing, testing), upward mobility system, wage and salary program, benefits, maternity leaves, and layoff and recall policy.

7. *Internal Audit and Reporting System*

Gather data and evaluate progress toward meeting goals on quarterly basis. Take corrective action where needed.

8. *Support of Company and Community Programs*

Train supervisors in affirmative action requirements and their implementation. Provide job and career counseling to employees. Cooperate with community institutions in regard to such matters as day care centers for children, transportation, and housing.

Enforcement Guidelines and Remedies

Because the standards used in Title VII and Executive Order 11246 cases are very similar, we shall discuss together (as one) the criteria used by the administrative agencies and the courts for deciding cases under these two regulations.

Top management's good intentions are not sufficient to avoid prosecution for discrimination. The results of a company's actions and *not* its intentions are what determine whether it is discriminating. It is illegal to continue company policies and practices that have an adverse impact upon protected groups unless the firm can demonstrate that a practice is necessary for the safe and efficient operation of the business. Once a plaintiff (the aggrieved individual or group) shows a prima facie case of discrimination by demonstrating adverse impact upon a protected group (blacks, women, etc.), the burden of proof shifts to the company to justify its employment practice.

What is adverse impact? It is a concept which relates to the entire employment process in the organization wherein the protected group is treated significantly worse than the majority group in the organization in regard to hiring, job assignment, promotion and other employment conditions. For example, the plaintiff may demonstrate that the firm has a disparate rejection rate for blacks compared to whites. Or the firm may be using a restricted policy to exclude members of a minority group. Or in a private, nonclass action case the aggrieved person must show that he was qualified for the job but was rejected by the firm that is still seeking other applicants whose qualifications are comparable to the complainant's.

Language in Title VII and court decisions allows companies charged with discrimination to offer four kinds of defenses. These are:

1. *Bona fide occupational qualification reasonably necessary to the normal operation of the enterprise.* This exception to the proscription against discrimination has been very narrowly construed by the EEOC and the courts.
2. *Bona fide merit or seniority system.* For example, it may be legal to promote men ahead of women if men rank higher in seniority under a union-employer agreement.
3. *Business Necessity.* Here the company must establish, via overriding evi-

dence, that the discriminatory practice is necessary for the safe and efficient operation of the business.

4. *No adverse impact.* The company may demonstrate with data that it has not rejected minorities or women at a significantly greater rate than nonminorities or men.

Remedies.   When courts have found that discrimination has existed in an organization, they have ordered that the employer must "make whole" and restore the rightful economic status to the individuals involved. A firm may be ordered to hire individuals or reinstate them with back pay and seniority, and to promote people. If pervasive discrimination has been found in an organization, the courts may order that the employer "make whole" *all* persons in the affected class, not only those who filed charges. The court may also require the installation of a comprehensive affirmative action program.

AT&T Settlement.   An idea of the kind of remedies that can be fashioned is given by an examination of the AT&T case. In 1973 the American Telephone and Telegraph Company entered into a consent agreement with the Equal Employment Opportunity Commission and the U.S. Department of Labor that has constituted the largest settlement action in terms of dollar costs and number of people involved under the anti-discrimination laws and regulations. The following are the main features of the agreement.

1. Each Bell System company agreed to set up an affirmative action program. The program included goals and timetables for increasing the representation of minorities and women in job classifications where they had been underutilized (such as craft and managerial jobs). The plan also required goals and timetables to increase the representation of males in telephone operator and clerical jobs.
2. Minorities and women were given special transfer and promotion rights, if basically qualified, to move into craft jobs. Lump-sum payments of from $100 to $400 were paid to at least 10,000 minority persons and women upon their successful movement into these jobs.
3. A large number of women college graduates who had been hired between 1965 through 1971 and been placed directly in first-level (lowest) management positions were given the opportunity for special evaluations at the corporation's assessment centers to ascertain their potential for promotion to middle-management jobs. These women had originally been denied the change to participate in AT&T's fast-track Initial Management Development Program.
4. The pay of many nonmanagerial women was raised to ensure equal pay for equal work.

The first-year cost of this settlement was about $38 million. Additional wage-increase costs of $25 to $35 million occurred over the next five years.[13]

[13] Information on AT&T settlement is given in Ruth G. Shaeffer, *Nondiscrimination in Employment, 1973–1975* Report No. 677 (New York: The Conference Board, 1975); also *Equal Employment Opportunity Agreement Between American Telephone & Telegraph Co. and Equal Employment Opportunity Commission and U.S. Department of Labor* January 18, 1973, Report 25 (Chicago: Commerce Clearing House).

OLDER WORKERS AND AGE DISCRIMINATION

There were 31.3 million persons, ages 45 and over, who were in the labor force in 1975. In comparison with the great public attention that has been focused upon the employment problems of women and minorities since the mid-1960's, only modest efforts have been directed toward the problems of older persons in the labor force. But this situation has been changing rapidly. With an aging population the interest groups representing older Americans have become stronger, more vocal, and more politically active.

Executives have traditionally preferred to hire and promote younger workers. Rosen and Jerdee devised a unique research design to uncover the biases and stereotyped views that managers hold of older employees. They presented *identical* case incidents to a large national sample of *Harvard Business Review* subscribers. The only difference in the incidents is that the central individual was labeled as a young person in the version sent to half the respondents and an older person in the version sent to the other half. The results of this survey study showed that the respondents perceived older employees to be inflexible and resistant to change. They were less likely to make efforts to retrain older employees. Also there was a tendency to deny promotions to older employees compared with identically qualified younger persons. Rosen and Jerdee concluded that some of the discriminatory bias was subconscious because a questionnaire filled out by the same respondents revealed rather supportive attitudes towards older employees in regard to management policies, affirmative action, and mandatory retirement.[14]

In his summary of research studies comparing older with younger workers on several dimensions, Fjerstad reports that older workers had fewer work injuries but they take longer to recover when injured. Productivity comparisons from various studies showed essentially no differences between younger and older office workers but they showed that among production workers, those under 25 and those over 55 produced slightly less than the 25–54 age group. Absenteeism and turnover were lower for the over 45 age group.[15]

National unemployment statistics reveal that males in the 45–64 age group have about the same unemployment rates as those in the 35–44 bracket. For women the 45–64 age group has a lower unemployment rate than the female segment of 35–44. To some extent seniority rules protect the older worker from layoff. However, those who do become unemployed have a much harder time finding a new job. The older workers have a much greater duration of unemployment than younger ones.[16]

Age Discrimination in Employment Act of 1967, as Amended

The Age Discrimination in Employment Act of 1967, as amended, covers workers and managers in any private business firm that employs 20 or more persons.

[14] Benson Rosen and Thomas H. Jerdee, "Too Old or Not Too Old," *Harvard Business Review*, Vol. 55, No. 6 (November–December 1977), pp. 97–106.
[15] Robert L. Fjerstad, "Is It Economical to Hire the Over Forty-five Worker?" *Personnel Administration*, Vol. 28, No. 2 (March–April 1965).
[16] Shirley H. Rhine, "The Senior Worker–Employed and Unemployed," *Conference Board Record*, Vol. XIII, No. 5 (May 1976), pp. 5–12.

It also covers actions taken by an employment agency and those taken by labor unions having at least 25 members. Also protected by the law are employees of state and local governments and those in the federal civil service. This law prohibits discrimination because of age against persons at least 40 but less than 70 years of age in regard to hiring, discharge, retirement, pay, conditions and privileges of employment. The law is administered by the Employment Standards Administration of the Department of Labor.

In the first few years after initial enactment of this law, there was relatively little litigation over age discrimination. However, in the severe economic slump of 1974–1975 companies laid off and discharged many salaried employees to cut payroll costs. Hourly paid workers were laid off too but union contracts required the process to be carried out according to seniority rules. Salaried employees often invoked the procedures of the law to try to protect their jobs.

Until the 1978 Amendments were enacted, the 1967 law protected employees in the 40-to-65 age bracket. The major purpose of the 1978 Amendments was to raise from 65-to-70 the age at which employees can be forced to retire. This provision became effective January 1, 1979. Excluded from the higher age limit for mandatory retirement are high-level executives who are entitled to annual pensions of $27,000 or more and tenured faculty members in college and universities. The extended age limit does become effective for such faculty members on July 1, 1982. For a great many years the mandatory retirement age for federal civil service employees was 70. The 1978 amendments eliminate this age limit entirely. Mandatory early retirement is allowed under the amended law, just as under the original 1967 Act, for bona fide occupational reasons. These exceptions are interpreted narrowly. Early retirements for air-traffic controllers, pilots, and agents of the FBI have been approved.[17]

Nearly all of private industry has used 65 as the normal and mandatory retirement age since the 1930's. The private sector geared its pension plans to retirement at 65. In doing so, it followed the example of the Social Security system which was enacted into law in 1935.

In Congressional deliberations in 1977 and 1978 proponents of raising the age for mandatory retirement to 70 argued that depriving older workers, who are still capable of productive work, of the right to work amounts to "ageism" which is discrimination akin to racism or sexism. Numerous medical authorities have stated that forced retirement often subjects workers to difficult adjustments that can have a negative impact upon health. A majority of workers in private industry aren't covered by a private pension plan. In 1974 only 21 million workers in the private sector were covered by pension plans. Thus, it is an economic necessity for many to work beyond age 65. Another reason for raising the mandatory retirement age to seventy is to induce more people to work beyond age 65 and not have them collect old age benefits under the Social Security system until a later age. This will reduce the heavy financial drain upon the system. A further reason for raising the mandatory retirement age is the increased life expectancy.

---

[17] Further information about the 1978 Amendments to the Age Discrimination in Employment Act can be found in "New 1978 Mandatory Retirement and Age Discrimination Rules," *Labor Law Reports: Employment Practices* (Chicago: Commerce Clearing House, April 6, 1978) and in Irwin Ross, "Retirement at Seventy: A New Trauma for Management," *Fortune*, Vol. 97, No. 9 (May 8, 1978), pp. 106–112.

In 1935 the average life expectancy at birth for both sexes combined was 61.7 years whereas by 1976 the figure had risen to 72.5 years.[18]

Despite the benefits of a higher mandatory retirement age, there are also some disadvantages. It will depress the employment opportunities for millions of young people who enter the labor market each year if older workers do, in fact, continue working five years longer. Within organizations promotion opportunities for young and middle aged personnel will be depressed if older employees and managers stay until 70.

In recent years there has been a pronounced trend toward early retirement, before age 65. In 1977, for example, 67 percent of all persons first receiving old age benefits under the Social Security system started collecting them at age 62.[19] Will this trend be reversed? Only time will tell. Very likely the percentage of the workers and managers who choose to continue after 65 will be modest for those working in organizations having adequate pensions benefits.

Organizations will have to face quite directly the problem of individual employees whose performance has declined materially with advancing age. Formerly if the individuals were in their early 60's, management could simply wait until age 65 when they had to retire. Now, if these individuals so choose they can stay until age 70 unless management decides to make a case against them and discharge them "for cause." In such instances management must carefully document its case in order to avoid a charge of discrimination under the Act.

THE HANDICAPPED

It is estimated that there are 12 million handicapped persons in the United States who are "employable." However, a large percentage of these are unemployed. The Rehabilitation Act of 1973 requires all private employers with federal contracts over $2500 to take affirmative action to recruit, hire, and advance "qualified" handicapped persons. Companies with 100 or more employees and holding a federal contract for more than $100,000 must maintain affirmative action plans for the handicapped. However, goals and timetables are not required.

Enforcement action by the Department of Labor in the first three or four years after enactment was slow. There has been confusion in the minds of employers as to just who is a handicapped person and how far they must go in accommodating their work places for such individuals. Questions such as these arise. What kind of jobs can an epileptic safely perform? Can a blind person do data processing work? How about an individual afflicted with cerebral palsy? What about mentally retarded persons?

With this law prodding them, companies have found that they can successfully utilize many handicapped persons that previously would have been turned away at the employment office door. Union Carbide Corporation is advertising sales-representative jobs in handicapped groups' newspapers and U.S. Steel Corporation has started recruiting at the National Technical Institute for the Deaf at Rochester Institute of Technology.[20]

---

[18] Labor Law Reports: Employment Practices, Ibid., p. 9.
[19] Irwin Ross, Ibid., p. 107.
[20] *Wall Street Journal* (January 27, 1976), pp. 1 & 11.

IMPACT OF EEO UPON PERSONNEL ACTIVITIES

Equal Employment Opportunity laws and regulations have had a profound effect upon the way companies, educational institutions, and public employers carry out their personnel functions. For the most part the standards for performance of such activities as recruitment, selection, and upgrading have been raised significantly. Many executives have resented the intrusion of the government into their human resource programs. However, EEO is firmly established as public policy and companies have found that raising the quality of their personnel programs to meet equal employment opportunity requirements has had generally beneficial effects in other areas as well.

To insure that EEO is really integrated into the fabric of an organization special efforts are required. The committment of top management and the requisite policies, programs and procedures must be communicated fully to all operating and staff managers. Training seminars should be given to familiarize key personnel with the laws, regulations, and important court decisions. Definite goals regarding hiring, placing, training, and promoting minorities and women can be set for each department of the organization. Audits should be conducted to ascertain progress toward meeting the agreed-upon goals. Then managers can be rewarded in relation to their achievement of these goals.

Recruitment

Many state anti-discrimination laws, with their enforcement regulations, are very explicit in prohibiting certain kinds of recruitment advertising and preemployment specifications. Title VII does not expressly prohibit specific kinds of specifications and inquiries; however, the EEOC and the courts look upon certain practices with extreme disfavor and their use may constitute evidence of intent to discriminate.

Help wanted advertising and specifications given to employment agencies or used internally in a company cannot indicate a preference or a limitation based on sex, age, race, color, religion, or national origin. An advertisement for "laborers under age 40" would be illegal. An airline cannot specify that it seeks only women for flight attendants. Likewise a company cannot advertise for women or female stenographers and thereby exclude males.

Companies should participate in career days and job fairs sponsored by schools and community agencies. To recruit blacks employers often find it advantageous to make special "outreach" efforts to attract inner city blacks. They can also make contacts with local chapters of the NAACP and the Urban League. Handicapped workers can be recruited through such establishments as sheltered workshops and aid-to-blind agencies. Word-of-mouth recruitment through present employees would not widen the employment base but it rather tends to perpetuate the current racial and ethnic pattern.

Selection

Personnel specialists must be careful, in designing an employment application form, that they do not include illegal questions. Likewise they and other managers must avoid unlawful inquiries in interviews. Among the inquiries ruled illegal by New York State's Division for Human Rights, for example, are the following:

- to inquire of a woman's ability to reproduce, and attitudes toward family planning.
- to require a photograph of applicant at any time before hiring.
- to inquire about religious affiliation.
- to ask age or date of birth, but it is legal to ask if person is between the ages of 18 to 70.[21]

It is of course reasonable to establish education and training requirements for jobs. But several court decisions and EEOC rulings have stated, loud and clear, that such requirements must have a manifest relationship to the jobs for which people are being hired. Subjective, unsupported judgments will not suffice. For example, an employer was guilty of racial job bias by reason of a requirement that applicants for a sales representative position must have a college degree. Business necessity was not demonstrated.[22]

Testing. Except for the more progressive and professionally managed organizations, a great many firms have accepted and rejected job candidates on the basis of arbitrarily set passing score cut-off points on tests when in fact management has not known whether those scoring above the cut-offs would be any more successful on the job than those scoring below. In short they haven't bothered to validate the tests they were using. They have exhibited implicit and unfounded faith in their tests.

Title VII, Equal Employment Opportunity does permit employers . . . "to give and to act upon the results of any professionally developed ability test provided that such test, its administration or action upon the results is not designed, intended or used to discriminate because of race, color, religion, sex or national origin."[23]

In order to provide guidance to employers the Equal Employment Opportunity Commission has issued guidelines for the use of testing. These provide that the use of a test that adversely affects hiring, promotion, transfer, or any other employment opportunity for those classes protected by the law constitutes discrimination unless the test has been properly validated and evidences a high degree of utility. The guidelines recognize three different kinds of validity (1) criterion-related validity; (2) content validity; and (3) construct validity. Criterion-related validity is the most widely used method of establishing the utility of selection tests. It requires the collection of job performance data and the correlation of such data statistically with test scores for a representative sample of people. The guidelines define the concept of "unfairness" and specify procedures to be followed to alleviate such a condition. "Unfairness" occurs when members of

---

[21] *Rulings on Inquiries Relating to Race, Creed, Color, National Origin, Sex, Age, Disability, Marital Status, or Arrest Record* (Albany: State of New York, Division of Human Rights, 1975).
[22] EEOC Decision, No. 70-402, January 19, 1970 as reported in *Labor Law Reports, Employment Practices Guide*, Vol. 1 (Chicago: Commerce Clearing House), paragraph 437.25.
[23] Section 703 (h) of Title VII of Civil Rights Act of 1964.

one race, sex, or ethnic group characteristically obtain lower scores on a selection procedure than members of another group and the differences in scores are not reflected in differences in a measure of job performance. When such a condition occurs, the selection procedure may unfairly deny job opportunities to members of the group obtaining the lower score. The guidelines cover not only traditional pencil and paper tests but also performance tests, training programs, probationary programs, interviews, and application forms.[24] If there are job progression structures for advancement, tests may be used at the entry-level grade to predict ability to perform at higher-level positions. But such testing is allowed only if there is a high probability that persons employed will in fact attain the higher-level job within a reasonable period of time.

In 1971 the U.S. Supreme Court issued a landmark decision in the Griggs v. Duke Power Company case. In 1965 the company had established a policy that to qualify for placement in any but the labor department an employee had to obtain satisfactory scores on both the Wonderlic Personnel Test (a mental ability test) and the Bennett Mechanical Comprehension Test, as well as have a high-school education. The required scores were set at the national median for high-school graduates on these two tests. A group of black employees challenged these requirements in federal courts on the basis that they were denied promotion opportunities because of these selection devices.

The Supreme Court ruled unanimously that the company had unlawfully discriminated against these persons. The court said that "if an employment practice which operates to exclude blacks cannot be shown to be related to job performance, the practice is prohibited." It further held that neither the school completion requirement nor the intelligence test was shown to bear a demonstrable relationship to successful job performance.[25]

In 1975 in Albermarle Paper Co. v. Moody, the Supreme Court handed down another important decision on testing that sharpens and strengthens the requirements. Albermarle Paper Company in North Carolina had been using for several years the Wonderlic Personnel Test and the Revised Beta (a non-verbal intelligence test) to select employees for admission into various skilled lines of progression from the unskilled labor pool. Four black employees had challenged the use of these tests in a class action suit. The Court specifically endorsed the EEOC Guidelines on testing and said that Albermarle's validation study was defective in four respects:

1. Use of a test in jobs for which it had not been validated. Each test had shown significant correlation for only a few of the eight lines of progression. But both tests were required for all jobs. A test may be used in jobs other than those for which it has been validated only if there are no significant differences between the studied and unstudied jobs. However, Albermarle had conducted no job analysis.

[24] *Uniform Guidelines on Employee Selection Procedures* (1978) adopted by the Equal Employment Opportunity Commission, the Civil Service Commission, Department of Justice, and Office of Federal Contract Compliance Programs, Department of Labor; effective September 25, 1978; Published in *Employment Practices Guide* (Commerce Clearing House, Chicago, Illinois). These guidelines supercede previous guidelines issued by the EEOC in 1966 and 1970
[25] Griggs v. Duke Power Company op. cit.

2. Using subjective supervisory ratings as criteria for test validation. Supervisory ratings can legitimately be used, but they must be used with far more care than was shown by Albermarle.
3. Usings tests for entry-level jobs that were validated only for upper level jobs.
4. Validating tests on a group of job-experienced white workers whereas the tests were given to new job seekers, who were younger, inexperienced and often nonwhite.[26]

It will be recalled from our discussion in the chapter on Selection Testing and Interviewing that there are four kinds of validity. They are (1) concurrent, (2) predictive, (3) content, and (4) construct. Concurrent and predictive validation techniques together are called "criterion-related" methods because they statistically correlate test scores with measures of job performance. No correlation studies are used for content and construct validity. The EEOC guidelines on testing express a decided preference for criterion-related studies and allow use of content and construct validity methods only when use of the criterion method is not feasible.

A criterion-related study must include (1) graphs and statistics showing relationship between tests and job criteria; (2) average test scores and criteria for all relevant subgroups, including minority and nonminority groups where differential validity is required; and (3) for each test a minimum passing score that is reasonable and consistent with normal expectations for the group being studied. In addition, where supervisory ratings are used for a criterion they must be founded upon careful job analysis information.

While criterion-related validity is preferred, content validity might be acceptable to the EEOC and the courts in those cases where there is too small a number of job holders, especially of different races and sexes, to obtain proper statistical data. Also, content validation is proper for an achievement or proficiency test. In this case the courts require a comprehensive assessment of duties and responsibilities of the job and an assessment of the required knowledges, skills, and other abilities required of the job incumbents. It must be demonstrated by systematic job analysis that the items on the test are actually derived from the job.

Although most of the attention by personnel people, the EEOC, and the courts has been directed toward validation of tests, it is well to point out that the rules on testing also apply to all formal, scored, or standardized techniques of assessing job suitability including personal history or background requirements, scored interviews, interviewer's rating scales, and scored application blanks.

The response of many companies to the high standards for testing imposed by the EEOC and the courts has been to abandon them. They just have not wanted to invest the time, talent, and money necessary to develop a testing program that meets professional standards. On the other hand, such a retreat does not really solve the problem because any selection technique can be challenged if it results in an adverse impact upon protected minorities and women. The burden of proof is upon management to show that it had rational reasons for rejecting job candidates. Such rational reasons may have been derived from tests that have

[26] Albermarle Paper Co. v. Moody 422 US 407, Reported in *Labor Law Reports: Employment Practices*, No. 86, (Chicago: Commerce Clearing House, June 30, 1975).

been professionally installed or from other sound evidence that relates job applicants' qualifications to job requirements.

Accommodating for the Handicapped. With the impetus given to companies by the Rehabilitation Act of 1973 to increase their hiring of physically and mentally handicapped persons, personnel officers need to reexamine existing hiring specifications to see if they can all be supported by accurate job analysis data or whether, in fact, deaf persons, persons with a missing limb, mentally retarded individuals, and persons with other handicaps could effectively do certain jobs. Would the modern bureaucratic organization have hired any of the following people?

- Tom was a young deaf man who liked to tinker with gadgets and who claimed he could invent new and wonderful things.
- Frank, a college graduate, could walk with leg braces only with great difficulty, but for the most part was confined to a wheelchair. Yet he had aspiration for executive leadership.
- Max lost both legs and one hand in a war, but he had a good education and a desire for a major executive job.

Because of arbitrarily established hiring standards, most firms probably would not hire any of these three individuals. Yet all were outstanding in their chosen fields of work.[27]

Training

Whether blacks, American Indians, women or the handicapped succeed on their assigned jobs after hiring is determined to a considerable extent by the kind of orientation, training, and supervisory leadership they receive. For employing disadvantaged blacks (as well as disadvantaged whites), many companies have developed very successful programs. Lockheed Aircraft Corporation, for example, found that a key to its success was careful attention to training. The people were trained for specific jobs and they were given more training than was generally required for the jobs involved. The instruction was by demonstration, doing, and by repetition. Small units of accomplishments were used and recognition was frequent. Also, a great deal of personal counseling was required. Lockheed noted that the trainees required an enormous amount of help with financial, family, and vocational problems.[28]

Women are of course no strangers to the world of paid employment. But the thrust in recent years has been to open up more opportunities in professional and managerial jobs. Hence, special attention should be given to offering them opportunities to participate in such higher level programs.

[27] The three individuals referred to are Thomas A. Edison, Franklin D. Roosevelt, and Max Cleland, Director of U.S. Veterans Administration in the administration of President Jimmy Carter.
[28] James D. Hodgson and Marshall H. Brenner, "Successful Experience: Training Hard-Core Unemployed," *Harvard Business Review*, Vol. 46, No. 5 (September–October 1968), pp. 148–156.

Performance Appraisal

Performance appraisal is really a systematic, organized way for making and recording judgments about the performance of employees. For those jobs in which the work is quantifiable and measurable, appraisals can be objective to a degree. Other jobs are difficult to measure, and the resultant evaluations of the job holders tend to be subjective. When it is used to select people for promotion or for layoff, companies can run afoul of the law of minorities and women are involved and they suffer an "adverse impact." The Zia Corporation, a contractor with the U.S. Atomic Energy Commission at Los Alamos, New Mexico was found by the court to have violated the law when it used supervisory ratings to decide whom to lay off and there was a disparate impact upon Spanish surnamed employees. The Court of Appeals held that Zia had violated the regulations because the ratings were not based on any definite identifiable criteria based on quality or quantity of work or specific performances that were based upon some kind of record. The ratings were faulted for being too subjective.[29]

The responsibility then rests with all organizations to insure that their employee appraisal systems are soundly designed and executed in order to satisfy the EEOC guidelines.

Promotions

Affirmative Action regulations require companies to keep adequate records to monitor upward mobility of "affected class" employees (those who suffer and continue to suffer effects of discrimination). Barriers to upward mobility must be identified and overcome. The selection standards and procedures for promotion should conform to EEOC guidelines. This means that there must be objective job descriptions and the standards required for promotion must be written and validated. The EEOC and the OFCCP have tended to hold that women and minorities should be given a chance at the better jobs if "minimally" qualified, even though they may not be "best" qualified (when competing with white males, for example).

Seniority

Seniority systems used for upgrading and promotion and for order of layoff have come under much attack by women and minorities in EEO litigation. Because these protected groups have moved into industry in large numbers only in recent years, it is obvious that they rank low on the seniority lists when it comes time to promote and layoff. Therefore, they will experience an adverse impact if employers abide by seniority rules as spelled out in union–employer contracts.

There has been some inconsistency in court rulings on seniority. In some cases they have ruled that seniority had a discriminatory impact and the seniority procedures had to be changed while in other cases they have upheld the rigid following of seniority rules.

For the use of seniority in promotion the Crown Zellerbach Company case served as a guide for several years. Here the company was ordered by the U.S.

---

[29] U.S. Court of Appeals, 10th Circuit, Brito v. Zia Company, 478F. 2nd 1200 (1973) as reported in Shaeffer, op. cit., pp. 27–28.

Court of Appeals in 1969 to give up its long established job lines of progression seniority system and adopt mill-wide seniority because the job-line seniority served to keep blacks in the lower paying jobs. Following this, many companies, for example, in the steel and trucking industries, negotiated agreements with their unions that provided for switching from job-line and departmental to plant-wide seniority. They also allowed greater transfer and promotion rights to all employees. More recently, in a case involving the Teamsters Union and a trucking firm, the U.S. Supreme Court in 1977 upheld a seniority system that resulted in whites having greater seniority rights for job upgrading than minority members where the system was created *before* Title VII was enacted in 1964. On the other hand in a case where discrimination arose *after* the law was passed, the Court did grant relief to the aggrieved employees.

The courts have rather consistently upheld "last-hired, first-laid off" policies that are spelled out in the seniority provisions of union–employer contracts. The Bureau of National Affairs reported in a survey of 300 organizations in a variety of industries that 88 percent of the companies did not give minorities or women any special treatment in determining the order in which employees would be laid off. Predominantly they used seniority as the guideline.[30]

REVERSE DISCRIMINATION

A few years ago a young man (an acquaintance of the author) applied to the telephone company for employment as an installer-repairman. He was turned down for this job but was offered a job as an office clerk—a job paying substantially less money than the craft installer-repairman position. He was told that the company had to increase substantially the number of women and blacks in its craft jobs, and hence was not hiring white males in the foreseeable future for these jobs, but he could have a clerical job because there were few white males in this job category. Because of examples like this, and countless comparable ones, many people have complained bitterly that companies are forced by government affirmative action rules to favor the hiring, job assignment or promotion of blacks over whites and of women over men.

Yet Section 703j of Title VII of the Civil Rights Act contains express language that seems to prevent preferential treatment for any individual or group on account of an imbalance which may exist in regard to the total number or percentage of persons of any race, color, religion, sex, or national origin in an organization in comparison to the number or percentage of such persons in the community or in the available work force. Despite this stated Congressional intent, the U.S. Department of Labor and the EEOC have required thousands of companies to hire and promote many more blacks and women in order to meet affirmative action goals and timetables. Most of the decade of the 1970's was a period of high unemployment. With scarce job opportunities this has meant that often whites and males were turned down in favor of blacks and females.

Advocates of affirmative action have asserted that "goals" are different from fixed, numerical "quotas" and hence are perfectly proper and legal. Laurence H.

---

[30] *Equal Employment Opportunity: Programs & Results*, Survey No. 112 (Washington, D.C.: The Bureau of National Affairs, 1976).

Silberman, who was Under Secretary of Labor from 1970 to 1973 and who helped devise minority employment goals for government contractors at that time, has had second thoughts about the value of affirmative action goals. He writes that the distinction between goals and quotas is more metaphysical than real. He claims that the elimination of goals or quotas would not wipe out the gains minorities have made over the years.[31]

If pressure from the government to increase the employment opportunities of women and minorities since the mid-1960's had not taken place, it is extremely doubtful whether any real change would have occurred. On the other hand, should a white person, who is better qualified than a protected minority person, be denied a job or a promotion simply because the company needs to meet a numerical quota or goal in order to retain its government contract? The problem of apparent reverse discrimination is very difficult to resolve. It is unlikely ever to be resolved to the full satisfaction of all contesting parties. The law says that employment decisions must not be made in favor of or against people on the basis of race, color, age, sex, or national origin. This still leaves employers considerable latitude to use other criteria in selecting people for hire or promotion. In the future when the various protected groups have achieved greater parity with non-minorities in employment status, there will be less pressure to give the minorities special preference to correct alleged imbalances.

In June, 1979 The United States Supreme Court ruled in favor of a racial quota in a case involving admission to a craft training program. Brian Weber, a white employee at the Kaiser Aluminum and Chemical Corporation plant in Louisiana had sued both the company and his union, the United Steelworkers, after he was denied admission to a craft training program. In 1974 the union and the company had signed a collective bargaining agreement that provided for creation of a craft training program and selection for the program on the basis of seniority. The agreement also provided that at least 50 percent of the trainees were to be black until the percentage of black skilled craft workers in the plant approximated the percentage of blacks in the community.

In reversing two lower Federal courts, the Supreme Court upheld the plan adopted at the Kaiser plant. Noting the narrowness of its inquiry, the Court held that Title VII does not forbid private employees and unions from voluntarily agreeing upon affirmative action plans that accord racial preferences in the manner used at Kaiser.

Questions for review and discussion

1. What reasons account for the generally lower earnings of black workers compared with white workers? Of women compared to men?
2. What is meant by the concept "culture of the poor?"
3. What steps must a company take to comply with government affirmative action requirements?
4. Some people argue that to change deep-seated beliefs such as racial prejudice or discriminatory attitudes toward women, it is better to reeducate the public and leaders of business rather than to force change by legal mandates and

[31] Laurence H. Silberman, "The Road to Racial Quotas," *Wall Street Journal* (August 11, 1977).

compulsion from government regulatory agencies. Discuss this issue of achieving change by education versus compulsion.

5. Are there any differences between the requirements of Title VII of the Civil Rights Act and Executive Order 11246? If so, explain.
6. How have equal employment opportunity regulations and court decisions changed the way employers carry out selection testing?
7. Give reasons for and against mandatory retirement at age 65 (or some other fixed age) for employees.
8. What changes have companies had to make in the various components of their personnel programs in order to conform to equal employment opportunity requirements?
9. Discuss the issue of possible reverse discrimination against nonminorities in order to meet mandated employment goals.

Case problem

THE ALTAMONT DIVISION

Most of the business of the Altamont Division of the Chittenden Corporation consists of contracts from the United States Department of Defense. The Division is located in a small eastern city of 40,000 population. Of this population, about 12 percent are blacks and 3 percent are Hispanic Americans. Altamont has total employment of about 1100. Only thirty-five of these are blacks, eleven are Hispanics, and one is physically handicapped. All of these are employed in lower level jobs. The total employment at Altamont has declined gradually over the past five years from a peak of 1400 to its present level because of cutbacks in government business. About 25 percent of the total employment is in scientific and technical jobs. There are no blacks or Hispanics and only fifteen women in these scientific and technical positions. The division employs many women but they fill primarily the clerical and blue collar assembly jobs.

Because it is a government contractor, Altamont is required to maintain an affirmative action program. On paper the program appears to commit the Altamont management to many activities to hire and improve the status of minorities, women, and the handicapped. Among the actions stated in the plan are:

1. Hire more blacks and Hispanic Americans.
2. Provide minorities, women, and handicapped equal opportunity to improve their qualifications for advancement and to participate in training and development for supervision. Likewise they will participate on an equal basis in training programs, reassignments, and temporary promotions.
3. There shall be no disparity in compensation received by minorities, women, and the handicapped in comparison with nonminorities for equivalent duties and responsibilities.
4. Sufficient resources will be provided to administer an effective EEO program.
5. There will be an EEO Committee whose function is to monitor and suggest changes in the program as required. Also an EEO Manager shall be appointed to coordinate the entire program. An important responsibility of the

Manager is to process employee grievances regarding equal employment opportunity. The EEO Manager reports to the Director of Personnel.

There is a pervasive feeling among many employees and managers in the Division that the affirmative action program exists only on paper and that little has been done to implement it. Privately the EEO Manager, who is black, says that top management has only given lip service to the program and doesn't really believe in EEO. He notes that no blacks have been hired in the past year. Only one black and one woman were permitted to be enrolled in the last supervisory training program and to date, neither has been appointed to a permanent supervisory position. (Both are being continued as acting-supervisors.)

The Director of Personnel retired two months ago. You have recently been hired as the new Director of Personnel and have been promised full support in your activities by the Division general manager. You find that the EEO program suffers because of budget limitations, a gradually declining level of employment in the Division, and a lack of understanding of EEO concepts throughout the organization generally. You have also determined that much of the EEO annual budget is spent by the EEO Committee (composed of the EEO Manager and five other management personnel) in attendance at training seminars and conferences given at resort hotels in Florida and California. You believe in managerial training but you wonder how much good has been accomplished from attendance at these conferences. Also, you have learned that women and minority employees have rarely filed discrimination complaints and grievances out of fear of being labeled troublemakers and thereby made more vulnerable to layoff.

Question

What actions would you, as the new Director of Personnel, take to improve the affirmative action program in order to have it meet its stated objectives?

Suggestions for further reading

DECKER, LOUIS R. and DANIEL A. PEED. "Affirmative Action for the Handicapped," *Personnel*, Vol 53, No. 3 (May–June 1976), pp. 64–69.

GATEWOOD, ROBERT D. and LYLE F. SCHOENFELDT. "Content Validity and EEOC: A Useful Alternative for Selection," *Personnel Journal*, Vol. 56, No. 8 (August 1977), pp. 402–407, 417.

GORDON, FRANCINE E. and MYRA H. STROBER. *Bringing Women into Management*. New York: McGraw-Hill Book Company, 1975.

HAUSMAN, LEONARD J. et. al., eds. *Equal Rights and Industrial Relations*, Madison, Wisconsin: Industrial Relations Research Association, 1977.

HENNIG, MARGARET and ANNE JARDIM. *The Managerial Woman*. Garden City, New York: Anchor Press/Doubleday, 1977.

HOLLANDER, JAMES. "A Step by Step Guide to Affirmative Action," *Business and Society Review*, No. 14 (Fall, 1975), pp. 67–73.

JACOBSON, CAROLYN J. "The Job Problems of Women Workers," *AFL-CIO American Federationist* (February 1977), pp. 12–16.

KREPS, JUANITA M. *Women and the American Economy: A Look to the 1980's,* Englewood Cliffs, New Jersey: Prentice-Hall, 1976.

PACE, LARRY A. and LYLE F. SCHOENFELDT. "Legal Concerns in the Use of Weighted Applications," *Personnel Psychology,* Vol. 30, No. 2 (Summer 1977), pp. 159–166.

PATI, GOPAL C. "Reverse Discrimination: What Can Managers Do?" *Personnel Journal,* Vol. 56, No. 7 (July 1977), pp. 334–338, 360–362.

SHAEFFER, RUTH G. *Nondiscrimination in Employment: Changing Perspectives 1963–72* (Report No. 589), New York: The Conference Board, 1973.

———. *Nondiscrimination in Employment: A Broadening and Deepening National Effort, 1973–1975* (Report No. 677), New York: The Conference Board, 1975.

WALKER, JAMES W. "Why Stop at 65?" *Management Review,* Vol. 66, No. 9 (September 1977), pp. 13–18.

Performance appraisal

In our daily lives we continually size up and form opinions of the people with whom we come in contact. In social relations this is done quite casually, often subconsciously, and rarely systematically. If one wishes to select a barber, dentist, physician, or a home builder, he may be somewhat more thorough in the manner in which he forms judgments. When we move into the area of cooperative group endeavors—in short, organizations—we find that supervisors must continually judge the contributions and abilities of their subordinates. Certain individuals are more adept at doing one type of work than another, certain ones cannot be depended upon to carry through an assignment to completion, others show great initiative and reliability and can take on projects with a minimum of supervision. The supervisor must frequently make decisions pertaining to the pay treatment of his employees, as well as employee placement, transfer, promotion, and individual development. Shall these personnel actions be based upon spur-of-the-moment decisions, or shall they be based upon carefully thought-out judgments made by a supervisor in collaboration with others and formulated in a systematic manner?

Because managers must make judgments of their employees almost constantly and for many reasons, the question naturally arises as to whether this should be formalized into a systematic performance appraisal program or whether it should be a haphazard, disorganized affair. Because evaluation goes on all of the time, the question is not whether to appraise employees. Rather it is *how* to evaluate people. The overwhelming weight of argument is in favor of the formalized performance appraisal approach.

Under a formalized appraisal system supervisors and managers are encouraged to observe the behavior of their people. They tend to be interested in their training and development. Judgments, often from many raters, are recorded on paper and placed in the individual's personnel folder. Decisions on personnel changes of status are not left to the vagaries of recollections of busy supervisors. Human memory is often unreliable. Hidden talents are sometimes uncovered, especially if a number of raters appraise the same individual. A formal rating procedure minimizes the likelihood of capable people being overlooked for training opportunities, pay raises, promotions, and new assignments. It is difficult to operate a large organization without some form of written appraisal plan. When comparing candidates for promotion from different organizational units, management must have written records of ratings so that sound decisions can be made. Sometimes the ultimate decisionmaker is high in the organizational hierarchy, and he does not personally know the individuals being considered for the post. He must rely heavily upon ratings, records, and written recommendations.

How widespread is the use of formal employee appraisal programs? In a survey of 426 manufacturing firms distributed across the principal manufacturing industries, the National Industrial Conference Board found that 67 percent had employee appraisal programs.[1] Another study of 567 firms known to have progressive personnel programs revealed that 60.5 percent had performance appraisal programs for supervisors and 45.3 percent had plans for executives.[2]

Evolution of Performance Appraisal

Systematic employee appraisal techniques came into prominence during and immediately after the World War I era. It was then that Walter Dill Scott succeeded in persuading the United States Army to adopt his "man-to-man" rating system for evaluating military officers. During the 1920's and 1930's, industrial concerns began installing rational wage structures for their hourly employees. They established the policy that in-grade wage increases would be based upon merit. The early employee appraisal plans were called merit-rating programs. Indeed, the term *merit rating* was by far the most widely accepted designation until the mid-1950's.

Most of the merit-rating plans from 1920 to the mid-1940's were of the rating-scale type with factors, degrees, and points. Indeed, the analogy between a point plan of job evaluation and a rating-scale plan of merit rating is very close.

Commencing in the early 1950's, great interest developed in the performance appraisal of technical, professional, and managerial personnel. This was tied in closely with the wave of interest in formal management development programs. It was recognized that appraisal, on a systematic basis, was an integral part of a well-designed development program.

[1] *Personnel Practices in Factory and Office: Manufacturing*, Studies in Personnel Policy, No. 194 (New York: National Industrial Conference Board, 1964).
[2] W. R. Spriegel and Edwin W. Mumma, *Merit Rating of Supervisors and Executives* (Austin: Bureau of Business Research, University of Texas, 1961).

At the same time that action in the area of performance evaluation of upper-level personnel has grown and intensified, interest in the rating of hourly paid workers has somewhat declined. A major resons for this is that in so many companies their pay and advancement are regulated by seniority. Management can still merit-rate the workers, but there is less opportunity to make use of these ratings.

Accompanying this change in emphasis has been a change in terminology. The older term, *merit rating,* has tended to be restricted to the rating of hourly paid employees. It has also been used more frequently when the object is to develop criteria for pay adjustments, transfers, and promotions. The newer terms *employee appraisal* and *performance appraisal* have the connotation of emphasis upon development of the individual. They are used more commonly to designate plans for white-collar, managerial, and professional personnel. They are broader in scope, because an appraisal interview with the ratee is almost always included in the appraisal program.

However, it should be pointed out that terminology in the personnel field is neither fixed nor rigid. Many other terms are commonly utilized in addition to the aforementioned. Among these are *personnel appraisal, personnel review, progress report, service rating, performance evaluation,* and *effectiveness report.*

Appraisal Defined

Performance appraisal is the systematic evaluation of the individual with respect to his performance on the job and his potential for development. Ordinarily the evaluation is made by the individual's immediate superior in the organization, and this is reviewed in turn by his superior. Thus, everyone in the organization who rates others is also rated by his superior. This is true for all except non-supervisory employees. As we shall see later there are some variations of this boss-rates-subordinate practice, but it is by far the most common arrangement.

Management by objectives has become very popular in recent years. The philosophy underlying this system is different from that of conventional appraisal. Management by objectives (sometimes called appraisal by results) emphasizes the setting of performance goals on a mutually agreeable basis by discussion between the individual and his immediate superior. The superior plays more of a supportive and coaching role than a judgmental one. This appraisal system is most commonly applied to managerial, professional, and sales personnel. In its broadest sense management by objectives is really a process of managing. It embodies the heart of the managerial art.

Applications of Appraisals

Employee appraisal is an essential part of effective personnel management. Its purpose and uses are as follows:

Employee Performance.   Appraisals are an aid to creating and maintaining a satisfactory level of performance by employees on their present jobs. When the actual evaluation process is followed up with an appraisal interview with each employee, it may contribute toward more effective or improved performance on the part of many individuals.

Employee Development.   The appraisal may highlight needs and opportunities for growth and development of the person. Growth may be accomplished by self-study, formal training courses, or job-related activities, such as special broadening assignments and job rotation. It should be clear that training and development of employees and managers strengthen the organization as well as aid the individuals.

Supervisory Understanding.   A formal and periodic appraisal encourages supervisors to observe the behavior of their subordinates. Encouraged by the proper top-management attitude, they can be motivated to take an interest in each person and to help him. If carried out properly the entire appraisal process can facilitate mutual understanding between the supervisor and his subordinates.

Guide to Job Changes.   An appraisal aids decision making for promotions, transfers, layoffs (where seniority may not be the controlling factor), and discharges (for inadequate performance). Systematic assessments of an individual by a number of raters, made over a period of time and recorded in writing, help to make this process reasonable and sound. It should give due consideration to the needs of both the organization and the individual.

Wage and Salary Treatment.   Many organizations relate the size and frequency of pay increases to the rating assigned to the employee in the performance appraisal.

Validate Personnel Programs.   The accuracy of predictions made in the employee selection process is often determined by comparing or correlating performance ratings with test scores, interviewers' evaluations, and so on. An indication of the worth of a training program can sometimes by determined by an analysis of employee performance after completion of a particular course of instruction.

In summary, the various uses for performance appraisal can be classified into two broad categories. One category concerns the obtaining of evaluation data on employees for decision-making for various personnel actions such as pay increases, promotions, transfers, discharges, and for selection test validation. The other main use is for employee development including performance improvement, training, coaching, and counseling.

BASIC CONSIDERATIONS IN APPRAISAL

When a rater evaluates someone, he tends to think in terms of what kind of a person he is and what he has done. Thus, appraisal plans require the rater to rate or score the employee on his personal traits and characteristics and on his contributions. Determination of the former is rather subjective, since different raters may appraise the same individual differently. Ann Smith's attitude toward the company may seem acceptable to one supervisor, but another boss may feel that Smith is a little too critical of company policies and scores her lower on that account. Employee contributions—what a person actually accomplishes on the job—can be more objectively ascertained. For many jobs the quantity of work produced is readily measurable, and it serves as an excellent gauge of the employee's performance. Such measures are available for a high proportion of direct labor jobs in industry. On the other hand, it is very difficult to measure the output of a receptionist, an engineer, a maintenance man, or a public relations director.

It might be readily conceded that an employer is primarily interested in assessing his employees' performance (that is, contributions), and therefore these factors should be counted most heavily. However, it is also apparent that such personal traits as cooperativeness, dependability, attitude, initiative, and ability to get along with others also have a bearing upon the employee's value to the organization. These characteristics affect a person's relations with his boss and with his coworkers, and they influence his effectiveness on the job.

In recent years management has tended to place the greatest weight in appraisal upon the actual results people achieve on their jobs. It is recognized that two people can have quite different personalities and yet be equally effective in their work. This can be true even on the same job or occupation.

Standards of Performance

In order to evaluate employees, it is necessary to have something against which to compare them. Thus, it is possible simply to compare one person with another. This in essence is the ranking method of rating. However, an approach that is likely to be more fruitful is to establish, in writing, definite standards of accomplishment employees can reasonably be expected to meet. Such a method makes it possible for both the supervisor and his subordinate to reach agreement on just what is expected in terms of performance.

A useful starting point for developing written standards is the job description. For professional and managerial personnel much can be gained by having the individual and his boss jointly develop the standard. For lower level employees, whose jobs tend to be very precisely defined and limited, the supervisor quite generally will inform his subordinate of his expectations in terms of quantity and quality of work, attendance, punctuality, job knowledge, and thoroughness.

The following are some examples of performance standards for management personnel. It will be noted that they are of necessity expressed in somewhat general terms. Judgment on the part of the rater is required to determine how well the individual meets these expectations.

For a controller: effectiveness of and improvement in accounting procedures; promptness with which management is informed of operating and financial results; soundness of policies and procedures recommended; quality, quantity, and timeliness of suggestions given to corporate office executives; quality, quantity, timeliness of suggestions and guidance given to plant management.

For a manufacturing manager: production schedules for his division are met; product meets established quality standards; injury frequency is less than 10.0 per hundred full-time workers; manufacturing overhead maintained within expense budget limits for level of operations; equipment down-time does not exceed 8 percent; efficiency of direct labor utilization is at least 90 percent of established standards; manager creates and maintains satisfactory level of morale within his division; manager provides adequate cross-training assignments for his personnel.

It should be pointed out that performance standards are relative to the group and to the organization. Not only are the needs of each organization different, but from one company to another the caliber of the manpower will vary. The expectations of management are higher in some companies than others.

Performance and Potential

Depending upon the purposes of the employee appraisal program, the evaluation may be directed toward the actual performance of the individual on his present job or toward his potential for promotion to a higher-level position. Quite often the rater(s) is asked to make judgments in both areas.

To determine a person's potential for taking on greater job responsibilities and for advancement requires a great deal of knowledge and skill on the part of the appraiser. The demands of the individual's present job may not give him an opportunity to demonstrate his full abilities. The question of a man's potential for growth can be answered fairly only when one considers "growth for what?" If an engineer is being considered for promotion to a supervisory position in the engineering department, he must possess a certain cluster of aptitudes and abilities. On the other hand, if he is being considered for a high-level staff position, he will need quite different qualifications. Thus, it would be folly to design an appraisal-rating form that simply asked the question "Potential for Promotion?"

Quite generally a supervisor can more accurately appraise the potential of a subordinate if he deliberately plans new and varied job assignments that will confront the person with a variety of problems and require him to demonstrate a number of his abilities.

Of course, the issue of employees' performance on their present jobs is often more urgent than that of advancement to higher-level ones. In this case the appraisal program will give major emphasis to contributions in comparison with established standards, to quantity and quality of work, to attendance, dependability, job knowledge, and to cooperation with others. Where present day-to-day job performance is more vital than the potential for future advancement, the appraisal program is more likely to be geared to improving performance on one's present job, wage and salary treatment, and training needs for the individual.

Who Does the Appraising?

The prevailing practice in nearly all private and public organizations is to have the supervisors and managers of each department evaluate the performance of each of their subordinates. Most commonly these ratings are reviewed by their immediate superiors. The presumption for such a procedure is that the person charged with responsibility for managing a department has the proper understanding of organizational objectives, needs, and influences. Being held accountable for the successful operation of his department or unit, he must, presumably, have control over personnel-administration decisions affecting his people.

However, there is another aspect to this picture. The view that a supervisor receives of his subordinates is not complete. Certain features of their behavior are unknown or only partially known to him. If given the opportunity, a person's work associates could supply considerable information and insight into his make-up. The military services of the United States use peer ratings in the service academies and in officer candidate schools. Peer ratings do not supplant ratings by superior officers; rather they supplement the customary types of rating in order to make decisions on promotions, job assignments, and selection for special training schools. In reviewing the many research studies conducted in connection with peer ratings in the military services, Hollander found that in some of the studies peer ratings were a more valid predictor of leadership performance than were ratings by superior officers. In summary he found that peer ratings yielded good reliability and validity and were a very useful appraisal method.[3]

Roadman reported on a research investigation in a large industrial corporation where peer ratings of managers, who participated in a 4-week middle-manager training program, were highly predictive of promotions two years hence. At the conclusion of the course the managers rated one another. The ratings were not available to the participants' operating divisions and hence could not have influenced the promotion decisions.[4]

Lewin and Zwany have reviewed the research on peer ratings. They state:

> In summary; peer evaluations are valid tools for predicting future success and are superior to all other measures available at the time of rating. The simplicity in administering and scoring peer ratings also results in a highly practical procedure.[5]

In summarizing fifteen selected studies of the predictive validity of peer evaluations, they determined that both the mean and median correlation coefficients were .41.

Peer ratings are widely used by professors in colleges and universities for promotion and tenure decisions. They are also used by physicians in clinics. However, peer ratings are rare in business and industry.

The group appraisal method, wherein each supervisor evaluates not only his own subordinates but also those working for other supervisors, can be very effective. This is especially true where the supervisors have interaction with one anothers' subordinates and have a chance to observe their behavior. Multiple judges can modify or cancel out a bias by the immediate supervisor (who makes the sole determination in most appraisal systems). Research experiments conducted by the Personnel Research Branch of the Department of the Army have demonstrated that the average ratings of a number of raters for each employee are more valid than a single rating.[6]

---

[3] E. P. Hollander, "Buddy Ratings: Military Research and Industrial Implications," *Personnel Psychology*, Vol. 7, No. 3 (Autumn 1954), pp. 385–393.
[4] Harry E. Roadman, "An Industrial Use of Peer Ratings," *Journal of Applied Psychology*," Vol. 48, No. 4 (1964), pp. 211–214.
[5] Arie Y. Lewin and Abram Zwany, "Peer Nominations: A Model, Literature Critique and a Paridigm for Research," *Personnel Psychology*, Vol. 29, No. 3 (Autumn 1976), p. 430.
[6] A. G. Bayroff, H. R. Haggerty, and E. A. Rundquist, "Validity of Ratings as Related to Rating Techniques and Conditions," *Personnel Psychology*, Vol. 7, No. 1 (Spring 1954), pp. 93–103.

Approaches to Appraisal

Over the years quite a variety of techniques have been created to appraise employees. These techniques can be classified according to the concept underlying each method. These approaches are as follows:

a. *Comparison against standards*
   The standards can consist of descriptions of various levels of behavior or the standards can consist of numerical scales. Examples are the various types of rating scales and check lists.
b. *Interpersonal comparisons*
   The ratee is ranked against others in his job or department on a global or overall basis. No written standards of performance are used.
c. *Setting of goals*
   Each individual's performance is compared against his agreed-upon objectives. This is the management-by-objectives method.
d. *Free-form essay*
   Performance is described and compared against generalized standards existing in the mind of the rater.
e. *Direct performance measures*
   Direct counts of output, quality, attendance, sales dollars, etc. are used. This approach tends to be combined with some of the other approaches such as comparison against standards and management by objectives. Direct performance measures account for only part of the total performance of most employees in most jobs. Qualitative gauges of performance are needed to evaluate the remainder.

APPRAISAL METHODS

We shall now examine the principal kinds of appraisal techniques that are in use. We shall also discuss their particular strengths and weaknesses.

1. Rating scales
   a. Personal traits and behavior scales
   b. Job dimension scales
   c. Behaviorally anchored rating scales
2. Management by objectives
3. Interpersonal comparisons
   a. Ranking
   b. Forced distribution
4. Check list
   a. Weighted check list
   b. Forced-choice
5. Essay
6. Critical incident

Rating Scales

Personal Traits and Behavior Scales. The personal traits and behavior scale technique is the oldest and most widely used of all appraisal methods. It is sometimes referred to as the conventional rating scale technique. Most commonly the rater, who is usually the ratee's direct supervisor, is supplied with a printed form, one for each person to be rated. This form contains a number of qualities and characteristics to be rated. For nonsupervisory workers typical qualities rated are quantity and quality of work, job knowledge, cooperativeness, dependability, initiative, industriousness, and attitude. For managerial personnel typical factors are analytical ability, judgment, leadership, creative ability, initiative, knowledge of work, and emotional stability.

Ratings scales can be continuous wherein the rater places a mark somewhere along a numbered line or they can have discrete steps, such as five steps ranging from poor to excellent. Figure 12-1 is an example of a conventional rating scale form that uses five discrete steps for each factor being rated.

One means of insuring that the rater has based his scoring upon substantial evidence is to leave space on the form after each factor and require that he explain the reason for each rating. In effect the rater is asked to give examples of the subject's behavior that justify the assigned rating. Also, sometimes certain direct measures of performance are asked for on the form such as number of absences or units produced.

One major advantage that all rating scale techniques have in common is that they require an evaluation of employee performance on several dimensions or factors. Research has demonstrated that one overall rating of work performance is not as effective in evaluating people as are several specific performance factors. Seashore et al. found a low degree of relationship among four individual job measures and overall job performance for 975 nonsupervisory employees working for a delivery service firm out of 27 locations throughout the country.[7]

The rating scale technique using personal traits and behaviors is relatively easy to construct and each rating form can apply to a wide range of job categories. Typically, a company will construct one form for managerial personnel, another for nonsupervisory office employees, and another for hourly workers. Rating scales are easy to use and understand. Various statistical summaries can be prepared from the rating sheets.

There are also serious disadvantages. The evaluation of the kinds of personal traits that are so commonly used—cooperativeness, personality, attitude, judgment, etc.—is a subjective process. Also, management is really concerned about job performance. This is the "bottom line" to use the financial analyst's term. People with different personalities may be equally effective in job performance. Numerical scoring gives an illusion of precision that is really unfounded. The rating scale technique is also subject to the well known errors of *halo effect, leniency or strictness, central tendency,* and *interpersonal bias.* These are described later under "Problems in Rating."

Job Dimension Scales. The job dimension technique requires that a different set of scales be constructed for each job or job family. The dimensions or factors

---

[7] Stanley E. Seashore, B. P. Indik, and B. S. Georgopoulos, "Relationships Among Criteria of Job Performance," *Journal of Applied Psychology,* Vol. 44, No. 3 (June 1960), pp. 195–202.

Job Knowledge

1	2	3	4	5
Serious gaps in his knowledge of essentials of job	Satisfactory knowledge of routine aspects of job	Adequately informed on most phases of job	Good knowledge of all phases of job	Excellent understanding of his job. Extremely well informed

Judgment

1	2	3	4	5
Decisions often wrong or ineffective	Judgment often sound but makes some errors	Good decisions resulting from sound analysis of factors	Sound, logical thinker	Consistently makes sound decisions, even on complex issues

Oral and Written Communication

1	2	3	4	5
Unable to express ideas clearly. Often misunderstood	Expresses ideas satisfactorily on routine topics	Generally expresses thoughts adequately	Consistently expresses thoughts clearly	Outstanding in written and oral expression

Attitude

1	2	3	4	5
Uncooperative, resents suggestions, no enthusiasm	Often cooperates, often accepts suggestions	Satisfactory cooperation, accepts new ideas	Responsive, cooperates well, helpful to others	Excellent in cooperation, welcomes new ideas, very helpful and enthusiastic

Quantity of Work

1	2	3	4	5
Falls below minimum requirements	Usually meets minimum requirements	Satisfactory quantity	Usually well exceeds minimum	Consistently produces superior quantity

Quality of Work

1	2	3	4	5
Poor quality, many errors or rejects	Quality usually o.k. Some errors or rejects	Satisfactory quality	Quality exceeds normal standards	Consistent high quality work

Overall Evaluation

1	2	3	4	5
Poor	Fair	Satisfactory	Good	Excellent

Figure 12-1
A Conventional Rating Scale Form Using Five Discrete Steps for Each Factor Being Rated.

used are taken from the job description. Each factor is a major job duty or responsibility. Thus, for a secretary, job dimensions might be: take dictation and transcribe, type letters and reports, schedule appointments and meetings, receive visitors, maintain petty cash fund, arrange hotel and travel reservations. Figure 12-2 is a job dimension rating form for an industrial nurse. Dimensional scales share many of the same strengths and weaknesses of trait and behavior scales. However, they do get away from the trait rating problem because they

JOB DIMENSION	Excellent	Good	Satisfactory	Fair	Poor
Render first aid and treat job injuries and illnesses.					
Operate therapy equipment.					
Provide medication for minor ailments such as colds and headaches.					
Teach first-aid classes.					
Dispense safety glasses.					
Maintain inventory of medical supplies and safety glasses.					
Keep records of treatment rendered.					
Drive automobile to transport employees to hospital.					

Figure 12-2
Dimensionalized Rating Scale for Industrial Nurse.

focus directly upon job duties. The rater is not asked to judge personality factors. Because a separate form must be created for each job it is more practical to use this technique in those organizations that have many employees in a very few job titles. Municipal police and fire departments would fit this criterion as would a district sales office or a restaurant.

Behaviorally Anchored Rating Scales.   The behaviorally anchored rating scale technique (BARS) is quite new. Development work by psychologists has been going on since the 1960's. The technique has considerable promise. It appears to overcome some of the problems inherent in regular or conventional rating scales. Because it is new and because considerable time and effort is required to construct a BARS, the technique has not been used much in industry as yet.[8]

A separate rating form must be developed for each job or job family. The rating form contains job factors or dimensions that are specific for each different job. Each job dimension contains seven or nine anchors which are specific statements that illustrate actual job performance.

To develop a BARS the active participation of the job holders and their supervisors is most desirable. First, the key job dimensions or areas of responsibility must be identified. Second, the job holders and their supervisors are asked to describe a great many examples of actual job behavior that pertain to various degrees of job performance. Third, these examples or incidents are classified under the various job dimensions or areas of responsibility. Fourth, these know-

[8] For explanations of development work and research into this method see: P. C. Smith and L. M. Kendall, "Retranslation of Expectations: An Approach to the Construction of Unambiguous Anchors for Rating Scales," *Journal of Applied Psychology*, Vol. 47 (1963), pp. 149–155; L. Fogli, C. L. Hulin, and M. R. Blood, "Development of First-Level Behavioral Job Criteria," *Journal of Applied Psychology*, Vol. 55 (1971), pp. 3–8.

ledgeable people are asked to rate each item of job behavior by assigning it a number on a scale from 1 to 7 or 1 to 9. A "1" would indicate the lowest level of job performance and a "7" or "9" would show the highest level. Then the average scale value for each incident of behavior is computed. If there is little agreement among raters on the scoring of particular items, then these are eliminated. The final seven or nine items of behavior (with their scores) become the anchors for each job dimension.

Figure 12-3 is the BARS for the job dimension "supervising sales personnel" for rating department managers in a retail store. In this situation comparable behaviorally anchored scales were prepared for the other eight job dimensions which were: handling customer complaints, meeting deadlines, merchandise or-

Figure 12-3
A Behaviorally Anchored Rating Scale for the Job Dimension "Supervising Sales Personnel" for a Department Manager of a Store. *From: J. P. Campbell, R. Arvey, M. D. Dunnette, and L. V. Hellervik, "The Development and Evaluation of Behaviorally Based Rating Scales."* Journal of Applied Psychology, *Vol. 57, No. 1 (1973), p. 17. Copyright 1973 by the American Psychological Association. Reprinted by permission.*

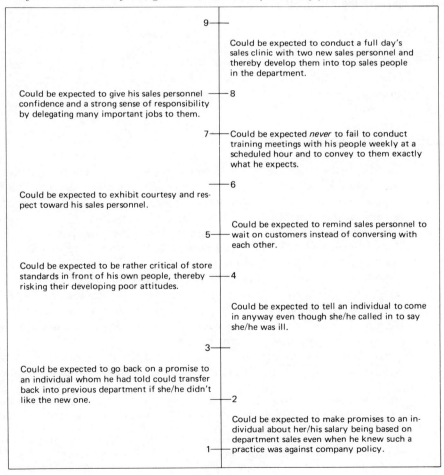

dering, developing special promotions, assessing sales trends, using company systems, communicating relevant information, and diagnosing problems.

An advantage of BARS is that the scales with anchor points are directly applicable to the jobs being evaluated. This aids feedback to the job holders for performance improvement and reinforcement for appropriate behavior. Because of employee participation in development they are better able to accept the feedback. Also the procedure for constructing the scales yields anchors that are very job specific and concrete. This contrasts with the often vague traits used in conventional rating scales.

On the other hand it is costly and time consuming to create BARS. It has been claimed that interrater reliability (that is, the degree to which different raters agree upon the proper assessment for a given set of appraisees) for BARS is better than for conventional rating scales. However, a review of several research studies has yielded mixed results in this regard. Likewise the results of leniency error investigations for BARS compared with conventional rating scales have been mixed.[9] Thus we can say that BARS holds promise but more development work needs to be done.

Management by Objectives

Management by objectives (MBO) has enjoyed wide acceptance in recent years. In fact, it has emerged as the most frequently used method for the appraisal of managers at all levels.[10] Because MBO is so very different in concept from the other evaluation methods we will discuss it later in the chapter after we have had an opportunity to explore problems that seem to be inherent in these other techniques.

Interpersonal Comparisons

Ranking. The ranking method requires the rater, who is usually the supervisor, to rank his subordinates on an overall or global basis according to their job performance and value to the organization. Thus, someone must end up as low person on the "totem pole" and someone must be high person. One aid to this ranking process is to have the rater choose the best and poorest performer first. Then he can select the best and poorest of the remaining employees and so on until he has evaluated all of his group. This is called *alternative ranking.*

Another ranking plan is to have the rater group his ratees into, say, the lowest third, the middle third (average performance), and the highest third.

The *paired-comparison* technique is basically a very organized way of obtaining a rank-order listing of employees. It necessitates the comparison of each employee with every other employee, one at a time.

An employee's standing in the final rank-order list is based upon the number of times he is chosen over the other individual in all the paired comparisons. If

[9] D. P. Schwab, H. G. Heneman III, and T. A. De Cotiis, "Behaviorally Anchored Rating Scales: A Review of the Literature," *Journal of Applied Psychology*, Vol. 28, No. 4 (Winter 1975), pp. 549–562.
[10] Robert I. Lazer and Walter S. Wikstrom, *Appraising Managerial Performance: Current Practices and Future Directions* (Report No. 723), (New York: The Conference Board 1977), p. 22. In this survey the essay method was second in frequency of usage and rating scales third.

there are N employees to be rated, then $N(N-1)/2$ separate comparisons must be made.

A major weakness of the ranking method is that it does not reveal the amount of difference between persons in adjacent ranks. Also, the technique does not consider specific components of behavior. Only the whole person is judged. There are no standards of performance. In addition it is difficult to integrate the rankings across several departments.

Forced Distribution. The forced distribution procedure has been designed to prevent supervisors from clustering their employees at the high end of the scale. Clustering at the high end has been a persistent problem, for example, in performance rating of military officers in the U.S. armed forces. Forced distribution also avoids clustering around the mid-point as occurs in some organizations.

The rater is required to distribute his ratings in a pattern to conform to a normal frequency distribution (or some other arbitrary distribution). Typically each supervisor must allocate 10 percent of his people to the highest category, 20 percent to the next, 40 percent to the middle bracket, 20 percent to the below average bracket, and 10 percent to the bottom grouping.

The forced distribution technique is based upon questionable reasoning. It would be a coincidence indeed if the *actual* distribution of performances in any given department conformed to a normal curve or any other arbitrarily set distribution. This technique brings to mind the college statistics professor who was teaching a graduate class of only four students. At the beginning of the semester he announced that there would be one A granted, two C's, and one F, and this is exactly how he assigned the grades at the completion of the course!

Check List

There are two kinds of check-list methods. One is the weighted check list, and the other is the forced-choice method. Both necessitate a considerable amount of developmental work within the organization.

Weighted Check List. A weighted check list contains a large number of statements which describe specific aspects of behavior that can occur in the job for which it has been designed. Each statement has a weight or score attached to it. In appraising an individual's performance, the rater checks those statements which accurately portray the behavior of the employee. Generally the check list given to the rater does not show the item weights. The scoring is done in the personnel office.

The weighted check list makes the supervisor think in terms of very specific aspects of behavior. However, the method is costly, in terms of staff developmental time, to install because a separate list must be constructed for every job or job family.

Forced Choice. One objective of the forced-choice method is to minimize rater bias. The rating form, which must be designed specifically for each general category of jobs, consists of several clusters of four statements each. Each statement describes an aspect of employee behavior. For each tetrad the rater must check the one statement that is most descriptive of the individual and one that is least descriptive. Within each tetrad two of the statements appear favorable and two appear unfavorable. The weightings are not known to the rater. Of the two positive statements only one actually is characteristic of high performers. If it is checked the ratee receives plus credit. Of the two negative appearing statements only one discriminates between high and low performers. If this one is checked as being least descriptive of the person, then he gets plus credit also.

Research studies have shown that there is less bias in the use of forced choice compared to the rating-scale procedure. Also when validated with other measures of job performance it has obtained good correlations. However, the forced-choice technique is seldom used by organizations. It is expensive to install. Also, the system frustrates or negates the supervisor's ability to discuss the rating with the employee. The scoring of the items is kept secret from the rater and he does not know which of the statements paired as to desirability actually counts positively for the individual.

Essay

In the essay method the rater describes the performance, traits, and behavior of the employee. The essay can be completely free flowing but more commonly the personnel office devises a form which asks each supervisor to answer in his own words such general questions as the strengths and weaknesses of the employee, leadership ability, technical effectiveness, promotion potential, and development needs. Very often the essay method is combined with the conventional rating scale form.

To do a sound job of appraisal, the supervisor must devote considerable time and thought to writing his analysis. This is both a virtue and a defect of the essay method. On the other hand it induces the rater to be observant in order to obtain sufficient information to write his essay descriptions. However, the technique demands more time than the average supervisor can (or will) spend. Also, the employee may receive a weak rating in comparison with others simply because his supervisor is a poor writer.

Critical Incident

In developing the critical incident system in a company, the major performance factors that are important for each broad grouping of jobs (e.g. sales, supervision, technician jobs) are first identified by persons who have close knowledge of the work. Then the supervisor is given a notebook containing these performance categories. Frequently throughout the year the supervisor must directly observe and record examples of behavior under the categories that indicate effective or successful action and those that show ineffective or poor performance.

This technique is a variant of the essay method. The rater obtains a great many specific examples of behavior so that his written evaluations for each factor can be factually documented. Vague generalities are avoided. This procedure can provide a sound basis for feedback to the individual and is thus valuable for developmental purposes.

A danger of this method is the very real possibility that it can lead to overly close supervision, with the boss "breathing down the necks" of his people. It may give the employees the impression that everything they do will be recorded in the boss's "little black book."

PROBLEMS IN RATING

Being conducted by humans, performance appraisal is frequently subject to a number of errors and weaknesses. Certain of these errors are more common in some appraisal methods than others, as will be revealed by the discussion to follow.

Halo Effect

The halo effect is the tendency of most raters to let the rating they assign to one characteristic excessively influence their rating on all subsequent traits. Many supervisors tend to give an employee approximately the same rating on all factors. The rating-scale technique is particularly susceptible to the halo effect. One way of minimizing its influence is to have the supervisor judge all of his subordinates on a single factor or trait before going on to the next factor. In this way he can consider all of the men relative to a standard or to each other on each trait.

Leniency or Strictness

Some supervisors have a tendency to be liberal in their ratings; that is, they assign consistently high values or scores to their people. This is a very common error in rating programs. Somewhat less common, but equally damaging to the usefulness of appraisals, is the tendency of some supervisors to give consistently low ratings. Both of these trends can arise from varying standards of performance among supervisors and from different interpretations of what they observe in employee performance. It is due to the subjectiveness of man. It can be partially overcome by holding meetings or training sessions for the raters so that they can reach common agreement on just what they expect of their men. Of course, if the employees in Department A are consistently judged higher than those in Department B, it is difficult to determine whether this reflects true differences in their abilities and contributions or whether it simply reveals leniency on the part of one manager and strictness on the part of another.

Central Tendency

Some raters are reluctant to rate people at the outer ends of the scale. Quite frequently this central tendency is caused by lack of knowledge of the behavior of the persons he is rating. He knows that management policy dictates that he must appraise his employees at periodic intervals. But if he should be unfamiliar with some of the individuals, he may play it safe by neither condemning nor praising. He would be hard pressed to substantiate such judgments. As we shall see shortly, under the heading "Organizational Influences," the way in which the appraisal information is handled by higher management sometimes induces supervisors to rate down the middle.

Interpersonal Relations—Bias

How a supervisor feels about each of the individuals working for him—whether he personally likes or dislikes them—has a tremendous effect upon his ratings of their performance. This is especially operative in those situations where objective measures of performance are either not available or difficult to develop.

In one working group consisting of professional employees in the government, there was a change of directors in charge of the force. A new director was brought in from a distant location when the previous head was promoted to another branch. Within the space of a few months, the new man had completely inverted the ratings of his people. Those who had been rated high by the previous director were rated unsatisfactory by the new man, and vice versa. One man who had been classified lowest in the group because the previous head had considered him unsatisfactory, was promoted to be second in command within the space of eighteen months. Although all the men were sincere, conscientious people, there was a difference in point of view and of personalities between the new director and most of them.

Experimental evidence to demonstrate the powerful force of interpersonal relations has been developed by Kallejian, Brown, and Weschler. In this experiment, which concerned a research and development laboratory, a clinically skilled interviewer interviewed 32 employees regarding their relations with their coworkers and superiors. On the basis of these interviews, he formulated an evaluation of the personality of the superiors who rated each group of employees. The interviewer then predicted how the superiors actually had rated these people. He did it on the basis of his knowledge of interpersonal relations because he was not familiar with the technical work of the laboratory. When his ratings were correlated with the supervisors' ratings on overall effectiveness the results were accurate at the 3 percent level of significance. When correlated for 17 specific characteristics of performance, his ratings were accurate at the 5 percent level of significance.[11]

Organizational Influences

Nowhere is the subjectivity of performance evaluation more glaring than when ratings change according to the way they are going to be used by management. Fundamentally raters tend to take into consideration the end use of the appraisal data when they rate their subordinates. Perhaps this is only natural.

If they know that promotions and pay increases hinge on the ratings, they tend to rate on the high side (they are lenient). Effective supervisors tend to go to bat for their employees. Besides it would look bad for a boss (and his relations with his subordinates would suffer) if other departments received higher pay increases than his group.

On the other hand, when appraisals are made principally for the development of the employees, supervisors tend to emphasize weaknesses. The whole focus is upon what is wrong with these people and what they have to do to improve.

[11] Verne Kallejian, Paula Brown, and I. R. Weschler, "The Impact of Interpersonal Relations on Ratings of Performance," *Public Personnel Review* (October 1953), pp. 166–170.

Actual experience with rating plans has demonstrated that supervisors will rate their people near the middle of the spectrum (average) if their bosses put pressure on them to correct the subpar performers (or get rid of them) and if they are called upon to really justify a rating of outstanding. In other words they will follow the path of least resistance, because they know that the "big boss" will be demanding of them in relation to those rated low or very high.

Experience has also shown that ratings tend to be higher when supervisors and managers know that they must explain their judgments to their subordinates.

APPRAISAL AND PERSONAL DEVELOPMENT

The appraisal process is quite properly viewed as an integral part of the development of people in the organization. Such development leads to improved job performance and the acquiring of new skills and knowledge by the individual. This qualifies him for broader responsibilities, more rewarding assignments, and promotion. A development plan should be tailor-made for each employee (whether he be an hourly worker, an engineer, or a manager).

A development program generally includes the following action steps by the supervisor or manager:

1. Analyze job duties and responsibilities. Discuss with employee to reach agreement upon these requirements.
2. Establish standards of job performance. Supervisor discusses these with employees so that there is common understanding and agreement.
3. Observe employee performance.
4. Appraise the employee. Judge potential for growth and advancement. Supervisor prepares appraisal report.
5. Supervisor conducts discussion of performance with the employee. May discuss the rating he received. Coaching and counseling may be done after filling out of periodic appraisal report (commonly annually). Often coaching is carried out informally on day-to-day basis as supervisor and subordinate interact on the job.
6. Establish a plan of action for employee development. Supervisor may initiate special assignments and projects, may send to formal training courses, may delegate more decision-making responsibilities and authority. Much of employee development must be self-initiated in a proper organizational and managerial atmosphere. Supervisor can stimulate growth by providing appropriate financial and nonfinancial incentives. Development plans should emphasize strengths upon which the person can build rather than trying to overcome weaknesses of character and temperament.
7. Periodically review progress with employee. Grant proper recognition for his accomplishments.

The foregoing process may be conducted with either little employee participation or with substantial participation. For example, does the subordinate have any say-so in setting the standards of performance or in creating a plan for his own development? Not only from the standpoint of respect for the dignity of the individual but also to gain commitment, the supervisor ought to involve his subordinates in the decision process.

A keystone of this developmental program for each employee is communication between the supervisor and the individual regarding his performance and behavior—in short, a discussion of the appraisal. Nearly all staff personnel men insist that every supervisor and manager must hold a postappraisal interview with each person to communicate the evaluation to him and to discuss plans and ideas for the future (especially improvement where such is needed). Yet most operating supervisors are very reluctant to conduct these postappraisal discussions. If company policy compels them to do it, they tend to do it sometimes informally so that the employee is not fully aware that it is an appraisal interview. Or some supervisors do it perfunctorily. Some do it only as long as the initial enthusiasm emanates from top management. Later they give only lip service to the discussions with their subordinates. Why does this reluctance exist?

Problems with Postappraisal Interviews

Operating supervisors and managers tend to resist postappraisal interviews because of the experiences they have had with them, both with their subordinates and with their superiors when they themselves have been appraised. Let us now look at the typical interview conducted according to the rules laid down in many company manuals.

Usually on an annual basis the boss calls his employees into his office one at a time for the appraisal interview. Both parties tend to build up emotionally for this. The boss plans what he is going to say, and the subordinate tends to be apprehensive about what he is going to hear. When the actual interview commences, the supervisor tries to put the individual at ease by talking about the weather, the latest big league ball game, golf, or his family. The employee knows this is just an interlude before getting down to serious business. Then the supervisor explains his overall evaluation in broad terms. He initially mentions some good aspects of the employee's performance. He may then give the employee a chance to express his views. Next the supervisor tells him his weaknesses and past failures. He allows the employee to explain himself. Then the supervisor explains what steps he must take to improve his performance. He may, at this point, ask for the employee's ideas on improvement. One variation of the procedure above provides an opportunity, before the boss announces his evaluation, for the person to tell how he would rate himself.

Let us now examine the sources of trouble with this approach. In the first place the employee is put on the defensive. He is on the "hotseat" and he knows it. When the boss, who is in a position of authority over the man, criticizes him, it is a threat to the employee's self-esteem and his integrity. His personal security may even be threatened by the process.

According to Douglas McGregor this conventional approach to the appraisal interview comes very close to a violation of the integrity of the individual. The boss is placed in the position of playing God. He is judging and at times criticizing the personal worth of the man.[12]

[12] Douglas McGregor, "An Uneasy Look at Performance Appraisal," *Harvard Business Review*, Vol. 35, No. 3 (May–June 1957), pp. 89–94.

There is a tendency for the supervisor to slip into the practice of criticizing those personality traits that annoy him. There is the case of the well-qualified and competent engineer whose boss picked on him in the interview because he did not smile more often. This trait did not affect his work performance, and being forty years old he would find it difficult to change anyway. The question may be further explored by asking what right the supervisor had to try to remake this engineer's personality. It is possible that in a few months time a new supervisor might have been put in charge of this man, and he would be perfectly content with his mannerisms.

The subordinate may disagree with his boss's rating and may fight back at the criticism leveled at him. But knowing the power his superior has over his job tenure, he will be at a disadvantage in doing so. In any case the interview will become unpleasant for both parties. If the employee is submissive, he may simply take the criticism with little visible reaction. The boss may misinterpret this passive behavior and assume the man fully agrees with him.

Employees and managers alike often say that they want to know where they stand in the eyes of their superiors. But what they really want is reassurance, approval, and support.

That a postappraisal interview is an emotionally charged experience and even a traumatic one for some is revealed by the following example:

> John, a man of 48, was clearly exhausted emotionally when we met at the restaurant. He had taught at this junior college for two years and had just, this morning, gone through his second appraisal interview with the director. John had been called on the carpet the previous year for the way he organized his courses. This time to prepare himself for the experience he had gone to his minister for words of advice on how to stand up to the criticism. Despite this encouragement and help John was clearly "beat" when I talked with him. His whole conversation was devoted to the way he had again been raked over the coals by the director.

Most personnel specialists would agree that the purposes of postappraisal interviews are to let a subordinate know where he stands in the eyes of his boss, to point out weaknesses so that the person can correct them, to point out strengths, and to show the person how to improve his performance. But research evidence shows that things often do not work out as planned. Based upon an investigation in a large industrial corporation that had prided itself for having a sound traditional performance appraisal system, Meyer, Kay, and French found that criticism has a negative effect on achievement of goals and that defensiveness on the part of the subordinate in the face of criticism causes deteriorated performance. In comparing actual interviews containing many criticisms with those having few criticisms it was found that goal achievement was poorer ten to twelve weeks hence for those receiving an above average number of criticisms. High criticism constitutes a threat to one's self-esteem and it prevents a meaningful, constructive relationship between superior and subordinate from emerging.[13]

[13] H. H. Meyer, E. Kay, and J. R. P. French, Jr., "Split Roles in Performance Appraisal," *Harvard Business Review*, Vol. 43, No. 1 (January–February 1965), pp. 123–129.

Approaches and Solutions to Appraisal Interview Problems

Nearly everyone agrees that there should be feedback from the supervisor to his employees. One of the very important responsibilities of a supervisor is to coach and counsel his subordinates. The most fruitful approach to the interview is dependent upon the situation, the job, the person, and the goals to be accomplished.

For the New Employee. If an employee is new to the company and if he is relatively inexperienced and untrained, he expects to have to learn a great deal before he is fully qualified and is accepted. Most organizations designate the initial learning time as a probationary period. The person knows he is on trial and so does his supervisor. If the probationary term is six months in length, the supervisor does not wait until the very end to talk to the person about his performance. On the contrary, from the very start he has made a concerted effort to orient the person to his new environment and to train him properly. In his day-to-day contacts the supervisor will coach the employee. He will give help on methods, techniques, and the details of the job. He will guide and mold his behavior to conform to the standards of the organization. If all of the foregoing is carried out with proper regard for the rights and feelings of the newcomer, he will readily accept the guidance and correction. He will be eager to be accepted. So this type of appraisal discussion should in ordinary circumstances post no great obstacles.

For Other Employees. For trained and experienced employees, for those who have worked for the organization for some time at whatever level they may be (worker or manager), certain general principles can be followed.

The success of the appraisal discussion depends to a large extent upon the climate that management in general and the supervisor in particular have established ahead of time. There must be an atmosphere of confidence and trust. The subordinate must know that his boss is *for* him, that he approves of him and supports him. In this kind of atmosphere, the individual knows that criticism and suggestions for improvement are meant to assist rather than damage him.

Prior to the discussion the supervisor must have done a very thorough job of evaluating the man's performance, so that he feels confident of his position.

The supervisor must concentrate upon results rather than personality traits. People can readily accept discussion of the objective facts of work schedules, outputs, accomplishments, reports completed, sales made, scrap losses, budgets, profits, and the like. Criticism and discussion of personality traits, mannerisms, and so on, are seldom fruitful. This usually causes resentment. Managers must recognize that a number of employees, each having different personalities, can all achieve satisfactory results. Suggestions for improvement should be directed toward the objective facts of the job. Develop with the individual joint plans for the future. Do not criticize the individual as a person.

The supervisor should try to capitalize upon a person's strengths. This may mean giving full range to a person's assets and skills. If a person is poor at doing detail work but good at assignments where breadth and vision are demanded, then it makes little sense to try to force him to be effective at detail work.

Finally the supervisor must recognize that he himself may have biases, idiosyncrasies, and faulty impressions. His concept of how people and things shape up is just one view. His concept is not the only one possible. There may be a number of ways of performing work and of reaching job and unit goals.

Frequent Coaching and Guidance.   The alert and effective supervisor does not wait until the end of the year to talk to his employees about their work and progress. As the needs of the situation dictate, he makes it a practice to praise Bill, who has done a fine job on his assigned project, to find out what help Henry needs because he has fallen behind, and to redirect Joe's seemingly scatter-shot types of efforts. On these occasions, if he deems it desirable, the supervisor may expand the discussion somewhat into other areas of the man's work and his interests and aspirations. Although not labeled as formal appraisal interviews, these conversations serve to regulate the work, motivate the individual, let him know where he stands, and provide an opportunity for the boss to coach his team members.

MANAGEMENT BY OBJECTIVES

Management by objectives has been designed to overcome certain of the inherent problems of traditional appraisal systems. It really constitutes a new way of managing. A major goal is to enhance the superior-subordinate relationship, strengthen the motivational climate, and improve performance.

The key features of management by objectives are as follows:

1. Superior and subordinate get together and jointly agree upon and list the principal duties and areas of responsibility of the individual's job.
2. The person sets his own short-term performance goals or targets in cooperation with his superior. The superior guides the goal-setting process to insure that it relates to the realities and needs of the organization.
3. They agree upon criteria for measuring and evaluating performance.
4. From time to time, more often than once per year, the superior and subordinate get together to evaluate progress toward the agreed-upon goals. At these meetings new or modified goals are set for the ensuing period.
5. The superior plays a supportive role. He tries, on a day-to-day basis, to help the man reach the agreed-upon goals. He counsels and coaches.
6. In the appraisal process the superior plays less the role of a judge and more the role of one who helps the person attain the goals or targets.
7. The process focuses upon results accomplished and not upon personal traits.

As it is applied in practice, certain variations from the methods, here described, occur. The procedure given here is closest to that formulated by Douglas McGregor.[14] It is also very similar to the work-planning-and-review method developed by a team of behavioral researchers at the General Electric Company.[15] The method recommended by the well-known management consul-

---

[14] McGregor, op. cit., pp. 89–94. See also Douglas McGregor, *The Human Side of Enterprise* (New York: McGraw-Hill Book Company, 1960), ch. 5.
[15] Meyer, Kay, and French, op. cit., pp. 127–129.

HIGH-PERFORMANCE TIRE & RUBBER COMPANY

Name: T. M. ROBBINS   Position: STORE MANAGER

| Area of Responsibility | Type of Measure | Levels of Performance | | Time Period | Plans for Meeting Objectives | Results Achieved |
		Present Level	Objective			
1. Retail sales	Units Dollars	350/mo. $25,000/mo.	450/mo. $32,000/mo.	1 year	Increase advertising flyers and newspaper ads. More customer safety checks in shop (tread wear, shocks).	
2. Operating Costs	Dollars	$7,000/mo.	$6,600/mo.	1 year	Control overtime and use of part time help; consolidate merchandise orders; reduce bad debts.	
3. Service Sales (Brakes, exhaust systems, shock absorbers, etc.)	Dollars	$5,500/mo.	$6,500/mo.	1 year	Increase advertising; use discount coupons for state inspections.	
4. Wholesale sales	# of tires	95/mo.	110/mo.	1 year	More contacts with dealers; discount and promotional allowances.	
5. Quality of Service	# of written customer complaints	7/year	3/year	1 year	Better training of mechanics; better scheduling of appointments; handle complaints more promptly.	
6. Safety	# of lost workday injuries	4/year	0/year	1 year	Safety training; maintain equipment better.	

Employee's Signature

Date

Supervisor's Signature

Date

Figure 12-4
A Management by Objectives Worksheet for a Tire and Rubber Company Store Manager.

tant Arch Patton is also similar, but it deviates in one important respect. Under Patton's formulation the superior does serve in the role of a judge. He rates his subordinate on how well he did in meeting the assigned targets and he tells him his rating.[16] Some writers emphasize that top executives meet with their immediate subordinates in groups to set goals for the company and for the major divisions. This process is carried on down the various echelons of the organization. Also the executives meet privately with their subordinates to establish individual goals.

Targets set can be both quantitative and qualitative. Thus, a manager of manufacturing for the ensuing year might set targets for himself (and his division) of a reduction in direct costs of 4 percent, reduction of spoiled product by 2 percent, and increase of return on investment to 14 percent. Qualitative goals may be to improve work flow, to institute better on-the job training, and to improve shop housekeeping.

Figure 12-4 is an example of an MBO worksheet that has been made out jointly by a store manager for a tire and rubber company and his immediate superior. The left hand column shows six major areas of the store manager's responsibilities. The present levels of performance are shown for each of these six areas. Next are listed the targeted objectives for each area. In this example the time period to reach each goal is one year. Finally, the worksheet shows some plans that have been discussed as possible ways of achieving these agreed-upon goals. In this particular illustration quantitative measures are available for each of the performance areas.

Management by objectives that involves mutual goal setting is most appropriate for technical, professional, supervisory, and executive personnel. In these positions there is generally enough latitude and room for discretion to make it possible for the person to participate in setting his work goals, tackle new projects, and invent new ways to solve problems. This method is generally not applicable for hourly workers because their jobs are usually too restricted in scope. There is little discretionary opportunity for them to shape their jobs. Their duties, responsibilities, and performance targets are imposed upon them by industrial engineers and supervision.

Management by objectives possesses a number of advantages. By participating in the setting of the goals, the individual acquires a stake or a vested interest in trying to meet them. The General Electric Company research referred to earlier revealed definitely greater accomplishment for those persons who set definite goals than for those who did not.[17] Both the superior and subordinate are on the same team working for a better functioning group. A person is not rated against a fixed rating scale. His targets and responsibilities are set and evaluated in terms of his particular situation and abilities. Defensive feelings are minimized because the superior is not a judge but a helper. Emphasis is on performance and not personality traits. The emphasis is also upon the present and the future, which can be controlled. In conventional appraisal the focus is upon the past, which cannot be altered.

However, it must be made clear that management by objectives is not a pan-

---

[16] Arch Patton, "How to Appraise Executive Performance," *Harvard Business Review*, Vol. 38, No. 1 (January–February 1960), pp. 63–70.

[17] Meyer, Kay, and French, op. cit., p. 127.

acea. A highly directive, authoritarian manager may find it difficult if not impossible to lead his people in this participative, human-being-centered, supportive style. The subordinate may try to set easily attainable goals in order to look good when he meets with his superior to review progress. If too much weight is placed upon quantifiable goals such as profits, costs, and efficiency, qualitative goals such as investment in human resources (training, health, and morale builders) may be downgraded.

Management by objectives has certain disadvantages when used for allocating salary increases and for promotions. Because goal setting and goal attainment is so individualized it is difficult to compare the performance of one person with another or to a standard to which everybody is held. Remember that in MBO performance standards are personal, not uniform throughout a department. Likewise MBO focuses upon short run goals and their attainment. It does not concentrate upon identification of traits that would qualify one for a new and different job.

Carroll and Tosi have summarized the conclusions of many research investigations into the MBO process. They report that the goal setting process is highly instrumental in gaining improved subsequent performance. The degree to which performance improves depends upon whether the goals are at the proper level of difficulty for the individual, whether proper time limits are set, and whether the goals are specific. Feedback information on performance is useful when it is timely, specific, and task relevant. Participation yields greater subordinate acceptance of decisions and with proper leadership can generate high quality decisions. Participation must be genuine not manipulative. Legitimate participation tends to yield higher satisfaction and performance.[18]

In the General Electric study referred to previously, the weight of superiority was on the side of the "work planning and review method" (appraisal by results). It proved to be far more effective in improving job performance than the traditional rating system. Attitudes and actions improved significantly. Subordinates stated that their managers gave them more help, were more receptive to new ideas and suggestions, and made greater use of their abilities and experience.[19]

A Conference Board investigation of on-going MBO programs in industry reveals that the most successful programs are those where it has become a pervasive approach in day-to-day management of the business. Companies that used management by objectives solely for performance appraisal, management development, or for compensation purposes were not as happy with the results achieved as those that used it as a total management system. The program, to be successful, must not be looked upon as an "add-on" concocted by the personnel department. It must be an integral part of the daily activities of operating managers.[20]

[18] Stephen J. Carroll, Jr. and Henry L. Tosi, Jr., *Management by Objectives: Applications and Research* (New York: Macmillan Publishing Co., Inc. 1973), ch. 1.

[19] Meyer, Kay, and French, op. cit., pp. 126–127.

[20] Walter S. Wikstrom, *Managing by and with Objectives*, Studies in Personnel Policy, No. 212 (New York: National Industrial Conference Board, 1968).

EQUAL OPPORTUNITY CONSIDERATIONS

The lessons derived from rulings by the U.S. Equal Employment Opportunity Commission and the courts are that organizations should design and operate their performance appraisal programs with far more care than they have in the past. If a personnel evaluation technique is used as an instrument to select people for promotion or layoff, then that technique may be considered to be an "employee selection procedure" which could come under the purview of the EEOC's "Guidelines on Employee Selection Procedures." If a company's promotion (or transfer, layoff, and discharge) actions result in a disparate or adverse impact upon any protected group such as minorities, women, or those in the ages of 40 to 70, then the burden is placed upon the company to justify its actions as a matter of business necessity.

Performance appraisal ratings can be used as criterion measures for selection test validation. In the landmark Albemarle Paper Company v. Moody Case (1975) the U.S. Supreme Court ruled that the supervisory ratings used by the company were not based upon well defined job related criteria.

Where performance appraisals were used as selection instruments for the purpose of personnel actions such as promotions or layoffs, several lower U.S. courts have held that these procedures violated Title VII of the Civil Rights Act of 1974. Conventional trait rating scale systems appear to be most vulnerable to legal challenge on the grounds of discrimination. This is because the traits are often vaguely defined, they are not specific to the jobs under purview and careful job analysis has not been done. Management by objectives systems appear to be most defensible because job performance criteria are integral to the method.[21]

ISSUES AND PERSPECTIVES

There is widespread acknowledgment among personnel specialists and upper level managers that sound performance appraisal programs can be beneficial to both the organization and the individual. However, there is also general recognition that many appraisal programs contain serious weaknesses. Principal weaknesses are resistance by supervisors to the devoting of adequate time and attention to appraisals, bias and favoritism in making evaluations, lack of reliability and validity in ratings, problems between supervisors and subordinates in discussing and acting upon the appraisals, and the tying of appraisals to the reward system.

Industrial psychologists and personnel specialists have strived mightily over the years to design appraisal systems that would yield good reliability and validity and that could be effectively used by managers. Progress has been made but the ideal system has not been found. The most appropriate system to use is governed by the specific objectives to be achieved. For development of the individual and performance improvement management by objectives has come to be recognized as the best system. MBO is very widely used especially for manage-

---

[21] Robert I. Lazer, "The Discrimination Danger in Performance Appraisal," *The Conference Board Record*, Vol. XIII, No. 3 (March 1976), pp. 60–64.

rial and professional positions. This system, however, is less useful as an evaluation technique to allocate rewards such as salary increases and promotions where interpersonal comparisons and comparisons against standards must be made.

If all categories of employees are considered, the conventional rating scale technique remains most popular. Its weaknesses can be alleviated by careful definition of the factors being rated, concentrating more on performance contributions and less on personality traits, including factors that can be objectively measured where possible, requiring written substantiations of the ratings, and using multiple raters.

Weighted check lists, forced choice, and behaviorally anchored rating scales all have considerable merit; however their acceptance by organizations is impeded greatly by their fairly high cost for development.

The interaction between the supervisor-rater and the subordinate-ratee is a critical part of the appraisal process. The discussion of the subordinate's performance is most effective when the supervisor is supportive, when the parties focus upon job results not personalities, and when there is openness and joint problem solving.

Should subordinates rate their supervisors? This is hardly ever done. In fact the issue itself is ignored in bureaucratic organizations. Yet very positive benefits could be obtained if management would work out procedures by which employees could fill out evaluation forms to rate their supervisors on those aspects of the work that can be directly observed by the subordinates. A prerequisite to success with such a program would be trust and honesty among management and the employees. Because subordinates view their supervisors from a particular perspective and because they may not appreciate all the demands placed upon their supervisors, ratings by subordinates should be properly viewed as only part of the input that makes up the total appraisal of the supervisors. Nevertheless it can be a valuable input that is totally ignored in most organizations.

Another issue for consideration is the relation of the annual salary interview and the developmental discussion. Current thinking suggests that appraisal discussions between the manager and his subordinate that are focused upon performance, development, and career goals should be conducted at entirely different times during the year from the discussion concerned with the individual's salary treatment for the ensuing period. The purposes of the two interviews are quite different. For salary administration a manager is normally provided a budgeted amount of money that he (or she) can allocate among the people in his department. He may use various criteria for assigning the different amounts of money. A significant factor is the performance of the employees compared with each other or compared with a standard. When the manager invites each individual into his office for the salary discussion, he has already made his salary decision. It has been approved by his boss. If there is disagreement between the manager and his subordinate as to the amount of salary increase, the manager tends to sell his decision. If the manager were to admit a mistake, he would have to go to his boss, acknowledge his error, and ask approval for an upward adjustment.

The atmosphere of the developmental interview should be totally different. Here the manager should be very supportive. There should be a free interchange of plans, suggestions, and goals. Neither party should be put on the defensive. Nor should bargaining for salary occur in a developmental interview.

Questions for review and discussion

1. What arguments can you give for the adoption of a formal employee-appraisal program in a business organization? Is such a program practical or necessary for a small organization of, say, 100 employees?
2. What objective measures can be used to evaluate performance in the following occupations: salesman of electronic computers, development engineer, foreman in a factory, machine operator in a factory, the president of a department store, stenographer?
3. Research studies have rather consistently shown that performance evaluation by one's peers yields good reliability and validity. Yet this appraisal method is rarely used in business, industry, or government. Why do you think this is so?
4. Explain the meaning of the following:
   a. Halo effect
   b. Central tendency
   c. Leniency or strictness
   How can these problems be overcome?
5. In some organizations the initial wave of enthusiasm upon the installation of a new appraisal program soon subsides. Appraisal forms are filled out by supervisors, filed in personnel folders, and then forgotten. Supervisors rarely conduct postappraisal interviews unless a person is doing very poor work. Supervisors look upon appraisal as an extra chore done somehow to satisfy the personnel department. What actions can you suggest to solve these problems?
6. Do you feel that every employee should be shown the appraisal sheet that has been made out for him? What are the advantages and disadvantages?
7. What are the problems involved in postappraisal interviews between superior and subordinate? How can these difficulties be alleviated?
8. Describe management by objectives. How does it differ from traditional appraisal methods? What are its advantages and possible limitations?
9. Why does current thinking indicate that appraisal for salary increases should be conducted entirely separately from appraisal for development of the person?
10. What are the advantages of Behaviorally Anchored Rating Scales compared with conventional rating scales?
11. In what ways might an organization carry out its performance appraisal program such that it conflicts with Federal equal employment opportunity requirements?
12. Employee appraisal systems utilize one or more of five basic concepts. One of these is comparison against standards. Name four others.
13. Why is the practice of having employees rate their supervisors so very rare? How might such rating be put to effective use?

Case problem

You are the director of employee relations for the McDavitt Manufacturing Company, which has annual sales of $25 million and total employment of 600. A little over a year ago you played a prominent role in the installation of a management-by-objectives program in the company. Among the main features of the program are setting of objectives, delineation of areas of accountability, adoption of performance measurement criteria, and appraisal discussions between superior and subordinate. You feel that your own department ought to be a model of the successful application of the program.

About a year ago objectives and plans were developed jointly by yourself and each of your subordinates. You are especially concerned at this time about the performance of the safety director, Henry Phillips. He has responsibility for organizing and directing the safety and health program. In carrying out his responsibilities he must work in close cooperation with the managers of the operating departments. Among the key components of the safety and health program are policies and procedures, engineering and hazard elimination, industrial hygiene, safety education and training, accident investigation and analysis, rules enforcement, and first-aid treatment.

Henry Phillips had been appointed safety director about a year and a half ago. At that time the accident frequency and severity rates were 60 percent above the industry average and an inspector from the Occupational Safety and Health Administration had cited the company for several serious violations of federal standards. When you held your first objectives-setting discussion with Phillips nearly a year ago, he had already made substantial progress toward improving the safety and health performance of the company. However, a great deal remained to be accomplished. At that time sound safety and health attitudes and behavior had not yet permeated all segments of management.

Shown below are the jointly established objectives set one year ago and the actual results achieved as of last month:

Objective	*Results*
1. Reduce number of lost workday cases incidence rate per 100 workers from 4.7 to 3.5.	Reduction to 4.2.
2. Reduce the lost workdays rate (severity) per 100 workers from 85 to 65.	Reduction to 75.
3. Personally conduct monthly safety meetings with plant supervision.	Goal has been met.
4. Insure that plant supervisors conduct short bi-weekly safety meetings with their people.	Only about 50 percent of meetings have been held.
5. Reduce health and safety grievances from 2 per month to 1 in 3 months.	Grievances average 1 per month.
6. Revise and update policy and procedure manual.	Completed.
7. Work with engineering department to correct noxious fumes in processing department.	Project initiated and one quarter completed.

You feel that Henry Phillips has the requisite job knowledge for his responsibilities. He performs well in developing plans, programs, and procedures, and in diagnosing problems. However, you feel that he should be more aggressive in selling his ideas to operating managers and in getting them to improve the safety performance of their units.

Henry Phillips will be coming to your office in about a half hour for an appraisal discussion.

Questions

1. How would you conduct the interview? What would you say? Work out a plan for this interview.
2. Role play this interview. Henry Phillips' viewpoint upon commencing the interview is that he has worked very hard during the past year to achieve the goals agreed upon and has made good progress. However, his efforts have suffered from a lack of full cooperation from many of the managers and supervisors in the operating departments. Safety and health of workers are usually given a low priority in competition with production and cost reduction goals.

MBO EXERCISE

A purpose of this exercise is to provide students an opportunity to learn how to develop performance objectives jointly by working with an individual job holder (student). Other purposes are to learn ways of measuring or evaluating job performance and to learn how to design an MBO worksheet that could be used in a real organizational situation.

Divide the class into groups of about 5-6 persons each. After each group is formed the members describe to one another a job that they have held or now hold. Then the group selects one person's job to be used for this MBO exercise. The group will interview the job holder and prepare an MBO worksheet.

The group should explore with the job holder the major responsibility areas of his job. A method for measuring or evaluating performance in each area should be identified. To enhance objectivity in performance evaluation it is advantageous to use quantitative measures of performance wherever possible. However some job components cannot be measured quantitatively so qualitative gauges to performance must be used.

Next, the current level of performance in each area of responsibility should be recorded. Then reasonable performance targets or objectives for the future should be jointly decided with the job holder. A time period (6 months, 9 months, one year, etc.) for achieving each objective should be agreed upon. There should be some discussion of possible ways of achieving each objective.

Each group should design and hand in to the instructor an MBO worksheet. Figure 12-4 may be used as a guide.

Suggestions for further reading

CARROLL, STEPHEN J., JR. and HENRY L. TOSI, JR. *Management by Objectives*. New York: Macmillan Publishing Co., Inc., 1973.

CUMMINGS, L. L. and DONALD P. SCHWAB. *Performance in Organizations.* Glenview, Ill.: Scott, Foresman and Co., 1973.

HAYNES, MARION G. "Developing An Appraisal Program," Part 1 and Part 2, *Personnel Journal*, Vol. 57, No. 2 (January, 1978), pp. 14–19; No. 3 (February, 1978), pp. 66–67 ff.

KELLOGG, MARION S. *What to Do About Performance Appraisal,* rev. ed. New York: American Management Associations, 1975.

KOONTZ, HAROLD. *Appraising Managers As Managers.* New York: McGraw-Hill Book Company, 1971.

LAZER, ROBERT I. and WALTER S. WIKSTROM. *Appraising Managerial Performance: Current Practices and Future Directions* (Report No. 723), New York: The Conference Board, 1977.

LEVINSON, HARRY. "Appraisal of *What* Performance?" *Harvard Business Review*, Vol. 54, No. 4 (July–August 1976), pp. 30–40.

OBERG, WINSTON. "Make Performance Appraisal Relevant." *Harvard Business Review*, Vol. 50, No. 1 (January–February, 1972), pp. 61–67.

ODIORNE, GEORGE S. "MBO in the 1980's: Will It Survive?" *Management Review*, July, 1977.

SCHWAB, DONALD P., H. G. HENEMAN III, and T. A. DeCOTIIS. "Behaviorally Anchored Rating Scales: A Review of the Literature." *Personnel Psychology*, Vol. 28 (1975), pp. 549–562.

WINSTANLEY, NATHAN B. "Performance Appraisals and Management Development: A Systems Approach," *The Conference Board Record*, Vol. XIII, No. 3 (March 1976), pp. 55–59.

Career
development

Traditionally employing organizations did little or nothing to help employees plan and develop their careers. The personnel management program focused primarily upon the needs of the organization in hiring, placing, transferring, promoting, and laying off people. This state of affairs has been changing in recent years.

Starting in the 1970's there has been concern by managers, employees, scholars, and public policy makers with improving the quality of working life. Working men and women, especially those who are young and those who possess post-secondary education, have expressed desires for meaningful jobs, increased personal freedom, better opportunities, and more say-so in matters affecting them in the workplace. Public policy in the area of equal employment opportunity has been causing companies to give greater attention to training and promotion opportunities for ethnic minorities and women.

In very recent years leading professionals in the field of human resource management have been creating career development designs and programs. There is a growing body of solid literature in the field of careers, career planning, and career management. Some of our leading corporations have set up career development programs. Among these are General Electric, Xerox, TRW, American Telephone and Telegraph, 3M Company, and Travelers Insurance Company.

Some organizations have concentrated their career development efforts upon management personnel only. But they would do well to broaden their activities to include nonmanagement employees as well. These comprise eighty to ninety percent of the total people in the typical organization. These people have development needs and aspirations, they experience transfers and promotions, and they often need to acquire new skills. They are essential to the success of any organization and they ought not to be neglected.

Why Have a Career Development Program?

There are several cogent reasons which explain why employers ought to establish career development programs. Whereas only the well-financed and larger organizations may have the resources and expertise to operate full-blown programs, even smaller companies can carry out simplified, but effective programs. We shall address the situation of the smaller company later in the chapter. The following are important reasons for adopting career development programs:

a. *Equal Employment Opportunity.* In order to provide better opportunities for minorities and women to move up in their organizations from entry level jobs, the Equal Employment Opportunity Commission and the Office of Federal Contract Compliance Programs of the Department of Labor have been requiring organizations to identify career paths and eliminate barriers to upgrading for minorities and women.

b. *Quality of Working Life.* Employees, especially younger ones, express desires to obtain greater control over their own careers. They are less willing than earlier generations of employees to simply accept the roles and assignments given them at the convenience of management. They want greater job satisfaction and more career options.

c. *Competition for High Talent Personnel.* Highly educated professionals and managers often give preference in selecting a company for which to work to those that are supportive of their career aspirations and have career development programs.

d. *Avoid Obsolescence, New Skills.* Rapid changes in technology, demographic changes, ups and downs in the economy, and changes in consumer demand can render obsolete the skills that employees in various occupations have acquired, often through years of training. Career development programs can assist individuals in anticipating changes and can help them gain new skills for which there is a real demand.

e. *Retention of Personnel.* By instituting career development programs in their organizations, management may reduce turnover of employees caused by frustration of individual career ambitions.

f. *Improved Utilization of Personnel.* Too often people are kept in jobs which they have outgrown or which are dead-end assignments. Performance is better when people are placed in jobs they like and which fit their ambitions.

CAREER DEVELOPMENT PROCESSES AND CONCEPTS

A career is a lifelong sequence of jobs integrated with the attitudes and motives of the person as he or she engages in these work roles. It is important to understand that a career is more than a group of jobs held by a person during his life-time. It also consists of the training the individual follows in preparation for his work roles and the aims, hopes, ambitions, and feelings he holds in regard to these work roles. In this book we are primarily concerned with paid jobs in a company, nonprofit organization, or governmental agency. However, a career, broadly speaking, can also comprise unpaid work such as homemaking or volunteer activities in the community.

One's career has importance for several reasons. It helps to establish the individual's identity and status. A career provides meaning and focus for one's life. Because most jobs are performed in proximity to others, work takes on a social meaning as well. Work can provide an opportunity for satisfying the employee's desire for recognition and achievement. Of course, one's job is also instrumental in providing money to obtain the necessities and luxuries for living.

Career Stages

Van Maanen and Schein have described the major stages of a typical person's career.[1] Their stages are expressed in broad terms.

1. *Exploration stage*
   Occupational images are obtained from mass media, books, and movies. Advice and example are provided by parents and teachers. Individual makes self-assessment of his strengths and weaknesses. Person makes choice of educational path through school and college (or many do). The individual tests his ability to work and accomplish real vocational tasks.
2. *Establishment stage (early career)*
   a. Job Seeking, Getting Hired
   b. Induction and Orientation
   c. First Job Assignment
      Often the new employee experiences reality shock at sub-stages (b) and (c). He faces unfulfilled expectations, anxiety, and disillusionment in his early job experiences. The employee must demonstrate his performance. Often times early assignments are hard, dirty, or unpleasant.
   d. Leveling Off, Transfer, and/or Promotion
      Supervisor tells employee he is succeeding or failing. If succeeding the person acquires feeling of competence and commitment to organization. If failing, he experiences insecurity and anxiety. May have to look for another job.
   e. Granting of Tenure
      If tenure is granted the person feels happy. He has "made it."
3. *Maintenance stage*
   a. Mid Career
      Person is given more important work assignments. This is a period of maximum productivity and value to the organization. Individual feels sense of personal growth and feels secure in his role.

[1] John Van Maanen and Edgar H. Schein, "Career Development," appearing as Chapter 2 in J. Richard Hackman and J. Lloyd Suttle, *Improving Life at Work* (Santa Monica, Calif.: Goodyear Publishing Co., Inc., 1977), pp. 54–57.

b. Late Career

Job assignments utilize individual's wisdom, perspective, and judgment. May teach younger employees. Person may face threats to his position from younger, better trained, and more aggressive employees. In late portion of mid-career stage or early part of late-career stage the person must work out his or her "mid-life crisis." The person adjusts his ambitions and goals to be realistic with what he can accomplish in the years remaining to him.

4. *Decline stage*

Planning for retirement. Learning to accept a reduced role. New accommodations to family, friends and community.

Career Success

Traditionally career success has been defined by people as having a job paying a good salary, having high occupational status, and moving upward to positions of greater responsibility, pay, influence, and prestige. The employee and manager alike have been expected to be committed to the organization. It has been assumed that if employees did a good job and were loyal, then management would reward them with job security, benefits, promotions, and respect. This traditional "organization man" orientation has been very widespread.

However, Hall and other authorities on career development have observed that many people nowadays—employees, professionals, and managers—have adopted a somewhat different orientation for themselves. The essence of this newer mode of thinking about one's career is personal freedom, self-determination, and a personal view of success. We will call this the *personal fulfillment* career orientation. Here are the main features of this newer pattern of thinking about career satisfaction:

a. The individual tries to control his own career development. The person, himself, decides whether to acquire additional training, to seek particular jobs, and perhaps, to move out of the organization.
b. Freedom, growth, and self-determination are important personal values.
c. The person seeks a healthy balance among job, organization, family, friends, and recreation. He is not a "workaholic."
d. Success is personally defined. This may include the traditional goals of money, advancement, and prestige but it also may include self-fulfillment, self-respect, strong friendship ties, and happiness gained through off-the-job activities.
e. The person is not passive and compliant. He (or she) plots his own course through life. He is not a conforming, organization man. Rather, he is mobile and assumes full responsibility for his own destiny.[2]

---

[2] Hall calls this mode the Protean career (after Proteus in Greek mythology). See Douglas T. Hall. *Careers in Organizations* (Pacific Palisades, Calif.: Goodyear Publishing Co., Inc., 1976), pp. 200–203.

Career Development

We shall now examine the meaning of the term career development along with its two components which are career planning and career management.

Career development is the planning of one's career and the implementation of career plans by means of education, training, job search and acquisition, and work experiences. If we look at the process more from the perspective of the organization, then career development is the process of guiding the placement, movement, and growth of employees through assessment, planned training activities and planned job assignments.

Career planning is a subset of career development. It is the personal process of planning one's work-life. This includes evaluating one's abilities and interests, examining career opportunities, setting career goals, and planning appropriate developmental activities. Although career planning is mainly an individual process, the employing organization can assist through career counseling offered by the personnel staff and the supervisors, through workshops to assist the people in evaluating themselves and in deciding upon developmental programs, through career planning workbooks made available to interested employees, and through the dissemination of information about jobs within the organization and outside the organization.

Career management is the other subset of career development. Whereas career planning is primarily a personal process, career management focuses more upon plans and activities done by the organization. In career management the management of the organization matches individual employee career plans with organizational needs and implements programs to accomplish these joint objec-

Figure 13-1
The Contents of Career Planning and Career Management as Components of Career Development.

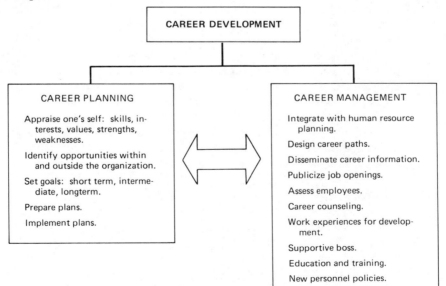

tives. The personnel department plays a central role in orchestrating this entire process. Individual career plans are related to the organization's human resource inventory and needs forecast. Management designs career paths. It provides information about job openings and makes career counseling available to the employees. Employee performance and potential is assessed. Management supports education and training programs. It provides for employee development on the job.

Figure 13-1 is a chart showing the content of career planning and career management and showing these as the two components of career development. The arrow connecting the two blocks signifies that career planning and career management are interrelated processes.

CAREER PLANNING

The steps in the career-planning process are: (1) Appraise one's self; (2) Identify opportunities; (3) Set goals; (4) Prepare plans; (5) Implement plans. Let us examine each of these steps.

Self-Appraisal

The starting point of career planning is get to know oneself. What kind of a person am I? What skills do I possess? What are my values and interests? What do I like to do? What do I dislike? What are my strengths and limitations?

Various self-directed career planning workbooks are available to help people assess themselves.[3] These contain text material plus exercises. A good introductory exercise is to ask the individual to write his own obituary as he would like it to appear x years hence upon death. The individual is asked to write down what he would like others to remember him by? What did he always want to do but never found time or opportunity to do? What are his life and career concerns?

Another exercise to assist in self-analysis requires the person to identify his or her strengths and weaknesses in regard to technical, interpersonal, communications, administrative, and personal skills. He is then asked to indicate the degree of importance he attaches to such job characteristics as autonomy, security, affiliation with others, financial rewards, and influence over others. Next he is asked to describe jobs he has held that are most and least rewarding. Finally, he is asked to describe his ideal next job.

Another means of finding out information about oneself is to take aptitude and vocational interest tests. These are administered by career counseling centers at schools and colleges.

Identify Opportunities

One's skills, interests, and values should be related to career opportunities. Although some would argue that there is always room for one more good person in

---

[3] Examples are: Walter D. Storey, *Career Dimensions I and Career Dimensions II* (Crotonville, New York: General Electric Company, 1976); Bernard Haldane, *Career Satisfaction and Success* (New York: AMACOM, 1974); A. G. Kirn, *Lifework Planning* (Hartford: Arthur G. Kirn & Associates, 1974).

a declining occupation, those choosing this course of action ought to recognize they will have a "tough row to hoe." This course is like trying to swim upstream. It is a good idea to study trends in the economy, population demographics, technology, and public policy because these shape the future job market. The aerospace program of the 1960's, for example, caused a high demand for physicists. A change in public policy in the 1970's caused a drastic decline in demand for persons trained in this profession.

In the society at large an excellent source of occupational information is the *Occupational Outlook Handbook* which is prepared by the U.S. Department of Labor. A new edition is published biennially. Also many technical and professional societies publish information about careers in their specialties.

The personnel office should publish information regarding jobs within the organization. This can take the form of organization charts, lists of titles and actual descriptions of jobs classified according to pay level, department, and location. The personnel office also should publish the requisite qualifications for each of these jobs. Job openings, as they occur, can be announced through bulletin board notices and inter-office announcements.

Opportunities within one's organization are influenced by the growth or contraction of the business, company policy regarding employee development and promotion from within, and internal office politics. Are people promoted on the basis of performance or on the basis of interpersonal politics and influence maneuvering?

Set Goals

After the individual has appraised his personal strengths, weaknesses, interests, and values and after he has obtained knowledge of job trends and opportunities, he can properly establish his career goals. This will require the setting of short-term, intermediate, and long-term goals. Goals that lead to growth should be challenging so that the individual gains new skills and outlooks. The goals should be consistent with one's capabilities and compatible with one's self-image.

Prepare Plans

In thinking through the measures one will need to take to meet his goals it is advisable to consult with one's supervisor and with the responsible member of the personnel department. Plans may be made for any of various actions designed to achieve the career goals. Reasonably one ought to start with feasible short-term on-the-job learning experiences and useful off-the-job training activities. As success is achieved on the early activities, bigger and longer run developmental projects can be tackled. The planning should take into account the special needs of the person such as skills and experiences required to reach the various goals.

Implement Plans

For implementation of one's plans it is most desirable that the organizational climate be supportive. This means that top level management must encourage all echelons of management to help their subordinates develop their careers. Actions to implement the plans may include special project assignments, temporary job transfers, filling in for the boss when he is on vacation, in-service training classes, self-study reading assignments, assignment to a special task force, and evening classes in an area college.

CAREER MANAGEMENT

Now we shall identify and explain the features of a rather complete career management system. The organization having limited resources may not be able to implement all of these features. It probably would have to do without an assessment center and may be able to offer only modest education and training programs.

The key ingredients of an effective career-management program are as follows: (1) Integrate with human resource planning; (2) Design career paths, (3) Disseminate career information, (4) Publicize job openings, (5) Assess employees, (6) Career counseling, (7) Work experiences for development, (8) Role of the boss, (9) Education and training, (10) New personnel policies and practices.

Integrate with Human Resource Planning

The proper starting point for career management is human resource planning. This is the foundation for most of a company's personnel programs. The human resource plan contains an inventory of current manpower (numbers of people, age distribution, skills, location, etc.), a forecast of manpower needs for various time points in the future, an analysis of the gap between needs (demand) and projected supply of manpower, and a set of implementation programs to meet human resource needs. The supply and demand portions of human resource planning deal with people in the aggregate. At the implementation stage individuals are hired, placed, trained, appraised, transferred and promoted, and supervised. It is at this implementation stage that career management intersects with human resource planning.

There must be a system of matching job openings with the skills and talents of present employees. What percentage of job openings are going to be filled by hiring from the outside and what percentage are going to be filled by transfers and promotions of present employees? What kinds of developmental experiences through work assignments will be offered to employees? What education and training programs will be offered?

The personnel staff must work with operating managers and with front-line supervisors to translate the human resource plans into employee development activities to meet present and projected manpower needs.

Design Career Paths

Lines of job progression to successively higher level jobs have evolved in a great many organizations over the years. Thus, lines of promotion for skilled craftsmen have been commonly regularized. An employee goes from apprentice or from helper to mechanic second class and then mechanic first class. In production departments of companies in heavy industries such as paper, chemical, and steel, many lines of progression have been formalized.

Despite the tradition among skilled crafts and in some heavy industries, most organizations have not systematically designed career paths for employee development. But they should do so. The starting point is the collection of job descriptions for all the jobs in the organization. Equipped with these, a committee of managers representing the various departments can be formed to design rational career paths. Career paths can be created for growth within various broad occupational groupings such as clerical-office, data processing, research laboratory, sales, personnel, engineering, crafts, and manufacturing. Each successive job in the path should contain at least one new skill requirement that wasn't present in the previous job. Furthermore, the jobs in each career path should bear a rational relationship to one another. Thus Job A, the first or lowest job in a career path, should contain many skill elements that are also present in Job B, the second job in the progression. Therefore, when an employee moves from Job A to Job B he doesn't have to learn an entirely new set of skills. Rather, he takes on more responsibility and adds one or two new skills to his repertoire of skills. Career paths for the development of managers and high level staff personnel should include jobs in several different functional departments to provide broad knowledge and perspectives of the business.

Many companies that employ large numbers of technical and professional personnel have designed career paths for these people that parallel the ranks in the management hierarchy up through the upper middle management level. This is desirable. Such professional career paths provide opportunities for progressively greater responsibility and also reward the individuals with more money and prestige.

Disseminate Career Information

The personnel department should prepare a written description, often in simple brochure form, of job and career opportunities in the organization. Many companies prepare such literature for use in their college recruiting programs. But such information ought to be prepared for other jobs and careers in addition to those for college graduates.

In designing career brochures it is important to be realistic. If there is no growth in some segments of the business, then the literature should point out forthrightly that job opportunities are scarce in those segments.

Publicize Job Openings

In far too many organizations information about the creation of new jobs and the opening up of existing jobs because of transfers, promotions, or terminations is kept secret among a small group of managers. Such a practice is unsound because too often qualified candidates are overlooked.

All job openings should be publicized by means of bulletin board announcements and interoffice news media. These announcements should give a condensed statement of job duties, indicate the qualifications needed, and indicate the pay grade and job location.

Assess Employees

For the benefit of both the employing organizaiton and the individual, employee performance and potential must be assessed. A well designed and implemented performance appraisal system can yield much valuable information for career development. Most performance appraisal reports are written by the employee's immediate supervisor. He should know each of his employees well. But his report is prepared from the perspective of just one person. It can be incomplete and biased. A more thorough, in-depth, and balanced evaluation of people can be obtained through use of an assessment center.

An assessment center is a system for evaluating a small group of persons by using several evaluation techniques such as simulation exercises, tests, biographical questionnaires, interviews, and observation by trained assessors. The assessment center method has shown good predictive validity for identifying potentially successful managers. It is, however, a costly method. For this reason its usage tends to be restricted to the selection of managerial personnel. It has been used successfully not only for selection but also for employee development. When used for employee development each participant is offered a counseling session at which he can see and discuss the evaluations made of his performance in all the exercises and tests.

Career Counseling

Career counseling can be conducted in three modes. In one mode it is conducted (hopefully) by each supervisor and manager when he engages in a performance appraisal interview with each subordinate. In this interview the two parties can discuss opportunities for career development such as special projects, new responsibilities, and training opportunities.

Often times a wider view of career opportunities can be provided by a career counseling resource person in the personnel department. This individual can help employees plan their careers and inform them of possible avenues for training and development.

A third mode for career counseling is that offered in a career workshop. A career workshop takes the participants through a series of planned exercises to help them plan their careers. It also can offer individualized counseling.

Work Experiences for Development

Probably the most powerful vehicle for employee development consists of planned work experiences to help the individual learn and master relevant knowledge and skills. These planned experiences can take many forms: challenging jobs, job rotation, temporary project assignments, assignment to a temporary task force, promotions, temporary lateral transfers, and even an occasional downward transfer to learn specific skills.

Role of the Boss

Unfortunately, most organizations do not train their managers to be developers of talent and they don't reward them for doing a good job in this area. For any career development program to work, this negative state of affairs has got to change. If managers are held accountable only for production and profits, these are the things they will emphasize. If top management really believes in "people development" it will reward those managers who do this well by granting pay increases, verbal recognition, and promotions.

Some managers hoard their good talent. They have spent much time and effort in developing good employees and they are reluctant to let them move on to bigger and better jobs. Top management, again, sets the policy and the climate in this regard. Lower level managers should not be allowed to block the progress of their people. If these managers are rewarded for developing strong contributors, they need not fear having them move on.

Education and Training

Many kinds of learning cannot be gained adequately on the job; hence employees must be enrolled in various educational and training programs. These programs can range from short in-service courses to teach a specific skill to week-long seminars at a training institute to regular college courses for academic credit. Contemporary thinking is that education and training opportunities ought to be made available to all levels and categories of personnel and not just to a few favored ones.

New Personnel Policies and Practices

The operation of a career development program brings out issues that some organizations may not have faced before. It may be desirable to involve the employee's family in certain career decisions such as new career directions, relocations, and promotions. If the employee's spouse has a job, a contemplated relocation can generate severe intra-family stress.

Not every individual who is promoted or transferred will succeed in his new position. The personnel department must work out a policy to take care of these people. Normally, they should have the right to move back to a job equivalent in rank and similar in nature to the one they gave up before taking the promotion.

Closely related to the foregoing is the desirability of granting tenure to those who are offered opportunities for various job rotation assignments, transfers, promotions, and training. Because the individuals involved in these experiences are moved about fairly frequently, they are required to make many adjustments in their patterns of behavior and may therefore experience some anxiety. To counter this problem management should announce to these people that they have been granted tenure or reasonable job security with the company. The individuals ought not be worried that one work failure will cause them to be discharged.

A career development system works best when there is a genuinely open internal labor market. This means that employees are adequately informed about careers, jobs, job qualifications, career paths, and job openings. They can apply for job openings and be judged on their merits. Selection of individuals for promotion and transfer opportunities is made on the basis of matching qualifications with job requirements and not on the basis of favoritism and political connections.

THE SMALLER ORGANIZATION

The typical smaller work organization ordinarily does not have the resources in talent, time, and money to plan and operate a complete career development program. What can the smaller organization realistically expect to do?

The smaller organization can adopt a policy of being supportive of its employees' career development. It can design rational career paths. Hopefully it already has job analysis information to aid this process. But if such data are lacking, meetings of managers can be convened to discuss and identify career progression sequences. Condensed descriptions of jobs and career possibilities within the organization can be prepared and distributed to all employees. Job openings can and should be posted on bulletin boards throughout the establishment.

Supervisors can be encouraged to adopt a supportive, developmental stance when they hold performance appraisal meetings with their people. Employees can learn new knowledge and skills by being given additional responsibilities and special projects while performing their present jobs. Transfers and promotions should be carefully thought out not only to meet the needs of the company but also to determine whether a contemplated move will really help the individual develop.

Normally the smaller enterprise does not spend much money and time providing formal education and training courses for its people. But the personnel director of the smaller firm can at least publicize the course offerings of area two- and four-year colleges and of technical schools. He may also be able to work with continuing education specialists from these institutions to offer occasional special courses for personnel within his firm to meet particular needs.

In summary, the management of the smaller enterprise can be sensitive to employee aspirations and can assist them in enhancing their careers. It can work to insure that it maintains an open internal labor market as we have defined the concept previously.

Questions for review and discussion

1. Explain the contemporary interest in the establishment of a career development capability by work organizations.
2. Define the following concepts: career, career development, career planning, and career management.
3. Describe the principal stages of a person's work-life.
4. Compare and contrast the traditional "organization-man" career with the newer "personal fulfillment" career orientation.
5. Give the principal components of career planning; of career management.
6. What kind of a career development program is feasible for the smaller enterprise?

Suggestions for further reading

BURACK, ELMER H. "Why All of the Confusion About Career Planning?" *Human Resource Management*, Vol. 16, No. 2 (Summer 1977), pp. 21–23.

DYER, LEE, ed. *Careers in Organizations.* Ithaca, N.Y.: N.Y. State School of Industrial and Labor Relations, Cornell University, 1976.

HALL, DOUGLAS T. *Careers in Organizations.* Pacific Palisades, Calif.: Goodyear Publishing Co., Inc., 1976.

———— and FRANCINE S. HALL. "What's New in Career Management?" *Organizational Dynamics,* Vol. 5, No. 1 (Summer 1976), pp. 17–33.

INTERNATIONAL LABOR OFFICE. *Career Planning and Development.* Management Development Series No. 12, Geneva, Switzerland: International Labor Organization, 1976.

WALKER, JAMES W. "Does Career Planning Rock the Boat?" *Human Resource Management,* Vol. 17, No. 1 (Spring 1978), pp. 2–7.

WELLBANK, HARRY L., D. T. HALL, M. A. MORGAN, and W. C. HAMNER. "Planning Job Progression for Effective Career Development and Human Resources Management," *Personnel,* Vol. 55, No. 2 (March–April 1978), pp. 54–64.

Promotion, transfer, layoff, and discharge

In the modern organization, whether it be a business or a charitable or governmental entity, there is frequent shifting of people from job to job both laterally and vertically in the structure. There is also considerable movement of people into and out of the organization as the volume of employment fluctuates. We shall be concerned in this chapter with the nature of these movements, management policies and procedures, criteria for decision making, and the effects upon the people involved. Specifically we shall study issues connected with promotion, transfer, layoff and recall, demotion and discharge.

The frequent shifting of employees, which necessitates changes in jobs and employees' status, is caused by many factors. Top management may decide that the business can be conducted more effectively by making certain changes in the organization structure. This may involve regrouping jobs, changes in departmental boundaries, elevation or lowering of jobs and functions, and physical relocation of people, jobs, and departments.

If there is an expansion in the volume of production and employment, this usually necessitates creation of new jobs and the promotion of some employees to positions of greater scope and responsibility. Often jobs are made more specialized as the volume of work and employment expands. Take the case of a personnel department as an illustration. In a very small company the personnel manager himself must handle employment, wage administration, training, benefits and services, labor relations, and safety. If the volume of employment should grow greatly, the personnel manager would have to choose someone to devote nearly full time to interviewing and selecting new employees. Likewise he would need the help of a training specialist to launch and coordinate training programs for the new employees. Conversely, as the size of the work force declines, there is often not enough work to keep a specialist busy all day at his specialty. Therefore, his job would be enlarged, and a number of functions may be assigned to him. This may be readily appreciated by examining the maintenance activity in a factory. A large plant would be able to utilize effectively the services of a number of specialized maintenance personnel, such as electricians, plumbers, carpenters, painters, millwrights, and the like. But if the volume of production should decline greatly, then each of these types of employees would not be busy enough to make a full work load, and their jobs would have to be combined. The excess personnel might be transferred to other jobs or laid off.

Another cause for changes of jobs and status is the introduction of new products, services, processes, and methods of operation. Reductions in force are occasioned by abandonment of product lines or services and by plant closings. General business conditions and the business cycle have a powerful effect upon the movement of employees in organizations. Those companies that are heavily involved in government defense contracts experience frequent extreme fluctuations in employment.

In addition to all of the foregoing, shifting of people is caused by retirements, quite, and discharges. When a top official of an organization retires or resigns, this may trigger a whole series of promotions if the organization has a policy of promotion from within the company.

PROMOTIONS

A promotion is a reassignment of the individual to a job of higher rank. Ordinarily this higher-level job will entail more demands on the individual. The scope of responsibility will be greater. Usually, but not always, the person's pay is raised at the time he is promoted. Quite frequently attached to the new position are symbols of higher status, such as a more important job title, more authority, a bigger desk, greater freedom of movement around the plant, and less close supervision of one's activities.

In our society promotions are much coveted. Most employees (but not all) have a desire to get ahead. They want the higher pay that accompanies a promotion in order to achieve a better standard of living. Their wives and children want more material possessions and conveniences around the home. The concept of starting at the bottom of the ladder when one is young and rising in status and income as one grows older is part of our culture. One's status in the neighborhood and the community is often gauged by his income level and the importance of his job. Some individuals who have a high level of aspiration set goals for themselves to reach certain positions in their companies at selected ages. If they do not achieve their objective, they may become severely frustrated. Because of the way advancement is looked upon by the majority in our society, it is important that companies and other work organizations adopt and follow sound promotion policies.

Promotion Systems

How much horizontal and vertical movement should be designed into career systems in organizations? While the nature of the work and technology strongly influence career paths, management choice also shapes them. Let us look at some examples of career systems. Industrial firms typically have the following loosely defined career systems:

1. *Unskilled and semiskilled hourly.* Entry is into labor pool. Upgrading occurs by seniority or seniority and ability to such jobs as machine operator, assembler, and tester.
2. *Skilled crafts.* Entry jobs are helper and apprentice. Then people move up to journeyman and top craft classifications. A few gain promotions to foreman, inspector, methods analyst, and production coordinator, which are salaried jobs.
3. *Clerical.* Entry-level jobs are clerk, typist, stenographer. Promotions are made to secretary, accounting clerk, and administrative assistant.
4. *Technician.* Technicians are support personnel for scientists, engineers, and other professionals. Examples are computer programmer, laboratory technician, and draftsperson. Promotions are made to higher grades in occupational classification and some obtain supervisory positions.
5. *Professional.* Individuals enter the organization in such classifications as assistant engineer or scientist. Promotion ladder is through such positions as associate engineer, engineer, senior engineer, and project engineer (or scientist). Some move into managerial positions.
6. *Managerial.* Entry occurs as a management trainee or assistant supervisor. Then people move horizontally and vertically through a variety of staff and line assignments to middle-management levels. A very few eventually reach top management.

In the foregoing, crossing over from one career path to another is rare except that some professionals do move into management.

In the military services there are two broad career systems—enlisted personnel and commissioned officers. Entry into enlisted ranks is through the recruitment offices of the various services. The entry rank is usually the lowest enlisted rank, such as private in the Army. Although some technicians are recruited directly into the higher enlisted ranks, most commonly the recruit is assumed to be unskilled and is sent to a service school to learn a specific skill. Sources of commissioned officers are the various military academies and the R.O.T.C. programs at colleges and universities.

In civilian employment in government, career systems tend to keep people within a particular department or service. Thus one's entire career will typically be within one of the units of government, such as the Foreign Service, Public Health Service, National Park Service, and the Federal Bureau of Investigation. There is little lateral movement from one service to another.

Rank in Job or Individual? Most career systems are based upon the concept of placing the *rank-in-the-job*. This means that the content of the job—the level of skill, effort, and responsibility—determines its pay classification and place in the hierarchy of jobs. This is a direct consequence of the modern emphasis upon rationalization of organization with its concepts of specialized competence, job analysis, job evaluation, and organization planning. To be promoted a man must move from his present job assignment to one of greater job demands and responsibility. A person can earn more money while retaining his present job but this is based upon an in-grade merit increase. The minimum and maximum pay allowable for a position are set by the job evaluation and pay grade system.

The other career system is known as the *rank-in-the-person* (or individual) or rank-in-corps plan. Here the rank is more tied to the person than to his job. It is widely used for professionals in both private and government employment and for faculties in universities. In the rank-in-the-person system the position levels in the career hierarchy are dependent more upon the levels of skill and performance of the professionals than upon objective differences in content of the jobs. A hierarchy of job titles such as assistant economist, associate economist, economist, and senior economist represents degrees of proficiency more than differences in basic job content. To some extent the rank-in-the-person concept intersects with the rank-in-the-job system because the higher-level classifications may involve more complex work and greater responsibilities.

Rank-in-the-person makes sense when it is difficult to objectively define and measure real job differences as is required in a job evaluation program. This situation applies to most professional categories of work. Rather than create one large all-inclusive classification such as accountant, attorney, or scientist, management sets up a series of ranks within each job family to provide an incentive for good performance and to grant recognition and status to those who have performed well.

Another reason for using the rank-in-the-individual system is to generate loyalty to a particular corps or organizational unit. This is a major factor in developing esprit de corps in the Army, Navy, Air Force, and the Marines. An individual will not hesitate to accept an assignment to a job of slightly lower responsibility because he carries his rank with him. Promotions are based upon seniority and long-term performance in a variety of posts, not upon performance in a single job.

Promotion of Management and Professional Personnel

This section deals with the promotion of professional and administrative personnel, of nonsupervisory persons into the ranks of management, and of managers to higher-level positions.

Promotion Planning. Many companies make no advance plans for administering promotions. When a vacancy occurs, they start searching for someone who is qualified to fill the post. This process is haphazard and often results in a hasty, poorly considered decision.

A carefully conceived promotion program consists of the following elements: (1) policy; (2) identification of promotion channels; (3) selection and appraisal; (4)

training and development; (5) communication; and (6) centralized records and coordination.

Among the policy issues that must be decided are whether to fill vacancies primarily from within the organization or to hire directly in the open labor market. Shall promotion opportunities be confined to a selected "elite" corps within the company? Many companies give special preference to those college graduates whom they have hired directly out of college and who have gone through a special program. These people are variously called the "crown princes" or the "fair-haired" boys. Is it sound to give special preference to a few and deny promotional opportunities to other qualified personnel? Another policy question is whether to grant an increase in pay at the time of the promotion, and if so how much? It seems sound to grant a significant increase in pay at the time a person is actually promoted. Otherwise, the promotion is hollow, and the individual resents management for being "cheap." If promotions are to be an incentive for improved performance on present assignments, there must be some financial reward to deserving individuals.

Promotion channels, stepping-stone jobs, and logical job sequences should be identified and recorded on paper. This process is intimately related to job analysis and to organization planning. Ordinarily these paper plans are to serve only as general guides. There will always arise special circumstances in which nonstandard routes up the organizational ladder are perfectly reasonable.

The selection of individuals for promotion is closely related to performance appraisal and to centralized records maintenance. The education, experience, skills, abilities, and evaluations of all employees should be recorded and maintained in central files in the personnel office. The actual procedure for selecting one individual from among several prospects will vary from organization to organization. Ordinarily labels are not placed upon each employee in the sense that he is tagged for a certain higher position far in advance. Rather, a committee of superiors in the organization in consultation with a personnel officer will commonly review the qualifications of a number of candidates. In some instances management personnel are invited to nominate, from among their subordinates, people whom they consider qualified for the vacancy.

Job openings should be announced to members of the organization via newsletters and bulletin board notices so that interested individuals may apply. These announcements should state job title, principal duties, and qualifications, and pay grade.

Official Selection Criteria.   For nonunion personnel nearly all organizations state that promotions are decided upon the basis of performance in one's present position and ability and potential to assume the responsibilities of higher-level positions. Sometimes other factors are considered, such as length of service,[1] education, training courses completed, previous work history, and the like. The rating that a person receives from his supervisor under a formal appraisal plan plays a significant part in the decision. But there are other, unofficial selection

---

[1] In some civil service systems a person must have served a minimum length of time at his present grade level before he can be considered for promotion. In the military services length of service is weighed along with other factors such as merit and ability.

criteria that are often employed. However, top management rarely talks about these factors.

Unofficial Selection Criteria.   An excellent source for gaining an insight into the sociological and interpersonal factors that so often determine who is promoted is the research of Melville Dalton.[2] Dalton conducted field studies into the behavior of managers in a number of companies.

Although company officials and policy manuals asserted that people were promoted on the basis of ability, hard work, honesty, cooperativeness, and merit, he found that many unofficial and informal influences were powerful determinants as well. Religion, national origin, and political affiliation were significant factors. Membership in the "right" social club was important. Family connections and personal friendships also were influential.

Dalton found a high correlation between years of schooling and rank in one's company. Yet there was little relationship between the individual's courses of study at college and his type of work in the company. Dalton theorized that the social and political skills that students acquire through participation in campus activities serve as a good background for later success in management.

In picking persons for promotion into responsible management posts, there is a tendency for the top executive to choose those who think and feel just as he does. He often values loyalty to himself and to the organization as being as important (or more important) as ability. He tends to select those who have social, political, economic, and religious interests that are similar to his own. In short, top executives tend to choose those who are carbon copies of themselves. Often this is done subconsciously. One of the reasons for the great emphasis upon these factors is the absence of clear-cut, objective measures of performance for most managerial positions.

All of the foregoing places the ambitious subordinate in the position where he feels he must ape the boss in order to be appraised favorably and be recommended for promotion. Organizations acquire a personality of their own, and the personality of the top executive sets the pattern for the whole group of management personnel. Those who do not match the attitudes, beliefs, and culture of the organization tend to leave. They will look elsewhere until they find an organization and a niche where they fit in well.

Assessment Centers.   Because thoughtful managers and personnel experts have long recognized that the traditional methods of selecting managers are highly subjective and fraught with error, many corporations have adopted the assessment center system. An assessment center is a place where a series of individual and group exercises are administered to a group of candidates who are seeking a given category of job. As generally used in business and industrial organizations the candidates are being evaluated for their potential for success in management. Assessment centers use multiple measurement or evaluation techniques such as simulation exercises, tests, biographical questionnaires, interviews, and observation of assessee behavior by trained assessors. The dimensions and qualities that

[2] Melville Dalton, *Men Who Manage: Fusions of Feeling and Theory in Administration* (New York: John Wiley & Sons, Inc., 1959).

are evaluated in the assessment center are determined by comprehensive analysis of the job demands and human behaviors required for the jobs involved. After the group of candidates have performed the various assigned exercises and tests, the assessors or observers meet to develop a pooled evaluation of each individual.

In recent years assessment centers have become very widely used, especially in larger corporations. Professionally designed centers have shown good results in identifying those who have the talent and skills for success in management or in higher level management.

The assessment center technique was first used by the German Army prior to World War II. The British used the procedure for selecting officers during that war. At that time also the United States Office of Strategic Services used assessment centers to pick undercover agents. The first application in American industry was by the American Telephone and Telegraph Company, which launched its Management Progress Study in 1956.

Bell System's Management Progress Study was a longitudinal research investigation into selection techniques and the careers of managers. The purpose of the project was to determine whether measurements and ratings made in the early phases of a person's career at an assessment center are predictive of his subsequent accomplishments five, ten, and twenty years later. In this study small groups of young men were brought to the center for three and a half days of intensive measurement, observation, and evaluation. A total of 422 men were assessed. Two thirds of these were college graduates who were assessed soon after being hired. The other third were former hourly paid craftsmen who had advanced to the lowest (foreman) level of management. They were not college graduates except for a handful who had earned degrees via evening school.

The techniques used for collecting information on the people included (1) a two-hour interview; (2) an in-basket exercise; (3) a business game involving a manufacturing problem; (4) a leaderless group situational exercise that involved the evaluation of foremen for promotion; (5) projective personality tests such as the Thematic Apperception Test; (6) pencil-and-paper intelligence, aptitude, and personality tests; (7) a personal history questionnaire and an autobiographical essay. In addition it should be pointed out that trained staff members observed each group problem and recorded impressions of each individual. In 1965 correlations were made between predictions made at the assessment center and criteria of performance in subsequent years. Specifically these criteria were management level achieved and current salary. In two of the groups who had the longest service in management from the date of original assessment, the assessors made accurate assessments of management level to be achieved in 78 percent of the cases. Of those people whom the raters judged would not reach middle management within nine to ten years, the raters were correct in their predictions in 95 percent of the cases.

Of the specific techniques used, the situational exercises and the aptitude tests exhibited the highest correlations with subsequent job performance. Among the aptitude tests the intelligence test, particularly the verbal portion, showed the highest correlation. The personality questionnaires showed the lowest correlations with performance.

It should be pointed out that the Management Progress Study was strictly a research endeavor. The information collected on each person and the predictions made were kept under strict control. They were not made available to line managers because this might influence their judgments on promotion of the people who had been assessed. The results of the Management Progress Study were so favorable that the Bell System established in the mid-1960's over fifty assessment centers throughout the country. The measurement techniques are essentially the same as those employed in the research project. But since the method has been proven, the results of the ratings and measurements *are* transmitted to operating management for actual use in making personnel decisions regarding those who have gone through the centers. The staffs of these centers are experienced Bell System managers of proven competence.

Another corporation to adopt the assessment center method is the Standard Oil Company of New Jersey. Their project is called Early Identification of Management Potential. It has included all ranks of management from the first-line supervisor up to the chairman of the board. Measuring instruments have included both published and custom-made pencil-and-paper tests, a personal interview, and a biographical questionnaire. Situational exercises were not employed. The best predictors in the Jersey Standard project have turned out to be the biographical data and the mental ability data.

An important component of a majority of assessment centers is the group discussion, often leaderless and with assigned roles. In such a simulation the group is given a problem to solve and is instructed to arrive at a group decision. Typical problems assigned to a group of candidates are a promotion decision, bonus allocation, discipline, or a production expansion plan. Figure 14-1 shows an assigned role group discussion with the assessors seated on the outer perimeter.

Figure 14-1
An Assigned Role Group Discussion Simulation in an Assessment Center. Performance of candidates is evaluated by observers. *Photo by permission from Development Dimensions International, Pittsburgh.*

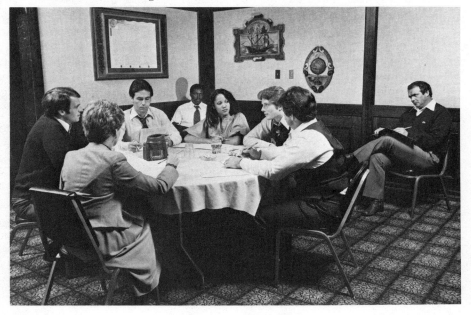

Because the assessment center method is costly and requires a fairly advanced degree of sophistication of personnel and psychological knowledge, so far it has been used primarily by large companies. But those using it have clearly indicated satisfaction with the results. And if one considers the cost of faulty selection of managers with its consequent effect upon performance, turnover, and morale, the cost benefit effectiveness becomes evident.[3]

Promotion of Organized Employees

Most unions, particularly the industrial type of unions, have taken an active interest in representing their constituents in regard to promotion practices. Among the things they have done is press for seniority as a major criterion for selection for a better job, insist that present employees be upgraded before hiring on the outside, adopt job-posting procedures, and make the choice of the individual to be promoted subject to the grievance procedure. As a result of their comprehensive survey of the effect of union policies and collective bargaining upon management, Slichter, Healy, and Livernash have stated:

> Although management once felt that promotion decisions were one of its most important prerogatives, it is now coming to realize that proper use of the seniority criterion in these decisions is not necessarily incompatible with efficiency and employee morale.[4]

This statement does not mean that merit and ability have been cast aside or that seniority is the only criterion for selection. But in recent years labor agreements and actual practice have given seniority an ever-increasing role in the selection of people for promotion.

Promotion Methods.   Generally speaking the employer administers the promotion system, and the union may submit a grievance if it is dissatisfied with the action management has taken. The right of the union to challenge an employer's decision is, of course, guided by the wording of the labor agreement. In some companies the employer may privately follow pretty much whatever selection scheme he wishes. It is only when he makes the formal announcement of an appointment that the union may step in. In other companies the job post-and-bid system is used, and this is spelled out quite specifically in the union agreement. Many employers have refused to accept a job-bid system because they feel they will be forced into a position where they must always assign the most senior employee to the new job. However, job bidding and ironbound seniority do not necessarily go hand in hand. In plenty of companies management has maintained its right to give primary weight to merit and ability.

A fairly common practice is for management (sometimes in consultation with

---

[3] Further information on the Bell System Management Progress Study and Assessment Center is contained in Douglas W. Bray and Donald L. Grant, "The Assessment Center in the Measurement of Potential for Business Management," *Psychological Monographs: General and Applied*, No. 625, Vol. 80, No. 17 (1966). See also Walter S. Wikstrom, "Assessing Managerial Talent," *The Conference Board Record* (March 1967).

[4] Sumner H. Slichter, James J. Healy, and E. Robert Livernash, *The Impact of Collective Bargaining on Management* (Washington, D.C.: The Brookings Institution, 1960), p. 181.

the local union) to establish, on paper, definite channels of promotion. These charts look like the typical company organization chart upside down. Often these promotional lines of progression are set up on a departmental basis. A man may start out as a laborer in a steel mill, for example. As time passes and vacancies occur he may move up any one of various channels, such as crane operation, furnace operation, rolling mill operation, materials handling, and the like. Each step in the various branches of these promotion "trees" serves as a learning post for the next higher job.

Seniority As a Factor in Promotions.   Many union–employer agreements specify that some weight must be given to seniority when selecting candidates for promotion. Simply defined *seniority is length of service*. When the term is used, it usually has the added connotation of certain rights or benefits attained on the basis of length of service. Some rights and benefits are based upon competitive seniority among the employees. Rights to promotion, transfer, order of layoff, and recall are examples of competitive seniority. Other benefits tied to seniority have nothing to do with one person relative to another. Thus, a person may be entitled to three weeks' vacation after ten years of service, a pension after thirty years, and a certain amount of sick leave after six months of service.

What are the arguments in favor of using seniority as a factor in selecting people for promotion? Seniority is impartial. It eliminates any possibility of favoritism influencing the choice. Because special favoritism to a few would soon disrupt the group, seniority helps maintain group solidarity. If promotion decisions are left solely to the discretion of management, there is a greater tendency for ambitious employees to apple polish and try to seek the favor of their superiors. Not only does this create dissension within the work group, but union leaders feel it weakens loyalty to the union.

Seniority fits in with the cultural expectations of mankind. From primitive tribal society through modern civilization, greater benefits, status, respect, and privileges have accrued to older people. We speak of elders in a tribe as being the leaders and decision makers. Likewise some present-day churches are governed by those called elders. Promotions in the lower grades of military ranks are based heavily on seniority.

Up to a certain point, employees increase their proficiency at work as their length of service increases. Of course, this does not go on indefinitely. But it would be fair to say that there is a very rough correlation between length of service and performance.

A final argument in favor of the seniority criterion is that it rewards loyalty. As many people work for an organization, they tend to build up a proprietary interest in their jobs, workplaces, and their departments. They tend to feel that the rewards of promotions should go to those who have been there the longest rather than to raw newcomers.

A principal argument against using seniority as a basis for promotion is that it may cause unqualified people to occupy important positions. If this occurs extensively throughout an organization, it can eventually lead to the organization's deterioration. In other words, efficiency may be seriously impaired.

The incentive to excel on one's present job is weakened if one knows it will not count toward advancement. Ambitious short-service employees are discouraged if they know they must wait many years before being promoted. Further, if grossly unqualified individuals are assigned to positions of influence, this can undermine the morale of the group.

Even if a man with long years of service exhibits superior performance on his present job, this is no guarantee that he has the skills, knowledge, and ability to perform some other higher-level job.

In balancing the equities, it is frequently the wisest choice to give consideration to both ability *and* seniority when choosing individuals for promotion.

Union Agreement Provisions.   The two most common union–employer contract provisions pertaining to promotion are (1) the most senior employee in the particular seniority unit will receive the promotion if he is qualified for the job, and (2) where ability, skill, and competence are relatively equal (as between two employees) then seniority shall govern in the applicable unit. Clause number 1 above means that the most senior employee in the appropriate seniority unit (occupation, department, or plant) will get the promotion if he can meet the minimum performance expected on the job. Clause number 2 above means that management has the right to select the best person for the vacancy if one is clearly well above the other possible candidates in ability. But if there is little difference in the skill and ability of persons in a group of two or more employees, then management must select the most senior employee for the job. This second clause is generally considered to grant greater flexibility to management in picking the most qualified individual.

Problems with Promotions

A great many administrative and human relations problems tend to arise through the application of a promotion program.

Disappointed Candidates.   There once was a man in his middle thirties who was a graduate of a prestigious men's college and who held a staff position in the personnel department of a large company. His post was roughly equivalent in rank to that of a shop general foreman. In other words, he was in lower management. The company was expanding rapidly, and most of this man's colleagues, who had been hired at about the same time he had been employed, had been promoted to positions of much higher status and authority. Coming from a socially prominent family, this man had high aspirations. Initially he had simply been overlooked for promotion. He had not been in the right spot at the right time under the right boss. He felt that he was losing out. He continually pressed his boss for a promotion. He eventually became embittered. Then his boss refused to recommend him for promotion because of his "bad" attitude.

This little story has a number of important lessons. First, top management must establish a clear-cut promotion program, and controls must be built into the system to insure that deserving candidates are not overlooked. Second, continual bypassing of an aspiring person can undermine his morale and his performance. The whole process may become circular. He may develop a "bad" attitude because he was not promoted when he thought he deserved it, and this attitude may be the very thing that prevents his advancement.

There is one further ramification. Most of us do not see ourselves as others see us. If a person has not been performing up to par, his supervisor should apprise him of the fact. On the other hand, if a person is clearly doing well on his present job but is not qualified to move up to the next higher position, his superior should discuss with him ways in which he can obtain the necessary qualifications. If he is in a blind alley, his supervisor should inform him of his chances and eventually try to move him into a department where opportunities are more favorable.

Some Refuse Promotion. Not everyone seeks advancement. Many people know their limitations and know that they might fail on a more difficult job assignment. A person may value his leisure more than material rewards associated with a higher-paying job.

Quite frequently blue-collar workers will refuse promotion to foremen because they are unwilling to give up the security of belonging to a union and being in a bargaining unit. If production cutbacks occur, workers will be laid off in inverse order of seniority. But having left the work group, foremen often have no seniority rights to displace other workers. To remove this impediment to promotion, management often insists, when negotiating a labor agreement, that a person promoted to foreman shall retain the seniority rights he had at the time he was advanced. Sometimes workers are reluctant to take a foreman's job because they will lose the protection a union affords them against capricious or arbitrary treatment by management. There are very few formal grievance procedures for non-union personnel in industry.

Supervisor Will Not Release the Employee. Sometimes a supervisor adopts the view that his subordinates are indispensable to his operation and he cannot possibly release anyone to take a better job in another department. This viewpoint may arise simply because the supervisor is selfish. It may come about also because some supervisors are good at training their subordinates, but as soon as a few superior employees are developed, they are transferred or promoted out of the unit. The supervisor may feel that the efficiency of his department may suffer if he loses his most capable people.

The solution to this problem rests with higher management. By giving credit to subordinate managers and supervisors for developing promotable employees, it can prevent the feeling that it is necessary to hoard good men to meet top management's expectations. If there is a balanced emphasis among all departments, then there will be little need for certain departments to hoard their best employees.

Promotion Opportunities Not Equitable. Often a company will drift into a situation in which it is favoring people from certain departments for promotion into the ranks of management. Over the years one large company has tended to give rapid promotion to college graduates who work in the production and sales departments while relegating those in the engineering department to positions of individual contributors. In fact quite often in industry the person with specialized technical training, such as an engineer, mathematician, or chemist, is not given equal promotion opportunities with the generalist who may rise through administrative posts at a rapid rate. The facts of life in many industrial corporations are such that the generalist may take on administrative and executive assignments in a large number of different fields, whereas the engineer or scientist tends to be considered for supervisory and executive positions only within his own technical department.

To correct this inequity and to provide incentives for engineers and scientists, some companies have established what they call "dual ladders." They have set up a number of high-level salary grades for functional individual contributors. These carry salaries equivalent to those paid middle-level managers.

TRANSFERS

A *transfer consists of a reassignment of an employee to another job of similar pay, status, and responsibility*. A transfer is a horizontal move from one job to another. It is to be distinguished from a promotion, which is a vertical move in rank and responsibility. A transfer may involve a slight change in level of responsibility and status, because ranks and grade levels in many organizations are defined very broadly.

Causes of Transfers

People may be transferred either because of the needs of the business or at their own request, because they feel they would be happier in a different job. The term *needs of the business* covers a multitude of reasons. Most shifts of personnel are occasioned by changes in volume of output, changes in organization, introduction or dropping of product lines, and similar adjustments in business operations. Absences of key employees from work make it necessary to reassign others to fill their shoes.

Quite often management will make a remedial transfer because an individual is not performing adequately on his present assignment, and an analysis of his qualifications causes management to feel that he would be more suitable in a different spot. Managers as a rule are not alert often enough to the fact that an employee who is a failure under one supervisor and on one kind of work might be very successful if he were transferred to a type of work suited to his aptitudes and interests. Too often managers will not take a second look at the person who is unsuccessful in his initial job assignment.

Sometimes employees request a transfer because they do not like their present work situation or because they feel that opportunity for advancement is better in some other department. The typical procedure for handling these requests makes it necessary for the man to discuss his desires with his present supervisor first. The personnel department coordinates such internal transfers. The employee, in effect, must apply for a job in another department. When an opening occurs, he must be interviewed by the manager of the department concerned.

Administration of transfers

Transfers are classified as temporary or permanent. Those caused by changes in volume of production and by absence of key employees are often of the temporary variety. Those caused by fundamental changes in the nature of a company's business, by reorganization, at the individual's own request, and in an effort to salvage a person who has been misassigned, are often of a more permanent nature.

If the employees are represented by a union, management may find that its freedom to shift people around as it sees fit is restricted. If the union contract specifies that job vacancies must be posted on the bulletin board so that interested employees may bid for them, this process may slow up the work of reassigning people. It may also prevent management from reassigning those it wishes to move. To overcome this problem many union–employer agreements provide that temporary transfers of, say, one or two weeks' duration can be made without posting the job on the bulletin board.

Unions over the years have sought to insure that their constituents are properly paid for the level of skill and effort they must exert in their jobs. They have pressed for a close matching of duties and responsibilities with pay. If management then wishes to shift certain people to somewhat different types of work, the union will be zealous to see that they are not then required to work harder or at a higher level of skill and effort for the same pay. Management sometimes feels that this hampers its efficiency, but in reality if a well-developed job-evaluation system is maintained, a proper matching of job titles, pay, and duties poses no serious administrative burden.

Another type of relocation is that caused by the closing down of one plant and the opening of a new one in a distant location. Most commonly in such circumstances the company moves only its executives and certain other key personnel. Hourly paid workers and clerical employees are left behind without jobs.

However in recent years courts have tended to rule that seniority and job rights become vested through the collective bargaining agreement and that the employer must offer jobs in the new plant to workers who wish to move to the new location.

LAYOFF AND RECALL

One of the disadvantages of our free enterprise economy is the fact that mass layoffs and unemployment occur frequently throughout the country. To be sure, we feel that the benefits of our free economy far outweigh its limitations. Nevertheless, the frequent ups and downs of product and financial markets, changes in the business cycles, and uncoordinated decisions of thousands of business firms often result in large-scale layoffs and rehirings of workers.

A layoff is an indefinite separation from the payroll due to factors beyond the employee's control. It is caused by such factors as loss of sales, shortage of materials, seasonal fluctuation in markets, production delays, and technological displacement. At the time a worker is laid off, the employer often does not really know how long it will be before he can recall the individual. Some temporary layoffs actually turn into permanent separations because the volume of production never picks up sufficiently to warrant rehiring laid-off workers. A layoff should be clearly distinguished from a discharge. When someone is discharged he is permanently separated from his job because of poor performance or violation of company rules of conduct.

Depending upon company policy and union–employer contract provisions, laid-off workers retain certain rights with their employer. In some instances they continue to accumulate seniority for a certain period of time, they may have certain recall rights, and time spent on layoff may count toward vacation, pension, and sickness benefits. Depending upon the circumstances, the employer often hopes that the laid-off workers will remain attached to his company rather than permanently sever the relationship. It will save the company the cost of training green help if all laid-off employees return to work when they are asked. Of course, the longer the duration of the layoff, the less likely it is that the separated workers will ever return.

Layoff of Unorganized Employees

When employees are not represented by a union, management is free to use whatever criteria it wishes in deciding whom to let go and whom to retain. Some companies see a layoff as a golden opportunity to weed out undesirable employees. But this should be the exception, because management that is enlightened and efficient should have continuously done a careful job of selection, training, placement, appraisal, and separation from the payroll where necessary, so that it does not need the excuse of a layoff to get rid of incompetent people. It must be agreed, however, that the performance of employees on any type of work will range along a continuum, and any organization will want to retain its top performers and drop those who contribute the least.

In actual practice in nonunion situations, management usually selects people for retention (or its counterpart layoff) on the basis of many factors. Among these are performance, age, length of service, number of dependents, financial obligations, and health. Job performance is usually given the greatest weight, followed next by length of service. The other factors reflect management's concern with what might be hardship cases if the individual is laid off.

A refreshing approach to the problem of surplus employees is that used by the International Business Machines Corporation. For more than 35 years this company has never laid off an employee for economic reasons. Instead, it retrains workers who are no longer needed in one job and assigns them to another job within the company. Since 1970 it has retrained and physically relocated 5,000 employees. IBM has a strong commitment to job security through retraining and reassignment. The management believes that its policy has paid off through better morale, less employee worry, and better cooperation.[5]

Layoff of Organized Employees

Layoff procedures have always been of utmost concern to unions. The goals of the union in regard to layoffs are to preserve the union as an institution, to maintain its organization structure, to protect the union members' jobs insofar as possible, to insure equitable and impartial treatment among individuals, to prevent divisive influences within the group, and to maintain certain re-employment rights for those who are laid off.

Forestalling and Minimizing Layoffs. Most union agreements contain provisions designed to forestall or minimize layoffs. The most common provision is

[5] *Business Week*, "How IBM Avoids Layoffs Through Retraining," (November 10, 1975), pp. 110–111.

some form of worksharing. A 1972 study by the U.S. Department of Labor of 1,845 major collective bargaining agreements, each covering 1,000 or more workers, revealed that just under 25 percent of the agreements provided for worksharing.[6] There are three types of worksharing procedures: reduction in hours, division of work, and rotation of employment. Reduction of hours, by far the most common method, requires that weekly hours of work be reduced below normal schedules to spread the work among all persons in the bargaining unit. Most agreements specify that hours shall not be reduced beyond a certain minimum, such as 32 hours per week. If further cut-backs should be necessary when this point is reached, then layoffs could occur.

Division of work means that all available work is divided equally among the employees. This mechanism is used mainly in the wearing apparel and textile industries, where workers are paid on piece work or by wage incentives. The emphasis here is on equal earnings rather than actual hours of work. Thus, fast workers may put in fewer hours of work per week but earn the same as slower ones.

Rotation of employment requires that short, specific periods of layoff be rotated equally among all employees rather than laying people off. In the Department of Labor study this method was used in only 5 percent of the agreements that had worksharing provisions.

Other supplementary methods of forestalling layoffs are by restrictions on the amount of overtime worked, restrictions on subcontracting, restrictions on new hires, and by specifying that the reduction in force shall be no faster than the rate of attrition via voluntary quits, retirements, discharges for cause, and transfers.

Seniority in Layoffs.   When layoffs actually take place, seniority is by far the most common criterion for determining the order in which people will be separated. In the Department of Labor study mentioned above, layoffs were handled with seniority being the sole criterion in 27.2 percent of the agreements, seniority being the primary factor in 44.2 percent, and seniority being a secondary factor in 19.5 percent.

When seniority is used as the primary factor in determining who shall be laid off, this means that seniority has a predominant role but that ability and other factors are also considered. Usually, this means that junior employees will be laid off provided that the senior employees can do the remaining work even if junior employees are more capable. A typical contract provision reads as follows:

> Length of service shall prevail in layoffs and rehiring, provided the senior employee can perform the work required.

When seniority is a secondary factor, this means it is only when ability and physical fitness are equal (when choosing among several employees), that length of service becomes the deciding factor.

[6] U.S. Department of Labor, Bureau of Labor Statistics, *Layoff, Recall, and Worksharing Procedures,* Bulletin 1425–13 (Washington, D.C.: Government Printing Office, 1972). The 1,845 agreements in this study include virtually all the major collective bargaining agreements covering 1,000 or more workers in the United States exclusive of railroad, airline, and government agreements.

Seniority Units.   The seniority provisions of a contract and their application in layoff, bumping, and recall often are exceedingly complex. When layoffs occur, employees may be able to exercise their seniority rights to protect their jobs according to job family boundaries, departmental boundaries, or on a plantwide basis. Seniority rights for bumping and layoffs on a companywide basis for multiplant companies are rather infrequent.[7]

If there are fifteen welders in a company and the lowest three in seniority are laid off when a plant reduction in force occurs, this is considered job or job-family seniority. It might be that the three welders possess much higher seniority than employees who are retained in other departments, but if the contract has set up seniority units on the basis of job-classification boundaries, then these three must be laid off. The same principle applies to a departmental seniority unit. With plantwide seniority the shortest-service employees are let go regardless of their jobs or departments.

Management usually favors narrow seniority units and as little bumping as possible in the interests of maintaining plant efficiency. Unions press for as wide a seniority unit as they can get in order to provide as much job protection as possible.

Bumping on Layoffs.   Exigencies of business operations may cause the elimination of the jobs of some very senior workers. Shall these people then be separated from the payroll? Most commonly the answer is no, because these employees are allowed to bump or displace the shortest-service employees in their seniority unit. These short-service workers may actually hold quite different jobs, but if the long-service people are capable of doing this work, then they can displace the newer workers. Heavy layoffs that extend over a period of weeks or months usually cause a chain reaction of displacements in which those who bump others are in turn bumped themselves a short time later. This process can disrupt plant efficiency to a considerable extent. It is for this reason that management tries to set up narrow seniority units.

There are a number of other restrictions on bumping that appear in some collective bargaining agreements. Bumping may be made inoperative for temporary layoffs of less than two weeks' duration. Certain employees (usually 2 to 5 percent of the labor force) may be declared by management to be "essential" and thus exempt from bumping. A man may be permitted to bump only into a job on which he has had previous experience. Or a man must possess a specified amount of seniority in excess of the person he seeks to displace. All these limitations serve to maintain plant efficiency while at the same time decreasing the job security of the senior employees as a group.

Recall from Layoff.   When the work force expands after a layoff, the general principle applies that workers will be recalled to work in inverse order of layoff or according to seniority. However, the process is not as simple as this implies. Certain operations and certain departments will expand their activities before others. The activities of those low-seniority workers who were first laid off may

---

[7] *Bumping* is the term commonly used in unionized companies to denote the displacement of one employee by another who has more seniority. The "bumped" worker may in turn displace another of lower senority or be laid off.

be the first to be resumed. So in practice recalled workers may be assigned to jobs different from those they previously held. In view of this, the majority of labor agreements specify that ability, skill, and physical fitness will be given consideration in addition to seniority.

DEMOTION

A demotion is the reassignment of an employee to a job of lower status and pay. Usually the level of difficulty and responsibility is lower on the new job.

Demotions may be caused by factors beyond the employee's control. This is the typical case when a reduction in force occurs. Although some employees may be laid off, often those who remain must take lower-level positions because departments may be combined and jobs may be eliminated. This can affect both managerial and hourly paid personnel. When large-scale layoffs occur and the bumping process is set into motion, workers pretty much expect that they will be forced to take lower-level jobs, at least until the level of plant activity picks up in the future.

The other major type of demotion is caused by some inadequacy (or alleged inadequacy) on the part of the individual in terms of job performance, attitude, and capability. He may have recently been promoted but failed to meet the standards of performance for the higher position. It often happens that technology, methods, and practices change but that old-timers are unable to adjust to the new ways. In other words, management has raised the requirements of their jobs substantially, and they cannot meet the new expectations. Should these long-service employees be demoted to less demanding jobs? People age at different rates. Occasionally the health and vigor of certain individuals have deteriorated before the customary retirement age, so that they can no longer do their work adequately. What action should be taken with these individuals?

A person's work career is often one of the most important things to him in his whole life. His hopes, pride, and joy may be wrapped up in his career. His job title, pay, and level of responsibility determine his social status and his living standard. A good job is a symbol entitling one to certain rewards and respect both within the organization and in the community. Thus, for some people, it can be a devastating blow to suffer a demotion. This feeling is not so likely to arise when the demotion is caused by a reduction in force, because this action is often taken impartially and objectively. It is not a black mark against the man. Furthermore there is the expectation that business will pick up again in the future, and one's old position can be regained.

For the long-service employee, for the ones who have performed effectively in the past, the most satisfactory solution is generally to make no demotion. Rather it is to keep the person in his present job but to take away some of his duties and responsibilities and assign these to someone else. Another solution is to create a position for the person at the same pay and status but with lowered job demands. Both these solutions permit the man to retain his dignity and the respect of others as well as his accustomed level of income.

Do Not Demote for Discipline

It is unwise for management to use a demotion as a penalty for violation of company rules of conduct. If a man has a poor record of attendance, has been insubordinate, or has come to work drunk, a demotion will not change his behavior. He may simply retain his old habits on the lower-level job. Discipline is a form of training and correction. If a person were to be demoted as a form of discipline, not only would he have to learn his new job, but he would have to learn to overcome his previous unsatisfactory behavior. In addition, he would have to make the psychological adjustment occasioned by the loss of pay and status.

Demotion in a work situation would be akin to putting a fourth-grade school boy back to third grade because of bad deportment in the fourth grade. The punishment is simply inappropriate for the offense.

TERMINATION AND DISCHARGE

A termination is a separation from the payroll or cessation of employment for whatever reason. A *discharge is a permanent separation from the payroll, usually because of some inadequacy or offense by the individual.* Traditionally employers have held that they had the absolute right to dismiss employees for any reason whatsoever. The common law of the nineteenth and early twentieth centuries buttressed this position. This viewpoint was rooted in the property rights of ownership and the notion of the personal liberty of the employer to run his business as he saw fit. An employee was always free to quit and the employer could not prevent this. Likewise an employer could dismiss an individual without recourse by that person.

But this once absolute right has been modified because of three institutions: (1) unions; (2) civil service systems; and (3) protective labor laws. Collective bargaining agreements specify that workers can be discharged only for "just cause," which means that it must be for good and sufficient reason. Workers, through their union representatives, are able to appeal a discharge through the grievance procedure to eventual binding arbitration.

Another major group of protected employees are those who work for government at the local, state, and Federal level. The Federal Civil Service Act of 1883 launched the merit system for Federal employees. Public administrators cannot fire employees without substantial evidence. Warnings must be given beforehand. Proper procedures as spelled out in the law must be followed in processing a dismissal. Further, the affected person has certain due process appeal rights.

Federal laws prevent discrimination by employers against employees for certain categories of people and for certain activities. Thus, as we have seen, the Equal Employment Opportunity provisions of the Civil Rights Act of 1964 ban discrimination in employment because of race, color, national origin, religion, or sex. The National Labor Relations Act, as amended (Taft–Hartley Act) bans discrimination because an employee engages in union activities.

However, the foregoing protections still leave large areas in which employers have a free hand to fire employees. Over 60 percent of the labor force is nonunion and nongovernmental. Most salaried employees in the private sector of the economy are unprotected and most hourly and salaried employees in the small business sector of the economy are not unionized.

Managers, administrators, and professionals are quite vulnerable to dismissal. If there is a cutback in sales and production volume, they may be laid-off. But for them there is no union or contract protection that determines the procedures for layoff. They may be discharged because of charges of inadequate performance, misbehavior, or simply because the boss doesn't like them. They can also be fired for asserting that some order of the boss is contrary to company policy or is illegal.[8]

Some progressive companies have put controls upon the firing of employees who aren't protected by a union. In essence these companies have set up written guidelines stating the allowable grounds for dismissal, procedures for deciding and processing a dismissal case, and providing for due process appeal procedures.

At the Xerox Corporation, for example, there is an ombudsman for handling employee grievances and no employee with more than eight years of service can be discharged without the written approval of the chairman of the corporation.[9]

Questions for review and discussion

1. What are the forces and factors in organizations that cause such job changes as promotions, transfers, and layoffs to occur?
2. In designing a career or promotion system, where would you use rank-in-the-job and where rank-in-the-person? What difficulties can occur in administering a rank-in-the-person system?
3. Describe the purposes and operation of an assessment center. What are the advantages of an assessment center over traditional methods of choosing persons for promotion? Disadvantages?
4. Explain the principal features of a sound promotion program.
5. The job post-and-bid system of filling job openings is most commonly instituted at the request of a union. Do you feel that such a system can be useful to an organization for filling jobs for nonunion groups?
6. Why is it that top management will announce that the official criteria for promotion are such factors as merit, initiative, and ability, but fail to give open recognition to the unofficial and informal factors, such as interpersonal and sociological influences? How important do you think these unofficial criteria are in the average company?
7. What are the relative merits of giving weight to length of service when selecting employees for promotion? Is seniority more appropriate at the worker level than at the manager level?
8. If a man is promoted or transferred on the initiative of management and he clearly fails to perform adequately on the new job, should he be returned to his old job? Demoted? Discharged? What if someone else has been promoted into his old job?

[8] For examples and a discussion of salaried employees being dismissed for challenging the propriety of orders they received from the boss, see "Fire Me?—An Employer Can Fire Anyone at His Slightest Whim," *National Observer* (April 29, 1972).
[9] "How Xerox Ombudsman Helps Xerox," *Business Week* (May 12, 1973), p. 188.

9. If a plant closes down and resumes operations in a new plant in a different section of the country, what rights to jobs in the new plant should rank-and-file employees have? What job rights should professional or technical employees have? Should job rights be accorded status similar to property rights? Discuss.
10. What part does seniority play in layoff of unionized employees?
11. In balancing the equities, does layoff according to seniority help or hinder management? The union? Individual employees? Employees as a group?
12. Prepare a set of policies and guidelines for handling the termination of non-union employees and managers.
13. Explain how a chain reaction of bumpings could occur with mass layoffs.

Case problems

PROBLEM 1

The ABC Company, a public utility, has an engineering department composed of 200 employees. The major share of the work involves cost estimation, specification writing, and equipment planning and ordering. Some of the work also involves basic engineering analysis and design. Over two thirds of the engineering force is composed of employees who possess only a high school education and who have served a number of years as mechanics, electricians, and other types of craftsmen before being promoted into the engineering department. Quite frequently foremen who had been inept at supervising people but who had good technical knowledge were transferred to the engineering department and classified as engineers. The one third of the engineering force that does possess college degrees in engineering are assigned to the more complex technical phases of the work, involving the application of engineering principles. Most of the supervisory positions in the engineering department are held by graduate engineers.

Over the years the company has placed major emphasis upon the operating phases of the business. Those recruited directly upon graduation from college are placed in a management training program of twelve months' duration. They are rotated through a number of assignments in various departments of the company including the engineering department. Only a small percentage of these "college hires" are assigned permanently to the engineering department, however. Of the total number of college graduates hired by the company each year, about one half hold engineering degrees and the other half are composed mostly of liberal arts and business administration graduates. Many of the engineers eventually attain managerial positions in the nontechnical phases of the business.

As technology has advanced, the top management of the ABC Company has experienced a real need for more graduate engineers in the engineering department. It feels that in the past it diluted the manpower in this department too thin by assigning too many nonengineers and nondegree holders to this type of work. In many instances the engineering department had become the dumping ground for misfits from operating departments. For these interdepartmental transfers the engineering department had had no practical selection methods. It had pretty much taken whoever was offered.

In recent years there has been a problem of low morale, particularly among those engineering personnel who have had an engineering education. They have noticed that promotions for engineers were few and far between, whereas those college graduates who had gone into other departments rose in the organization quite rapidly. The general attitude has evolved in the minds of higher management that engineers were best utilized as technical specialists—as functional individual contributors. There was also the feeling that engineers as a group are poor at dealing with people, and therefore they would make poor supervisors.

Recently the personnel department made an analysis of the salaries and rate of progress of all those college graduates hired fresh from college during the years 1970–1975. During these years engineers and nonengineers had been hired in about equal proportions. It was found that those persons who were now working in nonengineering departments (regardless of their college preparation) were receiving higher salaries and had attained higher-ranking positions than those who were doing engineering work.

Salary levels for engineering personnel are considered adequate in comparison with rates paid by other companies for the same occupations. The company conducts an annual salary survey and makes a sincere effort to keep its salaries competitive.

Questions

1. Assuming that you have been given the task of recommending a program of action to solve the problems contained in this case study, what would be your proposals for the following critical areas?
   a. Selection policies and procedures for transfers of employees to engineering jobs
   b. Low morale of graduate engineers within engineering department
   c. Inequitable promotion opportunities
   d. Using former craftsmen and foremen on engineering jobs
2. Should engineers look to their advancement primarily by going into administrative and executive work or by achieving status and economic advancement within the engineering profession itself?

PROBLEM 2

Ralph V., age 39, mill manager for The Pulp and Paper Company, arrived at his office on Friday morning as usual. Shortly after his arrival he received a telephone call from Mr. Jenkins, the executive vice-president of the company, asking him to come immediately to his office. Once in Mr. Jenkins' office, he was informed that he was being discharged effective as of the end of that day. Mr. Jenkins stated that he had been dissatisfied with Ralph V.'s performance for a long time and had been contemplating this move for many months. Ralph V. was stunned and visibly shaken. He protested that he did not believe his work had been unsatisfactory and that he had worked many long hours over the past five years to meet the multitude of problems encountered in running the mill. Mr. Jenkins stated that his decision was final. In fact a new mill manager had recently been hired to take Ralph V.'s place. The new man was going to report on the following Monday. Acknowledging the abruptness of this termination, Mr. Jenkins offered the mill manager six weeks' pay as a separation allowance.

Ralph had originally been hired five years previous as assistant mill manager. He was promoted to mill manager after one year when the old manager retired. The mill manager was in charge of all paper manufacturing operations in a mill employing 500 people. The functions of operations, maintenance, production control, and quality control were under his jurisdiction. Organizationally, the mill manager reported to the vice-president of the fine paper division, who in turn reported to the executive vice-president of the corporation. Ralph V. had originally been hired from the outside by Mr. Jenkins. He came well recommended.

A few days later in discussing Ralph V. and his termination the personnel manager said privately:

> He was a very affable guy. Very talkative and outgoing. He was popular with his foremen. Whenever I visited his office on business I found it difficult to get away because he had so many stories to tell that did not really relate to the job. Ralph also took pride in counseling and coaching foremen, group leaders, and hourly workers. There was many a man who probably should have been discharged for poor work or violation of plant rules whom Ralph reformed and saved for the company. Ralph "cooked his own goose," however, when he got into a serious argument with his immediate boss, Jake Richards, the vice-president of the division, about a year ago. Ralph was hired originally by the executive vice-president and he reported to him before Richards was employed. The new vice-president of the fine paper division was hired a little over a year ago to give the division more managerial attention and improve its profit picture. He became Ralph's immediate boss.

The director of engineering in commenting upon the situation made the following remarks:

> Ralph was just not on top of things. He tended to have a continuous stream of people in his office to get decisions on production problems and also to talk about social matters and trivia. He was active in various fraternal and civic organizations in town and spent a great deal of time on the telephone handling these matters. In fact he also lost some normal job time handling these outside affairs.
>
> He was lax about planning, anticipating problems, and knowing what was going on in his own mill. Oftentimes the foremen would run the production lines at only half or three-quarter speed because of troubles with the equipment or the product. Yet this could go on for a whole day or two and he would be unable to diagnose the cause of the trouble. Again, quality of the paper coming off the machines might be low, and Ralph would not take prompt corrective action. Also there were recurring problems with maintenance and housekeeping.
>
> However, I do say that many of the problems in the mill were not fully Ralph's fault. He was not given the essential services he required to run a tight ship. He should have had more support from higher management.

One of the long-service superintendents in the mill made these remarks about two months later:

> Things aren't noticeably different under the new mill manager than they were under Ralph. The new man has many good ideas, but we still have frequent breakdowns of

equipment, bottlenecks, and quality problems. I think Ralph was the "fall guy" for all that's wrong around here. Many of us have been wondering who is going to be fired next. I understand Jake Richards was determined to get rid of Ralph and never made an effort to help him.

The discharged mill manager, Ralph, was interviewed privately at lunch about two weeks later. He made these remarks:

> I'm somewhat bitter about this whole thing. I was never given any real signals that this was coming. I had been in Mr. Jenkins' office just a few days before that Friday morning talking about various production matters. He did not act unusual at that time. As a matter of fact I always got along fine with Jenkins. I will agree that on a couple of occasions in the past he told me that he was displeased with production levels in the mill. But I did not take that to mean any strong criticism because he knew (or I thought he knew) that I was trying to run the operation with some equipment that was old and subject to serious breakdowns. Besides he didn't always let me hire the people I needed. I had very few foremen who were fully qualified.
>
> I understand they hired my replacement behind my back and had been negotiating for months to get him.
>
> I think Jake Richards was working on Jenkins for a long time to have him fire me— that is ever since he and I had the squabble about my refusing to fire one of the group leaders about a year ago.

Questions

1. Evaluate the way in which Ralph was discharged.
2. Would you anticipate that the new mill manager would have any special problems upon commencing his new job? Discuss.
3. What do you think of the method top management adopted to assure continuity of operations, namely, timing the hiring of the new manager to coincide with the discharge of the old one?
4. If an executive is performing unsatisfactorily, what action should his immediate superior take?

Suggestions for further reading ———————————————————

BYHAM, WILLIAM C. "Assessment Centers for Spotting Future Managers," *Harvard Business Review*, Vol. 48, No. 4 (July–August 1970), pp. 150–160, 162–167.

FINKLE, ROBERT B., and WILLIAM S. JONES. *Assessing Corporate Talent*. New York: John Wiley & Sons, Inc., 1970.

FISHER, ROBERT W. "When Workers Are Discharged—An Overview," *Monthly Labor Review*, Vol. 96, No. 6 (June 1973), pp. 4–17.

HEISLER, W. J. "Promotion: What Does It Take to Get Ahead?" *Business Horizons*, Vol. 21, No. 2 (April 1978), pp. 57–63.

KEENY, JOHN. "Terminations: Bowing Out a Manager," *Personnel*, Vol. 48, No. 3 (May–June 1971), pp. 45–54.

KRAUT, ALLEN I. "New Frontiers for Assessment Centers." *Personnel*, Vol. 53, No. 4 (July–August 1976), pp. 30–38.

MINER, MARY GREEN. *Separation Procedures and Severance Benefits.* Washington, D.C.: Bureau of National Affairs, Inc., 1978.

MOSES, JOSEPH L. and WILLIAM C. BYHAM (eds.) *Applying the Assessment Center Method.* Elmsford, N.Y.: Pergamon Press, Inc., 1977.

SHAEFFER, RUTH G. *Staffing Systems: Managerial and Professional Jobs.* New York: The Conference Board, 1972.

SLICHTER SUMNER H., JAMES J. HEALY, and E. ROBERT LIVERNASH. *The Impact of Collective Bargaining on Management.* Washington, D.C.: The Brookings Institution, 1960, chs. 5, 6, and 7.

STEINMETZ, LAWRENCE L. "The Unsatisfactory Performer: Salvage or Discharge," *Personnel,* Vol. 45, No. 3 (May–June 1968), pp. 46–54.

Training

To operate organizations, large or small, requires staffing with competent personnel. Our public educational system is primarily oriented toward teaching broad knowledge and skills to enable people to cope successfully with their environment, to support themselves, and to help advance the society as a whole. Generally speaking, it is not designed to teach specific job skills for positions in particular companies or organizations.

About a million and a half young people enter the labor force each year. Because the vast majority of these are not prepared to perform jobs in work organizations, they must be trained by their employers. Even those who have studied a technical or professional field of work at college must receive some initial training in the form of orientation to the policies, practices, and ways of their specific employing organization. Moreover, because the technology of our productive processes is developing at such a rapid pace, there is also a need for continual retraining of experienced workers to perform new and changed jobs. The automation of recent years is but an advanced stage of the technological developments that have been taking place at an increased pace in recent decades.

Fifty years ago new workers were expected to pick up necessary job skills and knowledge from experienced fellow employees. The newcomers were typically called learners or helpers. Although it cannot be denied that this method of learning worked, it certainly didn't work well. It was quite haphazard and caused the learning process to be very slow. Many incorrect procedures were often acquired. Frequently old-timers would deliberately seek to protect their positions and status by hazing the new men and by confining the learners' activities to the menial parts of the work.

Large-scale systematic training activities in industry got their start during the periods of war production during World Wars I and II. Especially noteworthy were the Training-Within-Industry (TWI) and the Engineering, Science, and Management War Training (ESMWT) programs of World War II. The TWI program trained people in industry in procedures for teaching job skills to others (Job Instruction Training), in developing better work methods (Job Methods Training), and in industrial relations (Job Relations Training). The ESMWT program consisted largely of specialized technical courses offered by colleges and technical schools to employees in defense industries.

This chapter will explore the nature of training, objectives to be accomplished, organizational considerations in training, the learning process and learning principles, training methods, and training programs. Means of evaluating the effectiveness of training will also be discussed.

Training Defined

Training is the organized procedure by which people learn knowledge and/or skills for a definite purpose. The objective of training is to achieve a change in the behavior of those trained. In the industrial situation this means that the trainees shall acquire new manipulative skills, technical knowledge, problem-solving ability, or attitudes. It is expected that the employees apply their newly acquired knowledge and skills on the job in such a way as to aid in the achievement of organizational goals.

Training is often distinguished from education. Education is thought of as being broader in scope. Its purpose is to develop the individual. Commonly, education is considered to be formal education in a school, college, or university, whereas training is vocationally oriented and occurs in a work organization. Training usually has a more immediate utilitarian purpose than education. In practice, training and education frequently occur at the same time. This is to say that the distinction is not always necessary or appropriate. Some formal vocational school programs are quite immediately practical and job oriented, whereas some executive development programs in industry cover fundamental principles and philosophy, are broad in scope, and certainly should be designated as education.

TRAINING IN THE ORGANIZATION

Tangible Benefits of Training

Training is a vital and necessary activity in all organizations. It plays a large part in determining the effectiveness and efficiency of the establishment. Let us now examine some of the major contributions that training can make:

1. *Reduced learning time to reach acceptable performance.* By having qualified instructors and carefully controlled learning situations, management in countless cases has been able to obtain shortened learning periods and higher productivity from new employees.
2. *Improved performance on present job.* Training applies not only to new employees but to experienced people as well. It can help employees increase their level of performance on their present job assignments.
3. *Attitude formation.* A common objective of company training programs is the molding of employee attitudes to achieve support for company activities and to obtain better cooperation and greater loyalty.
4. *Aid in solving operational problems.* Training of both supervisory and hourly paid employees can help reduce turnover, absenteeism, accidents, and grievance rates. For example, inept supervision is often a cause of employee dissatisfaction and grievances. Supervisory training in such areas as labor relations, leadership, human relations, and administration may improve supervisor-subordinate relationships. Other operational problems that training can help solve are low morale, poor customer service, excessive waste and scrap loss, and poor work methods.
5. *Fill manpower needs.* One manufacturing company found it impossible to recruit sufficient skilled machinists and toolmakers. Hence it concluded that the best way to solve this manpower problem, in the long run, was to establish its own apprentice training program. A number of small manufacturers in the wearing apparel industry in an eastern city continually find difficulty in hiring adequate numbers of skilled sewing-machine operators. None of these firms has any type of organized training program. Yet a large company in the same city seldom is short of labor, because it operates a complete training school for sewing-maching operators. Consequently, it is able to recruit green labor and train these people to become experienced stitchers.
6. *Benefits to employees themselves.* As employees acquire new knowledge and job skills they increase their market value and earning power. The possession of useful skills enhances their value to their employer and thereby increases their job security. Training may also qualify them for promotion to more responsible jobs.

Organization for Training

In small companies training is, to a great extent, of the on-the-job variety, and it is done by line supervision. If personnel departments exist in these companies, the planning and coordination of training activities is typically one of the many responsibilities of the personnel manager. It is rare to find specialization carried to the point of having a separate training section within the personnel department.

On the other hand, the vast majority of larger companies have a separate training section within the personnel or industrial relations department. Organizationally the training and management development functions may be combined within one section.

The training activity is a staff function. It performs in the areas of policy formulation, advice, service, and control for organizationwide training activities.

More specifically the training director and his assistants must commonly perform the following functions: (1) determination of training needs; (2) development of overall plans, objectives, and assignment of responsibilities; (3) development of training programs in consultation with line executives; (4) collection and preparation of training materials, outlines, curricula, textbooks, and audiovisual aids; (5) instruction of certain courses (often orientation and supervisory development courses) and selection of qualified instructors for others; (6) training of certain operating personnel who are designated as instructors to develop teaching skills; (7) administration and coordination of all training programs; and (8) evaluation of effectiveness of training effort.

Line Training Responsibilities

Top line executive management (this may be the president or executive vice-president or a top division manager in a decentralized company) has the responsibility for authorizing basic training policies. Likewise it must review and approve the broad outlines of training plans and programs without, of course, concerning itself with details. It must approve the training budget. If, for example, the training director thinks it would be desirable to inaugurate a comprehensive executive development program, he would have to obtain the wholehearted support of the chief executive officer of the organization before he could undertake such an activity. It would be the training director who would formulate complete plans for carrying out an executive development program. However, these plans would have to be approved by top line management. A training director might feel that certain managers should be sent to one of the extended on-campus executive development courses given by a number of major universities. The actual selection of a person and the decision to release him from his present job for the duration of the course is a line management responsibility.

What are the training duties and responsibilities of lower line management? Foremen, general foremen, and office supervisors must be alert to recognize training problems that exist in their departments. They may participate in the creation of special tailor-made training programs to help solve specific problems in their units. They must bear direct responsibility for the successful conduct of an on-the-job training activity in their departments. If certain employees are to perform in the role of on-the-job instructors, the supervisor must insure that these employees have themselves been adequately trained in the principles of teaching. The supervisor must coach and counsel his subordinates in order to obtain adequate performance. In effect a supervisor is himself a trainer. He often is personally responsible for the orientation of new employees. He may conduct safety training meetings with his personnel. The supervisor selects, from among his subordinates, those who should participate in formal training programs. He is responsible not only for meeting production goals but also for developing his people.

Discovering Training Needs

Sometimes a manager decides to set up a training program because it is the popular thing to do and because other companies are doing it. However a company

---

can literally pour thousands of dollars down the drain unless it attacks its training problems on a more systematic basis.

Training programs should be established only when it is felt that they can aid in solving specific operational problems. Therefore, the rational way of deciding what kind of training activity to undertake is to make an analysis of the entire organization (people, jobs, technology, and so on) to identify trouble spots where training may help.

It should be pointed out at this time that training is not a cure-all. If employee output is low, this may be corrected by better skill training. On the other hand, the problem may not be one of inadequate training at all. It might be due to faulty material, process equipment, or engineering design. If it appears that the general caliber of the work force is low, this condition might be corrected by training. However, it could be that the general wage level is so low that the company cannot recruit good employees.

The identification of specific problem areas in the organization can suggest ways in which training may help toward a solution. The following are ways of discovering training needs:

1. Identify organizational and production problems
   a. Low productivity
   b. High costs
   c. Poor material control
   d. Poor quality, excessive scrap and waste
   e. Excessive labor–management strife
   f. Excessive grievances
   g. Excessive violation of rules of conduct, poor discipline
   h. High employee turnover
   i. Excessive absenteeism
   j. Delayed production, schedules not met
2. Analyze jobs and employees
   a. Job analysis
   b. Employee appraisal
   c. Testing
3. Collect employee and managerial opinions
   Interviews and questionnaires to obtain views regarding perceived problem areas and deficiencies which would indicate desirable training programs
4. Anticipate impending and future problems
   a. Expansion of business
   b. New products, new services
   c. New designs
   d. New plants
   e. New technology
   f. Organizational changes
   g. Human resource inventory—compare present human resources with forecasted needs

THE LEARNING PROCESS

Learning is really the core of the training process. When management installs a new training activity, it reasonably expects that through participation in this training employees will exhibit new or changed behavior. Indeed, *learning can be defined as that human process by which skills, knowledge, habits, and attitudes are acquired and utilized in such a way that behavior is modified.*

We know that a person has learned when he demonstrates it by performance. If John is studying German, he shows that he has learned by translating a passage in a book. A mathematics student, by solving written homework problems, has demonstrated that he has learned his assigned lesson. Likewise, a welding trainee reveals that he has learned to make a pipe weld by actually doing it.

Principles of Learning

Psychologists, primarily through experimentation, have developed a number of important principles of learning. These are equally pertinent for application by training directors who administer programs, for classroom instructors who teach employees, and for supervisors who train employees on the job.

Motivation. If trainees are not receptive to instruction, if they can see no reason to learn, then a training effort can hardly get off the ground. Adequate motivation is essential to the success of any learning situation. People are goal oriented in their behavior. They will exert themselves to fulfill a felt need. Learning is effective when the trainees perceive that they can satisfy some goal through participation in a training program.

There are two kinds of motives; intrinsic and extrinsic. In intrinsic motivation the work itself is satisfying to the individual. He takes pleasure in his work or schooling and derives a feeling of accomplishment upon successful completion of the work. Extrinsic motivation refers to the holding out of incentives or external rewards for the successful completion of a task. Such incentives may be praise from the boss or the instructor, higher pay, a bonus, prestige, better working conditions, and the like. Both types of motivation are important to the learning process. However, learning is quite difficult if the external incentives are available but intrinsic motivation is lacking. This situation can be illustrated by a college student who has chosen to enroll in an engineering curriculum because he knows that the salaries paid to graduate engineers are very good. However, this long-range goal is unlikely to motivate him to learn mathematics, physics, electronics, solid mechanics, and fluid mechanics if he dislikes these subjects. He may grit his teeth and force himself to get through these courses, but the learning will be quite painful. Conversely, learning engineering is easy for the student who has the aptitude plus the intrinsic interest in the subject matter.

Both rewards and punishment play a powerful role in motivation to learn. A reward for a desired response serves to stimulate a repetition of that behavior. Thus, students may receive praise from their parents for doing well in school, and this will motivate them to continue to do well. Punishment tends to inhibit a certain response, but it does not necessarily eliminate it. Mild punishment is effective if it is immediate and if the learner understands the reason for it. Supervisors and trainers must be very judicious in the way they administer punishment. If a learner has been doing poorly, threatening him with a discharge or reprimanding him may cause him to alter his behavior, but most generally such action will affect many other aspects of his behavior in addition to the learning situation. It may cause him to fear or resent his instructor or boss so much that he cannot concentrate upon learning the work at hand. Employees may learn to follow company rules of conduct because those who don't are clearly punished. But often an emphasis on punishment by management is only effective as long as there is repeated punishment or the threat of it. Employees will concentrate on avoiding punishment rather than doing the right thing. In the long run, people will learn to behave in a desired way if they understand the reasons for such prescribed conduct and if they are rewarded for such behavior.

Knowledge of Results. Somewhat related to motivation is knowledge of the learner's progress. Research experiments have demonstrated that people learn faster when they are informed of their accomplishments. After analyzing numerous research experiments concerning such diverse activities as line drawing, use of gun sights, dot-dash code receiving, and typing, Wolfe has concluded that it is essential that trainees be given knowledge of their efforts. He states that such knowledge should be automatic, immediate, and meaningfully related to the task at hand.[1] Thus in a training classroom students' examinations should be graded and returned to them so that they can know where they have erred and what they have done correctly. In on-the-job training the supervisor should inform the employee of his successes and failures so that he can adjust his efforts if necessary. People like to experience a feeling of progress. They want to know where they stand. If an instructor returns examination papers to a class of students with only the raw scores recorded, this knowledge will be meaningless until they are told how all the grades were distributed and how they stand in relation to expected performance. Learning is facilitated when the trainee has some criterion by which he can judge his own progress.

Learn by Doing. It is extremely difficult for a learner simply to listen to a teacher explain how to do something and then be able to do it solely from the explanation. It is by actually performing the task that a student really learns. The greater the number of human senses involved, the more complete is the learning. If one is teaching a physical task, such as operating a machine or sharpening a tool, it is easy to see how practice can be provided. But what if one is teaching theories and concepts? Actually a variety of techniques are possible. Laboratory experiments can be devised. Written problems can be assigned. Case studies and role playing can be utilized. Although not constituting full learning by doing, oral discussion and debate help to strengthen the learning of ideas.

When learning a task by practice, is it better to combine the total time devoted to practice into one concentrated session, or should the practice be subdivided into small time periods? The available research evidence seems to favor spaced practice sessions. Experiments with massed as opposed to spaced practice

---

[1] Dael Wolfe, "Training" in S. S. Stevens, ed., *Handbook of Experimental Psychology* (New York: John Wiley & Sons, Inc., 1951), pp. 1267–1286.

for simple motor skills and memorizing show that learning is superior for that type of practice that has a series of short rest periods.[2]

Whole or Part Learning?   In secondary school, when children learn to memorize a poem they do it one (or a few) stanzas at a time. Is this the way employees should learn to perform work sequences—one step at a time? Whether whole or part learning is preferable depends to a certain extent upon the nature of the learner and of the material to be mastered.

However, certain generalizations can be made. If the material to be learned is simple, if the task has few operations, then whole learning is superior. Where the different parts of the material are logically interrelated into a large unit, then the whole method should be employed. On the other hand, if the knowledge to be learned or the task to be mastered is very complex and long, then it should be broken down into parts so that the trainee can learn one section at a time.

Usually if part learning is primarily employed, the whole procedure can be presented in broad outline at the beginning and then periodically thereafter to orient the trainee to the whole subject. In fact, whole and part learning can be intermixed in the same training sequence to gain the benefits of both approaches.

Is Theory Desirable?   Does the chemistry laboratory technician need to understand why chemical reactions occur as they do? Does the process operator in an oil refinery need to know why he must turn valves and adjust temperatures and pressures? Do workers perform better if they understand the principles underlying the work they do?

The prevailing weight of evidence shows that learning is faster and can be applied better to new situations if the trainees understand the principles involved. This was found to be true for boys shooting at targets that were underwater: a knowledge of refraction increased the accuracy of shooting. It was also true for college students who had to solve simple reasoning problems. Those who were told the principles upon which the problems were based did better than those who were simply given sample solutions to a few problems. Those who were given a series of problems in such a manner that they could derive their own principles did still better in future problems.[3]

From the foregoing it is clear that a person who understands the theory behind his work is in a good position to readily adapt to a new problem situations as they arise. The person, however, who has simply been trained to perform as an automaton will be hopelessly lost when confronted with situations out of the ordinary. This principle of teaching theory as well as practice does not mean that we need a graduate electrical engineer to repair a television set. But it does mean that the TV repairman, for example, should possess a practical, working knowledge of electronics as it applies to television receivers.

In summary, employees should be taught sufficient theory to understand the principles and reasons underlying their work and to cope successfully with the general run of problems they may encounter.

[2] See E. R. Hilgard, *Theories of Learning*, 2nd ed. (New York: Appleton-Century-Crofts, Inc., 1956), p. 487. Also William McGehee and Paul W. Thayer, *Training in Business and Industry* (New York: John Wiley & Sons, Inc., 1961), pp. 151–153.
[3] Dael Wolfle in S. S. Stevens, op. cit., pp. 1277–1278.

Learning Motor Skills. In motor-skill work, muscular movement is prominent, but it is under sensory control. Examples of motor skills are skiing, skating, swimming, carpentry, setting up and operating machine tools, welding, glass blowing, using hand tools, and operating a sewing machine. The instructor must show and explain the materials, tools, and equipment that he will use. He should then demonstrate how to perform the activity. If the activity is complicated, the instructor should break the operation down into logical components, explain the steps involved, and then demonstrate. Next the learner should start practicing the operation. He should understand what he is doing and be able to explain the activity. The instructor should provide guidance and feedback. The learner must know if his performance is progressing properly or improperly. Generally after practicing for a period of time, a rest pause should be provided. Distributed practice periods are generally more fruitful than prolonged and concentrated practice.

Learning Concepts and Attitudes. This process is much more complex than learning motor skills. At one extreme is rote learning, where a person may have to memorize a poem, learn the names of the parts of a machine, or learn a computer language. At the other extreme one may learn for depth of understanding. There may be all sorts of interconnections and associations among the ideas he learns. He may learn the reasons why as well as beliefs, attitudes, and philosophies. He may search for general theorems, truths, and laws.

There are many ways to learn ideas and attitudes. We can learn by trial and error and personal experience. We can read and observe. We can learn by listening and talking with others.

The learning of ideas is enhanced when the students participate actively in the process. They may work on problems and exercises and ask and answer questions. This may be both written work and oral discussion in class. It is especially valuable to encourage students to explore problems and issues in some depth so that they discover relationships and principles for themselves. It may save time if the instructor organizes all the subject matter and explains it logically and clearly to his trainees. But, at least part of the time, opportunity should be provided for them to work on exercises, problems, and concepts and discover truths for themselves.

Indeed, a fundamental question in designing a classroom learning experience is whether to depend heavily upon the lecture method of instruction or to foster a high degree of group discussion and interaction. The answer to this question depends somewhat upon the objectives of the program of training or education. If the purpose is solely to provide information of a factual nature to the group, the lecture method, which is highly leader centered, is quite satisfactory. However, if the material to be learned is subject to varied interpretation and is not precise or explicit, then group discussion, with a group-centered method of conducting the class, is clearly superior. There is also evidence that retention of factual knowledge is greater in classes having a high degree of group-member interaction. This result appears to be caused by the learning reinforcement that comes from the testing of one's ideas with others and from the intellectual stimulation this generates.

Courses whose purposes are to modify attitudes, facilitate behavioral adjustments, aid interpersonal relations, and promote self-insight are clearly superior when the trainer adopts a democratic, participative leadership style. High member interaction is most conducive to these goals. A very authoritarian trainer tends to be ineffective in changing group attitudes, but a leader who generates high member involvement can more effectively modify opinions, prejudices, and emotions.[4]

TRAINING METHODS

Those who administer training programs have a great choice of methods for imparting learning in trainees. The particular method selected is determined by considerations of cost, time available, number of persons to be trained, depth of knowledge required, background of the trainees, and many other factors. The following is a listing of the major training methods:

1. On-the-Job
2. Vestibule
3. Classroom Methods
   a. Lecture
   b. Conference
   c. Case Study
   d. Role Playing
   e. Programmed Instruction
   f. Computer-Assisted Instruction
4. Other Methods
   a. Demonstration
   b. Simulation and Games

On-the-Job Training

The vast majority of all training carried on is of the on-the-job variety. Much of what passes for on-the-job training is extremely haphazard. For example, a young engineer fresh out of college took a position in a large corporation. He was immediately assigned to an application engineering job. For training he was told to read a stack of books describing company standard procedures and specifications. His boss assumed that by studying these he would learn his job. As another example, Bill was hired as a machine operator in a government arsenal. He was expected to turn out precision parts on milling machines and boring mills for military weapons. He had had machine experience in another company but had never worked on this specific product under these conditions. He was given no instruction by the foremen. What he learned he had to gain informally by asking help from experienced work associates.

How should on-the-job training programs be conducted? Primary responsibility rests with each departmental supervisor. If he understands training princi-

---

[4] A discussion of when to use leader-centered and group-centered training styles, based upon an extensive review of available research, is contained in Alan C. Filley and Franklin C. Jesse, "Training Leadership Style: A Survey of Research," *Personnel Administration*, Vol. 28, No. 3 (May–June 1965), pp. 14–21.

ples and methods and if he takes an interest in proper training of new employees, chances are that it will be done properly. The training may be done either by the supervisor himself or by a designated experienced nonsupervisory employee. The person doing the training must be given recognition for his work. He must not consider training to be an unpleasant chore that interferes with production. The instructor must himself first receive training in the principles and techniques of instruction. It is the responsibility of the training department to teach all on-the-job instructors how to instruct.

The instructor must assemble all necessary equipment, procedure sheets, working materials, and training aids. He must break down the material to be learned into meaningful packages and present it to the employee in a manner appropriate to the job to be learned. In many instances he will actually demonstrate how the work is to be performed. He will carefully guide and observe the trainee as he performs the work. Correction will be given as required.

A variety of training aids and techniques can be used in conjunction with on-the-job training. Among these are procedure charts, pictures, manuals, sample problems, demonstrations, oral and written explanations, and tape recordings.

On-the-job training is most appropriate for teaching knowledge and skills that can be learned in a relatively short time (a few days to several weeks) and when only one or at most a very few employees must be trained at the same time for the same job. If a great depth of theory must be acquired, then this can be accomplished more efficiently in a classroom. On-the-job training is useful for learning unskilled and semiskilled manual type jobs, clerical jobs, and sales work. For skilled, technical, professional, and supervisory jobs, the underlying educational background must be obtained by other means; however, the applied aspects of these jobs are quite generally learned right on the job.

On-the-job training has the advantage of permitting the trainee to learn on the actual equipment and in the environment of his job. He can actually experience a feeling of accomplishment as he produces useful products. If only a few are to be trained at one time, it is cheaper for the employer to resort to on-the-job training rather than to invest in a vestibule school or classroom setup. Quite often expensive manufacturing equipment cannot be duplicated in the classroom.

On-the-job training suffers from the fact that the instruction is often disorganized and haphazard. Learners are subjected to the distractions of a noisy shop or office. There is a tendency to slight the principles and theory in favor of immediate production.

Vestibule Training

Vestibule training is the term used to designate training in a classroom for semiskilled production and clerical jobs. It is particularly appropriate when a large number of employees must be trained at the same time for the same kind of work. Where it is used, there is a greater likelihood that management will have well-qualified instructors in charge. The emphasis tends to be upon learning rather than production. It has been used to train clerks, bank tellers, inspectors, machine operators, testers, typists, and the like.

In vestibule training an attempt is made to duplicate, as nearly as possible, the actual material, equipment, and conditions found in a real work place. Typically the learning time ranges from a few days to a few weeks. Theory can more easily be presented in a vestibule school than on-the-job. The learning conditions are carefully controlled.

Classroom Methods

Classroom instruction is most useful when philosophy, concepts, attitudes, theories, and problem-solving abilities must be learned. This means that a considerable depth of knowledge must be acquired. There are certain aspects of nearly all jobs that can be learned better in the classroom than on the job. Certain portions of company orientation and safety training can be accomplished most effectively in the classroom. Most commonly, however, we think of the various classroom methods being used for technical, professional, and managerial personnel, where a considerable grounding in theories, principles, and concepts is necessary. Let us now examine some of the principal classroom instruction techniques.

Lecture. The standard instructional method in colleges and universities—the lecture—is a formal, organized talk by the instructor to a group of students. The lecturer is presumed to possess a considerable depth of knowledge of the subject at hand. He seeks to communicate his thoughts in such a manner as to interest the class and cause them to retain what he has said. Quite often the students will take notes as aids to learning.

The principal virtue of the lecture method is that it can be used for very large groups, and thus the cost per trainee is low. It can be organized rigorously so that ideas and principles relate properly one to the other.

However, the limitations of this method may outweigh its advantages. The learners are passive. It violates the principle of learning by doing. It constitutes one-way communication. There is no feedback from the audience. The presentation must be geared to a particular level of knowledge and may bore the advanced student and be beyond the capabilities of the slow learner. It tends to emphasize the accumulation of facts and figures; however, this does not mean that the learners will be able to apply their knowledge. Because it is difficult to hold the full attention of listeners for a sustained period, lecturers are tempted to resort to anecdotes, jokes, and other attention-getters. This activity may eventually overshadow the real purpose of the instruction.

The most fruitful way to use the lecture is to combine it with other techniques. Thus, a teacher may conduct a class by the combined lecture–discussion method. He may then lecture only to add new information that the group does not possess. He may give formal reading assignments, present demonstrations, and show films.

Conference. A conference is a small group meeting, conducted according to an organized plan, in which the leader seeks to develop knowledge and understanding by obtaining a considerable amount of oral participation from the trainees or students. It overcomes certain of the disadvantages of the lecture, because here students play very active roles. They are not passive. In fact, the very success of any conference is dependent upon contributions from the students. Learning is facilitated through building upon the ideas contributed by the conferees. The people, to an extent, learn from one another.

There are three basic kinds of conferences: (1) the directed conference (also called the guided or instructional conference); (2) the consultative conference; and (3) the problem-solving conference. The directed conference is most commonly used for training purposes, because the instructor has certain concepts he wishes the class to absorb, and he guides the group carefully to insure that they cover these ideas. Conferences are not limited to training purposes, however. They are frequently used in all sorts of organizations to attack operating problems by bringing to bear the pooled thinking of a number of people. For solving business problems, either the consultative or the problem-solving method may be used.

Let us examine some of the features of a directed conference used for training purposes. Because it depends for its success upon the active participation of the conferees, the size of the group must be limited to fifteen to twenty persons. The people should sit facing one another around a conference table rather than theater-style, as in an ordinary classroom. The students should have some knowledge of the subject to be discussed before coming to the conference. This can be obtained from assigned readings or previous experience or both. The instructor introduces the topic and invites viewpoints from the group on problem areas related to this topic. He must, by the skillful use of questions, make sure that the class analyzes the topic thoroughly. Often he will record student responses on the blackboard. He will summarize progress made at pertinent points throughout the session. Points of disagreement will also be highlighted. In the directed conference the instructor or leader may introduce new material by occasional brief periods of lecturing.

In contrast to the lecture, the students play a very active part in determining the progress of the conference. They are not forced to submit passively to the instructor's viewpoints. They are expected to make assertive statements and to ask questions. They learn not only from the instructor but also from one another. It is rare for a trainee to become bored or to fall asleep in a conference, whereas this condition is common in the lecture. Interest tends to be high. The conference is ideally suited to tearing apart problems and issues and examining them from different viewpoints. It is an excellent procedure for reducing dogmatism and modifying attitudes. Because they have had a part in developing solutions and reaching conclusions, the conferees are often willing to accept these conclusions. The skilled conference leader is acutely aware that he must avoid imposing his opinions upon the group.

The principal limitations of the conference method are as follows: (1) it is limited to a small group, and (2) progress is often slow because all those desiring to speak on a point are generally allowed to do so. Irrelevant issues creep in easily.

Case Study. In the teaching of mathematics, it is almost universal practice for the instructor to assign problems for the students to work out to illustrate the principles previously taught. This method gives the student an opportunity to apply his knowledge to the solution of realistic problems. Likewise, this principle can be applied to the teaching of those subjects concerned with human affairs. Case studies are extensively used in teaching law, personnel management, labor relations, marketing, production management, and business policy.[5]

Cases can be used in either of two ways. First, as stated above, they can be used subsequent to the exposition of formal theory. In this way students must apply their theory and knowledge to specific situations. Second, they may be assigned to students for written analysis and/or oral class discussion without any prior explanation of pertinent concepts and theory. The students are expected to derive useful generalizations and principles themselves. This second approach places heavy demands on the student. It requires that the students have a good deal of maturity and some background in the subject area.

The case study method is very popular in graduate professional schools of law and business administration. It is also frequently used in supervisory and executive training in industry.

Case discussions in class are usually conducted in a conference atmosphere. Students soon learn that there is no single answer to a particular problem. Engineers who are used to a right and wrong dichotomy are often initially frustrated in case discussions because the instructor does not tell them what is the right solution.

The case study method of instruction provides for learning by doing. Good cases are usually based upon real experiences and problem situations; therefore, student interest tends to be high. They are excellent for developing analytical thinking and fostering problem-solving ability. Narrowmindedness is reduced because the trainees soon learn that others have studied the identical problem and come up with different patterns of analysis and solution. Students must often defend their proposals in the face of keen criticism from others. The case method is an excellent means for integrating the knowledge obtained from a number of foundation disciplines.

Role Playing.   Role playing is actually a technique that should be used in conjunction with some other instructional method such as the lecture or the conference. Originally developed by J. L. Moreno for group therapy for mentally disturbed people, it has been widely used for human relations and leadership training. It is primarily used to give trainees an opportunity to learn human relations skills through practice and to develop insight into their own behavior and its effect upon others.[6]

In role playing two or more trainees are assigned parts to play before the rest of the class. There are no lines to memorize and no rehearsals. The role players are provided with either written or oral descriptions of a situation and the role they are to play. After being allowed sufficient time to plan their actions, they must then act out their parts spontaneously before the group. Typical role-playing situations are a supervisor discussing a grievance with an employee, a super-

---

[5] For a discussion of the case method in teaching management and human relations, see Kenneth R. Andrews and others, *The Case Method of Teaching Human Relations and Administration* (Cambridge, Mass.: Harvard University Press, 1953).

[6] Excellent accounts of role playing are contained in Alex Bavelas, "Role Playing and Management Training," *Sociatry* (now *Group Psychotherapy*), Vol. 1, No. 2 (June 1947), pp. 183–191; Norman R. F. Maier, A. R. Solem, and A. A. Maier, *The Role-Play Technique: A Handbook for Management and Leadership Practice* (LaJolla, Calif.: University Associates, 1975); and in Corsini, R., M. Shaw, and R. Blake, *Role Playing in Business and Industry* (New York: The Free Press, 1962).

visor conducting a post-appraisal interview with an employee, an employment interviewer conducting a hiring interview, and a salesman making a presentation to a purchasing agent.

Role playing for developing human relations understanding and skills has a number of advantages. It provides an opportunity for students to actually put into practice the knowledge they have absorbed from textbooks, lectures, and discussions. It is learning by doing. They become sensitive to the way their behavior affects others. It helps people to appreciate other points of view as when roles are switched (that is, the boss plays the part of the worker). Knowledge of results is immediate, because the role players themselves as well as the class analyze and criticize the behavior of the players. Interest and involvement tend to be high.

Programmed Instruction.   Programmed instruction (sometimes packaged in a device called a teaching machine) was developed in the late 1950's for both school and industrial applications.

The key features of programmed learning are (1) students learn at their own pace; (2) instructors are not a key part of the learning; (3) the material to be learned is broken down into very small units or stages; (4) each step logically builds upon those that have preceded it; (5) the student is given immediate knowledge of results for each answer he gives; and (6) there is active participation by the learner at each step in the program.

Some types of programs take into account individual differences in background. If a student is unable to give the right answer to a question or a series of questions, he will be directed along a different branch of the program to provide him with the fundamentals he has missed.

To date, programmed instruction has been used primarily for teaching factual knowledge, such as mathematics, a foreign language, and job routines. It has not been used to develop philosophical concepts, attitudes, or clinical problem-solving skills. The cost of creating a single program is very great.

Computer Assisted Instruction.   Computer-assisted instruction is grounded in some of the learning principles employed in programmed instruction. It is often used to provide drill and practice to help students learn material that is well structured such as grammar, basic mathematics, and reading. It can also be used as an adjunct to other educational methods to develop problem-solving skills. Computer-assisted instruction is costly. It has been used mostly to teach basic skills in schools. Its adaptation to teaching job skills in industry has been slow.

Other Methods

Demonstration and simulation are other important instructional methods. Demonstrations may be carried out either on the job or in a classroom. Simulation is sometimes done in the classroom and sometimes in a laboratory type of situation.

Demonstration.   Of all the senses, sight is one of the best for learning. A demonstration in which the instructor actually shows the trainees how to do something has wide application. It is one of the key steps in much on-the-job training. The instructor may show an assembler how to put something together, a tester how to test an engine, a stitcher how to sew a seam, and a pilot trainee how to manipulate controls in an airplane. A sales manager may show sales trainees how to deal with a potential customer and how to explain the performance features of his merchandise. Soldiers in the army receive much of their training by means of demonstration.

Demonstrations are usually combined with some other techniques, such as a lecture, pictures, text material, and discussion. A demonstration is particularly effective for skill training. It has only limited usefulness for training management personnel. Because a demonstration emphasizes primarily knowhow, principles and theory must be taught by some other method.

Simulation and Games. A simulator is any kind of equipment or technique that duplicates as nearly as possible the actual conditions encountered on the job. Certain portions of the training of military and commercial aircraft pilots are conducted in flight simulators. Astronauts receive part of their training in simulators. Business games, to be described in Chapter 16, "Management Development," are a form of simulation. Student participants make various business decisions in a competitive market situation. They learn the consequences of their actions after their decision-data is fed into a computer which has been programmed with a model which is supposed to be a realistic representation of the economic market situation.

Trainee interest and motivation are normally high in simulation exercises because the actions taken closely duplicate real job conditions. Simulation is very useful (and even necessary) where on-the-job practice could result in a serious injury, a costly error, or the destruction of valuable material.

TRAINING PROGRAMS

Principles of learning and training methods are useful only insofar as they contribute to effective training in a specific program. We shall now examine the more important kinds of training programs found in work organizations.

Orientation

Although proper orientation is easily and often neglected, it is essential for insuring that new employees get off to the right start. Although other terms, such as *induction* and *indoctrination* are also used, *orientation* is most accurately reflective of the real meaning of the process. *Orientation is the guided adjustment of the employee to the organization and his work environment.*

The objectives of orientation are multifold. In carrying out such a program management seeks to create favorable attitudes toward the company, its policies, and its personnel. It can instill a feeling of belonging and acceptance. It can generate enthusiasm and high morale. Quite frankly many employers seek to mold employees' attitudes and behavior so that they fit in well with the organization and accept management policies and ethos. A well-run orientation program may minimize the likelihood of rules violations, discharges, quits, grievances, and misunderstandings.

After an employee is hired, both the personnel department and his supervisor play key roles in the orientation process. The relative part played by each depends upon management intention and the resources of the personnel department. In small companies, either having no personnel department or else having only a skeleton one, the major responsibility for new employee orientation falls upon the operating supervisor. Even in large companies with extensive personnel departments, there are certain orientation tasks that essentially belong to the employee's own department.

What is the role of the supervisor in orientation? He is responsible for making the newcomer feel he is wanted and needed. He should pave the way ahead of time by informing present employees that a new employee is going to work in their midst. He should give reasons for adding a new employee, so that any suspicion or resentment is allayed. The supervisor should review, with the new employee, the nature of his duties, introduce him to each person with whom he will come in contact, and show him the department or work area and its facilities. In introducing him to other employees with whom he will deal, the supervisor should make it a point to explain the function of these individuals, so that the new employee can properly deal with them in the future. Thus, a factory production worker should become acquainted with his group leader, inspector, maintenance man, setup man, union steward, timekeeper, and the like. The employee should be told what is expected of him in terms of performance and conduct. He must know what he can expect from the company regarding pay, pay increases, promotion opportunities, holidays, vacations, and benefit plans.

The personnel department is responsibile for seeing that the orientation program is initiated in the first place, and that it is carried out according to plan. It should train line supervisors in the performance of their orientation responsibilities. In some companies it exerts staff control over these line supervisors by requiring them to fill out a check list form that shows they have done specific orientation tasks for each new man.

The following is a listing of important content information and actions that may be included in an orientation program. It includes fundamental things that should be done with each new employee. However, the list is not conclusive, since every organization will make adaptations to fit its needs.

EMPLOYEE ORIENTATION CONTENT

1. Company history, policies, practices.
2. Company products and/or services.
3. Company plants and facilities.
4. Organization structure (in general).
5. Employee responsibilities to company.
6. Company responsibilities to employee.
7. Pay treatment.
8. Rules of conduct.
9. Tour of department.
10. Work schedules.
11. Collective bargaining agreement.
12. Benefit plans—life insurance, medical, hospitalization, pension, unemployment.

13. Safety program.
14. Training opportunities.
15. Promotion policy.
16. Introduction to fellow employees.
17. Establishment of a feeling of belonging and acceptance, showing genuine interest in new employee.
18. Employee appraisal system.
19. Work assignment.

Experimental evidence of the value of proper orientation of new workers is reported by Myers and Gomersall, who conducted the research at the Texas Instruments Company. Interviews with about 400 factory operators who had been on the job only about a month disclosed that (1) they felt very anxious the first few days on the job; (2) hazing by older workers intensified their anxiety; (3) turnover of new people was caused primarily by anxiety; (4) they were reluctant to discuss problems with their supervisors. As a result of this background information, Myers and Gomersall devised an experiment with a control group and an experimental group. The control group was given the conventional two-hour orientation consisting of a briefing on hours of work, insurance, parking, work rules, and the need to conform to the company expectations. The experimental group of new workers was given a full day's orientation. This included the same two-hour orientation provided the control group. But in addition they spent the remainder of their first day in a conference room with the trainers. There was no work the first day. Emphasis was placed upon getting acquainted with one another and the company. They were encouraged to relax. Four key points were emphasized: (1) their likelihood of success in the job was very good; (2) they should disregard hazing by older employees; (3) they were encouraged to take the initiative in asking questions of their supervisors; (4) they were told about their new supervisor and how he would behave. Then they were introduced to the supervisor and training operators. What were the results of this experiment? For the experimental group job-learning time was reduced, output was higher, and attendance was better. Waste and rejects were also lower for the experimental group. The researchers attributed this gain to lowered anxiety through better orientation. Supervisors were also aided in improving their role in the orientation process.[7]

Job Skills and Knowledge

When we speak of training for job skills and knowledge, we are not talking about any specific program. Rather we are referring to the variety of training programs, methods, and aids that have been established to answer particular training needs. Either on-the-job or classroom techniques may be employed. The subject matter will vary according to the training problem encountered. Although many who are unsophisticated regarding training tend to look upon it as primarily for new employees, in actuality a vast amount of training effort must be continuously expended on further education and retraining of old employees. The content and

[7] Earl R. Gomersall and M. Scott Myers, "Breakthrough in On-the-Job Training," *Harvard Business Review*, Vol. 44, No. 4 (July–August 1966), pp. 62–72.

demands of jobs change with time, the expectations of management change, and above all the technological revolution that is going on in our civilization means that old ways become obsolete and new skills must continuously be introduced. Quite frequently the best answer to a shortage of labor for particular kinds of work is to grow skilled workers from within.

Perhaps an illustration of a job-skill program may be appropriate. In the cutting and packing department of a paper mill, the foreman was plagued by low output, poor quality, and failure to meet schedules. He wanted to get rid of several of his workers. The assistant personnel manager asked him one day if he had ever actually taken the time to really train his people. The foreman said that no, he hadn't. Because they had been on the job when he took charge, he assumed they knew how to do their work. Working together, the foreman and the personnel man, developed an on-the-job training plan that drew heavily upon Job Instruction Training procedures of the Training-Within-Industry program of the World War II era. This training effort, when combined with improved work methods, was largely instrumental in raising the productivity level of the department to an acceptable level.

Apprentice Training

The apprenticeship system, which is a way of developing skilled craftsmen, is a descendant of the craft guild system of the Middle Ages. The apprentice in America before the Industrial Revolution generally lived in the home of the master craftsman to whom he was indentured and received no wages but simply was given his room, board, and clothing. Boys became apprentices at an early age—typically at the age of 14. Apprenticeships commonly lasted for seven years. The training was entirely of the on-the-job variety. Much of the work was very menial and routine.

In 1937 Congress passed a national apprenticeship law, popularly known as the Fitzgerald Act. Its purpose is to promote the furtherance of apprentice training and to extend apprenticeship standards on a voluntary basis throughout the United States. A Bureau of Apprenticeship was established within the United States Department of Labor. The act also reorganized and enlarged the Federal Committee on Apprenticeship. This committee has recommended certain essentials of an effective apprenticeship program. There should be a minimum starting age of 16, an approved schedule of work experience supplemented by at least 144 hours per year of related classroom instruction in subjects related to the trade, a progressively increasing schedule of wages, proper supervision of on-the-job training, and periodic evaluation of the apprentice's work.[8]

Apprenticeable trades are those requiring at least 4,000 hours (two years) of training experience through employment. Recognized apprenticeable trades exist in approximately 300 skilled occupations grouped by the United States Department of Labor under 90 general trade classifications. Typical occupations and their term of apprenticeship in years are airplane mechanic—4 years, carpenter—4 years, photoengraver—5–6 years, and rigger—2 years.

Quite frequently an employer can arrange through the local board of education

[8] U.S. Department of Labor, Bureau of Apprenticeship, *Apprenticeship Training* (Washington, D.C.: Government Printing Office, 1956), p. 6.

in the community to have the related classroom courses given in a high or vocational school. The related classroom instruction for a machinist, for example, would include the following subjects: safety, industrial and labor relations, blueprint reading and sketching, mathematics, trade theory, and trade science (cutting tools, heat treating, welding theory, and so on).

The apprenticeship system in this country is very loosely organized. Each employer is free to run his program as he sees fit (union participation especially in the building trades is often necessary). But there is no requirement to conform to state or Federal standards for the various trades. Thus an apprentice graduate from Company X may have received vastly inferior training to that of a graduate from Company Y. Some employers still look upon apprentices as a source of cheap labor, and their time is often occupied with menial tasks. Yet properly run according to state and Federal standards, countless apprentice programs are turning out well-qualified journeymen. For these companies skilled-labor needs are being adequately met. The advantages of apprentice training to the trainees are that they receive decent wages while learning and that they acquire a valuable skill that commands a high wage in the labor market. Skilled craftsmen in many industries earn as much or more than technicians, subprofessionals, and beginning professional employees, such as engineers and scientists.

Training the Disadvantaged

During the 1960's the American public—as well as business and governmental leaders—became aware that many hundreds of thousands of poor and disadvantaged people were unable to obtain and keep decent jobs in our industrialized society. Federal legislation was enacted to help these people obtain the skills needed to qualify for regular jobs and to encourage the private sector of the economy to hire them. Many cooperative programs were started between governmental units and businesses and among consortia of businesses. Many of these programs are still in operation and are successful.

A key component of these programs has been training for employment. Many disadvantaged persons not only lack useful job skills but they do not know the kind of behavior expected of them in the workplace. They do not understand proper grooming, how to deal with their supervisor and fellow employees, the need for steady attendance, and the necessity of good work habits. Therefore, orientation to industry is an important part of their training. Skill training must follow.

Opportunities Industrialization Centers, founded by Reverend Leon H. Sullivan in the early 1960's, is the largest private employment and training organization in the country. It operates 140 centers throughout the United States and has close ties with business firms, both large and small. It provides training for people where definite arrangements have been made for jobs at the completion of the training. This organization provides education and training in adult basic education, orientation to the world of work, and job skills.

Other organizations with on-going training programs for the disadvantaged are the Borg-Warner Corporation, Chrysler Institute, Control Data Corporation, Cummings Engine Company, IBM, and Levi Strauss.[9]

[9] David Robison, *Training and Jobs Programs in Action* (New York: Committee for Economic Development, 1978).

Special Purpose Programs

A wide variety of courses and programs can be and are provided by organizations for their employees. Many corporations reimburse their people for part or all of the tuition for courses taken in local colleges and universities as well as in proprietary technical schools. Safety training courses and meetings for hourly paid employees are almost universal among those organizations operating sound accident prevention programs. Courses in public speaking and effective presentation are quite popular.

EVALUATION OF THE TRAINING EFFORT

If management invests in training programs for employees, it understandably expects to see some tangible benefits derived therefrom. When a staff training director approaches top management for approval to establish a new training activity, the question reasonably can be asked as to what good the course will do and why the company should invest such and such a sum of money in it. In short the question is "How can we determine the value of a training program?"

Training directors use a number of techniques to evaluate the effectiveness of training programs. Generally speaking, the usefulness of these methods is inversely proportional to the ease with which the evaluation can be done. One approach is to pass out a questionnaire to the trainees at the completion of the program to obtain their opinions as to its worth. Their opinions could also be elicited by means of interviews. Another approach is to measure the knowledge and/or skill that employees possess at the beginning of training and again at the completion of training. This is accomplished by administering the same examination (or an alternate form of a single examination) before and after.

The real purpose of training is to cause a change in employee behavior on the job and ultimately to improve the effectiveness of the organization. The aforementioned evaluation techniques do not measure employee behavior on the job. Thus, if employees say they liked a course of instruction, this is not the real payoff. A comparison of before-and-after test scores does not really get to the point either. People may show that they have learned a lot on classroom examinations, yet they may not transfer this learning to the job.

A better way of measuring the worth of training is to use various indices of work performance and compare them after the course with measures before the course. In this manner the output and quality of work of production workers, salesmen, stenographers, and other workers can be used for evaluation purposes. Though at first glance this seems to be a fruitful approach to the problem of evaluation, there is a basic flaw in the method. We have no way of knowing whether the training activity caused an improvement in the performance index or whether it was achieved as a result of a combination of other factors. An improvement might have been caused by better production planning, better supervision, new work methods, and improved materials, as well as training.

The most refined method for evaluating training (and one that avoids the errors of other techniques) is to measure performance before and after training for both a control group and an experimental group. This procedure can be accomplished by selecting two groups of employees that are approximately equivalent in education, experience, skill, job conditions, and performance. Subject one group to the training program and give no training to the other (control) group. Some time after training is completed, choose relevant performance measures and compare results for the two groups. This method is somewhat cumbersome from the administrative standpoint; however, it is one of the most fruitful methods available. Unfortunately, such a rigorous experimental approach to training evaluation is seldom carried out in practice.

Questions for Review and Discussion

1. What contributions can an effective training program make to a business organization?
2. What are the duties and responsibilities of the following for training?
   a. The training department
   b. Line supervision
3. How can one determine what kind of training programs to offer?
4. Discuss the following concepts as they affect learning:
   a. Motivation
   b. Knowledge of results
   c. Learning by doing
   d. Whole or part learning
   e. Teaching the theory underlying the work
5. What considerations should be evaluated when deciding whether to train employees on the job or in a classroom?
6. A company has decided to set up formal courses for selected groups of its employees in the subjects listed below. Of the various instructional methods available, which would be most suitable for each course?
   a. Statistics and probability theory
   b. Maintenance of electronic equipment
   c. An attitude-building course for regular employees and supervisors on the employment of minorities and the disadvantaged
   d. Motion and time study
   e. Operation of a nuclear reactor
   f. Industrial safety
7. What constitutes a thorough apprenticeship-training program? What are the strengths and limitations of the apprentice-training system?
8. Quite commonly education and training courses are evaluated by means of brief questionnaires given to the participants at the end of a course. This is common in colleges and for employee and management training. How valid and useful is this method of evaluation? Are there better methods? Discuss.

Case problem

The Ajax Manufacturing Company is in a very competitive metal products business. It employs 4,000 people. Because the designs and prices for its products are quite similar to those of its competitors, it maintains its sales by emphasizing quality and service. About a year ago it lost two of its major customers, who had been dissatisfied with excessive manufacturing defects. The Ajax Company, upon studying the problem, decided that its basic engineering was sound but that carelessness and lack of quality consciousness on the part of production workers, inspectors, and manufacturing supervision were a prime cause of the trouble. Accordingly, it established a quality control course to solve the problem.

The course was given after working hours, from 7:00 to 9:00 P.M. each Thursday for ten weeks. Employees were not paid to attend. Technically, attendance was voluntary; however, management intimated that employees who attended faithfully would have the fact recorded in their personnel records. This fact would be considered in future pay raises and promotions. The course was taught by a staff engineer from the Quality Control Department. Consisting mainly of lectures, the course was varied at times to include movies on quality control and some discussions. The course covered such topics as the need for high quality, "quality can't be inspected into a product, it must be built in," conditions affecting quality, costs of poor quality, inspection standards, inspection procedures and methods, statistical quality control, sampling inspection, and control chart procedures. The course was open to all interested employees in the plant, including supervision. Attendance at the early sessions averaged around fifty. Toward the end of the course it had declined to about twenty-five.

The training director made the following comment at the conclusion of the course. "Frank Smith (the instructor) did a good job of lecturing. He was interesting, informative, and spiced his talks with humor at appropriate times. It was not his fault that attendance fell off."

Questions

1. Do you think this training program was organized and administered properly?
2. Are there other training methods that could properly have been used?
3. Evaluate this approach to improving product quality.

Suggestion for further reading

BASS, BERNARD M. and JAMES A. VAUGHAN. *Training in Industry: The Management of Learning*. Belmont, Calif.: Wadsworth Publishing Co., Inc., 1966.

BUREAU OF NATIONAL AFFAIRS, INC. *Technical Aids to Manpower Training*. Washington, D.C., 1970.

CARROLL, STEPHEN J., JR., FRANK T. PAINE, and JOHN J. IVANCEVICH. "The Relative Effectiveness of Training Methods—Expert Opinion and Research," *Personnel Psychology*, Vol. 25, No. 3 (Autumn 1972), pp. 495–509.

CRAIG, ROBERT L. (ed.) *Training and Development Handbook*, 2nd ed. New York: McGraw-Hill Book Company, 1976.

GARDNER, JAMES E. *Helping Employees Develop Job Skill: A Casebook of Training Approaches*. Washington, D.C.: Bureau of National Affairs, Inc., 1976.

LYNTON, ROLF P., and UDAI PAREEK. *Training for Development.* Homewood, Ill.: Irwin-Dorsey, 1967.

NASH, A. N., J. P. MUCZYK, and F. L. VETTORI. "The Relative Practical Effectiveness of Programmed Instruction," *Personnel Psychology*, Vol. 25 (1971), pp. 397–418.

PATTEN, THOMAS H., JR. "Relating Learning Theory to Behavior Change in Organizations," *Human Resource Management*, Vol. 13, No. 4 (Winter 1974), pp. 27–36.

THIS, LESLIE E., and GORDON L. LIPPITT. "Learning Theories and Training," (two-part article). *Training and Development Journal*, Vol. 20, No. 4 (April 1966), pp. 2–11; Vol. 20, No. 5 (May 1966), pp. 10–18.

U.S. DEPARTMENT of LABOR, *Apprentice Training.* Washington, D.C.: Government Printing Office, 1969.

YODER, DALE and HERBERT G. HENEMAN, JR. (eds.) *Training and Development.* Washington, D.C.: Bureau of National Affairs, Inc., 1977.

Management development

For some years now successful corporations have devoted special efforts to the training and development of their management personnel. There has been a recognition that qualified executives of the caliber and quantity needed throughout our society do not just emerge from the labor force without consciously planned action on the part of work organizations, large and small. When undertaking to establish a management development program, top management must fully understand just what it is trying to accomplish. What is management? What do managers do? What knowledge and skills must they possess? How can these best be acquired? What part does the individual play in the program? What are the merits of on-the-job development as contrasted with classroom training? We shall examine these and related topics in this chapter.

NATURE OF MANAGEMENT DEVELOPMENT

What Is Management Development?

Management development is a systematic process of training and growth by which individuals gain and apply knowledge, skills, insights, and attitudes to manage work organizations effectively. As explained in the previous chapter on training, training and the learning process really involve the implication that there will be changed behavior on the part of the individual. Managers develop not only by participation in formal courses of instruction but also through actual job experiences in a work environment. The role of the company is to establish the program and the developmental opportunities for its managers and potential managers. But it must be recognized that simply exposing employees to lectures, case studies, readings, job rotation assignments, and the like, does not guarantee that they will learn. An equal, and perhaps more important, counterpart to the efforts of the organization are those of the individual. There has been increasing recognition that the company can set the proper climate, but that the major effort must be made by the individuals themselves. Thus, self-development is an important concept in the whole program for management development. The participants must have the motivation and the capacity to learn and develop. They must make the requisite efforts to grow.

What Is a Manager?

Before one can obtain an adequate understanding of the principles and procedures of management training and development, he must know what a manager is and what he does.

Management is a process of utilizing material and human resources to accomplish designated objectives. It involves the organization, direction, coordination, and evaluation of people to achieve these goals.

The word *manager* has been used in a variety of ways by industrialists and theorists. To some the term *manager* means top executive. To others a manager is any person who supervises other employees. In fact, one large manufacturing company uses the term without any status connotations. In this firm a manager may supervise a number of managers, and he, in turn, may report to a manager. Thus, the organization structure contains a number of echelons, each level possessing the designation of manager.

The most commonly accepted view is to consider as members of management all those who coordinate and direct the activities of others plus all those administrative and staff people who deal with others outside their own group and who have a decided impact upon the organization. Thus, all supervisors from a foreman up through a corporation president are decidedly managers. Administrative personnel such as planners, coordinators, executive assistants, and the like are also members of management even though they do not supervise other employees. They are members of the management team because their work is related to or affects management policies, practices, and actions. Usually, engineers and scientists are considered to be professionals but not managers.

Another way of understanding what managing is and what managers do is to examine the functions of management. The process of management consists of planning, organizing, staffing, leading, and controlling. Planning encompasses looking ahead to the future, setting goals, and figurng out policies, procedures, and methods for accomplishing these goals. The cognitive and decision-making processes are heavily involved in planning. Organizing involves the breaking down of the total work to be done into jobs, groups, and departments and the establishment of workable relationships between these units. It includes such elements as grouping activities both by level and by type, setting up jobs, determining authority and responsibility relationships, setting up patterns of communication, delegating, and use of staff. Staffing refers to the process of recruiting and selecting people to run the enterprise. Leading is the motivation and direction of people to achieve a desired goal. It integrates the personal goals of the employees with the objectives of the enterprise. Finally, the control function of management includes measurement of work performed, comparison of actual performance with a predetermined standard, and then the taking of corrective action, when necessary, to insure that performance meets standard.

Knowledge and Skills of the Manager

Although a foreman is just as much a manager as a top executive officer, the nature of his work and the skills he must utilize to do this work are different from those of a major executive. A foreman must devote a majority of his time to leadership activities. He must be an expert at applied human relations. He must motivate, communicate, direct, correct, discipline, coordinate, teach, and reward his subordinates. He must also be able to teach his men the technical aspects of the products and processes with which they must work. He must effectively solve routine technical problems of the work processes. A foreman primarily carries out directions from above. The scope of his discretionary power is quite limited.

Top executives need very little technical skill pertaining to the products and processes of the business they manage. To be sure, they must have an appreciation or general knowledge of the capabilities and limitations of these technical processes, but these are the men who hire others to design, install, operate, and maintain the facilities. Major executives devote much of their time to forecasting, policy formulation, and planning. They deal, to a considerable extent, with forces and people outside their own organizations. They are concerned with the economic, social, and political environment. They must be adept at integrating the various functional branches of an organization, such as production, sales, finance, and industrial relations. Top managers spend a high percentage of their time interacting with other people in group conferences and two-person face-to-face dealings. Executives not only exert their authority and power to get things done through their subordinates, but also they frequently seek to persuade and influence others outside their own hierarchical sphere.

In analyzing the skills needed by an administrator (manager, according to our terminology), Katz speaks of three types: technical, human, and conceptual skills. Technical skill refers to proficiency in handling methods, processes, and techniques of a particular kind of business or activity. Human skill refers to the ability to work effectively with others and build cooperative group relations to achieve goals. Conceptual skill, as Katz describes it, is the ability to see the organization as a whole, to recognize interrelationships among functions of a business and external forces, and to be able to guide effectively the organization in consideration of the multitudinous forces affecting it. Coordination depends upon conceptual skill. Conceptual skills are concerned with the realm of ideas and creativeness. Technical skill is an essential ingredient of lower-level management, human skill is important at all levels of management, and conceptual skill is especially critical in top executive positions.[1]

Evolution of Management Development

It was not so many years ago that a man was selected to be a supervisor on the basis of his performance as a worker. High-producing workers who were aggressive and loyal to the organization were likely candidates for promotion into management. However, superior workers do not necessarily make superior managers. Corporate executives and high-level public administrators have come to recognize the need for planned programs for the selection, training, and development of managerial manpower.

Formal management development programs began to appear in large corporations in the late 1940's and early 1950's. Since then there has been growing sophistication in the organization and content of such endeavors. They have spread to smaller corporations and to governmental agencies at the Federal and state level. Several forces have operated to cause the expansion of management development activities.

There has been a pronounced shift from owner-managed to professionally managed enterprises. Management has been recognized as a distinct kind of occupation consisting of teachable skills and a unified body of knowledge. Management can be described as an emerging profession. Professions consist of two kinds: the learned (law, medicine, teaching, and so on) and the artistic (acting, music, and so on). We are here concerned with the learned professions. A profession has the following characteristics:

1. It requires advanced, specialized formal education and training.
2. It requires the consistent exercise of discretion and independent judgment.
3. It is based on a deep and organized body of knowledge. Efforts are continually made to expand the knowledge through research.
4. The members of the profession have a keenly developed sense of ethics and public responsibility.
5. The members of the profession have a sense of common identity and purpose. There is a professional organization that seeks to advance the field and uphold professional standards.
6. It demands certain recognized standards of competence in terms of education, training, experience, and human performance.

It must be recognized that management is still an emerging profession. It is not full-fledged, because of the lack of recognized standards of competence, and because the members have not created or adhered to any generally accepted code of ethics. There exists great variation in the routes people take to become managers and in performance after they acquire their positions. But the point being made is that management has been acquiring more and more of the characteristics of a profession even though it has still not arrived there.

Within the past few decades there has been an ever-increasing amount of

---

[1] Robert L. Katz, "Skills of an Effective Administrator," *Harvard Business Review*, Vol. 33, No. 1 (January–February 1955), pp. 33–41.

research-generated knowledge of the principles and techniques of administration. This applies both to general management and to its various functional fields, such as personnel and industrial relations, production, finance, marketing, and accounting. The universities through their schools of business, public administration, industrial management, and social science have carried on much of this research effort under both government and industry sponsorship. Generally the business community has looked favorably upon his knowledge and has tried to apply it in those situations where it is appropriate.

The rapid rate of technological and social change has made it imperative to have managers who are trained to cope with these developments. Among the manifesatations of this change are expansion into overseas markets and the rise of the multinational corporation, intense competition in the United States from foreign firms, and new products of greater technical complexity.

There has been increased recognition by business and industrial leaders of the social and public responsibilities of the corporation. Companies must now acknowledge their responsibility for minimizing environmental pollution and meeting the costs thereof. Organized consumer groups are demanding better products and services. Minority groups are demanding more and better job opportunities. And, as the representative of the public interest, government is regulating private business more closely. These public and social responsibilities require that managers in business have broader vision and a greater understanding of the interdependence of the institutions of our society. The older and narrower focus upon the firm as simply a profit-maximizing instrument is insufficient for present-day realities.

Recent Trends.   Formerly management training and development were provided primarily for an elite corps of "crown princes" and "fair-haired" boys. In more recent years industry has concentrated upon the development of *all* who are in management positions, both to improve performance in their present jobs and to provide a solid basis for those who move up. Also there has been increased recognition of the desirability of tailor-making development programs to fit individual needs. Not only do people differ in their capacities, experiences, and temperaments, but their positional responsibilities differ. Therefore, programs no longer seek to homogenize the managers. And finally, corporate leaders understand that management development must not be a one-shot affair. It must be integrated into the spectrum of required management activities. It is part and parcel of good day-to-day management.

Start at the Top

Management training and development can succeed best when they pervade the entire organization and when they begin with top management. This is a fundamental necessity for any program of this type to be successful. However, in actual practice this simple idea has not been grasped by top business and industrial leaders. Many thousands of dollars are spent annually on foremen's training conferences throughout this country, yet much of this effort is fruitless. A management development program can succeed only in a climate of sound management from the top to the bottom of the organization.

The author has been personally involved in teaching numerous supervisory courses where top management has said in effect "we think that the company could be improved if we could make better leaders of our supervisors and improve their management knowledge and skills." However, the realities of the situation are such that supervisors may learn the latest and soundest principles and techniques of management in the classroom but not be allowed to apply the knowledge of the job because, so often, higher management does not practice this pattern of management itself. The realities of the authority structure in industry are such that a supervisor must conform to the demands of his superiors. If this pattern of leadership is in conflict with the principles that the supervisor learned in his management course, he may experience serious frustration and impaired performance.

In a significant and pioneering research project aimed at evaluating the effectiveness of foreman-leadership training at the International Harvester Company, Fleishman, Harris, and Burtt found that foremen performed back on the job in a manner that conformed to the attitudes and behavior of their bosses. If their superiors rated high on what the researchers labeled a "consideration score," then the foremen also rated high on a "consideration score," and vice versa. Their ratings were irrespective of knowledge and attitudes developed during participation in the leadership course. The researchers concluded that foremen are more responsive to their day-to-day climate on the job than to any special course of training they may have taken.[2]

From this study and the evidence of other researchers, consultants, and management training specialists, it is clear that management training and development, to be effective, must begin with top executive officers of a firm. As they acquire new insights and skills and as they begin to practice these in their work, they are in a sound position to launch formal development activities for members of middle and lower management.

PLANNING AND ADMINISTERING THE PROGRAM

The inauguration of a management development program must be done by the chief executive officer of an organization, because it involves fundamental policy decisions, important actions by executives all down the line, and the expenditure, in some cases, of considerable sums of money. Ordinarily the planning and guiding of an executive development program is carried out by a committee composed of major executives, whereas the day-to-day administration is performed by the personnel department.

Let us now examine the essential ingredients of a management development program. The key elements are

1. Analysis of organization needs.
2. Appraisal of present management talent.
3. Management human resource inventory.
4. Planning of individual development programs.

---

[2] Edwin A. Fleishman, Edwin F. Harris, and Harold E. Burtt, *Leadership and Supervision in Industry: An Evaluation of a Supervisory Training Program* (Columbus, Ohio: Bureau of Educational Research, The Ohio State University, 1955).

5. Establishment of training and development programs.
6. Program evaluation.

Analysis of Organization Needs

After the key decision to launch a management-development program has been made, the first thing to do is organization planning. The organization structure must be studied to ascertain whether activities and functions are grouped properly. Forecasts must be made of the growth of the business. Projected new products and services must be identified. What will the organization consist of five or ten years hence in terms of functions, departments, and executive positions? Will any portions of the organization have to be reduced in size?

The next step is to prepare descriptions and specifications for all management jobs. The purpose is to obtain a record of the kinds of management work performed and the kinds of executives and administrators needed in the organization. It is necessary at this stage to highlight the kind of education, experience, training, special knowledge, skills, and personal traits required for each job. If the company already has in operation a comprehensive job-analysis program (as it should have), then it will be necessary at this point only to collect the job descriptions and job specifications for all management activities, review them, and make desired summarizations.

Top management must make a policy decision as to whether it wishes to fill contemplated vacancies in executive ranks from within the organization or whether it wants to hire from the outside. This decision will depend to some extent upon the caliber and number of present personnel in comparison with projected needs. Most commonly companies hire on the outside to fill their lowest-level positions and then promote from within. In effect they grow their own executives except where they have a critical shortage of specialized high-level talent.

Appraisal of Present Management Talent

The purpose of this part of the program is to determine qualitatively what the organization has in terms of management talent. Existing performance appraisal data should be examined to determine if they properly identify the developmental needs of individuals and if they contain estimates of their potential for moving ahead. If the existing appraisal information is inadequate then the appraisal system must be revised to meet the needs of the management development program. It is also appropriate to utilize data from an assessment center.

Management Human Resource Inventory

At this stage it is necessary to prepare an inventory of present management personnel. For each member of the management team, a card is prepared, listing such data as name, age, length of service, education, work experience previous to company employment, company experience, training courses completed, health record, psychological test results, and performance appraisal data. This information is often summarized and stored in a computer. If the data have been judiciously classified into categories, it then becomes possible to select via the computer all those individuals possessing a desired kind of background. For example, the computer may be set up to select all those who are college graduates, who have had at least 5 years' experience in the supervision of research and development projects, and who are rated above average by their bosses.

Some organizations go one step further than the preparation of a management inventory. They set up *replacement tables or charts* that show each individual, his background and rating, and projected promotions and transfers. Quite often this is prepared in organization-chart form with certain coding used to portray a man's rating and planned movement. For example, Mr. A, the plant manager may be 67 years of age and three years from retirement. Mr. B, the manager of manufacturing, may be 47, a college graduate, have 18 years of diversified plant experience, be rated outstanding in ability and potential, and be picked to fill the plant manager's position when Mr. A retires. The replacement chart may also show that there are several capable executives who will be given serious consideration for the plant manager's post at the time Mr. A actually retires.

Although the replacement chart is certainly a systematic way of mapping out plans for the utilization of management manpower, it must be recognized that conditions may change rapidly, so that the earmarking of individuals for particular jobs several years hence is highly speculative.

Planning of Individual Development Programs

This activity must be performed by each executive working cooperatively with each of his subordinates. The executive should be guided heavily by the results of the performance appraisal, which will indicate strengths and weaknesses for each person. Much has been said in recent years about the allegation that American industry has been molding a group of conformists and "organization men." In reality it is unwise to try to force every management person into the same mold. Each of us has a unique set of physical, intellectual, and emotional characteristics. Therefore, a development plan should be tailor-made for each individual. In setting up this development plan, each executive should give consideration to the expressed interests and goals of his subordinates as well as the training and developmental opportunities that exist within the organization.

Establishment of Training and Development Programs

This step of the broad management development effort involves the setting up of well-conceived training and development opportunities on a companywide basis. The personnel department or its training section will establish certain training programs—such as leadership courses, management games, strategic planning seminars, courses with local universities, and so on—as needs, time, and costs dictate. Top management may wish to send certain individuals to executive development courses at universities. It may establish a companywide system of job rotation or of multiple management.

The personnel department executives must take an active part in keeping abreast of new developments in the field of management education and development. They must carefully study training needs and recommend to top management that certain specific programs be set up as conditions dictate. These staff officers must continually work with line managers to insure that they are developing their subordinates and that they are not denying qualified candidates the opportunity to participate in formal courses. The staff training executives should keep adequate records to audit and control the management development activities throughout the entire organization.

Program Evaluation

Many organizations have undertaken vast programs of management development. Since these involve large expenditures of time and money, top management justifiably would like to know whether it is receiving its money's worth. Have the training and development improved individual and organizational performance?

It is exceedingly difficult to obtain definitive proof that such activities have accomplished their given objectives. A group of supervisors may take a course in human relations and leadership. After the program is completed, some may exhibit subtle changes in attitude and behavior; however, it is difficult to measure these. An executive may attend an in-residence advanced management course at some university; yet it may be difficult to observe a significant change in his work after he returns to the job.

When we discussed program evaluation in the previous chapter, it was pointed out that there were several methods that could be used. A test can be administered to the group being trained both before and after completion of the program, job performance can be measured both before and after the program, and experimental and control groups can be set up. A rigorous evaluation design, such as experimental and control groups, is costly and may disturb the people and the organization. Because an organization is an interacting system and because there are many factors affecting the performance of individual managers and their organizational units, it is difficult to isolate the changes induced by participation in the training activity. Also changes in managerial performance often occur gradually over a long period of time after exposure to many on-the-job, classroom, and life experiences.

Personnel executives are well aware of the difficulties involved in trying to evaluate management development and training activities. A survey of training directors and personnel executives revealed that only 15 percent of the companies represented in the study conducted some kind of limited cost/benefit analysis of their programs and another 10 percent examined such factors as improved sales results or increased longevity of productive employment for the individuals involved. Most respondents claimed benefits could only be measured in subjective terms and not in terms of dollars and cents.[3]

DEVELOPMENT THROUGH WORK EXPERIENCE

There are two principal methods by which people can acquire the knowledge, skills, and attitudes to become competent managers. One is through formal

[3] William H. Wagel, "Consensus: Evaluating Management Development and Training Programs," *Personnel*, Vol. 54, No. 4 (July–August 1977), pp. 4–10.

training and education courses; the other is through on-the-job experiences. Fifty years ago in the United States, almost all management development occurred on the job. (Most of the learning was unorganized and haphazard.) In the 1950's when the management development movement in industry was working up a "full head of steam," the major emphasis was upon taking managers away from their jobs for a period of time so they could attend executive development and supervisory training classes.

Now it is recognized that both classroom and on-the-job training are important. Formal course work is invaluable for learning new knowledge, new techniques, and broader concepts. Yet real learning can occur only when the learner has an opportunity to practice and apply his ideas. This must be done on the job. It must be further recognized that a manager, by the very nature of his position, serves as a teacher for his subordinates. The authority structure of the organization and the responsibilities of a manager cause him continually to guide and mold the behavior of his subordinates so that they conform to his expectations.

Of the two influences, formal training courses and on-the-job development guided by the boss, the latter is the most powerful. Yet it is totally unsound to place sole reliance upon on-the-job development because many executives and managers are themselves unqualified to carry out this important task. They may lack the skill, the interest, or the patience. They may possess wholly faulty notions of administration, and for them to impose such ideas upon all their subordinates would be tantamount to deliberately weakening the organization. Yet when on-the-job development is properly balanced with classroom training, and when both are carried out in an atmosphere of sound management emanating from the very top of the company, then we have a workable formula for management development.

We shall now examine some of the important techniques of management development.

Understudies

An understudy is a person who is in training to assume, at a future time, the full duties and responsibilities of the position currently held by his superior. It is a means of insuring that a fully trained individual is available to take over the job of a manager when he leaves his post because of promotion, retirement, or transfer.

There are several ways of arranging for understudies. A department manager may pick one individual within his unit to become his understudy. He will then teach him his own job and let him grapple with the problems that confront the manager daily. Or the department manager may choose several of his subordinates who will act as understudies. They may take turns at filling their boss's job when he is absent because of vacation, a business trip, or illness. Or the manager may designate one of his subordinates to be his administrative assistant. This assistant will handle a great variety of administrative matters that his superior may choose to delegate to him. Quite often the choice of an understudy is not made by a department head alone; he must consult with his superior.

An understudy can gain the requisite experience to take over his boss's job in a number of ways. When the manager is handling his daily operating problems, he may discuss these with his helper to get his ideas and give him experience at decision making. He may assign the understudy to investigate and make written recommendations regarding long-term problems. There may arise occasions when the understudy can be assigned direct supervision of a two- or three-person task force. This will give him an opportunity to try out his leadership skills. The understudy may also be sent to important executive meetings in place of or in attendance with his superior. He may be called upon to make presentations and proposals before higher executives.

The understudy method is a practical and fairly quick way of training designated persons for greater management responsibilities. It emphasizes learning by doing. Motivation of the learner tends to be high.

On the other hand, this technique has serious disadvantages. It insures that things will be done pretty much as they always have been. It does not infuse any new ideas into the unit. The understudy will have been picked in the first place because his way of thinking and acting is similar to that of his boss. The other major disadvantage of the understudy approach is that it destroys the incentive to get ahead for all the other employees in the unit who have not been made the understudy.

Job Rotation

The transferring of executives from job to job and from plant to plant on a coordinated, planned basis is a popular practice among industrial concerns. Under the typical arrangement a top-management committee oversees the operation of the program and makes the final decisions on the reassignment of executives. When a manager takes a new post on such a program, it is no mere orientation assignment. He is placed in an important line or staff position in which he must assume full charge and make regular management decisions. Quite often this executive on the rotational program will be back-stopped at each location by experienced, permanent personnel who will exercise a steadying influence and keep things running if the individual has difficulty. Job assignments under a rational scheme typically last from six months to two years. Sometimes the new job assignment will represent a promotion for the individual. The executives to whom these rotating managers report evaluate their performance and funnel appraisal reports back to the central coordinating committee.

In the modern corporation a high proportion of the entry jobs for junior executives and engineers demand a considerable degree of technical knowledge and specialization. As a person increases in stature with time, he can never acquire the broad perspective and diversified skills needed for promotion unless he is deliberately taken out of his speciality and placed in different types of situations. In order to obtain the generalists who are ultimately needed at upper-management levels, the enterprise must take action to provide a variety of job experiences for those judged to have the potential for major executive ranks. Job rotation answers this need. It also serves to break down departmental provincialism—the feeling that only my department is important and others' problems are not worthy of my concern. When a number of managers have served in one another's units, they can all understand the reasons why a certain function must be done in a particular way. Interdepartmental cooperation is enhanced.

Job rotation injects new ideas into the different departments of an organization. Under this system of management development, a manager is not destined to end up in just one spot. He is equipped to step into any one of several executive posts in any of various functional divisions. Thus, the organization gains management strength in depth.

However, job rotation is hard on those executives who are in the program, because they must periodically pull up stakes and move to a new location. This is upsetting to home and family life. It periodically tears the children out of school and forces them to make new friends in a strange town. The net result is such that the executive must, in effect, center his life upon the company.

Job rotation may undermine the morale and efficiency of the departments managed by these executives. Sometimes the rotating executives are viewed as an elite corps, somewhat apart from the other personnel. Their attitudes and expectations set them off from the other supervisors and administrators. If sharp cleavages arise between these groups, then cooperation is impeded and frictions occur.

Coaching

It is quite common for consultants and researchers to find, upon interviewing employees and managers alike, that they are rarely told by their superiors how they are doing. Their supervisors have not taken the time to sit down with them to discuss their performance on specific assignments or on their last few months' work. Yet, if properly done, coaching is something every supervisor can do. It costs little money, and it contributes toward improved performance by the individual and ultimately by the whole work group.

A manager should recognize an obligation to take a decided interest in the training and advancement of those who work for him. His coaching responsibility can be implemented by doing a number of things. He can delegate more. He can assign not only the routine chores, but he can invite his people to tackle some of the more complex problems, which he may have felt could be properly handled only by himself. An executive can give his subordinates an opportunity to participate in making important decisions affecting the department. This can be done either on an individual basis or else by a group conference of all management members in the department.

The effective coach avoids criticizing his subordinate's personality. He concentrates upon the work and the job. What constitutes a good or bad personality is a matter of opinion. Besides, it is extremely difficult to change another's personality. To do so would appear high-handed to many persons.

As a management development technique, coaching requires the least centralized staff coordination. Every executive can coach his people regardless of whether top management has set up any formal management development program. It can yield immediate benefits to the organization, the coach, and the individual. It constitutes learning by doing. The learner can experience a feeling of progress. He can see the fruits of his efforts.

Multiple Management

Multiple management is the designation given to the system whereby permanent advisory committees of managers study problems of the company and make recommendations to higher management. The concept of multiple management, or the junior-board-of-executives system, as it is sometimes called, was pioneered by Charles P. McCormick in 1932 when he established his Junior Board of Executives at McCormick & Company in Baltimore. McCormick went on to set up a Factory Board, a Sales Board, and the Junior Sales Associates. Although originally appointed by the president of the company, the Junior Board itself now rates its own members and sets up a membership committee to appoint new members. For each succeeding term of office, some of the old members must be dropped and new people added to the Board. At McCormick & Company the various boards are granted wide latitude to investigate problems in different facets of the business. When a board has arrived at a solution to a problem, the members must agree unanimously before the proposal can be submitted to the Senior Board of Directors (which is the regular stockholder-elected board). This insures that problems are throughly worked out. The latter board is under no compulsion to adopt proposals of the subordinate boards. Junior boards serve in an advisory capacity only. However, the vast majority of recommendations are adopted by the Senior Board. The junior-board-of-executives system has been used successfully by a number of companies in addition to McCormick & Company. Craf made a study of twenty-one companies that used this system of manager training. He emphasized that a junior board is different from the ordinary committee found in all businesses. Junior boards are formally organized under a set of bylaws. The members rate one another to decide which ones deserve to retain membership after their term of office expires and which should be dropped. Often board members are paid extra compensation for their service. Most importantly the boards do far more than merely discuss topics. Committees within the board are assigned definite projects by the chairman. They must conduct thorough investigations and submit written reports to the entire board. The junior boards ordinarily have broad authority to study nearly any phase of a company's business.[4]

As a management development technique, multiple management—or the junior-board-of-executives system—has several advantages: (1) it gives board members an opportunity to gain knowledge and experience in aspects of the business other than their own specialty; (2) it helps identify those who have good executive talent. Multiple judgments are obtained on each individual through the board rating system; (3) the members gain practical experience in group decison making and in teamwork. In addition, junior boards can make significant contributions to organizational performance.

Action Learning

Action learning was created by Professor Reginald W. Revans of Great Britain in the 1960's and has been used in many corporations throughout Europe. In action learning the participants work on real problems, most commonly from within their own companies but also sometimes from outside organizations. They do not tackle problems from their own job assignments. The learners or participants must formulate their own descriptions of actual, on-going problems. They must diagnose the problems and take action to implement their proposed solutions.

[4] John R. Craf, *Junior Boards of Executives: A Management Training Procedure* (New York: Harper and Row, 1958).

Each participant belongs to a group, called a "project set" which consists of four or five other trainees of diverse backgrounds plus two advisors, one from inside the company and one from outside. Typically, a project set (group) meets for one full day every week. The group reviews each member's progress on his project, discusses the member's diagnosis of the problem, and offers constructive criticism. Ordinarily the trainees work on their projects over a period of many weeks (or months). Each participant, in addition to the consultations within his own project set, works with a client–executive in whose department or company the participant's problem exists. This client–executive must be committed to working in a supportive way with the trainee on the project and to seeing it through to full implementation. The completion of a project is not the preparation of a technical report but rather the actual implementation of the recommendations.

When an action-learning program is first set up, the participants are brought together for initial orientation to play business games to develop a sense of working in teams, and to meet with the sponsoring executives who pay for the program and with the client-executives with whom they will work on projects.[5]

FORMAL TRAINING COURSES

Formal training courses for managers can be conducted in a number of ways and under a variety of conditions. Several of the training techniques discussed in Chapter 15, "Training," find important applications in supervisory and executive training. The conference method is probably used more than any other single technique. Role playing and written case studies are ideally suited for use within the conference type of classes. Extensive reading assignments in company literature, college textbooks, and journal articles are frequently given to middle- and top-management trainees. At the foreman level, reading assignments tend to be light. Professional training specialists tend to feel that foremen, because the majority lack a college education and because they are not required to read extensively on the job, would be frustrated by long required reading assignments.

The lecture method is employed in courses for all levels of management. However, it is rare to find any training course that consists entirely of lectures. Lectures are usually interspersed with discussions, films, case studies, role playing, and demonstrations.

Who does the teaching in management training courses? The answer is that practice varies considerably. Subjects dealing with the company, its policies, and organization are often taught by either a major line executive or a member of the training staff. Quite often a business organization will engage professors from schools of business administration and engineering to teach courses in statistics, operations research, production planning, and methods engineering. Or these management techniques may be taught by specialists within the company who are professionally qualified in these topics. Those courses concerned with the particular processes and technology of the industry, for example, metalworking in the metal fabrication industry and food processing in the canning industry, are most generally taught by qualified engineers and technicians within the organiza-

---

[5] Nancy Foy, "Action Learning Comes to Industry," *Harvard Business Review*, Vol. 55, No. 5 (September–October 1977), pp. 158–168.

tion. College professors and consultants are often hired by companies to teach courses in human relations, organization theory, industrial relations, report writing, public speaking and reading improvement.

Subject Matter and Course Content

The essential subject matter appropriate for management training is as follows:

1. The company or organization
   a. Objectives and philosophy
   b. Policies and procedures
   c. Products and services
   d. Organization structure and organization dynamics
   e. Plant facilities
   f. Financial picture
   g. The labor agreement and union-management relations
2. Management principles and techniques
   a. Organization principles
   b. Financial planning and management
   c. Management information systems
   d. Production planning and control
   e. Methods analysis and work measurement
   f. Personnel management
   g. Wage and salary administration
   h. Cost analysis and control
   i. Statistics and probability
   j. Operations research
   k. Data processing and computers
   l. Marketing
   m. Risk management
3. Human relations
   a. Fundamentals of human behavior
   b. Motivation
   c. Group dynamics
   d. Attitudes
   e. Conflict resolution
   f. Managing change
   g. Patterns of management
   h. Concepts of leadership
   i. Power, authority, influence
   j. Communication
   k. Personnel management responsibilities of supervision in such areas as selection, training, pay administration, counseling, appraisal, discipline, and grievance handling
4. Technical knowledge and skills
   These are peculiar to every type of business and to every type of work. Managers, of course, must have an adequate understanding of the technology, products, processes, and methods of their line of business.

5. Economic, social, and political environment
   a. Business ethics
   b. Economic system
   c. Relations with local, state, and Federal governments
   d. Community relations
   e. Social responsibilities
   f. Legal framework for business
   g. Business operations in foreign countries
   h. Environmental issues such as land use and pollution control
   i. Consumerism
6. Personal skills
   a. Speaking
   b. Report writing
   c. Conducting meetings
   d. Reading improvement
   e. Interpersonal skills, listening, feedback, communication

Any of these individual topics—for example, organization principles, statistics and probability, or reading improvement—might constitute an entire twenty to thirty (or more) classroom hour course. Because resources in any company are limited, the training department staff must decide in what subject areas the greatest needs lie. It can then establish courses to tackle these problems first.

The training needs of a newly appointed manager are somewhat different from those of experienced ones. The experienced person will need only a very light coverage of subject area 1 above, "The Company or Organization," whereas this is a logical starting point, and one that demands great emphasis, for the newcomer.

Emphasis Varies with Management Level. Although foremen, department heads, plant managers, and vice-presidents are all members of management, the nature of their duties and responsibilities differs rather substantially. The six main subject areas listed above are necessary for all levels of management. However, certain topics are more appropriate for one level than another. For example, foremen are not directly involved in the economic, social, and political environment of a corporation, whereas vice-presidents are. Not only the content but also the depth of knowledge and skill vary according to the level and nature of the personnel involved.

Courses for top management will emphasize such subjects as economics, finance, organization theory, human relations, policy formulation, administrative controls, business operations overseas, the business person in politics, labor relations, and public relations. Because top executives, to a large extent, control their organizations' relations with the outside world, there is usually considerable time devoted to topics concerned with the economic, social, and political environment. Courses for members of middle management tend to contain elements of both top- and lower-level management programs. They, of course, devote considerable time to human relations and personnel management principles because these are essential at all levels of management. Middle-level executives must often possess a solid grounding in such management techniques as cost analysis and control, data processing, production planning and control, and wage and salary administration.

Courses for first-level supervisors concentrate upon technical processes of the business, human relations, and personal skills. They tend to be immediately practical. They are closely related to the supervisor's day-to-day job.

University Nondegree Programs

Approximately forty colleges and universities offer residential programs in management for executives employed in industry. These programs are given on the college campus, and in most cases the participants are sent by their companies. The employer pays full tuition and living expenses plus the individual's salary. In addition to these broad-coverage management programs—they are often called advanced management or executive-development programs—there are literally scores of special-purpose programs given by universities. In the discussion that follows, we shall confine ourselves to the broad, residential executive-development programs.

The first university executive-development program was started in 1931 at Massachusetts Institute of Technology. This was the Sloan Fellowship program, which provided financial support for a few young industrial executives each year to spend a year of study in industrial management. The next program—and the first really large-scale one—was started in 1943 by the Harvard Business School at the request of the United States Office of Education to train executives in war industries. Terminated at the end of World War II, this program was soon reactivated and modified by Harvard because of strong requests from private industry. The Harvard Advanced Management Program is 13 weeks in length and is for top-level executives. The program is designed to handle two groups of about 160 people each year, one group starting in September and the other in February. Largely using the case method of teaching, the faculty offers the following courses in the program: business policy, marketing management, accounting and financial policy, finance, business history, problems in labor relations, business and world society, human behavior in organizations, mathematical concepts for decision making, and simulation.[6]

Corporate Institutes

A few of the very large American corporations have set up their own educational institutions to provide short programs of study for their management personnel. Among the firms having such institutes are General Electric, IBM, American Telephone and Telegraph, International Harvester, Johnson and Johnson, and Westinghouse.

Illustrative of these is the General Electric Management Research and Development Institute, established at Crotonville, New York, in 1955. This Institute offers a thirteen-week program, called the Advanced Management Course, which is designed primarily for the top four levels of management. The program

---

[6] Information on university executive development programs is contained in J. P. West and D. R. Sheriff, *Executive Development Programs in Universities*, Studies in Personnel Policy, No. 215 (New York: National Industrial Conference Board, 1969).

content includes management theory, business policies, general management, and economic, social, and political issues. It also includes job-related material designed to help in the management of a GE product department. A variety of instructional methods are used including case studies. Instruction is given by both GE executives and professors from leading universities.[7]

Management Games

A management game—also called a business game—is a classroom simulation exercise in which teams of students compete against each other or against an environment to achieve given objectives. The game is intended to be a close representation of real-life conditions. Often the controlling features of a game are expressed in the form of a mathematical model.

A typical top-management type game consists of three teams—each representing a company—that compete in producing and selling the same product in the same marketing area. Each company tries to achieve a good financial position, to increase its assets, to make a good return on investment, and to place itself in a strong position for the future. Each team or company makes quarterly decisions in regard to product price, advertising, production volume and cost, research and development expenditure, and investment in additional plant manufacturing capacity. These decisions are fed into a computer that has been programmed with a mathematical model that simulates a typical economic situation in the market. The computer then feeds back to each team its own performance data derived from the interaction with the other competing teams. Teams can change their strategies as the game progresses and determine the impact upon performance of such changes.

A game contains many, but not all, the variables present in real-life businesses. Student-managers can learn the consequences of their decisions in a classroom situation, which is a low-risk environment. Student enthusiasm tends to be high when playing management games. Students play different roles in their teams and they learn how to work together cooperatively. A game takes the learning situation a step farther than can be done in a case study. In addition to diagnosing a problem and deciding upon a course of action, the students can learn what happens when they implement their decisions.

A limitation of management games is that the mathematical model, practically of necessity, has to be a simplified representation of real life. Because it is simplified (or if it is inaccurate) it may generate erroneous learning for the students.

Transactional Analysis

Transactional analysis (TA) is a technique used to help people better understand their own and others' behavior, especially in interpersonal relationships. Courses in TA are given to managers, salespersons, and professionals to help them improve interpersonal communications and effectiveness.

Dr. Eric Berne is generally credited with developing the basic concepts and

[7] Thomas H. Patten, Jr., *Manpower Planning and the Development of Human Resources* (New York: John Wiley & Sons, 1971), pp. 430–433.

theory of transactional analysis. It is based upon concepts of psychotherapy; however TA concepts and formulations are expressed in layman's language so that it has become very popular in recent years. Besides Berne, others who have done important work in developing transactional analysis and in disseminating information about it are Thomas A. Harris, Muriel James and Dorothy Jongeward.[8]

The primary concepts in transactional analysis are ego states, transactions, strokes, and ways people spend their time.

There are three ego states: parent, adult, and child. The *parent* ego state of a person comprises the judgmental, value-laden, rule-making, and moralizing component of personality. It is expressed by advice, admonitions, "do's" and "don'ts." The *adult* ego state is authentic, direct, and reality-based. It is rational, fact-seeking, thinking, and problem-solving. The *child* ego state constitutes the emotional, creative, spontaneous, impulsive component of personality. It must be noted that ego states are not tied to one's chronological age. In the course of daily interactions adults are likely to display all three ego states, however, one state may predominate.

A *transaction* is a basic unit of social interaction. It consists of an exchange of words and behavior between two people. The heart of transactional analysis is the study and diagraming of the exchanges between two people. In this analysis the learner identifies the ego state that both the initiator and the respondent exhibit in the transaction.

A *stroke* is a unit of recognition, which can be positive or negative. People, generally, have a pervasive need for recognition and approval. Examples of positive strokes are: "You did a great job, Henry."; "Would you like to join us for lunch, Mary?"; "I admire you." Examples of negative strokes are: "You failed again."; "Why are you here?"; "You did that job wrong."

The ways in which people *spend their time* are classified into six categories: withdrawal, rituals, activities, pastimes, psychological games, and authentic encounters or intimacy.

Courses in transactional analysis have become quite popular and widely used in American industry. By exposing their managerial personnel to these courses, top management hopes to improve their self-understanding, interpersonnel effectiveness, communication, and leadership skills. The goals of TA are very similar to the goals of sensitivity training which is discussed in Chapter 17, "Organization Development." Transactional analysis generates much less tension in the learner and it is less threatening to him than is sensitivity training.

Management Development in Perspective.   Management training and development are intimately related to the entire system of management practice in an organization. If administration is disorganized, haphazard, and faulty, then sound management development will be extremely difficult to accomplish. Executives and supervisors learn, to a great extent, by precept and example while on the job.

Management development activities must be undertaken on behalf of and by all members of management, not just a chosen few. An organization stands or

---

[8] Eric Berne, *Transactional Analysis in Psychotherapy* (New York: Grove Press, 1961); Eric Berne, *Games People Play* (New York: Grove Press, 1964); Thomas A. Harris, *I'm O.K.—You're O.K.* (New York: Harper & Row, 1967); Muriel James and Dorothy Jongeward, *Born to Win* (Reading, Mass.: Addison-Wesley, 1971).

falls on the basis of the total efforts of the entire team. An effective, going concern cannot afford to neglect a large segment of its leadership in favor of an elite corps.

Those in charge of guiding the whole program can appropriately adopt an eclectic view toward the process. They must not place all of their eggs in one basket of, say, job rotation or coaching or management games; rather they must establish a multidimensional program that reaches to every manager and educates in a variety of ways for a variety of specific purposes.

Questions for review and discussion

1. What is a manager and what does a manager do?
2. What elements constitute the management process?
3. What knowledge, skills, and abilities should a manager possess?
4. Is management a profession? Discuss.
5. Why is it necessary that management training and development activities be started with top executives first?
6. What are the essential components of a comprehensive management development program?
7. What role should the following play in a management development program?
   a. The president of the organization
   b. The director of industrial relations
   c. The training director
   d. Individual supervisors and executives throughout the organization
8. How can one determine the value of specific management training and development programs?
9. Prepare, in outline form, a curriculum for a comprehensive series of training conferences for
   a. Foremen
   b. Vice-presidents of an industrial company
10. A major problem in management training activities is that of achieving real improvement or change by the participants on the job. Why is this a problem and what can be done about it?
11. What is transactional analysis? What are its basic concepts?
12. Which training techniques, of those discussed in Chapters 15 and 16 are most effective for accomplishing the following objectives?
    a. Imparting factual knowledge
    b. Inducing attitude changes
    c. Developing awareness of oneself and one's effect upon others.

Case problem

A SUPERVISORY TRAINING COURSE

James Westmore was contacted on the telephone by the Extension Director of State University Labor–Management Center. Westmore was a professor at a private university in a nearby city. The director invited Westmore to teach a ten-session supervisory training course to the shop foremen at the Peerless Machine and Foundry Works. He suggested that Professor Westmore visit the personnel manager at Peerless to become oriented to the company and its problems.

The Peerless company employed 300 people and produced heavy iron and steel products. The personnel manager told Professor Westmore that he liked to take advantage of State University's services by having it give one course for the foremen every year on some aspects of supervision and industrial relations. The full cost of these courses was paid by State University as part of its extension program for industrial, labor, and public organizations.

Inasmuch as the company could not spare the foremen during the working day, the course was given one afternoon each week for ten weeks from 4 to 6 P.M. The foremen came directly to the course from their jobs. They received time and one half overtime for these extra hours. Because the company lacked training class facilities, the personnel manager arranged that it be held in the quarters of a fraternal club a few blocks from the plant.

This fraternal club was situated in an old house in a declining section of the town. A makeshift classroom was set up in the former dining room of this house. Old card tables were placed back to back to make a conference type layout. The blackboard consisted of an old slate supported by a card table and leaned against the wall. Light was provided by an old-fashioned chandelier from which several bulbs were missing.

On the Monday afternoon of the first class Professor Westmore found that he had to introduce himself to the class of sixteen foremen. The personnel manager had left word with one of the men to say that he was busy and could not make it. Because there was no chalk for the slate board, one of the foremen volunteered to go to the store to buy some.

Professor Westmore had prepared a course outline that contained the following topics: (1) nature of a foreman's job, (2) what foremen expect from management, (3) what workers expect from their foremen, (4) elementary aspects of organization, (5) motivation, (6) making work assignments, (7) coaching, (8) complaints and grievances, (9) leadership, and (10) discipline. He made weekly assignments of about 25 to 30 pages in a textbook on supervision. The classes were conducted on a lecture-discussion basis with some case studies used.

Professor Westmore noticed that the men were always late for the class although they seemed to be in and about the building. Finally at 4:00 P.M. on the third week he decided to explore the building. To his surprise he found most of the men drinking beer at a bar located on the second floor. In class the foremen were courteously attentive on the surface but basically seemed unenthusiastic. In many of the discussions they stated that they had learned about various aspects of human relations and supervision in courses given to them by other instructors in previous years. Professor Westmore began to wonder if he had been hired to repeat instruction that had been given previously. The men said on more than one occasion that the ideas about leadership and human relations contained in the book and in Professor Westmore's talks were O.K. in theory, but they wouldn't work at the Peerless plant because of MacGregor, the factory manager. They claimed that MacGregor knew nothing about human relations and was tough to deal with, that the union always went directly to the personnel manager with the grievances, and that they, as foremen, had no authority. All discipline was handled by the personnel manager.

Westmore observed to himself that these foremen felt more like workers than members of management. They even dressed in blue jeans and shop work clothes. The pattern-shop foreman made the following statement to him one day: "I have worked here for twenty-five years and have been a foreman for fifteen. But maybe I should have taken a job somewhere else. One day I was standing on the street corner when a truck from the Acme Steel Company went by. The truck driver must have just gotten his paycheck, because he threw his checkstub out the window and I picked it up. He gets $300 a week, and that is lots more than I get as a foreman."

Questions

1. Was this training course launched properly?
2. What could foremen training accomplish in this company?
3. What do you think of the course content and method of instruction?
4. How do you account for the behavior of the foremen in this training program?
5. If you had free rein to make needed changes, what actions and what kind of management development program would you establish for this company? How would you carry out your program?

Suggestions for further reading

BASIL, DOUGLAS. *Managerial Skills for Executive Action*. New York: American Management Association, 1970.

BENNETT, DUDLEY. "Transactional Analysis in Management," *Personnel*, Vol. 52, No. 1 (January–February 1975), pp. 34–44.

BRAYTON, JAMES A., and RICHARD L. CHAPMAN. *Transformation of Scientists and Engineers into Managers* (National Aeronautics and Space Administration). Washington, D.C.: Government Printing Office, 1972.

DESATNICK, ROBERT. *A Concise Guide to Management Development*. New York: American Management Association, 1970.

KIRKPATRICK, DONALD L. *A Practical Guide for Supervisory Training and Development*. Reading, Mass.: Addison-Wesley Publishing Co., 1971.

LIVINGSTON, J. STERLING. "Myth of the Well-Educated Manager," *Harvard Business Review*, Vol. 49, No. 1 (January–February, 1971), pp. 79–89.

MINTZBERG, HENRY. "The Manager's Job: Folklore and Fact," *Harvard Business Review*, Vol. 53, No. 4 (July–August 1975), pp. 49–61.

PARLOUR, RICHARD R. "Executive Team Training," *Academy of Management Journal*, Vol. 14, No. 3 (September 1971), pp. 341–344.

TAYLOR, BERNARD and GORDON L. LIPPITT (eds.) *Management Development and Training Handbook*. New York: McGraw-Hill Book Company, 1975.

WEST, J. P., and D. R. SHERIFF. *Executive Development Programs in Universities*, Studies in Personnel Policy, No. 215. New York: National Industrial Conference Board, 1969.

WIKSTROM, WALTER S. *Supervisory Training* (Report 612). New York: The Conference Board, 1973.

YUILL, BRUCE and DANIEL STEINHOFF. *Developing Managers in Organizations*. New York: John Wiley & Sons, 1975.

Organization development

A host of problems that occur daily in the typical company tend to be ignored by the conventional improvement efforts of management development specialists, personnel managers, and management consultants. These are some common examples:

Professional staff members of the research and development department of a manufacturing firm feel that project teams do not communicate with one another effectively, laboratory leadership is too loose and sporadic, project funding procedures are inconsistent, and many scientists are underutilized in relation to their talents.

Administrators and staff specialists in Government Bureau "A" have learned that it is advisable for them to always record in writing their conversations and commitments made with other administrators, on a daily basis, as a defensive measure to protect their own positions. Many claim to have learned from bitter experience that higher-echelon administrators often look for scapegoats when programs are under criticism. They place the blame on lower-level functionaries.

Manager A vigorously opposes a proposal concerning new product development advanced by Manager B. A advances numerous arguments that have the aura of rationality but the underlying reason for his opposition is a personal animosity and suspicion of *B*. The culture of the organization does not permit such feelings to be recognized openly hence they surface indirectly.

Recent advances in behavioral science knowledge and techniques are being made available to corporate executives. There is now greater interest—and capability—in attacking human and organizational problems that were previously ignored. Attention is now being directed toward integrating the needs of individuals with the goals of the organization, creating mechanisms to reduce destructive conflict and produce genuine collaboration, adapting to changes in the social and economic environment, and revitalizing—or altering—existing bureaucratic structures.

Specifically, what is organization development (often called, simply, OD)? *OD is a planned process designed to improve organizational effectiveness and health through modifications in individual and group behavior, culture, and systems of the organization using knowledge and technology of applied behavioral science.* Frequently, a consultant (called a change agent) is used to assist in diagnosing the situation and in helping the client develop action programs to improve the organizational effectiveness. The change agent may come from outside the organization or he may be a full-time member of the organization but external to the particular client group he is helping. An important component of OD is the systematic assessment of the needs of the organization and the problem areas to be worked on. The client group normally plays an important role in carrying-out the assessment.

OD is a developing and evolving field of activity. It does not consist of a fixed methodology. The professional practitioners, including researchers, writers, and consultants, have created and applied a variety of approaches and techniques for organizational improvement. However there are certain commonalities. Most practitioners in this field have been trained in the behavioral sciences. Most tend to emphasize the people dimensions of organizational effectiveness, such as attitudes, norms, values, interpersonal skills, and behavior patterns. However, they do not ignore such elements as organization structure, reward systems, managerial control, and technology. Most lean philosophically toward a supportive, collaborative, and participative system of management.

VALUES OF OD MOVEMENT

Just as we can analyze the values of the American labor union movement and of the free-enterprise business system, so, too, can we investigate the values, ideals, and beliefs of the organization development movement. It is imperative that corporate executives, who are considering whether or not to launch an OD effort in their establishments, gain a full understanding of its underlying values because these values differ quite strikingly from those prevailing in work organization life generally. In some respects the OD values strike a responsive chord in many managers who believe these newer values represent what *ought* to be, even though day-to-day experience typifies an opposed set of values. Ordinarily, managers, being pragmatists not theoreticians, do not directly articulate the values that guide their actions. These values lie beneath the surface and the observer can infer their substance by noting the behavior of organization members. Let us now review the dominant values of the OD movement.

Man is Basically Good. If one considers that mankind is fundamentally evil, lazy, irresponsible, selfish, and destructive, then he copes with this situation by devising all sorts of controls and punishments that make people behave according to the code of the owner, master, or boss. On the other hand, if man is viewed as potentially good, responsible, helpful, and trustworthy, then one leads by being supportive and creating opportunities for growth, self-control, and personal responsibility. Employees then can make worthwhile contributions to the organization while fulfilling their own needs and aspirations.

Need for Confirmation and Support. So often organization members are conditioned to believe that "no news is good news." Supervisors pay attention to their people only when they make a job assignment or when they want to find fault for an alleged failure. Yet we all have a human need to be confirmed as a person and to know that the boss really does care about us.

Consider the case of a man who worked as a buyer in the purchasing department of a large manufacturing firm for ten years. During that whole period his supervisor never expressed concern for him as a person, never asked about his problems, never asked about his aims and aspirations. Feeling that he was not really wanted, this man resigned to take a job as purchasing agent in a small plumbing supply house at a lower salary. But here he was really needed and wanted. The owner paid attention to him and depended upon him. This individual continued until retirement knowing that he was a significant part of the company.

People Can Grow. The practitioners in the organization development field hold that people are capable of learning new ways of coping with situations and can develop new facets to their skills and personalities by being exposed to a variety of opportunities. While it may be true that people seldom change their core personality structure, it has been demonstrated that under the right environment they can adapt, grow, and learn.

Accept Differences Among People. The health of an organization can be enhanced if the managers and employees accept differences in personality, race, religion, and viewpoints. The conventional rule that subordinates should not openly disagree with the boss is challenged by organization development precepts. It is legitimate to raise opposing views in staff meetings. It is legitimate to take an unpopular stand and disagree with the group. The existence of employees having a variety of backgrounds, orientations, and perspectives strengthens the organization.

Express Feelings and Emotions. In our society children, especially boys, are taught to hide their tears and sorrows. In the business firm people think that they must exhibit only their rational side to others. To reveal emotion, sentiment, anger, or tenderness is viewed as a sign of weakness.

Yet high levels of motivation, commitment, and creativity depend, not upon detachment, but upon giving full range to one's feelings. We expect people in the performing arts to express their emotions because that is required in order to reach the peak of their talents. Would not encouragement of members of the business organization to apply themselves to the fullest lead naturally to some displays of anger, joy, and exhilaration? The repression of feelings, then, may be counterproductive.

It can be further argued that management ought to consider feelings and sentiments to be legitimate concerns in making decisions, just as are costs, profits, and efficiency.

Be Authentic, Open, and Direct. The average person may think that duplicity is solely the mark of politicians vying to retain or gain elective office. But actually such behavior is exhibited widely in work organizations and bureaucracies throughout the world. In the game of influence maneuvering that seems to go on continually, many managers feel that they must manipulate others, tell half-truths, withhold vital information, and mask their true motives.

Is such behavior truly productive? Organization development advocates think not. People should "tell it like it is." Honesty and directness enable people to put their energy into the real problems of the job rather than forcing them to waste their efforts in fending off the machinations of others.

Give Attention to Process Activities. In the ordinary situation when a project engineer, for example, is assigned the activity of putting his team to work on a new design project his manager expects him to forthrightly attack the tasks at hand. However, the project engineer may find that his entire program will run smoother if he will initially devote attention to the relationships among the people on his team and between his team and other departments within the company. But the training of both engineers and managers typically ignores the problem of work-facilitation processes.

Among important process activities are team building and maintenance, developing mechanisms for resolving disputes between units, creating organizational and workflow arrangements, building interpersonal rapport, and setting up decision-making guides.

Foster Cooperation. Some executives know of no other way to manage their people than to generate win-lose competition for salary increases, choice work assignments, and for the bestowal of their favors. From childhood they have been conditioned to view life as a raw struggle where only the fittest survive. But our industrial civilization has advanced to the state where much of the work of the world is carried on by groups. The work roles are highly interdependent. The older competitive strategy derived from a bygone era of self-employed shopkeepers and craftsmen is much less relevant for late twentiety-century institutions. People must learn that collaboration, that is, a helping relationship toward one another, produces a greater volume of goods, services, and rewards than does destructive interpersonal competition.

Confront Conflict. Rather than suppress conflict (we are talking about interpersonal conflict not violence), gloss it over, or ignore it, organization development professionals advocate that it be brought out into the open in order to identify root causes and to attempt a satisfactory resolution. Too often people divide into opposing camps over a knotty issue and assume that one party can gain only at the expense of the other. Actually this need not be the case. Creative problem-solving may help both parties gain or at least reach a compromise solution which may minimize losses or dissatisfactions.

Objectives

In a sense the objectives sought in an OD effort can be inferred from our foregoing discussion of values. The top managers who have decided to undertake organization development expect to change the ways in which organization members and groups have been operating in order to effect improvements in performance.

They aim to increase the openness of communication among people, levels in the structure, and departments, and to build into the system a process of feedback of performance and attitudes to aid in making adjustments.

Managers and employees can be expected to increase their degree of responsibility for planning and implementation. They ought to acquire a greater sense of ownership of the objectives of the organization. Basically, then, we can say that a major goal is to achieve a sense of commitment, self-direction, and self-control.

The customary modes of decision-making may be revamped so that decisions are made on the basis of information and knowledge by people who are organizationally close to the point of action. Rather than perpetuating the bureaucratic pattern of centralized authority and power at the top, organization members who have the relevant data will be encouraged to make their own decisions in the context of the agreed-upon objectives and policies of the establishment.

Another objective is to generate collaborative effort rather than destructive, energy-wasting competition. The power struggles which so often go on behind the scenes are dysfunctional from the standpoint of the organization as a whole and most of the members. This energy can be redirected to more constructive purposes.

The organization structure may be analyzed to ascertain whether it facilitates or hinders the work flow. Sometimes one finds that the structure has been put together to fit an arbitrary format rather than to conform to the functions to be carried out.

The underlying hostility and conflict that so often fester will be brought out into the open. The organization development effort will try to resolve the issues and redirect energies.

Whereas many writers assert that planned change is an overriding goal of organization development, Chris Argyris, one of the leaders of the OD movement, rejects the current idealization of change as an end in itself. Actually, human beings require a certain degree of equilibrium to be healthy.

Argyris asserts that the OD consultant must not force a goal of change upon a client. Rather the client must be helped to decide whether change is needed and, if so, to determine what kind. He sees the objectives of OD intervention activity as (1) the generation of valid information about the organization and its problems; (2) free choice for the client system so that it can select from alternative courses based on knowledge; and (3) internal commitment by organization members to the choice selected rather than coerced action.[1]

---

[1] Chris Argyris, *Intervention Theory and Method—A Behavioral Science View* (Reading, Mass.: Addison-Wesley Publishing Company, 1970), pp. 17–24.

THE OD PROCESS

Organization development starts with a perception by some responsible executive (or group of executives) that there are inadequacies within the organization that can probably be corrected by the introduction of organization development activities. If the requisite professional competence for OD is not available within the enterprise, then management will engage the services of a qualified outside consultant to help diagnose the organizational situation and to develop OD activities, called interventions, to solve the problems identified. In recent years many larger corporations have developed OD competence within their own personnel departments. Specifically these resource people are usually located within the management training or OD group of the personnel department. But, in any case, whether the OD specialist is obtained from the outside or from within, he performs in the role of a consultant or change agent to the particular organizational unit involved.

Role of Consultant.   The role of the organization development consultant is different from that of a traditional management consultant. The traditional consultation process begins when a top executive perceives a problem that he feels can be solved by an outside expert. The problem may be one of excessive costs, poor productivity, faulty product design, or high labor turnover. The consultant enters the organization, gathers information, makes a diagnosis, and designs a course of action based upon his experience and expertise. He prepares a written report and submits it to the executive who hired him. Implementation depends upon the client-executive. It is his decision to take steps to carry out the recommendations, to modify them, or to ignore the entire report. This kind of consultation involves a short term, intensive, "expert" type of activity.

A frequent problem with this traditional mode of consultation is that the client does not really understand the frame of reference of the consultant nor does he share in developing the diagnosis. When the consultant leaves, too commonly the client is insufficiently prepared to carry through the remedies recommended.

In contrast to the traditional consultation model, the OD change agent works closely with the management team in information gathering, joint diagnosis, and selection of the particular interventions or activities to be utilized to improve the functioning of the organization. The change agent is a skilled advisor who helps the whole management team recognize their problems, learn the skills to resolve them, and then work out solutions on the job.

Comparison with Management Development.   Further insight into the nature of organization development may be gained by comparing it with management development. These two strategies for making improvements and changes can be viewed as supplementing one another. They are not mutually exclusive.

Management development focuses mainly upon improving the performance of managers as individuals, whereas organization development seeks to improve the overall performance of entire groups, departments, and more broadly the organization as a whole.

The specific objectives of management development may include (1) indoctrination of company philosophy, (2) knowledge of the company, its policies, procedures, and technology, (3) learning human relations skills, (4) acquiring skill and understanding in such management techniques as cost control, data processing, management information systems, and financial planning, and (5) skill in actually performing various management positions in different functional specialties. Specific objectives of OD may be (1) to facilitate problem solving on the job and improve quality of decisions, (2) to accomplish changes more effectively, (3) to reduce destructive conflict and make it more productive, (4) to increase commitment to organization objectives, and (5) to foster collaboration among individuals and groups. In OD work, sentiment, emotions, and hopes are areas of legitimate concern.

Broadly speaking, the methodologies of management development can be classified under two major headings: (1) on-the-job and (2) classroom. Job rotation, coaching, understudy, and special assignments are examples of on-the-job methods. Lectures, case studies, readings, role playing, and written homework are types of classroom methods. In addition to these two broad categories, there may be individual psychological testing and counseling.

In contrast, the methodologies or interventions of organization development consist of such activities as survey feedback, process consultation, sensitivity training, managerial grid training, confrontation meetings, team building, goal setting, and interpersonal peacemaking. Like management development, OD may at times utilize certain classroom training techniques that emphasize experiential or learning-by-doing exercises.

Management development activities more commonly comprise a number of discrete programs, each of a rather short duration. On the other hand, organization development can be thought of as a long-term process that continues indefinitely. It also infuses the day-to-day activities of the organization members. It is not perceived as something apart from managers' and employees' normal job roles.

Elements of the OD Process

The OD process comprises the following five components:

1. Diagnosis
2. Selection and Design of Interventions.
3. Implementation of Intervention.
4. Evaluation.
5. Adjustment and Maintenance of System.

The *diagnosis* phase of organization development assesses the health (or illness) of the organization. It identifies problems and clues to the causes of these problems. The particular target unit may be the whole organization, a major division, a plant, a department, or a group of people within a department. The diagnosis typically focuses upon such organizational processes as communication patterns, goal setting, planning and decision making, conflict resolution, relations among different departments and groups, and superior-subordinate relations.

The tools that can be used for diagnosis are questionnaires, interviews, direct observation, and analysis of documents and reports. A questionnaire administered to all the personnel of a given department or establishment might ask such questions as:

1. To what extent do you feel free to talk to your superior about problems of your job?
2. How well are you kept informed of relevant matters in your department?
3. To what extent are promotions awarded to those who have performed well?
4. To what degree do the members of your department cooperate and help one another?

Whereas a questionnaire can be administered to large numbers of people, respondents can be anonymous, and it can be designed for objective scoring, an interview is a personalized face-to-face contact. It is useful for an in-depth exploration of information uncovered via the questionnaire.

Direct observation generally involves the observation of a group of people and the recording of their behavior on observation data sheets which list the various elements of behavior to be collected. A variant, which is really a combination of the questionnaire and observation, asks all those people within an organization who deal with a given department, say production, to record the experiences and impressions they have acquired in dealing with that department.

The final source of information about an organization's problems consists of documents and reports that may already be available. A study of existing reports may reveal those departments having excessive scrap, costs, turnover, absences, or grievances.

After the diagnosis phase of OD has been carried out, one turns next to *selection and design of interventions*. Indeed this step is intimately related to diagnosis. If it has been determined that the relations between Department *A* and Department *B* have been stormy and non-productive, then the consultant and the client managers may design an intergroup workshop involving members of both departments. If the diagnosis phase uncovers the fact that there is insufficient openness, trust, and cooperation within a department, then a laboratory training program may be designed.

Implementation of intervention is the third phase of the OD process. Implementation involves working with the people in the target organizational units. The intervention may take the form of workshops, feedback of data to participants, group discussions, written exercises, on-the-job activities, redesign of control systems, redesign of jobs and numerous other activities. It is important to recognize that OD is not a "one-shot, quick cure" for an organization's ills. Achieving real, lasting change in the attitudes and behavior of organizational members takes a great deal of effort and much time.

The fourth stage is *evaluation*. The OD efforts must be evaluated to determine what results are being achieved and to determine if these efforts must be redirected. Depending upon the nature of the problems to be corrected, the evaluation effort may be simple or complex. In some cases simple observation or interviews of the participants may be sufficient. In other instances more sophisticated evaluation designs may be needed. For example the same survey instrument may be administered before the OD intervention and six months after the intervention to detect changes. Or, experimental and control groups may be compared.

The fifth and final step is *adjustment and maintenance of the system*. This step is often omitted, but it shouldn't be. As evaluation information is received from step four, the change agent and his management clients should determine what changes, if any, should be made in the OD interventions. Are the intended results being realized? If not, why not? Have there been unintended results? Have other parts of the organization been changed by the OD efforts? Organization development is properly viewed as an on-going process. Adjustments are to be expected as the process proceeds.

INTERVENTIONS

The interventions of organization development are the planned activities that are introduced into the system to accomplish the desired changes and improvements. Interventions are the methods and techniques that have been created by OD professionals and others to achieve improvements in the functioning of organizations. The major kinds of interventions are as follows: survey feedback, process consultation, sensitivity (laboratory) training, managerial grid, goal setting and planning, team building, and interpersonal peacemaking. In addition, there are other kinds of interventions used by OD consultants which have been developed from somewhat different intellectual roots. Among these are changes in the organization structure, job enrichment, compensation systems, work flow changes, and participative management systems.

It ought to be clear that no single company and no single consultant would utilize all these techniques. The choice of a particular intervention strategy depends upon the diagnosis of needs and upon the particular orientations of the management of the client firm and of the consultant.

Survey Feedback

Attitude surveys have been used by progressive companies for many years to ascertain the viewpoints of the employees about such matters as wages, hours, working conditions, and the treatment they get from their supervisors. However, with the traditional attitude survey the analysis of the results and the development of action plans to correct the deficiencies is the exclusive province of the personnel department and upper management. Except for receiving a summary of the tabulated responses in the company newspaper, the employees have no involvement.

The OD way of handling attitude surveys is to feed back the results to all the people who filled out the questionnaires. The data is first provided to the top executive team. Then each executive holds a meeting with the people reporting directly to him to analyze and evaluate the survey results in a workshop setting. In these workshops plans are formulated to take actions to correct the problems identified by the survey. This workshop process proceeds downward throughout the entire hierarchy. Even rank and file workers are involved in discussing the survey results that apply to their own work unit. They can suggest solutions to problems. The workshop is conducted by the relevant manager or supervisor. Often the OD consultant participates in the workshops as a resource person.

Process Consultation

Although used by many practitioners the leading innovator and spokesman for process consultation is Edgar Schein.[2] The process consultant helps the organization members with whom he is dealing learn to develop the skills needed to diagnose and solve the on-going problems of their organization. He does not mastermind matters for them. The process consultant helps the people diagnose a number of important human processes such as communication, member roles and functions in groups, group problem solving and decision-making, group norms, leadership and authority, intergroup cooperation and competition, and conflict.

The process consultant meets with the department members in work teams, observes their interactions and problem-solving procedures, and feeds back to the teams his observations along the human dimensions mentioned above. He helps the team members understand the interaction, influence, and decision-making processes that have gone on in their work team meetings. He coaches and counsels individuals and groups to help them understand their behavior and help them work out more effective behavior. But he does not impose his own prescriptions.

Sensitivity Training

Sensitivity training (often called T-Group or laboratory training) is an experiential method using relatively unstructured face-to-face groups as the principal learning vehicle.

The objectives of sensitivity training are to help people understand themselves better, to create better understanding of others, to gain insight into the group process, and to develop specific behavioral skills. Many people go through life never really understanding why they feel and act as they do. They do not really know how others feel about them. They are insensitive to the effects of their behavior upon others.

Employees give great deference to their bosses. A supervisor may, year after year, issue orders to his subordinates and criticize them without ever fully realizing that many of them may fear or hate him. If such a boss has an opportunity to participate in a sensitivity training course, he can be expected to gain important insights into himself and his effect upon others. Quite often trainees are upset about what they learn.

T-group programs also seek to improve communication skills. They help the trainee become an active listener—to really learn through listening. When engaged in conversation, many of us concentrate upon what we are going to say rather than upon what the other fellow is saying.

Additional goals are to aid participants to work more effectively as group or team members and to perform leadership roles at times. Also one can see how informal groups coalesce, how people come to play different roles, how informal leadership may emerge, and how an organization actually takes structure and form. They can observe and experience interpersonal influence.

[2] See Edgar H. Schein, *Process Consultation: Its Role in Organization Development* (Reading, Mass.: Addison-Wesley Publishing Co., 1969).

How is sensitivity training carried on? Although methods vary somewhat depending upon the specific orientation of the program, the core of most programs is the face-to-face, largely unstructured (T-group). This group typically consists of from eight to about sixteen persons. At times there may be no leader, no agenda, and no stated goal for this small group. The group is left to its own devices to develop interaction and on-going experiences that serve as the real substance of the learning process. At other times the designated "trainer" introduces certain planned activities involving interaction between paired individuals and subgroups. The participants are encouraged to give feedback to each other on their personal feelings and reactions to what is happening in the group and on their reactions to one another's behavior. The emphasis is on the "here and now," not on the participants' experiences before they come to the program.

One or two professional trainers sit in with each T-group. However, the trainer tends to remain in the background. He does not lecture to them, does not rule certain conduct right and other conduct wrong, and does not pass out rewards and penalties (grades) as in conventional training courses. The role of the trainer sometimes seems ambiguous to the T-group members. At times he plays the role of a detached observer, at other times he acts as a group member, and at others he clearly introduces planned exercises for the group to engage in. His true role is to help the individuals and the group to learn from their own experiences in the group.

The emphasis in T-group work is not upon learning specific objective facts but rather upon gaining understanding of feelings, gestures, attitudes, and emotions—in short, sensitivity to oneself and others. There is a high degree of participation, feeling, and involvement in the typical session.

In addition to the T-groups, laboratory training also may include role playing, intergroup competitive exercises, self-insight questionnaires, theory sessions with lectures, background readings, panel discussions, and training films.

When used as part of a traditional management development program, sensitivity training has generally involved a group of strangers from different organizations who are gathered together at a resort hotel or training center remote from their home locations. There will be no continuing relationship among the people after the training is over. Thus, it is expected that the participants will feel safe and free to express themselves truly without fear of their behavior being reported back to their home organizations. Experience has shown that the impact of stranger laboratory training back in the companies that have sent the trainees is liable to be minimal, therefore sensitivity training when used as a key component of organization development frequently consists of people from the same organization. They may be arranged into *cousin* groups, which consist of members of the same organization but who have no working relationship with one another. Or the training design may consist of *cluster* groups. Here the T-Group will contain several clusters of three or four people who do have a working relationship with one another as peers or colleagues (not boss-subordinate). Another variation is to have a *family* group consisting of a manager and the people who work for him.

The major criticisms of sensitivity training have been that it generates too much emotional stress for the participants, that the process takes one's psychological defenses away (and thus constitutes an invasion of privacy), and that it is very difficult for the participants to carry-over the openness, trust, and equalitarianism from the T-Group to their ordinary job environment. Because of these problems, sensitivity training which emphasizes primarily introspection and interpersonal relations has declined drastically in usage over the past decade or so. Nowadays a sensitivity training group is generally composed of people from the same organization or department who are brought together to improve their understandings, attitudes and interpersonal relationships to solve real work problems. Sometimes the intervention may be called something other than sensitivity training. It might be called such things as team-building or Managerial Grid (phases 1 and 2).

The Managerial Grid

The managerial grid, created by Robert R. Blake and Jane S. Mouton, utilizes small face-to-face groups as the basic learning mechanism.

The theoretical formulation underlying a grid seminar is the "managerial grid." This is a graphic way of expressing underlying assumptions and theories about ways of managing people in work organizations. Blake and Mouton have synthesized and summarized the salient features of current theory in organizational behavior. They postulate that managers may evidence a concern for production or a concern for people (or a combination of these) in their styles of management. The graphic representation in grid form displays concern for production along the abscissa or X-axis on a scale from 1 through 9. The ordinate or Y-axis expresses concern for people and is also on a scale of 1 through 9. See Figure 17-1. A management theory that exhibits a maximum concern for production and a minimal interest in people (9, 1) is characterized by a high-pressure,

Figure 17-1
The Managerial Grid.

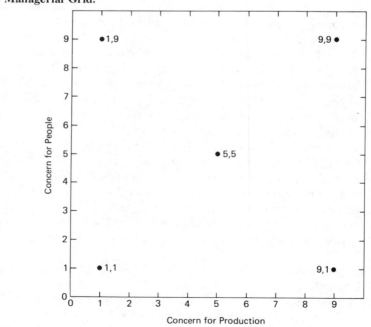

authoritarian style. The converse of 9, 1 management is 1, 9, which shows a low concern for production and a high concern for people. This has been labeled "country-club" management. Leadership that evidences a high concern for both people and production is labeled 9, 9. This is held to be a most desirable pattern of management from the standpoint of conflict resolution, creativity, commitment, morale, and productivity. In addition to these three positions on the grid, there is the 1, 1 theory of management wherein management basically abdicates its responsibilities for both people and productivity and the 5, 5 theory wherein management compromises and adopts an "organization-man" strategy. These five basic theories of management can be supplemented by eight other positions or combinations on the grid to make a total of thirteen formulations.

There are six steps or phases in grid organization development. Phase 1 consists of studying the managerial grid as a theoretical framework for understanding human behavior in the organization. The participants are pointed toward a full comprehension of 9, 9 management as a basis of organizational excellence.

A grid seminar, typically of one week's duration, is composed of a number of study teams of five to nine members each. Participants come from various organizations. The objectives of the one-week seminar include helping each person to recognize his own grid style, developing team action skills, facilitating interpersonal communication within a team, strengthening the use of the critique for problem-solving and learning, and helping the members analyze their own corporate work culture.

The work of the seminar is focused upon various team problem-solving projects involving a time schedule, scoring, comparison with other teams' performance, and critiques. Toward the end of the week each team member will receive a written description of his own managerial style prepared by the other members of the team working jointly. This is based on their observations of his behavior throughout the week. Also each participant prepares a diagnosis of his own company's culture by characterizing it as 9, 1; 5, 5; 1, 9; and the like.

Phase 2, called teamwork development, is a seminar of one week's duration consisting of the members of the management of a single company grouped into family teams. Thus, a plant manager and his immediate subordinates could constitute one seminar team. Each member's perception of the team's culture is developed and discussed in the context of the actual problems faced on the job, whether they be financial, market strategy, quality control, union relations, or the like. The teams also work on objective-setting and problem-solving projects related to their area of corporate responsibilities. Participants learn the benefits of openness and directness in introducing problems and working them through to solutions.

Phase 3, designated intergroup development, focuses upon the relationships between different divisions, departments, and units. Frequently marketing, production, and engineering departments exemplify contrasting orientations to the solutions of common problems. A major goal of Phase 3 is to develop improved ways of resolving differences. In this phase, departments or groups that normally interrelate on the job are brought together, two at a time, to identify features of an idealized relationship and of their actual relationship. The participants then recommend measures for improving the interworkings of their departments.

Phase 4 involves the creation of an ideal strategic model for the organization. The participants are primarily the chief executive and his immediate subordinates, although there is input from many other managers. These top executives study several books and articles written by successful business leaders who have described their corporate strategy problems and how they met them. When reading this resource literature the executives are provided with study guides that help them analyze the material according to six areas: financial objectives, nature of the business, nature of the markets, organization structure, policy, and development requirements. After completion of the above work, the team meets for essentially a full week of activity to relate the knowledge gained from the written sources to the formulation of an idealized corporate strategy plan. Although this seminar requires one full week, the actual creation of a complete strategy model may take many months of on-the-job activity.

Phase 5 is implementation of the strategic model. This is carried out by working through the natural components of the corporation, whether they be divisions, profit centers, or product lines. For each component a planning team is established whose function is to examine all the essential elements of its operations, such as raw material procurement, manpower utilization, production processes, and marketing channels, in order to insure that they are performed in the best possible way.

The sixth and last phase is a systematic critique of progress achieved using as a guide generalized criteria that Blake and Mouton have devised and presented under the designation Corporate Excellence Rubric.[3]

Goal Setting and Planning

Logically, many would hold that goal setting and planning ought to be an essential part of any organization improvement program. Indeed it ought to come near the beginning.

Whole-Organization Goal Setting. One method for accomplishing this is for top management to establish corporate and divisional goals for such items as return on investment, share of the market, new products, human resources, and community relations. Then each organizational unit working down through the structure, sets its own goals, independently of top-management goals, but with knowledge of them. Next the statements of these unit goals are sent to the top-management group. Analysis is made. If there are discrepancies top management may adjust its goals in the light of information from the various units. Also the discrepancies may be noted by top management and the unit goal statements sent back to them for modification. With successive interactions an agreed-upon set of organizationwide goals can emerge.

In applying this technique all units have some influence upon the final goals. The individual managers acquire a sense of ownership of the goals and a commitment to their attainment.

---

[3] This account of grid organization development is derived from Robert R. Blake and Jane S. Mouton, *Building a Dynamic Corporation Through Grid Organization Development* (Reading, Mass.: Addison-Wesley Publishing Company, 1969). The reader may also wish to consult Robert R. Blake and Jane S. Mouton, *Corporate Excellence Through Grid Organization Development* (Houston, Texas: Gulf Publishing Company, 1968). The theoretical formulation of the managerial grid is presented in Robert R. Blake and Jane S. Mouton, *The Managerial Grid* (Houston, Texas: Gulf Publishing Company, 1964).

Confrontation Goal-Setting Meeting. Richard Beckhard has created a one-day activity called the confrontation meeting. It can be used not only for goal setting but also for developing specific plans for change and solving operational problems. It can involve an entire management team of an organization of, say, 60 to 100 members. Following an introduction by the chief executive about the purpose of the meeting and the procedure to be followed, the people are divided into groups of five or six members each. These people come from different departments. No boss is in the same group with a subordinate. These groups are given about an hour to prepare a list of changes that would improve their own situations and the organization generally. The items can deal with procedures, policies, facilities, attitudes, managerial behaviors, and the like.

Next, the lists are placed upon chart pads and explained to the entire assemblage of all groups. Then the total group helps the leader assign category headings to each item on the list. Following an intermission the participants reconvene into new groupings comprised of organizational units—such as engineering, personnel, and marketing—chaired by the heads of these units.

The organizational unit groups survey the entire list, choose three or four items that affect their group, arrive at a course of action for these items, and prepare a timetable for doing the work. In addition, these groups examine the total list for items they think are important for top-management action. Then they prepare a plan for communicating the results of the confrontation meeting to the rest of the people in their units who were not in attendance.

Following the above, the entire 60 to 100-member meeting is reconvened to hear each subgroup's report. At this meeting the top executive makes a response to each item presented.

The final step consists of a follow-up meeting several weeks later at which each unit and the top executive report on progress.[4]

Team Building

The heart of team building is a series of off-site problem-solving sessions of two to five day's duration. These are usually for family groups, that is, a manager and all those reporting directly to him. Sometimes they are also conducted for two interacting departments. These sessions are normally conducted by a third party, either the external OD consultant or the internal staff consultant.

Team building meetings are undertaken to improve such things as performance, decision making, role clarifiction, communications, and operating procedures. By way of illustration, TRW Systems Group, an aerospace research and development component of TRW, Inc., utilizes the matrix form of organization. An individual engineer, for example, may be a member of several project teams simultaneously. When a new team is formed, for example to write a major proposal for funding, offsite team-building sessions are held to help people understand their respective roles and interrelationships. These are process type activities to help the project team function better when they attack the actual content of their tasks.[5]

---

[4] For more on the confrontation meeting see Richard Beckhard, "The Confrontation Meeting," *Harvard Business Review*, Vol. 43, No. 2 (March–April 1967).

[5] TRW Systems Group (B), ICH14H14 (Boston, Mass.: Intercollegiate Case Clearing House, 1969).

Part and parcel of the most team-building programs is the feedback of diagnostic data collected by the organization-development consultant. Before the meetings he may have discovered such dysfunctional aspects as employee alienation, overlap of responsibilities, missed deadlines, and destructive interpersonal conflict. The specific objectives of the team-building meetings are determined by the manager, key subordinates, and the consultant.

At the team-building meetings the objectives are discussed along with the diagnostic data provided by the third party. The group frames an agenda and gives the issues a priority ranking. The consultant encourages the people to behave in accord with T-Group dynamics. They are encouraged to take risks in what they do and say. Openness, trust, and full expression of opinions are urged. Actually, by his actions the manager tends to determine the level of candor and trust that the group will exhibit. The meetings are best used for issues of general concern to the unit members. They ought not be used to handle personal matters between the manager and one of his subordinates, for example.

Interpersonal Peacemaking

Richard Walton describes the work that he has done in interpersonal peacemaking and presents an analytical framework for carrying out such third-party consultation.[6] Walton's methodology is suitable for diagnosing and resolving conflict between two persons such as the managers of two interrelated departments, two members of the same department, or members of a standing committee.

At the outset it is important to identify the two basic (often interrelated) kinds of conflict. One concerns interpersonal disagreements over substantive issues such as policies, procedures, and the way a particular matter should be handled. The second concerns the personal and emotional conflicts arising between two interacting people. The techniques for handling these two issues are distinct. Conflict over substance requires bargaining and problem-solving measures between the individuals with the aid of mediative interventions by a third party. Emotional conflict requires a modification of a person's perceptions and the working through of feelings between the two people. The solving of substantive issues is more of a cognitive matter, while solving emotional controversies is more an affective matter.

Walton does not advocate the elimination of all interpersonal conflict. Rather he holds that a *moderate* amount can increase motivation and creativity. Also it can strengthen one's understanding of his own position about a problem and help him gain greater awareness of his own identity. Too much conflict, however, can drain the energy of all parties concerned, making it unavailable for real productive work. Also it can destroy teamwork and cooperation.

There are four operational strategies for handling conflict between two people. Three of these are methods for *controlling* the conflict, while the fourth can properly be called a method for *resolving* it. One control strategy is really that of avoidance. The parties reduce the frequency with which they deal with one another especially on issues where conflict could occur. An advantage is that this

[6] This explanation of third-party peacemaking is derived from Richard E. Walton, *Interpersonal Peacemaking: Confrontations and Third-Party Consultation* (Reading, Mass.: Addison-Wesley Publishing Company, 1969).

provides a cooling off period and it also protects the large organization system from disruption. A disadvantage is that the conflict may become indirect. Thus, the two people may attack one another through others or through roundabout procedures.

A second control strategy involves the use of constraints and regulations. There may, for example, be generally understood customs that limit the amount of direct criticism focused against individuals in group meetings.

The third control strategy consists of adopting any of various coping measures. Thus, a person may prop himself up emotionally by getting sympathy from a co-worker or his wife. Or he may create alternative ways of living and performing in the organization that allow escape from the conflict with his adversary.

The fourth strategy is one of resolution. This requires a direct confrontation between the parties. It involves clarification of the issues, understanding the underlying forces at work, and an analysis of the feelings of the persons involved. Such confrontation requires candor and openness. One must acknowledge his own personal needs, concerns, and doubts. This is of necessity a two-way mutual proposition.

Role of the Consultant.   The consultant or third party plays a key role in this conflict resolution. Most simply he can help get the people together and he can help them to recognize their interdependency and the need to reconcile differences. He can aid in establishing a climate of openness and can provide emotional support to the participants.

More active third-party interventions consist of interviewing the parties privately, structuring the meetings or confrontations, intervening in the ongoing process, and assisting in follow-up activities.

By interviewing the two persons privately, the consultant can judge their desires and feelings, obtain background information, explain the requisites for conducting the confrontation meetings, and inform them of the responsibilities of the consultant in the process.

In setting up the meeting (or meetings) he can pick a time and place appropriate to the situation (perhaps it could be an informal luncheon meeting). In special cases he may feel it appropriate to invite other involved persons at least for certain portions of the meeting.

During the meeting itself the third party may perform numerous functions. He can referee the discussion, focus on certain areas, terminate an unproductive avenue, support a reticent party so he can express his views, encourage the two parties to exchange personal impressions of each other, help them diagnose causes and develop solutions, and he may actually offer counsel.

Finally, he can help the two persons create a plan and a procedure for conducting future dialogues on their own, with the consultant, or with a different third party.

Other Interventions

The methodologies described above are the major techniques or interventions utilized by organization development practitioners. However, there are other important techniques that are used for organizational improvement and change. These other techniques have generally been created previous to the emergence of the OD movement or independent from it. They constitute worthwhile strategies and are often incorporated into OD programs. These other interventions, explained in other chapters of this book, are the following:

a. *Job enrichment:* the adding of decision-making, responsibility, challenge, and larger units of accomplishment to routine jobs.
b. *Management by objectives:* collaboration between manager and each subordinate in setting subordinate's work goals, evaluating progress, and setting new goals.
c. *Changes in organization structure:* introducing different organization designs such as project and matrix organization or decentralization.
d. *Participative management:* participative problem solving meetings, Scanlon plans, union-management cooperation.

CONCLUDING OBSERVATIONS

Organization development is most successful when there is a deep commitment to it on the part of top management. Further, since changing the culture of an organization to one of collaboration, openness, and trust is an integral part of OD, the OD effort must infuse the whole organization.

Because of the orientation and training of its leading proponents, organization development tends to focus upon changing attitudes, values, and enhancing interpersonal skills. However, OD professionals do recognize that structural changes in the system such as job redesign, organization redesign, and new compensation plans are also very important for achieving lasting improvement in the performance of an organization.

Finally OD, as stated before, should be viewed as a long term, continuing process rather than a short term "shot-in-the-arm" for the organization.

Questions for review and discussion

1. What are the philosophical values of the organization development movement? Are these values held widely by managers and other members of American work organizations?
2. Explain the role and characteristic mode of operation of the organization development consultant or change agent. Contrast this with the operating procedures of the typical management consultant.
3. Compare organization development with management development.
4. What is sensitivity (laboratory) training? What are its goals? Must it be an integral part of the overall OD activity? Give criticisms of sensitivity training.
5. What is the managerial grid and how is it used in OD work?
6. Think of some organization where you have worked or of which you are a member. How might it benefit from OD? What specific OD interventions would you recommend and why?
7. If an organization development effort is successful in a particular organizational setting, how would you know it? What measures or gauges could be used? Is it likely that the culture of that organization will have been changed?

8. Give and explain the five elements or components of the organization development process.

Suggestions for further reading ———————————————

BECKHARD, RICHARD. *Organization Development: Strategies and Models*. Reading, Mass.: Addison-Wesley Publishing Co., Inc., 1969.

BENNIS, WARREN, G. *Organization Development: Its Nature, Origins, and Prospects*. Reading, Mass.: Addison-Wesley Publishing Co., Inc., 1969.

BURKE, W. WARNER. *Current Issues and Strategies in Organization Development*. New York: Human Sciences Press, 1977.

FORDYCE, JACK K., and RAYMOND WEIL. *Managing with People: A Manager's Handbook of Organization Development Methods*. Reading, Mass.: Addison-Wesley Publishing Co., Inc., 1971.

FRAME, ROBERT M. and FRED LUTHANS. "Merging Personnel and OD: A Not-So-Odd Couple," *Personnel*, Vol. 54, No. 1 (Jaunary–February 1977), pp. 12–22.

FRENCH, WENDELL and CECIL H. BELL. *Organization Development: Behavioral Science Interventions for Organization Improvement*. Englewood Cliffs, N.J.: Prentice-Hall, Inc., 1973.

HUSE, EDGAR, and MICHAEL BEER. "Eclectic Approach to Organizational Development," *Harvard Business Review*, Vol. 49, No. 5 (September–October, 1971), pp. 103–112.

McGILL, MICHAEL E. *Organizational Development for Operating Managers*. New York: AMACOM, 1977.

MARGULIES, NEWTON, and ANTHONY P. RAIA. *Organizational Development: Values, Process, and Technology*. New York: McGraw-Hill Book Company, 1972.

———. *Conceptual Foundations of Organizational Development*. New York: McGraw-Hill Book Company, 1978.

RUSH, HAROLD M. F. *Organization Development: A Reconnaissance*. Report No. 605. New York: The Conference Board, Inc., 1973.

UNDERSTANDING AND MANAGING PEOPLE

Understanding people and motivation

Human beings, as individuals, are very complex in their psychological make-up. When they interact with one another in groups and in large organizations, the complexities are multiplied. Scientists still have much to learn about the nature of man. However, as a result of systematic experimentation, observation, and clinical studies, behavioral scientists have developed insights into the nature and conditions of human behavior.

This chapter is essentially concerned with an analysis of the reasons people behave as they do, and with an explanation of various means by which management can stimulate and guide the conduct and actions of members of its organization. We shall explore the subject of human motivation and look into some important theories of motivation. Why do people act as they do? What do they seek out of life? Why do some have high levels of aspiration and others not? Do most human drives and wants form a consistent pattern? We shall delve into the subject of human adjustment and the concepts of adaptive and maladaptive behavior. What are the characteristics of behavior induced by frustration? How can one's job induce frustrations?

Finally, and most importantly, we shall discuss ways in which motivational principles can be applied by management in the work situation. The concept of integration of goals—the joining together of the drives and wants of employees with those of the organization for which they work—will be examined.

HUMAN BEHAVIOR FUNDAMENTALS

In his efforts to guide and direct others, the manager must first of all acquire an understanding of the nature of human behavior and why people act as they do.

Self-concept and Personality

To understand another person, we must be aware of how he thinks and feels about himself. This image of himself that the individual holds may not be a fully accurate representation. Nevertheless, he will tend to behave in accordance with his own self-image. His actions are a function of how he views himself. His behavior will be logical from his point of view although it may not appear logical from our own perspective. Even though a person's knowledge about himself may be a little vague, he will strive at all times to be true to his own views of himself. Our opinion of this person may be quite an inaccurate picture of how he considers himself. To learn to understand him truly we must be less judgmental of his actions and more perceptive.

How does a person acquire his self-concept? The strongest influence is that in the home during one's formative years as a child. If a child is raised in a family where people are demonstrative, he will learn that this is approved behavior. If high but attainable standards of achievement are expected by his parents, he will tend to hold to such standards throughout life. Children in the family are rewarded or punished for all sorts of behavior. They learn to avoid physical and emotional pain and to repeat that behavior which gains approval and reward. In addition to the influences of the parents and brothers and sisters, are those of friends, associates, teachers, and other authority figures. As a child matures he gains a view of his personal worth on the basis of the way others respond to him and on the basis of his achievements. Thus, a person's sense of personal worth is conferred on him as well as derived in relation to his accomplishments. Gradually as maturation takes place, the individual acquires rather definite beliefs about what his behavior, values, and goals ought to be. These become internalized.

In addition to self-concept everyone also acquires a personal view of his world. He perceives and responds to other people, places, things, and events. His personal frame of reference is an amalgam of his self-image, his behavior, and his perception of the world about him. His perceptions and preconceived notions of his environment help determine whether he will be bold or meek, optimistic or pessimistic, trusting or suspicious.

Based upon his self-concept and his view of the world about him, each individual develops an accommodation and a characteristic way of acting. He will always behave in such a way as to protect and improve his adequacy in his world as he sees it. His behavior is internally logical and consistent as he sees it.

In talking about *self*, we have in a sense also been talking about personality. Personality is the sum total of the physical, mental, emotional, and social characteristics of a person. It is the integrating process by which all the physiological and psychological components of man are combined into the whole. Psychologists, in their research investigations, have devised many ways of quantifying bodily sensations, perceptions, intelligence, attitudes, and motives. However, these do not act singly. They are all contained within the unified whole of the person. Frank Edwards is the personnel director. It is not simply his intelligence alone nor his emotional state alone that is Frank Edwards. All of his attributes operate together to reveal his characteristic responses. The *self* and *personality* are one and the same. Personality is more than the sum of all the various attributes of a person; it is the organization of these parts.

When a human being is internally consistent within himself, we speak of him as having a well-adjusted personality. When he is externally adapted to his environment, we say he is well-adapted. When one is both adjusted and adapted, we say that he has an integrated personality.

A person may be at ease with himself but maladapted for his environment. Conversely he may get along well with others socially and in business but suffer from all sorts of internal tensions and anxieties in the process.

An individual continually strives to maintain his personality consistent and in balance. The basic parts of the adult personality are stable. In actuality we deduce an individual's specific personality from the stability of his characteristic way of behaving.

As a person matures, he gains more needs and abilities, and he also deepens many of those he already possesses. As new ideas, traits, and outlooks are gained, these are incorporated into the person so as not to upset his equilibrium. With maturation his private world expands. His perception of the world about him is always colored by his frame of reference and his self-image. Actually everyone, in a sense, lives in his own private world. The personality becomes complete and integrated only when it interacts with other people, things, and groups. The isolated individual cannot fully develop. We can understand ourselves only as we can understand others; conversely we can understand others only if we also understand ourselves.

Individual Differences

Beyond the more noticeable and obvious differences among people in physical appearance, voice, intelligence, race, language, and general habits, are the less readily apparent differences in emotional responses to various stimuli, and in motives, attitudes, and modes of thought.

There are vast differences among people of different cultures and subcultures even though biologically they are the same. For example, one can observe great differences in the competence, behavior, and attitudes between the subculture composed of corporate executives and that of the culturally deprived. If a manager tries to operate various personnel programs for a group of poorly educated, disadvantaged people in a factory setting, he soon learns that they do not respond to the same kind of communications and incentives that he is accustomed to. The culturally deprived are not verbally oriented. Some are illiterate, and others read with great difficulty. They will not react to the discipline of the factory in the same way as middle-class employees. When applying for jobs, they may not think in terms of the long-run future and prospects for advancement. One personnel manager stated that he has interviewed hundreds of disadvantaged persons applying for laboring jobs in factories and that they very rarely ask about opportunities for promotion.

Even within the same social milieu we find considerable variation in the abilities, attitudes, and temperaments of people. If a manager gives identical projects to two engineers, he will find that their modes of attack may be quite different. People react to praise, criticism, promises, frustration, and the like quite differently. A challenging assignment may frustrate one man but stimulate another.

The manager must be perceptive. He must be ever alert to the world and personality of his subordinates, peers, and superiors.

Human Behavior Is Caused

Initially it is important to know that all human behavior has a cause (or causes). There is a reason for a person's behaving as he does. A stimulus is present to initiate behavior on the part of the individual. For example, physiological changes in the body accompanying the passage of time since a person has had his last meal will give rise to a feeling of emptiness and discomfort in his stomach. There will be a feeling of hunger. We call this a need or a feeling of tension inside the person. The person will normally then seek food to alleviate his hunger so that he can again experience a feeling of well-being. To generalize, we can say that one or more stimuli may interact with an individual. The person will then experience a state of tension such that he seeks to fulfill his need and reduce the level of tension and discomfort. He adopts a type of behavior he feels will satisfy his need.

The cause for human behavior constitutes an interaction between a stimulus (noise, light, a threat) and the person's own internal interpretation of that stimulus. Thus, to one person a sound may be annoying, whereas another may consider it like soothing music. If one employee smiles at another, the second may view the smile as a leering smirk. On the other hand, someone else may consider it a smile of approbation. One's perception is determined by his background, personality, and the circumstances surrounding the event.

The actions of rational human beings are goal directed. Our behavior is aimed toward the fulfillment of basic wants, drives, and needs. The politician who does favors for his constituents hopes thereby to gain their votes at election time so that he can retain his office. The piece-rate worker in the clothing factory may work very hard to increase her earnings because she desires to buy a new coat or a car. It is important to understand that behavior is purposeful and that it is caused. People are not uncooperative just for the sake of being perverse. There are causes for such behavior. The successful leader is the one who can uncover these causes and take steps to correct them. Bawling out an uncooperative worker does not get at the cause. This constitutes treating the symptom only.

MOTIVATION

Motives are the mainspring of action in people. The leader who wishes to incite his followers to reach an objective must hold out the promise of reward once the objective is attained. What rewards do people seek in life? The answer is that they seek to fulfill their wants, drives, and needs.

The term *motive* implies action to satisfy a need. The term *need, want, drive,* and *motive* are often used interchangeably by psychologists. Motivation can be defined as a willingness to expend energy to achieve a goal or a reward. Let us look at the chart below in order better to understand motivation.

Need	Behavior	Reward
Respect from others	Outstanding work on the job	Praise, pay increase, status symbols

Assume that an engineer in industry seeks to win the admiration and esteem not only of his boss but also of his fellow engineers. This feeling on his part is called a need or a motive. Although there are perhaps a number of ways of achieving this, let us assume that our engineer chooses to work unusually diligently on a particular design project so that it becomes evident to his supervisor that he has made a major contribution. The supervisor may then choose to reward the engineer for his performance with oral praise, with a pay increase at salary review time, with certain formal recognition in the company newspaper, or by means of a letter of commendation to higher management. Depending upon how the individual perceives these forms of reward, his original need may be wholly or partially satisfied.

The psychology of learning tells us about the *law of effect, which states that behavior that is perceived to be rewarding will tend to be repeated, whereas behavior that goes unrewarded or is punished will tend to be extinguished.* This has great import for trainers, personnel directors, and managers. Over the long run they can induce desired behavior such as high quality workmanship, good attendance, loyalty, or initiative by their choice of rewards and the way they are administered. Unrewarded behavior tends to disappear, as evidenced by the example of a high-level engineer in the department of public works of a state government who worked out a plan for saving $250,000 for the government. He installed the plan on his own authority and then proudly informed his boss about his cost-saving. His boss showed not the slightest interest in this accomplishment. What his boss was interested in was new and bigger projects to expand the prestige of his department, not ways to reduce expenses. The engineer got the message and did not repeat his cost-cutting venture.

Classification of Needs

To understand human needs adequately, it is useful to classify them as to type. Thus we have innate or primary needs, such as food, shelter, water, rest to overcome fatigue, and so on. These are inborn needs. Generally speaking, they are not conditioned by experience. The innate needs are primarily physiological in nature. Gratification of these needs is vital to the survival of a human being as an organism.

The other major type of need is called an acquired or secondary need. These needs are dependent upon our experience. They are learned. They vary greatly from person to person and from one group to another. The need for a lady to wear white gloves and a hat at certain social gatherings in warm weather is certainly not inborn. It is culturally determined. It is acquired from her parents and friends. It is largely a manifestation of the desire to belong and be accepted by others. In the home the child feels a need to be wanted and loved. We are all familiar with the serious emotional problems that occur in children who are rejected by their parents. The same motives to be needed, to be wanted, and to belong are present in adults. An employee can readily sense when his boss disapproves of him. If a supervisor or manager, by his attitude and actions, makes it apparent that he dislikes one of his employees, this usually causes anxiety, tension, and frustration in the subordinate. If the supervisor's attitude is readily apparent to the other employees, his attitude often has an effect upon their relations with the rejected employee. Figure 18-1 presents a classification and listing of basic human needs.

The drive to obtain safety and security has several ramifications. Partly it is related to the innate physiological need for self-preservation. The aim is to avoid bodily harm, to avoid suffering, to continue to exist. The need for security is also social in context. The fact that one knows that others like him, respect him, and want him to continue to be a part of the group or organization, enhances his feeling of security. We can call it a feeling of emotional security. The struggle to achieve a measure of security is fundamental for most people. Some achieve financial security by means of hard work, superior ability, and fortuitous circumstances. Others turn to collective security from their group. Thus, we have various health and welfare programs to provide a measure of security for eligible members. These may take the form of a pension plan operated by a private employer for his employees, a group insurance program paid for by union members' dues, or a comprehensive social security program provided by a national government for its citizens.

The egoistic needs are concerned primarily with a person's view or conception of himself. Satisfaction of these needs tends to enhance one's ego. Some writers refer to the egoistic needs as *personal* drives. They are often called the higher needs, because a person is seldom motivated to fulfill them until after he has first

Figure 18-1
A Classification of Basic Human Needs.

met his physiological and social wants. Business executives and political leaders tend to be strongly motivated to meet their egoistic needs. They have a drive for power, prestige, and status. They seek to make their mark in the world. They want to accomplish and achieve. They want others to hear their words. But persons of lesser fame also desire satisfaction of their personal needs. The bookkeeper with forty years' service who has labored long and hard in the back room of a merchandising establishment feels a warm glow when someone praises him, and he feels very important if his boss asks him for his advice on an involved accounting problem.

Hierarchy of Needs—Maslow

The psychologist A. H. Maslow has developed a widely acclaimed theory of human motivation in which he postulates that there is a definite rank-order priority of human needs. Until the more basic wants are fulfilled, a person will not strive to meet his higher needs. Maslow classifies needs into five categories:

1. Physiological.
2. Safety, stability, and security.
3. Belongingness and love.
4. Self-esteem and the esteem of others.
5. Self-actualization, self-realization, and self-accomplishment.[1]

The implications of the hierarchical nature of human motivation are important for an understanding of why people behave as they do. If a person has barely enough food, water, and shelter to survive, his entire energies are devoted to eking out an existence. He is not interested in status, prestige, or making his ideas known to others. He cannot afford the luxury of engaging in ego-enhancing activities. Once the basic physiological and safety wants are met, then people strive for companionship, belongingness, love, affection, and the esteem of others. When he has a superabundance of food, clothing, and shelter, the fulfillment of these needs no longer motivates our hypothetical man. He turns to his higher needs. The higher needs are social and psychological in nature. They are less concrete and more nebulous than the survival needs. Particularly when we concern ourselves with the egoistic drives, we find that full satisfaction seldom occurs. People can always take more recognition, more praise, more status, and more adulation.

Characteristics of Acquired Needs

The strength and pattern of the acquired needs vary considerably from one person to another. The boy who is raised on a farm in Iowa will tend to seek somewhat different satisfactions in life from the boy whose father is a corporation executive and who lives in the suburbs of New York City. The former may cherish the values of family, neighbors, the soil, and the open air, whereas the latter may struggle hard to climb the corporate ladder and thereby achieve power and

[1] A. H. Maslow, *Motivation and Personality* (New York: Harper and Row, 1954). See especially ch. 5.

wealth. Therefore, we can say that when people exist in different environments and when their experiences are different, the pattern and intensity of their motives will vary. Anthropologists have observed that among some peoples on earth the great urge to acquire more goods and possessions that is so characteristic of Americans is totally absent. Likewise competition serves successfully as a motivator for company salesmen and for college athletes, but it is far less successful as a stimulus to higher production for blue-collar workers in the factory.

Acquired needs vary over time for the same individual. A young breadwinner raising a family has an urgent need for a higher income, whereas the same person, after his children have reached adulthood, finds a lesser need for material rewards but may seek more leisure time or pursue cultural activities.

Learned needs do not operate upon a person singly. They occur in groups. The desire to achieve a higher income may be based upon one's desire for greater status and respect in the company and the community at large as well as the desire to obtain more of the material comforts of life. Very frequently a person is not fully aware of why he behaves as he does. He is not able to say "I do this because I seek security." His motives are often hidden from conscious recognition.

Level of Aspiration

The degree to which a person will strive to achieve and accomplish is determined by his level of aspiration. Failure tends to lower what one feels he can do, and success raises his sights. The person who repeatedly fails to reach his goal must lower his sights (or change his methods) or else experience deep frustration. On the other hand, one young industrial relations director, who had risen very rapidly in the business world, was a member of top management in his company, had a good salary, and enjoyed considerable prestige and acceptance both in his company and in the community. Upon being asked if he were now satisfied, he replied, "No." He aspired to continue to go up in the business world. He hoped to become president of his company and obtain higher and higher financial rewards. Repeated success in this case gave rise to continually higher expectations.

There is another important determinant of one's level of aspiration. This is parental influence. Most of our values in life we gain from our parents. If a boy's father is a doctor, he would tend to experience considerable status anxiety if he were to hold only a minor clerical position as an adult. Conversely, if by example and preachment a father demonstrated that a foreman's job in a factory was the epitome of success, there would be a tendency for the son to let that be his standard of accomplishment.

One's associates also exert an influence upon the level of expectation. In seeking to win and maintain the approval of his friends, a person will try to behave as they do. In the factory individual workers tend to produce as much as the group to which they belong. If most of a college sophomore's friends own automobiles, he, too, will aspire to own one. If it is considered socially desirable for college freshmen to become pledged to a fraternity, then individual students will exert great efforts to achieve fraternity membership.

HUMAN ADJUSTMENT

Human adjustment is concerned with the way people react in the process of seeking to satisfy their needs. Some, whom we call well-adjusted individuals, are relatively successful in meeting and solving the myriad problems that the average person faces. We speak of them as possessing a mature personality. These persons are goal centered and adopt a flexible, resourceful, problem-solving form of behavior.

If an obstacle or barrier presents itself on the path to attainment of their goals, they are adaptive. They try other ways of relieving tension and satisfying their needs. They may intensify their efforts, they may reorganize their perception of the problem, and they may adopt substitute goals. Others, who are not so fortunate, may be poorly adjusted to meet the problems of life. They may exhibit what we call maladjusted or maladaptive behavior. They may be disorganized and unproductive in relieving tension and fulfilling their needs. Their actions take on the characteristics of frustrated behavior.

Now all persons cannot be conveniently classified into the two categories of well-adjusted or maladjusted. People fall along a continuum. The terms are relative. Many persons whom we would ordinarily consider to be well adjusted may in a particular situation lose their tempers, swear, or develop a tension headache. When goal-directed behavior is successful it leads to a reduction of internal tension and a satisfaction of needs. However, all of us experience situations that irritate, annoy, and vex us. John may have missed his usual train on the way to work in the morning causing him to miss an important business contact. Or if the boss is in a grumpy mood, the entire office force may become apprehensive.

Defense Mechanisms

When motivated behavior encounters an apparently insurmountable barrier, and when a problem-solving approach fails to achieve the goal, then frustration occurs. All of us encounter situations in which our self-integrity is threatened and we must find an outlet. We speak of the various forms of behavior that people may adopt in the face of frustration as *defense mechanisms*. Occasional resort to a defense mechanism as an outlet does not mean that a person is maladjusted. It is when frustration-directed behavior dominates one's whole life that we can say that a person is abnormal and needs expert help.

Now the barriers to the fulfillment of needs and wants can be both external and internal. If a boy who is sent to the store by his mother to buy a bottle of milk finds his way blocked by two neighborhood bullies, then the obstacle to the attainment of his goal is clearly external. If a salesperson continually repels potential customers because of his own antagonistic personality, then this barrier is internal to the salesperson. To a considerable extent the most difficult obstacles to surmount are those arising within the person himself. Likewise some barriers are "thing-type" obstacles; for example, it is too cold or the car has a flat tire. Others are "people-type" barriers. The most vexing type is that involving people. Executives whose jobs require that they try to persuade others to act know that this can be a very challenging assignment.

The defense mechanisms that people may adopt as an outlet from frustration can be classified into four broad categories:

1. Aggression.
2. Withdrawal.
3. Fixation.
4. Compromise.

Within each category are a number of subcategories. The particular form of reaction a person adopts depends upon his personality, the situation, and how he perceives the barrier. The frustration tolerance of people varies considerably. Some are much more susceptible to frustration than others. Different people will react differently under the same circumstances.

Let us now examine the various forms of frustrated behavior. One of the most common forms is *aggression*. This is primarily an attack response designed to inflict injury or damage. We see aggression nearly every day in one form or other. It is readily apparent in children, where it usually takes the form of a physical attack (for example, hitting another child because he has taken a toy). With adults, physical violence as an outlet for frustration certainly occurs too (for example, violence on union picket lines to prevent strike-breakers from going to work). However, education and training have taught most adults in most situations to channel their aggressive impulses into nonviolent forms. Thus we find a person spreading rumors about another whom he dislikes or uttering vituperative remarks against the source of a frustration. In labor–management relations examples of aggression are the firing of a worker because he is active in organizing a union, or, on the employee's part, a deliberate slowdown in protest against the actions of the company.

There are a number of kinds of *withdrawal* reactions that occur. Basically when a person withdraws, he seeks either physically or mentally to avoid the obstacle or situation. Thus, we find flights into *fantasy* and daydreaming. By so doing a person can obtain satisfaction through a temporary escape from reality. Physical *escape* or absence from the situation is another type of defense mechanism. The worker who continually changes jobs because of dissatisfaction with what he is doing at the time may simply be avoiding a sound appraisal of himself and a mature approach to his problems. *Regression* consists of adopting less mature, more childish behavior. Sometimes it signifies an attempt to return to the security and comfort of one's childhood. Symptoms of regressive behavior in adults are crying, pouting, horseplay, loss of emotional control, and homesickness. A continual longing for the good old days may be a reaction to frustration. Those who live in the past do so because the present is unhappy for them.

Still another form of withdrawal is *resignation*. This involves giving up the struggle. After repeated failure the individual may cease trying. The downtrodden worker who has lost all hope of better things from his job may have simply resigned himself to his unsatisfactory existence.

Fixation, the third major type of frustrated behavior, consists of a compulsion to continue repeatedly a type of behavior that does not result in the attainment of a goal. It does not reduce tension. The person is figuratively hitting his head against a stone wall. Persisting in the old way of doing things, even when unsuccessful, may be the only recourse that some people know. They are afraid or do not know how to try something else.

Compromise reactions, the fourth major category, consist of *sublimation, ratio-*

nalization, and *projection*. Compromise involves altering one's objectives either actually or symbolically. Thus in *sublimation* an individual will adopt a substitute goal, or behavior, generally one that is on a higher ethical plane and socially more acceptable. *Rationalization* involves protecting one's ego by claiming that he really didn't want something anyway. It may take the form of giving false reasons for one's conduct. Alibiing is a form of rationalization. Sometimes a person finds his own thoughts or actions so intolerable that he ascribes them to another individual. Such an action constitutes *projection*. Examples of this can be found in the unfaithful husband who accuses his wife of infidelity or in the irritable person who accuses others of being irritable. The person who adopts this form of defense machanism often believes his accusations to be true.

DISSATISFACTIONS ON THE JOB

In this chapter we have so far examined the needs and wants that human beings seek to satisfy in their quest for happiness and fulfillment in life. Then we have discussed ways in which people react when their motives and drives are blocked. We have discussed defense mechanisms and adaptive and maladaptive behavior. The employment situation provides abundant opportunities for need satisfactions for employees. Work can be meaningful; it can answer many (but not all) of employees' basic wants.

Yet we find in every organization countless individuals and groups who are dissatisfied and frustrated. It is true that some may have been maladjusted when first hired. Others may have been emotionally mature, well-adjusted individuals at the time of hiring, but over the ensuing years they may have experienced so many insurmountable obstacles on the job (inadequate pay, difficult boss, lack of advancement, and so on) that they acquired serious tensions and anxieties. A third category consists of those who have encountered severe disruptions in their private lives off the job (for example, family or financial problems). In actual practice it may not be possible to ascribe a person's source of discontent and frustration solely to personal background, to the job situation, or to home pressures. It may be a composite of many influences.

There is little doubt that in our society a person's job exerts a powerful influence upon his well-being. A wage-earner devotes about one quarter of his entire adult life to his job. His job establishes his economic and social station in life. Loss of a job can mean hardship and loss of status. The many anxieties and pressures encountered at work can have a profound effect upon one's personality and happiness.

Some people find themselves working on limited, short-cycle jobs which they find routine, repetitive, and boring. In many situations employees feel insecure because layoffs are frequent in their company and in their industry. Job insecurity occurs also, in some organizations, due to frequent and perhaps arbitrary discharges of individual employees over alleged infractions of the rules or due to personality clashes between supervisor and employee.

Various tensions occur in any organization in the course of daily interpersonal contacts. There may be jealousies and rivalries between individuals in the same office. A frequent source of anxiety is the relationship between an individual and his boss. The supervisor controls most of the rewards and penalties the employee receives on the job. Any feeling that one is being slighted or discriminated against can cause worry and frustration.

Another source of discontent for some employees is lack of progress in achieving the job promotions they desire. For many persons their career is the central focus of their lives. Failure to advance at the same rate as ones' contemporaries or in accord with ones' own standards for advancement can be a source of great frustration.

SIGNIFICANT MOTIVATION THEORIES

So far in this chapter we have studied motivation by examining basic human needs and wants and by discussing Maslow's hierarchy of needs. Let us now turn to four other important theories of motivation. The first has been formulated by psychologist Frederick Herzberg. It is a theory of motivation in the context of a work organization. That is, it is a theory of work motivation rather than a more general theory of human motivation. The second, by Harvard psychologist David McClelland, is concerned with achievement motivation, not only in the context of individuals but also in the context of achievement drives in entire societies. The third theory is behavior modification. Although relatively new to managers and to work organizations it is supported by over thirty years of experimental work by Harvard psychologist B. F. Skinner. The fourth is the expectancy model of motivation formulated by Victor Vroom.

Motivation–Hygiene Theory

In the late 1950's Professor Herzberg and his research associates conducted careful interviews with two hundred engineers and accountants who worked for eleven different companies in the Pittsburgh area.[2] This research endeavor was designed to test the concept that man has two sets of needs: (1) his lower-order needs to avoid loss of life, hunger, pain, and other deprivations and (2) his needs to grow psychologically. Included under his psychological growth needs are those of knowing more, seeing more relationships in what one knows, creativity, being effective in vague situations, maintaining individuality in the face of group pressures, and real growth through self-achievement.

The interviewers asked these men to tell about events in the course of their employment that caused them to feel a marked improvement in job satisfaction and also about those situations that caused a substantial reduction in job satisfaction. A great many probing questions were asked in each interview to pinpoint just how and why the people felt as they did and how their feelings affected their job performance and personal relationships.

When the results of the research were analyzed, the researchers found that one group of factors accounted for high levels of job satisfaction. These were labeled *motivators* because they seemed to be effective in motivating the indi-

[2] The original motivator-hygienic factor theory is presented in Frederick Herzberg, Bernard Mausner, and Barbara B. Snyderman, *The Motivation to Work*, 2nd ed. (New York: John Wiley & Sons, Inc., 1959). A more complete formulation and further research investigations are contained in Frederick Herzberg, *Work and the Nature of Man* (Cleveland: The World Publishing Company, 1966).

vidual to superior performance and effort. These factors were *achievement, recognition, work itself, responsibility,* and *advancement.* All of these satisfiers related to the job content.

Another group of factors, labeled *hygienic* or *maintenance* factors seemed to focus on discontent with their work situation. However, these factors were seldom mentioned by the respondents as causing positive job satisfaction. These factors pertained primarily to the job context or environment. These factors were *company policy and administration, supervision, salary, interpersonal relations,* and *working conditions.*

What are the practical implications of this research? The hygienic or maintenance factors provide an essential base on which to build. If employees' wages, fringe benefits, working conditions, eating facilities, job rights, and status systems are inadequate, they will feel uneasy and discontent. They may complain openly about job conditions and company policies. They may even become very antagonistic toward the company. However, if all these maintenance needs are taken care of adequately, the people will not necessarily work any harder. But these factors do serve as a base upon which to add the motivators to improve job performance.

It is true that certain people, in these studies, reported that they received job satisfaction solely from maintenance factors. Herzberg has asserted that such individuals show only a temporary satisfaction when hygiene factors are improved, they show little interest in the kind and quality of their work, they experience little satisfaction from accomplishments, and they tend to show a chronic dissatisfaction with various aspects of job context (such as pay, status, and job security).[3]

How can top management apply Herzberg's motivators—achievement, recognition, the work itself, responsibility, and advancement—in a practical way to create a high level of job performance? It must create a climate where employees and managers can reach satisfactions for their higher-order needs. Some of the specific leadership practices that it can institute are delegation of responsibility and authority, job enrichment, full utilization of employees' skills and training, establishment of an atmosphere of approval toward subordinates, granting of earned pay increases, and granting promotions when deserved.

Herzberg holds that motivation-seekers are motivated by the nature of the work itself, have a higher tolerance for poor hygienic factors, and show capacity to enjoy their work.

Although numerous researchers have independently replicated Herzberg's two-dimensional theory of work motivation, the theory does have its critics. Some scholars and researchers have commented that this two-factor explanation of job satisfaction is a great oversimplification of the whole motivational complex of the world of work. Also the Herzberg research technique does not include any statistical correlations between the *motivators* and actual job performance. Vroom has asserted that employees who are interviewed may attribute the causes of their satisfaction to their own achievements on the job while they ascribe their dissatisfactions, not to their own inadequacies, but to factors in the work environment (hygienic factors).[4] Some studies also show that hourly-paid blue-collar workers place more emphasis upon maintenance factors (such as pay

[3] Herzberg, *Work and the Nature of Man,* p. 90.
[4] Victor H. Vroom, *Work and Motivation* (New York: John Wiley & Sons, Inc., 1964), p. 129.

and job security) than do higher-level employees. In effect maintenance or hygienic factors may be considered as motivators by blue-collar people.[5] Regardless of the criticisms, however, the motivator-hygienic factor theory of Herzberg has received considerable support from independent investigators. Although not all employees are motivated primarily by job content (we already know that humans are very complex and variable), the theory does provide a very useful way of analyzing work motivation and of predicting the probable employee responses to managerial leadership practices.

Intrinsic and Extrinsic Motivation

Intrinsic motivation is that which occurs while a person is performing an activity in which he gains satisfaction from engaging in that activity itself. This is internal reward. It is directly part of the job content. Extrinsic motivators are the incentives or rewards that a person can enjoy after he finishes his work. This is related to the job environment or an external reward.

Traditionally work has been viewed as necessary drudgery. Rewards came in the form of pay, which was enjoyed off the job; holidays and vacations, which were enjoyed off the job; cafeterias and lounges, which were enjoyed away from the job; and pensions, which were received after retirement from work.

Modern behavioral research has tended to emphasize that work itself can be satisfying. This has been postulated in the writings of Herzberg, just discussed, and of other behavioral scientists such as Rensis Likert, Chris Argyris, and Douglas McGregor.

Managers in some of our more enlightened corporations have been applying this concept by placing people on jobs for which they are trained and are interested, by new concepts of job design and work flow, and by gearing recognition directly to the job.

Although there are those enthusiasts for intrinsic motivation who would substantially downgrade all efforts toward extrinsic motivation, in reality both are necessary. If working conditions, wages, job security, and fringe benefits are inadequate, a company will find it difficult to recruit and retain good people. Turnover, absenteeism, and grievances tend to be high where management ignores external forms of reward. Large bureaucracies, in both government and industry, tend to do quite well in meeting people's maintenance needs. What they so often lack is emphasis upon challenging assignments, an encouragement of innovation, and large rewards for achievement. By emphasizing job tenure, loyalty, and conformity, bureaucracies tend to repel those with an enterprising spirit and drive.

A sound motivational climate must provide both extrinsic and intrinsic motivators.

---

[5] Critiques of the motivator-hygienic two-factor theory are contained in Victor H. Vroom, op. cit., pp. 127–129; Lyman W. Porter, "Personnel Management," *Annual Review of Psychology*, Vol. 17 (1966), p. 411; A. Kornhauser, *Mental Health of the Industrial Worker* (New York: John Wiley & Sons, Inc., 1965); and Orlando Behling, George Labovitz, and Richard Kosmo, "The Herzberg Controversy: A Critical Reappraisal," *Academy of Management Journal*, Vol. 11, No. 1 (March 1968), pp. 99–108.

Achievement Motivation

Beginning in the 1940's, a group of researchers led by Harvard psychologist David C. McClelland began investigating the achievement motive in people. For a measuring instrument they used a projective test of personality, the Thematic Apperception Test. In this research, subjects were shown a series of pictures and then asked to tell a story about each picture. This technique reveals the inner dynamics of a person's personality. What does a man think about and what does he daydream about when he is not required to think about anything in particular? If a man spends his time thinking about doing things better—about building, creating, and doing—then psychologists say he has an achievement orientation. On the other hand if one spends his time thinking about his family and friends, he has an affiliation orientation. Of course, the reader will recognize that most people are not entirely achievement-oriented or entirely affiliation-oriented. They possess some of each. But there are people who lean much more in one direction than the other.[6]

McClelland's research, which has now been carried on for many years, has uncovered some important things about achievement-oriented people. They actually tend to translate their thinking into action. They are not idle dreamers. They place great demands upon themselves. They are persistent and they are realists. They are not romantics.

For the achiever accomplishment is often an end in itself. This is comparable to the mountain climber who was asked why he continually tried to scale Mount Everest. His answer, "Because it is there," has become classic.[7]

The achievement-oriented individual believes in moderate risk-taking. He is not a reckless adventurer. Rather he takes calculated risks. He also tends to be very sanguine about his likelihood of success. He is persistent for the long-term pull. Such individuals also seek concrete feedback on how they are doing.

How do high-achievement-oriented people get that way? Parental influence is paramount. The parents set high standards of accomplishment. They show warmth and encouragement. The father is not domineering or authoritarian. Discipline is consistent and specific, but it is neither harsh nor all-pervasive. Over-disciplined children tend to be overregulated and docile. McClelland found that middle-class parents—managers, professionals, and entrepreneurs—tend to impart a decidedly stronger achievement drive than do lower-class parents.

People also acquire their achievement drive (or lack of it) from the culture and predominant values of the society in which they live. McClelland has charted the tendencies of many societies throughout the world and for different periods in history. He did this by coding the contents of the literature of a people. Schoolbooks were especially useful. The values imparted to the youth are instrumental in shaping that nation's future. The United States scores high in achievement. Business careers offer abundant opportunities for realization of this motive. The Protestant Ethic helped shape this orientation in the population. In recent years the Soviet Union has also scored high in the achievement motive. McClelland

---

[6] David C. McClelland, *The Achieving Society* (Princeton, N.J.: D. Van Nostrand Company, 1961).
[7] This statement was made by the British mountaineer George Leigh Mallory, who tried to scale Everest repeatedly in the early 1920's. He tragically perished in 1924 when very near the top.

has found a positive coefficient of correlation of .53 between achievement scores derived from the literature of twenty-two nations and their subsequent economic growth rate.[8]

After people are on the payroll, management bears the responsibility of establishing a leadership climate that encourages the achievement motive to thrive in the organization.

Behavior Modification

In very recent years the work of Harvard psychologist B. F. Skinner has come to the attention of human resource specialists and managers in industry. Skinner's early experiments in the 1940's dealt with conditioning the behavior of pigeons. Later he investigated the shaping of human behavior in countless experiments. Until recently most of the applications of Skinner's principles had been in psychotherapy, in handling disturbed and retarded children, in schools, and in programmed instruction. Nowadays, business firms are learning how behavioral modification can be used in their establishments to motivate performance. The Emery Air Freight Corporation has been a leader in implementing Skinnerian psychology to boost workers' performance.[9]

Skinner is a leading proponent of the behaviorist school of psychology, which holds that behavior is caused primarily by externally induced stimuli. He asserts that behavioral scientists should give up their emphasis upon the inner life of man and upon free will. Rather they should concentrate upon relations between man and his environment.

Let us look at the basic concepts of behavior modification. Skinner and his disciples say that all behavior is shaped and maintained by its consequences. A man does something because of the reinforcement he received from similar behavior in the past. If the outcome of his action is pleasing to him, the likelihood of his repeating that same action is high. A reinforcer is something that increases the probability of a behavior occurring again. We can look upon a reinforcer as a reward or incentive to behave in a certain way. Reinforcers may be tangible like food or money and they can be intangible like praise and approval.

There can be three distinct types of reinforcement: (1) punishment or negative reinforcement; (2) extinction or neutral reinforcement; and (3) positive reinforcement.

Punishment is the most widely used technique in our society for controlling behavior. It can be done in two ways. The first is by inflicting physical or emotional pain and the second is by withdrawal of a desired stimulus such as food or water. The purpose of punishment is to decrease or stop the occurrence of a certain behavior. Skinner argues against punishment for controlling behavior for several reasons. When the punishing agent is absent, the individual may again exhibit the undesired response. Punishment tells someone what not to do but it does not shape his behavior in the desired direction. It shows him what is wrong but not what is right. A third disadvantage of punishment is that the person who

[8] David C. McClelland, "Business Drive and National Achievement," *Harvard Business Review,* Vol. 40 (July–August 1962).
[9] "At Emery Air Freight: Positive Reinforcement Boosts Performance," *Organizational Dynamics,* Vol. 1, No. 3 (Winter 1973), pp. 41–50; "Where Skinner's Theories Work," *Business Week* (December 2, 1972), pp. 64–65.

is being punished may strike back at the punisher. And finally it can cause psychological and physical damage to the punished individual.

Extinction consists of applying a neutral stimulus after the behavior occurs. The behavior is neither rewarded nor punished. This method has fewer undesirable consequences than punishment but it still does not induce or teach the desired behavior.

Positive reinforcement is most recommended by Skinner. It is efficient because it increases the likelihood of a desired response. Favorable emotions are aroused. The individual tends to develop favorable attitudes toward the person who applies the positive reinforcement. Also the physical and emotional discomfort of punishment is avoided.

Reinforcement can be applied according to three different schedules: (1) continuous; (2) fixed ratio but not continuous; and (3) variable ratio. A continuous schedule rewards a person every time he exhibits the desired behavior. Piece-rate wage incentive and salesmen's commission plans work this way. A fixed ratio schedule might reward the person, say, every second time he exhibits the sought-after behavior. With a variable ratio, behavior is reinforced randomly.

Another variable is the amount of time that elapses between the behavior and its reinforcement. Skinner says that reinforcement should be very prompt or immediate.

Behavior modification can be applied to such activities as employee training, job design, wage payment, supervision of workers, control of quantity and quality of output, and attendance control. Let us consider the supervision of workers and the regulation of their quantity and quality of work. It is desirable to set goals for individual and group output and quality. If possible these should be set in quantifiable terms. Measurement of performance and feedback of that data to the employees should be done on a daily or weekly basis as is appropriate according to work operation cycles of their jobs. The very process of informing employees how they are doing is a form of reinforcement. The supervisor should provide praise, recognition, approval, and personal interest in various ways to indicate reinforcement for what the individual is doing right. This positive reinforcement may consist of a smile, nod of approval, a specific statement that the person met a quota, and an offer to buy him a cup of coffee. Initially the reinforcement should come as soon as possible after the behavior and regularly. But as time goes on the reinforcement can be less often and of unpredictable frequency. In certain situations it may be practical to reward workers with free time. Thus, if they meet an agreed-upon daily output quota before the end of the shift, they can go home.

Behavior modification is not a panacea. Several motivational forces often affect an individual at the same time and these may conflict with one another. A direct piece-work wage incentive plan is a prime example. The worker is supposedly reinforced by management to maximize his output up to the limits of his skill and energy. However, the work group often pressures him to restrict output because of fear of a rate cut by management and because of a fear that very fast workers will "show up" the ordinary and slower workers. The work organization situation often is much more complex than the school or laboratory situation in which conflicting influences can be minimized.

Skinner's theory has also been criticized by some writers because it denies the existence of free will and the autonomous, inner-motivated man. These latter concepts are central to the constructs of Abraham Maslow and Douglas Mc-Gregor.

Expectancy Model

Formulated by Victor Vroom, the expectancy model of motivation is useful for analyzing and explaining the motivation of individuals in an organizational setting.[10] The model does not explain the factors or content of what motivates people to work as do the theories of Maslow and Herzberg. Rather it helps one understand the thought processes (which may be conscious and organized but which also can be subconscious or disorganized) that an individual goes through in deciding whether or not to exert the effort to try to achieve any of various possible goals. It is a useful tool for analysis and research. But the expectancy model doesn't offer specific substantive answers for managers who are trying to improve the motivational climate for their work units.

To understand the expectancy model, one must first learn the meaning of three concepts used in expressing the model. These are valence, expectancy, and instrumentality.

Valence is the degree or extent to which a person desires a particular outcome. It can be measured by asking an individual to state how important any of various outcomes or goals are to him. Other terms that can be used to represent the concept of valence are preference, expected utility, or affective orientation toward a particular outcome.

Expectancy is the perceived probability that effort or behavior by the person will yield a particular outcome or result. This probability is subjectively determined by the individual.

Instrumentality is the degree or extent to which the person believes the attainment of the first-level outcome will yield a second-level outcome (which is the ultimate goal of the person). A second-level outcome is a human need such as companionship, security, respect of others, or accomplishment.

Figure 18-2 shows how the elements in the expectancy model are tied together. Let us trace through the flow from element to element and relate the model to real behavior. Let us assume the case of a production engineer in a manufacturing plant who is responsible for the efficient and reliable operation of the production machinery. He feels a strong need for a substantial pay increase so that he can accumulate funds to make a down payment on a house for himself and his growing family. The engineer knows that his manager wants to increase the number of units per hour produced by production process number one. The engineer knows also that to increase productivity would require much ingenuity and effort on his part. He is not fully sure whether he can succeed in re-engineering the line to raise productivity. He thinks, but is not really sure, that if he can successfully raise productivity, his manager will reward him with a handsome pay raise. Applying these facts to the expectancy model we note that the engineer has a strong *valence* or desire for a higher income so he can buy a house. He thinks the probability of achieving the action (expectancy number 1) of reworking the process equipment and raising productivity is reasonably good. Multiplying the valence times expectancy number 1 gives us the strength of his

[10] Victor H. Vroom, *Work and Motivation* (New York: John Wiley & Sons, Inc. 1964).

Figure 18-2
Expectancy Model of Motivation.

motivational force to engage in the *action*. The engineer must also determine the probability (expectancy number 2) that his successful action will cause his boss to raise his pay (*organizational reward* or first-level outcome).[11] The instrumentality is the closeness of the relationship between the pay increase and the purchase of the house (satisfaction of personal need).

Vroom's expectancy model of motivation has been tested empirically by a great many academic scholars and researchers. The results of these investigations have generally been supportive of its theoretical constructs and formulation. Researchers generally determine the valences and expectancies by directly asking employees questions about their goals and perceptions of likelihoods of achieving them.

The practical value of the expectancy model for managers is that it demonstrates that motivation is highly individualized from person to person. The manager must know the special concerns and strengths of his people. If he desires to obtain particular kinds of performance from them, he must inform them of the connections between performance and reward. He must learn of their expectancies and valences and perhaps he can increase the motivational force of individuals through supportive performance appraisal discussions.

MORALE AND PRODUCTIVITY

For a great number of years, it has been assumed that a work force that possesses high morale is also likely to exhibit high productivity. It has seemed logical to managers that happy workers are also productive workers. However, research investigators have demonstrated that there is no simple relationship between morale and productivity. Enough instances of high productivity and low morale and of high morale and low productivity have been observed to cast doubt upon the once-assumed direct relationship. The heart of the matter is that morale is a complex concept. It includes many facets.

Some writers have emphasized the satisfaction of needs as a dimension of morale. Others have stressed the social approach by concentrating upon group bonds and friendships. Still others have emphasized attitudes toward supervision, the work, and the organization. And finally other writers have concentrated on the interaction of personality with the work situation. Recognizing that morale is multidimensional, let us define it as the *total satisfactions a person derives from his job, his work group, his boss, the organization, and his environ-*

---

[11] In general, organizational rewards could consist of many items such as a promotion, pay raise, assignment to more interesting work, and a news item about the employee in the company newspaper.

ment. It is also affected by his personality structure. Morale pertains to the general feeling of well-being, satisfaction, and happiness of people.

Productivity is output divided by input. Commonly, the productivity of an industry or of an establishment is measured by the total physical or dollar volume of output divided by the man-hours of input for a given time span. The productivity of a work group or of individuals is generally expressed in terms of the units produced during a given time period, say, a day, week, or month. Productivity of routine repetitive work is easy to measure. But the output of creative and intellectual efforts is very difficult to measure. Thus, professional and executive work accomplishments may have a long time span before completion and considerable judgment may be required to determine the real value of work done.

Vroom has tabulated the results of twenty investigations into the relationship between morale (job satisfaction in Vroom's terms) and job performance. These studies were made by many researchers working independently. They pertained to such diverse occupational groups as insurance agents, bus drivers, female office employees, sales clerks, farmers, and supervisors in a package delivery company. Statistical correlations between satisfaction and performance ranged from $+.86$ to $-.31$, with a median of $+.14$ for all studies.[12] Thus, there seems to be a low but positive relationship between overall morale or job satisfaction and productivity of various work groups in general. Yet there are enough instances of negative correlations to alert us to the act that intervening factors may be present.

For various reasons, productivity can be reasonably good while morale is low. Many industrial plants are highly engineered. Output may be high under machine-paced and assembly-line conditions. Jobs may have been carefully analyzed, improved, and subdivided by industrial engineers. Materials and parts may flow smoothly from work station to work station. Inprocess inventory may be kept at a minimum. Measured daywork standards may have been established for each worker's job. Under such conditions productivity of shop departments may be good even though employees dislike their jobs and their conditions of work.

Rensis Likert claims that the relationship between morale and productivity for complex and varied work such as research, engineering, and life insurance selling tends to be moderately high.[13] It seems that when the performance depends solely upon the man or the team and when the job cannot be engineered, then those employees who feel favorably disposed toward their job situation are also more likely to be motivated to produce.

Situations in which morale is high but performance is poor also occur with some frequency. This discrepancy can occur when a pleasant, social, country-club atmosphere is encouraged or permitted by supervision. The people may gain considerable pleasure from coming to the office each day to meet their friends and socialize. But the motivation to produce may be minimal.

Actually, job attitudes and morale can be quite positive for two reasons. The first has just been given above. Employees gain social satisfaction from interac-

---

[12] Victor H. Vroom, op. cit., pp. 183–185.

[13] Rensis Likert, *New Patterns of Management* (New York: McGraw-Hill Book Company, 1961), ch. 6.

tions at the workplace. Working conditions and supervision may be good. Second, high morale may result from high motivation to produce. Much recent behavioral research has demonstrated that when a leadership and work-group climate is structured to generate high work motivation, then employee satisfactions and attitudes are often positive. In other words, management should put its eggs in the basket that creates a highly motivated work force. Good morale and job satisfaction are likely to follow. But if top managmeent spends its efforts on morale-building programs *only*, for instance, wages, working conditions, recreation programs, and financial benefits, it will become disillusioned when work performance remains low. It should not be assumed, however, that money spent on morale-building programs is necessarily wasted. Numerous investigations have demonstrated that there is a positive correlation between high morale and low turnover and low absenteeism. Worker loyalty and stability are important.

APPLYING MOTIVATIONAL CONCEPTS

We have, so far, discussed a number of basic concepts and theoretical foundations for understanding individual behavior, motivation, and reactions to blocking of motives. The executive must be able to apply his knowledge of human behavior dynamics to real work situations in order to elicit acceptable performance from his work force. There is no simple formula to tell the manager how to lead and motivate his people. The executive must be perceptive with regard to the character of his people and the demands of the situation. He must be adaptable and flexible in applying motivational principles. Responses of employees are a function of the reward system and how they perceive the rewards as satisfying their needs.

Power and Force

The traditional method of motivating people to work in private business has been to apply the "carrot and the stick" from a strong power base. The manager who is unschooled in the fundamentals of human behavior feels this is the best way to move people. The carrot has been the weekly pay check, or direct wage incentives, or bonuses for managers. The stick has been the threat of demotion, transfer to an undesirable assignment, or discharge. Even though discharges may be invoked infrequently in a given organization, they occur just often enough to cause employees generally to be apprehensive about their job security. Another form of the carrot and the stick is to deny pay raises to individual employees or even to cut their pay at a time when the cost of living rises yearly.

The use of pay increments that are tied to performance is sound from the point of view of motivation theory. However, pay is seldom administered in a manner fully consistent with motivation theory. Hence, it does not commonly generate the kind of strong performance that it could. Also those managers who are philosophically addicted to the "carrot and the stick" do not understand the rich array of other positive reinforcers available to motivate people.

The use of threats or the "stick" suffers from all the disadvantages of negative reinforcers that we discussed previously under behavior modification. In addition, when employees are protected against arbitrary treatment by their union they are unlikely to jump whenever the foreman says jump. Our high standard of living, such that basic physical wants are met for most people, means that nowadays they are motivated more by social and egoistic drives than formerly. In addition the relatively high educational attainment of the labor force generates a desire on employees' part to participate in decisions at the work place and to have some measure of autonomy. Hence, autocratic leadership is less effective now than it was a generation or two ago.

Money As a Motivator

Money should be looked upon as one instrument among many for managing motivation. Managers in industry often tend to place major reliance upon pay, bonuses, and money incentives because they are easiest to manipulate. But the results do not always justify the efforts to use money as a motivator. There is abundant evidence that many blue-collar workers will deliberately restrict output even when working on a direct wage-incentive plan.

Yes, pay is important for providing the material necessities of life. But it is most important for what it symbolizes to the recipient. To use pay effectively as a motivational tool the manager must study his people, the conditions under which they work, and the tasks they perform. Many jobs require close team cooperation. For such jobs an individual pay-incentive plan can be destructive of group cooperation. On the ther hand, a wage-incentive plan that rewards all members of the group for increased team output can be effective.

The value of money is determined by what people have learned to associate it with. For the young female secretary, a good salary symbolizes stylish clothes in abundance. For the young married father it represents a down payment on a home. For the executive who has just been promoted, a substantial pay boost tells him that his company superiors think highly of him. It is an index of progress.

McClelland points out that several research studies have revealed that persons who score high in achievement motivation on psychological tests do not work harder for the prospect of making more money alone. They are motivated by the love of accomplishment, interest in their work, and by success itself. The money comes afterward and of course is appreciated. On the other hand, people with a low-achievement drive quite often will work for more money when it symbolizes something that they dearly want.[14] Such people tend to have no intrinsic interest in their work. But they will strive for the things money can buy, such as a new automobile, a new television set, or a vacation cruise in the Caribbean.

Competition

Competition as a form of motivation is widely used in our society. Examples that first come to mind for most of us are, perhaps, the competition that occurs in sporting events (both amateur and professional) and in games among friends, for example, a game of cards. In business, competition is most commonly used in sales departments. It is practically standard practice to have salesmen compete

[14] David C. McClelland, "Money As a Motivator: Some Research Insights," *The McKinsey Quarterly* (Fall 1967), pp. 10–21.

against one another for various awards and prizes. Another form of competition is that which takes place among members of the management hierarchy in most organizations for the prize of a promotion. Because there are fewer positions as one approaches the top of the organizational pyramid, the competition can get very intense and at times even vicious. If a number of people are striving for the same goal, and if that goal is attainable by only the one who wins, we know that such competition can motivate many people to give their maximum efforts.

However, competition has serious limitations when used within an organization. If, for example, all the members of one department are competing for a single promotion, considerable jealousy and hostility are bound to develop among the employees. Mutual cooperation will be poor. So in this case individualistic competition will, as in most cases, cause a destruction of teamwork. In this situation where people are competing for a promotion that can go to only one, the standards for selection of the winner can seldom be completely objective. Therefore, the losers may justifiably consider that bias and favoritism entered into the selection.

Another serious disadvantage of competition as a motivator is the frustration experienced by the losers. Any of the various forms of behavior induced by frustration may occur: aggression, regression, resignation, fixation, sublimation, and so on.

If the stakes are high, if the penalty for losing is great, then we find destruction of teamwork, lower morale, and frustration to be common consequences.

Cultural factors affect the attitude of different types of people toward competition. Blue-collar factory workers are less likely to respond to competition than executive and professional employees. Blue-collar employees often band together to protect themselves from the harmful effects of competition. Unions, for example, advocate seniority rules as a method of avoiding the loss of security that might occur as a result of competition.

Job Design and Work Flow

The nature of work itself strongly influences whether employees show interest and zest or whether they experience boredom and monotony. Actually the matter is determined by the nature of the worker himself (many seek challenging work; others accept routine, repetitive work), the nature of the job, and the leadership and social environment in which the employee performs. We examine the matter of job design and its effect upon worker performance in Chapter 7, "Job Design and Analysis," and Chapter 19, "Quality of Working Life."

Integration of Goals

A desirable and somewhat idealized system of work motivation is to provide opportunities for need-satisfaction through doing the job itself. The object of this pattern of motivation is to develop employee commitment to the objectives of the organization. Management sets up a system of rewards that causes high levels of job satisfaction at the same time that the employees are working productively to meet the objectives of their job, department, and plant.

Such a system of motivation is the essence of what Douglas McGregor called

Theory Y management.[15] Rensis Likert has called it System 4 management.[16] This approach holds that people will exercise self-direction and self-control in working for objectives to which they are committed. They will become committed to working for organization goals to the extent that they gain real satisfaction from doing so. This style of leadership has sometimes been called "management by integration and self-control."

It emphasizes openness and trust, supportive supervision, and participation in decision making. It activates all motives—economic, social, and egoistic. To a considerable extent employees can gratify many of their drives for security, belongingness, status, self-expression, self-significance, and achievement right on the job.

This system of motivation works best in situations where the people have some freedom to exercise their own initiative, where they can see a direct connection between their efforts and the performance of their organizational unit, and where their work careers constitute a dominant focus in their lives. These conditions fit many executives. They are dediated to their work and their organizations. They enjoy their jobs so much that the jobs do not seem like work to them. They adopt a proprietary interest in their companies. Not only is intrinsic motivation maximized but so is extrinsic motivation. These people exercise considerable influence and power. They can make things happen. They may command vast human and material resources. Their opinions mean much both in their organizations and in their communities. They enjoy prestige, high status, and high pay. They are operating at the high end of Maslow's hierarchy of needs.

Many other types of people in our society tend to enjoy this highly satisfactory motivational situation. This is true for many professionals such as college professors, attorneys, economists, engineers, and scientists. This integration of goals also tends to hold true for the self-employed and the small businessman.

However, it must be admitted that it is very difficult for workers on low-level, repetitive jobs to experience this form of motivation. They may have been conditioned by past experience to expect no real satisfaction from their work. They may stay on their jobs and perform solely for their pay. Their jobs may have been so highly engineered or regimented that there is no opportunity for growth, recognition, and achievement.

Participation

Participation means the physical and mental involvement of people in an activity. Specifically, in the field of personnel management, the term has come to mean the involvement of employees in decision making. In this sense it means primarily mental involvement and ego involvement. Many managers speak loosely of developing participation in their employees. They exhort employees to "put their shoulders to the wheel," to help management cut costs, to attend company social functions, and to give generously to the Community Chest drive. These activities do not constitute true participation. Genuine participation includes those situations in which management actively encourages employees and

[15] Douglas McGregor, *The Human Side of Enterprise* (New York: McGraw-Hill Book Company, 1960).

[16] Rensis Likert, *The Human Organization* (New York: McGraw-Hill Book Company, 1967.)

lower-echelon managers to help make decisions regarding the business and the work. Although it is top management's job to set policy and establish overall goals, there is plenty of opportunity for subordinate members of the organization to participate in decision making in such areas as production methods, materials handling, cost reduction, safety, employee relations problems, and working conditions.

Participation in decision making can take many forms: consultative supervision, democratic supervision, multiple management, labor–management cooperation, suggestion programs, and others.

Questions for review and discussion

1. Explain the meaning of the following concepts:
   a. Self-concept.
   b. Personality.
   c. Motive.
   d. Defense mechanism.
2. Explain Maslow's hierarchy of needs.
3. Explain Herzberg's motivation–hygiene theory.
4. What are the characteristics of high-achievement-oriented persons?
5. Do you think B. F. Skinner's behavior modification theory is compatible with Maslow's and Herzberg's theories?
6. Distinguish between morale and motivation. If workers have high morale, is their productivity also likely to be high?
7. How can individual motives and organizational goals be integrated?
8. Discuss the importance of money as a motivator.
9. Analyze the satisfactions you have obtained from the various jobs you have held. What differences do you note?
10. Explain the expectancy model of motivation.

Case problem [17]

A college senior related the following story to his professor:

PART I

Last summer I was hired by the Department of Public Works of my home city in Ohio (a city of about 25,000 population) to work as a combined crew leader–truck driver. I had worked the previous two summers as a laborer in the department.

The functions of the department were to collect garbage and trash from households and commercial establishments, to repair and resurface streets, and to maintain public buildings and parks. The department personnel consisted of a superintendent, two foremen, an office clerk, twenty-two regular employees,

[17] The author expresses his appreciation to Mark H. Baranello, a former student, for providing the essential features of this case.

and eight to ten temporary summer help composed of both college and high-school students.

At the beginning of the summer I was assigned as a crew leader–truck driver to collect brush, tree limbs, and garden trimmings set out at the street by residents of the city. I had a crew of four high school boys ranging in age from 16 to 18. The boys only worked four hours a day. Thus, I had two of them in the morning and two in the afternoon. Brush collection was regarded as a nuisance by the regular personnel in the department and they preferred to avoid this task. Therefore it was assigned to the summer workers.

From the start I had trouble getting the boys to really produce. The morning crew consisted of Edward and Thomas. Edward, age 17, was the son of one of the foremen in the department and was a high school football star. He did as little work as possible. Thomas, age 16, was a friend of Edward's and modeled his behavior after him. I spent considerable effort coaxing and prodding these boys to work harder. They were slow workers and took frequent rest breaks. The afternoon crew of Red and Alex was slightly more ambitious and output was somewhat better. In dealing with the morning crew I often pointed out that the afternoon boys had a better attitude and got more work done. This was supposed to improve their efforts but mainly it caused resentment and no more work output. In actuality I felt that neither the morning nor the afternoon crew was doing a good job. The boys were fully aware of my disappointment in their performance.

This was my first supervisory assignment and I was unsure of myself in how to handle the leadership role. I appealed to Edward's father, the foreman, to speak to his son. The father said he did this but it yielded no change in Edward's attitude and performance. I became worried that the superintendent would find out about the weak performance of my crews. My major leadership efforts were directed toward shaming the boys for shirking their responsibilities. However, because their pay rate was quite low it did not seem fair to baldly tell them they were not even earning their pay.

Midway through the summer a change took place. We were taken off the residential brush collection and given the job of working along the sides and beds of various creeks to remove debris and to cut down weeds and brush. At this time of year the stream beds were mostly dry. The debris had to be carried to the truck, which I parked at the nearest bridge. The four high-school boys were hired full time and given a raise from $2.80 to $3.30 per hour. Also two regular year-round workers were assigned to this project. These regular employees had reputations of being mediocre to average workers. Both had very limited educations.

Knowing that work attitudes had not been good in the first half of the summer and that I was having difficulty in supervising the boys, I consulted the superintendent and one of the foremen on how to organize and direct this new assignment.

Questions

1. Why do you think the crew leader was having difficulty in obtaining good productive effort from his crew members?

2. What plan would you recommend for organizing and directing the creek clean-up work in order to increase motivation and output?

PART II

We decided to group the six persons into two crews, each being assigned to a different section of a creek. A typical day consisted of entering a creek bed at a bridge and working down to the next bridge. Along the way the banks would be mowed with hand scythes. Any debris lying in the bed, on the banks, and under bridges would be picked up and carried to the dump truck parked at the next bridge.

Each crew consisted of two high school boys and a regular adult employee. Those who seemed to be compatible with one another were put together in a crew.

I altered my style of supervision from that used in the residential brush collection. I explained the work groupings and outlined generally how the work was to be done. I set only rough boundary conditions on work methods and scheduling and left the specifics to each crew. Each crew set its own work pace and decided when to take rest periods and coffee breaks. I did, however, tell them approximately how much of a creek ought to be completed in a day.

As truck driver, I dropped off each crew at different job sites along a creek. I spent much of my time shuttling back and forth between crews, loading the truck, and answering questions. I personally did not do any weed cutting and debris collecting. I tried to understand each person as an individual and to take an interest in him. I talked to Edward about his high school athletics and this pleased him. When someone handled a task well, I praised him. I no longer stood over them like a drill sergeant. In general, I changed from my previous style of frequent criticism to support, encouragement, and praise.

In some cases where the terrain was suitable I started the two groups at one bridge working on opposite sides of a creek. Their goal was to finish at the next bridge. Thus, we had some friendly competition. The boys seemed to look upon this as fun.

Within a few days after starting this new activity, work effort, cooperation, and output rose appreciably. They stayed at a fully satisfactory level throughout the remaining weeks of the summer. Instead of the resentment shown toward me in the first part of the summer the boys showed an attitude of friendliness and co-operation.

Questions

1. How do the organization and supervision of the work that was actually used compare with your proposed plan?
2. Relate motivational principles to the methods used in Part II of this case.

Suggestions for further reading

Dowling, William F. Jr., and Leonard R. Sayles. *How Managers Motivate: The Imperatives of Supervision*, 2nd ed. New York: McGraw-Hill Book Company, 1978.

Ford, Robert N. *Motivation Through the Work Itself*. New York: American Management Association, 1969.

Gellerman, Saul. *Management by Motivation*. New York: American Management Association, 1968.

———. *Motivation and Productivity*. New York: American Management Association, 1963.

Hamner, Clay W. and Ellen P. Hamner. "Behavior Modification on the Bottom Line," *Organizational Dynamics*, Vol. 4, No. 4 (Spring 1976), pp. 2–21.

Herzberg, Frederick. *The Managerial Choice: To Be Efficient and To Be Human*. Homewood, Ill.: Dow-Jones Irwin, 1976.

———. "One More Time: How Do You Motivate Employees?" *Harvard Business Review*, Vol. 46, No. 1 (January–February 1968), pp. 53–62.

Lawler, Edward E. III. "Developing a Motivating Work Climate," *Management Review*, Vol. 66, No. 7 (July 1977), pp. 25–28, 37–38.

Livingston, J. Sterling. "Pygmalion in Management," *Harvard Business Review*, Vol. 47, No. 4 (July–August 1969), pp. 81–89.

Locke, Edwin A., "The Myths of Behavior Mod in Organizations," *Academy of Management Review*, Vol. 2, No. 4 (October 1977), pp. 543–553.

Maslow, A. H. *Motivation and Personality*, 2nd ed. New York: Harper and Row, Publishers, 1970.

McClelland, David C. *The Achieving Society*. Princeton, N.J.: D. Van Nostrand Reinhold Company, 1961.

——— and David J. Winter. *Motivating Economic Achievement*. New York: The Free Press, 1969.

Roche, William J., and Neil L. MacKinnon. "Motivating People with Meaningful Work," Harvard Business Review, Vol. 48, No. 3 (May–June 1970), pp. 97–110.

Skinner, B. F. *Beyond Freedom and Dignity*. New York: Alfred A. Knopf, Inc., 1971.

Quality
of
working
life

Commencing in the early 1970's there has been a rising interest in the quality of working life for both blue and white collar workers. Managements of many leading corporations have been concerned to the point that they have launched comprehensive projects to improve work force productivity, organizational effectiveness, and the quality of working life. Although various leaders in management, labor, government, and the universities had in past years intermittently expressed concern about such matters as decent wages, hours, working conditions, and the problems of boredom, monotony, and fatigue, the issue of quality of working life did not become focused into a coherent thesis until the 1970's.

The single event that sparked public attention to this important issue was the strike in March 1972 of approximately 8,000 workers at the new General Motors' Lordstown, Ohio plant. Both workers and their union leaders charged, with considerable justification, that General Motors' management had cut the workforce and speeded up the pace of work on the assembly line. The national news media began to issue reports about the problems at this plant and in other companies throughout the country. These reports asserted that many American workers, especially young ones in the mass production industries, were experiencing a sense of frustration and alienation over their conditions of employment.

Leaders in many organizations have been studying the matter of quality of working life and how to improve it. Quite generally productivity improvement has been studied in concert with quality of working life. Among the concerned agencies and organizations have been the National Center for Productivity and Quality of Working Life (a Federal agency) and private organizations such as the Work in America Institute and the American Quality of Work Center. Scores of American and European corporations have on-going projects in this field. Among these are General Foods, American Telephone and Telegraph, Corning Glass Works, General Motors, and Texas Instruments in the United States and Volvo, Saab-Scandia, Norsk Hydro, and Olivetti in Europe. Also university scholars and researchers have been doing considerable work in the area of quality of working life.

In this chapter we shall investigate the meaning of work, conditions of working life facing many employees, the meaning of the concept "quality of working life," strategies for improving both quality of working life and productivity, case examples of successful industrial programs, union attitudes, and issues involved in implementation.

THE NATURE OF WORK

Historically, cultural values about work have shifted greatly over the years. In ancient times work was performed mostly by slaves. The Renaissance and Reformation brought great changes in prevailing attitudes toward work. Work acquired a moral dignity of its own. Hard work and frugality were a way of pleasing God and were the road to salvation. Max Weber, the German sociologist and historical scholar, explained that the rise of capitalism in the eighteenth century was related to the earlier glorification of the values of hard work, saving, and the accumulation of material wealth by the originators of Protestantism—Martin Luther and John Calvin. He labeled these values the Protestant ethic. The idea that work was virtuous was brought to North America from Europe.

Work is an activity that produces something of value for other people. It includes paid employment plus unpaid work in the household and on the farm by family members.[1]

Work serves many purposes. The economic function of work for producing goods and services is its most obvious value. In return for production the worker is paid wages that enable him to purchase food, clothing, shelter, plus other needs and luxuries of life. But work serves other values as well.

Part of the social needs of people are supplied at the workplace where they meet, converse, and share experiences. One's job connotes a certain level of social status both for the worker and his family. Work also contributes to an employee's self-esteem by reflecting his contribution to the work group, department, and company. If a person is competent and meets his own and his boss's expectations, this contributes to his sense of personal work. Also, an individual's occupation helps shape his or her sense of identity. He will often identify himself, when meeting strangers, by stating his occupation and name of his em-

[1] *Work in America*, Report of a Special Task Force to the Secretary of Health, Education, and Welfare (Cambridge, Mass.: The MIT Press, 1973), p. 3.

ployer. Thus, we learn that Maxine is a nurse at Tyler General Hospital, Frank is a machinist at U.S. Steel, and Edward is a professor at Cornell.

Let us now look at those features of work in modern industrialized society that tend to be common to a great many enterprises. Of course there are variations in the degree to which these factors are present from one establishment to the next. First we note that the work role is separate from the family role. Contrary to the situation in agrarian societies, work in an industrialized society is sharply separated from family life in orientation, content, time, and location.

Employees at all organizational levels are expected to be compliant and obedient to autocratic authority. The prevailing organizational ethic is that the boss knows best or, at least, that he has the right to impose his will upon subordinates on the job. Especially in larger organizations employees are subjected to strict discipline and regimentation. These organizations enforce a complex system of rules and require employees to perform (and rest) according to strict work pace and time controls.

Typically jobs are defined narrowly. This means that each job demands only a narrow range of skills. The conventional wisdom of industrial managers is that minute division of labor increases efficiency and output.

Another feature of work in modern society is the underlying threat of layoff. This has long been characteristic of employment in private enterprises because of fluctuations in market demand and layoffs due to technological changes. In recent years public sector employees have also had to face the problem of lack of job security. For example, declining student enrollments in many communities have caused teacher layoffs in public schools.

CONTEMPORARY PROBLEMS OF AMERICAN WORKERS

In this section we shall examine two contradictory viewpoints about the state of American workers' attitudes and satisfaction (or dissatisfaction) concerning their jobs. Each viewpoint has plenty of vocal and articulate proponents.

Workers Are Dissatisfied Thesis

We have seen that work manifests significance over and above its strict economic function by providing meaning, social relationships, self-esteem, sense of personal worth, respect from others, and a sense of identity.

Behavioral science investigators have detected substantial differences in the degree of satisfaction people in various occupations say they obtain from their jobs. When asked the question, "What type of work would you try to get into if you could start all over again?" a high percentage of those in professional occupations stated they would choose the same type of work again. On the other hand, few of the blue-collar workers said they would choose the same work. The percentages of professionals who would choose similar work again were as follows: urban university professors, 93 percent; mathematicians, 91 percent; biologists, 89 percent; lawyers, 83 percent; journalists (Washington correspondents), 82 percent. For white-collar workers (a cross-section), 43 percent would select similar work again. For blue-collar workers some of the results were as follows:

skilled printers, 52 percent; paperworkers, 42 percent; skilled autoworkers, 41 percent; skilled steelworkers, 41 percent; unskilled steelworkers, 21 percent; unskilled autoworkers, 16 percent. A cross-section of blue-collar workers (all occupations surveyed) was 24 percent.[2]

The reader can see from the foregoing that job satisfaction (as evidenced by the survey question) corresponds rather closely with the social status and prestige ranking of occupations. There is also a rather close correlation between the educational level required for an occupation and job satisfaction. People in the higher-ranking jobs have more autonomy at work, have greater influence over what they do and what happens to them at work, more commonly experience a sense of work accomplishment, and can feel they are making their "mark" in what they do.

Discontent is concentrated more among blue-collar workers and white-collar workers (white-collar as distinct from professional and managerial personnel). The causes of discontent are many and varied but can generally be related to the features of work in modern industrialized society discussed earlier.

Alienation. The term *alienation* is used by social scientists to designate the constellation of attitudes, frustrations, and behaviors of people existing under the conditions we are talking about. Alienation contains the following ingredients: (1) powerlessness, (2) meaningless, (3) isolation, and (4) self-estrangement.[3] *Powerlessness* means that the individual feels he has no capacity to affect management policies and rules, job conditions, and immediate work processes. *Meaninglessness* refers to the condition in which the employee derives no sense of meaning or accomplishment from the product or service he works on. *Isolation* designates the feeling of being socially isolated from others in one's place of employment. There may be little social contact and lack of membership in social groups. *Self-estrangement* consists of boredom and lack of ego-involvement in one's job.

Conditions of Work. Let us look at the conditions of work life of many workers. We shall start with the blue-collar worker. Blue-collar workers (often called hourly paid workers) are those who work in factories, construction, transportation, and service industries in unskilled, semiskilled, or skilled capacities. They generally must punch a time clock at the beginning and end of their daily shifts. Typical jobs are machine tender, janitor, assembler, sewing machine operator, laborer and production welder.

There are many sources for discontent and alienation with variation, of course, from one situation to the next. In their quest for efficiency industrial engineers have driven toward machine pacing of the worker in many factories. This is true of assembly lines along a moving conveyer belt and of production processes in which workers load and unload one or more machines in controlled sequence.

The automobile assembly line is the epitome of the fast paced, short cycle, repetitive production process in industry. See Figure 19-1. The assembly line does yield high productivity but this is achieved at a large human cost in terms of monotony, fatigue, and alienation.

[2] Ibid., pp. 15–16. This survey is taken from a report by Robert Kahn, "The Work Module," (1972).
[3] Robert Blauner, *Alienation and Freedom: The Factory Worker and His Industry* (Chicago: University of Chicago Press, 1964).

Figure 19-1
An Assembly Line in an American Automobile Factory.

The discipline of the industrial plant tends to be strict. In many plants an employee must get permission from his boss to leave his work station to go to the rest room. He must start and stop work by the plant whistle, cannot clean up at the end of the shift before a designated time, and cannot argue with his foreman. The pressure for production is often relentless.

Contrary to popular belief many people must still work amid conditions of dirt, noise, and danger in American industry. A *Wall Street Journal* article entitled "Brutal, Mindless Labor Remains a Daily Reality for Millions in the U.S." portrays striking examples of the adversities many must face daily. From midnight until 10 A.M. a foundry worker in Ohio works in an inferno of heat, filth, and noise. He shovels thousands of pounds of red-hot slag from beneath a furnace into large bins on wheels. He must, at times, crawl inside a cooled furnace to chip hardened slag with a hammer and chisel. Then he lines the furnace with blobs of thick, sticky mud before the furnace is fired again. The article also describes a coke-oven worker in Pennsylvania who ranges back and forth over the hot brick top of a battery of ovens wearing wooden pallets under his shoes and a rubber mask. His task is to pull off thick steel lids on the oven tops with an iron bar so he can dump in coal from "lorry cars" that move along the oven roofs on rails. The job is filthy, hot, monotonous, and dangerous. The man is surrounded by thick acrid smoke.[4]

Lack of task variety is a source of discontent for many. The extreme task specialization of modern production processes has contributed to boredom and monotony. Sometimes workers are less conscious of the repetitive nature of their jobs if they have opportunities for social interaction while they work. However, factory noise and physical separation of work stations frequently minimize the possibility of conversing, exchanging stories and experiences, and joking.

[4] *Wall Street Journal* (July 16, 1971).

For unskilled and semiskilled jobs, especially, there is little if any opportunity for the worker to express his own ideas and ingenuity. The planning of work methods and tooling is done by the engineer and the supervisor. The worker is simply a "hired hand." Many behavioral scientists contend that workers have a desire for autonomy and some degree of control over their jobs but that this desire is frustrated by ever–present bureaucratic controls.

What is the situation for white-collar workers? By white-collar personnel we mean such occupations as clerks, typists, stenographers, secretaries, record keepers, sales clerks in stores, and key punch operators. The proportion of these types in the labor force has been increasing. The routinization and regimentation of the factory have now invaded the office. There is little to distinguish the long rows of desk workers from the long rows of factory bench hands except for cleaner working conditions in the office. There is often extreme task specialization in the office. Many companies time study their white-collar workers and set time standards for their tasks just as they do for the factory jobs. A great array of business machines, copiers, and computers are in use. Many white-collar personnel are simply office machine tenders.

Job Pressures and Health. Evidence is being accumulated that job satisfaction or its opposite, job frustration, has a substantial effect upon health. A scientific investigation of aging revealed that the strongest predictor of longevity was work satisfaction. The second ranking factor was general happiness. These two factors were better predictors of longevity than a rating by an examining physician, a measure of smoking, or of genetic inheritance.[5]

Although it is well known that many factors such as smoking and excess body weight contribute to heart disease, scientists have also determined that certain factors in the work situation contribute to the risk of acquiring heart disease. These are job dissatisfaction (tedious work, lack of recognition, poor relations with co-workers, and poor working conditions), low self-esteem related to the job, and occupational stress (work overload and time pressures). Other factors contributing to heart disease are lack of stability, security, and support in the job environment. Peptic ulcers, arthritis, and stroke also have been correlated with job stress.[6]

Workers Are Satisfied Thesis

Several writers and investigators have disputed the claim that a large segment of American workers are alienated and derive little satisfaction from their jobs. To support their contentions, these critics cite data from both job satisfaction surveys and from statistical indicators of labor turnover, absenteeism, strikes, and productivity.

In a review of 2,000 surveys of job satisfaction of many groups in many industries conducted over many years, Robert Kahn reported that there is a consistency in response patterns. Few people were extremely satisfied, but fewer still were extremely dissatisfied. The modal response was on the positive side of neu-

---

[5] Erdman Palmore, "Predicting Longevity: A Follow-up Controlling for Age," *Gerontologist* (Winter 1969).

[6] *Work in America*, op. cit., pp. 77–81.

trality—"pretty satisfied." The portion dissatisfied was in the 10–21 percent range.[7] Measures of labor turnover, absenteeism, strikes, and productivity do show definite fluctuations from year to year but these fluctuations are more closely correlated with changes in other factors such as economic cycles, supply and demand for labor, and inflationary trends than with shifts in worker satisfaction.[8]

The critics also refer to periodic public opinion polls such as Gallup and Roper which have, for a good number of years, revealed that the majority of persons questioned say they are satisfied with their jobs.[9]

Analysis and Explanation

What are we to make of the contradictory views and evidence? It is inaccurate to make a sweeping statement that workers are or are not satisfied with their jobs. There is really considerable variation from individual to individual and group to group. University of Michigan survey data reveal that those most dissatisfied tend to be young (under 30 years of age), blacks, those earning low wages, and operators and nonfarm laborers. Blue collar workers are more dissatisfied than white collar personnel.[10]

Self-employed persons express greatest job satisfaction. They are their own bosses and have great autonomy. However, with each passing decade there have been fewer opportunities to be self-employed. In the mid-nineteenth century more than half of all employed persons were self-employed. By 1970 the percentage of self-employed had dropped below 10 percent.

Managerial, technical, and professional employees are more satisfied with their jobs than are lower ranking personnel. Information published by the Opinion Research Corporation demonstrates that discontent among hourly-paid and clerical employees has been growing in recent years. This conclusion is based upon questionnaire responses of 175,000 employees in 159 companies that have been surveyed many times since 1950. There is a "hierarchy gap" in the levels of job satisfaction between managers and those of hourly and clerical personnel.[11]

Job discontent and frustration can be caused by (a) jobs of limited scope and those having tasks of short cycle, jobs with no opportunity to exercise discretion and initiative, excessive bureaucratic controls, and oppressive supervision; or by (b) low wages, bad working conditions, and job insecurity. The key to the question of how working people view their jobs is simply this—What are their expectations from work? Do they want primarily, decent wages so they have adequate money to obtain their life satisfactions off the job? Or do they expect not only

[7] As quoted in Harold Wool, "What's Wrong with Work in America?—A Review Essay," *Monthly Labor Review*, Vol. 96, No. 3 (March, 1973), pp. 38–44.

[8] Ibid., pp. 41–42.

[9] For further information see Mitchell Fein, "The Real Needs and Goals for Blue Collar Workers," *The Conference Board Record*, Vol. X, No. 2 (February, 1973), pp. 26–33; H. Roy Kaplan, "How Do Workers View Their Work in America?," *Monthly Labor Review*, Vol. 96, No. 6 (June, 1973), pp. 46–47.

[10] R. P. Quinn, T. W. Mangione, M. S. Baldi De Mandilovitch, "Evaluating Working Conditions in America," *Monthly Labor Review*, Vol, 96, No. 11 (November, 1973), pp. 32–42.

[11] Michael R. Cooper, B. S. Morgan, P. M. Foley, and L. B. Kaplan, "Changing Employee Values: Deepening Discontent?" *Harvard Business Review*, Vol. 57, No. 1 (January–February 1979), pp. 117–125.

decent wages and working conditions but also a high quality of working life? Do they want interesting work, variety, challenge, and autonomy? People bring to the work place quite different value systems. These different value systems are culturally determined—family upbringing, education, peer group relations, and early job experiences.

Some persons have high aspirations, are career oriented, and seek intrinsic satisfaction from their jobs. However, they may find themselves in stifling bureaucratic job situations. The boss may not care to hear their ideas. Their jobs may be limited in scope and promotion opportunities could be rare. Such people tend to seek expression for their abilities and ambitions in off-the-job activities—social activities, professional societies, or part-time businesses.

Regardless of the contrasting theses on job satisfaction and conditions of work in America, there is widespread recognition that both productivity and quality of working life can and should be improved.

Productivity in an enterprise and in the economy as a whole is based upon a combination of human, organizational, technological, and capital investment factors. Over the past three decades in the United States there has been a pronounced shift towards labor intensive service industries in which technology plays a lesser role than does the labor of the human being. Examples of these sectors of the economy are education, health care, and government. Certainly in these industries innovative programs to raise human productivity can have a substantial payoff. Also, in manufacturing industries where machines and technology loom large, experiments have demonstrated that new designs for work systems and "people management" can yield substantial and lasting gains in productivity.

The percentage of the labor force which is college educated has been increasing rather steadily since the late 1940's. The big boom in college enrollments occurred in the 1960's. Ordinarily a college degree has served as a key to the door of opportunity and the good life in America. However, by the 1980's, we now have a glut of college educated people in the job market. Between 1974 and 1985 the number of graduates will exceed job openings that require degrees by some 950,000, according to the Bureau of Labor Statistics.[12] The college graduates are moving downward to lower-income and lower-status jobs. This condition is generating high frustration among college-educated young people. Employers can help alleviate this problem by establishing career development, job enrichment, and other innovative quality-of-working life programs.

Even those workers of lesser education and aspiration, who look upon their jobs simply as a way of making a living, can cultivate a taste for a high level of involvement in their work. Many experiments have shown that once given the opportunity, ordinary hourly-paid workers can make real contributions toward solving job problems and improving productivity.

QUALITY OF WORKING LIFE

The most widely quoted definition of quality of working life is that formulated by Richard E. Walton. Professor Walton explains it in terms of eight broad condi-

[12] *Business Week* (February 20, 1978), p. 78.

tions of employment that constitute a good or desirable quality of working life. Walton's features or conditions are as follows:

1. Adequate and Fair Compensation.
2. Safe and Healthy Working Conditions.
3. Immediate Opportunity to Use and Develop Human Capacities. This includes autonomy, work requiring multiple skills, information and perspective, whole tasks, and involvement in planning.
4. Future Opportunity for Continued Growth and Security. This includes expanding of one's capabilities, opportunity to use new knowledge and skills, promotion opportunities, plus job and income security.
5. Social Integration in the Work Organization. This includes freedom from prejudice, egalitarianism, supportive primary work groups, a sense of community, and interpersonal openness.
6. Constitutionalism in the Work Organization. This includes rights to privacy and free speech. It also includes equitable treatment of employees and "due process" procedures in handling employees and in appeal procedures.
7. Work and Total Life Space. Walton argues for a balanced relationship among work and nonwork and family aspects of life.
8. Social Relevance of Work. The employing organization should perform in a socially beneficial manner.[13]

Clearly, of course, many employers do provide a work life climate that meets several of Walton's criteria such as adequate compensation and safe working conditions. Some companies also have interesting, challenging jobs and offer many opportunities for training and advancement. However, it is rare to find work-life situations that satisfy all eight of Walton's criteria. We can view these eight features as goals to aim for.

Because of individual differences among people and because of differences in the opportunities for need-satisfaction from one department of a company to another, we should expect considerable variation in the satisfactions experienced by different employees in the same organization.

STRATEGIES FOR IMPROVEMENT

As stated earlier many employing organizations, both in the United States and abroad, have programs to enhance both the quality of working life and productivity. Especially in the private, competitive sector management is nearly always looking for ways to cut costs and increase output. Productivity could be improved in ways that reduce the quality of working life. Thus management could raise work loads, reduce the number of personnel, and fractionate jobs further. This might increase productivity in the short run but it would most certainly increase employee tensions. We are concerned here primarily with programs that have as their objective both worklife improvement and improvement in performance.

[13] Richard E. Walton, "Quality of Working Life: What Is It?" *Sloan Management Review*, Vol. 15, No. 1 (Fall 1973), pp. 11–21.

A variety of strategies or approaches have been devised by experimenters. We shall here describe the principal strategies that have been employed. Typically an organization uses one or possibly two strategies as its main theme and supplements this with one or more subsidiary approaches.

Self-Managed Work Teams

Self-managed work teams are also called autonomous work groups or integrated work teams. In this method work groups of say, ten to twenty employees, plan, coordinate, and control their own activities. They have a team leader who is often a worker, not a member of management.

Groups of employees are given the authority not only to perform direct production operations but also to do certain activities that traditionally are done by service and staff groups. Thus, an assembly group may take on the added tasks of planning work methods, inspecting output, maintaining equipment, and even selecting employees for the team. These groups have authority to regulate their own work tempo. Key decisions are often made as group decisions.

The objective in setting up self-managed work teams is to create teams around whole units of work wherein the components of the work and the processes are interdependent. Generally several different skills and jobs are combined into each team. The team is accountable for performance of its whole unit of work (e.g. making sub-assemblies, processing customer claims) and given the personnel and resources necessary to complete the work properly. The reward system (pay, recognition, promotion) is related to both group and individual achievement.

Job Redesign and Enrichment

The content and structure of jobs can be changed in various ways. Whereas sometimes jobs have been enlarged horizontally to add more task variety and sometimes employees have been allowed to rotate from one limited job to another to introduce variety and interest, the principal thrust of those companies having quality of working life programs has been to enrich jobs that had previously been set up on the basis of narrow division of labor. The basic research and theory on job enrichment has been done by psychologist Frederick Herzberg. It is based upon his motivator-hygienic factors theory explained in Chapter 18.

Guidelines for designing enriched jobs are as follows:

1. Form natural work units so that the employee can experience a sense of ownership of the work and a feeling of responsibility. These tasks then become significant to the employee.
2. Combine tasks into larger units of accomplishment to enhance skill variety and task identity.
3. Establish client relationships. The employee should have direct knowledge of and, if possible, direct contact with the person or group that receives his completed work. Examples of a client relationship are a secretary doing work for a supervisor and a draftsman preparing drawings for an engineer. In this way

Figure 19-2
An Enlarged Engine Assembly Job in a Saab Factory in Sweden. Formerly these workers performed very short cycle operations on an assembly line. Now they do many different operations requiring up to 30 minutes per engine. (*World Wide Photos*)

the employee can obtain feedback on how well his or her work meets the needs of those who use that work.

4. Load the job vertically. This means that "planning" and "controlling" tasks should be added to the job. In narrow fractionated jobs the planning and controlling is traditionally performed by the boss. In enriched jobs the employees make their own decisions on work methods, setting up of equipment and tools, work pace, and checking on quality of work produced. This process increases the person's sense of autonomy.

5. Provide direct information and feedback to the employee. This means that the individual must have full information necessary to do his job and that he should receive feedback on the quality and quantity of his performance. In traditional job designs the feedback is given to the employee by his boss and this is often viewed as an evaluation of one's character and is resented. The feedback should not be evaluative but rather should be objective.[14]

Figure 19-2 shows an engine plant job that has been enlarged by combining tasks into larger units of accomplishment. This enlargement also helps the employees develop a sense of ownership of their work. However the job pictured

[14] Principles and guidelines such as these for enriching jobs are contained in: J. Richard Hackman, "Work Design," ch. 3, in J. Richard Hackman and J. Lloyd Suttle, *Improving Life at Work*, Santa Monica, Calif.: Goodyear Publishing Co., Inc., 1977 and in Frederick Herzberg, "The Wise Old Turk," *Harvard Business Review*, Vol. 52, No. 5 (September–October, 1974), pp. 70–80.

does not represent true enrichment because the operator does not perform planning and controlling tasks.

Participative Management

By *participative management* we mean a system of management in which employees participate in making management decisions that effect them and their jobs. This process increases employee motivation, generates ideas that may not have occurred to management alone, and reduces resistance to new methods and processes. It helps meet the human needs for autonomy, achievement, and self-expression. Although participative management can be structured in a number of ways, typically it involves a departmental supervisor conducting meetings with his immediate subordinates to make plans and decisions regarding such matters as tooling, equipment, methods, safety, distribution of tasks, and working conditions. Generally the supervisor retains final decision-making authority but works closely with his people in getting ideas, testing their reactions, and shaping solutions. Because participative management is so different in concept from the traditional "boss-knows-it-all" style of leadership, front line supervisors require specific training in the theory and methods of participative management.

Behavior Modification

Behavior modification, also called operant conditioning or positive reinforcement, is a direct application to the work-organization setting of the theory and methods of noted psychologist, B. F. Skinner. Most behavior modification work has been done in schools, mental hospitals, and prisons but in recent years some disciples of Skinner have applied behavior modification to the management of people in work organizations.

Proponents of behavioral modification are essentially interested in controlling and shaping behavior. They want to increase productivity, cut costs, or reduce absenteeism. They make no claims about improving job satisfaction and attitudes. They are not humanistic in their orientation.

The essential idea of behavioral modification is that behavior is determined by its consequences. The behavior desired by management (e.g. high productivity, high quality, coming to work on time) is shaped by rewarding successive approximations of the desired behavior. Each small improvement is reinforced. Improper behavior is ignored rather than punished according to strict Skinnerian precepts, although some proponents do use punishment. Main ingredients of a behavior modification program are identification of key behaviors to be shaped, setting of new behavioral goals, providing feedback on performance to the individual, devising various forms of suitable reinforces (e.g. pay, recognition, free time, adoption of suggestions), and applying the reinforcers.

Effective Leadership and Supervisory Behavior

Although there is no formula that teaches one how to be an effective supervisor, research evidence accumulated over many years has uncovered many useful insights. Employees like to work for supervisors who show consideration for them, who are supportive, and who are fair and just in their treatment. The supervisor should create an atmosphere of approval in his relations with his subordinates. Employees' perception of their quality of working life is affected heavily by the treatment they receive from their supervisors.

The effective supervisor also must take actions to help get the work out. This dimension has been variously labeled "facilitation and goal emphasis," "initiating structure," and "production-centered" leadership. The supervisor must be able to organize and direct people who will produce work. He must possess technical knowledge in order to diagnose production difficulties. He must set challenging but attainable performance standards. In certain circumstances the employees themselves may participate in setting output standards. He must help his people solve work and equipment problems. He must also provide job instruction. In implementing this facilitation dimension of his job the supervisor should not be overbearing nor should he pressure his people around.

Another important dimension of effective leadership and supervision is the development of teamwork among employees. The supervisor should generate an appropriate degree of participation in day-to-day decisions on the part of his people. They should care about their work and about the department. They should be highly involved and not apathetic.

Career Development

To more fully utilize the talents of their people, to help employees realize their career ambitions, and to enhance their feelings of achievement and recognition, many of the more progressive corporations are nowadays carrying on systematic career planning and development activities. The principal components of a comprehensive career program within an organization are (1) human resource planning; (2) communication of job opportunities and career path information to employees; (3) career counseling both by the supervisor as part of performance appraisal and by the personnel department; (4) provision for education and training of employees both within and outside the organization; and (5) special broadening job assignments and job rotation. In addition to these basic components some organizations have formal assessment centers to analyze and evaluate the capacities and potential of their personnel.

"Second careers" is a concept that is gaining acceptance in recent years. Because of pronounced changes in the demand for occupations (for example, the demand for teachers is down now whereas the demand for health-care personnel is up) and because of the emergence of new occupations, working people should have opportunities to reassess themselves in mature life and make a start on a new and different career. To effectuate this our labor market and educational institutions should provide assistance to those seeking new careers. Personnel managers should also see that the career development programs in their organizations provide opportunities for employees to change their career paths, where feasible.

Other Strategies

Several strategies, in addition to those already discussed above, have been used in a good many organizations to improve productivity or the quality of working life or both. Certain strategies that follow have been designed to improve only specific facets of the quality of working life. Others are more broadly based.

Scanlon Plan. Named after the late Joseph Scanlon, its originator, a Scanlon Plan is a plant-wide or company-wide incentive plan that contains three integral features: (1) a pervasive philosophy of cooperation among management and the employees; (2) a suggestion system designed to cut costs and raise productivity; and (3) an incentive formula by which cost savings are returned to employees in the form of bonuses and to the company in lower costs per unit of production.

Profit Sharing Tied to Productivity. The leading example of success in linking profit sharing to high productivity is the Lincoln Electric Company of Cleveland, Ohio. This company has a direct wage incentive system and annual profit-sharing bonuses tied to employee performance. Other important features of the company's personnel program are guaranteed annual employment, a stock purchase plan, and an advisory board containing worker representatives.

Administrative Justice. Administrative or organizational justice insures that disciplinary and grievance handling proceedings are carried out according to recognized principles of due process. For example, in administering discipline and discharge the affected employee is given a written statement of the charges against him, he has the right to defend himself, he has the right of counsel or representation, and final appeal is before an impartial party such as an arbitrator.

Flexible Working Hours. Flexible working hours, also called flexitime, is designed to give employees more individual control over the hours they work each day. Every employee is required to work a given number of hours per week or per month. However, the individual is granted considerable discretion in the times he starts and stops work each day as long as he is on the job for a fixed band of hours during the middle of the day, commonly 10:00 A.M. to 3:00 P.M. A variation of flexible hours is the four-day work week. Typically all employees in the organization must work four 10-hour or four 9-hour days each week. This gives employees three-day weekends for leisure time activities.

SOME CASE EXAMPLES

To enhance the reader's understanding of the kind of quality of working life and productivity programs that have been carried on in industry, we shall give four case examples of successful programs. The examples given here are simply illustrative of the many that are going on in industry in the United States and abroad.

General Foods Plant

In 1971 the General Foods Corporation opened a new plant in Topeka, Kansas to process and package pet foods. It began as a small plant. The plant's food processing, packaging, and office functions are built around self-managed work teams. Each team contains seven to fourteen members including a team leader.

Although workers are assigned specific tasks within a team, they can rotate to other jobs or share tasks with other employees.

Teams are provided with managerial type information to aid them in making operating decisions. Teams make their own decisions on such matters as individual job assignments, filling-in for absent members, selecting new team members, evaluation of job performance, and pay progression. All sets of tasks making up jobs within a team are roughly equally challenging so that a single job classification can be used for all personnel. However, pay increases can be earned when employees successfully learn to do other jobs within the team and ultimately in the plant.

Teams solve their own production problems and are responsibile for maintenance of equipment, quality control, and housekeeping.

Status distinctions among different categories of personnel are minimized. Conference rooms are available to all. There are no time clocks or reserved parking spaces.

The tangible results have been generally positive. Costs have been lower and quality has been higher than for other plants in the company. The absenteeism rate has been only about 1½ percent. Employee turnover has been very low. The plant also has an excellent safety record. The workers have evidenced high job satisfaction. They have stated that the work is interesting and that they like the opportunity to make their own decisions. A problem has been that some of the managers have found it difficult to accept the fact that the rank and file workers have power and influence to make many decisions traditionally reserved for managers.[15]

American Telephone and Telegraph Company

AT&T's program has been built around the concept of job enrichment. A job enrichment experiment was launched in the mid-1960's in the stockholder correspondents section of the Treasury Department. This section contained about 120 women employees who answered stockholder complaints via letter and telephone.

To enrich the jobs they were vertically loaded. The correspondents signed their own names to letters instead of having the supervisor sign them as was done previously. Completed letters were sent directly to the mail room instead of going to the supervisor for checking. Correspondents were encouraged to answer letters in a more personalized way. Full responsibility for quality was placed on the individual correspondents. Supervision became less close. These job enrichment changes were designed to provide opportunities for achievement, recognition, and responsibility through performance of the work. Results were favorable in terms of both job performance indicators and attitudes. Job enrichment projects were then set up in several other company departments such as engineering, traffic, controllers, and commercial.

It ought to be pointed out that job enrichment, although successful in certain

---

[15] Richard E. Walton, "How to Counter Alienation in the Plant," *Harvard Business Review*, Vol. 50, No. 6 (November–December, 1972) pp. 70–81 and Edward M. Glaser, *Productivity Gains Through Worklife Improvement*, New York: Harcourt Brace Jovanovich, 1976.

activities at AT&T, has not become pervasive throughout all reaches of the corporation.[16]

General Motors Corporation

In some of its manufacturing plants General Motors has experimented with new organizational systems and with participative management. Its work has been based upon Rensis Likert's System 4 style of management which is, to a large extent, participative management.[17] The other three styles of management in Likert's typology are System 1, Exploitative-Authoritative; System 2, Benevolent-Authoritative; and System 3, Consultative. According to Likert, the causal variables in achieving real change in any organization are managerial leadership and organizational climate. These determine both the intervening variables of peer leadership and group processes and the end result variables of productivity, costs, and profits.

At General Motors' Lakewood, Georgia plant the corporation instituted System 4 management. Some key elements in GM's program were training in System 4 concepts for all managers; abundant training for all hourly personnel; full information to hourly employees about such matters as future products, facility changes, quality, and efficiency; employee participation in planning new model production changes; and self-managed work teams in certain departments.

Within a few months after the changes were introduced, measurements of such human dimensions as organizational climate, supervisory leadership, peer leadership, and employee satisfaction showed substantial gains. It required about two years before measures of labor efficiency and quality showed notable improvements. Such a lag time is typical according to Rensis Likert.

Comparable projects have been introduced at other General Motors plants.[18]

Donnelly Mirrors, Inc.

Donnelly Mirrors manufactures mirrors for automobiles. It is a small, family owned company located in Holland, Michigan. It established a Scanlon Plan in 1952 that provides for plantwide standards and improvement goals and sharing of the dollar gains from productivity improvements. In addition to its Scanlon Plan, Donnelly uses self-managed work teams. Each team member is encouraged to master every job performed in his team. Participative management is employed by means of employee committees that contain four hierarchical levels of the organization. In 1970 all hourly employees were put on salary and time clocks were removed. Long term gains in a variety of performance indices (productivity, quality, costs, attendance, return on investment, etc.) have been impressive. According to Glaser this company is one of the most successful examples in the United States of a long-term commitment (since 1952) to improving the quality of working life.[19]

[16] Glaser, Ibid., pp. 63–71
[17] System 4 management is described in detail in Rensis Likert, *The Human Organization: Its Management and Value* (New York: McGraw-Hill Book Company, 1967).
[18] William F. Dowling, "At General Motors: System 4 Builds Performance and Profits," *Organizational Dynamics* (Winter, 1975), pp. 23–38.
[19] Glaser, op. cit., pp. 47–52.

UNION ATTITUDES

On the surface one would expect that American labor union leaders would have warmly endorsed efforts by industry to improve the quality of working life. But such is not the case. Why is this so?

Unions have traditionally and rather consistently pressed for higher wages and fringe benefits, shorter hours, job security via seniority provisions, individual protections via the grievance procedure and arbitration, and maintenance of the union as an organization.

Union leaders are suspicious of such techniques as job enrichment, self-managed work groups, and participation because they consider these as management methods to extract more work from employees without paying higher wages. They lump these work motivation methods together with the much older management sponsored time and motion study and wage incentive techniques. It is true that the underlying philosophies of the older scientific management techniques and the modern quality of working life techniques are miles apart, but the unions don't view them that way.

Union leaders are also suspicious of humanization of work programs because they consider them a threat to the union as an organization. These programs are initiated by management, often without consultation with the local union leaders. They feel that these programs constitute an attempt to wean the employees' loyalties away from the union.

Also at issue is the question of whether the average worker really wants a job that is intrinsically interesting and challenging. Some union leaders argue that rather than management initiated schemes to raise productivity and work motivation, the worker would prefer longer vacations, more paid holidays, and a shorter work week with no reductions in pay.

CONCLUDING COMMENTS

Most quality of working life programs constitute an attempt to increase employee satisfaction and performance through increased intrinsic motivation. These programs seek to involve employees more thoroughly in decisions and activities of their jobs, work groups, department, and to some extent of the whole organization. These endeavors try to enhance the motivators as defined by psychologist Frederick Herzberg—achievement, recognition, work itself, responsibility, advancement, and growth.

These programs do not, by and large, try to improve all components of quality of working life. For example, largely missing from such programs is attention to employee privacy, due process and just cause, freedom of expression, and equitable treatment. Also absent from most programs is a mechanism to provide for job security.

Despite the foregoing omissions this author thinks that the quality of working life movement is generally on the right track. Much of the work is based upon sound theory and research of the behavioral sciences. It should be a continuing movement for many years.

Success in any program to enhance performance and the quality of working life requires a deep understanding of the entire process by top management of the organization. Likewise top officials must be thoroughly committed to the activity and must understand the investment required and the possible problems to be encountered along the way.

Questions for review and discussion

1. Based upon the working people who you know well, would you say that most persons are quite oriented toward their work? Are their jobs a central focus of their lives? What differences do you note among people?
2. What values does one's job provide the individual over and above the purely utilitarian one of earning a living?
3. What features of work in our modern organizations can cause frustration and alienation?
4. Why is the level of job satisfaction generally higher for managers, professionals, and self-employed individuals than for blue-collar workers?
5. Educational attainment of the workforce has risen steadily over the years. Also the percentage of college graduates in the workforce has increased substantially. How do these factors affect satisfaction with work?
6. What features comprise a high quality of working life?
7. Explain the following: self-managed work teams, job enrichment, participative management, behavioral modification, career development.
8. Why have union leaders in America been reluctant to support quality of working life programs?

Suggestions for further reading

BARBASH, JACK. "Humanizing Work—A New Ideology," *AFL-CIO American Federationist*, Vol. 84, No. 7 (July, 1977), pp. 8–15.

CUMMINGS, THOMAS G. and EDMOND S. MOLLOY. *Improving Productivity and Quality of Work Life*. New York: Praeger, 1977.

DAVIS, LOUIS E. and ALBERT B. CHERNS (eds.) *The Quality of Working Life*, Vols. I and II, New York: The Free Press, 1975.

GLASER, EDWARD M. *Productivity Gains Through Worklife Improvements*. New York: Harcourt Brace Jovanovich, 1976.

GYLLENHAMMAR, PEHR G. "How Volvo Adapts Work to People," *Harvard Business Review*, Vol. 55, No. 4 (July–August, 1977), pp. 102–113.

HACKMAN, J. RICHARD and J. LLOYD SUTTLE (eds.) *Improving Life at Work*. Santa Monica, California: Goodyear Publishing Co., Inc., 1977.

KATZELL, RAYMOND A. and DANIEL YANKELOVICH. *Work, Productivity, and Job Satisfaction*. New York: The Psychological Corporation, 1975.

LAWLER, EDWARD E. III. "The New Plant Revolution," *Organizational Dynamics*, Vol. 6, No. 3 (Winter, 1978), pp. 2–12.

SUOJANEN, WAINO W., et al (eds.) *Perspectives on Job Enrichment and Productivity*. Atlanta, Georgia: Georgia State University, 1975.

Work in America. Report of a Special Task Force to the Secretary of Health, Education, and Welfare. Cambridge, Mass.: The MIT Press, 1973.

Leadership, supervision, and management systems

A supervisor persuades his team of engineers that they must revise their procedures drastically in order to meet the scheduled delivery date in the space technology program. A young lady stenographer takes the initiative in making arrangements and getting the other young women to help in giving an office party for an associate who is moving to the West Coast with her husband. An engineer who senses strong discontent among his fellow engineers because they must constantly put in long hours of overtime discusses the matter with the others and agrees to act as their spokesman before the boss. A telephone lineman takes charge when his gang experiences difficulty running cable while the foreman is temporarily away from the job.

All of the foregoing acts are examples of leadership behavior. In the first situation the supervisor's leadership behavior was an integral part of his formal position of authority and command in the organization. In the other three instances the leadership acts were initiated by employees who volunteered their services. They exhibited actions of an informal leader. They were not endowed with formal authority by the organization.

Leading is the element of management that impels others to action. It is one of the essential functions that must be performed by all supervisors and executives—that is, by all who direct the work of other people. Leading, of all the key functions of management—planning, organizing, staffing, leading, and controlling—is one of the most difficult to understand, acquire, and evaluate. For centuries scholars have been speculating on the nature of leadership. Yet only in recent years have researchers conducted systematic investigations that have yielded useful insights into the dimensions of leadership.

Supervision is front-line management. The supervisor directs and controls the activities of non-supervisory personnel. We shall explore the nature of the supervisor's job and the pressures typically faced by a supervisor. We shall also look at those supervisory behaviors that have been found effective in achieving employee satisfaction and high unit performance.

Because the overall style of management and organizational climate are so influential in determining the performance of individual departments within an establishment, we shall examine, also in this chapter, different systems of management.

NATURE OF LEADERSHIP

Leading is the process of influencing others to act to accomplish specified objectives. A precise and comprehensive definition of leadership is that formulated by Tannenbaum, Weschler, and Massarik, who state that it consists of interpersonal influence, exercised in a situation and directed, by means of the communication process, toward the attainment of a specified goal or goals. They pointed out that leadership always involves attempts by a person (leader) to affect or influence the behavior of a follower (or followers) in a situation.[1]

The effective leader gets others (followers) to act. He may impel them to action by any of numerous devices: persuasion, influence, power, threat of force, and appeal to legitimate right.

The person who occupies a leadership position must transmit his feelings and exhortations to his followers by the process we call communication. Communication involves both the sending of messages and understanding by the receiver. The successful leader is the one who can appeal to his constituents in a meaningful way. He talks their language.

Among the objectives the leader seeks to have the group accomplish may be those of the larger organization, as when a foreman exhorts his workers to increase production to meet the schedule set by top management. The leader also is an agent of the led. He seeks to satisfy the needs of his followers. Thus, a foreman may go to bat for his men to obtain higher pay classifications for them because both he and they honestly believe the higher pay rates are justified. It should be emphasized that the leader of a group in a formal organization has the dual objectives of representing the interests of his group to higher management and of getting his subordinates to work for the goals of the enterprise as a whole. The problem of leadership is further complicated by the fact that individuals within his group of followers may (and usually do) possess varied and conflicting

[1] Robert Tannenbaum, Irving R. Weschler, and Fred Massarik, *Leadership and Organization: A Behavioral Science Approach* (New York: McGraw-Hill Book Company, 1961), p. 24.

goals. These may not always be compatible with the objectives of the total organization or of the immediate group.

Followership is intimately related to leadership. A person's attempted leadership is only effective insofar as he is able to cause others to respond favorably to his initiation of action. In fact, the way a subordinate reacts to his boss' directives affects the latter's manner of leading. A supervisor may learn from experience that it is unwise to assign John and Henry to work as partners on a maintenance repair job because John has previously said that he will not work with Henry. Of course, the supervisor could threaten to discharge John unless he works with Henry. But he knows that forcing the two men to work together is folly because their incompatibility prevents effective work cooperation.

FOUNDATIONS OF LEADERSHIP

For centuries writers, historians, and the public in general held to the notion that leadership was primarily exercised by great men, that they were "born" and not "made" (by education and training), and that real progress and change in civilization awaited the coming of such individuals.

Indeed even in the late nineteenth and early twentieth centuries in America, writers depicting the successes of great industrial giants asserted that their position of authority and power derived mainly from their superior birth, superior ability, and superior personal magnetism. These powers were possessed by only a fortunate few. But such theories have been largely discredited as a result of the scientific investigation of leadership by modern researchers.

Traits, Situation, and Group

In selecting supervisors from within the ranks of a company, can management identify those employees who will be good leaders by the personality traits they exhibit? Is there a distinct leadership type? Do leaders as a whole possess traits that distinguish them from nonleaders?

Over the years innumerable investigators have sought to answer such questions as these. They have employed such methods as observation of behavior in group situations, analysis of biographical data, psychological testing of persons occupying leadership positions, and ratings by observers. It has been asserted that a commanding voice, vigorous health, tall stature, a striking appearance, and dominance are common characteristics of leaders. However, the fact of the matter is that to a considerable extent these studies have yielded a confusing and often contradictory array of characteristics allegedly possessed by leaders. It has been found that the traits claimed to be possessed by leaders are also widely exhibited by followers as well.

As a result of a comprehensive investigation of leadership, Stogdill concluded that the pattern of leadership traits differs with the situation. There is no single personality configuration that typifies a leader. He observed that the evidence strongly suggests that leadership is a relationship that exists among people in a social situation and that a person who becomes a leader in one situation may not do so in a different situation.[2]

There are three main variables to be weighed when one analyzes the leadership process: (1) a *leader* operating in a (2) *situation* in relation to the (3) *personalities, attitudes, and abilities* of the followers. The present state of knowledge is such that it is not now possible to define with precision the specific leader qualities and behaviors required for effective performance in defined situations with particular types of followers. However, the general dimensions of the problem are known.

Different types of followers—the group that is led—respond to different kinds of leadership. Some have great initiative and self-confidence; they respond best when they can assert themselves and work on their own. Other subordinates by reason of their background and personality development must have everything structured for them. Otherwise they feel lost. They require close guidance. Some employees like to take on new and important responsibilities; others simply are willing to "put their time in" and are content to obtain all their satisfactions off the job. Some persons exhibit little identification with the goals of the organization. Again we find that some employee groups possess a high level of education. They accordingly will respond to a particular style of leadership that would be quite inappropriate for a group having little formal education.

There are innumerable situations in which leadership must operate. Variations exist in the nature of the tasks, organizational environment, time dimensions, and social and cultural environment. The relationship that a leader or supervisor has with his boss affects the way he deals with his subordinates. On the one hand, there may be mutual confidence and trust between them; on the other, the supervisor may himself feel insecure in respect to his boss. The insecure position of a supervisor is bound to transmit itself into his dealings with his subordinates.

Different jobs within the work organization require different abilities. The assertive, exuberant, outgoing, people-centered sales manager would find himself ill at ease and ill equipped to supervise a design engineering department. Likewise it should be apparent that the skills and behavior required by our industrial giants in the early twentieth century—the Rockefellers, Fords, and Carnegies—to found industrial empires were quite different from the coordinative and administrative skills needed by the present-day executive to guide a modern enterprise.

A business leader operating in a Latin-American cultural climate must behave differently from one operating the same kind of enterprise in New York State. Variations between these two environments exist in the customs and expectations of the people both within and outside the work organization.

---

[2] Ralph M. Stogdill, "Personal Factors Associated with Leadership: A Survey of the Literature," *The Journal of Psychology*, Vol. 25 (January 1948), pp. 35–71. Added evidence of the view that leadership is specific to the situation can be found in an experimental investigation by Carter and Nixon. See Launor F. Carter and Mary Nixon, "An Investigation of the Relationship Between Four Criteria of Leadership Ability for Three Different Tasks," *The Journal of Psychology*, Vol. 27 (January 1949), pp. 245–261.

Any Common Traits?

We have emphasized that there is no such thing as the "leader type." Different situations and different groups require different leadership abilities. Generally speaking there are considerable variations in the personality, ability, capabilities, and skills of successful leaders. Yet with all the research that has been done into this problem, it can reasonably be asked whether there are not a few characteristics of successful leaders that the practical executive can give attention to when he is selecting subordinate leaders. The answer is that yes, there are some traits that appear in a majority of the investigations of leadership. But it should be remembered that although the statistical correlations between these traits and leadership ability are positive, the correlations are often low. The correlations also do not prove a cause-and-effect relationship. It may actually require one set of traits to achieve a position of leadership and another, but related, set of abilities to maintain that position.

Intelligence.   Studies of leadership tend to show that a leader has somewhat greater intelligence than his followers. However, he will not usually have a great excess of intelligence over the average of his followers.[3] A manager of scientists would have, on the average, somewhat higher intelligence than his followers. But a person possessing the level of intelligence of a typical Ph.D. in physics would have far too much to supervise successfully a gang of laborers.

Social Sensitivity.   Because he deals constantly with others and achieves his own and group objectives through the efforts of other people, the successful leader must be accurately attuned to others. He must be aware of their feelings, goals, and problems. He must be able to sense and judge accurately human reactions in order to be able to influence others. The successful leader must also be able to sense the values of the whole group he directs. He must be socially perceptive.

Activity and Social Participation.   A man is unlikely to rise to a position of leadership and is unlikely to maintain that position if he is passive, apathetic, and aloof. The successful leader tends to initiate action for others. He is awake, alert, and enthusiastic. He proposes, suggests, and coordinates. Leaders tend to participate actively in group functions. Because leadership actions involve influencing other people, a successful leader must be skilled in working with people. Stogdill has reported positive correlation in a large number of investigations between leadership and the traits of social activity, biosocial activity, and social skills.[4]

Communication Skills.   Since a leader exercises his skills primarily by interacting with his subordinates and with others outside his group, he must be effective as a communicator. He need not be, in any sense, a silver-tongued orator; but he must have a sufficient range of communication abilities to transmit his messages accurately. Fluency of speech is especially important.

[3] Stogdill, op. cit., pp. 44–45.
[4] Stogdill, op. cit., pp. 56–59.

AUTHORITY AND POWER

In the formal organization—whether it be industrial, commercial, governmental, military, or philanthropic—leadership takes place in conjunction with authority and power. In fact, these are to a substantial degree necessary concomitants of leadership.

Authority is defined as the legitimate right to direct or influence the behavior of others. The legitimacy component of authority implies that which is morally or legally proper. This legitimacy may derive from the laws of the state, from the charter of the organization, and from rule and custom of the society.

In our economic institutions—factories, offices, stores, banks—authority is customarily viewed as flowing from the top of the organization structure downward through the hierarchy—from the board of directors to the president, to the various echelons of managers, to the front-line supervisors, and finally to the workers. Of course in the broad sense, authority in both public and private organizations emanates from the society as a whole. Our organizations exist and operate at the sufferance of the public.

As children are reared and as they mature, they are conditioned to accept the authority and directives of their parents, of their school teachers, and of various authority figures in the community. Indeed the school—beginning with the one-room school house—has served as both a seat of learning and as an institution in which children are trained to accept the kind of authority and discipline that will be imposed upon them when they participate as adults in an industrialized society.

Now it should be apparent that authority and obedience to it are not absolute. People may reject an order given by the leader, whether he be a corporate manager or the mayor of a city. In the ordinary course of events employees (and citizens) will follow most orders. However, they may reject—passively or overtly—some orders because they believe them to be unfair, unreasonable, or impossible. The followers may individually or as a group reject the person who issues the orders. Conflict, peaceful or violent, may follow. To preclude rejection and subsequent conflict the leader may consult, beforehand, his subordinates or certain trusted advisors to ascertain the attitudes of the followers. He may then modify his plans to try to gain a meeting of the minds and cooperation. Additionally the leader often has available for use, if need be, various elements of power that he can bring to bear to induce the followers to comply with his orders and policies. We shall discuss power shortly.

In membership organizations, such as unions, professional and civic organizations, and in democratic countries, the members elect their leaders for fixed terms of office. Thus, the authority of the leaders flows directly from the members. These elected leaders recognize the source of their legitimacy and authority. But there is a general consensus, often bolstered by constitutions, laws, and by-laws, that the members will accept the authority and leadership of these officials during their terms of office.

Power and Leadership

For leadership to be effective, it often must be supported by some measure of power. This is true for both the formal work organization and the informal social group. A leader tries to influence the behavior of other people. He may give them instructions, he may coordinate activities of specialists, he may seek to reconcile conflicting views, and he may seek to impel them to greater efforts to achieve higher productivity.

What is power? Power is the ability to achieve dominance of one's objectives and methods. It often involves the capacity to employ force if necessary.

French and Raven have postulated that there are five bases or sources of power. Although an understanding of the nature of power is facilitated by this categorization, it should be pointed out that more than one power element is often at work in any given situation. Their bases of power are (1) reward, (2) coercion, (3) legitimacy, (4) identification with the power figure, and (5) expertise.[5]

The arsenal of rewards the executive in industry can dispense to get his employees to work to achieve designated goals is well known. Positive leadership through rewards tends to develop a considerable amount of loyalty and devotion of subordinates toward their leaders.

Coercion is the application of actual force to secure one's way. In private industry, physical coercion is almost never used by management. But coercion is also punishment. And the business leader often obtains compliance simply by the threat (often implied) of demotion, transfer, layoff, or discharge. The supervisor who shuns and ignores a subordinate is also punishing him. So is the superior who berates his employees.

Legitimate power is analogous to authority in the organization wherein employees ordinarily accept orders from their supervisors because they accept the authority system when they decide to work for that company. Cultural values also provide a basis for legitimate power. Thus, a father in most societies throughout the world is looked upon as the head of the family. So that order and stability may be maintained, the members of an organization know they must abide by the reasonable directives of their officially designated superiors in the hierarchy. Repeated failure to follow legitimate authority would invite chaos.

Sometimes a follower develops a strong emotional attachment to a leader. There is a feeling of oneness between the two. Thus, the leader is able to influence and modify the behavior of the subordinate because the latter identifies strongly with the leader. This is called referent power or identification with a power figure. This type of power is less common in business and industry than any of the other four classifications.

Persons who possess a vast fund of knowledge and technical skill often have the power over others who are less well informed. Thus, when the respected physician suggests that people should get vaccinations against flu, his advice is usually heeded by the majority. When the lawyer formulates a procedure for handling litigation, the layman company president tends to adopt his advice. Power based on expertise is usually limited to a specialized area of activity—that of the expert's specialty, for example, law, engineering, physics, or medicine. The technical expert usually cannot extend his power to other spheres of activity.

[5] John R. P. French, Jr., and Bertram Raven, "The Bases of Social Power," in Dorwin Cartwright, ed., *Studies in Social Power* (Ann Arbor, Mich.: Institute for Social Research, 1959).

LEADERSHIP STYLE

When psychologists began to accept the fact that no single configuration of leader traits is predictive of successful performance, they turned their attention to investigations of leadership style. By style we mean the behaviors of the leader—what he does, what he emphasizes, and how he deals with subordinates.

An early significant experiment was that conducted by White and Lippitt under the direction of Kurt Lewin in 1938 at the University of Iowa.[6] Four groups of ten-year-old boys were each exposed to three different styles of adult leadership—autocratic, democratic, and laissez-faire. The four adult leaders were given training so that each was proficient in the three different leadership styles. The groups of boys were organized into clubs to carry on various craft activities such as carpentry, mural painting, wood carving, soap carving, and the making of plaster of Paris masks. In setting up these groups, the researchers tried to equate them in terms of scholarship and such interpersonal relationships as sociometric attraction or rejection, leadership, quarrelsomeness, obedience and social activity.

In describing the experiment, we shall concentrate upon the autocratic and democratic leadership patterns, because the laissez-faire style proved to be quite ineffective, as might be expected. In the autocratic situation all determination of policy was made by the leader; he dictated the activity steps one at a time; he dictated the particular work tasks and work companions of each member; he was personal in his praise or criticism; and he was aloof from active group participation. On the other hand, in the democratically led groups, policies were developed by group discussion. Activity perspective was gained during these discussions, and the leader gave alternatives when suggesting procedures. The boys were free to choose their own partners. The leader was fact-minded in his praise and criticism and tended to be a group member in spirit.

In the autocratic-leadership pattern the leaders spent a high portion of their time giving orders, making disruptive commands, and giving nonobjective praise and criticism. Conversely, the democratic leaders spent much of their time making guiding suggestions, giving information, and encouraging the boys to make their own decisions democratically.

What were the results of this experiment? As far as achieving work goals, the democratic and autocratic groups were about equally efficient. The autocracy created much hostility, aggression, and scapegoating among the boys. Several boys dropped out during the periods of autocratic leadership. There was more dependence and less individuality in the autocracy. In contrast there was more group-mindedness and more friendliness in the democracy. There was more mutual praise, friendly playfulness, and readiness to share group property in the democracy.

During the late 1940's and early 1950's investigators at Ohio State University, studying leadership in many different kinds of organizations, found that the many kinds of behavior exhibited by leaders could be conveniently classified into two categories. One category or dimension which they labeled "consideration" covered leader behavior in which there was a high degree of two-way com-

---

[6] Ralph K. White and Ronald Lippitt, *Autocracy and Democracy: An Experimental Inquiry* (New York: Harper and Row, 1960).

munication, mutual trust, rapport, and friendship between the leader and the group of followers. The other dimension which they called "initiating structure" included such leader behaviors as assigning tasks, emphasizing production goals, and defining the structure and ways of getting jobs done. Some leaders may be more oriented towards "consideration" whereas others may be more oriented towards "initiating structure." And of course, some may give a balanced emphasis to both dimensions.

Starting in the late 1940's and continuing through the 1950's the Institute for Social Research of the University of Michigan carried out many field investigations in a large variety of industrial, commercial, governmental and other types of organizations. These researches classified leader behavior into the two categories of "employee-centered" and "production-centered." These are basically synonymous with the Ohio State terms "consideration" and "initiating structure." Publications from the Michigan researchers in that era stated that supervisors or managers of high-producing departments were found to be employee-centered in their behavior towards subordinates and they practiced general (instead of close) supervision.[7]

Later work at Michigan resulted in the formulation by Bowers and Seashore that effective leadership is composed of the following four categories of leader behaviors: (1) Support of subordinates, (2) Facilitation of interaction among members of the group, (3) Emphasis upon meeting goals, and (4) Facilitation of the work (planning, coordinating, and providing resources).[8] In testing their model in 40 agencies of a life insurance company, they found that these four categories of leader behavior were significantly correlated with several measures of employee satisfaction and insurance agency performance. There was a somewhat greater relationship between leadership behavior and employee satisfaction than between leadership behavior and agency performance. They also found that the behavior of the employees towards each other was significant in determining the level of employee satisfaction and of performances. Further, the managerial leadership was primarily instrumental in shaping the degree to which the peer group was supportive toward its members and helped with the work. Although leadership style plays a major part in controlling work group satisfaction and performance, Bowers and Seashore pointed out that other elements such as power, work patterns, and personal and motivational factors are also significant in determining effectiveness.

SITUATIONAL FACTORS

Contemporary work into leadership has demonstrated that situational factors are very important in moderating the degree to which particular leadership styles are effective. As more and more research investigations have been made, we have learned that the analysis, explanation, and prediction of leadership are very

[7] See for example Daniel Katz, Nathan Maccoby, and Nancy C. Morse, *Productivity, Supervision and Morale in an Office Situation* (Ann Arbor, Mich.: University of Michigan, Institute for Social Research, 1950).

[8] David G. Bowers and Stanley E. Seashore, "Predicting Organizational Effectiveness with a Four-Factor Theory of Leadership, *Administrative Science Quarterly*, Vol. 11, No. 2 (1966), pp. 238–263.

complex. Current research is generally characterized as "contingency approaches to leadership." Let us now look at the more important situational factors.

Characteristics of Followers.   Studies have shown that subordinates who have strong needs for independence, who have confidence in their own abilities, and who believe that what happens to them occurs because of their own behavior, are more productive and more satisfied under participative leadership. Participative leadership is a style of leadership in which subordinates have a real say in decisions affecting them and their work. On the other hand, those who have dependent personalities, who have a low confidence in their own abilities to perform assigned tasks, and believe themselves to be controlled by chance factors are more receptive to authoritarian leadership.[9]

Task.   Some jobs and departments are highly structured and others are not. Much of the work performed by blue-collar workers in factories is quite structured and engineered. The work routines are carefully planned and laid out by industrial engineers. Vast numbers of workers in industry perform machine-tending and parts-assembly operations where the routines have been carefully spelled out. The army of clerks in the offices of the nation are also mainly engaged in specialized, structured tasks.

On the other hand, many jobs are and can be only loosely defined. The work is variable. Job procedures cannot be specified in advance. Such is the work of managers, engineers, scientists, doctors, salesmen, professors, staff specialists, and many skilled craftsmen and technicians.

The leadership style that is most fruitful for unstructured work tends to be different than that for structured jobs. House reports on one research study of 325 employees in a manufacturing concern. Regardless of differences in personality, those who were engaged in nonrepetitive, ego-involving tasks were more satisfied under a participative leadership style than under a non-participative style. In repetitive tasks, subordinates who scored low on authoritarianism were more satisfied under a participative style.[10]

Organizational Climate.   The overall organizational climate is a powerful determinant of both productivity and employee satisfaction, irrespective of the style of leadership practiced by front-line supervisors. Organizational climate is a composite of the system of management practiced by the top executives (for example, autocratic, paternalistic, or participative), the culture of the organization, peer group relationships, communication patterns, and motivational forces.

If an autocratic leader, for example, were to be appointed to the position of an academic dean in a university that had a strong tradition of professorial influence in the key decisions of new appointments, promotion and tenure, and curriculum design (collegiality), one could safely predict that this leader would continually face determined opposition from the faculty unless he altered his style to be compatible with participatory decision-making.

[9] Victor H. Vroom, "Some Personality Determinants of the Effects of Participation," *Journal of Abnormal and Social Psychology*, Vol. 59 (November 1959), pp. 322–327. Robert J. House and Terence R. Mitchell, "Path-Goal Theory of Leadership," *Journal of Contemporary Business*, Vol. 3, No. 4 (Autumn, 1974), pp. 81–97.
[10] House and Mitchell, Ibid., p. 94.

Power of Leader. The extent to which a leader has available for use the various elements of power (reward, coercion, legitimacy, identification, and expertise) frequently determines the degree to which he or she can obtain compliance from the followers. A manager in a company is endowed with many elements of power that help him get performance from his people. He or she can hire, fire, promote, and transfer (or effectively recommend these). He evaluates the performance of his people and grants or withholds pay raises. He possesses legitimate authority and the symbols of office (desk, title, high status).

At the other end of the spectrum is the informal leader who possesses fewer elements of power over his followers. He must gain cooperation by personal persuasion. He holds his position as long as the members feel that he effectively represents their interests.

Leader–Group Relations. One of the most critical aspects of leadership effectiveness is the relationship between the group members and their leader. Is the leader accepted by his or her followers? Do they like and trust him? Is he able to obtain their compliance without exerting a great deal of time and effort for each transaction? How readily do they respond to leader attempts to initiate action?

The effectiveness of the leader and his group is poor if they get along badly. Friction, hostility, and resentment can make accomplishing results difficult. Where the leader knows that his people resent him, he may still get compliance. However, he may resort to the use of threats to induce performance and under such conditions group performance tends to be minimal.

Relationship Among Key Dimensions

It is apparent from the preceding discussion that the effectiveness of a given leadership style is materially affected by the situational factors. Production (task)-oriented leadership may be effective under some conditions and employee-oriented direction may work better under other conditions. Behavioral scientists have been trying to determine, for about 25 years now, the true relationships among the major situational dimensions. A great deal of empirical and theoretical research addressing this matter has been carried on by Fred Fiedler and his associates.[11]

His investigations have sought to explain how certain situational factors interact with leadership style. These factors are (1) leader-member relations, (2) task structure, and (3) leader's power position. He and his associates have systematically investigated the performance of work groups under various combinations of leader's style (production-oriented or employee-oriented) and the three situational factors. Among the groups studied have been athletic teams, church groups, consumer-sales cooperatives, factories, aviation cadets, open-hearth steel crews, supermarket departments, and hospital nursing.

Fiedler has constructed a contingency model of leadership effectiveness based upon the degree of favorableness of the group-task situation. The favorableness of the situation is the degree to which the situation enables the leader to exert influence over his group. According to Fiedler, the most crucial element in lead-

---

[11] Fred E. Fiedler, *A Theory of Leadership Effectiveness* (New York: McGraw-Hill Book Company, 1967).

ership is the leader-member relationship, that is, the extent to which they trust him and will respond to him. Eight situational combinations have been studied and classified. These range from a situation most favorable to the leader (good leader-member relations, structured task, and strong power position) all the way to the most unfavorable situation (poor leader-member relations, unstructured task, and weak power position).

His theory predicts that production-oriented leadership works best under conditions that are either very favorable to the leader or conditions very unfavorable as defined above. The human relations or employee-oriented leadership style is most effective when the conditions are only moderately favorable or moderately unfavorable to the leader (the intermediate range on his 8 combinations of situational factors).

Although there has been some criticism by other psychologists of Fiedler's research constructs and methodology, his work represents a major step forward in our understanding of the relationship of the various situational factors involved in leadership.

Path-Goal Theory. Another contingency theory that has attracted considerable attention in recent years is the path-goal theory of leadership formulated by Evans, House, Mitchell and others.[12] It is based upon the expectancy model of motivation. This theory recognizes four kinds of leader style or leader behavior. These are (1) directive leadership, (2) supportive leadership, (3) participative leadership, and (4) achievement-oriented leadership.

The central propositions of the theory are (1) that the leader's behavior is acceptable and satisfying to followers to the degree they see such behavior as either an immediate source of satisfaction or as instrumental to future satisfaction, and (2) that the leader's behavior will generate performance by the followers to the extent that satisfaction of their needs is contingent upon effective work performance by them.

The path-goal theory recognizes two categories of situational variables. The first category which is labeled "personal characteristics of the subordinates" is composed of three sub-factors: (1) authoritarianism of followers, (2) belief in locus-of-control of one's life (controlled by one's self internally or subject to external events), and (3) subordinates' perception of own ability (high or low ability). The other situational variable is the "environment." This too, is comprised of three sub-factors as follows: (1) the nature of the task; (2) formal authority system; and (3) the character of the primary work group. Both sets of contingent factors must be assessed in order to predict the results on satisfaction and productivity of specific leader behaviors.

The theory postulates that directive leadership (authoritarian) has a positive correlation with satisfaction of subordinates who are engaged in ambiguous tasks and has a negative correlation with satisfaction for subordinates involved in clear tasks. Supportive leadership has its most positive effect on subordinate satisfaction for those engaged in stressful, frustrating or dissatisfying tasks. Achievement-oriented leadership is most effective in generating subordinate confidence that their efforts will pay off in effective performance where the tasks are ambig-

---

[12] M. G. Evans, "The Effects of Supervisory Behavior on the Path-Goal Relationship," *Organizational Behavior and Human Performance*, 55 (1970), pp. 277–298; House and Mitchell, op. cit.

uous and nonrepetitive. The theory also postulates several other relationships.[13]

To date, independent empirical investigations of the path-goal theory have been generally supportive of its concepts, formulation, and predictive capacity. But much more research needs to be done.

Conclusion. Leadership effectiveness is intimately tied to motivation, to relations between the leader and the followers, and to followers' perceptions that complying with the leader's directives will lead to satisfaction of their needs. Because of differences in follower perceptions and differences in the environmental situations, the results of any given leader behavior can be quite variable. Substantial progress has been made by researchers in formulating a useful theory of leadership but a great deal more work remains to be done. On the basis of the findings to date, it is clear that the many variables interact in a complex way. Hence no simple leadership prescription for the manager is likely to ever emerge.

SUPERVISION

Supervision is the function of leading, coordinating, and directing the work of others to accomplish designated objectives. A supervisor guides his or her subordinates so that they produce the desired quantity and quality of work within the desired time. He must also see that their needs are satisfied and that his group achieves its objectives with a minimum of friction and a maximum of harmony. In short, a supervisor seeks to have his group accomplish the required work and likewise seeks to promote need satisfactions and high morale among the employees.

A supervisor performs a leadership role. His behavior helps motivate employees to work toward approved goals. Without leadership, whether it be of the formal or the informal type, a mass of people are uncoordinated and can accomplish nothing. Supervision is crucial to all organized endeavor. The behavior of a supervisor is vital for determining the level of productivity and morale of his work group. In one research investigation of the attitudes and motivation of 200 accountants and engineers employed in nine companies, supervision was found to be one of the chief causes for dissatisfaction. The dissatisfaction related to such aspects of supervision as incompetency, poor scheduling of work, lack of teaching ability, unfriendly relations, lack of support, and unwillingness to listen to suggestions.[14]

Nature of Supervisor's Job

A very useful definition of a supervisor is that contained in the Labor–Management Relations Act of 1947 (Taft–Hartley Act). Section 101, Subsection 2 (11) defines a supervisor as "any individual having authority, in the interest of the employer, to hire, transfer, suspend, layoff, recall, promote, discharge, as-

---

[13] House and Mitchell, Ibid., pp. 90–91.
[14] Frederick Herzberg, Bernard Mausner, and Barbara B. Snyderman, *The Motivation to Work*, 2nd ed. (New York: John Wiley & Sons, Inc., 1959), chs. 8 and 13.

sign, reward or discipline other employees, or responsibility to direct them, or to adjust their grievances, or effectively to recommend such action, if in connection with the foregoing the exercise of such authority is not of a merely routine or clerical nature, but requires the use of independent judgment." In formulating this labor relations law the United States Congress decided that foremen and supervisors should be considered, in effect, as members of management and that they should not be entitled to representation elections and bargaining unit certifications conducted by the National Labor Relations Board, as are nonsupervisory employees. Because foremen are direct representatives of the employer in dealings with the rank-and-file worker, Congress evidently felt that it would be inappropriate for foremen and office supervisors to be union members as well.

Common parlance has tended to restrict the use of the term *supervisor* to those individuals who direct the activities of others and who are also in the lower ranks of the management hierarchy. If we divide the organization structure of a typical company into three levels of management—top, middle, and lower—then the word *supervisor* would apply to those at the lower level. In a very large corporation this lowest level would typically consist of two organization levels. Common job titles are foreman, assistant foreman, general foreman, and superintendent. For office and white-collar work the title *supervisor* is used, never foreman. The generic term is *supervisor*, and this can be properly used to apply to persons in charge of production workers as well as those in charge of office workers.

A front line supervisor must have very good understanding of the technology of his department. We are using the term technology in a broad sense to cover both machines and processes technology as well as the technology of "knowledge workers" or professionals which includes scientific and technical concepts and skills. The supervisor is not expected to be skilled in performing the various jobs under his direction but he is expected to understand the jobs in order to diagnose and solve work problems. In contrast to front-line supervisors, upper level managers do not need intimate knowledge of the multitudes of technologies of their organization. They need planning, administrative, and conceptual skills.

The supervisor also must be skilled in the various leadership and human relations functions. Among these are motivation, face-to-face communication, training, and coaching.

Duties and Responsibilities of a Supervisor

If we were to make an on-the-spot analysis of the activities of a supervisor during a typical work week, what would we find? Although we would find some variation from department to department and from company to company in the degree of emphasis devoted to the various supervisory tasks, we would find rather surprising agreement in the list of functions which a supervisor must perform and for which he is responsible. In a very hazardous industry, safety would require a great deal of attention from a foreman, whereas in a nonhazardous one this would be a minor part of his job. However, the maintenance of safe working conditions and adherence to rules of safety is definitely a requirement of the latter's job, just as it is with the foreman in the hazardous factory.

Let us now examine the particular duties and responsibilities of a supervisor. You will note that these items are classified as "duties and responsibilities."

There would not be enough hours in the day for a supervisor to perform personally all of these items himself. Therefore, in many instances he is responsible for seeing that these tasks are carried out by one or more of his subordinates. Thus, he may delegate to one of his employees the task of requisitioning materials and supplies or of instructing a new employee in the details of his job. Certain essential leadership functions, such as appraising, counseling, and disciplining, should not be delegated.

The order of appearance of the following duties and responsibilities does not indicate relative importance. They are all essential. For purposes of classification, certain responsibilities are listed under the heading "Personnel Management and Human Relations." However, it must be emphasized that in carrying out practically all the other responsibilities such as production, quality, and costs, the supervisor must deal with people and exercise human relations skills. It is really not possible, in the day-to-day activities of a supervisor, to make a strict line of demarcation between those duties involved in getting out the production and those involved in personnel management.

Production
   Requisition materials and supplies.
   Expedite the flow of materials and supplies.
   Plan utilization of machines and equipment.
   Schedule flow of work through department.
   Assign employees to operations and jobs.
   Check progress of employees.
   Help employees clear production problems.
   Maintain records of production.
   Meet production schedules.
Maintenance
   Check equipment for correct operation.
   Order repairs to equipment.
   Maintain clean and orderly working environment.
Methods improvement
   Devise new and improved work methods.
   Cooperate with staff groups such as industrial engineering in developing and
      installing better methods and procedures.
Quality
   Insure that quality standards are met.
   Analyze quality reports and take corrective action on defective work.
   Inspect incoming materials.
   Act on changes in quality standards.
   Cooperate and coordinate with quality assurance, engineering, and inspection
      personnel.
Costs
   Control and reduce costs.
   Analyze budget.
   Determine causes for variances from standard costs and budgeted costs and
      take corrective action.
Personnel management and human relations
   Request additional employees as needed.

Make final employee-selection decision.

Orient new employees to their environment, the requirements of the organization, and their rights and privileges.

Train employees.

Provide face-to-face leadership.

Appraise performance.

Coach and correct.

Counsel employees.

Recommend pay increases, promotions, transfers, layoffs, and discharges.

Enforce rules and maintain discipline.

Settle complaints and grievances.

Interpret and communicate management policies and directives to subordinates.

Interpret and communicate employee suggestions and criticisms to higher management.

Motivate subordinates; provide rewards for good performance and behavior.

Eliminate hazards and insure safe working practices.

Develop own skills and abilities through self-development activities and participation in company training programs.

Cooperate and coordinate with personnel department in administering the company personnel program within own department.

POSITION AND PROBLEMS OF THE FOREMAN

A foreman is the head of a department or section involved in production or maintenance operations (as distinct from white-collar office activities). He supervises, typically, anywhere from five to forty blue-collar, rank-and-file workers. Within the management hierarchy the foreman occupies a unique position in that he supervises nonmanagement personnel, whereas all the other managers direct other managers. His job is unique because the attitudes and expectations of rank-and-file workers are quite different from those of managers. The workers have less upward mobility. They perform more narrow, restricted jobs. They possess less education. To a considerable extent they obtain fewer need satisfactions on the job. They tend to gain most of their ego satisfactions through off-the-job activities. The foreman is the connecting link between management and labor. It is through him that the policies and directives of upper management really become operational.

Pressures on the Foreman

Being a front-line leader of employees at the point where all prior management planning and decision making is translated into the actual fabricating of a product or the rendering of a service, the foreman is a key person in the organization. Yet he is subjected to unremitting pressures from a number of sources. See Figure 20-1 for a graphic representation of the demands and forces impinging upon the typical foreman.

First and foremost the foreman must please his immediate line superior in the organization. There is a tendency in industry for line superintendents and pro-

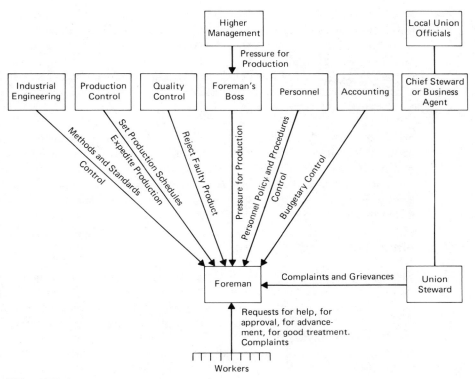

Figure 20-1
A Schematic Organization Chart Showing the Pressure and Demands Made upon a Manufacturing Foreman by His Boss, His Subordinates, Staff Departments, and the Union.

duction managers to be primarily interested in getting out the production. The foreman often interprets this pressure as a demand to meet the production goals even if it is necessary to sacrifice human values in dealing with his men. He knows he will be called upon the carpet if there are delays in meeting scheduled delivery dates or if his costs are excessive, but he also knows that there is less likelihood of criticism from above for overriding human relations values.

The various specialized staff departments, such as industrial engineering, production control, and personnel, exist to help line departments do a better job. They provide technical knowhow and specialized services and guide and regulate the activities of line departments. However, to the foreman the behavior of people from these departments often appears as intrusion, interference, and trouble. The industrial engineer tells him how his operations must be performed as well as how fast individual workers must work; the production control specialist tells him on what dates he must complete certain work and then rides herd on him to see that he meets these due dates. Quality control sets quality standards and rejects certain items as unsatisfactory. The personnel department sets hourly wage rates for his subordinates, hires workers for his department, and sometimes overrules his decisions on grievances filed by the union. Accounting establishes budgets and standard costs, and the foreman's line boss criticizes him if he exceeds these estimates.

A foreman is also subjected to pressures from his immediate subordinates. The employees expect supportive, favorable treatment from their foreman. They want him to help them with their work problems and to go to bat for them to obtain necessary tools and equipment, pay raises, promotions, better working conditions, and the like. Basically they want their supervisor to help them obtain satisfaction for many of their physical, social, and egoistic needs insofar as these can be provided in the working environment.[15]

If employees are represented by a labor union their problems, complaints, and grievances are brought to the foreman's attention with persistence backed by power. Most unions will not dally long if they do not receive satisfaction from the first-line supervisor. They will go over his head to higher line management or to the personnel department. Sometimes the foreman finds that his decisions on grievances are overruled by the personnel department, and sometimes he is criticized by the line management for having too many labor problems.

Background, Outlook, and Status

Foreman quite generally acquire their positions as a result of promotion from the ranks of the workers. In other words, a foreman was previously a blue-collar worker himself. Whereas in years gone by management tended to promote the skilled worker who was at the same time hard-driving, aggressive, and company-minded, today managers are more sophisticated. They know that skill as a worker does not necessarily mean skill as a supervisor. In picking a person to be foreman, companies look for administrative ability, leadership, and human-relations skills, as well as technical ability.

In recent years many of the large companies engaged in manufacturing technical products have tended to hire college graduates for jobs as foremen. Usually this is looked upon as a beginning job for a young person who will rise in operating management. In many cases young engineers and business administration graduates are assigned jobs in production supervision as part of their company training programs. This practice of utilizing college graduates for careers in production management means that promotion opportunities for hourly production workers are materially reduced, and it also means that noncollege foremen find it exceedingly difficult to meet the competition for advancement to higher levels in the organization. In essence it means that the majority of these up-from-the-ranks foremen can go no higher in the organization.[16]

In many plants the foreman is not really treated as a manager. He is primarily a transmitter of orders. He is somewhat like a policeman in that he simply enforces schedules, work methods, rules, and directives established by others. His authority and discretion are severely limited.

Although many organizations have done an excellent job in providing the

---

[15] Documentation of this point, based upon a research investigation, can be found in Edwin A. Fleishman, Edwin F. Harris, and Harold E. Burtt, *Leadership and Supervision in Industry* (Columbus, Ohio: The Ohio State University, 1955), pp. 59–60. It was found that workers expected the ideal foreman to rate high on a "consideration" score. They preferred less "initiating structure" on the part of their foremen.

[16] For an analysis of the use of college graduates as foremen see Kenneth Hopper, "The Growing Use of College Graduates As Foremen," *Management of Personnel Quarterly*, Vol. 6, No. 2 (Summer 1967), pp. 2–12.

foreman with the status symbols of management—exempt payroll, a desk, an office, clerical assistance, partipation in management training programs—others treat him as a glorified worker or a "pusher." He may wear a blue collar, punch a time clock, and for his office have little more than a high stool and table in the corner with a bare light bulb suspended overhead. Here he may have a clip board hanging from a nail in the wall where he keeps the day's work tickets.

If a reduction in force occurs due to production cutbacks, the foreman is vulnerable to being "bumped" back to a production job as an hourly paid worker. Foremanship is not a profession like engineering or law. A person may have worked his way up to this position with one employer, but if circumstances cause him to seek employment in a different industry, chances are he will have to start at the bottom as a worker. Then, too, a foreman lacks the protection against arbitrary treatment that a union affords the production worker in the factory. For the hourly worker layoffs are by seniority, and discharges are almost always appealed by the union. His pay raises are uniform and regulated by the union contract.

Implications of the Foreman's Position

The net result of all of the foregoing facts regarding the position and problems of the typical foreman in industry means that he is not secure in his status. He does not have a full measure of control over the departmental operations for which he is held accountable. He is subjected to a multitude of pressures from higher management, his workers, the union, and from staff departments. Being insecure he must be cautious. He has to play it safe. He is ever perceptive to the feelings and inclinations of his boss; yet he cannot succeed as a leader if he ignores the needs of his subordinates. As an individual he is readily replaceable. He does not always know where he stands.

PATTERN OF EFFECTIVE SUPERVISION

The front-line supervisor plays a significant part in influencing the performance of his work unit. He or she also exerts a major influence upon the job satisfaction and morale of the employees. The questions of what kinds of supervisory practices generate high work group performance and what practices contribute to high employee satisfaction have been the subject of numerous research investigations over many years. Certain general principles and concepts have emerged from these studies. It ought to be pointed out before discussing these principles that they are generalizations. Particular circumstances in individual situations may call for exceptions and deviation from these general guidelines.

Supportive Behavior

Extensive investigations performed by researchers at the Institute for Social Research of the University of Michigan and others has established the importance of supportive behavior by the effective supervisor.[17] What is supportive

---

[17] See, for example, Rensis Likert, *The Human Organization: Its Management and Value* (New York: McGraw-Hill Book Company, 1967), ch. 4.

behavior? The supervisor who is supportive displays confidence and trust in his subordinates. He shows concern for each employee as a person. He keeps the employees properly informed of events in the department and the organization. He solicits ideas from the employees. He gives help in solving work problems and gives credit for good work. The supportive supervisor creates an atmosphere of approval towards his people. And finally, the supervisor treats his employees fairly and equitably.

Supportive supervisory behavior has quite consistently correlated positively and highly with the satisfaction of subordinates.[18] Supportive supervisory behavior, of and by itself, does not consistently generate high performance from a work group. However, when supportive behavior is combined with supervision that acts to facilitate the work and acts to set challenging performance goals, as discussed below, then productivity tends to be high.

Facilitation of Work

The effective supervisor provides adequate tools, equipment, and materials so that the employees can do their jobs properly. He or she also provides proper job information, production plans and schedules. The supervisor gives help in diagnosing technical problems when requested. He insures adequate liaison with other departments so that the work flows smoothly and so that necessary cooperation is obtained from other supervisors.

In providing technical help and job instruction the supervisor must exercise care not to supervise the employees too closely. Inexperienced workers and those unsure of themselves do need close guidance, but for experienced and trained personnel, general, rather than close, supervision is advisable.

Performance Goals

Performance goals which are challenging but attainable contribute to high work-unit productivity. Employees need to know what is expected of them in terms of units to be produced, due dates, reports to be completed, sales to be made and the like.

Traditionally goals and standards are established by the boss and by upper management. However, goals may also be set jointly by discussion between the boss and his subordinates. Thus, in "management by objectives" performance targets for several months ahead are commonly determined mutually. Also, in some organizations participative management techniques are used to set short term production targets.

Livingston has argued persuasively and has offered evidence to show that those managers who display confidence in their subordinates and who communicate an expectation of high performance, tend to manage work units that consistently outperform units run by managers who show little confidence in their employees' capacity to produce.[19]

[18] Gary Yukl, "Toward a Behavioral Theory of Leadership," *Organizational Behavior and Human Performance*, Vol. 6, No. 4 (July 1971), pp. 414–440.
In his writing the author uses the term "consideration" to designate supportive behavior.
[19] J. Sterling Livingston, "Pygmalion in Management," *Harvard Business Review*, Vol. 47, No. 4 (July–August 1969), pp. 81–89.

Influence in Hierarchy

Several research investigations have demonstrated that the really effective supervisor is able to exercise considerable upward influence in dealings with his or her boss.[20] This upward influence impacts upon both productivity and employee satisfaction. The front-line supervisor's authority is usually rather limited. To obtain sufficient resources for his department and in order for the higher level manager to come to really understand the problems of his department, the supervisor must have influence with that manager. Sometimes, upper-level managers issue orders without having a full understanding of the likely effect upon each and every department. If a given department may have special problems implementing an order from above, the effective supervisor who has upward influence will work out an accommodation with his immediate organizational superior. The ineffective supervisor who has little upward influence may do little to make an accommodation or, if he tries, he may be unsuccessful.

Closely tied to upward influence is the willingness and ability of the supervisor to go to bat for his people. The successful supervisor recommends pay raises, promotions, training opportunities, needed improvements in working conditions and the like for his people and he is effective in gaining these items for them. Such positive and successful behavior not only strengthens employee morale, but also improves employee motivation and effort. In effect, when such rewards are deserved, the granting of these benefits serves as positive reinforcement for the work behavior of the employees.

Group Relationships and Participation

Some supervisors feel that they are directing primarily a collection of very separate individuals. They tend to deal with each of their subordinates as individuals and to downplay the relations of the people with one another. They seek to build strong lines of communication and loyalty between themselves and each individual worker, but discourage bonds among the people in the group. Such supervisors foster competition among the men and women for the rewards that they can dispense. This competition, although it may increase individual performance temporarily, tends to generate mistrust, conflict, and lack of cooperation among the employees.

In direct opposition to this foregoing pattern of supervision, the research evidence shows that the best supervisors build up group pride and loyalty. They involve the group as a whole in the problems of the department. They encourage the men and women to interact and help one another. The effective supervisor also engenders a feeling of group responsibility for the success of the whole section or department. Supervisors should be careful not to play favorites or to discriminate against any persons in the work unit.

Closely related to the development of teamwork is group participation in decision making. Participative management is anathema to the authoritarian boss. However, very considerable research evidence supports the view that,

[20] Donald Pelz, "Influence: A Key to Effective Leadership in the First-Line Supervisor," *Personnel*, Vol. 29 (1952), pp. 209–217; K. M. Rowland and W. E. Scott, "Psychological Attributes of Effective Leadership in a Formal Organization," *Personnel Psychology*, Vol. 21 (Autumn 1968), pp. 365–377.

under proper conditions, employee participation in departmental decisions (i.e. those under the control of the departmental supervisor) contributes to high unit performance as well as group satisfaction.[21]

Concentration Upon Management Functions

Some supervisors, especially new ones, believe that they can increase the total volume of output of their sections by pitching in and doing direct production work. This may be appropriate for emergency situations, but for day-in and day-out behavior it is counter-productive. The most successful supervisors are those who devote their attention to their management responsibilities of planning, organizing, leading, and controlling. They see to it that the direct production work gets done, but they themselves do not do it. They devote their time to planning, anticipating and preventing crises, coordinating, motivating, coaching, training, deciding, organizing, measuring performance, and taking corrective action where necessary.

It ought to be mentioned here that there are positions in many organizations called working foreman or group leader. These people *do* perform direct production work, but they are not really true members of management. A working foreman or group leader is a nonsupervisory employee who receives extra compensation for performing limited supervisory duties. Ordinarily these consist of such things as assigning workers to operations, clearing difficulties, checking on quantity and quality of output, answering technical questions, and instructing new employees. They do not have the authority to discipline, handle grievances, select new employees, or effectively recommend merit pay raises.

Organizational Climate

We said earlier, in our discussion of leadership, that organizational climate is a powerful determinant of both productivity and employee satisfaction. Its influence is so strong that it can outweigh the impact of the quality of frontline leadership. The climate of an organization is created by the overall system of management that is practiced. Let us now turn to a discussion of differing systems of management.

MANAGEMENT SYSTEMS

Although several writers have created classification schemes to depict different kinds of management systems, the one formulation that has been built upon years of careful empirical research is that developed by Rensis Likert. His Systems 1, 2, 3, and 4 are based upon work at the Institute for Social Research (which he headed for many years) of the University of Michigan.

When we speak of a system of management, we mean something broader than leadership style. Leadership style is a characteristic of an individual leader,

---

[21] See for example, Likert, op. cit., ch. 4; Alfred J. Marrow, David G. Bowers, and Stanley R. Seashore, *Management by Participation* (New York: Harper and Row, Publishers, 1967); and J. B. Ritchie, "Supervision," ch. 3 in *Organizational Behavior: Research and Issues* (Madison, Wisconsin: Industrial Relations Research Association, 1974).

whereas a management system is a style of management composed of a complex of practices and actions that pervades an entire organization. The system of management practiced by the top officials really establishes the organizational climate. The climate of organization A may be distinctly different from organization B. On who works in A and then in B can sense the differences.

In assessing organizational climate, it is desirable to administer questionnaires to both managers and employees. Sometimes there is a distinct difference between the managerial system that the upper level managers *think* they are using and the one that employees *perceive* them to be using. Organizational climate is a composite of the organizational structure, system of motivation, leadership style, communication patterns, quality of interpersonal relationships, peer-group relationships, quality of discipline, and general treatment of employees. The system of management determines the character of the organization and determines, ultimately, the outcomes such as profits, output, costs, and employee satisfaction.

Likert's Systems

Let us now look at the four systems of management articulated by Rensis Likert.[22]

System 1.   System 1 is an exploitive authoritarian system of management. Management endeavors, mainly by tight discipline and force, to extract production from workers with little or no regard for their well-being. The employees fear the bosses and are subservient. The bosses want it this way in order to keep the subordinates "in line." The bosses are aloof from the workers. Employees are competitive and often hostile towards each other. Practically all decisions are made at the top. Punishment for mistakes is emphasized rather than corrective discipline.

This is basically a harsh organizational climate. Employees are used in a bad way.

System 2.   System 2 is really benevolent autocracy or paternalism. The employees are expected to be subservient, compliant, and reasonably productive. They are also expected to be loyal. In return management treats them decently—perhaps even kindly. But decision making is centralized at the top. The social atmosphere is harmonious but employees are not involved in plans and decisions. Not only employees but also lower-level managers are expected to do as they are told, to be loyal and dependent.

Managers are oriented toward human relations but are not disposed toward such practices as job enrichment or genuine consultation.

System 3.   System 3 is consultative management. Management sometimes solicits ideas from employees to help solve problems. But management itself makes all the decisions. Suggestion plans may be used for upward communication. The motivational system provides rewards, occasional punishments and some ego in-

[22] Likert, op. cit., ch. 3 and Appendix II; and Rensis Likert and Jane G. Likert, *New Ways of Managing Conflict* (New York: McGraw-Hill Book Company, 1976), ch. 5 and Appendix.

volvement. There is a moderate amount of cooperative teamwork. Performance goals are usually accepted by the employees but there is occasional resistance. Control is primarily performed by upper management but with some shared responsibility at the middle and lower levels.

System 4.   With System 4 or participative management, supervision exhibits supportive behavior toward employees quite consistently. There is extensive friendly interaction among supervisors and employees and a high degree of trust. A great deal of the decision-making is by group participation. There is a full flow of information upward, downward, and horizontally in the organization. All human motives are activated and members of the organization are strongly motivated to achieve the organization's goals. Performance data is given directly to the lower levels so that these people can control and adjust their own performance.

Likert argues that the more effective organizations operate more closely toward the System 4 side of the spectrum. He states that three kinds of factors or variables describe an organization. These are causal, intervening, and end-result variables. *Causal variables,* which are responsible for much of the variation in performance from organization to organization, include managerial leadership and policies, information processes, performance goals, technological adequacy, decision-making processes, and extent of utilization of organizational principles. *Intervening variables,* which are shaped by the causal variables, include peer group leadership, influence, and coordination; group processes such as planning together and sharing information; and confidence in others. The *end-result variables* or outcomes are such things as profits, output, costs, and efficiency.

Based upon research Likert has found that a System 1 style of management may yield favorable end results in the short run but at the expense of a deterioration in the intervening variables. Over a longer time span, the decline of the intervening variables will cause a fall-off of the outcomes. If a System 4 style is then introduced into this establishment, it will take a great many months to turn around the intervening variables. Eventually, System 4 will impact pervasively and organizational performance will improve.

Actual organizations in America, of course, are distributed across the entire spectrum of these four systems. There are some small businesses in which the owner-manager works to maximize his gains, to squeeze his employees, and to discard them when they are no longer useful for his purposes. The owner is exploitative and predatory. Probably, the majority of organizations in both the private and public sectors operate around System 2 with a moderate percentage possessing some of the characteristics of System 3. True System 4 organizations are quite rare.

CONCLUDING OBSERVATIONS

Both students and practitioners of management know that the quality of leadership powerfully shapes organizational effectiveness. Variations in organizational performance and employee satisfaction from one organization to another are primarily caused by the quality of the management, especially top management.

The critical importance of leadership is illustrated by an experience which

General Omar N. Bradley relates in his book, *A Soldier's Story*. His book describes the campaigns of the Allied military forces in Europe during World War II to defeat the German forces and liberate the European people. The 90th Infantry Division had performed badly during the early weeks of the invasion of France. When his staff recommended the break-up of this division and the dispersal of the men to other divisions as replacements, Bradley resisted. He asserted that man for man, one division is just as good as another. Divisions varied only in the skill and leadership of their commanders. Bradley replaced the commanding general of the division and gave him authority to remove ineffective officers. The new commander replaced only 16 officers out of a total of 781 officers. Within three months, this division had been transformed into one of the finest divisions on the allied front.[23]

Leader effectiveness is conditioned by the unique interaction of leader, followers, and the situation. Important situational variables which influence the effectiveness of a given leadership style are characteristics of the followers and of the task, organizational climate, power available to leader, and leader-follower relationships. Significant research by Fiedler, Evans, House and others has helped to uncover and clarify the specific relationships among leaders' style and the situational variables.

We have explored the role and responsibilities of the frontline supervisor and the pressures upon this individual. Then important generalizations about the pattern of effective supervision were discussed. We noted that effective supervisors are supportive towards their subordinates, facilitate the work, set challenging performance goals, exhibit upward influence in the hierarchy, develop strong peer group relations and participation, and concentrate upon management functions.

Finally, we examined Rensis Likert's typology of management systems and noted the critical influence of the overall management system upon organizational performance.

Questions for review and discussion

1. "A successful leader is an unusually talented individual who is endowed through birth and otherwise with those traits that induce others to follow him. He is born to command." Discuss and evaluate this statement.
2. Give and briefly explain important situational factors which influence leadership effectiveness.
3. Think of situations in which you have observed leaders who fail and situations in which leaders succeed. What factors seem to account for failure and success?
4. Give and explain the principal kinds of supervisory behaviors that tend to generate favorable employee satisfaction and good work-unit performance.
5. Why is a first-line supervisor unique in his position as a member of management? What are the pressures and forces impinging upon the foreman in a typical industrial plant?
6. Explain how the system of management utilized by upper management can

[23] Omar N. Bradley, *A Soldier's Story* (New York: Henry Holt and Company, 1951), pp. 297–298.

substantially influence the ability of supervisors to be effective in achieving good unit performance and employee satisfaction.

7. Contrast Likert's System 1 from System 4 management. Explain causal, intervening, and end-result variables.

Case problems

PROBLEM 1[24]

Mr. Johnston, a new man from another department of the company, was appointed supervisor of the instrumentation repair and calibration section. This section was part of a large development-engineering and manufacturing laboratory.

The people in the section consisted of three engineers and nine highly skilled technicians. Their job was to repair and calibrate all electronic laboratory equipment and special manufacturing test equipment, most of which was originally designed by the development engineering group.

Mr. Johnston was introduced to the group by Mr. Foster, his predecessor, during the last two days of the latter's stay on the job. Mr. Foster emphasized the difficult nature of repairing the highly complex electronic equipment. He also noted that in his opinion the human relations aspects of the supervisory job were the most important ones. He felt that letting people work independently and at their own pace would result in their learning from their own mistakes.

During his first few weeks on the job Mr. Johnston made no changes in established procedures but concentrated on getting acquainted with the people, watching them work, and sometimes working with a technician or engineer to find the cause of a difficult instrument repair problem.

He soon realized that the total amount of work performed was rather low. There constantly remained a huge backlog of repair and calibration work to be done. Yet relations with other departments requesting the work were fairly good. In fact, people from these departments did not hesitate to bring in personal television or radio repair work.

Mr. Johnson found that through his working together with someone in his group, the trouble in a piece of equipment was usually located more quickly. He concluded that the men were not working very efficiently or exerting their highest efforts.

Rather than telling them this opinion, he decided to require individual rather than group reports on a weekly basis. These reports were to include the number of instruments repaired, causes of trouble, and the time spent on each piece of equipment, as well as a detailed explanation of the calibration activities of the individual.

Mr. Johnson was pleased to notice an immediate increase in the total number of instruments repaired with a resulting reduction in the backlog of work.

However, there seemed to develop a more strained and formal atmosphere between the supervisor and the group.

Two months later, two competent technicians who had been in the section five

[24] The author expresses his appreciation to Carl H. Rosner for the essential features of this case.

and eight years respectively, requested a transfer to another department in the company. They cited the pressure of work as a reason for the request.

Mr. Johnston realized that the request might be due to his increased demands on his people.

Questions

1. Diagnose the situation in this case.
2. What steps should Mr. Johnston take to retain the new, higher level of performance and also restore the friendly atmosphere and high morale previously present in the section?

PROBLEM 2: THE LABORATORY TECHNICIAN[25]

The story that follows was related by a young woman, a college graduate in biochemistry, who had been employed as a laboratory technician, first at Dansville Chemicals, Inc. and second at the Wheeler Chemical Company.

Part I. Dansville Chemicals, Inc.

My first job after graduation from college was that of a laboratory technician at Dansville Chemicals, Inc., a manufacturer of industrial chemicals and certain consumer products. My job involved the analysis of various random samples of products in the quality control laboratory. The technicians worked in individual cubicles which were located in a large room. The quality control laboratory was under the direction of a manager. Under him were two supervisors who directed the work of the technicians.

The manager prided himself on running a "tight ship." He pressured the supervisors to control the work pace and they constantly pressured the technicians to work at a faster pace. He did not like to see the technicians chew gum on the job, engage in social conversation, or ever look idle (even though the technician might be waiting for a chemical reaction to be completed). He rarely talked informally with the technicians and in fact did not know or bother to learn their names. Likewise, the immediate supervisors seldom initiated any conversations on a personal basis. Interaction among the technicians was made difficult because of the physical arrangement of the cubicles. The partitions made it impossible for the technicians to see one another.

Despite the fact that the analytical work was somewhat varied, I felt that it was boring and tedious.

Employees were allowed to take a combined rest and coffee break twice per day, at 10 A.M. and 2:30 P.M. The starting and ending times were announced by the ringing of a bell. Free coffee was provided by the company. Often, the testing activities of the technicians would not permit stopping precisely at 10 A.M. and 2:30 P.M. However, they lost their break time if they did not stop at these

[25] The author expresses his appreciation to Joanne Chin for providing the essential features of this case.

times. Management did not allow breaks at other times. During the breaks, the technicians congregated in one area and the supervisors clustered in another. There was practically no socializing between the technicians and the supervisors.

Employees and supervisors ate lunch in the company cafeteria. The social and physical separation of the different employee groups was very noticeable here. The hourly paid production workers ate apart from the clerical and secretarial personnel. The quality control technicians sat apart from the research technicians. And separated from all of these people were the managerial and professional personnel. Lunchtime for the technicians was over at 12:45 P.M. and their supervisors always insisted that they be back at their work stations promptly.

There was practically no chance for the technicians to be promoted to better-paying and higher-ranking jobs. During the two years I was employed at Dansville, I never knew a technician to be promoted. Although most of us possessed four-year college degrees (a few had two-year associate degrees), we were treated as decidedly inferior by the supervisors and by management generally. There was no program for employees to obtain training to qualify for higher rated jobs. The jobs were rigidly defined and there was no opportunity for us to take on more responsibilities in the laboratory.

Absenteeism tended to be fairly high. Supervisors expressed open annoyance about time missed from work. When some of the employees were absent, the supervisors demanded that those who were there proceed at a faster pace to make up the work lost due to absenteeism. We technicians resented both the aloofness and the constant pressure of the supervisors.

I found that I was often very tired after a day's work. Because I came to dislike conditions on my job, I welcomed any excuse to take time off. After two years I quit my job.

Questions

1. Why do you think management treated the laboratory employees the way it did? What assumptions about human behavior and the conditions of human performance did management appear to hold?
2. Is there anything that employees, individually or as a group, could do to change the way in which management treated them in this company?
3. We are given very little information about job performance and productivity in this case. Do you think it was high, average or low? Explain.

Part II. Wheeler Chemical Company

After quitting my job at Dansville Chemicals, Inc. I obtained a job at the Wheeler Chemical Company. This job was in the research laboratory but its content was similar to what I had done at Dansville.

Soon after starting work I noticed a very friendly and communicative relationship among the employees. Everyone was on a first name basis including the supervisor, the department head, and the director of the laboratory. Many times the department head as well as the director stopped to chat with us. Each technician had his or her own desk. Technicians did not have assigned laboratory stations. Rather, they worked at various stations as required by their particular projects. The supervisors, who had glass-enclosed offices out in the laboratory, were easily accessible to their people. The department head's office was centrally located. He maintained an open door policy such that we were welcome to discuss our problems with him without a formal appointment.

The company did not have a cafeteria. Some employees brought their lunches and ate at their desks. Others ate together at near-by restaurants. During lunchtime, certain games such as bridge were played. When the weather was good some employees played volleyball on the lawn outside. Supervisors and employees often mingled together in these activities. The company sponsored an annual Christmas party and a summer picnic. These events were well attended by all levels of personnel.

The supervisors often called group meetings to inform the people of progress toward work-unit goals, to find out if there were problems, and to solicit suggestions for solving these problems. We were encouraged, on the job, to develop a team effort to accomplish the work and to figure out the most efficient way of doing it. Because we shared a social closeness, we did not hesitate to voice both suggestions and criticisms.

The research department scheduled many informal seminars during working hours as well as formal seminars in the evening to keep the employees abreast of new developments in their technical fields. Although technicians were encouraged to attend, attendance was not compulsory.

My supervisor encouraged me to take additional college courses in the evening. In accordance with policy, my tuition costs were reimbursed by the company.

There were no time clocks. Work hours were flexible. Sometimes, people came to the laboratory in the evening to work on important projects.

Even though the work tasks were sometimes routine, my job did not seem tedious or boring. I found the team work and social activities stimulating. While I had felt very tired at the end of the work day at Dansville, here at Wheeler Chemical Co., I felt physically and mentally better at the end of the day.

Questions

1. Contrast the managerial styles and organizational climates at Dansville Chemicals, Inc. and Wheeler Chemical Company. What assumptions about people and performance seem to guide the thinking of management at Wheeler Chemical Company?
2. Do you think the management system at Wheeler Chemical could be applied successfully at Dansville? How could this system be introduced at Dansville?

Suggestions for further reading

ARGYRIS, CHRIS. *Increasing Leadership Effectiveness*. New York: John Wiley & Sons, 1976.

BENNIS, WARREN. *The Unconscious Conspiracy: Why Leaders Can't Lead*. New York: American Management Associations, 1976.

DOWLING, WILLIAM F., JR., and LEONARD R. SAYLES. *How Managers Motivate: The Imperatives of Supervision,* 2nd ed. New York: McGraw-Hill Book Company, 1978.

FLEISHMAN, EDWIN A., and JAMES G. HUNT (eds.) *Current Developments in the Study of Leadership.* Carbondale, Ill.: Southern Illinois University, 1973.

FULMER, WILLIAM E. "The Making of a Supervisor 1977," *Personnel Journal,* Vol. 56, No. 3 (March 1977), pp. 140–143, 151.

LITWIN, GEORGE H., and ROBERT A. STRINGER. *Motivation and Organization Climate.* Boston: Graduate School of Business Administration, Harvard University, 1968.

RITCHIE, J. B. "Supervision," ch. 3 in *Organizational Behavior: Research and Issues.* Madison, Wisc.: Industrial Relations Research Association, 1974.

SARTAIN, AARON Q. and ALTON W. BAKER. *The Supervisor and the Job,* 3rd ed., New York: McGraw-Hill Book Company, Inc., 1978.

STOGDILL, RALPH M. "Historical Trends in Leadership Theory and Research," *Journal of Contemporary Business,* Vol. 3, No. 4 (Autumn 1974), pp. 1–17.

————. *Handbook of Leadership.* New York: The Free Press, 1974.

STRAUSS, GEORGE. "Managerial Practices," ch. 6 in Hackman, J. Richard and J. Lloyd Suttle (eds.), *Improving Life at Work.* Santa Monica, California: Goodyear Publishing Co., Inc., 1977.

VROOM, VICTOR H. "Can Leaders Learn to Lead?" *Organizational Dynamics,* Vol. 4, No. 3 (Winter 1976), pp. 17–28.

Participative management

The maintenance superintendent in a steel mill calls a foreman into his office to obtain his suggestions on the most efficient and safest way to dismantle an obsolete overhead crane. A service-engineering manager in the home office of a computer manufacturer calls a meeting of his engineering staff to discuss ways and means of improving service for installations of equipment on customers' premises. Ideas are freely submitted by the engineers. A standing committee composed of both union and management representatives in a machine tool manufacturing company reviews cost reduction and methods improvement suggestions submitted by rank-and-file employees. These three examples illustrate some of the kinds of participation activities that occur in industrial enterprises.

Participation is the term used to designate the process by which people contribute ideas toward the solution of problems affecting the organization and their jobs. The people exercise some degree of influence in the decision-making process. Participation is ego- and task-involvement of an individual or group. It includes not only the physical contribution of the person but also his intellectual and emotional involvement in the affairs of the organization.

When managers establish means, on either an informal or a formal basis, for obtaining help from subordinates in the making of plans and decisions, they are tapping the knowledge and creativity of others. Because managers can't possibly know all the answers to all the problems and issues connected with the work of their departments, they can often obtain valuable advice and assistance from their subordinates. The process of participation brings into play the higher drives and motives of man: the drives for self-expression, accomplishment, autonomy, and self-assertion. It lets the employees know that their contributions are sought and appreciated. Great benefits to the company and its members can derive from such leadership; however, participation is not a cure-all or necessarily the most appropriate style of management for all circumstances.

Some writers have proposed that participatory management has positive values over and above its effects upon productivity and morale. In a society such as that in the United States, where the concepts of political democracy and the rights and duties of the individual to take an active part in the affairs of his country are cherished, it is held that the environment at one's place of employment should be fully compatible with these democratic ideals. To put the matter more directly, democracy should be practiced in the factory and office as well as in the outside civic and social life of American citizens. In point of fact, most business and industrial organizations tend to be quite authoritarian in the internal relations between superiors and subordinates. The system is rather autocratic. Yet this is a basic contradiction, because the executive who practices autocratic leadership at the office preaches the need for maintaining individual freedom in the American society as a whole. To him it is self-evident that citizens should have a say-so in the shaping of laws and policies that affect them. But often this executive does not know how to apply this democratic value system to his own company. Therefore, many spokesmen maintain that participation programs in work organizations derive positive support from the cultural heritage prevailing in the United States of America.[1]

ROLE OF PARTICIPATION IN THE ORGANIZATION

Participation is appropriate for all levels in the organizational hierarchy. In practice in industry it takes place only rarely at the level of the blue-collar and white-collar nonsupervisory employee. Many executives have the notion that these people would have nothing worthwhile to contribute. Participation activities via committees and meetings occur more often at middle and upper levels of management and with professional and technical groups of employees.

A program of management in which employees are invited to contribute ideas and suggestions concerning the running of the business must be distinguished from a system of democratic government. In a democracy the citizens—the people—set up their own governing body and make their own laws through elected representatives. The people have the power at stated times to elect, re-elect, or reject their representatives and executive leaders. However, in a work organization the employees do not select their leaders. Supervisors and managers are appointed from the top of the organization. Only in a very broad sense do these managers rule with the consent of the governed. If a manager is totally ineffective as a leader, he may be removed by his superior in the organization

[1] For another statement of this proposition see Walter Sikes, "The Paradox of Participation," *Personnel*, Vol. 39, No. 1 (January–February 1962), pp. 35–38.

because he observes that this manager cannot win the support and cooperation of his subordinates. But the subordinates do not directly exert control over their supervisors and managers.

Now when a manager consults his subordinates and shares some of his decision-making authority with them, he does this voluntarily. He still retains the final authority and most of the power to make and implement these decisions. He can rescind his sharing of decision making at any time.

Most of the participation methods and programs that exist in private enterprises in the United States are discretionary on management's part. Management can create the program and it can also abandon it. Exceptions to this primacy of management control are collective bargaining, in which management and union jointly bargain wages and conditions of employment, and union-management cooperation which is established under a collective bargaining framework.

Workers' participation in Europe, often called industrial democracy, has developed over the years from different philosophical roots than participative management in America. European-style participation is based upon Socialist political ideologies and is commonly woven into the laws of the various European countries.

Barriers to Participation

There are several possible barriers to effective participation that may exist in an organization.

A common barrier is a manager who has an authoritarian personality. Many managers possess a strong power motive. The very idea of consultation with subordinates is anathema to them. Such personalities will not accept suggestions from people beneath them in the hierarchy.

Another possible barrier is the phenomenon of pseudoparticipation. For a good number of years both serious scholarly works and popular management literature have discussed the concepts and advantages of participative management. Some executives have picked up some of these ideas and have tried to apply them in their own establishments. But often their efforts have contained a few surface "trappings" of participation without a genuine sharing of decision making. Some managers speak of developing a "sense" of participation among their employees. They exhort them to put their "shoulders to the wheel and all push together." They try to persuade them to work more enthusiastically to perform activities designed and regulated by management. This type of participation is task involvement but not ego involvement. It is not true participation.

Manipulation of the subordinates is another form of pseudoparticipation. In conducting meetings with subordinates, ostensibly for the purpose of joint consultation and problem solving, some managers try to manipulate their subordinates to get them to support a preconceived plan that was developed by that manager. Commonly the subordinates can see through such schemes. They may go along with the boss' game because of his power position but not necessarily because they believe in his plans. If the boss wishes to sell his plan to the department members, he should approach the matter from the standpoint of selling and persuasion. He should not pretend that they will have a role in shaping the plan.

Another potential barrier to participation is the power position of the supervisor who is conducting a problem-solving meeting with his subordinates. This situation can be accentuated if the subordinates are timid in their relations with their supervisor and if they sense that the supervisor is not fully receptive to their true feelings and suggestions. The subordinates know that he makes decisions regarding pay raises, promotions, and work assignments. Furthermore, the supervisor can subtly (or overtly) reward or penalize them in various ways on a day-to-day basis. Because of these circumstances the subordinates often tend to speak less freely in the presence of the boss. They know well enough not to trod on his pet ideas. And some individuals, seeking to ingratiate themselves with their supervisor, may express views designed to support viewpoints they know he already possesses. It is, perhaps, human nature for a person to feel more at ease among those who agree with him than among those who challenge him. Managers are no exception to this generalization.

If a group of people are called together to participate in a problem-solving conference, their responses may vary appreciably, depending upon whether the meeting is led by the boss or whether it is led by a peer or colleague. Assuming that both individuals are skilled conference leaders, the leader who is an organizational equal to the participants will tend to obtain more spontaneous participation from the conferees. The wise manager who is leading a discussion will carefully refrain from announcing his own personal opinions if he wishes to obtain genuine, uncolored contributions from his subordinates.

Another barrier to effective participation that manifests itself in many situations is the pressure to conform to the common beliefs of the group and of the larger organization. This phenomenon occurs in both the informal friendship and work groups that exist in all work organizations and also in formal groupings of people such as departments, divisions, and companies. This pressure for conformity tends to emerge and develop in order to protect the stability and security of the group or of the formal organizational unit.

Social psychologists and others have investigated many aspects of group conformity. One fascinating analysis of conformity in group decision making is that done by Irving Janis. He uses the term "groupthink" to refer to a mode of thinking that people engage in when they are heavily involved in a cohesive group and when the members' desires for unanimity or consensus override their motivation to realistically examine alternative courses of action. Janis examined the existence of a "groupthink" phenomenon in four decision-making situations of the administrations of four United States presidents—Franklin D. Roosevelt (failure to be prepared for the attack on Pearl Harbor), Harry S. Truman (invasion of North Korea), John F. Kennedy (the Bay of Pigs invasion), and Lyndon B. Johnson (escalation of the Vietnam War). Janis identifies a number of symptoms of "groupthink" in cohesive bodies. Among these are an illusion of invulnerability; unquestioned belief in the group's inherent righteousness; pressure against any group member who expresses strong arguments against the group's stereotypes, illusions, or commitments; and self-censorship of deviations from apparent group consensus. To minimize the possibility of a "groupthink" mentality from developing, Janis gives several suggestions. The leader should assign the role of critical evaluator to each member. The leader should refrain from stating his own preferences at least during the early stages of the deliberations. He should accept criticism of his own judgments. At least one member should be assigned the role of devil's advocate in examining alternative courses of action. Also, trusted outsiders should be consulted or invited to participate in the discussions.[2]

RESEARCH INTO PARTICIPATION

Most of the research investigations into participative management have focused upon those situations in which a leader develops a collaborative relationship with his or her subordinates, consults them from time to time on matters of concern to the work group, shows genuine interest in the people and their suggestions, and allows them discretion in carrying out their duties. Most studies also have dealt with situations in which the group members directly participated in the decision-making process rather than through representatives.

The pioneering research experiment into the effects of democratic methods of leadership was conducted by Lewin, White, and Lippitt at the University of Iowa in 1938. In this study, the effects of autocratic, democratic, and laissez-faire leadership climates upon groups of boys were contrasted. This research was discussed in Chapter 20, Leadership, Supervision, and Management Systems."

Cummings and Molloy have reviewed the findings of seven different rigorously designed experiments into participative management. These involved a variety of work activities such as a laundry, garment making, footwear assembly, clerical work, and maintenance. Generally in these experiments (but with some exceptions), both productivity and employee satisfaction increased under participatory leadership. The authors noted that management's willingness to allow employees to participate in important work decisions lets them know that they are considered competent and valued partners in the organization. This satisfies their needs for recognition, independence, and appreciation by others. Also when employees plan and put into effect their own decisions, satisfaction of the needs and values tied to those decisions is dependent upon effective execution of those decisions.[3]

In reviewing six research experiments that examined the relationship between participation in decision making and member satisfaction, Yukl found that in all studies there was a positive correlation between participation and subordinate satisfaction. In examining seventeen projects that had investigated the relationship between participation and group productivity, he found that eleven had shown a positive correlation between participation and productivity, three found no correlation, two found a negative correlation and one had mixed relationships for two groups.[4]

The Harwood Manufacturing Company, which makes clothing, has long been famous for its continuing commitment to participative management as a basic strategy for operation of its plants. Starting in the late 1930's the owner-president, Alfred J. Marrow, brought in consulting psychologists to develop ways

---

[2] Irving Janis, *Victims of Groupthink* (Boston: Houghton Mifflin Company, 1972), pp. 9, 197–198, 209–218.

[3] Thomas G. Cummings and Edmond S. Molloy, *Improving Productivity and the Quality of Work Life* (New York: Praeger Publishers, 1977), Part III.

[4] Gary Yukl, "Toward a Behavioral Theory of Leadership," *Organizational Behavior and Human Performance*, Vol. 6, No. 4 (July 1971), pp. 414–440.

of improving productivity, reducing labor turnover, and overcoming resistance to changed work methods through use of group problem-solving meetings with the employees. The early activities were controlled experiments. But these were so successful in solving the given problems that top management adopted participative management as a day-to-day way of life.[5]

Evaluation

The weight of evidence supports the conclusion that group participation in decision making often increases group performance and member satisfaction or morale.

Participation also facilitates acceptance of change. People tend to resent change that is forced upon them. How are they to know whether their interests have been adequately considered? In a conference discussion where the people work out the nature and mechanics of a proposed new system, they can analyze all the possible objections and ramifications and decide for themselves whether it is feasible.

Employee development is also enhanced by participative management. Employees, professional personnel, and lower-level administrators get an opportunity to learn about and solve a variety of problems that they would never encounter under conventional authoritarian management, until *after* they might be promoted to higher positions.

However, participation is definitely not a panacea. Participation works best where there is a firm commitment to it on the part of top management and where employees and supervisors have been taught how to participate. Also, it should be noted that there are some situations in which unilateral decisions by the boss are quite appropriate. The manager can't call a meeting every time he is confronted with a decision. In the next section we shall talk about conditions required for effective participation.

CONDITIONS FOR EFFECTIVE PARTICIPATION

Participation is not a magic solution to all the problems encountered in managing a business. Nor can it be used willy-nilly. Procedures for utilizing participation have their time and their place. Let us now examine the factors that determine how, when, and where participation can be effectively and practically employed.

Characteristics of Subordinates

Independence Needs.   Research has demonstrated that subordinates who have strong needs for independence react more favorably toward the opportunity to participate in decision-making activities than do those who have low independence needs and who score high on the authoritarianism measuring scale. By "need for independence" it is meant that the employees have strong drives to

---

[5] Alfred J. Marrow, *The Failure of Success* (New York: American Management Association, 1976) and Alfred J. Marrow, David G. Bowers, and Stanley E. Seashore, *Management by Participation* (New York: Harper & Row, 1967).

express themselves in their work, to exercise their own judgment, to assert themselves, and to figure things out for themselves. Thus participation appeals to persons having this type of personality structure more than it does to those having little interest or desire to exercise their own initiative and assert their independence.[6]

Desire to Participate.   This characteristic is related to the preceding one. Some employees and supervisors are quite content to operate in a framework in which practically all the decisions are made for them. They are content to work in a rigidly structured environment. But for participation to succeed, the people must become interested in the wider ramifications of their jobs, their departments, and their organization. They must want to contribute. They must be motivated in that direction. Of course, proper leadership can stimulate this desire. Employee attitudes toward participation are not immutable. A positive urge in this direction can be cultivated over a period of time by management.

Intelligence and Knowledge.   Subordinates must possess a certain minimum amount of intelligence and knowledge for any participation program to succeed. In other words they must first be capable of contributing, and then they must have something worthwhile to contribute. Because management sets the selection standards for employment, it can control the level of intelligence (generally) of those it puts on the payroll. In the short run, employees may lack the necessary information, background, and knowledge to make worthwhile contributions in any program of participation in decision making. However, information and training programs instituted by management can, in the long run, substantially raise the level of knowledge of the work force so that it can make useful contributions.

Organizational Climate

It would be pretty difficult for a supervisor, on his own initiative, to launch a comprehensive program of consultation or democratic supervision with his men if he were the only supervisor in the entire company who was so inclined. The employees would tend to misunderstand and misinterpret his efforts. If this supervisor's boss were unsympathetic, he would tend to feel that the supervisor was abdicating his leadership authority and responsibility, didn't know his own job, and was generally wasting time.

Basically, then, participation is most likely to succeed when top management (starting with the board of directors and the president) believes in it, encourages it, and practices it in its day-to-day relations with subordinate executives. The pattern of management established at the very top of an organization tends to be transmitted down through successive echelons to the lowest-level supervisors. Executives tend to reinforce and support those of their subordinates who think and act as they do and penalize those who do not conform to their modes of action.

[6] Victor H. Vroom, "Some Personality Determinants of the Effects of Participation," *Journal of Abnormal and Social Psychology*, Vol. 59 (November 1959), pp. 322–327. The subjects of this investigation were 108 first-, second-, and third-line supervisors in a large company whose basic activity was the delivery of packages from stores to private residences.

Problem Must Be Appropriate

An indecisive supervisor who cannot make decisions on routine administrative matters should not waste the time of his subordinates by calling meetings to get opinions on these run-of-the-mill problems. A manager is paid to run his department, to apply his knowledge and judgment, and to make decisions affecting his unit and its employees. It would be ineffective for him to, in effect, look upon his subordinates as a senate continuously in session to help him resolve daily problems. Participation should be utilized for those situations and problems that are important and that have a material impact upon the people involved and the organization.

A manager should not waste the time of all of his subordinates if a particular problem clearly concerns only one or two of his men. He should bring into the picture only those who have an interest and a legitimate concern for the topic. Of course, there are some occasions in which employees and managers may not themselves be directly involved in a problem area but the executive in charge values their counsel or wants them to be informed of what is going on.

Training for Participation

Not only do managers need to learn how to delegate, consult, lead conferences, encourage suggestions, and so on, but also employees need to learn how to work cooperatively and effectively in such situations. If a shop supervisor calls a meeting of all his machine operators and service personnel to figure out better production methods and ways of cutting costs, the employees must be told just what their roles are to be. Is the supervisor simply calling them together to have them serve as a sounding board for a program he has already designed? Or does he want them to assume the major share of the responsibility for improving methods? Will the supervisor be bound by any consensus decision? How should the group view vigorous dissent by a minority? Does the boss expect the employees to do advance preparation before coming to the meeting? How does he expect them to behave in the meeting? What is the role of the union steward?

The point being made here is that management cannot switch from an authoritarian to a participative pattern of leadership overnight and expect employees to respond instantly to the new program. They must be taught just what is expected of them and how they are expected to perform. If employees have been expected to be yes men for years, they cannot suddenly transform themselves into independent, thinking, creative people.

Scope of Authority and Responsibility

Managers should generally invite participation from their subordinates only on problems within their sphere of authority and responsibility. It would invite frustration for a low-ranking supervisor in a shop department to call his people together to arrive at decisions regarding company wage or vacation policy because this is clearly beyond his power to control. Policy questions are primarily the responsibility of top management. It would be very pertinent, however, for the supervisor to invite participation regarding such subjects as work flow, methods, quality, safety, cost control, employee discontents, and housekeeping.

There are some exceptions to the foregoing principle. Sometimes participation programs are set up to create ideas and proposals at lower levels in the organization. These must then be transmitted up through several levels in the structure before a final authoritative decision can be made. In this case the participation may serve as a method of upward communication, as a way of uncovering information and trouble spots that would be otherwise overlooked, and as a means of developing subordinates. In this case the supervisor of the employees who developed the proposal may have to recommend it to his superior before it can be adopted. However, if the participation program is to operate in this way, it is vital that the people involved fully understand just where the final decision-making authority resides.

Time Available

Emergency situations may preclude any consultation with others. A decision on a rush shipment of goods, a tactical action in a strike, a pressing action to meet a short deadline, and an act to avert serious damage to equipment or injury to personnel, may clearly require authoritarian behavior.

TYPES OF PARTICIPATION

As an aid to understanding the various kinds of participation programs and activities that can be utilized, it is helpful to classify them into two broad categories: (1) informal and semiformal methods and (2) formal programs.

Informal and semiformal methods
    A. Individual.
    B. Manager with Group of Subordinates.
Formal programs
    A. Committees.
    B. Junior Boards of Executives.
    C. Collective Bargaining.
    D. Union-Management Cooperation.
    E. Suggestion Plans.
    F. Workers' Participation-European Style.

Informal and Semiformal Methods

The informal and semiformal methods essentially involve relations between a supervisor (or manager) and his or her subordinates. These participation activities tend to take place at irregular intervals. When a specific issue arises, the manager may discuss the matter with one or more of his direct subordinates. In some departments the manager may schedule regular weekly or biweekly meetings with his staff. These meetings may be partially for the purpose of passing on information to the people and partially to involve them in group discussion and decision making.

Individual Participation.   Individual participation can occur in a variety of ways. A manager may invite one of his subordinates to his office to obtain his thoughts regarding a contemplated job assignment. The manager may walk through a production department and stop to chat with one of the employees about different ways of performing the work. An employee may seek out his supervisor to exchange views on a new project. In some relationships a subordinate may initiate actions and issues for his supervisor and they may jointly discuss operating problems almost as equals.

Individual participation occurs in an atmosphere of mutual respect and trust. Both the manager and the subordinates feel that they and the work unit have something to gain by a frank exchange of viewpoints regarding operating problems.

The manager who delegates a considerable amount of responsibility to his subordinates and who practices general and supportive supervision is, in effect, establishing a climate in which his employees feel free to make important decisions regarding their work. This is a form of individual participation.

Individual participation can be very effective, but it has its limitations when compared with group participation. In group discussion the process of free association can take place. A thought contributed by one person sparks an idea in another, and so on in a chain-reaction fashion. Because there are more minds involved in a group discussion, because the people may have specialized knowledge to contribute, and because the people may represent varied backgrounds and interests, the likelihood of developing a group solution that takes into account various special concerns is much higher than with individual one-on-one discussion.

Manager with Group of Subordinates.   Group participation can occur at any level in an organization. A foreman may convene a meeting of hourly paid production workers to discuss safety problems. A personnel director may call his staff together to lay plans to implement a newly developed affirmative action program. The president of a corporation may call a meeting of all the executives reporting to him to work out strategy to deal with an impending strike of the unionized workforce.

In group meetings the manager may allow different degrees of influence by the subordinates. In one case he or she may have already arrived at a tentative decision. He presents it to the assembled group for analysis and discussion and indicates that his decision is subject to change based upon ideas developed in the meeting. A somewhat greater degree of subordinate influence occurs when the manager has not made a decision beforehand. He presents a problem to the group, invites suggestions and analysis, and then makes a final decision. In both these forms the group may be able to propose a greater number of alternatives and trace through more consequences than could the manager working alone. Both of the foregoing degrees of participation are commonly called *consultative management*. The manager reserves final decision-making authority to himself. In practical operation of consultative management, the leader will tend to adopt, in a great majority of cases, the decision that has evolved in the group deliberations. Because he is consulting his subordinates, he must value their collective wisdom. But on rare occasions he may consider it necessary to render a final decision that is in opposition to the consensus of the group.

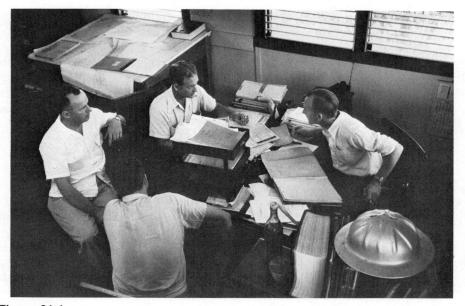

Figure 21-1
An Informal Consultative Management Meeting of a Superintendent and Three Foremen.

Figure 21-1 depicts an informal consultative management meeting of a superintendent with three of his foremen.

Some managers, on some occasions, may choose to allow their subordinates to exercise even greater influence in the decision-making process. They may outline the dimensions of a problem (or group of problems), explain the general limits of authority they and the group possess such as funds available or time constraints, and then ask the group to develop a course of action to solve the problem. With this form of subordinate involvement, the manager serves as a conference leader and perhaps also as a resource person to provide information not already possessed by the group. But he lets it be known that he is seeking a solution developed by the group as a whole. He also indicates that he will support the solution worked out by the group. The manager plays a role in the discussions but he does not dominate them. Some writers call this more advanced form of subordinate influence *democratic management*.

This form of participatory management does not stop at the exit door of the conference room. The leader, on a day-to-day basis, is receptive to suggestions from his people. He encourages them to take the initiative to plan and control their own work. He also develops a collaborative team relationship within the department. Employees trade ideas and help one another.

Formal Programs

Formal participation programs require the creation of organization structures and formal procedures to carry them out. There tends to be a degree of continuity and permanence to these programs. Certain participants acquire formal positions and titles over and above their regular jobs as employees or managers.

Committees. Committees are ubiquitous. They exist in all kinds of organizations and serve many different purposes. A committee is a group of persons, either elected or appointed, created to perform some function or mission. A group of people called together for one meeting does not constitute a committee. A committee has an existence of its own, a chairman, designated members, a defined purpose, and often an agreed-upon set of operating procedures. It may be a temporary or ad hoc committee formed to accomplish a specific mission and when its goal has been accomplished, it goes out of existence. Or a committee may be permanent. An example of a temporary committee is one formed to investigate sites for the building of a new facility. When the property is finally selected and purchased, the committee goes out of existence. An example of a permanent committee is a corporate board of directors.

Although the committee system is subject to faults and although the potential weaknesses of committees have been highly publicized, they can serve a very useful purpose. Many authorities feel that complex organizations cannot be managed successfully without the use of some committees which can be used to tap the expertise of people from varied backgrounds in such activities as planning, policy making, and solving of difficult problems. Good staff units can do a lot of investigative, analytical, and evaluative work, but they cannot fully substitute for the interactive deliberation and testing of ideas among people that goes on in committees.

In addition to the problem-solving contributions that committee members may make to the organization, their involvement in committee work can also provide valuable training and self-development. The members acquire specific knowledge about organizational matters, they gain perspective and understanding, and they may improve their skills at the give and take of group interaction.

Junior Boards of Executives. The junior board of executives system, by which standing committees of managers carry out studies and make recommendations to top management, is also known as multiple management. The idea of junior boards of executives was first installed in American industry by Charles P. McCormick in 1932 at McCormick & Company in Baltimore, Maryland. This system of management has since spread to a number of other companies. Most commonly these boards are composed of members of middle management, with some system existing by which members are rotated into and out of the board.

Generally these junior boards of executives have wide latitude to undertake the study of practically any type of problem area affecting the company's business. Within the board itself there will be committees that carry out investigations in project areas. Typical topics for investigation are company organization, executive compensation, automation, foreign markets, personnel policies, warehousing operations, and use of wage incentives. When the board has reached a decision, a recommendation is sent to top company management, which can accept or reject the proposal.

A junior board of executives can be looked upon as a standing advisory committee to top management. It is a type of "senate" representing middle (and in some companies lower) management in the conduct of the business. The selection of the board members and the choice of subjects for investigation are determined by the board itself. There is little or no dictation from the president of the company regarding the conduct of the board's business. A prime requisite for success of the junior board of executives system is top-management support and encouragement for the whole concept.

In addition to McCormick & Company, some other firms using junior boards of executives are Inland Division of General Motors, Kemper Insurance, Motorola, Fox Grocery, Barber-Greene, Cincinati Enquirer division of Combined Communications, and Memphis Publishing. The president of McCormick & Company believes that the junior boards system has substantially contributed to the company's ability to maintain a 16 percent-a-year growth in profits. The general manager of GM's Inland Division has stated that its middle management team system has been an unqualified success.[7]

Collective Bargaining. Collective bargaining, which occurs when a union represents the employees, is a type of participation program distinctly different from all the other participation methods. Collective bargaining is not instituted by management (except in special circumstances), whereas all of the other programs of participation are discretionary on management's part. Bargaining relationships usually commence as a result of a union organizing campaign and an election conducted by the National Labor Relations Board to determine whether the employees wish to have a union represent them in negotiations with the employer over such matters as wages, hours, and other conditions of employment. Although it must be admitted that in some instances a union and an employer may sign an initial labor agreement over the heads of the employees (that is, without a National Labor Relations Board election to determine employee sentiments regarding unionization), and it must be further agreed that a few unions are not democratically run, in the vast majority of cases unions do solicit member opinions at regular meetings regarding bargaining demands to be made of the employer and regarding the handling of day-to-day problems in the shop. The Labor–Management Reporting and Disclosure Act of 1959 (Landrum–Griffin Act) contains strong provisions to ensure union democracy.

Thus, it can be accurately said that employees through their elected leaders do participate on an equal basis with company representatives in negotiating labor agreements, in administering the agreement, and in processing grievances. The local union leaders, who are usually company employees as well, help make decisions regarding pay rates, seniority rules, pension plans, order of layoff, vacations, holidays, grievance procedures, benefit plans, and hours of work.

Union–Management Cooperation. Historically, the term *union–management cooperation* has meant a formal program of cooperation and consultation between management and union to solve production problems jointly and to devise improvements in plant efficiency for the mutual benefit of both the company and the employees. In recent years joint union–management committees have expanded their areas of activity into health and safety, employee morale, training, pensions, drug addiction and alcoholism, preretirement counseling, and energy conservation. Generally, the proposals generated in these joint committees are looked upon as suggestions to management. This means that management can accept or reject the proposals, and therefore it retains most of its traditional prerogatives. However, a management that is unusually sensitive about placing a

---

[7] "More Power for the Middle Manager," *Dun's Review*, Vol. 111, No. 6 (June 1978).

wall around its inherent rights is unlikely to enter into a cooperation program. The spirit of collaboration, conciliation, and give and take must prevail in order for a program of union–management cooperation to succeed.

A very early program was that begun in the 1920's by the Baltimore and Ohio Railroad and the Machinists union to figure out ways to increase efficiency, reduce waste, improve working conditions, and expand the business. Several thousand joint labor–management committees were established in defense industries during World War II to work on ways of increasing production and employee morale. But nearly all these committees were abandoned at the close of the war.

In the early 1940's a plan was created in the Tennessee Valley Authority upon the suggestion of local union leaders of the Tennessee Valley Trades and Labor Council. This plan has local committees at the various TVA plants plus a central committee to cover the entire system. The TVA plan has been unusually successful. A 1965 study by Patchen of the TVA experience in terms of its impact upon employees revealed that this program of labor–management consultation increases employee feelings of solidarity with the organization and with management and that it increases employee acceptance of work changes. The workers viewed work changes not as something imposed upon them but rather as products of joint consultation.[8]

An unusual form of labor–management cooperation is that established in Jamestown, New York in 1972. This program is unusual because it is a community-wide effort. Prior to the establishment of this program, many manufacturing firms had moved out of Jamestown and the unemployment rate was high. In 1972 a community-wide labor–management committee was formed. Eighteen companies and eleven unions are affiliated with the central committee. Each participating company has an in-plant committee. Committees have worked to raise plant efficiency, train workers, improve labor–management relations and improve the quality of work life. The community committee has also worked to attract new industry to Jamestown. To date, the efforts in Jamestown have been quite successful.

Another form of union–management cooperation is the Scanlon Plan. The Scanlon Plan (named after Joseph Scanlon, who originated the plan in the late 1930's) contains an incentive feature whereby any reduction in plant payroll costs below an agreed-upon standard or norm is passed on to the employees (or shared with them) in the form of a bonus. The standard is expressed as total payroll cost divided by the sales value of the product. Each department has a two-man committee composed of one management and one union representative (usually the foreman and the shop steward). It reviews suggestions obtained from the employees of that department. A larger plantwide screening committee acts upon the suggestions from all the departmental committees. Where it has been installed, the Scanlon Plan has generally worked well. It depends upon a genuine spirit of cooperation for its success. Experience has shown that with such a program the workers are more willing to accept technological change than in the typical company. There is a greater interest by the workers in the problems of management, the employees tend to help one an-

[8] Martin Patchen, "Labor–Management Consultation at TVA: Its Impact on Employees," *Administrative Science Quarterly*, Vol. 10, No. 2 (September 1965), pp. 149–174.

other to a considerable extent, and foremen actively seek (instead of resent) suggestions for improvement from the workers.

Although the idea of union–management cooperation is very appealing, it has not achieved wide acceptance in American industry. Workers often fear that cooperation on cost-cutting campaigns will endanger their own jobs. Union officials sometimes feel that cooperation programs may weaken their bargaining position to press for economic gains. Some executives fear that union–management cooperation will open the door to union invasion of traditional management prerogatives. Cooperation works best when all parties are secure in their relationships with one another.[9]

Suggestion Plans.   A suggestion plan is a formalized system established by an employer to encourage employees to submit ideas that will result in improvement for the business and the organization. The payment of monetary awards for accepted suggestions is a fundamental feature of these plans.

A well-run suggestion program can achieve a number of real benefits for the organization. It provides an additional avenue of upward communication. This is especially important, because higher management, in many organizations, is insulated from the problems and viewpoints of the employees. It provides a means by which employees can achieve some measure of participation in the affairs of the business. A suggestion system is looked upon by some people as a technique for improving employee relations and morale. A primary gain from a properly conducted program is the significant reduction in production and operating costs that can acrue. In addition, employees receive money awards and recognition from management.

Although there is considerable variation from organization to organization as far as the mechanics of their suggestion plans are concerned, the essential features of most plans have much in common. Typically, companies will recognize those ideas that will achieve measurable dollar savings in labor and/or material costs through new methods, procedures, materials, and equipment. They also welcome ideas proposing improvements in safety, housekeeping, employee relations, public relations, and those that aid the organization in general. For these latter types it is usually not possible to calculate a definite dollar benefit that will accrue to the organization from adoption of the suggestion. In this case, token awards are granted.

Suggestions are put in writing on special blanks supplied at convenient locations throughout the working area. These are then dropped into suggestion boxes. They are processed by a suggestion secretary, who may be a member of the industrial relations or industrial engineering departments. Many companies utilize the services of suggestion investigators, who collect all the facts needed to evaluate the ideas adequately. Final decisions on whether to accept, reject, or defer judgment until later are generally made by a suggestion committee, which is usually composed of middle-management individuals. Cash awards are computed on the basis of net annual savings in material and labor costs. Commonly

[9] Sources on union–management cooperation are William L. Batt, Jr. and Edgar Weinberg, "Labor–Management Cooperation Today," *Harvard Business Review*, Vol. 56, No. 1 (January–February 1978), pp. 96–104 and Charlotte Gold, *Employer-Employee Committees and Worker Participation*, Key Issues No. 20 (Ithaca, New York: New York State School of Industrial and Labor Relations, Cornell University 1976).

an employee will receive an award equal to a percentage (often 10 or 15 percent) of the first year's net savings.

As a means of developing employee participation and involvement in the thinking required to run an organization, a suggestion plan is less comprehensive than consultative management, democratic supervision, and union–management cooperation. It relies almost entirely upon written communication. There is little or no opportunity for groups of people to put their heads together to jointly evolve an idea and a plan. If an employee's idea is rejected because the suggestion committee misunderstood his meaning, there is little chance for him to explain it in face-to-face discussion.

However, the record does show that many companies have operated successful programs in the sense that a reasonable portion of the employees do contribute written suggestions and that 20 to 25 percent of these earn cash awards. The claim is not necessarily made that the suggestion plan is a broad comprehensive participation system.

WORKERS' PARTICIPATION—EUROPEAN STYLE

The movement toward participation by employees in organizational decision making has progressed farther in European countries than in the United States. In Europe this process is designated by such labels as industrial democracy, self-management, workers' participation, or the works council system. Whereas participative management in the United States tends to be rather informal and dependent upon the inclinations of managers in their particular organizational units, the process in European countries is much more highly structured. In many countries it is mandated by law.

The central core of the various systems consists of the works council, which is comprised of worker representatives elected by the employees in each plant or by the union. Large multi-unit companies also have central councils composed of representatives of the various plant councils. These councils articulate employee interests in discussions with management.

Although the organizational arrangements for workers' participation vary from country to country, a brief look at the mechanisms in two countries—West Germany and Yugoslavia—will be illustrative.

The works council system in Germany evolved over a period of about a hundred years but it did not achieve fully functioning status until after World War II. The West German Codetermination Law of 1951 established substantial employee influence in the direction of companies in the coal, iron, and steel industries. Under German corporation law most companies have two directing boards. The upper board is called a supervisory board and the lower board is called the management board. The Codetermination Law stipulates that in the coal, iron, and steel industries shareholders shall appoint five members of the supervisory board, the employees shall select five members (two appointed by the works council and three by the trade union), and one member shall be chosen by the board itself as a neutral. This eleven-member supervisory board then selects a three-member managing board, consisting of a commercial director, a technical director, and a labor director. In actual day-to-day practice the employee representatives on the two boards tend to concern themselves with employee-relations matters and do not try to actually manage the companies. This is left to the management representatives. But the labor representatives do possess considerable power, which is brought into play upon occasion. Although judgments on the values of codetermination vary depending on their source and the particular feature under scrutiny, the overall evaluation is positive. Rank-and-file workers strongly approve of it. The harsh authority relationships in the mines and steel firms that existed through World War II have disappeared. A 1968 survey of employee attitudes reported better social services as the primary benefit, followed, in descending order, by higher pay, improved working conditions, increased influence in personnel and business policies, and job security.[10]

The Works Constitution Act of 1952 extended workers' participation to all other private companies having 500 or more employees. Under this law employees in each enterprise elect one third of the members of the supervisory board while the shareholders choose two thirds. This board then selects the three-person managing board which runs the company.

Demands by German labor unions for parity membership in supervisory boards throughout industry led to the enactment of the Codetermination Act of 1976 which became fully effective on July 1, 1978. This law represented a compromise between the position of the unions and the position of businesses which feared that true equality of representation would cripple the decision-making process in companies. This new law partially supercedes the 1952 law in that all companies having 2,000 or more employees have approximate (but not full) parity between worker and stockholder representatives on the supervisory boards.[11]

Under the 1976 law the number of supervisory board members is determined by the total number of employees in the corporation. For companies which regularly employ up to 10,000 people, there must be twelve board members and those with up to 20,000 employees must have sixteen members. Companies larger than this must have twenty member boards. In a sixteen member board there are eight shareholder representatives and eight employee representatives. The law provides that two of the employee representatives must be selected by the union. The remaining six employee members are composed of both blue-collar and white-collar representatives in the same ratio of these two categories as they exist in the total employment of the company. The chairman and vice-chairman are chosen by a two-thirds majority. If such a majority cannot be obtained, a second balloting within the board is conducted. In this case the chairman is chosen by the stockholder members and the vice-chairman is chosen by the employee members. In conducting its business, decisions of the board are made by a simple majority vote. In the event of a tie, the chairman has the power to cast one additional vote to break it. So we can see that the stockholder voice has a slight power advantage. The actual day-to-day management of a company is handled by the management board, which is appointed by the supervisory board.[12]

[10] Heinz Hartmann, "Codetermination in West Germany," *Industrial Relations*, Vol. 9, No. 2 (February 1970), pp. 137–147.

[11] Full parity continues to exist in the coal and steel industries provided by the 1951 Codetermination Law. Workers in other industries continue to have one-third representation on supervisory boards in companies having from 600 to 2000 employees.

[12] Klaus E. Agthe, "Mitbestimmung: Report on a Social Experiment," *Business Horizons*, Vol. 20, No. 1 (February 1977) pp. 5–14.

Although it is too early to tell the full impact of the 1976 law, the system of codetermination that has existed in Werst Germany since 1951 has been met with general approval. Some experts have credited the workers' participation system with contributing toward the peaceful labor-management relations that occurred in West Germany for many years.[13]

The Yugoslavian system is called self-management. It was set up in 1950 after Marshall Tito broke away from the Soviet Union's style of central control of the economy and moved to decentralize decision making to the level of the enterprise. In this country most of the nonagricultural labor force works in enterprises whose policies are set by worker-elected councils. In every firm the workers elect a workers' council that consists of from 15 to 120 members, depending upon the size of the enterprise. This council selects a managing board whose membership includes the managing director. It is his job to really manage the business. His term of office is four years but he can be removed from office during that period by action of the council. To make the system work effectively, the Yugoslavs have found it necessary over the years to officially endow the managing director with considerable authority. Thus, the charters of most enterprises now state that the managing director has the power to coordinate all the affiliates of a firm in the interests of the whole organization, to ask the councils to annul acts by their management boards if he considers them unsound, and to choose his own advisory body composed of his top executives and technical specialists.[14] Most observers feel that the Yugoslavian system of self-management has been reasonably successful both from the economic and worker satisfaction standpoints.

Strauss and Rosenstein have classified the European (and Israeli) participation systems into three types according to their decision-making processes. First is the joint consultation model, in which management makes the final decisions but employee representatives are heard. This system is used in Sweden, Great Britain, and France. The second model is the joint decision-making model, in which worker representatives and management are jointly represented on a decision-making body (with the employee representatives often in the minority). Illustrative of this pattern is codetermination in West Germany and the Histadrut's joint management plan in Israel.[15] The third model is the workers control model, where final decision-making authority resides in the elected representatives of the workforce. This is the system used in Yugoslavia.[16]

For the present there seems to be no attempt to import European-style participation into the United States. In a sense the works council system fills a void in Europe that is met by the local union in the United States. Trade unions in Europe commonly bargain only at the level of the whole industry, where the

[13] Time lost and workers involved in strikes are very low in West Germany compared with other industrial countries in Europe and with the United States and Canada. See Burton Teague, "Can Workers Participate in Management Successfully?" *The Conference Board Record*, Vol. 8, No. 7 (July 1971), pp. 48–52.

[14] Gilbert Burck, "A Socialist Enterprise That Acts Like a Fierce Capitalistic Competitor," *Fortune*, Vol. 85, No. 1 (January 1972), pp. 82–91, 126.

[15] Histadrut is both a very powerful trade union and the operator of major economic enterprises in Israel.

[16] George Strauss and Eliezer Rosenstein, "Workers Participation: A Critical View," *Industrial Relations*, Vol. 9, No. 2 (February 1970), pp. 197–214.

broad structure of wages and terms of employment are settled. They do not participate in day-to-day labor affairs at the shop level as do American unions. However, European workers do have an advantage over their American counterparts in that their works councils are integral parts of their enterprises and that their structure for participation in enterprise decisions is written into law in most instances.

Questions for review and discussion

1. What is meant by the term participation? Distinguish between genuine and pseudoparticipation.
2. Traditionally why is participation carried on more frequently at higher levels in a business organization than at the foreman-worker level?
3. What are the advantages of participation to the organization? To the individual employee?
4. Give some examples of situations in which it would be inadvisable to invite participation from subordinates.
5. "The position of a leader is weakened if he consults his subordinates. They tend to acquire doubts as to his command of the situation, and this causes him to lose control." Discuss this viewpoint.
6. Why has the committee method of deliberation and decisionmaking been subject to so much criticism? Despite their shortcomings, committees are widely used in both the private and public sectors. Why to you think this is so?
7. In what ways does collective bargaining differ from the other kinds of participation activities and programs discussed in this chapter?
8. What is meant by the term union–management cooperation? What forces have impeded the adoption of these programs throughout industry?
9. Compare and contrast systems of participation in management in Europe and the United States. How would you account for the differences?
10. Explain the system of Codetermination used in West Germany. Do you think such a system would work in the United States? Why or why not?

Suggestions for further reading

BERNSTEIN, PAUL. *Workplace Democratization: Its Internal Dynamics.* Kent, Ohio: Kent State University Press, 1976.

CHANEY, FREDERICK B. and KENNETH S. TEEL. "Participative Management-A Practical Experience," *Personnel*, Vol. 49, No. 6 (November–December 1972), pp. 8–19.

EWING, DAVID W. "Who Wants Corporate Democracy?" *Harvard Business Review*, Vol. 49, No. 5 (September–October, 1971), pp. 12–14, 16, 18–21, 24–28, 146–150.

FOY, NANCY and HERMAN GADON. "Worker Participation: Contrasts in Three Countries," *Harvard Business Review*, Vol. 54, No. 3, (May–June, 1976), pp. 71–83.

FURLONG, JAMES C. *Labor in the Boardroom.* Princeton, N.J.: Dow Jones Books, 1977.

JANIS, IRVING L. *Victims of Groupthink.* Boston: Houghton Mifflin Company, 1972.

JENKINS, DAVID. *Job Power: Blue and White Collar Democracy.* Baltimore: Penguin Books, Inc., 1974.

WEINBERG, EDGAR. "Labor-Management Cooperation: A Report of Recent Initiatives," *Monthly Labor Review,* Vol. 99, No. 4, (April, 1976), pp. 13–22.

WILLIAMS, ERVIN (ed.) *Participative Management: Concepts, Theory, and Implementation.* Atlanta: Georgia State University, 1976.

Discipline

Discipline is essential to all organized group action. The members must control their individual urges and cooperate for the common good. In other words they must reasonably conform to the code of behavior established by the leadership of the organization so that the agreed-upon goals can be accomplished.

If the membership of any organization, whether a club, company, union, or nation, will not abide by some code of rules or laws, then that organization faces imminent collapse. Anarchy and chaos ensue. Repeatedly the world has witnessed the tragic spectacle of anarchy, mutiny, terrorism, and social disintegration in such countries as Zaire (formerly the Belgian Congo) in the early 1960's and Lebanon, Northern Ireland, and Cambodia in the 1970's.

In the work organization, skill in achieving a healthy state of discipline is an important qualification for the supervisor. Some supervisors have the knack of developing a willing conformance with the rules of the plant among their people. The employees cooperate, conform, and regulate themselves almost without their noticing any ostensible imposition of authority by the supervisor. On the other hand, other supervisors can rule only, it seems, by frequent resorts to threats and punishment. And with still other supervisors, the people do as they please and violate rules apparently with impunity.

The Meaning of Discipline

Webster's Dictionary gives three basic meanings to the word *discipline*. First it states that it is training that corrects, molds, strengthens, or perfects. The second meaning is that it is control gained by enforcing obedience. The third meaning is punishment or chastisement.[1] If we combine meanings one and two we can say that discipline involves the conditioning or molding of behavior by applying rewards or penalties. The third meaning is more narrow in that it pertains only to the act of punishing wrongdoers.

The first dictionary meaning will be treated in this chapter under the heading "Positive Approach." This is the kind of discipline that all managements should seek to create. Positive discipline is actually broader and more fundamental than the dictionary phrase *training that molds, corrects, strengthens, or perfects* implies. Positive discipline involves the creation of an attitude and an organizational climate wherein the employees willingly conform to established rules and regulations. It is achieved when management applies the principles of positive motivation, when sound leadership is exercised by supervision, and when the entire organization is managed efficiently.

The second meaning of discipline encompasses the use of penalties or the threat of penalties to cause people to obey orders and to live up to the rules of the game. Often force is employed. This is the kind of discipline exercised by sea captains over sailors since the earliest days of civilization and the kind used in military forces the world over. This form of discipline is explained in this chapter under the heading "Negative Approach."

In all organizations, regardless of whether positive or negative discipline is utilized, some individuals will, upon occasion, break the rules. They are then brought to see the error of their ways and the need for improving performance by applying some form of punishment. This is the third dictionary meaning described above. Under the concept of positive discipline the punishment is administered to correct and rehabilitate, not to injure. Under the concept of negative discipline the punishment is for retribution and to scare others so they will not commit the same crime. Administering the program, handling violators, and assigning penalties are covered in this chapter under the heading "Administering the Disciplinary Program."

APPROACHES TO DISCIPLINE

Because the objective in any organized group endeavor is to develop in the participants such an attitude and behavior that they conform to established norms of conduct, the question is how this can be achieved. On the one hand, those in charge can rule with an iron hand, punish rule violators severely, and, in general, force the members to obey and conform. This mode of leadership has variously been called negative discipline, punitive discipline, autocratic discipline, or rule through fear. The other approach is to develop in people a willingness to obey and abide by the rules and regulations. They do so because

[1] *Webster's New Collegiate Dictionary* (Springfield, Mass.: G. & C. Merriam Company, 1953), p. 236.

they want to, not because they are afraid of the consequences of disobedience. This form of discipline has been called positive or constructive discipline. Let us now examine the methods and implications of each type of discipline.

Negative Approach

This is basically the "big stick" approach to leadership. In industry this brand of disciplinary control was prevalent in the handling of hourly workers prior to the widespread growth of unions in the late 1930's. The union movement has been very successful in providing a considerable measure of security for the workers by granting them protection against arbitrary treatment by management. Disciplinary penalties are often appealed through the grievance procedure. If necessary these may be taken to arbitration for impartial review.

Of course, unions represent only a minority, albeit a large minority, of the employed persons in this country. The threat of punishment is employed by many managements to keep people in line. Although it may be infrequent that a person is suspended or discharged, the power of the boss to impose such penalties is kept ever present in the employee's minds. Written warnings may be handed out extensively to those who fail to meet the established standards of production or to those who are absent from work. The foreman may threaten individuals who do not respond as he expects. And of course during periods of business recession, the likelihood of being weeded out is prominent in employees' minds (especially in those companies in which management has considerable discretion as to whom it terminates).

The basic fallacy in negative discipline is that it achieves only the minimum performance necessary to avoid punishment. The people are not given a say-so in formulating the rules, and they are not taught the reason why. They are taught only that they will be punished if they break a rule. The rule-through-fear approach puts the emphasis upon avoidance of punishment, not upon enthusiastic, wholehearted cooperation.

Those who base their leadership upon rule through fear count upon making an example of violators. Public knowledge of the punishment (usually severe) is expected to serve as a deterrent to others. Yet in the whole history of crime, punishment has never been demonstrated to be a truly effective deterrent. The man who breaks the rules does not plan that far ahead. He is not thinking of the consequences. He is thinking only of his immediate wants.

As a philosophy of management for the long run and for the vast majority of followers, the practice of rule through fear can have only limited success. But this does not deny that for certain subordinates at certain times power and force may be the only answers. Some employees, as a consequence of their background and personality development, may respond only to the supervisor who uses a policy of "be tough."

Positive Approach

Positive discipline, often called constructive discipline, consists of that type of supervisory leadership that develops a willing adherence to the necessary rules and regulations of the organization. The employees, both as individuals and as a group, adhere to the desired standards of behavior because they understand, believe in, and support them.

Discipline must take the form of positive support and reinforcement for approved actions. This is fundamental to all learning. Punishment may be applied for improper behavior, but this is carried out in a supportive, corrective manner. There is no vindictiveness. The aim is to help, not harm, the individual. The supervisor lets it be known that he approves of the violator as a person but that he is training the employee in regard to a specific action.

A necessary prerequisite for the positive approach to discipline is communicating the requirements of the job and the rules and regulations to the employees. Every man must know, when he is hired and henceforth, just what management and his immediate supervisor expect of him. The performance standards (that is, workloads) must be fair, attainable with reasonable effort, and consistent from job to job. The rules likewise must be reasonable and few in number. Supervision must communicate the kind of positive behavior expected of employees rather than dwell upon an exhaustive list of detailed prohibitions.

In creating a climate of positive discipline, the supervisor seeks to build in his people a sense of personal responsibility and self-discipline. He applies principles of positive motivation and enlightened leadership. He recognizes individual differences among his subordinates and varies his methods and appeals as necessary.

When people are well trained so that they know how far they can go and what the limits of tolerated conduct are, they acquire a sense of security. They know the rules of the game, and they know where they stand.

In orienting a new person to his job and the company, the supervisor should explain what work performance is expected and what help is available to achieve it. He should then discuss the principal standards of behavior expected. This will ordinarily include such items as good attendance, notification when justifiably absent, punctuality, cooperation with the supervisor and fellow employees, standards of morality and honesty, and wakefulness throughout the work shift (no sleeping on the job). Particular circumstances in certain shops may require special no-smoking and other safety regulations.

To achieve constructive discipline, a supervisor must set a good example. For example, if he expects his employees to arrive at work every day on time, he must also arrive on time.

Group Responsibility.   If a supervisor takes the proper steps to build a cohesive, loyal work group, he will find that the group members will generally act to support and augment his disciplinary efforts. To do this he must first recognize the existence of the informal group and consult with his subordinates as a group in departmental meetings. He can lead discussions covering the plant rules and regulations as well as the need for them. The people can discuss how these apply to them in their own work situation. If the group understands and believes in the rules, it will often exert social pressure upon its members to insure that they live up to the rules. The group in an informal way may supplement the supervisor's efforts in such areas as prevention of horseplay, achieving good attendance, doing one's fair share of any team work, and controlling the length of coffee breaks.

In formal work organizations employee acceptance of rules and regulations could be greater if they were given a voice in their formulation. This could be accomplished in group meetings where the supervisor encouraged the people to agree upon those minimum norms of conduct which they felt were necessary for effective functioning of the group. Presumably these norms would be those of particular relevance to that group. They would be but a part of the overall regulations of the total organization.

In actual industrial practice management rarely involves the employees in either the formulation or the enforcement of plant rules and regulations. Management almost universally considers discipline to be a management prerogative and responsibility. It is reluctant to share this responsibility with employees or with the union.

ADMINISTERING THE DISCIPLINARY PROGRAM

Even under the best conditions and with excellent supervisory leadership and employee training, somebody is bound to step over the traces now and then. When this happens what action should management take? Are there in existence any generally accepted principles to guide management? Will certain measures be more effective in correcting the errant employee? Will certain actions have harmful repercussions upon future discipline in the organization?

Administrative Justice

Well-established principles and procedures for the handling and adjudicating of civil and criminal offenses against society have evolved in our legal system over a great many years via both common and statute law. Although administrative justice within private organizaitons has not developed to as advanced a state as in the public law field, certain powerful forces have been operating to create a body of fairly well accepted principles and procedural requirements.

Probably foremost as a positive force in this direction has been the impact of unionization upon employers and the work force. The presence of a union in a company means, almost invariably, the installation of a formal grievance procedure and generally arbitration as the final step in settling unresolved grievances. It is now about forty years since unions have become widespread in industry. We have accumulated forty years of arbitration experience that has hammered out certain guidelines for the administration of employee justice within the organization. One might say that we have developed an industrial code of common-law principles and precedents. The essence of the matter is that establishments should follow "due process" procedures.[2] Due process means that management must provide the individual with a written statement of the charges against him together with the reasons for the penalty. The individual must have full opportunity to defend himself and to utilize the formal grievance procedure. Grievance and arbitration procedures have developed over the years to the point that man-

---

[2] A full exposition of due process in industrial discipline is given in Orme W. Phelps, *Discipline and Discharge in the Unionized Firm* (Berkeley and Los Angeles: University of California Press, 1959), pp. 2–4, 141–143.

agement must bear the burden of proof to show both the fact of wrongdoing and the need for punishment.

It is important to note that disciplinary procedures and grievance procedures interact. Discipline administered by the first-line supervisor is one principal cause for later grievance appeal by the employee and the union. The disciplinary penalty may have been applied for a variety of alleged infractions such as tardiness, absenteeism, low output, excessive defective work, intoxication on the job, insubordination, horseplay, or violation of safety rules. If management takes proper care to administer its discipline fairly and with due concern for procedural safeguards that are designed to protect the rights of the parties, then there is less likelihood of subsequent charges by the employee or union of injustice or discrimination.

Another force that has stimulated the adoption of sound administrative justice and "due process" has been the growing bureaucratization of modern organizations. Systematic, formal procedures have been established to preserve the soundness of the organization and to protect the rights of the members. Employees often spend their entire work careers with one or two organizations. They must be assured that they will be treated fairly by management. They cannot continually quit to escape oppressive conditions.

Still another force leading to the practice of administrative justice has been the modern human-relations movement, which has emphasized concern for individual dignity and rights, sound leadership and managerial climate, positive motivation, and a concern for job satisfaction and the well-being of employees.

It is paradoxical to note that although collective bargaining has had a powerful influence upon the handling of discipline in industry, labor–management agreements contain very little on the subject. It is very rare to find the company rules and regulations with their accompanying penalties shown in the labor agreement. Traditionally management initiates the disciplinary policy and administers the program. The employees and the union have the right to submit a grievance if they do not like the way a case has been handled.

As far as contract language is concerned, most contracts merely state that management has the right to discipline, suspend, or discharge for *just cause* and that employees have the right to submit grievances if they consider an action unfair. Just cause means for good and sufficient reason.[3] Some contracts specify the powers of the arbitrator in ruling on discipline cases. Usually he can reverse a penalty if he does not believe there has been just cause for the punishment. He can also modify penalties that he considers too severe for the offense. Even when the contract language is silent on these matters most arbitrators assume that they have the right to do the foregoing things.

Principles for Administration of Disciplinary Action

In administering discipline and penalizing employees, management must constantly be aware of the dual objectives of preserving the interests of the organiza-

---

[3] In determining whether an employee has been disciplined for "just cause," arbitrators consider the following three factors: (1) Did the employee in fact commit the improper act? (2) If he did, should he be punished for his behavior? (3) Does the penalty assigned by management fit the nature of the offense?

tion as a whole and protecting the rights of the individual. Unless sound policies are adopted and orderly procedures followed, there is a danger that management will look at a case solely in terms of its own needs at the moment rather than in terms of the needs of the employee as well as the organization. Short-run expediency might prevail over long-run considerations. Let us now examine the principal ingredients of a sound disciplinary system.

Definite Policy and Procedure

It is the responsibility of top management to give serious consideration to the need for achieving a healthy state of discipline throughout the organization. It must decide what kind of behavior it expects from its employees and how it hopes to achieve this. Presumably the objective is to create a positive, constructive form of discipline through sound leadership and adequate training of all employees.

Top management must carefully think out the issue of the role of the first-line supervisor in the disciplinary system. Because of the need for consistency of action throughout the company and because the union will generally appeal the penalty over the foreman's head if it is dissatisfied, most industrial concerns have tended to centralize a considerable amount of authority in the hands of the industrial relations (or personnel) director. This can be carried too far however.

> The personnel manager of a small manufacturer proudly displayed his book of rules and penalties and announced (to the author in an interview), "I handle all disciplinary problems in my plant. The foremen bring the violators to my office, I listen to both their stories, collect further evidence where necessary, and then announce my decision. The foremen in this plant are not able to make proper judgments regarding these cases. Therefore, I handle the whole thing."

With such a policy as followed in that company the foremen are bound to lose respect and control of their employees.

The need to maintain consistency of action throughout the organization is not incompatible with the need to preserve the authority and position of the foreman. How can this be done? The foreman must be fully instructed regarding the rules and regulations, behavior expected from employees, progressive disciplinary penalties, and the rights of all parties—management, employees, and union. The foreman should be given the authority to issue oral and written warnings on his own. For cases that he thinks are serious enough to warrant suspension and discharge, he should consult his line superior or the industrial relations director before taking action. This not only insures consistency of action throughout the company but also prevents a worker from being fired because of capricious or ill-considered action by the supervisor. In these more serious cases, after all the pertinent facts have been brought out and a decision agreed upon, the first-line supervisor should announce the action to the affected employee.

To insure that the discipline policies and procedure are carefully formulated, that no essential elements are overlooked, and that members of management will support the program, there is considerable merit to involving representatives of middle and lower management in the process of developing the system.

Communication of Rules

Employees must have knowledge of the rule before they can be held accountable. Arbitrators have rescinded penalties when such was not the case.

The most commonly used method of informing employees about company rules is to include a list of the rules, penalties, and explanations thereof in the employee handbook. This is usually handed to a person at the time he is hired. This can be followed up with oral explanations of the more important rules during the initial orientation program. Usually this explanation is given in the department by the employee's supervisor. The reasons behind the rules should also be explained.

In addition to the statement in the handbook and the explanation by the supervisor, the list of rules and penalties may be posted on the bulletin board.

Burden of Proof

The principle of law underlying the English and United States legal systems, that an individual is presumed innocent until proven guilty, applies to industrial discipline cases as well. The burden of proof is upon the employer to show that the worker is guilty of the alleged offense. The degree of proof tends to vary with the seriousness of the charge. If there is serious doubt, arbitrators tend to give the employee the benefit of the doubt.

Consistency of Treatment

This is one of the most important principles and one that is too easily ignored. Management must not punish one man for an offense and ignore the same offense committed by another (often, more favored) employee. This kind of inconsistency can happen because supervisors in different departments have different standards of what they expect and have different tolerance limits when employees deviate somewhat from the standard. Thus, one supervisor may overlook the occasional taking of a few pencils by an office employee, whereas another considers such action to be stealing and grounds for discharge. In addition to this, a supervisor may have a grudge against one of his men and seize upon any plausible pretext to punish him, whereas a more favored employee may be granted wide latitude.

The best way to achieve consistency of treatment and application of the rules is through supervisory training courses and by consistent action by higher management on a day-to-day basis as cases are brought up.

Consider Circumstances of the Case

The need for consistency does not mean that two persons committing an identical offense must always receive identical penalties. The background and circumstances of each case may call for differential treatment. But consistency does require that both employees know that they have violated a rule. Management must not condone an infraction by one and not the other. Both must be handled with equal gravity. But it is in deciding the severity of the penalty, or indeed whether there should be any punishment at all, that management must grant due consideration to the full circumstances surrounding each case.

Company policy may specify that any employee who is absent for five consecutive days without notifying the company as to his reason is automatically terminated. Such discharge may actually be invoked in the case of a worker who has had a bad record of unjustified absences. However, a long-service employee with a good employment record may suffer no penalty at all when it is demonstrated that he was absent and did not call in only because he had gone to his hunting camp on an island in the north woods for the weekend and had become bound in by severe storms and a breakdown of his motor launch.

Therefore, extenuating circumstances can modify or dismiss a penalty in a particular case.

Progressive Penalties

Industrial disciplinary penalties have become fairly well standardized as a result of custom and practice. In ascending order of severity these are as follows:

1. Simple oral warning.
2. Oral warning that is noted in the person's employment record.
3. Written warning noted in employment record.
4. Suspension from the job, usually varying in length from one day to two weeks.
5. Discharge

Sometimes demotion is used as a penalty as is, also, the withholding of a scheduled pay increase. In industrial employment a monetary fine is almost never employed, although this practice is very common in professional team sports, such as baseball, football, and hockey.

In accordance with the concept of positive, corrective discipline, only oral or written warnings are assigned for minor offenses. For the average person such knowledge is sufficient to prevent a repetition. If minor offenses occur again and again, the penalty becomes more severe. A very serious first offense (such as stealing a substantial amount from the employer) usually brings immediate discharge.

The slate is normally wiped clean at the end of one or two years. This makes sense. There is no justification for holding against a man, in perpetuity, his indiscretions of past years if he has reformed himself in the meantime.

Reasonable Rules and Standards

The rules and standards of conduct should be reasonable. The plant conditions and management climate must be such that they are capable of attainment. Thus, if a supervisor plans to penalize an employee who does not produce up to standard, he must first of all determine whether the standard of output is attainable by the average employee and whether the individual is capable of producing to standard.

One plant has rather poor working conditions. The employees consistently break a company rule against littering the stairways with trash and bottles; yet the rule is difficult to enforce because there are no lunch room or locker room facilities. Hence, the employees have no other place to eat lunch or to take their rest breaks.

Right of Appeal

Whether a person has actually committed an infraction of the rules may be a matter of opinion in certain instances and depend on the frame of reference of the person making the accusation. For example, if a man disagrees with his boss vigorously on how to carry out an assignment, does this constitute insubordination? For this reason the accused employee should always have the right to appeal to higher authority. Even if the man is truly guilty as charged, it may be best to hold a full hearing before higher authorities to satisfy all parties to the case that the employee has been justly treated.

Now it is a well-established principle of law that a person must not be judged by his accuser. The prosecution and judicial functions must be separated. The judge should not be a party to the dispute or issue. But in work organizations this principle is not fully adhered to. Line managers usually determine whether a violation has occurred, decide its severity, and invoke a penalty against the involved employee. If the employees are represented by a union, a worker who feels that he has been disciplined unjustly can appeal the case through the successive steps of the grievance procedure. He may, if the union officials think he has a strong case, have the full power of the union behind him. Presumably as the case is appealed to successively higher levels of managers, these will take a more detached and broad view than would the man's immediate supervisor. The first genuinely neutral review of a discharge case comes if the union takes it all the way to arbitration. The arbitrator serves as a judge or impartial umpire. Of course, the mere fact that a case can be appealed to arbitration causes both the union and company to sit back and examine a case from all sides to judge in advance how an arbitrator *would* decide such an issue if it were actually brought to him.

Nonunion companies can also set up a formal appeals procedure. However, arbitration is practically never used as a final step. The chief executive officer serves as the final appeal step. His objectivity and impartiality will largely depend upon his philosophy of management, his personality, and the circumstances in the particular situation. A distinct separation of the judicial review from the executive function would require wholly different organizational arrangements than exist in most business firms.

RULES AND PENALTIES

Sound management requires that a reasonably comprehensive list of rules and regulations be adopted and reduced to writing. This should be done initially when management formulates its disciplinary policy. The very existence of a carefully developed schedule of rules signifies that management has given reasonable consideration to its disciplinary program. If a company has never thought out its disciplinary code, it can some day find itself in the very awkward spot of creating a rule after someone has done something that displeases management. In civil affairs a person cannot be prosecuted for a law that was legislated only after he committed an act.

Below is a listing of most of the common rules adopted in work organizations. They are grouped into two broad categories: (1) minor or moderate offenses, and (2) serious offenses. Of course, the specific situation in a particular establishment may cause an offense listed as "minor or moderate" to be so serious as to justify discharge. Thus, this listing should be viewed as illustrative only. It should also be noted that circumstances in a department or plant may require the adoption of many special rules. Safety rules are a good example of items that must be tailor-made to the situation:

I *Minor or Moderate Offenses*

Oral or written warning may be assigned for first offense; penalties will become progressively stiffer with repeated violation. Eventual discharge can result.
  a. Habitual tardiness
  b. Unexcused absence on one or more scheduled work days
  c. Failure to report accidental injury
  d. Leaving job or work area without authorization
  e. Loafing
  f. Individual gambling on company property
  g. Fighting
  h. Horseplay
  i. Unauthorized selling or canvassing on company property
  j. Sleeping on the job
  k. Smoking in a prohibited area
  l. Failure to obey safety rules
  m. Reporting for work or being on duty while intoxicated
  n. Clock-punching of another's time card
  o. Concealing one's defective work
  p. Work output below standard
  q. Excessive defective work due to employee's own errors

II *Serious Offenses*

First offense can bring suspension or discharge
  a. Malicious damage or destruction of company property
  b. Gross insubordination
  c. Gross immoral, indecent, or disgraceful conduct
  d. Stealing
  e. Carrying concealed weapons
  f. Promotion of gambling on company property
  g. Attacking another with intent to seriously injure or maim
  h. Deliberate falsification of company records

A Uniform, Published Scale of Penalties?

Opinion differs as to the desirability of fixing in advance a uniform scale of penalties for the various offenses. Those who oppose such a practice claim that the circumstances of each case are different, and it is impossible to decide ahead of time an appropriate penalty that would fit every instance of a particular offense. In some cases extenuating circumstances would justify a lighter penalty, whereas in others a harsher penalty might be called for. Is it as serious for a file clerk to sleep on the job as it is for a plant guard or watchman? If stealing is grounds for discharge, would it be fair to fire an office worker who takes a few wooden lead pencils?

There are some powerful arguments in favor of adopting a schedule of penalties for each offense. It insures consistency of treatment throughout all divisions of a company. Consistency is also achieved over time. An offense today is treated the same as the same offense a year ago. Employees have memories and equitable treatment appeals to them. Employees know where they stand and what to expect if they kick over the traces. A published list of penalties adds an aura of legitimacy to management enforcement action. Excessive or unusual penalties cannot be put into effect by ill-tempered or vindictive supervisors.

A written scale of penalties can be wholly compatible with the logical need for giving full consideration to the severity and circumstances of each offense. Consider the following example:

Penalties and Occurrences

Offense	First		Second		Third	
	Min.	Max.	Min.	Max.	Min.	Max.
Loafing on job	oral warning	1-day suspension	1-day suspension	3-day suspension	3-day suspension	discharge

With each occurrence of the act of loafing, management has reasonable latitude in choosing a penalty. If a man were caught loafing when the work demands were very light, he might be given a simple oral warning by his supervisor. On the other hand, if products are coming off a production line and an operator is making no effort to handle his assigned items and this causes damage or serious delay, he might be suspended without pay for a full day for the first occurrence.

Discharge As a Penalty

Discharge is the supreme punishment in industrial discpline. Some writers have called it industrial capital punishment. Where progressive penalties are assigned for repeated minor offenses, the threat of discharge often serves to "sober up" errant workers. Discharge may be the only feasible course of action in the case of employees whose behavior is so bad as to make their presence in the plant a threat to other employees or to the effective operation of the business.

Arbitrators are reluctant to order discharge unless the evidence is incontrovertible and unless efforts at correction have been tried and have proven unsuccessful. Discharge is particularly grave for a worker with considerable length of service, for he loses his accumulated pension and group insurance benefits plus extended vacation rights. With rigorous employee selection procedures and a careful weeding out of undesirable workers during the initial probationary period, management can almost elminate the need for discharges of permanent employees.

Questions for review and discussion

1. Why is discipline necessary to any organized group activity?
2. Distinguish among the various meanings of the term *discipline*.
3. Evaluate the implications and consequences of maintaining discipline by force or the threat of force.
4. What is positive or constructive discipline? What are the goals of the supervisor in instituting a pattern of positive discpline? How can positive discipline be achieved in a work force?
5. Do you think the local union leadership can or should play an active part in the disciplinary process in a company?
6. Describe the impact of collective bargaining and arbitration upon the handling of disciplinary problems in industry.
7. What should be the role of the first-line supervisor in handling employees who break the rules?
8. Do you think the dual goals of maintaining consistent treatment of all employees and adjusting the penalty to fit the circumstances of the particular case are compatible? Discuss.
9. Why are penalties often of the progressive type?
10. What should be the rights of an employee who has been charged by his supervisor with a rules violation?
11. Do you think a company should adopt a uniform scale of penalties for all offenses? Should these be announced to the employees?
12. Under what circumstances should discharge be used as a penalty?

Case problems

PROBLEM 1

Frank is an operator in a textile mill. Recently his foreman told him that the company was starting a regular program of monitoring the static-eliminator bars mounted on all carding machines.[4] The operation was to be performed monthly and would require about eight hours time each month. The work involved an inspection and cleaning of the bars plus wiping of each bar with special paper that was then sent away to a laboratory for measurements of any radiation leaking from the unit.

Frank refused to do this new work. He stated that he had been hired as a machine operator, not as a maintenance mechanic or radiation technician. He said that the maintenance mechanic job paid twenty cents more per hour and

---

[4] A static-eliminator bar is an aluminum bar containing a strip of foil that is composed of a radioactive substance. The emission of certain rays from the foil prevents the fibers in the product from clogging the machine.

that such work was outside his job classification. Further, he had heard via the grapevine that it was hazardous to touch the static-eliminator bars.

His foreman told him that he must either perform the duties assigned to him or face immediate discharge. The work was not of a higher skill than his regular job, and it occurred only once per month. The foreman further explained that handling these bars was not hazardous, because they had been used in the mill for two years and no one had been injured from the radiation yet.

Frank still refused to do the work and said he was going to see his union steward. With that the exchange between the foreman and the worker terminated.

That afternoon the foreman went to see his superior, the superintendent, about the matter. The superintendent viewed it as a clear case of insubordination, for which immediate discharge was provided in the rules. He advised the foreman to send Frank to his office, at which time he, the superintendent, would give the man one last chance to comply or be discharged.

Questions

1. Do you think this case involves a straightforward issue of insubordination? Are there any other important issues involved?
2. Can a man ever justifiably refuse to carry out a direct order from his supervisor? Discuss.
3. How would you handle this case if you were the superintendent?
4. What course is open to an employee who feels his boss has given him an order that he cannot or should not carry out?

PROBLEM 2

The ZYZ Company employs a large force of draftsmen of various classifications. The draftsmen are represented by an independent draftsmen's union at this company. The job title of Detailer 3 is an entry classification ordinarily assigned to new, relatively inexperienced detail draftsmen. Normally at the end of one year a Detailer 3 is upgraded to Detailer 2 if his work is satisfactory and if he demonstrates that he can do the slightly higher-level work of a Detailer 2.

On March 12, 1973, Mrs. Mary M., a Detailer 3 hired on January 8, 1972, submitted the following grievance to her superior:

> I request that my rating be changed from Detailer 3 to Detailer 2. I have been doing Detailer 2 work for about six months. I have always turned in jobs on time and in cases of rush work I have always had them in before they were promised. The designer that I work for and my drafting representative (union representative) both agree I am doing Detailer 2 work.

In discussing the grievance in the industrial relations office her supervisor made several assertions. He stated that he hired Mrs. Mary M. with the understanding that her job would involve a lot of short-promise work. A person doing such work must have a good attendance record. He said that she told him that her home problems would not interfere with her job.

The supervisor went on to say that he had spoken to her three times for talking too much and about her habitual tardiness. On February 26 he gave her a written warning notice because of excessive lateness, excessive absenteeism, and too much social conversation on the job.

The supervisor further stated that she was capable of doing Detailer 2 work. In fact, she has been doing some of it for the past six months. When she is on the job, the quality of her work is entirely satisfactory. The problem is that she is late and absent entirely too much. When she is here she talks too much with the other employees.

The absence record for Mrs. Mary M. is shown below:

5/8/72	½ day	Son sick
5/23/72	1 day	Out of town
6/14–15/72	2 days	Personal business
7/16/72	1 day	Illness in family
8/20/72	½ day	Alleged personal illness
8/29/72	½ day	Alleged personal illness
9/20/72	1 day	Personal illness
10/29/72	½ day	Car trouble
11/19/72	1 day	Car trouble
12/10–11/72	2 days	Illness in family
1/2/73	1 day	Personal business
2/18/73	1 day	Illness in family
2/24/73	1 day	Personal business

The supervisor said he would not promote a person with such a record.

Questions

1. Since Mrs. Mary M. has already demonstrated that she has done Detailer 2 work, do you think she should be upgraded?
2. If you were her supervisor, how would you handle this employee?
3. If one's actual work performance is of a higher grade level, does this justify a promotion regardless of excessive tardiness, absences, and talking on the job?
4. How appropriate is a denial of a promotion as a means of discipline?
5. If you were the manager in charge of the drafting department, how would you resolve this problem?

Suggestions for further reading

BAER, WALTER E. *Discipline and Discharge Under the Labor Agreement*, New York: American Management Association, 1972.

BEHOHLAV, JAMES A. and PAUL O. POPP. "Making Employee Discipline Work," *Personnel Administrator*, Vol. 23, (March 1978), pp. 22–24.

BLACK, JAMES M. *Positive Discipline*, New York: American Management Association, 1970.

GRAGG, CHARLES J. "Whose Fault Was It?" *Harvard Business Review*, Vol. 42, No. 1 (January–February 1964), pp. 107–110.

HANDSAKER, MORRISON. "Arbitration of Discipline Cases," *Personnel Journal*, Vol. 46, No. 3 (March 1967), pp. 153–156, 175.

HUBERMAN, JOHN. "Discipline Without Punishment," *Harvard Business Review*, Vol. 42, No. 4 (July–August 1964), pp. 62–68.

JONES, DALLAS L. *Arbitration and Industrial Discipline*. Ann Arbor, Mich.: University of Michigan, Bureau of Industrial Relations, 1961.

MAIER, NORMAN R. F. "Discipline in the Industrial Setting," *Personnel Journal*, Vol. 44, No. 4 (April 1965), pp. 189–192, 213.

PFIFFNER, JOHN M., AND MARSHALL FELS. *The Supervision of Personnel*, 3rd ed. Englewood Cliffs, N.J.: Prentice-Hall, Inc., 1967, ch. 7.

PHELPS, ORME W. *Discipline and Discharge in the Unionized Firm*. Berkeley and Los Angeles: University of California Press, 1959.

SLICHTER, SUMMER H., JAMES J. HEALY, AND E. ROBERT LIVERNASH. *The Impact of Collective Bargaining on Management*. Washington, D.C.: The Brookings Institution, 1960, ch. 21.

Grievance handling

In the course of human events in even the best-managed company, employee discontent, gripes, and complaints will certainly arise. Thus an employee may feel that his foreman assigns him to do all the dirty and heavy jobs. A clerk-typist may discover that the new girl—also a clerk-typist—has just been hired at a salary ten dollars a week greater than she is getting after a full year on the job. She goes to see her supervisor about her own salary. An hourly production worker may have been handed a written disciplinary warning by his foreman because he refused to work overtime last Saturday. The worker thinks it is unfair to be disciplined for this, and he goes to see his union steward.

The foregoing are but brief examples of the myraid situations that can give rise to employee anxiety and complaint. For the sake of justice to the individual and the smooth functioning of the whole organization, it behooves management to get at the root of employee dissatisfactions and to take corrective action wherever possible.

NATURE OF COMPLAINTS AND GRIEVANCES

If some problem or condition bothers or annoys an employee or if he thinks he has been unfairly treated by someone, he may express his discontent to someone else. When he vocalizes his dissatisfaction, we can then designate such action a complaint. Usually, but not always, when a person "sounds off" about something that bothers him, he hopes that the listener (a fellow employee or his supervisor) will do something to correct the difficulty.

But an unexpressed dissatisfaction can be just as worthy of consideration by the supervisor as the spoken complaint. Just as an untreated wound can cause dire consequences for a human being, so can a festering discontent in the shop lead to grave results.

There are many reasons why an employee may keep his problem "bottled up" inside himself. He may simple have a high tolerance limit for frustration. Or he may feel that the condition may soon change in such a way that the problem will then be corrected. He may have found from past experience that it does no good to complain to his supervisor. Sometimes a person may even feel that others will criticize or condemn him if he complains. By establishing a sound and healthy relationship with his people—one of mutual trust and confidence—the supervisor can do much to dispel employee fears and encourage free expression of feelings.

What Is a Grievance?

Viewpoints as to just what constitutes a grievance vary among personnel management and industrial relations authorities. According to some a grievance is any discontent or sense of injustice, expressed or not, felt by an employee in connection with his employment in an organization. This is a very broad conception. Such a definition includes all states of dissatisfaction or unhappiness whether they have been vocalized or not and whether they can be substantiated by facts or not.

A very narrow definition of a grievance is that adopted in many unionized companies. Here the labor policy may hold that a grievance is genuine only if there has been some alleged violation of the labor agreement. According to this view the only rights possessed by employees are those specifically spelled out in the contract; hence they can legitimately grieve only issues involved in the application and interpretation of the union–management agreement. As we shall see later in this chapter, such a narrow view has serious weaknesses. It is akin to a housewife's sweeping the dirt under the rug and pretending it doesn't exist.

Still another way of viewing this issue is to consider the act of expressing one's dissatisfaction with his supervisor as a complaint. It only becomes a true grievance if the supervisor is unable to settle the problem satisfactorily and then the employee appeals the case to the next higher level of management according to the steps in a formal grievance procedure. Thus, some labor–management agreements specify that a complaint that has not been settled on the basis of informal discussion between foreman and worker must be put into writing and then submitted to the second step of the grievance procedure, at which point it becomes a true grievance.

The concept that will be used throughout this chapter is that a *grievance is any dissatisfaction or feeling of injustice in connection with one's employment situation that is brought to the attention of management.* This is a reasonably broad definition, but it does exclude the unexpressed dissatisfaction. It is difficult for management to act on an employee's problem if he does not call the matter to their attention. The emphasis on management's part should be to create a proper leadership climate, so that employees who feel they have a justifiable complaint feel free to inform management of this fact.

WHY HAVE A GRIEVANCE PROCEDURE?

Some employers, especially in nonunion companies, take the view that there is really no need for establishing a formalized grievance-handling system. They hold that all their first-line supervisors are trained to hear employee complaints and to take prompt action to settle them. As a further argument they add that the company is well managed, it has an enlightened human-relations program in operation, and employees are generally satisfied, because very little evidence of dissatisfaction or complaint ever reaches the ears of top management. Of course, to the informed student of personnel management such contentions do not really prove much.

Why is it desirable that work organizations adopt a formal means for handling employee grievances? There are a number of sound reasons.

All employee complaints and dissatisfactions are, in actual practice, not settled satisfactorily by the first-level supervisor. There are many possible reasons for this. The supervisor may lack the necessary human relations skill to deal effectively with his people. He may lack the authority to take the action that is really necessary to properly solve the problem. He may even agree with the substance of the employee's grievance but know, from past experience, that it is futile for him to try to get higher management to act. Some supervisors may suppress the expression of grievances by their men. In those cases where the employee feels that his immediate supervisor has discriminated against him, he may feel that the supervisor can never, during a grievance discussion, fairly and objectively judge him and the situation. In this situation the employee must be able to appeal his case to some higher official.

Another justification for having a formal grievance-handling system is that it brings employee problems to the attention of higher management. The procedure serves as a medium of upward communication. Higher management becomes more aware of employee frustrations, problems, and expectations. It becomes sensitive to employee needs and well-being. Therefore, when higher management is formulating plans that will affect employees (for example, a plant expansion or contraction, company reorganization, or installation of new labor-saving machinery), it will have become fully cognizant of employee needs and reactions; hence complaints and grievances will be less likely to arise.

A grievance-handling system serves as an outlet for employee frustrations, discontents, and gripes. It operates like a pressure release valve on a steam boiler. Employees do not have to keep their frustrations bottled up until eventually seething discontent causes an explosion. They have a legitimate, officially approved way of appealing their grievances to higher management. If dissatisfied with initial attempts to iron out the difficulty with the supervisor, employees do not have to feel that they are going over their boss's head surreptitiously, as often happens in plants lacking a grievance procedure.

The existence of an effective grievance procedure reduces the likelihood of arbitrary action by supervision, because the supervisors know that the employees are able to protest such behavior and make their protests heard by higher management.

The very fact that employees have a right to be heard and are actually heard helps to improve morale. An employee's conception of his problem may be quite biased. He may even lose his case. But the very fact that one or more management representatives have listened attentively to his story serves to demonstrate that the individual worker is important to management and somebody cares about him. A helpful listener can often aid the employee to view his problem in a new light and sometimes help him solve the difficulty.

NEED FOR A JUDICIAL BODY IN WORK ORGANIZATIONS

The issue of the handling of employee grievances regarding management actions or oversights reaches to the heart of a basic deficiency in modern work organizations. It is a well-established principle of democratic government that there be a clear separation of legislative, executive, and judicial bodies within government. No one branch of the government should serve dual roles or dominate another branch. In work organizations line executives decide when employees have violated the rules of the organization, decide whether a person is guilty or innocent, select the penalty, and administer the penalty. They even sit in judgment upon their own actions when employees protest that something has been done unfairly. Now in the lowest ranks of any organization, supervisors must, in the interests of efficiency and the maintenance of order, administer discipline and handle employee complaints and grievances. But when employees appeal a decision of their immediate superior to some higher level in the structure, a clear need for an impartial and independent judiciary becomes evident. Under most existing systems employees must take their appeals to higher line executives. Although these executives may be more detached and broader in their outlook, they certainly cannot be wholly impartial. Their position in the organization causes them to seek to preserve the authority of their subordinate line supervisors. In many companies the first-level supervisor will not answer an employee's grievance until he has first consulted his immediate superior. Thus, both of the lower levels of supervision really think as one on the typical grievance.

It is only when a grievance is appealed to an impartial arbitrator (as provided for in most collective-bargaining agreements) that we can say a truly impartial and independent judicial body is being brought into the picture. But as we shall see later in this chapter, arbitration is rarely used in nonunion establishments.

The problem of the establishment of a judicial review body or system in business has just not been met. Indeed, most managers are hardly aware of the problem, because they have accepted, without question, the traditional ways of settling disputes by informal discussion between employee and boss as the principal and, often, only approach to the problem.

One approach to the establishment of a judicial review system is the public review board which was created by the United Automobile Workers Union in 1957.[1] This board is composed of independent and eminent citizens to which

[1] See the booklet published by the United Automobile Workers Union entitled *A More Perfect Union. The U.A.W. Public Review Board—Why, What, How* (Detroit: U.A.W. Publications Department, 1960).

members of the union can appeal their grievances against decisions of union leaders. The decisions of the board are final and binding.

Approaches such as this might be tried in a business corporation. Because there is practically no past experience in this realm, there needs to be some experimentation to find out what specific organizational arrangements will work best. The members of a judicial body or review board might be appointed by the board of directors of a corporation for a fixed term of office, say five years. Or they may be appointed by an employer or trade association to serve all member companies. If the members of the board served on a part-time basis, held other regular full-time jobs, such as that of college professor, attorney, or consultant, and were appointed in the manner just described, we could expect the board to function with a good deal of independence.

A great variety of methods might be used as far as manner of appointment of the members, term of office, means of hearing cases, method for removal, and means for implementing decisions are concerned. The simple point being made here is that there is a clear need for the establishment of a judicial system within work organizations. The specific means for achieving this objective will depend upon the circumstances and the philosophy of top management in the particular organization involved.

Some very fruitful insights into the issue of appeal systems established unilaterally by management (as opposed to those bilaterally bargained between union and management) have been provided by William G. Scott.[2] Scott studied appeal systems in nonbusiness organizations such as unions, the United States government, the Roman Catholic Church, and the United States Army, and business corporations in six major industrial categories. Scott concludes, on the basis of his research, that appeal systems tend to be established in large organizations which must of necessity formalize their personnel handling procedures. His data also support the proposition that organizations establish grievance procedures for their members where there exist, by rule or common practice, restrictions upon the freedom of the members to leave that organization if they find conditions unsatisfactory. And increasingly in both the government service and in the modern corporation, employees tend to make a career with the employer. Accrued fringe benefits operate in such a way as to reduce labor mobility. Although he grants that formal appeal systems may be established as a by-product of unionism and in recognition of the influence of industrial humanism (the modern human relations movement) upon managerial thought and practice, Scott has ascribed the most powerful influence to be that of the process of bureaucracy. Large complex organizations must adopt, for the sake of effectiveness and justice to the members, formal administrative justice systems.

GRIEVANCE SETTLEMENT FOR UNIONIZED EMPLOYEES

It is when a union organizes the employees that demands are made by the union to establish a formal grievance procedure. Practically all labor–management

[2] William G. Scott, *The Management of Conflict: Appeal Systems in Organizations* (Homewood, Ill.: Irwin and Dorsey, 1965).

agreements contain procedures for the handling of grievances.[3] It is understood by union and management alike that the signing of a labor contract does not automatically take care of all labor-relations problems that will arise during the life of the agreement. Therefore, a grievance procedure provides one means of settling such difficulties.

With the presence of a union, employees know that it is fully legitimate to submit complaints and grievances to management. Often the union officials will encourage the expression of grievances. This may be done to bring to the surface all underlying discontents, to demonstrate to management that all is not well in the plant, to identify issues that can strengthen the union's hand, or to show the employees that the union can successfully help them achieve their needs and wants on the job. The economic and social power of the union commonly serves to prevent lower-level supervisors from taking punitive action against those workers who have submitted grievances against management actions.

The Grievance Procedure

The general pattern for handling grievances in unionized establishments has become rather standardized, although specific details, of course, vary from company to company.

Because management is presumed to possess full authority to operate its business as it sees fit (subject of course to legal, moral, and labor agreement controls), the reasoning is that a grievance represents a request by an employee, group of employees, and/or the union for a change in some management action or lack of action. In effect management administers the business and applies the provisions of the union–management agreement. If the employees or the union do not like the way this is done, they must submit a grievance according to the procedure outlined in the labor agreement.

Figure 23-1 is a diagram depicting a typical grievance procedure for a medium- or large-size company. Instead of a five step procedure as shown, many union-employer procedures contain only four steps. In these cases one of the intermediate steps between the front line supervisor and arbitration is eliminated.

There is variation from company to company and union to union in the titles of the officials who handle grievances above the first step. A large local union in an industrial plant would typically use a chief plant steward and/or a plant grievance committee at the second step. A craft union would often involve the business agent at the second and higher steps. In presenting the case to an arbitrator at the final step, unions generally use field representatives or international representatives who work out of the unions' regional offices. In companies the labor relations or personnel office plays a major role in representing the employer's interest. When a grievance is appealed by an employee or the union beyond the first-level supervisor step, it is the responsibility of the personnel office to investigate the facts of the case. This involves gathering written documentation and interviewing concerned persons and witnesses. The personnel or labor relations

[3] A 1964 study of 1,717 collective-bargaining agreements, each covering 1,000 workers or more, representing almost all agreements of this size in the United States (exclusive of railroad, airline, and government) showed that 99.4 percent of these agreements contained grievance procedures. *Major Collective Bargaining Agreements: Grievance Procedures*, Bulletin No. 1425-1, U.S. Department of Labor (Washington, D.C.: Government Printing Office, 1964).

STEP	REPRESENTING THE EMPLOYEE OR UNION	REPRESENTING THE EMPLOYER
FIRST	EMPLOYEE ALONE OR UNION STEWARD ALONE OR BOTH TOGETHER	EMPLOYEE'S FOREMAN OR SUPERVISOR

If foreman's action is not satisfactory, the grievance is expressed in writing and appealed to second step.

SECOND	CHIEF PLANT STEWARD OR BUSINESS AGENT	SUPERINTENDENT OR INDUSTRIAL RELATIONS OFFICE

If management's action is considered unsatisfactory, union may appeal to third step.

THIRD	PLANT GRIEVANCE COMMITTEE (International Representative may assist)	INDUSTRIAL RELATIONS DIRECTOR OR PLANT MANAGER

If management's action is considered unsatisfactory, union may appeal to fourth step.

FOURTH	REGIONAL OR DISTRICT REPRESENTATIVES OF INTERNATIONAL UNION	TOP CORPORATE MANAGEMENT

If management's action is considered unsatisfactory, union may appeal to fifth step.

FIFTH	ARBITRATION BY IMPARTIAL THIRD PARTY

Figure 23-1
A Typical Grievance Procedure for a Medium- or Large-Sized Company.

manager must decide the response to be made to the grievant by testing the events and circumstances of the case against the meaning and language of the union–employer contract. He will also test the response against past practice and personnel policy. In deciding the proper answer to give the grievant the personnel or labor relations manager will generally consult closely with appropriate line executives such as superintendents, department heads, and plant managers. It is important for the personnel office to take a lead position in handling the employer's responses at the various steps of the grievance procedure. If this were not done, then each manager throughout the organization would develop his own answer to the grievances originating in his division. Such a procedure invites inconsistency of treatment and inequities. This could be disastrous not only to union–employer relations but also to plant human relations.

In handling grievances both union and employer representatives should view the grievance process as a means of developing solutions to problems. Oftentimes creative solutions and compromises will satisfy the grievant, the union, and the employer. Unfortunately, in too many instances the union and the management adopt a "we win/you lose" strategy. Such an attitude does not enhance the quality of labor-management relationships.

Over 90 percent of all collective-bargaining agreements in the private sector and about 75 percent of those in the public sector provide for binding arbitration as the final step in the grievance procedure.[4] This is the peaceful method of settling an unresolved grievance. The alternative, which does exist in some agreements, is a strike. The topic of arbitration will be covered later in this chapter.

The Clinical Approach to Grievance Handling

A fairly common view, especially among business executives, is that the labor agreement is a legal document that spells out the rights and obligations of the company, the union, and the employees. In complaining about conditions in the plant, the employee really has a right to submit a grievance concerning only those matters that have been specifically covered in the contract. In short, as explained earlier, the contract specifies the rights of the union and the employees; hence an employee can grieve only about some alleged violation of these rights. According to this conception of the grievance process, an employee who claims that he should be classified into pay grade 7 instead of his present grade of 6, on the basis of enlarged job responsibilities, would have a legitimate grievance, because the labor agreement specifically covers the matter of job classification. On the other hand an employee who complains that his foreman has picked on him and called him nasty names would have no right to submit a grievance, because there is no provision in the contract covering such an issue.

The procedure just described has been called a legalistic approach to grievance handling. Many union–management agreements conform to this narrow concept of what is a proper grievance by stating that a grievance must be an issue that *relates to the interpretation and application of the agreement*. Other kinds of complaints are ruled out as being illegitimate or unjustified.

Benjamin Selekman has stated eloquently the argument for adopting a clinical rather than legalistic approach to the handling of grievances. The emphasis in the clinical approach is upon getting to the root of the employee's dissatisfaction regardless of whether his grievance, as expressed, fits some narrow mold as defined by the labor agreement. Selekman points out that emphasis should be placed upon the problems of treating grievances rather than upon the mechanics of accepting or dismissing them. In answer to the question "When is a grievance not a grievance?" Selekman says, "Never."[5] Although the grievance on its surface may not fit a strictly defined mold of what constitutes a legitimate grievance according to a contract definition, it behooves management to make every reasonable effort to find out what is bothering the employee in order to take steps to rectify the trouble. Discontent, unhappiness, and unrest do not disappear just because a supervisor pronounces them irrelevant and outside the scope of the contract.

A further argument for following a clinical approach is that numerous problem situations are bound to arise that were not foreseen at the time the company and union negotiated the contract. These trouble spots cannot be swept under the carpet until it is time to bargain the next agreement one or more years later. The labor law of the United States (for example, Taft–Hartley Act) requires bargain-

---

[4] Daniel Q. Mills, *Labor–Management Relations* (New York: McGraw-Hill Book Co., 1978), p. 211.
[5] Benjamin M. Selekman, *Labor Relations and Human Relations* (New York: McGraw-Hill Book Company, 1947), ch. 5.

ing between management and union at all times to settle joint problems. This supports what common sense tells us anyway, namely that there must be a good faith attempt to solve difficulties and disputes as they arise. The grievance procedure provides an effective instrument for accomplishing this objective.

In conformity with this liberal view of grievance handling, foremen and higher-management personnel should wholeheartedly undertake to investigate and act upon *all* grievances. If a grievance cannot be tied to some provision of the labor agreement, it can certainly be judged according to psychological or sociological principles, principles of equity and justice, or according to established personnel policies of the company. This all-inclusive approach to grievances can be applied at all steps of the procedure save the last one—arbitration. Because arbitrators' decisions are generally final and binding and because management and the union, as a rule, do not choose to have arbitrators legislate for them by creating new policies and contract provisions, it seems reasonable that at this last step the arbitrator be empowered to settle only questions of contract interpretation or application. Hence use the clinical approach through all the lower stages of the grievance procedure, but be legalistic at the final arbitration step.[6]

Role of the Supervisor

The first-line supervisor in whose department a grievance originates should take the major responsibility for trying to reach a settlement that is acceptable to all parties concerned. However, all too often in actual practice his role becomes a minor one. When unionization became widespread in the mass production industries in the 1930's and 1940's, top management in many companies feared the consequences of faulty action by foremen in handling grievances, so it centralized all grievance-handling authority in the industrial relations department. On paper the foreman was the first step in the grievance procedure. In practice the industrial relations department answered all grievances. This could be done in a number of ways. In one way the foreman might actually give an answer to the worker and/or steward, but it would be an answer he obtained as a result of consultation with the industrial relations department. Sometimes foremen would get in the habit of rejecting any and all grievances, and these would then be appealed to the industrial relations office, which appeared in the second or third step of the procedure. Often the local union would sense that the foremen were powerless and would skip the first step and immediately take its cases to the office that had the authority. In this same vein the plant industrial relations director of a large corporation once said to the author somewhat proudly, "For each and every grievance, I write out the answers that my foremen give to the union. I would no more trust them with such an important responsibility than I would a child."

It is fully sound to enter a grievance at a higher step in the regular grievance procedure if it has broad policy implications for which no precedents have been established. But for practically all other types the foreman must be granted the necessary authority to make at least an initial settlement on his own. He must be

[6] This is essentially the approach recommended by Harold W. Davey in his *Contemporary Collective Bargaining*, 3rd ed. (Englewood Cliffs, N.J.: Prentice-Hall, Inc., 1972), pp. 144–146.

fully trained in labor policy, contract interpretation, and human relations so that he can properly carry out this responsibility. In recent years many companies have swung around to this way of thinking.

In the face-to-face dealings between the aggrieved employee and the foreman, the foreman must listen attentively in order to obtain the man's full story as he sees it. Depending upon the nature of the grievance and the circumstances, this may be an ideal occasion for the supervisor to employ the nondirective technique of interviewing. This technique is most appropriate if the supervisor perceives that there may be underlying causes related to the psychological or social adjustment of the individual to his work environment.

Because worker grievances are often intimately related to the activities and pressures involved in getting out production (for example, work assignments, transfers, workloads, job classifications, overtime distribution), the foreman is in the best position to make a full investigation of the facts of the problem. He can collect written data and examine records as well as interview union representatives, employees, and management staff personnel to compile a full account of the facts and history surrounding a case. When a supervisor does not feel sure of himself, he should certainly consult his immediate superior or the industrial relations department. But he should never become merely a messenger boy, a front, or a figurehead. Grievances tend to be settled most expeditiously and to the satisfaction of all parties concerned in those companies when the front-line supervisor plays an important role.

Role of Shop Steward and the Union

The position of a union steward is a difficult one. One of his prime duties is to represent workers and the union in the processing of grievances. Shall he look upon himself as a shop lawyer who goes to bat for every worker on each and every complaint? Shall he make no attempt to reject those he honestly believes have no merit? In most industrial unions the steward is elected by his fellow employees in the department where he works. They are his friends. If he wants to keep his steward's position and get re-elected, he has a powerful urge to simply go to bat for his colleagues on all complaints.

Yet there are serious disadvantages to this approach. A steward is a union leader, and he has to stand up and be counted on important issues. He must be strong enough to say no when the facts demand such a position. Most union leadership manuals for stewards tell them to perform, at least partially, a judicial role in handling employee grievances. A union's position vis-à-vis the company can be seriously weakened if it loads up the grievance machinery with a lot of cases that are so weak that the union loses them at the higher stages.

Sometimes the union steward concludes that he has a thankless job. He may overextend himself to push faithfully a large number of worker grievances to a successful conclusion. Yet once he tells the men that they are wrong on an issue and he cannot in all fairness push their complaint, he often finds that they are vitriolic in their abuse of him.

Actually much of the legalism that has crept into collective agreements and union grievance-handling procedures has been created by union leaders to insulate themselves from rank-and-file pressures.

Political struggles within a union often have a profound effect upon the number of grievances submitted and the vigor with which union officials push them. If there is a sharp contest for some important union office, the competing candidates will often try to demonstrate how much they can do for the rank and file by vigorously digging up issues and pursuing them to a successful conclusion. Pressure tactics such as slowdowns and brief walkouts may even be employed to force management to back down. The same kind of grievance activity may take place if the union that is "in" the company is being threatened by an outside union that seeks to win bargaining rights and unseat the incumbent union.

GRIEVANCE ARBITRATION

In the vast majority of union-employer relationships management has accepted binding arbitration as the terminal point in the grievance procedure even though this means that management does not have the "last say" in determining the outcome. In return for granting binding arbitration, management customarily receives a written "no-strike" pledge (incorporated into the agreement) from the union during the term of the union-employer agreement.

There are two basic ways of employing an arbitrator. One is the permanent arbitrator or umpire system, and the other is the *ad hoc* (from the Latin, meaning "for this case alone, or special") system. Some large corporations, such as General Motors and United States Steel, and certain trade associations, such as the needle trades in New York City, employ full-time arbitrators on a salaried basis. When the caseload is heavy there is some justification for having a permanent arbitrator. Further he can become expert in the particular problems of the industry, and there is no delay in engaging his services. Notwithstanding these considerations, however, the most common method is to engage arbitrators on an *ad hoc* basis. An *ad hoc* arbitrator will hear either one case alone, or he may hear several cases during the course of one or two days. An advantage of the *ad hoc* system is that the individual can be selected on the basis of his expertise for the type of case to be heard.

The procedure for selecting an arbitrator is commonly spelled out in the labor agreement. Often the arbitrator is selected from a panel of qualified arbitrators listed by either the Federal Mediation and Conciliation Service or by the American Arbitration Association. If the two parties are unable to agree upon an individual, the contract will often state that an arbitrator shall be appointed by one or the other of these agencies. It is almost universal practice for the union and the company to share equally the arbitrator's fee for his services.

Labor agreements generally specify that the decision of the arbitrator shall be final and binding upon all parties concerned—the company, the union, and the employees. Further they state, usually, that the arbitrator shall have only the authority to interpret, apply, or determine compliance with the provisions of the union–management agreement. He shall not add to, subtract, or alter the provisions of the agreement. This simply means that the parties expect the arbitrator to act in the role of judge and not a legislator.

An arbitration hearing is a quasi-judicial process. It may be conducted quite formally, or the entire process may be rather informal. The desires of the arbitrator himself and the custom of the parties determine whether the hearing will be run formally, or informally. But even a formal hearing ordinarily is much less strict and structured than is a hearing in a court of law.

Quite often after the hearing has concluded both the union and the company will file a post-hearing brief with the arbitrator to summarize facts and arguments of each side. Typically then the arbitrator has thirty days to make his decision and prepare his award and supporting opinion. The award is the decision of the arbitrator regarding the issue submitted to him. The opinion summarizes the positions of the two parties and explains the reasoning of the arbitrator in arriving at his decision.

GRIEVANCE SETTLEMENT FOR NONUNION EMPLOYEES

Relatively few companies provide a viable mechanism for handling grievances for their nonunion employees. A survey of 793 companies in the early 1960's by William G. Scott revealed that only 275 of these firms (35 percent) had some kind of program for handling employee complaints. However, only 91 of these 275 companies had a formal grievance system. The remainder had informal arrangements that were mostly rather loosely applied "open door" policies.[7]

A 1977 survey by Ewing of 1,958 subscribers to the *Harvard Business Review* (the vast majority of the respondents were managers in private firms distributed throughout the country) showed that 14 percent were employed in organizations having a management grievance committee and 11 percent were employed in firms having an ombudsman. But the majority of persons (63 percent) stated that their companies simply had an informal "open door" policy.[8]

By and large American managements have chosen either to ignore the problem of providing a means for solving nonunion employee grievances or they have relied upon quite informal measures. But the need for programs in the nonunion sector of the working force of business firms is nevertheless pressing.

Approaches to the Problem

In comparison to the well-defined procedures and the extensive experience of American industry in grievance handling for unionized employees, the procedures for nonunion personnel are either nonexistent, or else they are ill-defined, vague, and seldom employed. We shall explore the various approaches that have been or can be instituted for nonunion people.

Open-Door Policy.   Many top executives who have a genuine concern for the well-being of their employees have set up an open-door policy to solve employee grievances. The open-door policy means that any rank-and-file worker has a full right to go to the office of the chief executive officer of that company or plant to discuss his complaint. Under such a program, the executive promises to make

---

[7] William G. Scott, op. cit., pp. 56–89. Scott surveyed companies in these six categories: manufacturing, finance, retail, transportation, extractive, and public utilities. The 91 companies with formal programs represented only 11 percent of the total of 793 that responded to the survey.

[8] David W. Ewing, "What Business Thinks About Employee Rights," *Harvard Business Review*, Vol. 55, No. 5 (September–October 1977), pp. 81–94.

himself available for such contacts with the employees. He further implies that he will investigate every grievance and take appropriate action. Although some open-door programs permit the employee to go immediately to the chief executive with his problem, it is much better to require that he discuss the issue with his immediate superior first. This procedure will solve the majority of grievances at the bottom level and will keep the supervisor fully informed of what is going on in his own department.

Although on the face of it the open-door policy may seem like a good system to some, it seldom works out successfully in practice. There are a number of reasons for this. The social and organizational distance between the worker in overalls and the company president in the thick-carpeted office is so great that the worker is generally fearful of going to see the "big boss." He feels that he may not express himself well or that the "big boss" may not understand his point of view.

If the president should overrule the first-level supervisor, the latter will tend to lose face in front of his men. If the president does not act judiciously, he can seriously weaken the position of the supervisors.

If an employee feels that he has been mistreated by his foreman, he may get the action reversed by appealing to the chief executive. But the worker may find that although he has won that particular case, in the long run his supervisor may bear resentment against him and put him in an even worse position than he was originally.

The Inspector General Method.   The military system of providing a means of correcting injustices by having a representative from the Inspector General's office visit each unit once per year to hear and investigate soldiers' grievances is an approach that is rarely employed in private industry. One large company that for many years had an open-door policy decided to establish a special vice-presidential position to relieve the president of the load of hearing and investigating worker grievances. This vice-president visits every plant at least once per year and more often if necessary. He in effect performs the functions of an inspector general in the military establishment.

Ombudsman.   The concept of an ombudsman to process complaints of citizens against the government was first devised in Sweden in 1809. Finland also established this office in 1809 as a protector of the people. But it has not been until the 1950's and 1960's that the concept has really spread elsewhere in the world. In its most precise meaning an *ombudsman* is an independent and politically neutral officer of a governmental legislature. His function is to handle appeals by ordinary citizens against the executive bureaucracy. He has the power to investigate, has access to government documents, has the right to prosecute officials for illegal acts, and can publicize his findings.

In its more general and looser meaning, the term ombudsman has recently been applied to any official of an organization charged with the responsibility of investigating and settling member complaints. The inspector general system of the military is a form of the ombudsman. Many universities have created ombudsman systems to handle student grievances and employee grievances.

Although this concept is just now beginning to be applied to nongovernmental organizations, its success in government–citizen relations in the Scandinavian countries reveals that it is certainly worthy of trial in private establishments.[9]

The Xerox Corporation set up an ombudsman system in 1972. The ombudsman reports directly to the president, who is the only man who has authority to reverse his decisions. In creating the position officials at Xerox were convinced that only someone outside the corporate chain of command could insure fair treatment for employees.[10]

Multistep Grievance Procedure. Some companies have established official multistep grievance procedures patterned somewhat after those for union personnel. The last avenue of appeal is generally the chief executive officer of the company, or of the division, if the company is composed of semiautonomous divisions. Arbitration is seldom provided for. There are a number of reasons for this. Management is unwilling to dilute any of its powers by having an outside party review (and perhaps reverse) its decisions. The individual employee is often ill-equipped to prepare adequately and to present his case before the arbitrator. He generally cannot afford to pay one half the arbitrator's fee, as is customary in unionized establishments. If management assumes the burden of assigning a man to represent the employee and if it pays the full cost of arbitration, then the claim that both the company and the individual are on an equal footing before the arbitrator can no longer be made.

Although there are plausible reasons why arbitration is not more widely used, there is still considerable justification for having some impartial and independent agency serve as a final judicial body to review the decisions of top management. Some writers have proposed a board of review or a board of neutrals.[11]

The personnel management literature contains a number of references to multistep procedures for nonunion people. In most of these procedures the employee can appeal his case to successively higher levels of managers in his direct chain of command. The industrial relations department usually plays a key part in the proceedings. Sometimes this office is the next step of appeal after the supervisor. In others, a representative from industrial relations acts in an advisory capacity to the employee.

Grievance Committee. Some organizations have created a committee of management personnel and others have set-up a committee of non-management personnel to hear employee grievances on appeal from lower levels. The decisions may merely be advisory to the chief executive officer or they may be final and binding. Ewing reports that the H. P. Hood Company in Boston and the Polaroid Corporation have such procedures.[12]

---

[9] For an explanation of the ombudsman concept in government see Stanley V. Anderson, ed. *Ombudsmen for American Government?* prepared by the American Assembly, Columbia University (Englewood Cliffs, N.J.: Prentice-Hall, 1968).

[10] "How the Xerox Ombudsman Helps Xerox," *Business Week* (May 12, 1973), also "Where Ombudsmen Work Out," *Business Week* (May 3, 1976).

[11] See, for example, Walter V. Ronner, "Handling Grievances in a Non-Union Plant," *Proceedings of the Fourteenth Annual Meeting of the Industrial Relations Research Association* (Madison, Wis.: IRRA, 1961), pp. 306–314; Dale S. Beach, "An Organizational Problem: Subordinate-Superior Relations," *Advanced Management*, Vol. 25, No. 12 (December 1960), pp. 12–16.

[12] David W. Ewing, *Freedom Inside the Organization* (New York: McGraw-Hill Book Co., 1978), p. 161.

In order for a grievance system to work successfully in a nonunion organization, the employees must be assured, by both pronouncement and actual experience, that there will be no retaliation against them for submitting and pushing a case up through the successive steps in the system. Because of the great imbalance of power between management and the worker, employees naturally tend to have a deep-seated fear of retaliation by the boss or the other members of management. In fact, this is one of the principal reasons grievance procedures for nonunion people are seldom used. The danger is that top management will thus delude itself into thinking that everyone is content, because few if any grievances are submitted.

Questions for review and discussion

1. What is a grievance?
2. Why is it desirable that all work organizations have an established system for hearing and adjusting employee grievances?
3. What are the arguments in favor of establishing a judicial body within corporations and other work organizations with a clear separation of powers between the executive and judicial branches of the organization?
4. Explain how an employee's grievance would be processed through the grievance procedure in a typical large unionized company.
5. According to modern organization theory the industrial relations department should act primarily in a staff capacity. Is this principle violated if this department appears at the second or third step of the formal grievance procedure and takes on major responsibility for answering grievances? Discuss.
6. What is meant by the "clinical approach" to grievance handling? Contrast it with the legalistic approach. What are the arguments in favor of using a clinical approach?
7. Should all grievances be put in writing before management acts upon them? Discuss.
8. Discuss the proper role of the foreman in grievance settlement. Why has the foreman become powerless and a mere figurehead in grievance handling in some companies?
9. Describe the role of the union steward in grievance handling. What pressures play upon the steward?
10. Briefly describe the process of grievance arbitration. Include in your discussion the method of selecting an arbitrator, his authority, method of compensation, and hearing procedure.
11. Why do you think most companies have done little or nothing to establish a grievance-handling system for their nonunion employees?
12. What is the open-door policy? What are its merits and shortcomings?

Case problem

The ABC Textile Company employs 550 production and maintenance workers who are represented by a union.

The grievance procedure in the union–employer agreement provides that the aggrieved employee and/or his union steward shall first submit the matter to the department foreman. If it is not settled at this step, it must be put in writing on a standard grievance form and submitted to the plant superintendent. Representing the union at this second step is the local union grievance committee and/or the business agent. The third step is the company president and a representative of the international union. The fourth and final step consists of binding arbitration. The company personnel director acts in an advisory capacity to plant management at all stages. In actual practice he is particularly instrumental in shaping the decision on a grievance at the second, or superintendent, step of the procedure.

During the past three months the following cases arose:

1. The company had been plagued with chronic worker absenteeism. The procedure for keeping track of absences was to have each foreman record the names of all those who were absent each day in a notebook. In an attempt to correct the problem, the superintendent and the personnel manager made a quick check of the various foremen's notebooks and then discharged six of the most serious offenders. The union immediately filed a grievance charging discrimination because some of the six men who had been fired had better attendance records than some other workers who remained on the payroll. At the second step of the grievance procedure, management decided to reduce the penalty to a one-week suspension without pay. In commenting upon the case later, the personnel manager said he expected that worker attendance would improve since the employees had learned that management was serious about improving attendance and that serious offenders might be discharged. However, several of the foremen grumbled that the incident had undermined their authority with their men because management had backed down. They said that the six men involved were poor performers and should have been fired.

2. A foreman in one of the production departments asked a machine operator to operate a different machine to fill in for a worker who was absent that day. When he refused, his foreman told him to punch out his time card and go home. He would not be paid for the rest of that day. The union filed a grievance in the man's behalf charging a violation of the labor agreement. According to the contract the machines and processes are grouped into categories. An employee cannot be assigned to a machine outside his category without his consent. In this particular case the machine involved was outside the employee's regular category. However the skill and knowledge requirements for the two different machines were essentially the same. Also the rate of pay for both operations was the same. The labor contract stated that the least senior employee in the department could be compelled to move to the other machine if more senior workers were unwilling to do so. However the foreman was unaware of this contract provision and workers had not refused him in the past. At the second step of the grievance procedure, management decided that the foreman had erred and the man was paid for the time lost.

3. A man wearing canvas sneakers was told by his foreman not to come to

work again dressed in sneakers. Rather he must wear leather shoes as a safety measure to protect his feet against cuts and wounds from wire, nails, sharp projections on machines, and floor splinters. Before giving this oral warning, the foreman had consulted the superintendent and received full approval for his action. Despite the warning the man appeared for work the next day again wearing sneakers. He was sent home immediately, without pay, for the rest of the day. When he appeared for work the following day he was wearing leather shoes. However, the union filed a grievance charging discrimination because some workers in other departments had worn sneakers and had not been disciplined. The grievance was rejected at the first two steps of the grievance procedure and is now pending at the third step.

Many of the foremen complain that they repeatedly lose face in front of their employees because higher management gives in too frequently in the face of union pressure in grievance cases. The union business agent has claimed that management provokes most of the grievances by its own actions.

Questions

1. What seems to be wrong here? What measures should be taken to improve employee–management–union relations?
2. What do you think of the foremen's complaints about "undermining their authority" and "losing face in front of the employees"?

Suggestions for further reading

BEAL, EDWIN F., EDWARD D. WICKERSHAM, and PHILIP KIENAST. *The Practice of Collective Bargaining*, 5th ed. Homewood, Ill.: Richard D. Irwin, Inc., 1976, ch. 13.

EWING, DAVID W. "What Business Thinks About Employee Rights," *Harvard Business Review*, Vol. 55, No. 5 (September–October 1977), pp. 81–94.

———. *Freedom Inside the Organization*. New York: McGraw-Hill Book Co., 1978.

MICHAEL, STEPHEN R., "Due Process in Nonunion Grievance Systems," *Employee Relations Law Journal*, Vol. 3 (Spring 1978), pp. 516–527.

MILLS, DANIEL Q. *Labor–Management Relations*. New York: McGraw-Hill Book Company, 1978, ch. 14.

THOMSON, ANDREW W. J. *The Grievance Procedure in the Private Sector*. Ithaca, N.Y.: New York State School of Industrial and Labor Relations, Cornell University, 1974.

TROTTA, MAURICE S. *Handling Grievances: A Guide for Management and Labor*. Washington, D.C.: Bureau of National Affairs, 1976.

U.S. GENERAL ACCOUNTING OFFICE. *Grievance Systems Should Provide All Federal Employees an Equal Opportunity for Redress*. Report to Congress by the Comptroller General of the United States, Washington, D.C.: Government Printing Office, 1978.

VI

FINANCIAL COMPENSATION

Compensation administration

Wages, as a means of providing income for employees and as a cost of doing business to the employer, constitute one of the most important subjects in the field of personnel management. Wages can provide a source of motivation for employees to perform effectively. The wage rate offered is one of the most important considerations to a person who is contemplating taking a new job.

Formerly wage rates in organizations, whether in industry or in government and nonprofit institutions, tended to be established in a haphazard fashion, with little consideration given to consistency within the organization according to differentials in job requirements or to consistency with prevailing wages paid in other establishments. The movement in industry for the development and adoption of sound principles and practices of wage and salary administration had its infancy in the 1920's and 1930's, expanded greatly during and immediately after World War II, and in the 1950's became more mature with the general acceptance of the ideas and methods initiated earlier.

This chapter explores the subject of compensation administration. We shall examine rationales for financial compensation, wage criteria, wage policy and principles, job evaluation systems, establishing the pay structure, administration of pay, wage surveys, and compensation practices for professionals and managers.

Viewpoints of Wages

Employers consider wages as a cost of doing business. They are interested in labor cost per unit of output (whether the work is a unit of product or a unit of service). Wages, viewed broadly, constitute the largest single cost item for most firms. Even for the firm in which raw materials purchased from suppliers may amount to over half the total unit costs, it may be seen that to the supplier himself much of his costs were labor, and so on back to the original source of the raw material. When an employer contemplates an adjustment of his wage level, he considers the effect upon his total costs in relation to income. Through experience, employers have learned also that to attract and hold competent employees in a free labor market they must pay adequate wages and pay one worker properly in relation to other workers within their establishments.

On the other hand, employees view wages as a means of providing for their wants and needs according to certain general standards that they may consider. They may believe that they should get paid as much as others receive for doing the same kind of work in the same organization or in other companies in that locality of which they may have knowledge. They may believe that they should get paid according to the union scale or enough to maintain a differential over those doing work requiring less skill, experience, and education. Other informal criteria that employees adopt to judge the adequacy of their pay are whether it is enough to support themselves and their families at a level comparable with their friends, enough to save a certain portion in the bank, and enough to keep up with increases in the cost of living.

Compensation Administration

The term *compensation administration*, or alternatively, wage and salary administration, has come to be accepted as the designation for that field of endeavor concerned with the establishment and implementation of sound policies and methods of employee compensation. It includes such areas as job evaluation, development and maintenance of wage structures, wage surveys, wage incentives, wage changes and adjustments, supplementary payments, profit sharing, control of compensation costs, and other related pay items.

The term *wage* is commonly used for those employees whose pay is calculated according to the number of hours worked. Thus, the weekly paycheck will fluctuate as the number of hours actually worked varies. The word *salary* applies to compensation that is uniform from one pay period to the next and does not depend upon the number of hours worked. *Salaried* often implies a status distinction, because those on salary generally are white-collar, administrative, professional, and executive employees, whereas wage-earners are designated as hourly or nonsupervisory, or blue-collar. Some of the distinctions between wage-earners and salary-earners have tended to disappear in recent years because wage-earners in some organizations do receive full pay if they are absent for such reasons as sickness, whereas salaried employees, especially at the lower levels, often receive overtime pay when they work over the standard work week. In this book the word *wage* will be used as the general term and will include salary except where it is desired to highlight salary in its more specific context.

RATIONALE OF FINANCIAL COMPENSATION

To design, from scratch, a comprehensive program of financial compensation for an organization requires that the designer have a rationale—a set of goals and underlying principles about compensation and how it should work. In actual practice compensation programs in the majority of establishments have grown up over the years by additions, patches, and trial and error—but without any overall grand design. Nevertheless, whether programs have been consciously planned or whether they have grown by trial and error, we can take a detached view and analyze what on-going programs seem to be designed to accomplish.

There are four principal goals that compensation programs may seek to accomplish.

First they seek to serve a labor market function of allocating people among firms according to the perceived attractiveness of jobs as expressed by the rate of pay and associated pay supplements. Thus, wage and salary levels are an adjunct to employee recruitment. Firms must be reasonably competitive in their rates to entice job applicants to the employment office door.

Second, carefully designed compensation programs—with job evaluation, pay scales, and employee classification procedures—enable management to control wages and salaries and control labor costs. Supervisors are not allowed to pay their people above the job rate. Many firms carefully control the distribution of rates within a given rate range. Tight controls may be placed upon the frequency and size of pay increases. A tight table of organization may be constructed for each department. Thus, a particular department manager may be permitted to have only so many machinists first class, technicians second class, and so forth. He cannot pad his payroll or build an empire.

A third major objective of wage and salary programs is to keep employees content, to minimize quitting, and to reduce employee complaints and grievances due to inadequate or inequitable wage rates. It is hoped that a rational program of pay administration can satisfy employees that their pay is fair and that favoritism and discrimination have played no part in the allocation of money. Basically we are saying that management is using pay as a satisfier or as a hygienic factor. A satisfier (hygienic factor) must be distinguished from a motivator. A satisfier affects the feeling of well-being and contentment. If a satisfier such as pay is inadequate, employees may grouse, complain, quit, or agitate for a union. On the other hand, if the pay is perfectly proper and adequate, they may not be motivated to work any harder. A motivator, on the other hand, is something that induces one to consciously change his behavior.

A fourth and final goal of compensation is to induce and reward better performance. In other words, pay is looked upon as a motivator. It is a deeply cherished belief among American managers, generally, that increases in pay should be granted primarily on the basis of performance. Those who produce more should be paid more. Superior output and superior creativity must be rewarded. American business executives have asserted this loudly and often from Chamber of Commerce and National Association of Manufacturers platforms, via internal house organs for their employees, and to assembled union leaders. Executives have often railed against the leveling effect of union-imposed, seniority-dominated job and pay structures.

In brief, then, wage and salary programs can have four major purposes: (1) to recruit people to the firm; (2) to control payroll costs; (3) to satisfy people, to reduce quitting, grievances, and frictions over pay; and (4) to motivate people to superior performance. The weight of evidence shows that goals 1, 2, and 3 are accomplished reasonably well in the better managed organizations but that goal 4—motivation—is very poorly accomplished.

Patten studied the actual distribution of pay rates of thousands of nonunion salaried employees in a conglomerate type corporation. He compared performance ratings with the positions of the people within their pay-grade ranges. He found that length of service and age were much stronger correlates of a person's pay than his proficiency rating. He found that people with extensive years of service almost invariably drifted into the top quarter of their rate ranges regardless of their efficiency rating.[1] Lawler found a similar result in his study of the compensation of managers in a variety of organizations. There was very little relationship between their pay and their rated job performance. Yet the top executives of these firms claimed that pay was administered as an incentive.[2] In one large national company Mason Haire found very little correlation between past performance (as measured by salary) and recent raises in pay for middle and top managers. He concluded that raises were almost randomly distributed.[3]

Piece-rate and other incentive schemes for factory workers are widely used and are supposed to induce superior output. Yet widespread restriction of output exists in American industry. This phenomenon will be dealt with more fully in Chapter 25, "Individual and Group Incentives."

Can pay be used as a motivator? Yes it can. Frederick Taylor and his followers who constructed the scientific management movement looked upon the worker pretty much as an "economic man." They viewed money motivation as paramount. Elton Mayo discovered the social and belongingness motives of man in the world of work. Recent behavioral scientists have emphasized the needs for power, achievement, and self-actualization. Some management practitioners and some of the interpreters of the behavioral writers have erroneously understood these human scientists to say that money is not and cannot be a motivator. This is not what they actually said.

They actually said that there are many bases for motivation: money, job security, emotional security, respect, social acceptance, power, achievement, and so on. They said that money was erroneously viewed as *the* prime mover in the past. They downgraded money as a motivator but did not eliminate it. At times nonfinancial incentives are most important to the individual. At other times economic incentives occupy the spotlight. For the young professional who is raising a family and who has just entered industry, the need for more money to pay off a home mortgage, for the material wants of his family, and later to educate his children, may be very pressing. Yet at other times in his life cycle the goals of recognition, status, and achievement may be most important to him.

Pay is important for providing the material necessities of life, yes. But it is also

[1] Thomas H. Patten, Jr., "Merit Increases and the Facts of Organizational Life," *Management of Personnel Quarterly*, Vol. 7, No. 2 (Summer 1968), pp. 30–38.

[2] Edward E. Lawler III, "The Mythology of Management Compensation," *California Management Review*, Vol. IX, No. 1 (Fall 1966), pp. 11–22.

[3] Mason Haire, "The Incentive Character of Pay," in Robert Andrews, ed., *Managerial Compensation* (Ann Arbor, Mich.: Foundation for Research on Human Behavior, 1965), pp. 13–17.

important for what it symbolizes. For some people, money symbolizes security. For others it represents success. High pay may permit one to join the country club and the yacht club. If the boss grants one a sizeable pay increase, this may show the subordinate that the boss likes him and approves of his behavior.

Pay, especially earned and deserved pay increases, can satisfy higher order needs. Pay can be a motivator if geared to achievement.

In actual fact, though, in industry, pay administrators and top-management policy setters have given only lip service to the concept of pay as an incentive. The overwhelming emphasis, in practice, has been on designing and operating wage and salary systems that would keep people satisfied and insure continued membership in the organization. And both workers and managers alike have observed this to be true, too often. The clerical employee who works her heart out soon finds that she gets an increase of $10 per week, whereas her co-worker who slacks off much of the time gets a $7 increase. The extra dollars weren't worth the effort. The same is true for exempt personnel. The engineer who created three patentable designs over the past year is rewarded with a $700 increase, whereas the plodders and the followers receive $500. The union wins a 6 percent across-the-board increase for the production workers. To insure equity for the nonunion salaried personnel, management budgets 6 percent that is to be distributed selectively on the basis of merit. But when all the raises have been granted, employees get to comparing paychecks. They soon conclude that, although individual differences exist, the major thrust has been an across-the-board increase. Rigidly drawn salary structures, narrow pay ranges, and close limits on the frequency and amount of pay increases all serve to reinforce the control and the equitability functions of a pay system. This also dampens any motivational impact of pay. The goal of equity to keep people satisfied is overriding and perhaps with considerable justification. Many times the contribution of individuals cannot readily be identified as in term activities or in process-paced work. The appraisal of human performance is highly subjective. Management may not always be able to justify significantly different pay to employees assigned to similar duties. General economic conditions, supply and demand for labor, changes in competitive rates and in the cost of living—these all may necessitate a general across-the-board pay increase. There may then be very little left over in the budget for selective motivational increases in pay for deserving individuals.

Although specific research evidence is not totally clear on just how pay can be allocated so that it has the greatest motivational impact, it is probable that the size of a person's increase must be large in proportion to his base pay; that the increase must be determined by an appraisal plan perceived to be fair by all concerned; that the increase must be in some reasonable relationship to the value of the person's contribution, both in size and timing; and finally that the entire pay-for-performance plan have the full approval of management and the groups of employees involved.

PRINCIPAL COMPENSATION ISSUES

Discussion of the multitude of topics and problems of wage and salary administration can be most conveniently organized around seven distinct but related issues. These are as follows:

1. *Pay levels.* This refers to whether the entire structure is high, average, or low. It is determined by competitive rates in the labor market and industry, financial strength of the company, management policies, and other factors.
2. *Internal pay structure.* This concerns the hierarchy of pay rates, pay grades, and job classifications. Normally job evaluation constitutes the heart of this process.
3. *Individual pay assignment.* This involves classifying people into job titles and pay grades. It also means determining how much money each person is entitled to if the pay grades comprise a range of pay for each grade. Performance appraisal, a topic covered in Chapter 12, is intimately tied to the process of individual pay assignment in those organizations that relate pay to performance.
4. *Pay by time or by output.* Most people are paid by the hour, week, or month according to elapsed time on the job. However, some people are on piecework and are paid according to units of output. This topic is covered in Chapter 25, "Individual and Group Incentives."
5. *Special problems of professionals and managers.* Various incentive, tax-saving, and fringe-benefit plans are in common usage for corporate executives. For professionals there is a tendency to assign the pay rank to the person based upon his qualifications and performance, whereas for most other occupational categories, the pay rank is based primarily upon the intrinsic job content.
6. *Fringe benefits and pay supplements.* Such items as insurance, pensions, paid vacations, bonuses, profit-sharing, and the like are properly considered part of total employee compensation. They are a part of the company's labor costs, and they constitute part of the attractiveness of a job. These topics are covered in Chapter 25, "Individual and Group Incentives," and Chapter 27, "Benefits and Services."
7. *Control of wages and salaries.* Wage and salary administrators have devised a variety of techniques for regulating payroll costs. A table of organization may dictate just which job classifications are permitted in each operating department of the business. Job classifications may be audited annually to insure that the job descriptions and pay grades accurately reflect the current level of work performed. Incentive earnings may be reviewed to detect loose incentive rates. Pay increases may be carefully budgeted or limited.

WAGE CRITERIA

The determination of the wages for jobs and people has reached the stage where it can be very logical, consistent, systematic, and explainable, but it is not an exact science and never will be. For one reason the give and take in the labor market and the forces of supply and demand prevent this.

Let us now examine those factors that help establish wages in individual organizations. These factors do not operate alone but usually work together in determining wage rates, levels, and wage increments.

Prevailing Wages

Most firms decide whether their wages are right or not be ascertaining what other firms are paying for the same class of work in the same labor market or sometimes in the same industry regardless of where it is located. Although the firm can attract labor by paying somewhat less, in the long run it has to come reasonably close to its competition in order to obtain labor in sufficient quantity and of proper quality. The familiar economic price determinant of *supply and demand* is really intimately related to the prevailing wage concept. If the supply of a particular labor skill, say that of a machinist, becomes scarce, the buyers bid up the price in the labor market, and the prevailing wage rises. Likewise the reverse can happen. If an organization finds that it is unable to attract and retain the labor it desires, it may be that its wage level is too low.

Ability to Pay

The ability of the employer to pay affects the general level of wages in an organization relative to the prevailing level in the labor market or industry. It does not establish rates for individual jobs or people, as such. Within the same industry, firms that are enjoying good sales and profit pictures over the long run tend to pay higher wages than those having difficulty making ends meet. Marginal firms usually pay wages lower than the average for their labor market or industry.

Cost of Living

By the late 1970's about nine million employees were working under union-employer agreements in which wages were adjusted automatically up or down in conformance with changes in the Consumer Price Index prepared by the Bureau of Labor Statistics of the United States Department of Labor. Such union contract provisions are commonly called escalator clauses. Used in this way, the purchasing power of employees' wages is maintained approximately constant, regardless of changes in the general cost of living for the country as a whole. Where there is no automatic formula for adjusting wages according to the cost of living, individual employees, unions, and employers nevertheless do give consideration to these changes and use the fact that prices are rising or falling to bolster their positions in wage discussions and bargaining.

Related to the cost of living is the concept of a "living wage." How much money does it cost a wage-earner and his family to live per year at an adequate level of living? In a comprehensive research program, the United States Department of Labor determines each year what it would cost a city worker, his wife, and two children to live per year at lower, intermediate, and higher standards of living. For the autumn of 1977, it would cost this family of four living in an urban area $17,106 per year to sustain the standard of living defined as the intermediate level. This figure includes costs for food, housing, transportation, clothing, personal care, medical care, recreation, insurance, and taxes. The cost for this defined intermediate budget varied a good deal from city to city. For example the cost was $20,609 in Boston, $19,972 in New York–Northeastern New Jersey and only $14,776 in Austin, Texas.[4]

Generally employers do not favor using the concept of a living wage as a guide to wage determination, because they prefer to base wages upon employee contribution rather than need. Also they feel that the level of living prescribed in worker-budget studies is open to argument and is somewhat a matter of opinion.

Productivity

The key to the high standard of living that we in the United States enjoy in comparison with many other peoples of the world is our high level of productivity in the economy as a whole. Productivity is commonly measured in terms of goods and services produced or performed per employee-hour of labor. From 1947 to 1966 in the private economy in the United States, productivity increased at an average annual rate of 3.2 percent. However, from 1966 to 1975 the annual growth rate dropped to 1.9 percent.[5] Productivity improvements are generated by a combination of factors. These include technological improvements, greater capital investment, better methods of production, better education and job training of workers, improved worker ingenuity and skill, and more effective management.

In general highly productive industries and companies tend to pay higher wage rates than do low productivity industries and firms. Wage increases in excess of increases in prices—that is, increases in *real* wages—can be obtained if productivity increases are greater than the rate of inflation. During the period 1947 to 1962 real hourly earnings of nonsupervisory workers in the private nonfarm economy increased at an average rate of 2.5 percent annually. However, from 1962 to 1976 real wages increased an average of only 1.2 percent a year.[6] This lower rate of improvement in real wages in more recent years has been caused by the generally lower rate of productivity growth and high rate of inflation during this period.

Productivity can be looked at in another way also. When operating under a wage-incentive system in a plant, greater productivity by individual employees is recognized in the form of higher wages. Increased skill and effort cause higher productivity, which results in higher earnings.

Bargaining Power

When employees organize a union for purposes of collective bargaining with their employer, they often are able to obtain larger wage concessions than they would as unorganized individuals. The economic benefits to be gained by a strong organization are certainly attested to by the results achieved by many of

[4] U.S. Department of Labor, Bureau of Labor Statistics, *Autumn 1977 Urban Family Budgets and Comparative Indexes for Selected Urban Areas* (Washington, D.C.: Government Printing Office, 1978).

[5] Gordon F. Bloom and Herbert R. Northrup, *Economics of Labor Relations*, 8th ed. (Homewood, Ill.: Richard D. Irwin, Inc., 1977).

[6] H. M. Douty, "The Slowdown in Real Wages: A Postwar Perspective," *Monthly Labor Review*, Vol. 100, No. 8 (August 1977), pp. 7–12.

the larger and powerful labor unions in this country. Although a good argument can be made that forcing wages up faster than increases in productivity causes unemployment (as many believe has occurred in the coal industry) or higher prices and inflation, nevertheless, for those remaining on the payrolls a real gain is often achieved as a consequence of stronger bargaining power. Although the problem of comparing union and nonunion wage levels is a complicated one, the Bureau of Labor Statistics has compiled data in broad occupational categories that show that annual earnings of unionized workers are generally higher than those of nonunion workers. For example, in 1970 the median annual earnings of white-collar workers in the United States who belonged to labor unions were $8,609, whereas the annual earnings of nonunion white-collar workers were only $7,452. Unionized craftsmen, foremen, and kindred workers had median annual earnings of $10,034, whereas nonunion workers earned only $8,558. In manufacturing industries assemblers, checkers, examiners, and inspectors who were unionized had a median of $7,450, while nonunion workers had a median of only $5,693.[7]

Job Requirements

For ascertaining the relative value of one job to another within an organization, measures of job difficulty are frequently used. This is the basis for the many job-evaluation plans in use in industry. Jobs are graded according to the relative amounts of skill, effort, and responsibility required, and the adversity of the job conditions. The subject of job evaluation will be examined in detail later in this chapter.

Federal and State Laws

Federal and state labor laws affect wage and salary rates and structures. The Fair Labor Standards Act of 1938, as amended in 1977, provides for a minimum wage of $2.65 per hour effective January 1, 1978; $2.90 on January 1, 1979; $3.10 on January 1, 1980; and $3.35 on January 1, 1981. Nearly all employees in private business and industry are covered by this law. Excluded are employees of small farms and very small or intrastate businesses. This Act has special provisions which permit employers to exclude executive, administrative, and professional employees from overtime pay rules if certain conditions are met. In addition to the Federal law, 42 states have their own minimum wage laws.

For years many companies tended to pay women less than men for the same classifications of work. This practice was outlawed by the Equal Pay Act of 1963, effective June 1964, which amended the Fair Labor Standards Act and prohibits discrimination in wage payments on the basis of sex.

Observations Concerning These Criteria

These factors that determine wages do not operate in an isolated, distinct manner. Rather several criteria usually interact at the same time to influence wage

[7] U.S. Department of Labor, Bureau of Labor Statistics, *Selected Earnings and Demographic Characteristics of Union Members, 1970*, Report 417 (Washington, D.C.: Government Printing Office, 1972).

determination. For example, ability to pay and productivity are very closely related. In manufacturing, one company may have greater profits and lower costs because it has developed and invested in labor-saving machinery that has increased its productivity. Job requirements are listed as a wage criterion. One element of this is skill. High-skilled jobs pay more than low-skilled ones within the same company. But probably the reason more money is assigned to a high-skilled job is that there are fewer people available to fill such jobs (supply and demand).

WAGE POLICY AND PRINCIPLES

The wage policies of different firms vary somewhat. Marginal companies pay the minimum necessary to attract the required amount and type of labor. Often these companies pay only the minimum wage rates required by Federal or state law. With these rates they tend to be able to recruit only marginal labor.

At the other extreme some organizations pay well above the going rates in the labor market. They adopt such a policy because they seek to attract and retain the highest caliber labor force obtainable. By paying high rates, management is able to demand superior performance from its employees. Some managers believe in the economy of high wages. They feel that by paying good wages they can attract superior workers who will produce more than the average worker in industry. This greater production per employee, in effect, means greater output per man-hour. Hence labor costs may turn out to be lower than those existing in firms hiring only marginal quality labor.

Some companies also pay high wage rates because of a combination of favorable product market demand, superior ability to pay, and bargaining power from a strong union. This situation has characterized the basic steel industry for many years.

We have been talking about the extremes to this point. It is fair to say that the vast majority of companies seek to be competitive in their wage program. That is to say, they aim to pay somewhere near the going rate in the labor market for the various classes of labor they employ. Realistically they expect to employ a reasonably good quality of labor and to pay people fairly, with respect to one another, so that the employees feel they are paid properly. They do not want wage inequities to be a source of employee discontent. Thus, most firms give major weight to two wage criteria: job requirements and prevailing rates of pay in the labor market. Other factors, such as changes in the cost of living, supply and demand, ability to pay, and productivity are accorded subsidiary status, although special circumstances (for example, if the firm has been losing money for several years) may force one of these factors to the fore in the short run.

A generally sound policy is to adopt a job-evaluation program in order to establish fair differentials in pay based upon differences in job content. Employees are in a reasonably good position to judge whether their jobs are paid correctly in relation to other jobs in the plant. Job evaluation insures internal consistency of wage rates within the plant. External consistency—that is, reasonable equality with going rates paid by other companies in the community—can be achieved when a firm periodically surveys community rates and adjusts its general level of wages as required.

Principles of Wage and Salary Administration

The field of wage administration has been sufficiently well developed so that certain generally accepted guidelines and principles can be formulated.

1. There should be a definite plan in which differences in pay for jobs are based upon variation in job requirements, such as skill, effort, responsibility, and job conditions.
2. The general level of wages and salaries should be reasonably in line with that prevailing in the labor market. In some instances equality with pay levels in the industry is used instead of the labor market. The labor market criterion is most commonly used.
3. The plan should carefully distinguish between jobs and employees. A job carries a certain wage rate, and a person is assigned to fill it at that rate. Exceptions sometimes occur in high-level professional and executive jobs in which the job holder may make the job large or small, depending upon his abilities and contributions.
4. Equal pay for equal work. If two jobs have equal job difficulty requirements, the pay should be the same regardless of who fills them. This principle does not prevent having a rate range with individuals receiving different compensation within the range.
5. An equitable means should be adopted for recognizing individual differences in ability and contribution. For some concerns this may take the form of rate ranges with in-grade increases; in others it may be a wage-incentive plan; and in still others it may take the form of closely integrated sequences of job promotion.
6. The employees, and the union if there is one, should be adequately informed about the procedures used to establish wage rates. Every employee should be informed of his own position in the wage or salary structure. Secrecy in wage matters should not be used as a cover-up for a haphazard and unreasonable wage program.

JOB EVALUATION

Job evaluation is a formalized system for determining the relative money value of jobs within an organization. It involves the analysis of jobs for the purpose of writing job descriptions and specifications, rating of these jobs through use of a job evaluation plan, and conversion of relative job values to definite wage rates.

Historically, early attempts at job analysis and job evaluation were begun for the Civil Service Commission of Chicago in 1909 and shortly thereafter at the Commonwealth Edison Company in Chicago. A prototype of the modern systems of job evaluation was developed in 1924 by Merrill R. Lott, who created the first real point system for use by the Sperry Gyroscope Company. In 1926 Eugene Benge and Associates developed the factor-comparison method for the Philadelphia Rapid Transit Company.[8]

The adoption of job evaluation programs by industrial concerns increased in

[8] E. Lanham, *Job Evaluation* (McGraw-Hill Book Company, 1955), pp. 6–8.

the late 1930's and became very widespread by the late 1940's. Factors inducing companies to adopt wage rationalization programs were the rise of industrial unions in the 1930's, decisions of the National War Labor Board during World War II, and internal recognition by management of the need for orderly, logical means for establishing wage rates. Management has learned that it must have some means for explaining how it has arrived at wage-rate decisions when it is negotiating with unions.

Figure 24-1 explains in chart form the various elements of job evaluation and their interrelationship.

Certain basic principles must be followed when evaluating jobs. First it must be noted that those who are doing the evaluation must rate the job, not the employee. In deciding how much money a particular job is worth, there is always a temptation to be influenced in one's judgment by the qualifications and caliber of the individual who is presently performing the work. But he may be either over- or underqualified. It is the assignment of those doing the rating to be guided by the requirements of the job. It may be that an error has been made in placing individuals on particular jobs, but this is a responsibility of supervision and the personnel department.

A second guide to keep in mind is that, whenever possible, the pooled or combined judgments of several persons should be employed in evaluating jobs. Job evaluation is a systematic, orderly, logical way of setting rates of pay within an

Figure 24-1
The Elements of Job Evaluation.

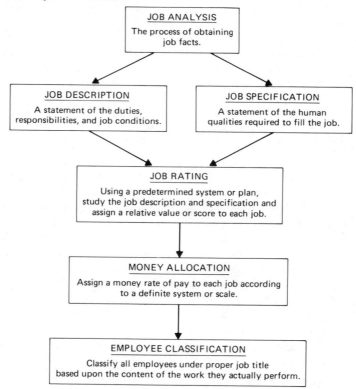

organization or company; however, it is not exact measurement; it is grading or rating. The decisions of a number of qualified persons will reduce the likelihood of serious errors.

A third factor to bear in mind is that the accuracy of job rating is determined primarily by the accuracy of the basic job facts available. A comprehensive program of job analysis must serve as a basis for any job-evaluation program.

JOB EVALUATION SYSTEMS

There exist in current usage four main types of job evaluation methods or systems. These are as follows:

Nonquantitative systems
1. Ranking or job comparison.
2. Grade description.
Quantitative systems
1. Point.
2. Factor comparison.

Although it is true that various practitioners and management consultants have from time to time developed modifications of one or a combination of two or more systems, the basic ways of evaluating jobs can be fully analyzed and understood by concentrating our attention on these fundamental types.

Ranking System

The ranking or rank-order system is suitable for small companies having a limited number of jobs. Although theoretically the method could be used for large organizations as well, it then becomes much too cumbersome for attaining a reasonable degree of accuracy. As for all four systems, accurate and complete job-analysis data are fundamental to the success of the ranking method. The procedure involves obtaining descriptions for all the jobs under consideration and ranking these from low to high job requirements. If the organization is small, with only two or three departments involved, management can satisfactorily dovetail the jobs from the departments to come up with a master list, as illustrated below:

High Job	12. Electrician		6. Drill-Press Operator
Requirements	11. Toolmaker		5. Punch-Press Operator
	10. Machinist		4. Spray Painter
	9. Millright		3. Materials Handling Man
	8. Fitter	Low Job	2. Laborer
	7. Assembler	Requirements	1. Floor Sweeper

Presumably the jobs will already have wage rates attached to them; the ranking system is being used to judge whether these are equitable. By arranging the jobs in an array such as this and with a committee of competent management personnel, necessary adjustments can be made in wage rates to correct any apparent discrepancies.

However, the ranking method has serious disadvantages that limit its usefulness. Judgments are frequently strongly influenced by present wage rates. The ranking process does not tell one how far apart the jobs are in job difficulty and content. The procedure is very cumbersome when jobs from a larger number of departments must be dovetailed together. The procedure likewise does not provide any means for recording on paper the substantiations for the ratings. Its principal virtue is that it is easy to apply to organizations having no more than, say, fifteen to twenty jobs.

Grade-Description System

The grade-description system, also called the classification system, is the one that was used for classifying jobs in the United States Civil Service for many years. Essentially it involves dividing up the job hierarchy into a number of pay groups or grades, developing written definitions for each grade, and then assigning every job to a particular grade.

In order to construct a grade-description scale, the basic information must come from descriptions of all the jobs involved. As in much job evaluation work it is best to use a committee to take advantage of pooled judgment in arriving at decisions. The committee must actually set up a rank-order list of a large representative sample of all the jobs in the organization, giving consideration to duties, skills, abilities, responsibilities, and other differentiating qualities. These jobs are then grouped into classes or grades that represent different pay levels ranging from low to high. By analyzing the job descriptions for those jobs slotted into each grade, common types of tasks, skills, knowledge, responsibilities, and job conditions can be identified and written in somewhat general language, so that these statements then become grade descriptions. When these have been developed for all grades they can then be used as a standard for assigning all other jobs to a particular pay grade.

Below are printed the first three grade descriptions for what is called the General Schedule (GS) covering professional, scientific, clerical, and administrative positions of the United States Government as defined in the Classification Act of 1949.

General schedule.

Grade GS-1 includes all classes of positions the duties of which are to perform, under immediate supervision, with little or no latitude for the exercise of independent judgment, (1) the simplest routine work in office, business, or fiscal operations, or (2) elementary work of a subordinate technical character in a professional, scientific, or technical field.

Grade GS-2 includes all classes of positions the duties of which are (1) to perform, under immediate supervision, with limited latitude for the exercise of independent judgment, routine work in office, business, or fiscal operations, or comparable subordinate technical work of limited scope in a professional, scientific, or technical field, requiring some training or experience, or (2) to perform other work of equal importance, difficulty, and responsibility, and requiring comparable qualifications.

Grade GS-3 includes all classes of positions the duties of which are (1) to perform, under immediate or general supervision, somewhat difficult and responsible work in office, business or fiscal operations, or comparable subordinate technical work of limited scope in a professional, scientific, or technical field, requiring in either case (a) some training or experience, (b) working knowledge of a special subject matter, or (c) to some extent the exercise of independent judgment in accordance with well-established policies, procedures, and techniques; or (2) to perform other work of equal importance, difficulty, and responsibility, and requiring comparable qualifications.

The assignment of a wage rate for each grade can be accomplished by taking an average of the existing rates for all the jobs in each grade or by following a procedure similar to that of the point system, which will be described later in this chapter.

In the mid-1970's the Federal government adopted and began to install the Factor Ranking system of job evaluation in place of the long-used grade description method. Factor Ranking is a combination of the point and factor comparison systems.[9]

In assessing the merits of the grade-description system, we can see that it is a definite improvement over the ranking method, because here we have a fixed written scale against which to compare all jobs. The process of rating jobs in the grade-description system involves a job-to-scale comparison. Because jobs often change in content over a period of time, one can readily see that the use of a scale is more durable and standardized. Also jobs are grouped into pay grades for administrative simplicity. A serious fault of the classification plan is that the grade description must of necessity be rather general and abstract in order to be applicable to a great variety of jobs. Also, like the ranking method it provides no way of weighting the compensable factors that make up jobs. How does one determine the worth of one job having high-skill requirements and low-job hazards in comparison with one having high hazards and low skill?

Point System

The point system is, by a wide margin, the most commonly used method of job evaluation in the United States. It is more complicated than either of the preceding two that have been described. If a company chooses to adopt the point system, it can either select a universal type of plan, such as that developed by A. L. Kress for the National Electrical Manufacturers Association, or it can tailor-make a plan to suit its own particular needs. If the decision favors a custom-designed plan, the company can either have personnel from within its own organization do the work (commonly this would be either the personnel department or the industrial engineering department), or it can engage an outside management consultant to plan and direct the installation. Initial discussion here will explain how to rate jobs by using a point plan that has already been established in an organization. After this some important considerations involved in constructing a point plan will be given.

Every point plan consists of a number of compensable job factors or characteristics. These can be classified under the four headings of skill, effort, responsi-

---

[9] Harold Suskin, ed., *Job Evaluation and Pay Administration in the Public Sector* (Chicago: International Personnel Management Association, 1977) ch. 5.

bility, and job conditions. Examples of factors or job attributes that are frequently used are listed below.

Factor Categories

	Skill	*Effort*	*Responsibility*	*Job Conditions*

Factors	Education
	Experience
	Training
	Judgment
	Analysis
	Mental
	  complexity
	Manual
	  dexterity
	Adaptability
		Physical
		  demand
		Visual effort
		Concentration
		Mental effort
		Muscular
		  coordination
		Alertness
			For preventing
			  monetary loss
			For direction
			  of others
			For machines
			For materials
			For safety
			  of others
			For policy
				Working
				  conditions
				Hazards

Of course, no single plan utilizes all these factors. Eight to twelve factors are common. Each factor is subdivided into degrees that define the relative amount of that factor that may be required for each of a series of jobs. Thus experience, which is almost universally employed as a factor, might be subdivided into five degrees: first degree, zero up to three months; second degree, three up to six months; third degree, six up to twelve months; fourth degree, one year up to three years; and fifth degree, three years and over. A scale of points is assigned to the degrees of each factor. Every point rating plan consists of factors with definitions for these factors, and each factor is broken down into degrees with written definitions for every degree. Figure 24-2 shows a complete point plan for nonmanagerial salaried positions. In rating a job, the proper degree for every factor is selected, and the corresponding points are tabulated to obtain a total score. This point sum corresponds to a particular wage or salary grade level, which in turn signifies a particular wage.

The process of developing a new point plan is rather involved. Initially a significant sample of the jobs for which the plan is to be used must be analyzed and job descriptions and specifications prepared. Usually one plan is designed for hourly paid production or shop type jobs, another for clerical jobs, and a third for professional, technical, and managerial jobs. Those developing the plan must decide what job attributes or factors the employer wants to pay for (that is, what factors are significant for the type of jobs under consideration). Then these factors must be rather precisely defined. Each factor is then divded into a number of degrees, degree definitions are developed, and then the factors must be given a weighting. For example, experience is generally weighted much heavier than physical effort. After the weightings have been arrived at, point progressions must be given to the degrees for each factor. Although judgment plays a part in setting up the point scales, certain statistical techniques (notably linear correlation and multiple correlation methods) are often employed in addition. The method used to convert points to money will be discussed later in this chapter under the heading "Establishing the Pay Structure."

The strengths of the point system are numerous. First of all, it breaks jobs down into factors or attributes, and this is certainly an aid to evaluation. The fac-

Factors	Degrees and Points							
	1	2	3	4	5	6	7	8
I Education	20	40	60	80	100	120		
II Training and Experience	10	30	50	70	90	110	130	150
III Decisions	10	30	50	75	100			
IV Responsibility for Loss	5	15	25	35	45	60	75	
V Relations with Others	10	30	50	70	90			
VI Job Conditions	5	15	25	40				

I EDUCATION

This factor evaluates the general educational development, whether acquired through formal schooling or informally through life experiences, required to perform the job.

Degree	Definition	Points
1	Follow simple oral one- and two-step instructions; add, subtract, multiply, divide and count whole numbers; read and write simple sentences.	20
2	Carry out detailed but simple written or oral instructions; add, subtract, multiply, and divide including use of decimals and fractions; read simple drawings and memoranda; fill out standardized routine forms.	40
3	Compute such items as discount, interest, percentage, ratio, volume; use elementary algebra or plane geometry; draw simple graphs or charts; read mechanical drawings instructions, and specifications; write routine reports such as production and quality reports; write routine correspondence.	60
4	Use algebra including linear, quadratic and exponential functions; use plane and solid geometry; use shop mathematics including proportions, and trigonometry; prepare correspondence of a non-routine or elementary technical nature; prepare reports requiring explanations of information; apply principles of such subjects as bookkeeping, electrical wiring systems, drafting, nursing.	80
5	Use advanced algebra, calculus, statistics; apply the sciences such as biology, chemistry, physics, or economics; apply general accounting principles; read complex drawings and specifications; prepare correspondence and reports of an involved or technical nature.	100
6	Apply specialized and advanced theory in mathematics, the physical sciences, or behavioral sciences; prepare reports concerning technically involved subject; apply principles of logical and scientific thinking to a broad range of problems; deal with a variety of abstract and concrete concepts.	120

Figure 24-2
A Point Plan of Job Evaluation for Nonmanagerial Salaried Positions Including Clerical, Technical, Service, and Professional.

tors are fixed and preweighted in such a way that all those doing the rating are forced to consider each job on the same factors and in the same way. The margin for differences of opinion, which is quite great in both the ranking and grade-description methods, is considerably narrowed. The likelihood of continuing or pyramiding errors over a period of time is minimized, because new jobs are rated against a fixed scale rather than against other jobs. The job-rating substantiation sheets, which are customarily used, provide a means for permanently

Figure 24-2 (Continued)

recording the reasons for each rating. Also points permit a ready and logical conversion to money. The principal disadvantage of the system is its greater cost of development and installation as compared with ranking and grade description. However, the greater accuracy possible with its use usually justifies the larger expenditure of time and effort.

Factor Comparison System

Being the second most popular system after the point method, the factor comparison method is often used for evaluating white-collar, professional, and managerial positions, although it is equally suitable for grading others as well. It is es-

Degree	Amount	Points	Degree	Amount	Points
1	Up to $25	5	5	500 – 999	45
2	$25 to $49	15	6	1000 – 1999	60
3	50 – 99	25	7	2000 – and over	75
4	100 – 499	35			

V RELATIONS WITH OTHERS

This factor evaluates the nature and complexity of relationships and contacts with other persons.

Degree	Definition	Points
1	Dealings limited to employees and supervisor within own work unit.	10
2	Deal with persons both within own department and in other departments or organization; give and receive routine information.	30
3	Deal with persons in other departments and in other organizations; give and receive various oral and written information; tact required to obtain cooperation.	50
4	Deal with persons both within and outside the organization involving discussions, explanations, and agreements on matters of importance to the functioning of the job or department.	70
5	Deal with persons both within and outside the organization including company managers, customers, or government officials; often involves negotiation, persuasion, and making agreements affecting welfare of organization.	90

VI JOB CONDITIONS

This factor evaluates both the quality of working conditions and hazards which might cause injury or illness.

Degree	Definition	Points
1	Normal office conditions.	5
2	Infrequent exposure to one or two disagreeable conditions such as noise, heat, cold, or dirt. Little or no exposure to accident hazards.	15
3	Occasional exposure to two or more disagreeable conditions such as noise, heat, cold, dirt, fumes. Exposure to injuries such as cuts, burns, or abrasions which would require absence up to two weeks.	25
4	Frequent exposure to two or more objectionable conditions such as noise, heat, cold, fumes, vibration, etc. Frequent exposure to serious hazards such as broken bones or hernia requiring absence of two weeks or more.	40

Figure 24-2 (Continued)

sentially a combination of the ranking and point systems. Like the rank-order method, it rates jobs by comparing one with another; like the point system, it is more analytical in the sense of subdividing jobs into compensable factors, and final ratings are expressed in terms of numbers. Actually ratings give us money directly.

In examining this method, we will first see how to rate jobs in an existing installation—that is, after the plan has been established. Figure 24-3 shows a job comparison scale or ladder diagram containing key jobs. This together with the job descriptions and specifications for these jobs constitutes the tools necessary

Cents Per Hour Per Factor	Mental Requirements	Skill Requirements	Physical Requirements	Responsibility	Working Conditions
170	Electronic Tech.	Tool Maker Machinist			
	Tool Maker				
160	Electrician	Electronic Tech.		Inspector Electronic Tech. Tool Maker	
150	Machinist				
				Electrician	
140	Inspector	Electrician			
130		Engine Lathe oper.	Laborer		
				Machinist	
120		Turret Lathe oper.	Assembler Fork Lift oper.	Engine Lathe oper.	Laborer Fork Lift oper.
	Engine Lathe oper.		Turret Lathe oper.		
110		Inspector	Electrician Machinist		Assembler Janitor
100	Turret Lathe oper.		Janitor	Fork Lift oper. Turret Lathe oper.	Machinist Turret Lathe oper. Tool Maker
90	Assembler Fork Lift oper.	Assembler	Tool Maker Engine Lathe oper.	Assembler	Engine Lathe oper. Electrician
80					Inspector
		Fork Lift oper.			Electronic Tech.
70			Inspector		
	Laborer				
60	Janitor	Laborer Janitor	Electronic Tech.	Laborer Janitor	
50					

Figure 24-3
An Illustration of a Job Comparison Scale for Shop-Type Jobs—Factor Comparison Method.

for rating. Key jobs serve as standards against which all other jobs are compared. A key job is defined as one whose content has become stabilized over time, whose wage rate management officials agree is presently correct (if a union is involved, it, too, must agree as to the correctness of the rate), and which is important to the organization. A job is important if a large number of persons are performing it or if it represents a significant skill in the company. Many may wonder how we can know whether the present wage rates for key jobs are correct. Information to help guide these decisions can be obtained by making job-to-job comparisons and by conducting an area wage survey.

The factor-comparison method customarily has about five compensable factors on which all jobs are rated. This is considerably fewer than the point system, but is nevertheless sufficient, because they are each defined more broadly. It is not absolutely necessary that the particular ones given in Figure 24-3 be the only ones that are used; nor need they be confined to five in number. The ones listed in this example are generally employed in this method, however.

In rating a new job, it is necessary that it be compared with all the other key jobs, one factor at a time. It is then assigned a money value in cents per hour for each factor according to the point on the scale at which this job best fits. This process is repeated for all of the other factors. The total money value obtained by adding the selected amount for each one individually is the wage rate for the job being evaluated. Essentially, then, the process of rating involves comparing the job description and specification for each job to be rated with all of the descriptions for the key jobs, working one factor at a time.

One may properly ask where this job-comparison scale comes from, so we shall now turn our attention to the problem of constructing a particular factor-comparison plan. Because it requires the use of key jobs from within the company for which the plan is being established, it must always be tailor-made. It is not possible to use a universal type of plan, as may be done with the point system. Let us examine Figure 24-4 to learn how to build a factor-comparison scale. This is a very simplified example, for in actual practice twenty or more key jobs are used, the number depending upon the total number of jobs involved.

Figure 24-4
A Factor Comparison Work Sheet Used in Setting Up the Key Job Rating Scale. *R* stands for rank; *M* stands for money. Rank number 1 is for the job having the highest amount of the factor, and 4 is for the lowest.

	Mental Requirements		Skill Requirements		Physical Requirements		Responsibility		Working Conditions	
	R	M	R	M	R	M	R	M	R	M
$6.40/hr. Electrician	1	158	1	140	3	110	1	144	4	88
$5.40/hr. Engine Lathe Operator	2	113	2	130	4	87	2	120	3	90
$4.95/hr. Assembler	3	90	3	85	2	125	3	85	2	110
$4.40/hr. Laborer	4	65	4	60	1	130	4	62	1	123

The work should be done by a committee of executives and administrators to take advantage of pooled judgment. The first step requires a ranking of the jobs, one factor at a time, until all the rankings have been agreed upon for all five factors. Then working horizontally, the present wage rate is allocated among all the factors. It will be remembered from what has been stated earlier that a characteristic of key jobs is that, by means of some other criteria, management is satisfied that the wages are correct. After all of the horizontal distributions among the factors have been completed, the money assignments must be reconciled with the vertical rankings. Thus if a particular job, such as electrician, is ranked number one on mental demand, it should receive more money than the engine lathe operator, which is ranked number two. When all discrepancies have been ironed out and the rating committee is in agreement, these key jobs can then be placed in the comparison chart as depicted in Figure 24-3. This key job comparison chart is analogus to the factors and degrees with corresponding points in the point system.

Advocates of the factor-comparison system point out that it is flexible and has no upper limit on the rating that a job may receive on a factor (the point system does have ceilings on the factors). Another advantage of this method is that it utilizes few factors and thereby reduces the likelihood of overlap—that is, two factors measuring the same quality. The procedure of rating new jobs by comparing with other standard or key jobs is logical and not too difficult to accomplish. Set against these, however, are certain disadvantages. The use of present wages for the key jobs may initially build errors into the plan. Likewise, the content and, therefore, the value of these jobs may change over a period of time, and this will lead to future errors. In other words, the standard is not fixed.

ESTABLISHING THE PAY STRUCTURE

Regardless of which method of job evaluation is used, the ultimate objective is to ascertain the proper rates of pay for all the jobs. In other words the job structure must be priced. Because both the ranking and grade-description systems are qualitative and do not arrive at number designations for the job ratings, the procedure for conversion to money is somewhat more inexact and may be handled in a variety of ways. For ranking, the existing rate may be compared with the new rankings and discrepancies corrected. It might be well to decide upon certain key job rates that are fair and correct, and then the other rates can be adjusted and slotted into the hierarchy. Under the grade-description system the jobs can be tabulated together with their present rates. Then judgments can be made as to proper rates for the grades. It will be recalled that the jobs are already grouped into grades; therefore, it may be considered sound to compute the arithmetic means of the present rates and let that serve as the new grade rate. These means could be adjusted by judgment to make a smooth or straight-line progression from grade one to the highest grade.

The factor-comparison system of conversion to money is quite simple because the method itself establishes pay directly in the rating process. Because it is desirable for administrative convenience to group jobs together into pay grades, averages of the newly determined rates can be found to give a figure for each grade.

With the point system a graph is plotted of all the points on the abscissa and the existing or old rates of pay on the ordinate. If the existing rates are reasonably correct and if the rating of the jobs under the point plan has been done carefully, we can expect these points to fall along a trend line with very little dispersion. On the other hand, if the existing structure is loaded with inequities and errors, we will find considerable dispersion or scatter from the trend line. There are a number of procedures available to ascertain the best-fitting trend line. The most common is to draw it by eye, carefully trying to insure that about the same number of points fall below as above the line. The other principal method is to use the statistical technique of "least squares." This is the most accurate way of finding the best-fitting straight line. For a straight line, $Y = a + bX$, where a is the Y intercept and b is the slope of the line, it is necessary to solve these two normal equations to determine the value of these constants.

$$\Sigma Y = Na + b\Sigma X$$
$$\Sigma XY = a\Sigma X + b\Sigma X^2$$

In these equations N is the number of jobs, Y is the wage for each job, and X is the point value. It must be noted that even if the points actually fall along a curve, these equations will give us the very best-fitting straight line. A similar statistical procedure can be used to find the best-fitting parabola, for example, if visual inspection leads one to suspect that the points would more faithfully be represented by such a curve. It would be best to consult a statistical textbook for the details of the exact procedure involved.

Figure 24-5 shows a trend line that has been drawn for a plotting of present wage rate against job evaluation points for seventeen hourly paid jobs. Our ob-

Figure 24-5
A Graph Showing a Trend Line Drawn Through a Plot of Points Versus Wage Rates for 17 Jobs with Single Rate Grades Constructed Thereon.

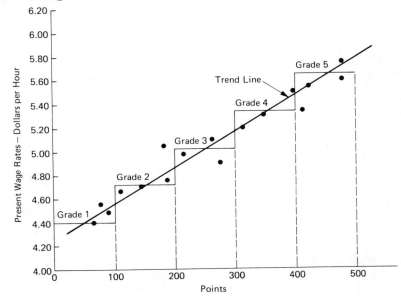

jective is to use this graph as a worksheet for constructing a wage structure with jobs grouped into labor grades. In this illustration vertical dashed guidelines have been drawn in order to divide the points into five groups or grades. Horizontal lines have been drawn though the midpoints of the trend line in each grade in order to arrive at a single rate of pay for each grade. This would be the simplest kind of structure, as shown in Table 24-1.

Table 24-1

Grade	Point Range	Hourly Wage Rate
1	0–100	$4.40
2	101–200	4.71
3	201–300	5.02
4	301–400	5.33
5	401–500	5.64

Commonly a range of money is established for each wage grade. The content and difficulty of the job are used to decide into which grade the job falls. The skills, abilities, and lengths of service of the different employees on each job determine how much money within the grade limits a particular employee receives.

Figure 24-6 is an example of how a rate range can be set up using the same data as in Figure 24-5. In this case we have five wage grades and a vertical spread of approximately 17 percent from the minimum of each grade to the maximum as shown in Table 24-2. It will be noted that the structure provides for overlap between adjacent grades. This means that the maximum rate for one

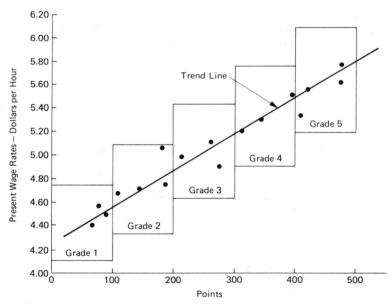

Figure 24-6
A Graph Showing a Trend Line Drawn Through a Plot of Points Versus Wage Rates for 17 Jobs with a Rate Range Established for Each Grade.

grade level is higher than the minimum rate of the next higher grade. The type of arrangement is almost always used for white-collar, professional, and administrative types of jobs. It is also sometimes used for hourly paid jobs, although in this latter case single or flat rates for each grade level are often employed. The reason for having overlapping rate ranges is that they provide greater flexibility for management in transferring an employee from a job in one grade to a job in an adjacent grade without changing his pay. This is especially true for temporary transfers. In addition, overlapping ranges are practically necessary if one wishes

Table 24-2

Grade	Point Range	Hourly Wage Range
1	0–100	$4.05–4.75
2	101–200	4.33–5.09
3	201–300	4.62–5.42
4	301–400	4.90–5.76
5	401–500	5.19–6.09

to have a reasonable vertical spread from minimum to maximum within each grade to properly compensate employees as they increase in skill and contribution during the years they may be assigned to a particular job.

Flat or single rates for each grade are useful for administrative simplicity and in situations in which the differences in merit and contribution of all employees assigned to particular jobs are slight. Unions usually demand wage uniformity within each grade in order to eliminate favoritism and discrimination in pay treatment of employees. It must be admitted that the rating of the worth of employees by their supervisors is a rather subjective process in many instances.

Over- and Underpaid Employees

Whenever a new pay structure is adopted, management is inevitably faced with the problem of how to deal with those employees whose present rates are outside the limits just established. If single rates for the grades are used, then the vast majority of employees will be off the line. A rate-range system, especially with wide limits, will reduce the number of adjustments that must be made. One approach to the problem is immediately upon installation of the new structure to raise all employees whose present rates of pay are below the new minimum for their particular grade up to that minimum. Because a primary purpose for the adoption of a job evaluation program is to eliminate inequities, this solution seems sound. Should a great number of jobs require increases thereby making the cost to the employer quite expensive, it might be practical to raise them in steps over a period of a few months. "Red circle" is a designation usually applied to those employees who are receiving more than the maximum for their grade. Mechanistically one might argue that these rates should be immediately lowered to their proper level. However, this would tend to cause a hardship for the employees affected. It certainly is no fault of theirs that management has decided to adopt a job evaluation program. They did not set the job rates in the first place. A reasonable solution would involve informing the "red circle" employees that they are being paid more than the proper rate, that they personally will continue to receive the same pay as they are now getting, but that all new persons assigned to their jobs will be paid within the grade limits. Thus, as employees are promoted to higher level jobs, and as some may eventually leave the company for reasons of retirement, resignation, and layoff, these wage rates will in the course of a few years fall into their proper slots. In addition to this solution to the problem, some organizations, when raising the entire wage structure across the board due to union bargaining or other reasons, will not grant any increases to "red circle" employees. Thus, the structure will catch up to these, and eventually they will fall within their proper limits.

Employee Classification

Regardless of which system of job evaluation is used, a decision has to be made regarding the job title to assign to every employee in the organization. For clear-cut, easily definable jobs the problem of employee classification is easy. If an employee operates a single-spindle, sensitive drill press and does nothing else, his title is self-evident, and his pay is tied to his job title.

However, many concerns have job families, such as the typist, clerk-typist, stenographer, secretarial group. A woman employed in an office may do typing, take dictation by shorthand and transcribe it, answer the telephone, sort and distribute the mail, compose routine letters for her boss, and so on. Shall she be classified as a stenographer or as a secretary? The pay differential may be $10 to $15 per week. The decision is of vital concern both to the employee and the employer. An additional example from the skilled trades should serve to emphasize the point fully. It is common in many factories to have such occupational sequences as millwright A and millwright B or machinist A and B, with the A designation receiving the higher pay and requiring somewhat greater skill and responsibility than the B.

Present Rates or Prevailing Market Rates

It should be emphasized that the entire preceding explanation concerned with establishing the pay structure has involved using existing wage rates as the basis for the new wage plan. Essentially the objective (in theory) is to iron out existing inequities and have all the rates fall upon a line when money is plotted against job difficulty points as in Figures 24-5 and 24-6. Because jobs are grouped into grades and special action is required for "red circle" rates, this theoretical goal is not achieved. However, the thoughtful reader may well question the wisdom of using present wages as a basis for building a better wage structure. If the level of the present wages is approximately correct and all that is required are some moderate adjustments of individual rates, then this procedure is sound. But if all the existing rates are out of line with the average rates prevailing in the labor market for the same class of work, then clearly it is folly to spend a large sum of money to install a job evaluation plan when the critical step of conversion to money results in the wrong answer.

A choice of one of two approaches can be used when existing rates are far apart from market averages. The first involves setting up a new structure based upon present wages, as has been already described. Then if the resultant wage rates are clearly below the average paid in the community, a policy decision must be made by top management. If it wishes to be fully competitive in the labor market, then the structure must be raised so as to achieve this goal. But the important point being emphasized here is that with such a solution the question of internal wage equity and the establishment of the structure is being treated separately from the question of the proper level and slope to the wage-trend line. The second alternative requires that wage rates for key jobs be surveyed in the labor market and that these rates be plotted against job evaluation points on the same graph as the one showing existing company rates against points for all jobs. With this approach, management is called upon to make a decision as to which trend line it wishes to use as a basis for constructing its grade levels. It may indeed choose to compromise between the present company line and the trend line for the area average key job rates. If this second alternative method is utilized, the structure is established directly upon the particular trend line selected.

ADMINISTRATION OF PAY WITHIN RANGES

It is almost universal practice to provide for a range of pay rates for each pay grade for clerical, administrative, professional, and managerial employees. Sometimes rate ranges are used for hourly workers as well, but often single rates are adopted in response to union pressure for uniformity of treatment of all employees. The rationale for paying people classified into the same grade different rates (within the limits of the grade) is that pay should closely reflect the value of an employee's contribution. It must be admitted that among a group of people all of whom are classified into pay grade 12, for example, there is likely to be a considerable variation in the quantity and quality of work produced.

The size of pay increases to advance an employee through his range may be based upon either predetermined fixed-step rates or upon individual decisions related to the individual employee's merit. Steps are commonly employed for hourly and clerical employees in industry. The pay schedules for government employees at the federal and state level are usually set up with predetermined steps. Public school teachers also have definite steps in their pay schedules. Where no definite steps are used, as is usually the case with administrative, professional, and managerial personnel, the personnel office and top management will often assign percentage limits to the pay increase. Thus the smallest increase might be 2 percent, and the largest might be 10 percent.

There are basically three methods of determining pay progression through a rate range: (1) length of service, (2) merit, or (3) a combination of merit and length of service.

Progression by length of service is also called automatic progression. For example, the progression for clerical employees in pay grade one might be as follows: Hiring rate—$140.00 per week. At the end of six months all persons would automatically be raised to $150.00 per week. At the end of the first year, the rate would be $160.00. From then on all persons in this grade could expect an increase of $10.00 per week each year until they have reached the maximum of $190.00 for that grade. In this example the length-of-service progression has used predetermined step rates. This combination is very common in industry.

In actual practice many length-of-service increases are only semiautomatic.

The individual employee must exhibit at least average work performance to receive his increase on schedule. If his performance is unsatisfactory, he may be denied an increase. The compensation policy of most organizations having length-of-service increases specifies that a man cannot be repeatedly denied his increase. If his supervisor can definitely establish that a man's performance is decidedly unsatisfactory on a continuing basis, he must be discharged or else reassigned.

When the salary policy states that progression within a range is based solely upon merit, the company must have some formal program for appraising the performance of all employees on a regular basis. Some firms have clear-cut formulas for translating an individual's performance rating score to a definite pay increase. Other companies are quite informal about the whole process. They leave both the frequency and the size of the pay increase pretty much up to the individual manager.

Especially in large organizations the problem of administering pay increases for thousands of people on a fair and honest basis has caused many managements to give some recognition to length of service. Philosophically most executives are opposed to the seniority principle, but when dealing with a very large work force, they are often forced to grant some recognition to this factor. One way of handling this problem is to count years of service as one factor in the rating plan used to set salary increases. Another method is to provide for automatic progression (length of service) to the midpoint of each range and merit progression above that point. Only those whose performance is decidedly above average can recieve pay increases above the midpoint.

UNION CONSIDERATIONS

According to the National Labor Relations Act, an employer is required to bargain rates of pay with the union that has been certified as the sole and exclusive bargaining agent for its employees in a particular bargaining unit. Because a company cannot avoid negotiations over wage rates for individual jobs with its union, the question resolves itself into whether the job evaluation procedure that management uses shall be open to join participation. It would be futile for an employer to spend a great sum of money installing a plan only to have the union refuse to accept the resultant job rates so determined. Before the program is initially established, union and management must agree upon the desirability of job evaluation and the general procedures to be followed. Various degrees of union participation may exist. It may range from simply a periodic review by the union of the work that management is doing in developing a program to full partnership participation all the way from the analysis of jobs through to pricing the job structure. Likewise in operating a going program, participation can range from a union review of the rates established by management (if the union is dissatisfied it will turn in a grievance) to equal partnership through a joint union–employer evaluation committee that rates all jobs. There is no single answer to the question of union participation. It depends primarily upon the attitudes and relationships between the two parties.

WAGE SURVEYS

If the wage policy of a firm is to keep competitive in the labor market, that is, pay rates that are at least approximately equal to those prevailing in the community, then it must collect accurate wage and salary data and make changes in its pay structure as may become necessary. Whereas job evaluation establishes pay differentials based upon differences in job content, wage-survey information provides a means by which management can determine whether its entire wage level is competitive.

In collecting wage data, management wants to find out the going rates for its key jobs in the area from which it recruits labor. This area is its labor market. A labor market is a geographical area within which employers recruit workers and workers seek employment. It is usually thought to consist of a central city or cities and the surrounding territory in which persons can change their jobs without changing their place of residence. This definition is expecially appropriate for hourly and clerical workers. On the other hand, the labor market area for engineers, scientists, and executives tends to be regional or national in scope. This is because such individuals are much more likely to be willing to relocate if they can find a good job in another city even though it may be far removed from their home town.

Although conducting one's own survey will probably yield the most satisfactory and accurate results, this rather costly procedure is not always necessary. There are other sources of reliable information. The Bureau of Labor Statistics of the United States Department of Labor conducts comprehensive surveys at regular intervals in the larger labor markets. Many trade and professional associations conduct wage and salary surveys and publish the results for their members. Local Chambers of Commerce and personnel managers' associations sometimes conduct pay surveys.

If a company conducts its own survey it must select a representative sample of its own jobs, carefully describe these jobs, and then visit other organizations in the labor market to find out what they pay for the same jobs. While job-rate information is being obtained, it is advantageous to also collect information on fringe benefits and personnel practices. The ability of a firm to attract and retain employees is influenced not only by direct wage rates but also by such items as overtime and premium pay policy, paid holidays, vacations, shift differentials, pensions, health insurance benefits, and employer-financed services.

COMPENSATION FOR PROFESSIONALS

In both absolute and relative numbers professional people in the labor force have increased greatly over the past several decades. The work of a professional requires knowledge of an advanced type in a field of science or learning acquired by a prolonged course of specialized instruction and study. The work requires consistent exercise of discretion and judgment and is predominately intellectual and varied in character. Among the professsional occupations are engineer, mathematician, physicist, biologist, attorney, economist, and accountant.

Job Descriptions

One approach to the design of job descriptions for professional positions is to prepare rather detailed *functional descriptions* which list and describe all of the specific duties and responsibilities of each position. If one uses this approach there would be several different categories, for example, of design engineer, each assigned to different kinds of projects. Also, there would be many levels of design engineer to reflect the gradations of complexity of projects worked on. A problem with this approach is that the work of a professional employee tends to be quite variable as to its nature and complexity over a relatively short period of time. A detailed job description would be too restrictive to adequately reflect the broad scope of activities. Another problem is that it is very difficult to find enough words and phrases, whose meanings are clear to all, to express the large range in complexity and scope of responsibilities from the very junior professional to the senior project professional within each job family.

Because of these problems many companies use very broad *general job descriptions*. Separate descriptions are prepared for the different functional categories of professional work such as research biologist, investment analyst, and manufacturing engineer. The general nature and scope of responsibilities are spelled out. The organization also identifies a limited number of position levels within each job family such as assistant engineer, engineer, senior engineer, and project engineer. Language is developed to reflect these broad differences. For example the project engineer might have overall responsibility for project planning and design for projects of $500,000 in value and he would direct the work of several lower graded engineers. At the other end the assistant engineer would help an engineer in design and development work on specific project components.

Salary Structure

Some companies evaluate their professional jobs with a point or factor comparison plan of job evaluation in pretty much the same manner as they evaluate hourly and nonsupervisory office jobs. The evaluation plan would be especially constructed for use with professional positions. Often a single plan appropriate for both managerial and professional jobs is employed. If detailed functional job descriptions were used, then a large organization would have scores or hundreds of different jobs which would be evaluated and points would then be assigned to them. All these jobs would then be grouped into, lets say, 10 to 15 pay grade levels. When an individual's assignment is changed, he or she would have to be classified under a new job title and perhaps into a different pay grade.

On the other hand, if general job descriptions were used, each broad job family such as accountant, engineer, and economist would be classified into 3 to 5 levels of job complexity and money worth. Thus, in a pay structure containing 12 grades for professional and managerial (lower and middle) personnel, the assistant engineer might be assigned to grade 3, the engineer to grade 5, the senior engineer to grade 7, and the project engineer to grade 9. The assignment of these general job descriptions to the different grades could be accomplished by a quantitative job evaluation plan or more simply by a ranking or grade description evaluation plan. The salary surveys of professional occupations prepared by the

Bureau of Labor Statistics of the U.S. Department of Labor show these occupations grouped into several levels. Hence, a company which uses these broad categories for their professional jobs can obtain market salary data summarized in a similar fashion.

Salary administration for professionals often means rank-in-the-person more than rank-in-the-job. As a junior professional employee develops and demonstrates successful mastery of gradually larger and more complex projects, he is given recognition of his greater worth by merit pay increases within the grade and then by promotion to a higher job title and grade level. This is a further reason why some organizations use broad general job descriptions.

Career Salary Curves

Career salary curves—also called salary maturity curves or professional maturity curves—have been used for many years by companies employing large complements of engineers and scientists, such as those firms in the aerospace industry. Career salary curves are used in place of functional job descriptions and job evaluation. Based upon salary survey data and internal company data and policy decisions, management draws curves that relate salary to years since receipt of the appropriate college degree (baccalaureate, masters, or doctors). An average curve is drawn for those who are judged to exhibit average proficiency. Other curves are drawn for those of above and below average performance. Job titles are used only for identification and status distinctions. Figure 24-7 is an example of a career salary structure.

The use of salary maturity curves combines the issues of salary structure and individual pay allocation into one step. Those who employ them admit frankly

Figure 24-7
Career Salary Curves Which Relate Annual Salary to Years Since Graduation from College and to Performance Rating.

that they cannot measure work content and create explainable job distinctions based upon differences in job duties.

The use of career salary curves has been fostered partly by the many market salary surveys which express salary data in this way. The Engineers Joint Council, which is supported by all the major engineering societies, publishes its salary survey data in the form of career curves.

A variation of the career curve approach we have been describing is to plot curves of salary vs. years in pay grade. Thus some universities prepare career curves, based upon survey data and their own salary policies, for the various academic ranks of assistant, associate, and full professor.

COMPENSATION FOR MANAGERS

The broad outlines of salary systems for managers are similar in their elements to those for lower level groups. There are job descriptions, job evaluation, pay grades with a range of pay for each grade, and salary surveys. The specifics of course, are quite different from employee wage administration and there are special features of managerial compensation that set it apart.

Job descriptions for management are often called position guides or responsibility guides. They do not contain detailed statements of duties and operating procedures. Rather, they cover areas of responsibility, scope of authority, and relationships with other positions and organizational functions.

Job-evaluation plans are usually tailormade to the special requirements of the organization. Sometimes point plans are used, but more commonly combination point-and-factor-comparison plans are employed. One well-known plan is the guide chart-profile method developed by Edward Hay & Associates, a management consulting organization.[10] There are three main compensable factors in the Hay system. The first factor is "know-how," which is the sum total of the knowledge and skills required for acceptable performance. The second factor is "problem solving," which is the degree of original thinking required for analyzing, evaluating, creating, reasoning, and arriving at conclusions. The third factor is "accountability," which is answerability for an action and its consequences.

After all the management positions have been evaluated and points assigned, it is necessary to group these into grades. This process is guided somewhat by the hierarchy depicted in the organization chart. In a 25-grade-level system the president would be at grade 25, the executive vice-president at grade 24, and so on down to the lowest level of management. Of course, the points assigned to positions would determine in which grades particular positions belonged. An assistant plant manager might come two grades below the plant manager position and would not necessarily occupy the next grade in descending order.

To "price" the salary grade structure it is necessary to obtain salary survey data. Well-known salary services provided by management and trade associations and by consulting firms classify managerial salaries by company size, by industry, and functional responsibility. Some surveys also indicate the relationships among different jobs within firms. Thus, they may show that in a given industry the top

---

[10] This job evaluation method is described in articles in *Personnel:* (September 1951, July 1954, and January–February, 1958).

operating executive gets, on the average, about 85 percent of the chief executive officer's salary.[11] Salary survey data is useful as a guide in setting the pay rates for "bench-mark" positions within one's own company. A bench-mark position is one which is important in one's company and for which reliable survey data is available. The pay rates for other positions and for the salary grades can be set with reference to the rates for the bench-mark jobs. It should be clear that management does not merely mimic the prevailing rates in its particular industry. It considers other factors such as the financial strength of the company, supply and demand situation for executives, and geographical variations in salaries.

Salary ranges for middle and upper level managers typically provide a spread from minimum to maxiumum of from 30 to 70 percent. There is usually considerable overlap from one grade to the next higher one.

In-grade raises in pay are almost always based upon evaluations of the performances of the managers, usually by means of formal appraisal plans. The total sums available for raises are often tempered by the profitability of the firm from year to year.

Supervisory Pay Issues. As the wages of hourly paid and nonexempt office personnel rise due to inflationary pressures and union contract settlements, management must pay attention to the pay rates of its foremen and office supervisors to maintain a fair differential between the supervisors and the employees whom they supervise. The issue of maintaining a differential also surfaces when the nonexempt personnel work over forty hours a week at premium rates.[12] The incentive to continue in supervisory positions may be reduced if highly paid nonsupervisory employees earn as much or more than their immediate superiors in the organization.

To prevent such possible salary compression many companies have a policy of maintaining the salary grades of front-line supervisors about 15 percent (on the average) above the pay grades of the highest paid employees that they supervise. Also these companies pay their supervisors extra money for working scheduled overtime.[13]

Top Management Compensation

There is some evidence that companies are nowadays placing greater emphasis in pricing the pay of their top executive positions upon external salary comparisons and somewhat less emphasis upon the neat calculations of an internal job evaluation plan. This is occurring in a climate of strong competition for talented major executives, price inflation, and rapidly rising salaries. These firms may use a job evaluation plan for guidance but it will give way to strong market evidence that certain positions are being paid too little or too much. Basically many orga-

---

[11] One prominent source of salary information is the Executive Compensation Service of the American Management Associations.

[12] Ernest C. Miller, "Settling Supervisors' Pay and Pay Differentials," *Compensation Review*, Vol. 10, No. 3 (Third Quarter 1978), pp. 13–27.

[13] Under the Fair Labor Standards Act exempt personnel are executives, administrative employees, and professionals. These do not have to be paid time and one-half for hours worked in excess of 40 in a week. Nonexempt employees on the other hand, must receive time and one-half.

nizations are combining market pricing with the ranking method to set top management salary scales.[14]

For lower- and middle-level managers, salary and earned salary increases constitute the principal forms of financial compensation. For top executives, pay supplements in the form of year-end bonuses, stock options, performance stock shares, and various perquisites comprise a very large share of their total annual compensation.

Corporate compensation specialists design executive incentives to attract and retain highly qualified talent, to induce superior performance, and to generate greater profits for the firm. Because executives must pay a high percentage of their salaries to the government in income taxes, compensation experts have tended to devote considerable (and perhaps too much) attention to tax-saving features of stock options, deferred compensation, and fringe benefits.

Here is a listing and brief explanation of the principal forms of financial incentives and supplements to direct salary that are provided for many top executives in private industry.

Incentive Bonuses.   Year-end cash bonuses are a very popular form of compensation. The fund of money from which bonuses are paid is often a predetermined portion of profits. The amount granted to each executive is based upon the individual's performance and upon his salary level.

Qualified Stock Option.   From the early 1950's qualified stock options were a favorite way of providing executives with the opportunity for extra income while saving on income taxes at the same time. However, the Tax Reform Act of 1976 ruled that all such options must cease by May 20, 1981.

Nonqualified Stock Option.   When an executive buys shares of his or her company's stock under a nonqualified option plan, there is no favored tax treatment from the Internal Revenue Service. However, there is great flexibility in using such options. The option can be granted by the corporation at any price, it can be exercised any time within 10 years, and the stock can be sold by the executive after holding it only six months.

Restricted Stock Plan.   With a restricted stock plan the corporation transfers stock to the manager, subject to a restriction of some kind that limits the stock's value during the period of the restriction. A typical restriction is that the individual is not allowed to sell the stock for a designated period, say five years. The executive is not required to pay income tax on the stock awarded to him until the point in time at which his rights to the stock become transferable.

Performance Shares.   A performance share is a stock bonus that is paid to the executive several years in the future if his preestablished goals for, say, two or more years are met.

[14] "How Companies Set Top- and Middle- Management Salaries . . . A Compensation Review Symposium," *Compensation Review*, Vol. 9, No. 1 (First Quarter 1977), pp. 32–46.

Deferred Compensation.   Deferred compensation usually takes the form of a bonus in cash or stock or a pension supplement. These are paid after retirement when the person's income tax bracket is lower.

Perquisites.   Perquisites include such benefits as personal use of a company automobile, personal use of a company-owned apartment, lodge, or yacht, and free medical examinations.

Questions for review and discussion

1. Explain why prevailing wage rates within a labor market are such an important factor influencing wages in individual companies.
2. What are reasonable goals for a comprehensive program of employee compensation? Why does compensation seldom really motivate improved performance?
3. If you had the task of persuading union officials in your organization to agree to the adoption of a job evaluation program, what arguments would you give?
4. A company president makes the statement that he or she sees no need for introducing a job evaluation plan into his company. He feels that if he conducts an annual wage survey and adjusts his own rates accordingly, there will be no need for a costly job-rating program. Do you agree or disagree? Why?
5. What criteria could you develop that would serve as a guide to decide the amount of vertical spread to be used for a pay structure having pay ranges for each grade?
6. Many companies have a practice of keeping wage and salary policies, rates, structures, classifications, and so on, secret. How much information would you provide the employees? Explain.
7. Explain the process involved in evaluating a given job using a point plan; also using a factor-comparison plan.
8. Compare the point system with the factor-comparison system on the following factors:
   a. Factors used.
   b. Degrees used.
   c. Method of expressing final rating.
   d. Usage of key jobs.
   e. How ratings are recorded and explained.
   f. Flexibility for meeting changing conditions and significantly different types of jobs.
9. Assume that you have been appointed to write a fact-finding report in a contract negotiation dispute over salaries between a local union of engineers and the company management. The union is asking for an across-the-board increase of 12 percent and the management offers to grant only 4 percent to be distributed only as merit increases to deserving persons. What factors would you use in deciding upon the size of the increase and how it should be distributed?
10. Compare the use of job evaluation using functional job descriptions with ca-

reer salary curves in determining the pay of professional employees. Give advantages and disadvantages of each method.

11. Compare salary administration for managers with wage administration for hourly paid employees. Explain the reasons for the differences which exist.

Exercises

WAGE LINES AND WAGE STRUCTURE

The data in Table 24-3 show the job titles and points assigned to these jobs under a newly installed point plan of job evaluation. The jobs are of the non-supervisory office and technical type. The wages shown are the present average weekly wages in this company and the average wages paid in the same labor market for these jobs as found from a carefully conducted area survey.

You are to plot a graph of points versus present company wages. You can show the average area rates on the same graph or on a separate one. By the method of "least squares" or some other appropriate procedure, obtain trend lines for both the company rates and the area rates. Then construct a wage structure having a rate range for each grade. This problem requires decisions to be made on which line to use, how many grades, the vertical spread in money within the grades, action to be taken on jobs now paid above and below the newly established limits, and method of in-grade progression.

Write a report showing your plottings of the wage lines, your proposed wage structure, and explanations for your decisions on the matters of which line you used, number of grades, vertical spread of money within grades, et cetera.

Table 24-3 Chart of Job Titles, Points, and Wages.

Job Title	Number of Employees	Points	Present Average Weekly Wage	Average Wage in Area
Clerk, Mail	2	93	$122.00	$117.00
Typist	3	98	123.00	133.00
Clerk, Typist	3	118	135.00	151.00
Bookkeeping Machine Operator	2	123	142.00	130.00
Switchboard Operator	2	128	163.00	156.00
Stenographer	5	145	160.00	165.00
Clerk, Billing	2	148	158.00	153.00
Clerk, Payroll	3	153	188.00	177.00
Key Punch Operator	2	163	165.00	170.00
Secretarial-Stenographer	7	168	180.00	185.00
Bookkeeper	2	178	156.00	180.00
Secretary	8	196	190.00	200.00
Buyer, Assistant	1	208	210.00	225.00
Nurse	2	216	216.00	247.00
Cashier	1	223	220.00	255.00
Draftsmen, Layout	12	256	236.00	260.00
Accountant, Assistant	3	266	260.00	276.00
Draftsman, Design	4	321	282.00	310.00

EVALUATING A JOB

Using the point plan shown in Figure 24-2, evaluate a job with which you are very familiar. This could be a job you have held, now hold, or one you have had a chance to observe closely. Alternatively work in groups of two to four persons. Interview one student to obtain all the essential facts about a job he has held —then evaluate it. In assigning the proper degree for each factor, select the degree which represents the highest level of job demand for the factor.

For the job that you rate, prepare a job rating substantiation sheet. List the job title and for each factor give your selection of degree and points. Add points to obtain total. Explain with one or two sentences your reason for selecting the particular degree for each factor. Your substantiation should relate elements of job content to degree definitions.

Suggestions for further reading

BELCHER, DAVID W. *Compensation Administration*. Englewood Cliffs, N.J.: Prentice-Hall, Inc., 1974.

BERG, J. GARY. *Managing Compensation*. New York: American Management Associations, 1976.

ELLIG, BRUCE R. "Compensation Management: Its Past and Its Future," *Personnel*, Vol. 54, No. 3 (May–June, 1977), pp. 30–40.

EPPERSON, LAWRENCE L. "The Dynamics of Factor Comparison/Point Evaluation," *Public Personnel Management*, Vol. 4, No. 1 (January–February, 1975), pp. 38–48.

HENDERSON, RICHARD I. *Compensation Management*. Reston, Virginia: Reston Publishing Co., Inc., 1976.

LAWLER, EDWARD E., III. "New Approaches to Pay: Innovations that Work," *Personnel*, Vol. 53, No. 5 (September–October, 1976) pp. 11–23.

MAHONEY, THOMAS A. "Justice and Equity: A Recurring Theme in Compensation," *Personnel*, Vol. 52, No. 5 (September–October, 1975), pp. 60–66.

MARSHALL, DON R. *Successful Techniques for Solving Employee Compensation Problems*. New York: John Wiley & Sons, Inc., 1978.

ROCK, MILTON L. (ed.) *Handbook of Wage and Salary Administration*. New York: McGraw-Hill Book Company, 1972.

SIBSON, ROBERT E. *Compensation*. New York: American Management Associations, 1974.

WINSTANLEY, NATHAN B. "The Use of Performance Appraisal in Compensation Administration," *The Conference Board Record*, Vol. 12, No. 3 (March, 1975), pp. 43–47.

ZOLLITSCH, HERBERT G., and ADOLPH LANGSNER. *Wage and Salary Administration*, 2nd ed., Cincinnati, Ohio: South-Western Publishing Company, 1970.

Individual and group incentives

Wages to employees for services rendered can be paid according either to the time worked or to the amount of work produced. Those whose pay is based upon time are paid a certain sum of money per hour regardless of how productive they may be—this is commonly called daywork or time work. Usually employees receive their paychecks once each week, and pay is calculated according to the number of hours the particular employee worked during that week. If, on the other hand, pay is computed according to how much work is produced (units, pounds, dozens, assemblies, tons, and so on) and if employees can earn extra money for producing more than a certain quota or norm, we say that this is a wage-incentive-payment method. If top management decides to adopt a wage-in-centive program, its objectives are generally to reduce unit labor costs by increasing man-hour output, to raise worker income without increasing labor costs, and to acquire a means of effectively controlling the production process. Features that most incentive plans have in common are measurement by management of the amount of work done, establishment of a quota or standard output, and the utilization of a formula for relating pay to production or performance.

In this chapter we shall investigate direct wage incentive programs and issues. We shall look at conditions conducive to the establishment of wage incentives, work measurement techniques, requirements for sound incentive programs, types of incentive plans, problems caused by incentive system operation, and approaches to solutions of these problems.

In direct wage incentive programs there is a close relationship between the amount of work produced by the individual employee and his pay. For the most part, engineering work-measurement techniques are used to establish the production standard upon which pay and output calculations are based.

Another whole category of incentives consists of plant- and companywide incentives that have objectives somewhat broader in scope than the higher-output-per-unit-time objective of the traditional wage-incentive installation. These plantwide and companywide incentives are based upon the concept of cooperation among management, employees, and the union (if the employees are represented by one). The objectives may be manifold. Included among typical objectives are a plantwide reduction in labor costs or total payroll costs, reduction in material and supply costs, fostering of greater loyalty towards the company, improved cooperation between labor and management, and lower turnover and absenteeism.

We shall discuss three kinds of plant- or companywide incentive programs. These are the Scanlon plan, profit sharing, and the Lincoln Electric Company's Incentive Program which is really an integrated system using several kinds of incentives.

DIRECT WAGE INCENTIVES

Wage Incentive or Daywork?

The percentage of production and related workers in the United States who are paid on an incentive basis has declined since the early 1960's. U.S. Department of Labor figures show that about 27 percent of production and related workers were on incentive payment in 1945 and 1946 and again in 1959 when another study was made.[1] The figure stood at 26 percent during the 1961–1963 period.[2] However, a study of payment methods for plant-workers (a somewhat broader category than just production and related workers) in all metropolitan areas in 1961–1963 compared with 1968–1970 showed that the percentage on incentive payment dropped from 20 to 14 percent. This study also showed that office workers on wage incentives were less than 0.5 percent during both periods.[3]

Among the reasons for the decline in utilization of incentives are (1) automation and machine-paced processes reduce the need for incentives; (2) the percentage of indirect workers is increasing while direct labor has been decreasing; (3) labor costs have increased over the years in some plants due to loosening of rates and inattention to auditing of standards; (4) union pressures and grievances over rates and earnings have caused problems for management; (5) supervisors complain about added administrative burden caused by incentive installations;

---

[1] L. Earl Lewis, "Extent of Incentive Pay in Manufacturing," *Monthly Labor Review*, Vol. 83, No. 5 (May 1960), pp. 460–463.
[2] John H. Cox, "Wage Payment Plans in Metropolitan Areas," *Monthly Labor Review*, Vol. 87, No. 7 (July 1964), pp. 794–796.
[3] John H. Cox, "Time and Incentive Pay Practices in Urban Areas," *Monthly Labor Review*, Vol. 94, No. 12 (December 1971), pp. 53–56.

and (6) some managements feel that good productivity can be achieved by other methods and with fewer problems.

Despite this gradual drift away from incentives in favor of time payment some industries still retain a strong attachment to wage incentives. Industries with a high percentage of production and related workers on incentive are men's work clothing, men's shirts and nightwear, men's suits and coats, men's and women's hosiery, footwear, basic iron and steel, and glass products.[4]

The decision to place work on an incentive basis of payment depends upon a number of factors. The following conditions must apply in order to utilize this form of wage payment.

1. The output of employees either individually or in groups must be measurable and suitable for standardization. By standardized we mean that the work methods, materials, tooling, and the operations are uniform from one unit or cycle to the next. If there is great variation in the work requirements themselves or in the conditions under which the work must be done from unit to unit, it may still be possible to measure the work in terms of time or some other criteria of performance, but any averages or norms so determined would be inherently of little value as far as standards go.
2. There must be a consistent relationship between the amount of skill and effort exerted by the employee and the output. Some processes are machine controlled entirely; thus, greater employee application can have little or no effect upon production. It is true that even in situations like this, however, some companies set up an incentive or bonus plan so that the employees will be diligent in supplying and servicing the machine to avoid shutdowns.
3. The work can be readily counted and credited to the proper individuals. If the cost of determining how much each individual employee has produced at each step in a production process is excessive, the alternative is generally either to utilize a group or plantwide incentive plan or to use daywork.
4. There must be an opportunity for reducing the unit cost of the product or service. Or expressed in another way, an increase in productivity should be attainable. Indeed a primary reason for an employer even to contemplate the installation of a pay incentive is his expectation that it will result in increased productivity, improved performance and efficiency, and lower unit costs.
5. The employees (and the union if the employees are organized) must accept, support, and cooperate in this method of wage payment. The reward that employees can expect to receive from participation is higher earnings than they would receive under the daywork or timework method of payment. But if such support is lacking, the incentive program will rest on a shaky foundation.

The five foregoing conditions indicate when the adoption of the incentive method of wage payment is practical and desirable. On the other hand, payment according to time worked is clearly preferable when these requirements cannot be met. Process-controlled operations, such as are found in most of the pulp and paper and chemical industries, are more properly paid by daywork. Most clerical, technical, engineering, and scientific occupations are not under incentives.

---

[4] George L. Stelluto, "Report on Incentive Pay in Manufacturing," *Monthly Labor Review*, Vol. 92, No. 7 (July 1969), pp. 49–53.

However, salesmen are typically paid by commissions or at least by a guaranteed base salary plus a commission. Many organizations pay their top executives according to a salary-plus-incentive-bonus arrangement, because there is a reasonable relationship between the performance of a company president, for example, and the profits of his company.

Thus, when the work is inherently variable, when it cannot be accurately measured, standardized, and counted, when productivity is not closely related to employee skill and effort, when employees and unions strongly oppose incentive payment, and when the employer can realize no potential gain from wage incentives, it is preferable to employ time wages. Time wages have the added advantage of simplified payroll computation. Likewise employees can readily ascertain their earnings for a given pay period (the same statement cannot be made for many incentive installations). A primary disadvantage of time payment is that the labor cost per unit is variable. The employer cannot as readily control or fix his direct labor costs, since different workers on the same job receive the same pay regardless of how much they turn out.

Work Measurement

Most commonly "time" is used as the standard for measuring performance of work that is on an incentive (time per piece, time per pound, time per assembly, time expressed as a percentage of maximum possible operating time for running mechanical equipment, and so on). Other bases or standards against which performance can be compared may also be used. The amount of finished or good product from a given quantity of material can give a standard expressed in terms of a percentage of maximum possible yield. Also, employees can be rewarded for a reduction in the usage of costly supply materials; in this case the standard is expressed as a budgeted money figure determined by accounting procedures. Or rewards can be tied to an improvement in quality, in which case the standard would be a permissible percentage of imperfections or rejects.

The time required to perform a given amount of work is, as was stated above, the most generally used measure upon which to base an incentive system. There are a number of methods available for establishing standards. These are (1) past performance; (2) bargaining between employer and union; (3) time study; (4) standard data; (5) predetermined elemental times; and (6) work sampling. Each of these methods will be discussed briefly.[5]

Past Performance.   Industrial engineers almost universally agree that past performance is a poor way of deciding what future performance should be. Standards derived from past performance when employees were on day work usually are much lower and easier to attain than those developed through time study and other engineered work-measurement techniques. Because no complete analysis has been made of work methods, delays, allowances, and of the skill and effort of those employees upon whom the past performance records are based, management cannot justifiably say what standard or normal performance should be.

[5] Full explanations of work measurement methods can be found in Delmar W. Karger and F. M. Bayha, *Engineered Work Measurement*, 3rd ed. (New York: The Industrial Press, 1977); Benjamin W. Niebel, *Motion and Time Study*, 6th ed. (Homewood, Ill.: Richard D. Irwin, Inc., 1976).

Bargaining Between Employer and Union.   Bargaining is the method followed in the men's and women's wearing apparel industries to a considerable extent. The facts upon which the negotiators base their judgments may be either past production records, their own experience, or actual time study. In the New York dress industry, as an illustration, samples of new dresses are submitted by employers to the price settlement department of the International Ladies' Garment Workers Union. The experts in this department analyze each garment in detail. Industrial engineers in the union conduct time and motion studies to provide standard time information, which is then used as a guide by the rate experts in the determination of an actual money piece rate for each garment. Then these persons meet with representatives of the manufacturers. If agreement is reached, the matter is settled. However, if there is a dispute, the office of the permanent impartial chairman (arbitrator) is requested to assign an impartial adjuster to study the garment and decide upon a piece price. Although his word is usually taken as final, appeal may be made to the impartial chairman himself.

Time Study.   The principal method used in industry to set work standards is stopwatch time study. The more modern and refined techniques of standard data and predetermined elemental times depend upon and are adaptations of basic time-study principles.

The basic task that is measured and standardized is the operation. An operation may consist of drilling four ½″ diameter holes through a piece of ⅜″-thick steel on a sensitive drill press; or in a garment factory it might consist of sewing a pocket on a man's white dress shirt; or in the electrical industry it might consist of spray painting the case for a circuit breaker as it hangs suspended from an overhead conveyor. In analyzing an operation, the time-study engineer will subdivide it into work elements. He will seek to find the most efficient way to perform the work. In some cases extensive redesign of the work place layout and revamping of the hand motions may be in order. The training of the time-study engineer causes him continually to seek a better way to perform an operation or sequence of operations.

After the most efficient method has been developed (of course, in the future a still better way may be found), one or more qualified workers is timed with a stopwatch while he is following the prescribed work procedure. A separate time reading is taken and recorded for each work element. Since different employees exhibit considerable variation in the pace at which they work, it is necessary for the time-study engineer to adjust the actual observed time by a percentage factor to arrive at the time it should take a normal worker exhibiting normal skill and effort to perform the given operation. This process of adjusting the observed time by a percentage factor to yield a normal or base time is called leveling or performance rating. Thus, if an operator spent 0.20 minutes to perform one element of his total operation and if the time-study engineer rated his performance (that is, skill and effort) at 20 percent above normal, the normal time for that element would be 0.24 minutes (0.20 x 120 percent). To the sum of the times obtained for the individual elements are added allowances to compensate the employee for necessary personal time, unavoidable delays, and for rest to overcome fatigue. The resulting figure is the standard time for the operation. Time-study authorities and practitioners claim they can achieve an accuracy of plus or minus 5 percent of the true standard time. The true standard, of course, is never really known.

Standard Data. When similar operations have been studied repeatedly by means of stop-watch time study, it soon becomes apparent that certain patterns and uniformity of times develop for individual work elements. By tabulating and classifying times taken from a large number of studies of similar work, the initial steps toward the development of standard data are made. By use of these data it is not necessary to make a stop-watch time study in order to arrive at the proper standard time. What is required is that the engineer observe the job in question to fully comprehend what is involved (noting machine, workplace, layout, parts, fixtures, and so on). By knowing what elements are required to perform the work, the engineer can select the standard times corresponding to these elements from tables of previously prepared standard data.

Predetermined Elemental Times. Predetermined elemental times are basically a form of standard data; however, the elements of work are of the general type or order called *therbligs*. Therbligs are elements of work that were first identified and analyzed by Lillian and Frank Gilbreth in their pioneering work in motion study. Therbligs are basic finger, arm, hand, and body motions, often called basic divisions of accomplishments. Reach, move, hold, grasp, position, preposition, inspect, assemble, and select are some illustrations of these elements. Use of ordinary stop-watch time-study procedures does not permit the measurement of work elements as short as therbligs. Standard time values for these are obtained by studying a large sample of diversified operations with a timing device, such as the motion-picture camera, that is capable of measuring very short elements.

There are a great many different predetermined elemental time systems from which to choose. A considerable number have been developed as proprietary systems by industrial engineering consulting firms; others have been created by industrial companies for their own use. In order to set a standard for an operation by using such systems, it is necessary for the engineer to make an extremely detailed analysis of the motions involved and to record these on paper. He must properly classify each motion and then take the time from a table of standard times. An ordinary operation having a work cycle of one minute could very well contain over a hundred basic elements of work. The great advantage of using predetermined elemental times is that the process of establishing a standard requires that the engineer make a very detailed analysis of the motions involved. This procedure often uncovers inefficiencies and leads to significant improvements.

Work Sampling. Work sampling requires that the engineer take a great number of observations of a worker at random times throughout the working day. He records precisely what the employee is doing at the time he is being observed. No stop watch is used. The objective is to find the frequency of occurrence of every work element. Even though the worker is not under observation constantly, by adequate random sampling of his activities, the engineer can ascertain within limits of accuracy that can be calculated statistically the percentage of time that he spends on each portion of the operation. Delays, allowances, and infrequently occurring noncyclic elements can also readily be measured this way. In order to set a standard by the work sampling procedure, it is necessary to level or rate the performance of the worker being studied (as with stop-watch time study) and to count the actual number of units produced during the period under study. Advantages of work sampling are that it is possible to study a considerable number of different operations at the same time, the psychological problems presented by standing over a worker for a considerable period of time as in stop-watch time study are avoided, and considerable statistical reliability can be achieved through the process of taking many observations over a period of several days.

Essential Requirements of a Sound Wage Incentive Program

Based upon the experiences derived from study of successful and unsuccessful programs in various industries through the years, writers, researchers, and others have concluded that if certain general principles or guides are followed by management in installing and administering a wage incentive plan, the chances for success are good. A successful plan is one that achieves its purpose. This is usually to increase productivity, reduce costs, improve efficiency, and increase employee earnings while at the same time maintaining or enhancing employee morale and employee relations.

1. Management, employees, and the union (if the employees are organized) should understand and support the incentive program. Since the procedures involved in methods analysis, time study, base-rate setting, and bonus calculation when taken collectively are rather complicated, explanations and training by management for employees and union leaders are essential. Discussion and participation with lower-level supervisors and union officials in the initiation and the development of the program are advantageous in creating the kind of support that is necessary for success.
2. Methods analysis of each operation should be undertaken before a work standard is established. The optimum methods and procedures for doing the work should be devised first. A standardized method should be followed. Employees must be taught how to perform the work according to this standard procedure.
3. The standard upon which the wage incentive is based should be arrived at by carefully applied work-measurement techniques, such as time study, standard data, work sampling, or predetermined elemental times. If piece rates are bargained collectively between management and union, the decisions should be guided by engineered work-measurement techniques. Standards should not be based upon past performance. If this were done, those employees who had loafed in the past would be rewarded with easy-to-achieve standards, whereas those who had previously given an honest day's work would be penalized with a difficult-to-meet quota.
4. Each job on incentive should have a guaranteed minimum or base rate. Even if output drops to a low level, the employee can depend upon earning at least a certain minimum amount of money. Normally this base rate will be determined by job evaluation. Differences in base rates among jobs will reflect dif-

ferences in skill, effort, responsibility, and job conditions. Maintenance of proper differentials between these base rates will insure that employees on jobs having low requirements will not earn more than employees on highly skilled jobs when both are on incentive.

5. The work standard (whether it be expressed in time or money per unit) should be guaranteed by management against change unless there is a change in the method, tooling, equipment, materials, or design of the product. The employee must know that his work standard or quota will not be increased just because he starts to make large bonus earnings. A change in the work standard is legitimate if the method of doing the job is altered. If management simplifies the operation in such a way that the time per unit is less than the previous standard, the worker should be able to earn as much money as before, provided he exerts equivalent skill and effort. If the employee, through his own initiative and ingenuity, figures out a better way, he should be rewarded.

6. It should be easy for employees to calculate earnings. Even with a complicated incentive formula, management with its specialized knowledge and calculating machines can generally compute employee earnings readily. However, employees need to be able to verify the payroll department's calculations. This builds confidence and trust in the program.

7. An effectice grievance procedure must be available to handle dissatisfaction and complaints on the part of employees. Grievances over incentives usually are concerned with charges by the employees that the rate or standard is too "tight" (that is, too difficult to meet) or that the time standard has been cut in violation of the labor agreement.

TYPES OF INCENTIVE PAY PLANS

Although literally scores of incentive plans have been used over the past seventy years, only a few primary types are in common usage at present. Those that will be explained here are measured-daywork, piecework, standard-hour, and gains-sharing plans.[6]

Measured Daywork

The measured-daywork plan is in the twilight zone between a true direct incentive plan and regular time payment or daywork. A work standard is set through time study or some other work-measurement technique. The worker is expected to meet this quota. If he exceeds the standard or falls below, he still receives his regular hourly rate of pay. From management's standpoint, the plan has the advantage that unit labor costs are much more predictable than with ordinary daywork, because there is considerable emphasis placed upon meeting the standard. In some installations merit rating is employed. This is the classical and historical type of measured daywork. Every three months each person is rated on

---

[6] Many of the numerous other plans were created by industrial engineering consultants. Some like the Taylor Differential Piece Rate plan are of historical interest but no longer in use. Other plans are the Gantt Task and Bonus, Rowan, Barth, Emerson Efficiency, Merrick, Hayes-Manit, and Dyer.

four factors: quantity of work, quality of work, dependability, and versatility. A high score yields an increase in hourly pay for the ensuing three months, whereas a low score results in a decrease in pay. The employee's rate of pay actually consists of two parts: a basic or guaranteed portion, which normally approximates 75 percent of the total rate, and the personal portion, which is subject to fluctuation every three months. As an incentive plan this particular type of measured daywork has the disadvantage that the reward for improved performance is not directly and proportionately related to that behavior. The pay adjustment is too remote in point of time. Also the instrument for relating pay to performance—that is, the foreman's judgment in merit rating the employee—is subjective. On the positive side the system does encourage (in fact, it requires) the foreman to become well acquainted with every employee in order to rate him. Also management has greater control over labor costs than is true under ordinary daywork.

There is another kind of measured daywork program that is becoming increasingly popular in industry. Indeed, it has tended to supplant the type just described. According to Slichter, Healy, and Livernash, the kind employing merit rating that adjusts the employee's hourly rate in accordance with his performance over a period of time has become quite rare.[7] More commonly at present measured daywork involves simply pay by the hour accompanied by control of worker efficiency by means of production standards. The hourly rate is not adjustable. Emphasis is placed upon the establishment of accurate standards of output through time-study, standard-data, or other procedures. Then pressure is placed upon the worker to meet the standard consistently. If his performance falls below standard, the industrial engineer and the supervisor investigate to determine the cause. If the materials, equipment, or process are faulty, corrective measures are taken. But if the worker is at fault, he is subject to disciplinary action (assuming the standard is fair and he has the basic capacity to do the work).

There is some evidence to indicate that measured daywork in contrast to piecework and other incentive plans results in less worker resistance to the introduction of changed methods. Also management encounters fewer union and worker grievances over the fairness of production standards. There is less likelihood of measured daywork causing sharp controversy between labor and management than with ordinary incentive arrangements, because there are fewer sensitive issues over which to clash.

Piecework

One of the simplest and most commonly used of all incentive plans is piecework. The standard is expressed in terms of a certain sum of money for every unit produced, such as $0.10 per piece or $0.77 per pound or $1.31 per dozen. The earnings of the employee are directly proportional to his output. This is what industrial engineers call a 1-for-1 plan—for each 1 percent increase in production the worker is paid a 1 percent increase in wages. If the basic hourly rate of pay of a given job is $4.00 (as established by job evaluation) and if the industrial engineer has set a standard time of 0.2 hours per unit (therefore 5 units per hour),

[7] Sumner H. Slichter, James J. Healy, and E. Robert Livernash, *The Impact of Collective Bargaining on Management* (Washington, D.C.: The Brookings Institution, 1960), p. 490.

we find that the piece rate then becomes $4.00 per hour divided by 5 units per hour, which is equal to $.80 per unit. Although in the early days workers were paid only for the actual work they turned out, with no guaranteed minimum, modern practice requires the payment of a certain minimum wage if the employee has not produced enough units to meet that base. Thus, as in the example just cited, if the guaranteed minimum were $4.00 per hour and if the worker's output was less than the 5 units necessary to earn the minimum, he would still be paid $4.00 per hour. With straight piecework (without a guaranteed minimum) many of the risks of factory management are transferred to the shoulders of the employee, because even if there are production delays, faulty materials, and machine breakdowns, the direct labor cost per unit to the employer is fixed.

For a piecework plan that has a guaranteed minimum, Figure 25-1 shows graphically the relationship between output of an individual employee and his total earnings. The direct labor cost to the employer per unit of output is shown on the ordinate at the right of the graph and is portrayed by the dashed line.

The advantages of piecework are its simplicity and ease of understanding by the employees. It is eminently fair in its rewards, since earnings are directly proportional to output for all output levels in excess of standard. The guaranteed minimum protects the employee's basic income should output fall below standard due to production delays or inexperience on the employee's part. Cost accounting and control by management are facilitated by the fact that labor cost is constant for output above standard.

However, the piecework system does have serious disadvantages. If a general wage increase is put into effect for all employees, this necessitates changing all the piece rates on the books. This is a very cumbersome clerical task. Usage of piece rates for a group incentive where different employees have different hourly

Figure 25-1
Piecework with a Guaranteed Minimum. The standard is $.80 per unit. For an output of 5 units or less per hour the employee is paid $4.00 per hour. For 6 units the pay is $4.80 and so on. In practice pay is calculated on basis of daily output.

base rates is very cumbersome. Piece rates often lead to confusion in the minds of both management and labor in that time study is here linked rather directly with money rates. To insure objectivity, the money rate should be arrived at for every job by an evaluation of its relative amount of skill, effort, responsibility, and job conditions, whereas the standard time should be determined by an objective study of the quantity of work that can be reasonably expected from a normal worker working under standardized conditions. The money level and the work standard should be considered separately.

Standard-Hour Plan

Sometimes called the 100 percent bonus or standard-time plan, the standard-hour plan expresses the work standard in terms of time. It features a guaranteed base rate that the worker receives if he fails to meet standard performance. This plan is very widely used, and it overcomes all the disadvantages of the piecework plan while retaining its advantages. It is essentially the same as piecework with a guaranteed minimum, with the exception of the fact that the standard is expressed in time instead of money. As defined by the Society for the Advancement of Management, it is a pay plan in which the percent performance over standard is rewarded by an equal percent premium over base pay.[8] An example will reveal more clearly how the system works. Assume that the base rate for a job is $6.00 per hour and that the time standard for the operation upon which the employee is currently working is ¼ hour per unit. Pay would normally be calculated separately for each day. If 40 units are produced in one day, the employee would have earned 10 standard hours of pay, or $60.00. If the work day were 8 hours long, he would then have earned 10 standard hours of pay, although his clock hours were 8. His efficiency is thus 125 percent. If, for some reason, the employees' output for the day were only 24 units (6 standard hours), he would be paid his base rate for the full 8 clock hours worked.

Advantages of this plan are that it is easy for employees to understand, and earnings are directly proportional to production above standard. a change in hourly wage rates for all employees has no effect upon the standards, because they are expressed in time units (rather than money units as in the piecework plan). It is readily suitable to group-incentive applications where the group may include employees on various base rates. Further it facilitates the utilization of accounting controls and departmental measures of efficiency. There appear to be no disadvantages to this system; in fact, many companies, having tried other more cumbersome plans, have dropped them in favor of the standard-hour plan.

Gains-Sharing Plans

A gains-sharing plan is one in which the money paid for increasing output above standard is not in direct proportion to the increment in production. The worker receives less than 1 percent increase in pay for each 1 percent increase in production. The "gains" are shared with the employer. All the gains-sharing plans are based upon the premise of rewarding the employee for saving time in the performance of his job. In one well-known plan, the Bedeaux plan, named after

[8] Society for Advancement of Management, *Glossary of Terms Used in Methods, Time Study, and Wage Incentives* (New York: The Society, 1953).

its creater Charles Bedeaux, 75 percent of the gain went to the worker and 25 percent went to indirect labor and supervision. In 1940 this plan was revised so that 100 percent of the gain went to the worker. The Halsey 50–50 bonus plan paid 50 percent of the value of the time saved (when a worker completed his units in less than the standard time) to the worker and 50 percent to the company.

Because the incentive payments are in less than direct proportion to output, both workers and unions have opposed gains-sharing plans. They are seldom used nowadays.

Group Incentives

Group incentives for work that is measured and standardized can be paid under any one of the foregoing types of incentive plans. Earnings are determined from the total number of units produced by the group. However, the group approach does not obviate the necessity of analysis and standardization of each job within the group. Where the workers are quite interdependent and where clear cooperation and coordination are vital to success, a group incentive plan makes a great deal of sense. On a production line, where one employee cannot get ahead of the person who precedes him, a group plan may work well. If there are a number of different jobs within the group, each having a different basic hourly rate of pay, the standard-hour plan works quite well. Here the percentage increase in output above standard for the entire group can be added to the base rate for each employee to determine the amount of his bonus for that pay period.

HUMAN AND ADMINISTRATIVE PROBLEMS

The usage of wage incentives in an industrial organization often achieves management's goal of higher productivity and lower direct labor costs. Further, the total cost per unit may very well decrease too. If a particular machine or work center has an overhead (or burden) costing rate of $16.00 per direct labor hour and if output is increased, then the overhead cost per unit is decreased, because the overhead rate, within limits, does not go up if production rises. Employees, too, stand to gain from the installation of a wage incentive system. Commonly their pay will average 20 to 30 percent higher. So far, so good.

However, the introduction of incentives brings about many administrative and human relations problems that either are not present at all under daywork or are present to only a minor extent. A larger industrial engineering staff is needed to devise the incentive plan, set work standards, and develop controls. Greater attention must be devoted to obtaining accurate piece counts of each worker and to maintaining quality and safety standards. And above all, serious human relations problems are created. Experience shows that grievance and arbitration activity is higher in plants using incentives than in nonincentive plants.

Role of the Industrial Engineer

The process of work measurement used to set standards generally requires that the engineer closely observe the detailed motions of the employee for a considerable length of time (anywhere from one half to a whole eight-hour day). The engineer often tells the employee to change his method of doing the work. To an experienced worker who feels he already knows his job well, this detailed observation and correction often cause tension and antagonism toward the engineer. But in reality this is only the start of a human relations conflict. The worker knows that the engineer is going to set a time standard on his job. This standard will determine his wages. If the rate turns out to be "tight," he will be unable to exceed standard performance, and he will only be paid his hourly base rate for the time he has actually worked. Workers tend to feel that if they can make the work look more difficult and take longer than really necessary, they can fool the engineer and thus get a "good" or a "loose" rate. However, the engineer is often aware of the worker's objectives, so he adjusts the actual observed time by a percentage factor to rate or level his performance. So if the employee stalls in doing his job and takes 5 minutes to perform a unit of work and if the engineer judges his skill and effort to be 75 percent of normal, he will allow only 3.75 minutes for the operation. Sometimes in spite of his awareness, the engineer is "fooled," and he does establish a loose rate. On the other hand, if the resultant rate should turn out to be "tight," not only will the worker who has been studied be dissatisfied, but also his fellow workers who perform the same operation will blame him for the bad rate.

The industrial engineer, trying to do a professional job, is many times caught between two fires. There is pressure from higher management for greater efficiency, higher production, lower labor costs, and the placing of as many jobs as possible on incentive in a limited amount of time. If the engineer establishes "loose" standards, he is criticized by management. Because he is dependent upon management for his job tenure, salary increases, and progress in the organization, he must conform to management's expectations. However, there are pressures on the other side of the fence too. The workers will turn in rate grievances and express resentment against him if they are not satisfied with the standards. Since the engineer must frequently mingle with the employees, he seeks at least their pasive good will and cooperation. If the employees should file a great number of grievances over the rates set, management may express dissatisfaction with the caliber of his efforts.

Restriction of Output

Restriction of output is a phenomenon that occurs with both union and nonunion employees and under both daywork and incentive situations. The problem is accentuated under an incentive system. Restriction of output means that informal group pressures and sanctions are imposed to prevent employees from producing as much as they are capable of. From the early days of the scientific management movement through to the present day, industrial engineers and management-engineering consultants have tended to believe that the installation of a wage incentive program would cause employees to try to maximize their earnings by maximizing their production. Certain individual employees indeed do just this. They work to the limit of their endurance to earn as much money as possible. But the majority control their output; they do not produce as much as they could if they worked to the limits imposed by bodily fatigue. Usually they work well below this point. In one factory the employees in the punch press department systematically produced at 27 percent above standard, never more. This restriction was achieved through group controls. When he was confronted with the evidence of restriction, the informal leader, who in this case was the shop steward, vehemently denied any planned effort on the employees' part to restrict work.

Why does this phenomenon occur? There are many reasons to explain it. First, employees tend to believe that if they earn more money than management thinks they should, the piece rate will be cut. Rate cutting is a practice that arose in industry many years ago. Ill-trained "efficiency experts" who served as consultants to employers often adopted this practice. At the present time all reputable industrial engineers and employers frown upon the practice. However, it still occurs often enough to arouse the employees' fears.

Even if the employer does not intentionally cut rates when earnings reach too high a level, sometimes a worker thinks he does. This comes about through the continued auditing and re-examination of operations that some companies undertake. In the effort to reduce costs still further, operations with established rates are many times restudied for further methods improvement, and then a new and lower rate is set. Strictly speaking the employee should have as good an earnings potential as before, but frequently management's motives are mistrusted. The employees may interpret this as a form of disguised rate cutting.

There are social reasons for restriction of output also. According to the logics and management and its engineers, employees should engage in individualistic competition, should work hard, and take pride in doing a good day's work for their employer. Primary emphasis should be upon the acquisition of more money as the fruits of hard labor. This is considered a major virtue. Concern with the reactions of one's associates to this competitive drive for more and more should not bother the individual. Yet many workers are not so strongly motivated in this direction. They are sensitive to what others in their work group think. They want to acquire and maintain the respect and friendship of their fellows. They feel that group acceptance, social participation, and group solidarity are important values. Those who seek to maximize their earnings by exceeding the group-imposed quota are labeled rate-busters. They generally are set apart from the group and its social activities. I was once employed in a shop where one employee beat up another worker because the latter was working too fast.[9] Rate restrictors sometimes feel they are "shown up" in the eyes of management by the high output of the "rate-busters," and they resent the latter. Workers often believe that slow workers will be discharged. Thus, in many factories there are conflicts between the restrictors and the rate-busters.

Wage Inequities

Work measurement techniques such as time study have a margin of error. Authorities claim that a well-qualified engineer can set standards that are within ± 5 percent of the true or correct values. Many critics challenge this assertion. But regardless of this controversy, it is a fact that nearly every industrial establishment has a fair number of loose and tight rates. These may be caused by inexpe-

[9] The victim, only slightly bruised, was transferred to another plant. The aggressor was a local union committeeman. Management, not wanting to upset good union relations, took no disciplinary action against him.

rienced engineers, by workers figuring out short cuts so that the rates become loose over a period of many months, or because the job conditions (adjustment of machine, quality of the materials, and so on) have changed with the passage of time. The fact that the earnings potential will vary significantly from one job to another causes anxiety and jealousy among the employees. They naturally compete to get the jobs with "loose" standards.

Then there is the perennial problem of equity between the semiskilled worker, who is on incentive, and the highly skilled employee, such as the tool and die maker, who is paid by the hour. Industrial engineers find it very difficult to put nonrepetitive, highly variable, and complex jobs on incentive. In one electronics factory, male machine-shop craftsmen went on a one-day strike because semiskilled women on incentive in the same plant had higher take-home pay.

Fluctuations in Earnings

A common source of frustration to workers is the variation in earnings from one week to another. This is prevalent in shops where there are short runs and new operations must be continually mastered, where workers are transferred from one operation to another frequently, and where the process equipment breaks down often (down-time). In job-order shops where new and different products are continually being introduced, there naturally is a lag from the introduction of new operations until they have been placed on incentive. If workers are paid daywork rates for this interim period, they will experience a temporary lowering of their pay.

Rewards for Methods Improvements

The typical incentive plan rewards employees for physically working harder but gives them nothing for greater ingenuity and new ideas on how to improve their jobs. If employees develop methods improvements that make the work easier and reduce the time per unit, they are faced with a dilemma. If they notify their supervisor or the industrial engineer of the improvement, there is every likelihood that the operation will be changed to conform to the better method. Then a new and lower time standard will be established. Employees often feel that their "reward" for passing on their ideas to management is a lower piece rate that will require harder work to earn as much money as they obtained previously. Even if the new rate should provide them with as much money as before the change (equivalent earnings for equivalent skill and effort), they tend to feel that they are exposing themselves to the risk of a tight rate. So we find that in many shops workers devise jigs, fixtures, and other simple methods improvements and keep them secret from management. By so doing they can increase their incentive earnings substantially without increased physical exertion. Or if they suspect that earnings of, say, 50 and 60 percent above base rate will arouse the industrial engineer's suspicions, they use their labor-saving devices to give themselves more free time during the working day.

Many companies attempt to solve this problem by encouraging employees to submit their proposals for methods improvements and cost reductions through a formal suggestion system in order to receive monetary awards. In theory this is fine. However, the typical suggestion plan pays the employee who submitted an idea 10 to 15 percent of the first year's net dollar savings. Many employees conclude that they will make more money by concealing their ideas from management and thereby obtain higher incentive earnings through utilization of jigs and fixtures of their own making. The central problem, in summary, is this: Should an incentive plan reward employees only for the exertion of greater physical skill and effort, or should it reward them for their own ideas and initiative as well? Would it be better to incorporate rewards for ideas into the basic incentive plan itself, or should this objective be met by means of a separate program? Possible solutions are the payment of much more liberal awards under a suggestion system or the adoption of a plantwide incentive system, such as Scanlon Plan.

Meeting the Problems Imposed by Incentives

Although no magic formulas exist that can solve the human problems imposed by incentives, there are certain sound approaches that, if followed, can ameliorate them. There is need for more research and experimentation to find full answers.

By assiduously applying the principles enunciated earlier in this chapter for the successful operation of an incentive program, some of these difficulties can be overcome or greatly modified. For example, employees' fears of rate cutting can be prevented by guaranteeing standards. Tight rates can be adjusted if an effective grievance procedure exists. Careful administration of the program can reduce fluctuations in earnings (for example, some firms pay the average incentive earnings that an employee has built up during the preceding three months when he is transferred to an unfamiliar operation or for machine down-time). If the employer adopts an easy-to-understand incentive system and if a training program is instituted to teach the employees how the plan operates, confidence will be built up and distrust and suspicion allayed.

Antagonisms between the industrial engineer and employees can be considerably reduced by a full recognition of the staff nature of the engineer's position in the organization. The employee is accustomed to having interaction originated for him by his foreman. In his approach to the employee for making a time study, the engineer should first obtain the authorization of the foreman. If the employees are represented by a union, the shop steward should be notified also. The foreman, steward, and engineer as a group would then approach the employee to explain the work measurement assignment in relation to his job. After the work standard has been determined, the engineer should present it to the foreman for his reactions and approval. It should be the foreman who announces the standard to the employee. The shop steward should also be informed of developments to obtain his reaction.

There are still other possibilities for overcoming many of these human relations problems. When employees are represented by a union, there is considerable merit to the idea of having a degree of union participation in the time-study and rate-setting process. Union participation through union-employed time-study men and bargaining of piece rates accounts, in no small measure, for the full acceptance by the workers of the piecework method of payment in the garment industry. It is not proposed here that work standards and piece rates should be bargained throughout industry. Employers typically hold that setting of workloads is a management prerogative. The money paid for each job is, of course, a bargainable issue. However, there is considerable merit to the proposal that local union officials and stewards receive training in the fundamentals of time study and incentives—even to the point where the union would have one or more fully qualified time-study experts in its membership. Various procedures could be followed for implementing this. Standards set by management would be put into effect except for those that workers have found by trial to be incorrect or unjust. They would then file a grievance. If a restudy of the operation were deemed by both parties to be advisable, it would be carried out by both the industrial engineer employed by the company and the time-study specialist working for the union. The dispute would then be resolved by a meeting of the minds of all parties involved: management as represented by the foreman and the industrial engineer and the employees as represented by the steward and the time-study specialist. Disputes unresolved at this level could be processed through the regular grievance procedure and eventually taken to arbitration if necessary.

The adoption of a plantwide incentive plan based upon the essential concept of cooperation between labor and management is another method of attemptng to overcome the multitude of human problems created by wage incentives. The Scanlon Plan is one well-known method. It does not involve individual job rates but rather a standard expressed in terms of labor costs as a percentage of the sales value of the product for the plant as a whole. Employee participation in reducing costs is actively encouraged. Teamwork and cooperation instead of individualistic competition are emphasized.

INCENTIVES AND LABOR–MANAGEMENT COOPERATION

An incentive system that departs considerably from commonly accepted notions of what an incentive plan should be is the one developed by Joseph N. Scanlon. The plan is generally known as the Scanlon Plan.[10] Mr. Scanlon was an official of the United Steelworkers of America in the late 1930's and early 1940's; later he joined the faculty of the Massachusetts Institute of Technology.

The plan consists basically of two parts: (1) a plantwide wage-incentive arrangement for which the standard is set by accounting methods and not by time study; (2) a program for implementing cooperation among the employees, the union, and the management to solve production and efficiency problems. This is accomplished through a unique suggestion plan. Although the details of the Scanlon Plan vary from one installation to another the essential features are the same. Even though the plan can work successfully in a nonunion company, Scanlon felt that if employees were represented by a union, the greatest advantages of employee participation could be obtained.

[10] Descriptions and analyses of the Scanlon Plan can be found in a number of articles and books. Among them are William Foote Whyte, *Money and Motivation* (New York: Harper and Row, 1955); "Productivity and Incentive Pay," *Management Record*, Vol. 19, No. 10 (October 1957); Russell W. Davenport, "Enterprise for Everyman," *Fortune*, Vol. 41, No. 1 (January, 1950), pp. 55–59; F. G. Lesieur and E. S. Puckett, "The Scanlon Plan Has Proved Itself," *Harvard Business Review*, Vol. 47, No. 5 (September–October 1969), pp. 109–118.

Labor-Cost Norm and Incentive Bonus

Cost accounting records are examined to arrive at a labor-cost norm. This norm is expressed as a percentage of the total sales value of the product shipped by the company. Usually direct and indirect labor as well as supervisory payroll are included in the figures for labor cost. Sometimes even executives are included in the incentive plan. Scanlon generally recommended that all employees from worker to major executive should participate. An example will show how the plan works. Assume that labor and management after a careful examination of accounting records arrive at a labor-cost norm of 40 percent of the sales value of the product. This figure then becomes the standard for the ensuing year. Calculations are then made on a monthly basis. If cooperative efforts reduce the actual payroll costs below that 40 percent figure for any one month, the employees will then receive a bonus.

It has been found practical to reserve a portion of the monthly savings (25 percent in Table 25-1) to balance against those months when the actual is in excess of the norm or standard. Likewise it should be pointed out that in some companies using the Scanlon Plan, a certain percentage of the savings is retained by the company. If major changes occur in basic wage rates, in the selling price, or in the cost of raw materials, or if the company invests in substantial technological improvements, a re-examination of the labor-cost norm may be made. A change in the percentage would be by mutual agreement between management and labor.

Suggestion Plan and Production Committees

It is through the suggestion plan that ideas are handled that make it possible to improve work methods, redesign products, reduce or simplify paperwork, and improve machine utilization. Every department has a production committee composed of a management representative (commonly the foreman) and an employee or union representative. The function of these committees is to process and evaluate employee suggestions. Some are accepted and put into effect at the department level. Those considered worthwhile for the entire plant or those in-

Table 25-1

Sales shipped for month	$125,000
Less decrease in value of finished goods in inventory and in process	25,000
Total production value	100,000
Labor cost allowable (40%)	40,000
Actual payroll for month	36,000
Savings from improvement in production efficiency	4,000
Less 25% for contingency reserve	1,000
Net available for distribution to employees	$ 3,000

Each employee receives a bonus of 8.33 per cent for the month ($3,000 divided by actual payroll of $36,000).

volving major expenditures and changes are passed on to an administration or screening committee composed of an equal number of management and employee (or union) representatives. Suggestions approved by the screening committee are passed on to top management for a final decision. Because management is represented on the screening committee, it generally approves at this point. There are no individual awards under the Scanlon Plan. The payoff comes from cost-cutting ideas that benefit the organization as a whole and thus contribute to the plantwide bonus. Benefits of this participative form of suggestion plan are threefold. (1) It emphasizes cooperation between management and labor. They work together in production and screening committees to solve problems. (2) Teamwork means that often a problem that could not be solved by one person alone is successfully handled by the combined brains of a group. (3) Genuine participation by employees in the affairs of the business reduces the likelihood of restriction of output and resistance to change on their part. They tend to support that which they have initiated and designed.

It is interesting to point out the contrasts between the traditional type of suggestion plan used in industry and the type that is part and parcel of the Scanlon Plan. In the standard suggestion plan individual employees write their ideas on suggestion blanks and drop these in suggestion boxes scattered throughout the plant. The suggestion box coordinator generally either assigns the suggestions to a specialist (such as an engineer) who then studies their feasibility, or he turns them over to a suggestion committee that evaluates them. If, after thorough investigation, management considers a suggestion useful, it will calculate the annual dollar saving that could be realized through adoption of the idea. Then a percentage of this amount will be awarded to the employee (usually in the form of cash but sometimes in merchandise). If an employee's idea is rejected, he generally is notified by means of a form letter.

So we see that in the traditional suggestion system the emphasis is upon the individual, whereas in the Scanlon Plan it is upon group cooperation and group sharing in the benefits. Formal written communication is utilized in the traditional plan, whereas social interaction and discussion are key features of the Scanlon method. In the traditional setup, first-level supervisors sometimes are jealous of workers who submit cost-cutting ideas, because they fear that higher management will criticize them for not thinking of the idea themselves first. This problem is not present under the Scanlon arrangement, because both supervisor and employee work together in the production committee to initiate ideas jointly.

Evaluation of the Scanlon Plan

The Scanlon Plan is not a panacea. Just as the success of other incentive plans depends to a large extent upon the way they are administered and upon the attitudes of the parties involved, so it is with the Scanlon Plan. This plan requires a high degree of mutual confidence and cooperation between labor and management. It places a premium upon group cooperation and the initiation of ideas among the employees. If individual workers are unproductive, they will still share in the bonus earned by the entire plant. If no bonus is earned for several months running (as happens in some companies), employee dissatisfaction can mount. The underlying philosophy of the Scanlon Plan is different from that of the traditional type of incentive program. It overcomes many of the inherent difficulties of the traditional approach, but it raises new problems.

PROFIT SHARING

The concept of a company sharing some of the profits of its business with its employees is not new. The practice had its beginning in America in the late eighteenth century and in England and France in the middle nineteenth century. Albert Gallatin, Secretary of the Treasury under Presidents Jefferson and Madison, initiated a profit-sharing plan in 1794 at his glass works in New Geneva, Pennsylvania. Horace Greeley had a plan for certain employees of the *New York Tribune*. Pillsbury Flour Mills in Minneapolis set up a plan in 1882. In 1878 the Procter and Gamble Company adopted a plan that is still in operation although in a revised form.[11]

Profit Sharing Defined

The first formalized definition of profit sharing was that adapted by the International Cooperative Congress, Paris, France, in 1889. It reads as follows: "Profit-Sharing is an agreement freely entered into, by which the employees received a share, fixed in advance, of the profits."

The Council of Profit Sharing Industries, which promotes the profit-sharing movement gives the following definition: "Any procedure under which an employer makes available to all regular employees subject to reasonable eligibility rules in addition to prevailing rates of pay, special current or deferred sums based on the profits of the business."[12]

For those plans that defer the distribution of benefits to employees until some future date, the regulations of the United States Internal Revenue Service must be adhered to if the employer wishes to avoid paying a tax on the profit-share sums. Among these requirements are the following. (1) There must be a predetermined formula for allocating the funds to the participants. (2) There must be a trust fund established, and this must be used for the exclusive benefit of the employees or their beneficiaries. (3) The plan must be in writing and communicated to employees.[13]

A profit-sharing plan, then, distributes part of the profits of the business to the employees. The earlier definition of the International Cooperative Congress specifies that the plan must have a definite formula or method for determining the amount that goes to the employees. The definition of the Council of Profit Sharing Industries omits any mention of an agreement by which shares are computed. Thus, under the latter's definition the percentage share going to the em-

---

[11] Some of the many companies that now have profit-sharing plans are Bell and Howell Company, Dow Chemical Company, Eastman Kodak Company, Kellogg Company, The Kroger Company, The Lincoln Electric Company, S. C. Johnson and Son, Inc., Sears, Roebuck and Company, and Tappan Stove Company.

[12] Council of Profit Sharing Industries, *Profit Sharing Manual*, rev. ed. (Chicago: The Council, 1957).

[13] F. B. Brower, *Sharing Profits with Employees*, Studies in Personnel Policy, No. 162 (New York: National Industrial Conference Board, 1957).

ployees might vary from year to year. Presumably the exact amount would be determined by the board of directors. The great majority of plans actually do have a systematic formula for computing the employee's share. It is logical that greater faith and confidence will tend to be created where the employees know exactly how their shares are figured.

Objectives of Profit Sharing

Why would an entrepreneur or the board of directors choose to share some of the fruits of a business enterprise with the employees? Although in practice the motives are many and varied, a fundamental purpose is to create a sort of proprietary interest on the part of the employees in the business organization. The belief is that they will be more loyal and devoted. Presumably the prospect of a profit bonus at the end of the year will motivate the employees to work harder in the hopes of increasing the profits of the company. They will become more cost conscious, try to reduce waste and scrap.

Other objectives are to improve employee morale, enhance employer–employee relations, and aid the public relations image of the corporation. A few companies, particularly in the past, looked upon profit sharing as a means of paying low wages and yet providing for adequate total employee income when profits were good. This in effect introduced a flexible wage structure to correlate with the profitability of the company. The rigidities of adequate wages through good times and bad could be avoided. Experience has shown that such plans based upon low wages (below prevailing rates for the given class of work) are generally unsuccessful.

For those plans that defer the payment of benefits until some future date, the objectives are modified somewhat from the foregoing. These plans typically provide benefits upon termination of employment, retirement, death, or disability. The goals here are to provide some financial security to meet certain risks of employment and life. Also management frequently feels that putting off the payment of the profit shares until many years in the future reduces the likelihood of employees leaving the company.

Types of Plans

Profit-sharing plans can be conveniently classified according to when the benefits are paid out to the employees. There are three categories:

1. Current Distribution—This is the oldest method historically and still quite popular. Under it benefits are paid monthly, quarterly, semiannually, and annually.
2. Deferred Distribution—Growing rapidly in popularity in recent years, this arrangement sets up a trust fund with benefits to be paid out for such contingencies as retirement, permanent disability, death, and termination of employment. In some instances the money is set up as a savings fund with employees having the right to withdraw certain portions after having been on the payroll for a specified number of years.
3. A Combination Plan—Some organizations have attempted to gain the advantages of both the current and the deferred distribution plans by paying out

part of the profit share in the year earned in cash to the employees. This is a tangible reward in the present that people can fully realize and appreciate. The rest of the money is placed in a trust fund to be paid out at some future date according to the provisions of the plan.

A 1965–1966 study by the Bureau of Labor Statistics of 12,771 establishments employing 8.9 million workers showed that 12 percent of plant workers and 22 percent of office workers were under some form of profit-sharing plan. Of these workers, 81 percent were under a deferred distribution type plan, only 8.7 percent were under current distribution, 7 percent were under combined plans, and 3.7 percent were under elective plans.[14] Bert Metzger of the Profit Sharing Research Foundation states that as of 1972 approximately 8 million employees participated in 122,962 deferred and combination profit-sharing programs and another one million persons participated in 80,000 to 90,000 cash-type programs in the United States.[15]

Figuring the Share

Most often the share of the total profits to be distributed to employees as a whole represents a fixed percentage of corporate net profits. In some cases it is a percentage of profits before deduction for dividends and taxes, and in others it is a percentage after deduction for dividends and/or taxes. In some cases the sum paid to participants is expressed as a percentage of the dividends to stockholders.

After the size of the total fund for any one year is computed, the allocation to individuals must be made. Usually each person's share is based upon the amount of his annual earnings in relation to the total payroll of those participating in the plan. Very commonly, also, the size of the share is related to one's length of service as well as his wage level. Occasionally each person's portion is based upon a performance-rating (merit-rating) score assigned by supervision.

Requirements for a Sound Plan

Based on a relatively long history accompanied by many successes and failures of various plans, certain helpful guides can be offered to insure a successful program. Profit sharing cannot be installed as a substitute for adequate wage rates. The wages paid must be comparable to the prevailing rates for the same class of work in the labor market. The profit share distributed to each employee must be something extra. Only then will it be an incentive; only then will be develop loyalty and a proprietary interest in the success of the business.

Before the plan is instituted the state of employer–employee relations must be satisfactory. Profit sharing cannot be expected to restore an unhappy situation. The entire personnel-management program should be up to date and sound. The company must already be doing the right things as far as wages, hours, working conditions, fringe benefits, supervisory climate, and employee communications are concerned.

[14] Gunnar Engen, "A New Direction and Growth in Profit Sharing," *Monthly Labor Review* Vol. 90, No. 7 (July 1967), pp. 1–8.
[15] Bert L. Metzger, *Socio-Economic Participation: Key to a Better World of Work in the Future* (Evanston, Ill.: Profit Sharing Research Foundation, 1972), p. 23.

There must be some profits available to distribute to the employees. If a company is unfortunate enough to have a number of years of financial losses or of very small profits, there will be discontent with the program. An occasional loss will not ruin a firmly rooted plan, but continued losses have been a major factor causing the abandonment of many plans.

If the employees are represented by a union, the full support and cooperation of this organization is essential for success. According to decisions of the National Labor Relations Board, profit sharing is a bargainable issue. An employer cannot install and operate a plan unilaterally if the employees' representatives choose to bargain the point.

Some Conclusions on Profit Sharing

A fundamental weakness of profit sharing is that employees' earnings are tied to profits—something over which they have only modest control. Profits are affected by general business conditions and the state of the business cycle, extent of competition, luck, caliber of top management, and other factors beyond the control of the employees. Of course, employees as a group do have some effect upon profits to be sure. But if top management wishes to adopt such a program primarily for its incentive aspect, then this objective can be only partially realized. Nevertheless the record through the years, while fraught with ups and downs, reveals that great numbers of programs have been successful. They satisfy management. They satisfy the workers.

LINCOLN ELECTRIC INCENTIVE SYSTEM[16]

The Lincoln Electric Company of Cleveland, Ohio, is one of the world's largest producers of electric arc-welding equipment and supplies. It also manufacturers electric motors. Its unique incentive plan has been in operation since 1934 with enduring and outstanding success. There is no union at Lincoln Electric. The incentive system at Lincoln has been so successful that one wonders why other companies have not been able to imitate it with corresponding success.

The program—which is really a systems type program because it encompasses a number of integrated elements—was started in 1934 by the late James F. Lincoln, the company president. He formulated the following principles as a basis for the company's incentive program:

1. Each employee's job security must be fully protected; his increased productivity must not threaten his job.
2. Employees must learn that their increased productivity and identification with company goals lead to increased take-home pay, enhanced job security, and significant profit-sharing payments.
3. Improved productivity and lower costs shall be passed along to customers in the form of price reductions to strengthen the company in the marketplace and to thereby further enhance job security.

[16] Much of the information on the Lincoln Electric Incentive System is derived from Bert L. Metzger, op. cit., pp. 12–15.

4. Management should continue to plow back earnings to develop the plant and the company's position in the market.

The incentive management program at Lincoln Electric contains the following elements:

1. *A piecework wage incentive plan with a guaranteed day rate.* Rates are set by motion- and time-study specialists. A worker can challenge a piece rate if he thinks it is unfair. The rate is then reviewed by a special committee. If the worker is still not satisfied, the time-study man runs the job himself for a day or two. His reestablished time is then accepted as the correct standard.
2. *Job-evaluated base rates.* Base rates upon which the piece rates are built are established by a committee of supervisors using a job evaluation procedure. The basic wage rates are competitive with other area companies.
3. *Merit Rating.* Each employee is merit rated twice per year on four equally weighted factors: workmanship (quality), output, ideas (improvements), and supervision required. The merit-rating score substantially determines each person's portion of the annual profit-sharing fund.
4. *Cash profit sharing.* The profit fund available for distribution to all employees is equal to the total annual profit less taxes, reserve for reinvestment in the business, and a 6 percent dividend for the stockholders. The size of an individual's profit share is equal to his annual salary times his merit-rating score times the profit-sharing factor (profit-sharing pool divided by annual payroll). Thus, in a given year if the profit-sharing factor is 105 percent, a $12,000-per-year employee with a merit-rating score of 120 percent would receive an annual cash bonus of $15,120.
5. *Job security.* Lincoln guarantees annual employment of at least 32 hours per week for fifty weeks a year for each employee after two years of service. This is a precondition for employees to expend their best efforts toward maximum productivity.
6. *Stock purchase plan for employees.*
7. *Advisory board.* There is an advisory board of elected employee representatives who suggest changes and operating policies to management.
8. *Promotions.* Promotions are primarily made by selection from within the organization. They are based upon merit not seniority.
9. *Job enrichment.* Many factory employees function almost as independent subcontractors. Each person does his own set-ups, his own inspection, and is responsible for his own production and product quality.

Results and evaluation

As of 1972 Lincoln Electric was selling its welding machines and electrodes at the same (or *slightly* higher or lower) prices as in 1934 when the comprehensive incentive-management program was begun. This has been achieved despite the fact that all cost elements such as labor rates and raw materials were three to six times as high in 1972 as in 1934. In 1969 the year-end profit-sharing fund totaled $16,544,000. This was divided among the total of 1,973 employees, making the year-end bonus equal to about 100–105 percent of annual pay on the average.

Zollitsch and Langsner have made a tabulation comparing average hourly earnings of production workers at Lincoln (including overtime premium, annual bonus, and vacation pay) with those in all manufacturing industries for the period 1956 through 1968. The Lincoln earnings are more than double the all-manufacturing average for each of these years. In 1968 for example, Lincoln workers earned $7.20 per hour, whereas the all-manufacturing average was $3.01.[17]

CONCLUSIONS

The purposes of pay incentives are to generate increased productivity as well as higher take-home pay for the employees. Each technique for achieving these objectives has its advantages and disadvantages.

The historical record in countless plants shows that direct wage incentives do raise output per direct employee hour, often significantly. However, these incentive programs demand close attention to day-to-day administration. Grievances over production standards tend to be frequent and there tends to be much conflict between management and labor in incentive shops.

Scanlon plans have shown a good record over many years. However, they tend to work best in smaller establishments. Labor-management cooperation is an essential ingredient. It seems that the collaborative spirit can be engendered more readily in the smaller organization than in the large impersonal bureaucracy.

Profit sharing rewards employees either with a year-end bonus or with a contribution to their deferred profit share fund when the profits of the corporation are good. Profit sharing helps to generate good will and loyalty to the company. It may also keep employee turnover low. However, profit sharing, alone, does not induce superior day-to-day performance.

The Lincoln Electric System, combining as it does many incentive elements, would seem to be the ideal mechanism for obtaining both high productivity and high employee satisfaction. Indeed, the program works well for Lincoln. However, hardly any other firms have been able to duplicate the Lincoln system. Part of the reason is that other managements have not been willing to include all the elements of the Lincoln formula. For example, they won't provide the essential job security which serves as a foundation stone at Lincoln. Also, part of Lincoln's success is due to the culture of the organization. The work pace is fast. People who aren't willing or able to work at a sustained fast pace year after year don't apply for employment at Lincoln. Or if they do apply and get hired, they find that the work demands aren't to their liking and they leave.

Can good job performance be achieved when employees are paid by the hour instead of by the piece? A great many managers say yes. Measured daywork is one answer. Other answers are good supervision, a supportive and effective managerial system, and sound motivational practices. We discussed principles and practices of effective managerial leadership and motivation in earlier chapters.

[17] Herbert G. Zollitsch and Adolph Langsner, *Wage and Salary Administration*, 2nd ed. (Cincinnati: South-Western Publishing Company, 1970), p. 500.

Questions for review and discussion

1. What considerations would guide your decision to pay employees according to an incentive pay plan or a daywork plan?
2. Give a list of occupations for which you feel it would be very difficult to develop a fully fair and equitable incentive plan.
3. From the standpoint of employees, what are the possible advantages of working under an incentive payment plan? Disadvantages?
4. Explain the meaning of the following:
   a. Time study.
   b. Predetermined elemental time systems.
   c. Standard hour plan.
   d. Performance rating (or leveling).
5. What are the causes of organized restriction of output that often develops among work groups in industry? How can the problem be alleviated?
6. What are the relative merits of individual incentives based upon engineered time standards as compared with a plantwide incentive, such as the Scanlon Plan?
7. Explain the principal features of the Scanlon Plan. Do you feel it can be operated successfully in a large multiplant company?
8. What might motivate an employer to install a profit-sharing plan?
9. Do you feel that a deferred profit-sharing plan will appreciably alter employee productivity or attitudes? Explain.
10. How would you explain the great success of the Lincoln Electric Incentive System over such a long span of years? Why do you think it has not been copied as successfully by other firms?

Case problems

PROBLEM 1

The Automotive Supply Parts Company is a well-established, profitable manufacturing concern located in a large eastern city. It makes a variety of products for the automotive industry. These are sold to the automobile manufacturers as original equipment and also sold through distributors throughout the country as replacement parts.

For several years the company had had a major portion of its production operations on individual incentives. A large, well-trained staff of industrial engineers is employed to analyze and improve production methods, standardize operations, and set time standards for individual operations by means of time-study procedures. Base rates of pay for every job are bargained with a local independent union. A standard-hour incentive plan is used throughout the plant. For output in excess of standard, the plan pays employees in direct proportion to the increase in productivity. Thus an employee whose average production for a day is 25 percent above standard receives a 25 percent bonus above his base pay. If an operation is shut down due to a machine breakdown or lack of materials, the operator is paid his guaranteed basic hourly rate for the actual hours involved.

The incentive program works fairly well in most production departments of the plant. If an employee feels that a particular standard is unjust, he can file a grievance with the union time-study stewards, who will investigate and retime the job if necessary. The union time-study stewards (three in number) are members of the union who have been trained by management in the intricacies of the time-study system used. They are paid by the company but do in fact effectively try to look out for the workers' interests when a time standard is in dispute.

In one large department, the punch press department, which contains sixty employees, there is continual conflict over the operation of the incentive program. In fact, the average number of grievances over time standards emanating from this department each year is more than are filed in all of the other departments combined. The union steward in this department is very aggressive in presenting grievances to management. Those in the industrial engineering department feel that a large part of the continuing controversy over time standards is due to the rabid antagonism of this one union steward. They feel that he keeps the workers continually stirred up and suspicious of the integrity of the industrial engineering department. However, the employees feel that he effectively represents their interests, so they have repeatedly reelected him to office throughout the years.

The employees complain that there is too much down-time, for which they receive only their base pay. They also do not like the fact that new operations or new parts are being continually introduced. Sometimes they must work several weeks on daywork wages on these new operations before the industrial engineer who is assigned to that department gets around to timing the work and placing it on incentive. They complain, through this steward, that the standards are too "tight." They can't make a suitable bonus. There is considerable animosity toward the industrial engineering staff members. One employee has stated, "Every time I see you time-study guys, I get so mad I see red."

The departmental foreman, who firmly allies himself with the industrial engineer assigned to his department, makes a practice of demonstrating to workers who complain about rates that the rates are in fact fair and just. He does this by sitting down at a punch press, producing at a furious pace for perhaps five minutes, and then announcing that he has no trouble meeting the standard. They complain that he could not keep up such a fast pace all day long, as they must do.

For its part the industrial engineering department feels that the work standards in the punch press department are fair. The head of the industrial engineering department becomes very annoyed with workers who deliberately hold back production on an operation for which the rate is in dispute. He has noticed that on more than one occasion when the standard (expressed in units per hour) has been lowered as a result of a grievance and consequent retiming of the operation, the employees have "gone to town" on the operation and produced far more than the original (disputed) standard. When workers restrict output on operations having rates they think are unfair, this also makes it very difficult, if not impossible, for the company to meet its production schedules.

On more than one occasion certain high producers (the rest of the workers call them rate-busters) have been physically shoved around and punched by other employees because the latter consider such activities detrimental to the security of the group.

With the exception of the punch press department, relations between the top leadership of the union and management are reasonably amicable. The president of the union is an electrician who remains rather aloof from the constant strife in the punch press department.

In summary, then, the employees, led by an aggressive shop steward, feel that the work standards are too tight to make a decent incentive bonus. (They have averaged 27 percent bonus over the previous six months' period on those operations having a time standard.) Further they claim that they receive only their base rate of pay for too large a portion of the time because of down-time and delay in establishing standards on new operations, and in general they resent the close controls that the incentive system imposes on their jobs. The industrial engineering department seeks to establish accurate standards, to prevent loose rates from being created, and to have the incentive system serve as an instrument of management control. It is willing to restudy operations over which grievances have been filed and make adjustments if they are fully justified. It never loosens a rate just because of worker and union pressure—only when the objective facts justify it.

Questions

1. Diagnose the situation presented in this case.
2. What can the industrial engineering group do to improve relations?
3. What can management do to alleviate the problem? What can the union leadership do?
4. Are problems such as these inherent in the operation of an incentive system?

PROBLEM 2

You are the president of a small manufacturing company which has total employment of 900 persons. You have been disturbed for some time about the inability of the company to earn profits on sales and on investment as good as the average for your industry as a whole. You have had a preliminary study of the problem conducted and it has been determined that your plant and equipment, while not as modern as the best firms in your industry, are at least as good as the average firm. You know that costs are too high and productivity is mediocre. You have convened a meeting of your department heads to try to figure out how to raise the performance of the company. A summary of their remarks follows.

Manager of Industrial Engineering: We should install a direct wage incentive system for all of our production operations. We should conduct a thorough methods analysis and time study of each and every operation. We should standardize in writing the detailed work methods to be followed by the worker in performing every operation. Then we should use a standard hour wage incentive plan.

Manager of Manufacturing Engineering: This is an era in which some other companies have been successful in introducing more mechanization and automation. I recommend that we do the same. I have begun to install several machine-paced operations in the plant. With machine-paced operations direct wage incentives are of no value. However, I favor the use of a measured daywork plan to keep people at their machines and to insure that they service them promptly.

Personnel Manager: The era of close worker control and regimentation by time and motion study and wage incentives is passé. I propose that we use job enrichment. We need to upgrade our front-line supervisors through better selection and training. We need better and more supportive supervision. We need more teamwork.

Manager of Manufacturing: I favor tighter controls to reduce worker absenteeism. We also need to reduce slipshod workmanship through better inspection and quality checks. I also think a profit sharing plan would improve employee attitudes and performance generally.

Manager of Management Development: I recommend two solutions to our problem. I think we could improve cooperation and productivity throughout the plant by the installation of a Scanlon plan. For the office and supervisory personnel I recommend training in the Managerial Grid and in team building.

Questions

1. Analyze the advantages and disadvantages of each proposed solution.
2. Can certain of the proposed solutions be used in combination? Are some incompatible with others?
3. What solution(s) would you favor and why?

Suggestions for further reading

BELCHER, DAVID W. *Compensation Administration.* Englewood Cliffs, N.J.: Prentice-Hall, Inc., 1974, ch. 13 & 14.

FEIN, MITCHELL. "Restoring the Incentive to Wage Incentive Plans." *The Conference Board Review*, Vol. IX, No. 11 (November 1972), pp. 17–21.

————. "Improving Productivity by Improved Productivity Sharing." *The Conference Board Record*, Vol. XIII, No. 7 (July 1976), pp. 44–49.

HENDERSON, RICHARD I. *Compensation Management.* Reston, Va.: Reston Publishing Co., Inc., 1976, ch. 17.

LINCOLN, JAMES F. *A New Approach to Industrial Economics.* New York: The Devin-Adair Company, 1961.

METZGER, BERTRAM L. *Profit Sharing in 38 Large Companies.* Evanston, Ill.: Profit Sharing Research Foundation, 1975.

MOORE, BRIAN E. and T. L. ROSS. *The Scanlon Way to Improved Productivity.* New York: John Wiley & Sons, Inc., 1978.

SHWINGER, PINHAS. *Wage Incentive Systems.* New York: Halstead Press (Div. of John Wiley & Sons, Inc.), 1976.

VII
SECURITY

Health
and
safety

In 1976 5,164,000 occupational illnesses and injuries occurred in the *private* sector of the economy of the United States. Of this total nearly 2,000,000 involved lost workdays, which is to say they were serious. In the same year 4,500 persons lost their lives in injuries and occupation illnesses in the private sector. These statistics should be interpreted in the context of total private sector employment of 65 million people in 1976. Thus, one out of every eleven employed persons experienced a job related injury or illness in 1976. These figures are generally typical of the work injury and illness experience that has occurred for all the years of the 1970's.[1] For the year 1971 the National Safety Council estimated the aggregate cost of work injuries and illnesses at $9.3 billion. This figure includes the costs of lost wages, medical expenses, insurance claims, production delays, lost time coworkers, and equipment damage.[2] After a moment's reflection it must be evident that these figures represent a serious problem in terms of human anguish, loss of income to affected workers, and cost to employers. A half-century ago American industry did very little to protect the health and

[1] *News* bulletin (U.S. Department of Labor, Bureau of Labor Statistics, December 1, 1977).
[2] Nicholas A. Ashford, *Crisis in the Workplace: Occupational Disease and Injury* (Cambridge, Mass.: The MIT Press, 1976), p. 17.

safety of its employees. Today a large portion of employers (especially medium- and large-sized organizations) operate extensive health and safety programs. Still there is a great deal more to be done among all employers, large and small, to improve the health of their employees.

For many years employers have had two reasons for making active efforts to reduce work injuries and advance the health of their people. One is the humanitarian concern for the well-being of their employees. The other reason is cost. It is more economical to maintain an accident-free plant and to have full attendance on the job than it is to have extensive lost time due to job-connected injuries and illnesses and to non-occupational sickness. In point of fact, the real impetus for the introduction of safety programs throughout industry was the passage of workmen's compensation laws (now generally called workers' compensation) in the various states, principally between the years 1910 and 1925. These laws hold employers financially responsible for injuries incurred on the job regardless of the specific cause of any accident. Business executives may have deplored the human damage suffered in unsafe plants prior to the passage of these laws, but they were actually prodded into action, for the most part, only because of them.

Until 1971 the responsibility for regulation of health and safety in industry was vested solely in the states. But this was all changed with the passage by Congress of the Occupational Safety and Health Act of 1970, commonly called OSHA. Thus, we can say that OSHA is the third major reason for employers to take positive action for the protection of the health and safety of their employees. (This act is comprehensive and has strong enforcement powers.)

In addition to individual companies and now the Federal government since the enactment of OSHA, there are other organizations that play important roles in workplace safety and health. The National Safety Council works actively in the field of research, education, and the compilation and publication of information. Casualty insurance companies that sell workmen's compensation insurance to firms generally offer certain accident-prevention consultation services to their clients. Many states maintain workplace safety inspection services within their departments of labor. Several professional societies are active in the occupational health and safety fields. Principal among these are the Industrial Medical Association (physicians), American Industrial Hygiene Association (industrial hygienists), and the American Society of Safety Engineers.

In this chapter we shall investigate the Occupational Safety and Health Act, the very serious national problem of occupational disease, occupational safety, factors in accident causation, components of a sound safety and health program, workers' compensation, health services, mental health, and alcoholism.

OCCUPATIONAL SAFETY AND HEALTH ACT

Background

As a result of the efforts of the organized safety movement,(that is, employers, insurance companies, the National Safety Council, and state labor departments) substantial and steady progress was made throughout the country in reducing work injuries, both their frequency and severity, and death rates. Although there were continuing problems such as the high injury rates in small business generally and in certain industries such as longshoring, roofing, meat products, and lumber and wood products, by and large, professionals in the safety movement were rather satisfied with the progress that had been made. And it is fair to say that the public at large had come to believe that the problem of job safety and health had been largely solved.

But problems were brewing! During the 1951–1961 period the injury frequency rate for all manufacturing industries, combined, had declined from a high of 15.1 in 1951. However, beginning with 1961 when a rate of 11.8 was recorded, the trend was steadily upward. In 1970 the injury frequency rate was 15.2.[3] Safety professionals and government experts were never able to definitely explain why the safety record in industry had deteriorated so badly after showing rather steady improvement since the beginning of the organized safety movement in the 1915–1925 era.

Disasters in the mines stirred public concern for workers' safety. In 1968 a disaster in a mine of the Consolidation Coal Company in Farmington, West Virginia took 78 lives. In that year one man died for every 550 men employed in coal mining in the country.[4] In the 1960's the problem of black lung (pneumoconiosis) came to public attention. A medical officer of the United Mine Workers Union was quoted as saying an estimated 100,000 miners (including those no longer working in the mines) had evidence of the disease.[5] Congress tried to meet the serious problem of coal-mine hazards by passage of the Coal Mine Health and Safety Act of 1969, which provides for rigorous federal standards and inspections as well as for federal benefits for victims of black lung disease.

Testimony by workers and union leaders before a subcommittee of the Senate Committee on Labor and Public Welfare, 91st Congress emphasized worker anxiety over the insidious health effects of exposure to dusts, fumes, gases, chemicals, and physical agents. Worker witnesses also complained about the failure of state laws to provide authority for entry into plants, inadequate state funding and staffing of the enforcement agency, obsolete standards, and failure to furnish inspection reports to employees affected.[6]

Evidence began to surface in the late 1960's concerning the pervasiveness of occupational diseases that have been previously unrecognized. Among these were pneumoconiosis (black lung), byssinosis (from cotton dust), mesothelioma (cancer from asbestos), and diseases caused by heavy metals such as lead and mercury.

Because of the foregoing conditions, Congress passed the Occupational Safety and Health Act of 1970. It became effective April 28, 1971.

---

[3] Data from *Injury Rates by Industry*, BLS Report 406 (Washington, D.C.: U.S. Department of Labor, Bureau of Labor Statistics, 1972).

Injury frequency is equal to the number of disabling injuries times 1 million divided by employee-hours of exposure. This was defined by the American National Standards Institute in its Z16.1 standard. This method of measuring injury rates has been largely superceded by the OSHA system of incidence rates.

[4] *Business Week* (December 14, 1968), p. 176.

[5] *Wall Street Journal* (December 3, 1968), p. 1.

[6] George Perker, "A Labor View of the Occupational Safety and Health Act," *Proceedings of the 1972 Annual Spring Meeting* (Madison, Wisc.: Industrial Relations Research Association).

Provisions of the Act

The declared Congressional purpose and policy of the act are "to assure as far as possible every working man and woman in the Nation safe and healthful working conditions and to preserve our human resources." The act authorizes the Federal government to establish and enforce occupational safety and health standards applicable to private business. Essentially, all private business firms affecting interstate commerce, even very small firms, are covered. Such coverage is broad. At the time the law became effective in 1971, it was estimated that 57,000,000 employees in more than 4,000,000 establishments were covered.

Administration and enforcement of the act are vested primarily in the Department of Labor, specifically a new agency within the Department called the Occupational Safety and Health Administration. The act established the National Institute for Occupational Safety and Health within the Department of Health, Education, and Welfare. The Institute conducts research and carries out experiments and demonstrations relating to occupational safety and health, sets up criteria for the establishment of standards in the field, publishes data on occupational illnesses, and conducts inspections necessary to carry out its responsibilities. There are approximately 13,000 potentially hazardous substances in use in industry. NIOSH has the responsibility to conduct research, or contract for the research, in order to set standards controlling the use of these substances.

The act states that each employer "shall furnish to each of his employees employment and a place of employment which are free from recognized hazards that are causing or are likely to cause death or serious physical harm to his employees." The employer has the specific duty to comply with safety and health standards promulgated under the act.

The law requires that each employee comply with occupational safety and health standards and all rules, regulations, and orders issued pursuant to the act that are applicable to his actions and conduct. Penalty provisions of the act apply only to employers. However, the wording of the law presumably strengthens the employer's right to discipline workers who violate safety rules. Employees are given certain rights. They can request a government inspection if they believe imminent danger exists or that there is a violation of a standard that threatens physical harm. An employee representative may accompany a federal compliance officer during an inspection of the establishment.

Perhaps the heart of OSHA is the system of health and safety standards. Standards are regulations for avoidance of hazards that have been proven by research and experience to be harmful to personal health and safety. For example, OSHA has set a limit for industrial noise of 90 decibels where there is continuous 8-hour per day exposure. Interim standards covering thousands of items and conditions were issued in 1971. These were based upon existing national consensus standards, such as those formulated by the American National Standards Institute and those applying to Federal contractors under the Walsh–Healey Act. Permanent standards are to be set according to the rather eleborate procedures provided in the act and according to the Administrative Procedure Act.

Enforcement is accomplished through a system of inspections, citations, and penalties (with provisions for appeals). Labor Department representatives may enter, without delay and at any reasonable times, any establishment to inspect the premises, and all pertinent conditions, structures, machines, apparatus, devices, equipment, and materials. They may also question the employer, employees, and employee representatives. If there is a violation of one of the standards, a written citation is issued and a reasonable time is allowed for correcting the condition. There are various classes of citations and monetary penalties depending upon the seriousness of the infraction. The act provides for both civil and criminal penalties. An employer who willfully and repeatedly violates requirements of the law can be assessed a civil penalty of not more than $10,000. Criminal penalties could go as high as $20,000 and/or one year in prison. In actual practice the penalties assessed have been quite modest.

Employers have a right to contest a citation or penalty by filing an appeal with the Department of Labor within 15 days from receipt of the citation. They can also request a variance from a standard upon showing that the working conditions provided are just as safe and healthful as the conditions required by the standard.

All covered firms must maintain detailed injury records in the manner and form specified by the Department of Labor. The Department of Labor in consultation with the Department of Health, Education, and Welfare is required by the law to develop and maintain an effective program of collection, compilation, and analysis of statistics on work injuries and illnesses.

The states can enter into agreements with the Secretary of Labor to develop and enforce their own standards. These programs must be at least as effective as the Federal program.

Issues and Controversies Over OSHA

Since its inception a great many company managements and industry associations have been vehement in their criticism of the Act and especially its administration. They have challenged the constitutionality of various sections of the law (the courts have generally upheld the law) and the engineering standards which the Occupational Safety and Health Administration has issued and required employers to meet. They have also charged that the economic cost of meeting OSHA standards is often too great and that the agency ought to consider economic impact as well as worker safety when it orders an employer to correct a particular hazard.

On the other side American unions have charged that the Occupational Safety and Health Administration has been underfunded, under-staffed, and negligent in setting standards for toxic substances, carcinogens, dusts and other disease producing agents.

The vast majority of safety and health standards used by the OSHAdministration are known as "consensus standards." They were developed gradually over a good many years by professional engineering societies, industry and trade groups, labor, and public interest groups. In this standards setting process, management and the engineering professions had the dominant voices and the greatest expertise. Ironically it is these very standards that many company officials have objected to. Some of these long existing standards dealt with somewhat trivial matters. For example, often mentioned standards were the requirement that toilets have open-front seats and that fire extinguishers be hung an exact number of inches above the floor. In 1978 the OSHAdministration revoked a great many standards considered trivial and not essential to worker safety and health.

Should employers be required to meet a safety or health standard even if the cost is high? How many lives and broken bodies should be traded off for a given dollar saving in costs? When Gerald Ford was President, he required that an economic impact analysis be made and considered in the setting of safety and health standards. The Federal courts have also ruled that economic considerations must be weighed in the establishment of standards. This is a difficult issue for which there exist no ready criteria or guidelines for balancing human life against cost. Congressional intent has seemed to favor worker safety and health over economics; however, actual implementation of the Act has elevated economic considerations so far that the setting of new standards has been dreadfully slow.

Some critics of the Act have argued that the whole concept of safety and health standards, inspections, and possible fines for violations is wrong. Rather, public policy should simply provide financial incentives and penalties for employers to induce them to create a safe and healthful workplace. This is really a free-market, free-enterprise model. However, this is precisely the program that employers have operated under with the workers' compensation insurance system for some sixty years. Insurance premiums are increased if payments to injured workers go up and premiums go down if employers operate safe establishments and payments to injured workers are low. However, experience has demonstrated that this financial incentive induces only *some* employers to install a sound safety program. The incentive applies after the fact of injuries and losses, and it works better for measurable injuries than for diseases, which are harder to trace.

What induces an employer to comply with the Act? Is it the possibility of incurring financial penalties for violations of specific standards? Barnum and Gleason have studied the role of penalties in inducing changed behavior on the part of employers. For the period of July 1972 through December 1974, the mean fine assessed for "nonserious violations" was only $14.99. Of all violations reported during that period, 98.53 percent were classified as nonserious. For the same time period "serious violations" resulted in an average penalty of $618.66. Only 1.22 percent of total violations were classified as serious. Again for the same period the average penalty for "willful violations," comprising .25 percent of the total, was $866.44. The authors determined that the average company is likely to be inspected only once in every ten years. Also some violations will be undetected. Because the probabilities of being inspected and fined for a violation are so slight and because the actual fines levied have been so low, the authors conclude that the purely rational economic employer (who would not be motivated by humane considerations) would find it to his advantage to accept the low risk of getting caught rather than expend, perhaps, considerable money correcting the hazard.[7] Hopefully other motivations are affecting managements in American industry to induce them to work positively and effectively for safe and healthful workplaces.

[7] Darold T. Barnum and John M. Gleason, "OSHA Sanctions: Implications for Public Policy," Proceedings of 28th Annual Meeting (Madison, Wisc.: Industrial Relations Research Association, December 1975), pp. 84–92.

Injury and Illness Experiences Under OSHA

Employers are required to record and report injuries and illnesses in accordance with procedures established by the Occupational Safety and Health Administration. Recordable cases include all work-related deaths and illnesses and those injuries which result in one or more of the following: loss of consciousness, restriction of work or motion, transfer to another job, or medical treatment beyond first aid. Employers must record each occurrence as fatality, an injury or illness with lost workdays, or an injury or illness without lost workdays. A case classified as a lost workday case involves one or more days following the day of injury or onset of illness on which the employee was unable to perform the duties of his regular job. These days count as lost workdays even if the employee comes to work but can only do restricted activity or is temporarily assigned to a less demanding job. Also, lost workdays—not calendar days—are counted.

The OSHA formula for calculating incidence rates is as follows:

$$\frac{N}{EH} \times 200,000$$

where

N = number of injuries and illnesses, or lost workdays.

EH = total hours worked by all employees during calendar year.

$200,000$ = base for 100 full-time equivalent workers (working 40 hours per week, 50 weeks per year).

This one formula serves to give the rate for frequency of injuries and illnesses (number of cases) and the severity of injuries and illnesses (lost work days).

Nationally, including all industries, have incidence rates improved since OSHA became operative on April 28, 1971? Figure 26-1 shows incidence rates per 100 full-time workers for the entire private sector for the years 1972 (the first

Figure 26-1
Occupational Injury and Illness Incidence Rates by Year for the Private Sector of the United States. The data exclude self-employed individuals, farmers with fewer than 11 employees, and employees in federal, state and local government. *Source: Annual News bulletins, "BLS Reports on Occupational Injuries and Illnesses," U.S. Department of Labor, Bureau of Labor Statistics.*

Year	Incidence Rates per 100 Full-time Workers			
	Lost Workday Cases	Nonfatal Cases Without Lost Workdays	Total Cases 1/	Lost Workdays (Severity)
1972	3.3	7.6	10.9	2/
1973	3.4	7.5	11.0	53.3
1974	3.5	6.9	10.4	54.6
1975	3.3	5.8	9.1	56.2
1976	3.5	5.7	9.2	60.5
1977	3.8	5.5	9.3	61.6

[1] Includes fatalities. Because of rounding, the difference between the total and the sum of rates for lost workday cases and nonfatal cases without lost workdays may not reflect the fatality rate.

[2] Figure not available.

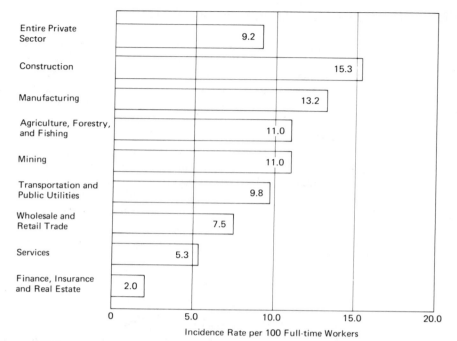

Figure 26-2

Injury and Illness Incidence Rates for Entire Private Sector and by Industry Division, 1976 (total cases). *Source:* News Bulletin, *U.S. Department of Labor, Bureau of Labor Statistics, December 1, 1977.*

full year of using the OSHA method of collecting statistics) through 1977. The table shows that lost workday cases have fluctuated from 3.3 to 3.8. Nonfatal cases without lost workdays (the less serious cases) have declined from 7.6 in 1972 to 5.5 in 1977. On the other hand, the number of lost workdays per case has increased. So, the evidence is somewhat mixed.

The early years of the existence of OSHAdministration have been fraught with intense controversy. The agency was underfunded and understaffed. Nicholas Ashford, a health and safety expert, has charged that OSHA was engineered to fail from the start by the Nixon administration. A strong commitment by the U.S. Department of Labor to occupational safety and health only began, according to Ashford, when John Dunlop was Secretary of Labor (1975).[8]

Variation by Industry and Firm Size. Figure 26-2 shows the very considerable differences in injury and illness incidence rates of the major industry classifications for the year 1976. The construction industry was the most hazardous whereas the finance, insurance, and real estate industries (largely white collar occupations) were the least hazardous.

If one looks at statistics showing severity of injuries (excluding occupational ill-

[8] Nicholas A. Ashford, "The Role of Occupational Health and Safety in Industrial Relations: Where We Are and Where We're Going," *Industrial and Labor Relations Report,* Vol. XV, No. 2 (Spring 1978), p. 25. (New York State School of Industrial and Labor Relations, Cornell University).

nesses) by specific industry classification, he finds that for 1976 the most hazardous industries in lost workdays per 100 full time workers were: water transportation (280 days), anthracite mining (229 days), lumber and wood products (165 days), trucking and warehousing (156 days), and oil and gas extraction (135 days).[9]

Historically, small companies have had higher injury rates than large firms. For example, for the year 1976 companies having from 100 to 249 employees had an injury incidence rate of 12.6 and those with 250 to 499 employees had a rate of 12.0 injuries per 100 full time workers. However, establishments having 2,500 or more employees had a rate of only 7.3.[10]

Why does small business, rather generally have a poor accident record? The fundamental reason is that owners and top executives in small businesses are not as safety-conscious and do not give as much effort to accident prevention as do managers of large corporations. The typical small businessman does not even compute his injury rate. The guide that he uses is the size of his workers' compensation insurance premium. The small employer does not employ a safety director and often he may not even have a full-time personnel manager. In his mind, the pressing problems of production, sales, and finance overshadow the importance of workplace safety and health. His accounting system does not isolate all those costs that are directly and indirectly caused by accidents.

OCCUPATIONAL DISEASE

There is a time bomb ticking away inside the bodies of hundreds of thousands of American working men and women. That time bomb is occupational disease. Only in very recent years has the truly enormous magnitude of the problem been recognized. Occupational disease tends to be understated in the statistics of individual companies and industries because very often the diseases manifest themselves only many months, or even years after worker exposure to the causative agents. By then the employees may be working for different companies, may have retired, or, if still in the same company, the cause-effect relationship may go unrecognized.

The Public Health Service estimates that each year 390,000 new cases of occupational diseases appear and 100,000 workers die from them.[11]

Illustrative of the seriousness of the problem is the following sample of headlines, with stories, which appeared in national news media in recent years:

1. *"A Grim Legacy from World War II"*

This article explains that many of World War II's 3 million shipyard workers may have a fatal, asbestos-caused cancer. Millions of pounds of asbestos were used to insulate pipes and valves in ships. Mesothelioma, a cancer that

[9] *News* bulletin, "BLS Reports on Occupational Injuries and Illnesses for 1976," (U.S. Department of Labor, Bureau of Labor Statistics, December 1, 1977), Table 2.

[10] U.S. Department of Labor, Ibid., Table 3.

[11] Comptroller General of the United States, *Delays in Setting Workplace Standards for Cancer-Causing and Other Dangerous Substances* (Washington, D.C.: General Accounting Office, May 10, 1977), p. 10.

strikes the stomach lining and chest cavity has been showing up in those people who worked in the shipyards over three decades ago.[12]

2. *"Study Indicates Anesthetic Gas Imperils Health of Operating-Room Personnel"*

   A research study has indicated that those people who are long exposed to gases such as nitrous oxide, ether, and halogenated hydrocarbons have a higher incidence of spontaneous abortions, birth defects, cancer, and liver disease than do nonexposed people.[13]

3. *"Seminar Focuses on Cancer Risks from Working with Vinyl Chloride"*

   Vinyl chloride exposure has caused liver cancer among plastics plant workers.[14]

4. *"Workers' Exposure to Carbon Disulfide Should Be Cut Sharply, Safety Aides Say"*

   Chronic exposure causes cardiovascular disease, neurological abnormalities, and possible effects on the reproductive system.[15]

Occupational health hazards are classified into four general types: 1) physical such as noise, heat, vibration, and radiation, 2) chemical such as dusts, poisonous fumes, gases, toxic metals, and carcinogens, 3) biological such as bacteria, fungi, and insects, and 4) stress such as physical, psychological, and ergonomic factors. The effects of health hazards can be slow, cumulative, and irreversible. Also, they are complicated by nonoccupational factors such as smoking and stress.

Public health scientists have estimated that more than 80 percent of all cancers are caused by environmental factors to which man is exposed. Precisely how much is occupationally caused is unknown. Cancer is the second leading cause of death in the United States. The rise in the incidence of cancer is rather closely correlated with the growth of industrialization. In 1900, 3.5 percent of all deaths were caused by cancer, whereas in 1968, the figure had risen to 16.5 percent. Because the production of petrochemicals has doubled every five years since the end of World War II, the incidence of cancer characterized by long latency periods can be expected to grow significantly over the next twenty to thirty years.[16]

It would be comforting if we could say that government officials, managers in industry, and occupational health scientists were now getting this gigantic problem under control. But in fact this is not the case. The Comptroller General of the United States has reported that about 13,000 known toxic substances are commonly used and about 500 new toxic materials are introduced by industry each year. As of 1976 the OSHAdministration had established permanent standards on only fifteen toxic substances: vinyl chloride, asbestos, and thirteen other chemicals considered to be carcinogens. Based upon this rate of progress, it would take over 100 years to establish needed standards on existing sub-

[12] *Business Week* (September 29, 1975), p. 31.
[13] *Wall Street Journal* (October 15, 1974), p. 8.
[14] *Buffalo Evening News* (March 23, 1974).
[15] *Wall Street Journal* (May 10, 1977).
[16] Ashford, *Crisis in the Workplace*, op. cit., pp. 10–11.

stances. But 500 new substances are introduced yearly.[17] So the job will never get done at the present rate of action. OSHAdministration is hampered not only by lack of funds, lack of manpower, and by industry resistance but also by the fact that insufficient basic research has been done in the areas of toxicology and occupational diseases.

OCCUPATIONAL SAFETY

Accidents

What is an accident? Most of us tend to think of an accident as some event that causes a personal injury. But in point of fact an *accident is really an unexpected occurrence that interrupts the regular progress of an activity.* In effect it is any unplanned or uncalled for break or deviation from the expected. It is a negative or unfortunate event. Many accidents take place without an injury resulting. A man may stumble while walking along an aisle yet suffer no injury. A rigger may drop a tool and narrowly miss a worker below. Both of these are accidents without injuries.

In industrial practice attention tends to be focused primarily upon accidents that cause injuries. But injury prevention should be accident prevention as well. The author is familiar with an accident involving an in-plant lift truck operator. He was using his truck, which contained a squeeze mechanism, to remove the top bale of textile fibers from a stack piled three high. The bale weighed about 1,500 pounds and was about 12 feet above the floor of the warehouse. His squeeze mechanism did not grasp the bale properly and the bale came tumbling down on top of the truck. The operator jumped to safety without a scratch. Damage to the truck was extensive. Here clearly was a serious accident calling for corrective measures by management. A commercially available protective cage was installed over the cockpit of the truck to protect the driver in the future.[18]

Costs of Accidents

In addition to the anguish and suffering experienced by injured employees, accidents are very expensive to the employer. Many executives simply look at their charges for workmen's compensation insurance and lose sight of the fact that the indirect costs of an accidental injury are considerably greater than the direct costs.

Accident costs are classified into two categories. First are the insured costs. The insured cost is the money paid for doctor and hospital bills, for weekly benefits while the injured employees are absent from work, and for any scheduled payments due to death, accidental dismemberment, or permanent disability. This cost is readily apparent and is met by the insurance premium.

The second category of costs due to accidents is called the uninsured costs. Some authorities call these the indirect costs of accidents. These costs are not ap-

---

[17] Comptroller General of the United States, op. cit., pp. 9–11.
[18] A protective cage had previously been installed on the truck but was removed when the foreman deemed that it slowed up production.

parent to top management unless it assigns somebody to conduct a specific research project to isolate them. What are these uninsured costs? They include lost time of injured worker, lost time of fellow employees who render aid to the injured person, time spent by supervisory personnel to assist the injured man and to investigate the cause of the accident, lost production, possible damaged matrial or equipment, and administrative expenses to process paper work connected with the accident.

The ratio of the uninsured to the insured costs varies widely from factory to factory according to the particular situation. However, investigators have found that these uninsured costs tend to average about four times those of the insured costs. In other words the insured or direct costs represent only about 20 percent of the total costs on the average.[19]

For some companies in high-risk industries the premium for workers' compensation insurance may run as high as 15 to 20 percent of payroll. If one estimates that the total cost for accidents in any one year is five times this figure, it can be readily appreciated that the accident rate can spell the difference between profit and loss for a company.

In addition to the financial burden imposed by accidents upon a company, those workmen who are injured bear a substantial cost also. Most workers' compensation laws specify a waiting period of one week before an injured worker can collect weekly benefits to make up for his loss of wages. Therefore, those who lose only one to seven days from work, receive no wage compensation whatever. The typical compensation law specifies that weekly benefits shall be only two thirds of the injured's wage up to a certain maximum. For permanent partial dismemberments the scheduled benefits are rarely adequate to compensate a worker for his future loss of earning power.

CAUSES OF ACCIDENTS

In order to prevent accidents from taking place it is necessary, first of all, to gain an appreciation of the causes of accidents. Accidents may at times seem to occur because of chance factors that are unavoidable. But digging beneath the surface one will find that in nearly every instance measures could have been taken to prevent the accident.

Accident causes can be classified into two major categories:

1. Unsafe chemical, physical, or mechanical conditions.
2. Unsafe personal acts.

Examples of unsafe chemical, physical, or mechanical conditions are the following:

1. Inadequate mechanical guarding.
2. Defective condition of equipment or tools (for example, worn electrical insulation, cracked ladder, split drive belt).

---

[19] See, for example, H. W. Heinrich, *Industrial Accident Prevention: A Scientific Approach*, 4th ed. (New York: McGraw-Hill Book Company, 1959), pp. 50–51.

3. Unsafe design or construction (for example, a pressure vessel that is too weak).
4. Hazardous atmosphere (for example, toxic substances in air, poor ventilation).
5. Inadequate or improper personal protective equipment.

Examples of unsafe personal acts are as follows:

1. Failure to follow established safe working procedures.
2. Horseplay, fighting.
3. Taking an unsafe position, such as under a suspended load.
4. Failure to use designated protective clothing.
5. Removing safety devices or making them inoperative.

Sometimes the physical or mental condition of the person involved may contribute to the accident. Thus, a worker may be emotionally upset, inattentive, or fearful. Or he may be extremely fatigued or suffer some physical defect that makes an accident more likely.

Unsafe Condition or Human Error. Over the years attempts have been made by various groups to classify industrial injuries according to whether they were caused by an unsafe physical condition or by an unsafe personal act. Some of the earlier studies purportedly showed that 85 to 90 percent of all injuries were caused by human error and only 10 to 15 percent by hazardous conditions. If one did not study the matter further, one might jump to the erroneous conclusion that management could obtain the greatest gain from the dollars it spends on accident prevention by devoting its efforts to employee education and ignoring the engineering aspect of safety. But such is not the case. More recent analyses of accident statistics reveal that the vast majority are due to a combination of unsafe physical conditions and unsafe personal acts. Basically if the hazard were not present in the first place, an injury could not occur. The traffic safety records of the modern divided, limited-access superhighways furnish ample evidence that good engineering design can reduce accident rates significantly. The people who drive on these highways are no different from those who drive on ordinary roads, so the personal behavior factor is essentially constant for both superhighway driving and ordinary driving.

A sound industrial-safety program must emphasize both the engineering aspects of safety (hazard elimination) as well as employee education and training (showing people how to work safely in the presence of certain hazards).

Accident Proneness

For years industrial psychologists have been intrigued with the empirically observed fact that certain individuals have more accidents than could be expected on the basis of chance and that accident rates in factories could be reduced if accident-prone workers were identified and rejected during the employment-selection process. Some of the earliest research to establish the fact of accident proneness was done by Greenwood and Woods in a British shell factory. Newbold also carried out one of the early investigations.[20]

Psychologists have given intelligence, aptitude, and personality tests to large numbers of people in a variety of occupations and industries. They have then correlated test scores with accident rates. The object has been to identify the specific traits that might be useful in predicting accident proneness. It has been shown that there is a definite relationship between accident rates and scores on motor sensory tests, emotional stability tests, muscular and perceptual speed tests, and visual tests in certain occupations. Above a certain minimum level no relationship has been found between intelligence-test scores and accident rates.

A Balanced View of Accident Proneness.   Despite the fact that the phenomenon of accident proneness does exist, many investigators and writers have been much too loose in their claims regarding the matter. It has been observed in many establishments that a small percentage of the workers have a high percentage of accidents; but this fact alone does not prove accident proneness. According to the laws of probability we would *not* expect all workers to have the same number of accidents. In any given year or other time period, some persons can be expected, by chance, to have several accidents, whereas others will have none. Mintz and Blum have done a scholarly job of setting the record straight regarding accident proneness. They conclude that this has been a much overemphasized factor and that it really accounts for only about 20 to 40 percent of the total variance of accident records.[21] Willard Kerr claims that the factor of accident proneness really accounts for only 1 to 15 percent of the total variance in individual accidents.[22] In actuality true accident-prone people are rather rare. To be accident prone, one must have a constitutional tendency to engage in unsafe behavior. What actually happens is that people who are apparently accident prone have only a temporary tendency toward frequent accidents, but if their performance were to be viewed over a long time span, it would be found that they settle down to an accident rate no different than that of the general population. Basically these people are in a transient stage. The group of accident-liable members is constantly gaining new members and losing old ones.

Thus, although the theory of accident proneness seemed for many years to be a promising solution to the problem of work injuries, in actuality, when put in proper perspective, it contributed but little to the overall problem.

Arbous and Kerrich have added their voices to those who have rigorously reduced the significance of accident proneness as a causal explanation of accidents. They assert that both laymen and accident prevention specialists have continued to try to account for work injuries on this basis even though researchers have long since revealed the weaknesses in the argument. In contradiction to the concept of accident proneness that deals with the statistical experi-

---

[20] M. Greenwood and H. M. Woods, "The Incidence of Industrial Accidents upon Individuals with Specific Reference to Multiple Accidents," Report 4 (London: Industrial Fatigue Research Board, 1919); E. M. Newbold, "A Contribution to the Study of the Human Factor in the Causation of Accidents," Report 34 (London: Industrial Fatigue Research Board, 1926).

[21] Alexander Mintz and Milton L. Blum, "A Re-examination of the Accident Proneness Concept," *Journal of Applied Psychology*, Vol. 33, No. 3 (1949), pp. 195–211.

[22] Willard Kerr, "Complementary Theories of Safety Psychology," *Journal of Social Psychology*, Vol. 45 1957, pp. 3–9.

ence of groups, they do say, however, that the individual clinical approach to accident proneness may have some merit. The clinical approach requires that an examination be made of individual accident repeaters from the standpoint of the whole man. This requires an investigation of each person's personality, emotional makeup, family background, physical condition, and so forth, in the context of the job demands and environment in which he works. Training, medical treatment, better supervision, and reassignment all may be required to generate a change in the person's behavior. Such an attempt at individual diagnosis could be very expensive and has seldom been applied in practice, although the concept appears to have merit.[23]

Accidents and Environment

The physical, psychological, and organizational environment in a plant has a powerful effect upon injury rates. Keenan, Kerr, and Sherman correlated accident rates of 7,100 personnel in a large tractor factory over a five-year period. They found that a comfortable shop environment (good working conditions) was the single most significant factor relating to a low accident rate. These researchers believe that bad working conditions (noise, dirt, heat, and so on), although not directly causing accidents, cause worker tension and frustration. This physical frustration distracts the workers, causing them to have more accidents.[24] Many practicing safety engineers have for years felt, on the basis of experience, that plant housekeeping and decent working conditions are a positive encouragement to safety. Thus the research evidence supports this belief.

Substantial evidence exists to demonstrate that the total stress (internal and external) that impinges upon a worker has a strong influence upon his likelihood to have accidents. Internal stress consists of such conditions as disease, alcohol, anxiety, or worry, whereas external stress is built up from noise, heat, dirt, fumes, and excessive physical strain.[25] Positive action by management to maintain not only good working conditions but also good employee health (physical and mental) is bound to pay dividends in terms of fewer accidents and lower charges for workmen's compensation. The initial cost of establishing a good work environment and an occupational health program often discourages management from making the investment. Although one may fail to persuade top management to invest in such programs on the basis of their contribution to employee morale and the humanitarian objective, quite often the prospect of a long-term reduction in the cost of accidents may provide the impetus to adopt such a comprehensive program.

Management action in another broad area can have a very beneficial effect upon safety. When management directs the organization in such a way that employees have real opportunities to get ahead, to be promoted, to exercise some initiative and responsibility, to participate in controlling their own jobs, and to

[23] A. G. Arbous and J. E. Kerrich, "The Phenomenon of Accident Proneness," in Edwin A. Fleishman, *Studies in Personnel and Industrial Psychology*, rev. ed. (Homewood, Ill.: The Dorsey Press, 1967), pp. 615–626.
[24] Vernon Keenan, Willard Kerr, and William Sherman, "Psychological Climate and Accidents in an Automotive Plant," *Journal of Applied Psychology*, Vol. 35, No. 2 (1951), pp. 108–111.
[25] Kerr, op. cit.

gain job prestige and other rewards, then accidents tend to be lower.[26] Thus, it can be concluded that the positive, supportive, need-satisfying, autonomy-enhancing leadership that is quite generally advocated by modern researchers and writers in the field of human relations in industry is just as successful in promoting occupational safety as it is in promoting productivity, loyalty, and high morale. In other words, the elements that constitute good management in other spheres of a business enterprise also constitute sound safety management.

Age, Training, and Work Experience

Available research evidence shows quite conclusively that young workers, untrained workers, and workers who are new on the job have substantially higher frequencies of work injuries than older workers, trained workers, and more experienced workers. Van Zelst investigated the effect of each of these factors separately in a large plant in Indiana. He found, for example, that the average monthly accident rate of about 1,200 workers declined steadily for the first five months on the job, after which the rate remained nearly constant for approximately a five-year period. When newly hired workers were given formal job training, Van Zelst found that the initial accident frequency was lower for this trained group and that the group declined to a normal expected level of accident frequency in three months instead of the five months for untrained employees. In the third and final part of his investigation, he found that a group of 614 persons of average age 29 years and 3 years' job experience in the plant had a significantly greater accident rate than a roughly comparable sized group age 41 years, also with three years of job experience. Van Zelst observed that age actually had a stronger effect upon accident rate than did time on the job. He tentatively concluded that immaturity of the employees was a large factor in explaining the accident experience of young workers.[27]

Management can profit from findings such as these by instituting proper job-training programs, exercising special safety monitoring of new employees, and by giving attention to the possible immaturity of workers in making hazardous job assignments. A company with high labor turnover is especially vulnerable to accidents. Management is well advised to take steps to reduce such turnover. A continuous parade of new workers is a sure invitation to a high injury rate.

Matched Pairs Research

In the early 1970's Shafai-Sahrai investigated 22 pairs of companies in eleven different industrial classifications in Michigan. Within each industry, two firms of similar size but markedly different injury rates were selected. All the firms studied had between 80 and 650 employees. He concentrated upon small companies because traditionally small firms have had high injury rates. He found several factors that correlated significantly with either good or bad safety performance.

In the firms that had lower injury rates there was high interest and involvement by top management in the safety activity. Top management involvement

---

[26] Ibid.

[27] R. H. Van Zelst, "The Effect of Age and Experience upon Accident Rate," *Journal of Applied Psychology*, Vol. 38 (1954), pp. 313–317.

included such behaviors as planning for achieving safety objectives, holding review and analysis sessions to compare results with objectives, and including safety reports on agenda for company board meetings.

Companies that had comprehensive accident record keeping systems in which accident costs were shown had better safety records than those firms that did not keep good records.

Good plant working conditions correlated positively with good safety performance. These included roominess, lighting, temperature, noise level, and cleanliness. Those companies that had better and more numerous safety devices and guards on machines had lower injury rates.

Shafai-Sahrai found that in firms with more married employees work injury rates were lower. Firms in which the average age level was high and worker years of service were high had lower injury rates than those firms with younger workers and fewer years of service.[28]

COMPONENTS OF SAFETY AND HEALTH PROGRAM

Assume that a company has a high workmen's compensation costs, and an inadequate safety and health program. What are the principal elements of a sound program that top management should consider for adoption? The details of course would have to be adapted to fit the circumstances of company size, number of plants, nature of the industry, technology, and organization structure. But the content of the program could be included under the elements discussed below.

Key Elements of Program
1. Objectives and policies.
2. Top-management support.
3. Organization.
4. Establishing responsibility for safety.
5. Engineering.
6. Job-safety analysis.
7. Analysis of accidents.
8. Education and training.
9. Enforcement.
10. Healthful work environment.
11. Adequate medical treatment.
12. Rehabilitation.

Objectives and Policies

When top management decides that it wants to take steps to obtain a safe organization, it must determine just how far it wants to go and what it wants to accomplish. Does it want to have a company that ranks with the best in its industry in terms of low injury frequency and severity? Or does it simply want a safety ef-

---

[28] Yaghoub Shafai-Sahrai, *Determinants of Occupational Injury Experience* (East Lansing, Michigan: Graduate School of Business Administration, Michigan State University, 1973).

fort that will reduce workman's compensation costs to a tolerable level. Is it willing to invest sufficient money to achieve a really nonhazardous plant? Or does it want to concentrate upon training the workers to cope moderately well in a basically dangerous environment? What policy will be adopted for those situations in which a production-oriented decision clashes with a safety-oriented decision?

Top Management Support

Top management sets the safety objectives and policies in the first place; and how top management chooses to support and implement its own policies is crucial to the effectiveness of these policies. It is top management that decides, ultimately, how extensive a safety organization to set up, the caliber of safety personnel that will be employed, and how much money, in total, it will invest in safety. The single most important element in the success or failure of any companywide program, whether it be safety, training, research, or maintenance, is the emphasis given to that program by top management.

Organization

The organizational arrangements that are created are conditioned by the size of the firm and the nature of its safety problems. In firms too small to justify a full-time safety director, the assignment may be given to the personnel director, to the plant superintendent, or to the head of industrial engineering. Larger companies will employ a full-time safety specialist. Usually he is part of the personnel department. Very large corporations, especially those in hazardous industries, will employ a whole staff of safety engineers, safety inspectors, and industrial hygienists.

Success in accident reduction and control requires the active involvement of operating management and of workers. Hence companies with successful safety programs usually create safety committees in each organizational unit. The principal managers in these units serve on the management committees and help in the planning and implementation of the program. Worker committees, often with rotating membership, are a useful way of identifying specific safety problems in the plant and of gaining worker support for the safety effort.

Close collaboration with the local union officers and shop stewards is desirable. In too many companies the sole involvement of the union is through the submitting of grievances about job hazards. Worker health and safety are so important that a mutuality of interests should be recognized. Shop stewards can advantageously serve on company safety committees.

Establishing Responsibility for Safety

Some industrialists think that with the appointment of a safety director they can "wash their hands" of all responsibility for safety and get on with their main business of obtaining high production, low costs, and adequate quality. Nothing could be further from the truth. The only way to achieve and maintain a safe plant is to place responsibility for safety on an equal status with responsibility for production, cost control, quality, and profit making. Whenever the responsibility for maintaining a safe plant is relegated to the position of a frill that can be attended to only after the more important objectives of production, costs, and efficiency are achieved, then injury rates will be excessive and will remain so until line management at all levels devotes adequate attention to accident prevention. The basic responsibility for injury prevention rests with line management. It starts with the company president and goes vertically downward through the entire hierarchy to the actual worker.

What then does the safety director do? Is he not responsible for safety? Yes, the safety director bears very important responsibilities for injury prevention. But he serves in a staff, not a line, capacity. He basically serves as an innovator, organizer, creator, advisor, teacher, analyzer, investigator, stimulator, and (at times) a prodder. He must organize the safety program throughout the plant, collect accident data, investigate accidents, help develop engineering applications (guards, and so on), conduct safety training and information meetings for management personnel, analyze jobs to develop safe working procedures, and prepare instructional material for use by foremen in conducting meetings with their men.

The staff safety director rarely has line authority to order supervisors and workers to take a particular action in regard to safety. But he often acquires considerable influence in the establishment of plant safety policies, procedures, and the development of engineering standards for safety. He works closely in these areas with other line and staff officers. But because they recognize his proficiency and specialized competence in the field of safety, the views of the safety director are given considerable weight.

Engineering

Proper engineering to remove work hazards is fundamental to any organized safety effort. If one were to look at the typical mill of 1910 and compare it with the typical mill of the 1980's in the same industry, he would immediately perceive the vast advances that have been made in elimination and guarding of dangerous mechanical, electrical, and chemical conditions. The typical mill of 1910 was a maze of exposed pulleys, belts, chains, gears, cutters, punches, and levers. Today technology has advanced to the point where many hazardous conditions have simply been designed "out" of the equipment and processes, and most of the remaining ones have been adequately guarded. But this statement should not be interpreted to mean that further engineering for safety cannot be done. Many factories are still behind the times as far as hazard elimination is concerned. New products, processes, and machines are constantly being designed, and full attention must be given to safety engineering in both design, layout, and installation.

The most foolproof way of engineering for safety is simply to eliminate the hazard from the machine, process, or structure. If, for example, a particular substance or material has been put into large heavy containers for movement from one operation to another throughout the plant (batch production) and if materials handlers have suffered many hernias and back injuries from lifting these containers, a basic engineering redesign of the production processes might eliminate the batch approach and substitute continuous-process production. In this case the physical handling of the containers by human labor will have been eliminated because the material will flow from one piece of equipment to another by mechanical conveyor or by blowing the substance through large pipes.

If it is not feasible to carry out a basic redesign of the production process to eliminate the hazard, then the next stage is to design and install a guard to prevent workers from coming in contact with moving parts or point of operation elements. Thus, gears on a machine are usually guarded to prevent human contact while the machine is in operation.

If it is not possible to eliminate the hazard or to guard the equipment itself, it may be possible to have the workers wear and use protective clothing and equipment. Thus, construction workers and those working around overhead cranes generally wear hard hats, machinists wear goggles, and welders wear face shields and gloves.

Job-Safety Analysis

Although job analysis for purposes of improving work methods, setting production standards, and determining pay rates is commonly carried on in many organizations, these investigations are rarely done for the purpose of identifying the hazards and figuring out ways of overcoming them. But job-safety analysis is very useful for hazard elimination and for designing safe work methods. By such study the safety engineer may note that a change in workplace layout, in the operating controls of the machine, or in work procedures may eliminate or reduce the possibility of injury to the operator.

Unfortunately most accident prevention work takes place after someone has been injured. Then the job is studied to make necessary changes to prevent a recurrence.

In addition to hazard elimination through changes in workplace, equipment, and methods, job-safety analysis produces a written statement of safe operating procedure.

Analysis of Accidents

Every accident that results in a personal injury, or could have resulted in a serious injury, whether it be simply a first-aid case or a more serious disabling one, must be investigated by the injured employee's supervisor to ascertain the cause(s) and to determine what specific remedies are required to avoid a recurrence. Although the primary reason for accident investigation is to find out what action must be taken to prevent a recurrence, accident information provides excellent case study material for use in training meetings.

Although every accident must be investigated and reported by the foreman, a more intensive investigation should be conducted by the staff safety specialist for all but the very simple and elementary accidents. This is necessary so that he can be fully cognizant of the accidents occurring in his plant and so that he can apply his technical skill to uncover elements of the case possibly overlooked by the foreman.

The safety department should periodically summarize all injuries that have occurred and classify them by plant, department, shift, cause, type of injury, and whether disabling or not. Injury statistics are valuable for revealing where further effort must be exerted to achieve improvement in the safety performance, for comparing the record from one year to another, and for apprising management of needs for further action.

Education and Training

Safety education for all levels of management and for employees is a vital ingredient for any successful safety program. Education in this context concerns the development of proper perspective and attitudes toward safety. It deals with basic fundamentals and the reasons why. Training is more concerned with immediate job knowledge, skills, and work methods.

Top and middle management require education in the fundamentals of safety and the need for an effective accident prevention program. The costs of accidents, both human and dollar costs, must be brought to the attention of line management. Top management in large- and medium-sized companies does not need to concern itself with the detailed mechanics of accident prevention, but it must acquire a sufficient awareness of safety fundamentals so that it will actively support the work of the safety department and of middle and lower management in carrying out the program.

The safety director and his staff must undertake to provide extensive education and training for first-line supervisors. The supervisors must understand their key role in the safety effort, namely, that they are primarily responsible for preventing accidents (assuming they have adequate support from above). Each supervisor must conduct his own safety training for his employee. This takes the form of both individual on-the-job training and periodic safety meetings held right in the department.

At the employee level there are two principal objectives: (1) to develop safety consciousness and favorable attitudes toward safety and (2) to achieve safe work performance from each employee on his job. To achieve these goals, a number of things must be done. At the time a person is hired, orientation by both the personnel manager and the person's supervisor should cover such areas as the need for safe work performance, the hazards in his own department and job, the necessity for prompt reporting of any personal injuries, desirability of reporting unsafe conditions to the supervisor, and the general causes of accidents. Each new worker must be taught how to perform his job safely. This frequently takes the form of on-the-job training. Instruction in safe working procedures must be integrated with instruction designed to achieve acceptable output and quality performance.

In addition to individual on-the-job training, successful safety practice in countless organizations has demonstrated the value of periodic safety meetings conducted by the supervisor. Among the topics that may be covered are the following: how to prevent accidents, accident causes, importance of good housekeeping, handling materials safely, first aid, machine hazards, fire prevention, use of hand tools, and protecting the eyes.

Enforcement

Primary responsibility for enforcement of standard operating procedures and safety rules lies with the first-line supervisor. When he observes employees who are not performing their jobs in the approved manner he calls this to their attention and corrects them. This can apply to countless situations such as the operation of in-plant trucks, fire protection, wearing of safety glasses, horseplay, and removal of machine guards. With adequate indoctrination and training there should seldom be need for punitive measures for violation of safety regulations. However, when individuals deliberately refuse to cooperate, then they need to be disciplined as they would for other rule violations.

If the employees are represented by a union, one can normally expect union cooperation in these matters if there has been full communication, documentation, and proper warning of the employee.

Healthful Work Environment

Simply stated, the objective of environment control is the prevention of occupational disease. The possible causative agents in the plant environment—dusts, fumes, toxic chemicals, noise, etc.—must first be identified. Then corrective action must be taken. There are many corrective methods that may be used. The best, from a worker health standpoint, is usually to eliminate or contain the agent at its source. For example, a completely closed system may be installed to prevent the release of toxic materials into the work environment. Equipment and processes can be reengineered to, say, cut down noise, eliminate leaks, or reduce vibration. The environment around the source can be improved. For example better plant ventilation can reduce the concentration of dust or fumes. Accoustical enclosures can be built around noisy machinery. A less expensive way of alleviating the health hazard is to provide personal protective equipment to the workers—respirators, eye goggles, gloves, and ear plugs.

The diagnosis and correction of health hazards often requires the services of an industrial hygienist. Industrial hygiene is the science and art devoted to the recognition, evaluation, and control of environmental factors and stresses associated with the workplace that may cause sickness, impaired health or significant discomfort and inefficiency. An industrial hygienist typically has a university bachelor's degree in engineering, chemistry, physics, or the biological sciences plus a masters degree in industrial hygiene.

Adequate Medical Treatment

Every establishment, whether large or small, should have adequate facilities and trained personnel for rendering first aid to injured employees. The small company should have a clean, adequately equipped first-aid room. Its supervisory personnel and key hourly employees should receive first-aid training so that they are skilled in rendering help to the injured. Larger establishments have need for the full-time services of an industrial nurse and a physician. The providing of first-aid treatment is but a part of a comprehensive industrial health program as described in a later section of this chapter.

Rehabilitation

If an employee has suffered a serious temporary disabling injury or a permanent disability, it behooves the employer and the workmen's compensation insurance company to exercise every effort to rehabilitate that unfortunate individual. This includes helping him to learn how to care for his daily needs of living, learning how to acquire and reacquire useful job skills, helping him make a positive mental adjustment to his new situation, and then finding a new position for him in the company (if he cannot return to his old job).

WORKERS' COMPENSATION

Unlike most social insurance programs in the United States, workers' compensation has been almost the exclusive province of the states rather than the Federal government. The first compensation law was passed by New York State in 1910. By 1920 all but six states had passed such laws. Mississippi, the last state to do so, passed a compensation law that became effective in 1949.

Workers' compensation laws place the financial responsibility for work injuries upon the employer without regard to who was at fault or who caused the accident. The costs associated with industrial accidents are considered simply as a cost of doing business that the employer must bear. Prior to the enactment of these laws, injured workers generally had little effective recourse. They had the right to sue their employer in a court of law to try to obtain compensation for wage loss, medical costs, and compensation for the damage suffered. However, workers fared very poorly in such court actions, because they possessed insufficient funds to pursue the cases and because the common law of the period favored the employer in such cases. This sad situation has largely been changed as a result of workmen's compensation legislation.

Benefits

All the compensation laws require that medical service be provided to injured employees. Although full medical treatment without any dollar limit is provided in the majority of states, about one fourth of the states place a limitation on the amount and on the period during which medical, surgical, and hospital services must be provided. In earlier years many state laws provided compensation for accidental injuries but not occupational diseases. This has changed so that all states now have coverage for occupational diseases although a few have specified limitations.

In addition to medical benefits the laws provide partial recompense for loss of wages during the period the worker is away from his job. In most jurisdictions the individual is paid two thirds of his average weekly wage up to a designated maximum, which is typically between $120 and $160 per week. To escape the administrative costs of handling numerous short disablements and to discourage employees from feigning an injury just to obtain a holiday, practically all states pay nothing to compensate for wage loss for periods of seven days or less. In other words there is a seven-day waiting period.

Permanent partial disabilities, such as the loss of use of an arm or the actual amputation of an arm, are paid according to a specific schedule given in the state law. Likewise benefits are paid for permanent total disability and to beneficiaries for death. State laws vary widely in providing for rehabilitation services. The trend is for increased payments in this area. The Federal government reimburses states for 50 percent of the monies they spend for rehabilitation.

Administration and Financing

To make certain that funds are available to meet a company's obligation for paying claims, state laws require either that it carry compensation insurance or that it put up a bond to demonstrate financial responsibility if it wishes to be self-insuring. A company that is self-insuring pays all benefits required by the law directly out of its own pocket. Because only large companies can assume the risk involved in self-insurance, the vast majority of employers insure with either a state insurance fund or with a private insurance company.

The basic premium charged an employer is called the manual rate. This rate is based upon the various industrial classifications and occupations that exist in the establishment. This manual rate is uniform throughout a state and is set by the insurance rating board. It is based principally upon the injury experience of each industry group and upon the dollar losses (costs for claims). This basic manual rate is adjusted upward or downward annually under a system called merit rating to make the cost to the employer closely representative of his true charges for payments to his injured employees. The merit rating feature of the state laws is undoubtedly a powerful stimulus to the employer to take affirmative action to reduce accidents.

HEALTH SERVICES

Historically, company health programs were inaugurated as a result of the passage of workmen's compensation laws with the attendant obligation to provide first-aid treatment for work injuries. Sometime later companies began to give pre-employment physical examinations both to insure that those hired could meet the physical demands of their jobs and to prevent being charged with a compensation claim for a pre-existing ailment. Company medical services then evolved to the point that if a physician was on the premises, it was only natural that he would be called upon to treat minor ailments not caused at work, such as colds, sore throats, skin disorders, headaches, and gastrointestinal upsets. Industrial medicine has grown to the point where the large corporation having a progressive personnel philosophy now takes positive steps to maintain good employee health off the job as well as on the job. Some companies have also established programs in the field of mental health. There has been a recognition by some corporate managements that it has a stake in the "whole person," not only his physical health but his mental health as well, both on and off the job. This concern for the health of employees has not led to the establishment of company clinics to provide broad treatment of nonoccupational illness. Most generally it has taken the form of health information and education services, individual counseling by physicians, referrals to private specialists, and action by management to improve hospital and doctor services in the community. Not only do comprehensive industrial health programs help the employees, but they also often result in reduced absenteeism, lower sickness insurance costs, higher productivity, and improved morale.

A comprehensive company health program will include the following features:

1. A professional staff of physicians and nurses.
2. Adequate facilities for emergency care of work injuries and for conducting pre-employment and periodic medical examinations.
3. Proper first-aid treatment for occupational injuries and diseases. Serious cases are referred to private practice physicians and hospitals.
4. Pre-employment medical examinations and periodic examinations for those exposed to special occupational hazards.
5. Reasonable first aid to employees for nonoccupational illness while on the job.
6. Information and education services for the personal health of employees.
7. Consultation with those suffering physical or emotional maladjustment to the work situation. The company medical personnel may offer advice, refer the individual to a private specialist, work with the person's supervisor, or refer the man to an appropriate community agency.
8. Adequate and confidential medical records.
9. Cooperation by the company physician or medical director with those responsible for accident prevention and control of the work environment to achieve an integrated employee health program.
10. Cooperation with public health authorities in regard to mass inoculations and other measures for the prevention of communicable diseases.
11. Advice and supervision, where necessary, to maintain proper company sanitation.

Although the foregoing health program is most feasible for the medium-and large-sized company, the small firm can carry out many of these elements by engaging the services of a qualified physician on a retainer or consulting basis.

MENTAL HEALTH

Mental health can be defined as a state wherein a person is well adapted, has an accurate perception of reality, and can reasonably successfully adjust to the stresses and frustrations of life. Solley and Munden asked fourteen senior psychiatrists and psychologists of The Menninger Foundation to describe people they knew whom they considered to be mentally healthy. From their responses five major characteristics were abstracted. First, mentally health persons respected others as individuals and were able to establish good relationships with them despite individual differences. They recognized that others may have different values and did not try to impose their own on them. Second, they were flexible and adaptable under stress. Third, they obtained gratification from a wide variety of sources—a variety of people, things, and events. Fourth, they accepted their own capabilities and weaknesses. They had a realistic self-concept and did not over-value or under-value their capacities. Finally, they were active and productive. They used their abilities for their own self-fulfillment and to serve others.[29]

---

[29] C. M. Solley and K. J. Munden, "Toward a Description of Mental Health," *Bulletin of The Menninger Clinic*, Vol. 26 (July 1962), pp. 178–188.

Relatively few companies employ professionally trained personnel—that is, psychiatrists, clinical psychologists, and psychiatric social workers—on either a part-time or full-time basis to provide mental health services for their personnel. Those that do tend to be the very large organizations. However, quite commonly the plant physician serves as a resource person in identifying mental illnesses and referring patient employees to qualified personnel in the community. Alan McLean, a psychiatrist, asserts that there is a trend toward *some* acceptance by employers and by unions of reasonable responsibility for providing treatment for mental disorders of employees.[30]

Mental disorders are complex as to cause. They may arise from disturbances in childhood, from physical illness, from relationships with others off the job, and from interaction with the work situation. Mental illness derives from the individual personality interacting with the total life situation. Sometimes executives feel that the state of human relationships in their organizations could be enhanced if only the problem employees—the malcontents and troublemakers—could be cured by referral to counselors and psychiatrists. But as Temple Burling, a psychiatrist, has pointed out, the problems are in the relationships among people and not simply *within* the people themselves. In asking the specialist to cure his problem employees the industrialist is sometimes expecting him to cure them of their human nature.[31] Therefore a major thrust in a mental health program should be upon the creation of sound supervisor–subordinate relations, elimination of festering conditions causing discontent, and the development of a favorable motivational climate.

Kornhauser reports on a study of the mental health of 655 workers (mostly production workers but including some office personnel as well) employed in various firms in Detroit. In relating mental health to occupational level he found that it becomes poorer among factory workers as one moves from skilled, responsible, varied types of work down to jobs lower in these respects and that the relationship apparently is not caused in any major sense by differences of prejob background or personality of the men involved. The relationship of mental health to occupation seems to be genuine and not dependent on selection effects. Recognizing that mental health has many roots, Kornhauser demonstrates a positive correlation between job level, education, and favorable childhood economic conditions. Job characteristics relate importantly to mental health. Kornhauser found that good mental health is correlated positively with jobs that give a man a chance to use his abilities, to perform a worthwhile function, to fulfill a role as a competent human being, and where a man can find interest in his work and experience a sense of accomplishment. Wage rates, job security, and physical conditions of work had little or no explanatory value in accounting for poorer mental health of lower versus upper job levels.[32]

The plant physician should play a key role in the mental health program. A major responsibility is to identify persons requiring help. Because employees almost never go to him and directly state that they have a mental health problem,

[30] Alan A. McLean, "Who Pays the Bill? A Clinical Perspective," *Journal of Occupational Medicine*, Vol. 9, No. 5 (May 1967), pp. 244–250.

[31] Temple Burling, "Psychiatry in Industry," *Industrial and Labor Relations Review*, Vol. 8, No. 1 (October 1954), pp. 30–37.

[32] Arthur Kornhauser, *Mental Health of the Industrial Worker* (New York: John Wiley & Sons, Inc., 1965.

he must take the lead in training supervisors and the plant nurse to spot these problems. He can observe employee behavior during visits to the medical department. Physical complaints and emotional ailments are often intertwined. In these relationships confidentiality must be assured. The employees should not be placed in the position of jeopardizing their jobs by seeking help and acknowledging that they have an emotional, stress, or anxiety problem. If the plant doctor should find a case that calls for treatment beyond his resources, he should refer the patient to a psychiatrist in the community. He should offer information to the latter about the individual's job requirements and relationships in the organization. In some cases he may have to arrange for a leave of absence for the person.

Supervisory personnel bear important responsibilities in identifying problem employees and offering emotional first aid. They should look for signs of prolonged or excessive anxiety. An employee's usual behavior may become exaggerated. A quiet person may become more withdrawn. When the person's customary mode of response proves ineffective he may become edgy, unable to concentrate, or panicky. In a very acute condition the employee may become noisy, aggressive, or even irrational. The supervisor must be supportive in his relationships and serve as a helpful listener in trying to counsel the individual. If improvement cannot be achieved with a moderate amount of counseling, the supervisor must refer the person to professional talent.

The Utah Copper Division of Kennecott Copper Corporation, employing 8,000 people, established a psychiatric counseling service in 1970 that has yielded very positive results. The program is conducted by a psychiatric social worker who provides prompt confidential help to employees. A simple phone call brings aid. The program has had considerable success with alcoholics but the counseling service deals with all sorts of problems, such as potential suicides, homosexuality, racial discrimination, and drugs.[33]

Alcoholism

The National Council on Alcoholism estimates that there are about 4.5 million alcoholics in the labor force. This is about 5 percent of the nation's work force. Trice and Roman state that between 3 and 4 percent of an average organization's work force are deviant drinkers.[34]

Because the problem is serious more and more companies are setting up formal programs to alleviate the problem. DuPont and Eastman Kodak have long-established programs. More recently General Motors and United Auto Workers Union created a joint program covering 400,000 workers. Some other companies with programs are Lever Brothers, General Dynamics, Merrill Lynch, American Motors, and American Airlines.[35]

What is an alcoholic? Trice and Roman explain the matter by identifying three categories of drinking behavior. The first is normal drinking, which does not impair functioning nor interfere with efficient performance of role assignments and

---

[33] *Business Week* (April 15, 1972), pp. 113–114.
[34] Harrison M. Trice and Paul M. Roman, *Spirits and Demons at Work: Alcohol and Other Drugs on the Job* (Ithaca, N.Y.: Cornell University, 1972), p. 2.
[35] *Business Week* (November 11, 1972), p. 168.

obligations. The second category is deviant drinking, where a person regularly drinks to excess to the point that his role performance is impeded. He is impeded because of a hangover or because he tries to function while under the influence of alcohol. The third category is alcoholic addiction, which is defined as a physiological loss of control over drinking behavior. Long-term, regular drinking increases physiological tolerance so that the person must drink more to achieve the same psychological effects. Eventually the human body cannot function without the ingestion of alcohol. Deprivation of alcohol causes harsh physiological withdrawal symptoms.[36]

Whereas alcoholism at one time was treated as a moral and penal problem (throw the town drunk in jail overnight to dry out), the modern theory is that it is a disease. This approach tends to absolve the individual of personal responsibility for his behavior, at least partially. It is viewed more as a medical and a social problem. However, the cause or causes of alcoholism have not been found. A great many theories have been advanced and much research has been done but the root explanation is still lacking. Nevertheless some treatment programs have demonstrated real success, so we can see that therapy need not wait for the ultimate scientific explanation.

Deviant drinking has pronounced negative effects upon work output and quality. Sometimes the drinkers work for short periods at a fast pace but this is followed by sharp declines in performance. Absenteeism is a pronounced problem. Professional and managerial personnel often go to work even when not feeling well but their performance suffers. Hourly workers tend to just stay away from the job when under the influence of alcohol. Trice and Roman report that poor work performance and absenteeism represent the principal negative impacts upon the organization. Surprisingly, turnover and accident rates are no higher for heavy drinkers and alcoholics than for ordinary employees.[37]

Alcoholics exhibit a pervasive tendency to conceal their drinking and deny that they have a drinking problem. Because drinking is socially accepted in our society, problem drinkers and alcoholics often become adept at manipulating their colleagues and sometimes even their supervisors to cause them to cover up their behavior.

The key to correcting the problem is to confront the deviant drinker with his poor work performance and attendance. If he is directly accused of being an alcoholic, he will invariably deny it. Therefore the supervisor must confront him with the results of his alcoholism, namely poor work performance. The individual must be brought to the point at which he acknowledges that he does have a drinking problem. This may require several discussions. The man may have to be told that he will suffer a disciplinary suspension or even loss of his job if he does not respond by changing his behavior. Experts in alcoholism control and therapy state that fear of job loss is generally the only deprivation that is strong enough to cause the individual to give up the pleasures of alcohol.

The supervisor plays the central role in confronting the employee with his problem, getting him to recognize it, and in helping him take corrective action. This process must be done in a constructive way. The individual must know that management wishes to help him overcome his dependency upon alcohol.

[36] Trice and Roman, op. cit., pp. 16–117.
[37] Ibid. pp. 121–144.

Trice and Roman assert that management, in formulating an alcholism control program, should avoid labeling alcoholism a disease because this tends to give the individual the impression that his behavior is out of his control. Management efforts should be directed toward getting the man or woman motivated to correct his or her own problem and to improve job behavior. If this effort fails, then full-scale medical treatment may become necessary and the condition ultimately may have to be handled as a sickness.[38]

The major components of an alcoholism control program consist of the following:

1. *Policy Statement*

   Coming from the chief executive this commits the organization to a program, outlines the content of the program, and assigns responsibilities to appropriate parties in the organization. It indicates the willingness of the organization to help those in need.

2. *Union Cooperation*

   Where the employees are represented by a union this feature is important. By being brought into the program early the union can play an important part in gaining cooperation and support from the employee group.

3. *Education*

   An organization-wide program of information and education covering the dimensions of the alcoholism problem and the features of the organization's control program is desirable.

4. *Training*

   Supervisors and managers at all levels (and union stewards, where a union is involved) must be given full training in the program and their responsibilities in it. The supervisor bears prime responsibility for identification of the problem and for working with the affected individual.

5. *Professional Services*

   Provision must be made for professional services. This may involve a nurse, counselor, personnel specialist, plant physician, or a psychiatrist. It may also involve outside medical services in the community.

Questions for review and discussion

1. What factors led to the passage of the Occupational Safety and Health Act?
2. Outline the principal features of the Occupational Safety and Health Act.
3. Explain the reasons for the great controversy over OSHA that has developed since the enactment of the Act.
4. What is an accident? Do all accidents result in injuries? Why must all be analyzed for effective safety effort?
5. Why is the injury experience of small companies typically worse than that of large companies in the same industry?

[38] Ibid. pp. 173–175.

6. Are most injuries caused by unsafe physical or mechanical conditions or by unsafe human acts? Discuss.
7. What part do accident-prone people contribute to the total problem of industrial work injuries?
8. How do the work environment and opportunities for recognition, advancement, and autonomy relate to accident rates in industry?
9. Give the components of a complete safety and health program.
10. Why has the seriousness of the occupational disease problem in industry been recognized only relatively recently? Why is control and reduction of the incidence of occupational disease so difficult to achieve?
11. What part does line supervision play in achieving good safety performance? What are the responsibilities of the safety department?
12. What behaviors and responsibilities must top management of a company adopt in order to achieve good occupational safety and health results?
13. Do you think an employer should acknowledge any responsibilities toward his employees in the area of mental health? Discuss.
14. Discuss the responsibilities of the supervisor in an alcoholism control program.

Case problem

In early February 1979 Frank Bradford, personnel manager of the Glen-More Processing Company, received a detailed analysis of injury experience for the period 1/1/78 through 12/31/78 for the company from the insurance company that provides workmen's compensation coverage. The most striking feature of the report was the great difference in work injury rates between Plants 1 and 2, which were located directly across the street from one another. He had known for quite some time from his own data that the injury frequency rate for the company was high both in comparison with the average for all manufacturing industries and with the textile industry in particular. In addition the company president had recently been expressing concern about the high dollar losses for workmen's compensation claims. Frank decided to convene a meeting of concerned management personnel to review the accident problem.

The Glen-More Processing Company produces nonwoven textile products and has been in business for over fifty years. It has a total employment of 450, of whom 397 are factory personnel including factory supervision. Plant 1 produces garnetted synthetic stock (polyester, nylon, and acrylic fibers). Raw material is purchased from various large manufacturers of synthetic filaments. The plant building and processing equipment are old. Many of the machines are driven by leather belts attached to pulleys on overhead lineshafting. Operations require the employees to put certain of the belts on pulleys while the garnett machines are running. Bales of stock weigh from 400 to 1,000 pounds and are handled both by power industrial trucks and by two-wheeled hand trucks. Plant 2, although located in an old, multistory brick building, contains fairly modern production machinery. The final product consists of rolls of bonded synthetic fibers that are sold to firms making outerwear clothing, sleeping bags, and upholstered furniture. The raw material moves through several kinds of equipment in essentially a continuous process (although there are certain batch operations as well). In certain respects the equipment in Plant 2 contains fewer hazards than that of Plant

1. Most of the machinery is driven by electric motors with enclosed "V" belt drives that are guarded. A few machines do require operators to feed material into in-running rolls and this brings their hands close to these "nip" points. Both Plants 1 and 2 have attached warehouses for receiving and shipping.

Frank showed the report from the insurance company to the general manager. They decided to use it as a resource document at the forthcoming meeting. At this meeting they hoped to uncover the causes for the high accident rate and develop a plan of corrective action. Copies of the report were given to all concerned members of top and middle management. Attending the meeting were the general manager, Frank Bradford (personnel manager), the plant managers of Plants 1 and 2, the chief engineer of the company, and the factory superintendents of Plants 1 and 2 (directly under the plant managers on the organization chart).

The salient information in the report "Accident Cause Analysis 1/1/78–12/31/78" prepared by the insurance company is shown below:

Total Work Injuries

	Plant 1	Plant 2
First aid only	13	25
Medical treatment only	18	68
Injuries with lost workdays	7	35
Total	38	128
Total days for all lost workday injuries	140	843
Average days/lost workday case	20.0	24.1
Incidence Rates:		
Lost workday cases	3.94	15.9
Lost workdays (severity)	78.9	383.2
Total employee hours for year	355,000	440,000
Average employment	177	220

1978 Averages for This Industry	
Incidence Rates:	
Lost workday cases	3.1
Lost workdays (severity)	65.4
Average days per lost workday case	32

Injuries by Type

	First Aid & Medical		Lost Workday	
	Plant 1	Plant 2	Plant 1	Plant 2
Struck against	7	11	2	7
Struck by	14	18	2	6
Caught between	8	18	2	6
Falls		8		6
Improper handling	2	4	1	4
Improper lifting		3		5
Foreign body in eye		31		1
Totals	31	93	7	35

Including *all* injuries in Plant 1, 60 percent involved injury to the hands, 12 percent to trunk of body, 8 percent to arms, 8 percent to head, and 12 percent to legs or feet. In Plant 2, 33 percent involved tiny particles of dust or dried chemical in eyes, 20 percent to trunk of body, 26 percent to hands, 8 percent to arms, 6 percent to head, and 7 percent to legs or feet.

The general manager opened the meeting by explaining that the accident problem was serious, that dollar losses had mounted, and that top management, while lax on safety in the past, wanted to cut its losses. He said that the Occupational Safety and Health Act placed direct responsibility upon management to maintain a safe and healthful work environment. He encouraged everyone present to speak freely.

Here follow key excerpts of remarks by the participants:

Personnel Manager: Our wage rates are about 20–25 percent below the going rates in the local area for occupations similar to ours. However, we are in line with other textile firms. For years we have only been able to hire people who can't qualify for jobs in other better-paying companies. The average education level of our hourly paid work force is tenth grade. We tend to hire mainly young people in the 18–25 age range. Older people usually hold better-paying jobs elsewhere and don't look for work here. In 1978 turnover of hourly help in Plant 1 was about 50 percent while in Plant 2 it was nearly 100 percent. The average length of service and age of employees in Plant 1 is higher than that of Plant 2. The operations in Plant 2 are rather seasonal. In that plant we lay off about 25 percent of the force every November and rehire in the spring. Seldom do those laid off in the fall come back with us in the spring. Absenteeism is about the same for both plants and averages about 8–9 percent.

Plant 1 Manager: We cut our accident rate quite a bit over the past couple of years by doing a number of things. We follow up vigorously on every accident. If it is due to a physical hazard we try to install such devices as machine guards, interlock mechanisms on access covers, and shut-off bars as required. If due to a human error we talk to all employees working on that kind of operation and explain what was done wrong and how to do it right. We also follow up closely on injured employees. We see that they get proper medical treatment. Sometimes a man gets a minor injury and uses it as an excuse to take a few days off. I send my superintendent (or a foreman) directly to the employee's home to investigate all questionable cases. We have been quite successful in preventing minor injuries from becoming lost-time cases. Our foremen are supposed to run short monthly safety meetings with their people but they don't do a good job of this and often won't do it at all unless I insist upon it.

Plant 2 Manager: The data from the insurance company show that we had a very bad year in 1978 in incidence rates. But I don't really know why. I conduct a safety meeting with my superintendent and foremen about once every month or two to discuss machinery and equipment items that need repair or replacement and go over general safety matters. Also we try to get the foremen to conduct brief safety meetings with their people about once per month. But it is hard to get them to do this. Most claim they are unable to speak in front of a group and get their message across. A few of the foremen do tour their departments and speak to individual employees about safety matters from time to time.

Superintendent, Plant 2: I think we have too many accident-prone people working here. Jake Ambrose had five accidents last year and one of these was a lost-time case. Frank Wilson had four accidents, one of which was a lost-time case where he was out for nearly a month. These are but two of the cases that come to mind now. Also our high turnover creates a serious problem. As you all know, we do not have a formal training program here for new workers but we do spend some time discussing safety rules and other matters at the time a new man is hired. I personally give each new hire a copy of the safety rules. During the first couple of days we assign new people to work under the direction of old-timers. We just about get a new man broken in on his job when he quits. Then we must start all over again breaking in a replacement. Sometimes I think we scrape the bottom of the manpower barrel when we hire people. Not only do we have a high turnover problem due to quitting but we also have to fire lots of new hires during the six-week probationary period, usually because of excessive absenteeism.

Personnel Manager: I think a serious problem in both plants is that we have a lot of people on our payroll who just don't want to work. Some will fake an injury just to get a few days off. Or if they actually do get hurt on the job they may stay out for a week or two even though it is a minor injury. We must police such cases better.

Superintendent, Plant 1: We have been trying to meet this problem for the last year or so. As you know we don't have a plant nurse or doctor. We are located only a half mile from the hospital. On any injuries more serious than a first-aid case we rush the person directly to the emergency room of the hospital and we stay there until the doctor has treated him and we learn exactly how serious his condition is. If someone doesn't show up for work some day and phones in saying he was injured the day before, we investigate thoroughly. We check with his foreman to verify or refute the claim. We even go to the worker's home if necessary. We have found some fraudulent cases and we take disciplinary action on them. Sometimes we find that a foreman has been careless and failed to make out an accident report on a real accident.

Chief Engineer: The record shows that a lot of injuries occur in the shipping and receiving operations of Plant 2. These include such things as dropping a dock plate on the foot, falling off the loading dock, getting hit by a lift-truck, and getting hit by a carton. In the operations around the processing machinery we get finger and hand injuries around the machines, slips and falls on stairs and catwalks, injuries from hand tools, and particles of dust and dried chemical in the eyes. It is true we conduct our manufacturing operations in two very old multistory buildings and some of our machinery is old and not of the most modern design. Perhaps we have some inherent hazards in our materials handling and machinery operations. However, I think human error and carelessness are a major cause of our problem. I think our foremen do not do a good job of teaching safety to the men and women here.

General Manager: We have discussed many aspects of our safety problem this morning but have not reached any definite conclusions. Perhaps we must reorganize our whole safety effort. As you know we do not have a safety director as such. We are not large enough for that. Frank Bradford handles the general direction of the program as part of his personnel responsibilities. In addition to the many aspects of the problem that were discussed this morning there may be others that we haven't identified yet. I am asking Frank to make a full investigation and to prepare a report that spells out just what we must do to cut down our dollar losses to a more reasonable figure. I doubt if we will ever achieve an outstanding performance here but we can certainly make improvements. Frank, I would like to know why there is such a great difference in accident frequency between Plants 1 and 2. Was this also true for 1977? Also, you might want to contact Fritz, the local union president, to get his views. I will call another meeting after we receive your report, say in about a month or so.

After the meeting Frank checked his injury records for 1977. The incidence of lost workday cases per 100 full-time workers was 8.1 for both plants combined. Plant 1 was 3.94 and Plant 2 was 11.4.

He then invited Fritz, the union president, in for a discussion of the accident problem. Fritz was quite blunt in stating that the foremen pushed the employees very hard for production but seldom took action to correct safety hazards when these were brought to their attention by the employees. This "brush-off" practice was especially common in Plant 2. Safety meetings for the employees were held only two or three times a year in either plant. The foremen and superintendent in Plant 1 were somewhat more effective in correcting hazards than were the foremen and superintendent in Plant 2. They were more safety conscious generally. He then itemized ten separate safety problems that had not been taken care of. These ranged from lax enforcement of the safety glasses program in Plant 2 to the need to repair two plant lift-trucks that had bad brakes. He also complained about the dirty and poorly equipped lunch and locker room facilities in both plants. He felt that the better safety record in Plant 1 was due to a more conscious practice of pressing for safety by supervision on a day-to-day basis.

Questions

1. What is wrong here? Has management identified the root causes of its serious safety problem? What do you consider are the principal causes?
2. Outline a program to reorganize and improve the safety effort and include the principal action steps to be taken. What elements ought to be given first priority?

Suggestions for further reading

ASHFORD, NICHOLAS A. *Crisis in the Workplace: Occupational Disease and Injury.* Cambridge, Mass.: The MIT Press, 1976.
————. "Worker Health and Safety: An Area of Conflicts," *Monthly Labor Review*, Vol. 98, No. 9 (September 1975), pp. 3–11.
BRODEUR, PAUL. *Expendable Americans.* New York: Viking Press, 1974.
"The Evolution of America's Industrial Safety Movement 1776–1976," *Occupational Hazards*, Vol. 37, No. 9 (September 1975), pp. 51–100.

FOLLMAN, JOSEPH F., JR. *Alcoholics and Business: Problems, Costs, Solutions.* New York: American Management Associations, 1975.

Guidebook to Occupational Safety and Health. Chicago: Commerce Clearing House, 1974.

KOCHAN, THOMAS A., LEE DYER, and D. B. LIPSKY. *The Effectiveness of Union–Management Safety and Health Committees.* Kalamazoo, Michigan: W. E. Upjohn Institute for Employment Research, 1977.

MCLEAN, ALAN A. "Job Stress and the Psychosocial Pressures of Change," *Personnel,* Vol. 53, No. 1 (January–February 1976).

MCLEAN, ALAN A. *Mental Health and Work Organizations.* Chicago: Rand McNally & Co., 1970.

PAGE, JOSEPH A. and MARY-WIN O'BRIEN. *Bitter Wages.* New York: Grossman Publishers, 1973.

TEPLOW, LEO. "Comprehensive Safety and Health Measures in the Workplace" in *Federal Policies and Worker Status Since the Thirties.* Madison, Wisc., Industrial Relations Research Association, 1976.

Benefits and services

Nearly every organization in this country provides its employees certain tangible benefits over and above the basic pay check. These benefits may supply financial protection against such risks as illness, accident, unemployment, and loss of income due to retirement. They may provide extra leisure, extra income, and a better work environment. Some benefits help fulfill the social and recreational needs of employees. Although benefits and services are not directly related to the productive effect of the workers, management often expects to aid its recruitment effort, raise morale, create greater company loyalty, reduce turnover and absenteeism, and, in general, improve the strength of the organization by instituting a well-conceived program in this area.

Although the term *benefits and services* is very widely used to designate this area of personnel management practice, other terms, such as *fringe benefits, employee services, supplementary compensation, indirect compensation,* and *supplementary pay* are also used. The frequently used term *fringe benefits* originated during World War II. Many management practitioners now object to this expression on the grounds that nowadays these benefits represent a very substantial portion of the total labor cost for a firm. They are no longer merely fringe costs or fringe items. They are important to management, employees, and unions alike.

The terms *benefits* and *services* are often used interchangeably by some writers. To others the word *benefit* applies to those items for which a direct monetary value to the individual employee can be rather easily ascertained, as in the case of a pension, separation pay, major medical insurance, or holiday pay. The word *service* applies to such items as a company newspaper, athletic field, Christmas party, or company purchasing service, for which a direct money value for the individual employee cannot be readily established.

Growth of Benefits and Services

With the exception of a very small minority of companies that had adopted progressive personnel programs in the 1920's, American industry, by and large, did not provide benefits and services for hourly paid workers prior to the World War II period.[1] Pension plans were rare before 1940. By 1975 more than 30 million people were covered by private pension plans. Paid holidays and vacations were almost nonexistent before World War II; nowadays employees typically receive eight to nine holidays per year and from one to four weeks of vacation annually, depending upon their length of service with a particular employer. Prior to 1940 very few employees were covered by hospitalization and medical insurance; now such protection is widespread throughout industry. Some employers now provide dental insurance and prescription drug insurance.

Benefits and services represent a tangible gain to employees that is either monetary or nonfinancial, depending upon the particular item involved. They also represent a labor cost for the employer. When viewed as a cost, the dramatic increase in benefits and services over the years can be appreciated by noting benefit cost data compiled by the Chamber of Commerce of the United States. For the economy as a whole the Chamber has estimated that the total cost to employers of employee benefits (not including services) averaged 3.0 percent of direct wage and salary payments in 1929, 17.0 percent in 1955, 21.5 percent in 1965, and 30.0 percent in 1975.[2]

Causes of Growth. Several factors account for the significant increase in fringe benefits over the past fifty years. Public policy is perhaps one of the most fundamental reasons. The Social Security Act of 1935 requires employers to share equally with employees the cost of Old Age, Survivors, and Disability Insurance. Employers pay the full cost of unemployment insurance.

The great increase in fringe benefits in the United States has coincided with the growth of unionism. Union demands at the bargaining table have often forced management to grant additional benefits. Unionization combined with National Labor Relations Board and court interpretations of the Wagner and Taft–Hartley Acts have broadened the scope of mandatory bargaining, so that management must bargain such issues as pensions, Christmas bonuses, vacations, profit sharing, stock-purchase plans, and group-insurance plans.

---

[1] Salaried white-collar and managerial employees fared slightly better, because they often received paid vacations and were paid when they were absent because of illness. With these exceptions these employees generally received no more benefits and services than hourly workers during this period.

[2] *Employee Benefits 1975* (Washington, D.C. The Chamber of Commerce of the United States, 1976), Table 21, p. 30.

The advanced stage of industrialization in the United States, the increasing interdependence of the people, the vital need for keeping one's job, and the general affluence and prosperity in the economy, all have served to make it both necessary and possible for employers to provide a measure of financial protection for workers against the risks of unemployment, sickness, injury, and old age.

Furthermore, employees have asked for and received longer vacations and more holidays to enable them to have time to enjoy the fruits of their good wages in leisure time activities.

TYPES OF BENEFITS AND SERVICES

Employee benefits include programs that help provide for *employee security*. These programs provide financial reimbursement to employees and their families for costs associated with both occupational and nonoccupational injuries and illnesses, unemployment, retirement, and death (life insurance). Another category of employee benefits is *paid leave*, which includes such items as paid holidays and vacations. A third category is *premium pay* which covers extra pay for working overtime on holidays and weekends, and for shift differentials. A fourth category is *bonuses and awards* which aren't related to employee production. These include profit-sharing bonuses, Christmas bonuses, and scholarships for employees and their family members. *Savings and thrift plans* comprise the last category of benefits. Some employers provide small supplements to the sums that employees voluntarily have deducted from their paychecks to be deposited in an employer-run savings plan.

Figure 27-1 is a table, from a U.S. Department of Labor survey, showing employer expenditures for the principal categories of employee benefits in the economy as a whole (all industries) in 1976. The items are expressed as percent of total compensation and as dollars per work hour. The reader will note that pay for time worked was 76.7 percent of total compensation. Thus, employee benefits comprised 23.3 percent of total compensation. Expressed differently, this 23.3 percent represented 30.4 percent of direct wage payments.

Employee services include *social and recreational programs* and facilities that are provided or subsidized by the company. Services also include a variety of *special aids and services* such as credit unions, loan funds, medical treatment for minor illnesses, and child care centers.

Although some businessmen classify such items as rest periods, clean-up time, rest rooms, parking lots, and first-aid services as employee benefits, this author would not classify them as such. These things are directly associated with work activities and the needs of people in a work setting. They are essentials, not extras.

The following tabulation gives the principal kinds of benefits and services commonly found in work organizations.

Employee benefits and services
A. Employee Security (financial protection against certain risks)
    1. Legally required employer contributions.
       Old Age, Survivors, Disability, and Health Insurance.
       Unemployment Insurance.
       Workers' Compensation.

Compensation Item	1976 All Industries	
	Percent of compensation	Dollars per work hour
Total compensation.	100.0	$7.53
Pay for time worked.	76.7	5.77
Straight-time pay.	74.7	5.63
Premium pay.	1.9	.15
Overtime, weekend, and holiday work.	1.6	.12
Shift differentials.	.3	.02
Paid leave (except sick leave).	6.1	.46
Vacations.	3.5	.26
Holidays.	2.3	.17
Civic and personal leave.	.2	.01
Employer payments to vacation and holiday funds.	.2	.02
Employer expenditures for retirement programs.	8.6	.65
Social security.	4.3	.32
Private plans.	4.3	.32
Employer expenditures for life insurance and health benefit programs.[1]	6.0	.45
Life, accident, and health insurance.	4.1	.31
Sick leave.	.9	.06
Workers' compensation.	1.1	.08
Employer expenditures for unemployment benefit programs.	1.3	.09
Unemployment insurance.	1.1	.08
Severance pay.	.1	.01
Severance pay funds and supplemental unployment benefit funds.	.1	([2])
Nonproduction bonuses.	1.1	.08
Savings and thrift plans.	.2	.01

Figure 27-1
Table Showing Employee Benefit Categories as Percent and as Dollars per Work Hour of Total Compensation, Private Nonfarm Economy–1976. *Source:* Employee Compensation in the Private Nonfarm Economy, 1976. *Washington, D.C.: U.S. Department of Labor, August, 1978, Table 3.*
[1] Includes other health benefit programs, principally State temporary disability insurance not presented separately.
[2] Less than $0.005
Note: Because of rounding, sums of individual items may not equal totals.

State disability insurance.
Railroad Retirement Tax, Railroad Unemployment Insurance.
2. Pensions.
3. Life insurance.
4. Hospitalization.
5. Medical and surgical payments.
6. Dental insurance.

7. Paid sick leave.
8. Supplemental unemployment benefits, separation pay, and guaranteed wages.
9. Accident insurance.
B. Paid Leave
   1. Holidays.
   2. Vacations.
   3. Personal business leave.
   4. Military service allowance.
   5. Jury duty.
   6. Voting time.
C. Premium Pay
   1. Overtime, weekend, and holiday work.
   2. Shift differentials.
D. Bonuses and Awards (Not related directly to employee output)
   1. Profit-sharing bonus.
   2. Christmas bonus.
   3. Anniversary awards.
   4. Tuition refunds, scholarships.
E. Savings and Thrift Plans
F. Service Programs
   1. Social and recreational programs, such as parties, picnics, athletic facilities, clubs, and dances where wholly or partially financed by the employer.
   2. Special aids and services such as credit unions, loan funds, company purchasing service, medical treatment for minor sickness, subsidy for food service, discount on purchase of company products, employee newspaper, child care center.

WHY ADOPT BENEFIT AND SERVICE PROGRAMS?

Let us examine the reasons that individual companies install benefits and services. We shall also note the forces causing the expansion of existing benefits and the introduction of new ones.

A primary reason explaining why an individual company institutes certain benefits and services is competition for employees. Starting in the early twentieth century a few progressive companies in various sections of the country established such programs as private pensions, group life insurance, and profit sharing, as well as various social and recreational activities. These firms soon become known as "good" places to work. In order to recruit and retain workers, other companies began following suit.

However, the really substantial growth of various forms of supplementary compensation and benefits is due, as we have noted, to union bargaining power. Private pension rights were enjoyed by only a very small percentage of the nation's labor force prior to 1949. In that year, the United Steelworkers of America won the right to bargain for pensions in the United States Supreme Court (Inland Steel Case). Since that time most unionized workers have obtained pension rights in their collective-bargaining contracts. Unions have also taken the lead in obtaining paid holidays and vacations, health insurance, supplemental unemployment insurance, and separation pay. In recent years provisions for dental insurance, prescription drug insurance and payments for eyeglasses have been appearing in labor–management agreements.

Some kinds of benefits are established to recruit and retain certain kinds of personnel. The opportunity to pursue advanced education programs at the master's and doctoral level is especially important to engineers and scientists. Hence, companies frequently establish tuition refund programs and will arrange for special courses and programs with nearby universities. Many firms pay membership dues to the professional society of an individual's choice and will pay his expenses to attend out-of-town society conferences. In another sense, money spent for the development of professional talent ought to be viewed as an investment by the company. This should pay off in the long run in improved performance. Viewed in this way, these items are not fringe benefits but things that should be an integral part of the operation of the business.

Some benefits are provided by employers because of a concern for the welfare of their employees and because they can best be provided through the employer. Blue Cross, Blue Shield, and health insurance plans offered by insurance companies are designed primarily for groups. Costs are lower this way. Enlightened self-interest is a motivating force here also. Employers know that prompt and proper medical treatment of illnesses yields a healthier work force.

The top management of an organization may establish a comprehensive program of benefits and services because it feels this will enchance employee morale, generate greater loyalty toward the firm, and provide a positive public relations image.

When faced with the question of whether to establish a particular new benefit or service, management must weigh the following factors:

1. *Cost and ability to pay.* Will the firm be able to pay the cost of the item in both the short and long run?
2. *Union demands and power.* Both the wishes of employees as expressed by their union representatives and the bargaining power of the union are realities that must be considered.
3. *Need.* Does the contemplated program answer a real need? Is it necessary in order to recruit employees?
4. *Tax consideration.* Most benefits and services are legitimate company expenses. If employees had to use part of their wages to purchase the same benefit, say from an insurance company, they would have already paid income tax on that income. Thus, for a given dollar cost it may be cheaper for a company to purchase the benefit.
5. *Administration.* Will the program be manageable or will it be unwieldy to administer?

SIGNIFICANT BENEFIT AND SERVICE PROGRAMS

Space does not permit an explanation of all the multitude of benefits and services that exist in business and industry. We shall concentrate upon those that are very widespread in usage.

Life Insurance

Group life insurance is one of the oldest and most prevalent kinds of employee benefits. The first group life-insurance policy written by an insurance company was for the Pantasote Leather Co. of Passaic, New Jersey in 1911.[3] As of 1975, 77.3 percent of all wage and salary employees, including both private and public sectors of employment, were covered by life insurance and death benefits through their employers.[4]

Group insurance, which includes life, health, disability, and pensions, operates according to principles different from individual insurance. With group insurance the insurance company makes no selection of individuals whom it will insure. The insurance carrier sets its premium according to the characteristics of the group as a whole. Most insurance companies require a certain minimum number of persons in the group, typically twenty-five people, to guard against adverse selection of risks and for lower administrative costs. The group to be insured must have been formed for some purpose other than to seek group insurance protection. This is to avoid a group made up solely of those in poor health or who might, for some other reason, represent expensive risks.

Group life insurance is written without a physical examination. Usually it is term insurance. This means that it has no cash surrender or paid-up value and no loan provisions.

In its survey of group life insurance practices in 1600 firms across a variety of industry classifications, The Conference Board found that life insurance benefits are usually tied to salary level. The median benefit is two times the employee's base salary. Most commonly the company pays the full premium for the coverage (this is called a noncontributory plan).[5]

Health Insurance

Private group health insurance plans pay part or all of the hospital and doctor expenses arising from illness and injury which is not job connected. (Workers' Compensation covers expenses of occupational injury or illness). Often the employees' dependents are also covered.

There are two kinds of health insurance plans: a base plan and a major medical plan. Often a company will have both plans. The base plan pays expenses for listed health services within the defined limits for each service. For example the base plan will typically pay for a hospital room, bed, board, and general nursing care included up to a certain dollar amount per day and up to a given maximum number of days. Some insuring organizations such as Blue Cross, established by the American Hospital Association, pay for a specified service such as semiprivate room accommodations without specifying a dollar limit.

Major medical insurance, available for an additional premium, covers a whole array of physician, hospital, laboratory, and nursing services beyond the limits of

---

[3] Robert I. Mehr and Emerson Cammack, *Principles of Insurance* (Homewood, Ill.: Richard D. Irwin, Inc., 1961), p. 553.

[4] Martha R. Yohalem, "Employee Benefit Plans, 1975," *Social Security Bulletin*, Vol. 40, No. 11 (November 1977), pp. 19–28.

[5] Mitchell Meyer and Harland Fox, *Profile of Employee Benefits* Report No. 645 (New York: The Conference Board, 1974).

the basic plan. Generally, there are no dollar limits for specific services but there is a total dollar limit of say, $50,000 for any benefit period. The individual must typically pay the first $50 or $100 of expenses (the deductible amount). Beyond this figure the insurance company pays 80 percent of all expenses and the employee pays 20 percent (the coinsurance feature).

In the vast majority of organizations the employer pays the full cost of the health insurance for the employee while the premium for dependents is shared by the employer and the employee.

Dental insurance has been emerging as a new benefit over the past ten years. In The Conference Board survey mentioned earlier 13 percent of the companies provide dental insurance for their nonoffice employees and 9 percent provide coverage for office employees.[6]

Another new development has been health service through a Health Maintenance Organization (HMO). A health maintenance organization provides comprehensive health services for enrolled members for a fixed prepaid annual fee. Examples are the Kaiser Foundation Plans in California, Oregon, and Hawaii which have been operating for many years. More than 7 million Americans obtain health care from HMOs.[7] The Health Maintenance Act of 1973 requires employers of 25 or more persons to offer membership in an HMO as an alternative to the existing health insurance plan if such a plan is available within the area.

Disability Insurance

Disability insurance compensates employees for wage loss due to nonoccupational illness and injury. There are two forms of disability insurance. The older and much more prevalent type is accident and sickness insurance. This typically pays from 50 to 70 percent of the worker's pay for up to 26 weeks of disability. A formal disability insurance plan is most common for hourly paid workers. White collar and managerial employees in industry are often granted sick leave at full pay by the company for a limited number of weeks. This is often done on an informal basis and the program is not insured.

A recent trend has been the introduction of long-term disability insurance to partially compensate for wage loss due to protracted or permanent disabilities. Generally employees contribute toward the cost of this insurance. Typically after a six-month waiting period, the plan will pay 60 percent of the individual's wage up to $1500 per month.[8]

Pensions

The Social Security Act, enacted in 1935, provides basic retirement income benefits to those who have worked in covered employment for the required number of years. Over 90 percent of the labor force are covered by old-age insurance under this law. The old-age pension program is but a part of the comprehensive Old Age, Survivors, Disability and Health Insurance system of the Act.

---

[6] Meyer and Fox, Ibid., pp. 14–15.
[7] George E. Rejda, *Social Insurance and Economic Security* (Englewood Cliffs, N.J.: Prentice-Hall, Inc., 1976), p. 218.
[8] Meyer and Fox, op. cit., p. 38.

Retirement benefit levels are insufficient to support retired workers and their dependents at an adequate level of living; hence, retirees must augment their Social Security payments with funds from personal savings or with funds from a pension plan through their employer or both. In January 1978 the average Social Security benefit received by a retired worker was $243 per month; for a retired worker and dependent spouse the benefit was $367.[9]

In 1975 46.2 percent (30.3 million persons) of all wage and salary workers in the private sector were covered by pension plans operated by employers and by unions.[10]

How much does it cost a retired couple to live? Annually the U.S. Department of Labor surveys the annual costs for a retired husband and wife, age 65 or over, who are self-supporting and living alone in their own home in an urban area. In the Autumn of 1977 the U.S. average annual cost for a lower-level budget amounted to $5,031; at an intermediate level the cost was $7,198 and at a higher level it was $10,711.[11] The family in the lower budget, compared with the intermediate budget, relies heavily on public transportation, supplemented where necessary by the use of an older car; it performs more services for itself; and it utilizes free recreational services in the community. The life style in the higher budget includes some new car ownership, more household appliances, and more paid-for services.

Pension Benefits.   There are two principal kinds of pension plans: *defined benefit* and *defined contribution*. The defined benefit plan is much more prevalent in both private industry and governmental units than is the defined contribution plan. Under the defined benefit plan the employee's retirement benefit is usually tied to years of service and earnings. A very popular formula specifies that the person shall receive 1½ percent (the usual range is 1 to 2 percent) times his or her years of service times average pay for the five years immediately preceding retirement. Whereas most organizations compute the pension benefit on the basis of the final three to five year's earnings, some companies base it upon career average earnings. This would yield a smaller benefit because of lower earnings early in the person's career. Whereas the white collar employees overwhelmingly have their pension benefits related to pay, hourly paid workers often receive a fixed amount of pension per year of service. In The Conference Board study, 37 percent of the firms do not relate benefit amount to pay for nonoffice workers.[12]

The money-purchase plan is a common type of defined contribution plan. This arrangement is established under a group annuity plan underwritten by an insurance company. The employer (and sometimes the employee, too) contributes a definite percentage of the individual's pay into a retirement fund. Upon retirement the principal and interest accumulated are used to pay the monthly pension. Under money purchase the contribution is fixed but the benefit varies. The variation is principally caused by changes in the interest earned on the fund over the years.

[9] Social Security Bulletin, Vol. 41, No. 5 (May 1978), Table M-13, p. 52.
[10] Yohalem, op. cit., pp. 20 and 22.
[11] *Three Budgets for a Retired Couple*, Autumn 1977 (Washington, D.C.: U.S. Department of Labor) August 13, 1978.
[12] Meyer and Fox, op. cit., p. 52.

Pension benefits are sometimes also built up from deferred profit sharing plans, savings plans, and stock bonus plans. Generally these arrangements are used to supplement a basic pension plan.

In an era of continual high price inflation, retirees find their private pension benefits have eroded quite rapidly. Seldom, however, are private pension benefits adjusted upwards for inflation. The Conference Board found that only 4 percent of the firms surveyed do this.[13] Fortunately, retirement benefits under the U.S. Social Security system are adjusted upwards annually according to changes in the Consumer Price Index.

Vesting Rights.   Vesting is a nonforfeitable right to pension benefits from the employer's contributions even if the employee should terminate his employment before retirement age. Years ago the majority of pension plans granted no vesting rights to workers who were permanently laid off or who quit. By the 1960's there was a pronounced trend toward granting vesting rights after employees reached a specified age, generally 45 or 50, and had accumulated a given number of years of service, typically 15 to 20 years. Vesting much sooner is now required by the Employee Retirement Income Security Act of 1974 (ERISA) to be discussed later.

Methods of Financing.   Prior to the enactment of ERISA a pension plan could be either unfunded or funded. The law requires all plans to be adequately funded. Benefits in unfunded plans were paid out of current operating income of the company. However, this was extremely risky. If the firm experienced a decline in revenue or went bankrupt, pension payments to retirees were often slashed or abolished. Many companies have funded their pensions but at an inadequate level to meet accrued liabilities.

There are two types of funded plans: *trusteed* and *insured*. A trusteed plan is administered by trustees who may be appointed by the company or jointly by the company and the union. Often a bank or trust company will administer the fund. In any case an actuary must be engaged to determine the amount of money that must be set aside each year to meet pension obligations.

Insured plans are underwritten and administered by an insurance company.

Who Pays?   Predominantly the employer pays the full cost of the pension benefits. In The Conference Board survey of 1600 companies 80 percent of the plans for office employees and 81 percent of the plans for nonoffice personnel were noncontributory. Company contributions to pensions, and the various insurances (life, health, and disability) tend, in recent years, to be viewed as a form of deferred compensation.

Retirement Age.   Sixty-five has been almost universally accepted as the normal retirement age ever since that figure was adopted by the Social Security Act in 1935 as the age for commencing old age benefit payments. Prior to this, the ordinary worker couldn't afford to retire. He worked until infirmity prevented working or until death.

Beginning in the 1960's a widespread movement toward early retirement

[13] Meyer and Fox, Ibid., p. 52.

began. Whereas there are no accurate national statistics on retirement age, there are measures that show a pronounced early retirement trend. For example, the labor force participation rate of male workers aged 60 to 64 has been dropping rapidly in nonfarm industries for 20 years. In 1977 only 62.9 percent of all men in that age group held jobs, compared with 82.6 percent in 1955. Experts believe that the average American retires at about age 62, the age at which he or she first becomes eligible for reduced Social Security benefits. In the basic steel industry the average hourly worker retires at age 61. At General Motors Corporation the average retirement age is 59. In both the steel and auto industries the unions have negotiated pension plans providing for early retirement.[14]

In 1978 Congress amended the Age Discrimination in Employment Act of 1967 in order to ban mandatory retirement before age 70. Prior to this a majority of employers required that their employees retire when they reached 65. (Many plans allow retirement as early as age 55 with reduced benefits.) Will many Americans now opt for retirement between ages 65 and 70 now that this right is protected by law? Only time will tell. Experience shows that those possessing modest educations and holding unskilled and semi-skilled jobs generally choose early retirement if their benefits are adequate. Professional and managerial personnel, who often derive intrinsic satisfaction from their jobs, will probably tend to work beyond age 65. Or they will retire early and pursue "second careers."

Employee Retirement Income Security Act of 1974 (ERISA)

Background. Enactment of the Employee Retirement Income Security Act of 1974 was preceded by several years of study by Congressional committees and by the U.S. Labor and Treasury Departments. Many serious abuses and problems were uncovered. A study by the Labor and Treasury Departments for 1972 found that 1,227 pension plans terminated that year with almost $50 million of lost benefits to about 20,000 workers.[15] A U.S. Senate Labor Subcommittee in 1972 reported that many pension plans were scrapped or benefits were greatly reduced when one company was acquired by or merged with another. Workers often lost all their accumulated pension benefits when they were laid off before reaching retirement age. Some companies dipped into their pension funds when they were in need of money for acquisitions, expansion, or just for operating cash.[16]

As workers have changed employers, they have often lost pension rights built up with the former employer. The United States Senate Subcommittee on Labor in 1971 determined that, as a result of harsh vesting rules, only about one person in ten would collect pension benefits from his employer.[17]

In summary, the principal reason why Congress passed ERISA was to overcome problems caused by inadequate pension funding, plan terminations, restrictive vesting rules, business failures, and just plain failure of employers to provide promised pensions when workers retired.

[14] *Business Week* (June 19, 1978), pp. 73–74.
[15] *Wall Street Journal* (August 28, 1974), p. 1.
[16] *Wall Street Journal* (March 7, 1972), pp. 1 and 20.
[17] George E. Rejda, op. cit., p. 78.

Provisions of the law. At the outset it should be noted that ERISA does not require employers to offer or set up pension plans. But if a plan is in existence or if a new one is established then the plan must meet certain minimum standards contained in the law.

Many of the provisions of the Act also apply to employee welfare plans such as those providing benefits for health care, accident and sickness, disability, death, and unemployment. This is especially true in regard to the fiduciary provisions and the reporting and disclosure requirements. However, we will focus our discussion only on the pension features of the law.[18]

A brief summary of the provisions of this very complex law follows:

Coverage and Administration. The Act covers pension and welfare plans established and maintained by employers engaged in interstate commerce or in an industry affecting commerce. It also covers plans run by unions alone or jointly with employers. The Act is administered by both the Department of Labor and the Internal Revenue Service of the Treasury Department. The newly established Pension Benefit Guarantee Corporation handles the pension plan termination insurance program.

Participation. A plan must allow an employee to participate when he or she has completed one year of service and is at least 25 years old.

Vesting. Any employee contributions must be vested fully and immediately. Employer contributions must vest at least as fast as one of the following schedules:

1.   Full (100 percent) vesting after 10 years of service.
2.   Graduated vesting. 25 percent vesting after 5 years of service, increasing yearly until 100 percent after 15 years.
3.   50 percent vesting as soon as the sum of age and years of service equal 45, plus 10 percent for each year thereafter.

Funding. The plan must fund the current year's benefit accruals. It must amortize any unfunded costs over 30 years for new plans and over 40 years for existing plans and multi-employer plans.

Fiduciary Standards. The "prudent man rule" (a legal concept) is imposed upon all persons who administer or provide investment advice for a plan. The fiduciary persons are to discharge their duties solely in the interests of the participants and beneficiaries. Various conflict of interest transactions are outlawed.

Reporting and Disclosure. Plan administrators must furnish each employee a summary plan description in easily understandable language. Administrators must also give the Department of Labor annual reports on various operating and financial details of the plan.

Termination Insurance. A termination insurance program is set up through the Pension Benefit Guaranty Corporation. The program pays benefits up to $750 per month to those who had vested rights in plans that were terminated with insufficient assets. Insurance is funded by an annual premium on all pension plans of $1 per participant. The Guaranty Corporation can recover benefit

---

[18] Further information on ERISA may be obtained by consulting the following: BNA Editorial Staff, *Highlights of the New Pension Reform Law* (Washington, D.C.: The Bureau of National Affairs, Inc., 1974); *Often-asked Questions About the Employee Retirement Income Security Act of 1974* (U.S. Department of Labor, Labor–Management Services Administration, 1975); Peter Henle and Raymond Schmitt, "Pension Reform: The Long, Hard Road to Enactment," *Monthly Labor Review* (November 1974), pp. 3–12.

costs from the defaulting company up to 30 percent of the firm's net worth.

Portability. Although Congress considered making it possible for employees to take their pension credits with them when they went to a new employer, the law as enacted does not provide for true portability. It does provide that a worker, if the employer agrees, can withdraw his or her pension credits from a plan and shift them either to an Individual Retirement Account or to another employer's plan without incurring a tax liability.

Widow-Widowers' Benefit. Unless the employee specifically elects otherwise, a married person must receive a pension benefit payable for his or her lifetime with a surviving spouse to receive at least 50 percent of that amount.

Enforcement. Both civil and criminal actions may be brought for violation of the law. Criminal penalties include fines or imprisonment or both for violations of reporting and disclosure provisions and for embezzlement, kickbacks, or false statements.

Employee Stock Ownership

Employee stock purchase plans have been around for many years. Such plans went out of favor during the great depression years of the 1930's because many workers, who could ill afford it, lost money as the market value of their companies' shares declined drastically. Over the past twenty-five years or so there has been a resurgence of interest in employee stock purchase plans. Many companies operate such plans. In the typical program the corporation sets up a payroll deduction arrangement in which an employee may voluntarily have a sum of money, up to an established limit, deducted from each paycheck. This is used to purchase shares of the company's stock, in the employee's name, through a broker. Usually the only company contribution is to pay the administrative costs and the broker's fee. Sometimes stock purchase plans are combined with employee savings and thrift plans via payroll deduction. Here some companies make an added contribution of a predetermined amount in the form of cash or company stock to the individual's savings. Purposes of employee stock ownership and savings plans are to enhance employee loyalty to the corporation and to build employee savings.

ESOP. The term "employee stock ownership plan" or ESOP has come to mean, in recent years, the kind of plan devised and promoted by Louis O. Kelso, a California attorney and executive of an investment firm. Although legally possible since 1942, ESOP's did not achieve any prominence until they were given favored treatment by the Employee Retirement Income Security Act of 1974 and the Tax Reduction Act of 1975. An ESOP has particular appeal to a small- or medium-sized company that wishes to raise equity capital.

The company sets up a trust under an agreement by which the trust buys shares of the company itself. The trust borrows from a bank a sum of money sufficient to purchase an agreed number of shares of company stock which are for the benefit of participating employees. The company issues shares of its stock to the trust and receives money from the trust thereby increasing its equity capital. Generally, the bank requires the trust to turn over the shares of company stock to it as collateral for the loan. The company pays into the trust, over an agreed time period, funds to pay off the bank loan and interest. When the loan is paid off, the bank returns the stock to the trust which then credits shares to each employee's account according to a given formula (generally related to employee's salary). When the employee retires or otherwise leaves the company, he takes possession of the stock shares or he may sell them back to the trust.

The principal advantage to the company is that it can obtain loan funds indirectly through the trust which it pays back with pre-tax dollars. The principal of a direct bank loan would have to be paid back out of taxable earnings. Presumably the company also gains because the employees acquire an ownership stake in the business. The employees' benefit is the stock they receive without any monetary expenditure.

Employment Security and Unemployment Pay

A protracted period of unemployment can spell severe hardship for the individual and his family. Except for periods of wartime, the United States has been plagued by chronically high unemployment. Economists have generally considered full employment to mean an unemployment rate in the range of 4.0–4.5 percent. Yet during all the years 1970 through 1979 the unemployment rate in the country as a whole never dropped below 4.9 percent. Mostly it fluctuated in the 6 to 7 percent range.

Basic protection against income loss is provided by the unemployment insurance system created by the Social Security Act of 1935. This law provided an incentive for all states to adopt unemployment insurance laws that met Federal standards. The Federal guidelines allow the states considerable latitude in setting benefit levels and durations as well as eligibility requirements. Benefits average about 50 percent of the individuals' previous earnings up to a maximum specified in each state's law. In 1977 these maximums varied among the states from $80 to $150 per week. The maximum benefit duration in most states is 26 weeks. Unemployment insurance is financed by a payroll tax paid by the employer. In five states the employee also pays a small tax on his earnings. "Experience rating" is used to adjust each individual company's payroll tax rate. If the company has stable employment with no layoffs the rate becomes quite low (say 1.0 percent). If an employer has unstable employment with large layoffs, his tax rate can jump up to 3–4 percent.

Some companies have established programs to supplement the modest benefits paid by state unemployment insurance. Often these have been created as a result of union bargaining demands as in the steel and automobile industries where layoffs occur rather often. In some other firms the managements, on their own initiative, have set up guaranteed employment plans to remove the specter of unemployment from the workers' minds.

Supplemental Unemployment Benefits. About two million employees in the automobile, steel, farm equipment, can manufacturing, rubber, and glass industries are covered by supplemental unemployment benefits (SUB) plans. These plans add to the amount of money an unemployed worker receives from the regular state unemployment compensation program to bring his total benefit up to a specified percentage of his regular wage.

There are two types of SUB plans: the insurance fund and the individual account or income-security plan. The latter is principally found in the glass industry; most of the others are insurance-fund plans.

In an insurance-fund plan the company contributes a certain number of cents per hour for all labor hours worked to a trust fund. Company contributions continue until the trust fund reaches a designated maximum level. If withdrawals to pay benefits reduce the amount in the fund below this level, then company contributions are resumed. The liability of the employer does not extend beyond the assets in the fund and the cents per hour contribution. Benefits vary somewhat from industry to industry. The plans in the automobile industry add to the states' unemployment compensation payments to bring the laid-off worker's combined income to 95 percent of his after-tax pay (less $7.50 for work-related expenses such as transportation and work clothing that are not incurred during layoff) up to a maximum of 52 weeks. The number of weeks of benefit each worker receives depends upon his length of service and upon the company's trust fund position (the amount in the fund compared to its maximum). Benefits are paid for a genuine layoff. Employees are not paid if suspended or discharged for cause, or if out on strike. The auto industry plans also provide for lump-sum separation payments for those on layoff at least 12 months. Depending on one's length of service this can vary in amount from 50 hour's separation pay on up to 2,080 hours after 30 years of service.

The individual account plans, also called income security or savings plans, provide for an individual account being set up for each employee. A specified number of cents per hours is contributed to the account for each hour worked. Each person has a vested right to the money in his or her account and may withdraw it if he is laid off or sick, retires, or leaves the company. These plans are in no way related to the benefits received under state unemployment compensation.

SUB plans are of greatest value to employees possessing a moderate amount of seniority. Very low-seniority workers obtain either no benefits or else benefits of very limited duration. Long-service employees are rarely laid off anyway, so they have little need for a SUB program.

Separation Pay. A survey by The Conference Board of 1600 companies distributed across various industrial classifications showed that 56 percent of the firms had separation pay plans for their office employees and 35 percent had plans for their nonoffice personnel. Such plans were more prevalent in large than small firms.[19] To obtain separation pay the termination of employment must usually be permanent, it must be initiated by the company and it will not be paid if the individual was discharged for just cause. Separation pay benefits tend to be quite modest. For those having less than five years of service the allowance is typically just two weeks pay. For longer service personnel the benefit is most often one week's pay for each year of service.

Guaranteed Employment and Wage Plans. So far we have been talking about private company and union programs to provide payments to unemployed workers. Now we shall talk about plans designed to keep people on the job or to provide them with a guaranteed annual wage.

[19] Meyer and Fox, op. cit., pp. 78–80.

Only a few corporations have seen fit to offer their employees either a guaranteed annual wage or guaranteed employment. Three long-standing and prominent plans are those of George A. Hormel & Company, the Nunn-Bush Shoe Company, and the Procter and Gamble Company. These plans were established in the 1920's. In the 1950's the Lincoln Electric Company established a guaranteed employment plan. Although several other companies have plans, we shall discuss only these.

The Hormel Company is a meat-packing concern in Minnesota. About 80 percent of the employees are covered. The employees are assured 52 regular, almost equal, weekly paychecks each year regardless of the fact that their hours of work may fluctuate from week to week. Overtime in excess of 40 hours in a week is paid at straight time under the guaranteed annual wage provisions of the Fair Labor Standards Act.

The Nunn-Bush Shoe Company has a flexible wage plan combined with guaranteed employment. Those having five or more years of service are guaranteed 52 weeks of employment a year. Those with less service receive a lesser guarantee. Each worker is assigned a yearly wage. He receives 1/52 of this each week. The total labor cost of the company is standardized, on the basis of past experience, as a certain percentage of the value of production for the year.

The Procter and Gamble plan guarantees 48 weeks of employment each year to all hourly workers having at least two years of service. Subtracted from this 48 weeks is time lost due to holidays, vacations, disability, voluntary absence, and emergencies. The company also has the option to reduce hours of work to 75 percent of normal. The plan makes no guarantee of an annual wage.

The Lincoln Electric Company, previously mentioned, has long been famed for its unique and highly successful wage incentive and profit sharing systems. Less known is its guaranteed annual employment plan.

After a seven-year test of a no-layoff policy, in 1958 the Lincoln Electric Company issued a formal guarantee of continuous employment for all its regular employees. This guarantee promises 49 weeks of work each year, of at least 30 hours per week. The remaining three weeks are a paid vacation. Employees are not guaranteed a particular work assignment or wage rate. The company commitment covers all full-time employees having at least two years' continuous company service. The company has always honored this guarantee of employment. Since 1958, working hours have averaged about 2,000 per year per employee. Among the many techniques the company utilizes to maintain full employment when sales volume temporarily declines are the introduction of new products, building products for inventory, and transferring workers to other jobs.

From 1958 to 1971 productivity at Lincoln Electric grew at the rate of 5.5 percent a year, well above the average of all manufacturing industry. Lincoln's management believes that the guarantee of annual employment stimulates workers to cooperate with management in raising productivity. They do not have to worry about being laid-off as a result of cost saving improvements.[20]

[20] Further information on Lincoln Electric Company's program is contained in Robert Zager, "Managing Guaranteed Employment," *Harvard Business Review*, Vol 56, No. 3 (May–June 1978), pp. 103–115.

Other Benefits and Services

In the aggregate a large number of benefits and services are provided employees, with considerable variation from organization to organization in the items offered. We shall mention here some of the more prevalent ones.

Cafeterias. Employers very commonly operate cafeterias for their employees especially where the location of the organization is not proximate to regular commercial restaurants. Often the employer will subsidize the cafeteria in order to keep food prices reasonable. Management recognizes the contribution to employee health and morale that can result from a well run food service.

Moving Expenses. Whenever a company transfers employees to jobs at a company facility in another geographical area, it almost always pays the moving expenses of the employee and his family. Many employers also pay the moving expenses for newly hired employees (especially salaried ones) who must relocate to take the job.

Credit Union. A credit union is a cooperative association designed to promote thrift among its members and to make loans to members. It is similar to a bank. There are over 23,000 credit unions in the United States. Credit unions under Federal law are classified as nonprofit cooperatives and are tax exempt. Although a credit union is organized and operated primarily by a group of employees, it is considered to be a company service because management often supplies free office space and encourages its establishment and operation.

Service Awards. To reward loyalty and to build commitment to the organization many companies award jewelry items (lapel pins, watches, rings, silver bowls, etc.), usually inscribed with the company name or logotype, upon the attainment of significant numbers of years of service such as 10, 20 and 25 years.

Social and Recreational Programs. The extent of social and recreational programs can range from establishments that have a simple Christmas party each year to those that offer a vast array of athletic facilities, hobby clubs, socials, open houses, and family get-togethers. The purpose of having such activities, from management's viewpoint, is usually to generate an enhanced feeling of belonging, to improve morale, and to develop greater company loyalty. Experience reveals that social and recreational programs are most successful when interested employees play an active part in organizing and running the individual activities.

Holidays and Vacations

The historical trend in America has been one of declining hours of work per week and per year and greater leisure time. In the 1870's the average work week was about 53 hours. In 1930 it was 47.7 hours. After the passage of the Fair Labor Standards Act in 1938, which requires payment of rate and one half for all hours over 40 worked in one week, the work week has tended to be standardized at 40 hours.[21] During wartime periods the average work week has gone above 40 hours. During business recessions it has dropped below this figure. But it has tended to hover about the 40-hour figure for over forty years.

Prior to World War II, hourly employees were generally granted three to five holidays per year but without pay. Directives by the National War Labor Board in labor-management dispute cases during the 1942–1945 period brought about the practice of paid holidays. According to a Conference Board survey of 1900 companies distributed among many industrial classifications, the typical company in 1974 granted its employees nine paid holidays.[22]

Before 1940 paid vacations for hourly employees in private industry were uncommon. If they received a vacation, it was usually for one week without pay. Office and managerial personnel generally did receive a one- or two-week paid vacation in that era. Nowadays the practice of granting paid vacations in all types of employment and industries (except agriculture and construction) is nearly universal. Hourly workers usually get a one-week paid vacation after one year of service and two weeks after two or three years of service. Both hourly paid and office workers typically are entitled to three weeks paid vacation after ten or fifteen years of service and four weeks after twenty years. Some companies grant five weeks vacation after twenty-five years of service and six weeks after thirty years.

Since 1963 employees in bargaining units covered by the United Steelworkers Union in the steel, aluminum, and can manufacturing industries have been entitled to thirteen-week sabbatical leaves once every five years.

Cafeteria Benefits

The cafeteria approach to benefit plan administration has been proposed as a way of meeting the differing needs and wants of employees. Under this concept each employee is granted the right to select his own benefits from among all those offered by the company. For example, a young employee with a wife and children might wish to have the most comprehensive health insurance coverage available including major medical, dental, eyeglass and prescription drug options. On the other hand an older employee may wish to avail himself of a supplement to the normal retirement benefit. Some individuals might also choose to take cash in place of a given benefit.

Certain constraints may be imposed. The sum total of benefits available to an individual must be within a uniform dollar limit (or percentage of salary limit) applied to all employees. Also, all employees may be required to take certain basic benefit coverages such as life insurance.

Although the idea of individual choice is intriguing, the cafeteria approach to benefit-plan administration has attracted very few corporate adherents to date. Three organizations that do have such programs are the American Can Company, TRW, Inc., and the Educational Testing Service.[23] Deterrents to the es-

---

[21] Geoffrey H. Moore and Janice N. Hedges, "Trends in Labor and Leisure," *Monthly Labor Review*, Vol. 94, No. 2 (February 1971), pp. 3–11.

[22] Meyer and Fox, op. cit., pp. 95–97.

[23] "New Life for Flexible Compensation," *Dun's Review*, Vol. 112, No. 3 (September 1978), pp. 66–70.

tablishment of these flexible programs have been restrictive Internal Revenue Service regulations and the administrative complexity of allowing individual choice among a broad array of benefits and options.

ALTERNATIVE WORK SCHEDULES

Ever since the enactment of the Fair Labor Standards Act in 1938, the 5 day-40 hour workweek has been widely accepted as standard in the United States. When the volume of work becomes heavy for a few weeks or months, management may require employees to work more than 40 hours or more than 5 days per week, at overtime rates of pay. Or when work is slack, a firm may reduce the hours per week below forty. But both of these conditions are considered temporary. Five days and forty hours have been still considered the normal work week. However, commencing in the late 1960's and early 1970's many private companies and government agencies have experimented with alternative work schedules. We shall discuss three of these: flexitime, compressed workweek, and job sharing.

Flexitime

Flexitime, sometimes called flexible hours, was first introduced in 1967 at the Messerschmidt Research and Development Center near Munich, Germany. It has spread fairly rapidly throughout European countries. It is estimated that about one third of the labor force in Switzerland, 5 to 10 percent of the white-collar labor force in West Germany, and a total of about one million workers in England, France, Scandinavia, and other European countries work under a flexitime system. Most applications in the United States have occurred since 1973.[24] In the United States flexitime is used by many companies, including Control Data Corporation, Northwestern Mutual Life Insurance Company, and the Nestle Company[25] and in many governmental agencies, including the Social Security Administration.

Flexitime works this way. Within a prescribed band of time in the morning, usually between 7:00 and 9:30 a.m., employees are free to choose their own starting time. Also they are free to leave within a prescribed band of time at the end of the workday, usually between 3:00 and 6:00 p.m. All employees are required to be at work during a core time of say 9:30 a.m. to 3:00 p.m. This means that the workday can vary from day to day in its length as well as the time at which it begins and ends. Each worker makes an agreement with his supervisor to put in the total required number of hours per day, per week, or per month. This time period varies from one installation to another.

The initiative in launching programs for flexible hours of work has generally come from management. Labor union leaders, particularly in the United States, have been wary of it. Because of overtime regulations of the Fair Labor Standards Act (time and one-half after 40 hours in one week) and the Walsh–Healey

[24] John D. Owen, "Flexitime: Some Problems and Solutions," *Industrial and Labor Relations Review*, Vol. 30, No. 2 (January 1977), pp. 152–160.
[25] *Wall Street Journal* (April 13, 1976), p. 1.

Act (time and one-half after 8 hours per day and 40 hours per week for government contractors), the flexibility of hours worked is more limited in the United States than in many European countries.

Management's purposes in introducing flexible hours are generally to raise employee morale and to cut down on tardiness and absenteeism. Various research investigations into flexitime applications have nearly always revealed strong support from employees who have worked under the system. They can set their working hours to avoid the traffic crunch of commuters, they are better able to attend to personal business such as shopping, banking, and dealing with public agencies during regular work days. Working mothers are better able to get their children off to school in the morning. Employees like the opportunity to control their own hours of work. Several studies show that the introduction of flexitime has reduced tardiness and absenteeism.

Management is best able to apply flexible hours of work in departments where there does not need to be a continuous flow of work from one employee to another. This means that it is often easier to use in white collar and service type jobs than in direct production work.

Compressed Workweek

In the early 1970's there was a flurry of interest in the compressed workweek–often called the 4-day or occasionally the 3-day workweek. In going to a 4-day week some companies retained weekly hours at 40 (thus ten-hour days), whereas others scheduled eight- or nine-hour days.

By 1972, 1,000 organizations had adopted the four-day work week.[26] However, interest soon leveled off and by mid-1974 only about 2 percent of full-time employees of U.S. firms were working on compressed work weeks.[27]

Just as with flexitime, the principal impetus for shifting to a compressed work week has come from management. Managers have sought to reduce costs through higher productivity by reducing the percentage of total working time devoted to start-up and shut-down activities. In some instances ten-hour work days have nicely corresponded to the pattern of workload demand, as in the case of certain retail and service establishments. Other objectives have been to reduce absenteeism and turnover and to raise employee morale.

Employees have often preferred a four-day work week because this gives them three-day weekends. Also, they make fewer round trips to work each week. Thus, total commuting time and cost is reduced. Early experience with the four-day week was positive in many companies. There was better morale, lower absenteeism and turnover, higher productivity, and lower costs. However, longer trials for some organizations demonstrated that it was really the Hawthorne effect they were witnessing.[28] The benefits were temporary.

[26] *New York Times* (July 16, 1972).
[27] U.S. Department of Labor, Bureau of Labor Statistics. *The Revised Workweek: Results of a Pilot Study of 16 Firms*, Bulletin 1846 (Washington, D.C.: Government Printing Office, 1975).
[28] This term comes from the Hawthorne studies at the Western Electric Company during 1927–1932, where gains in productivity, which had been initially attributed to improvements in working conditions, were later found to have been caused by workers' sense of involvement in a novel experiment.

Job Sharing

Job sharing is a pattern of work in which two employees, each working one-half time, share responsibility for performing one full time job. Each person has a permanent, part-time job. Salary and fringe benefits are prorated according to the number of hours worked.

Job sharing is new. To date it has been applied in only a few organizations. It appeals to married women with family responsibilities who can really only work a few hours per day. For employers this pattern of shared jobs makes sense in times of labor shortages for particular skills and as a way of accommodating to needs of certain employees. It has been successfully used by local governments in the San Francisco Bay area for such jobs as secretary, librarian, social worker, and receptionist.[29]

Questions for review and discussion

1. What factors have caused benefit and service programs to grow substantially since the period around 1940?
2. Do you believe that benefits and services should be considered a part of compensation that employees have earned by working at their jobs, or do you feel that they represent something extra that the employer is giving his employees? Justify your position.
3. Classify and give examples of the principal kinds of employee benefits and services.
4. What factors motivate the top management of a company to adopt benefit and service programs? What a factors must be weighed when deciding whether a particular program should be established?
5. For a given cost for a particular group insurance program, why might it be cheaper for the company to pay the cost than for the employees to do so?
6. What factors led to the passage by Congress of the Employee Retirement Income Security Act of 1974? Give the principal provisions of the Act relating to vesting, funding, reporting and disclosure, and plan terminations.
7. What is an ESOP (Kelso plan)?
8. How does group insurance differ from individually purchased insurance?
9. Discuss the contradictory forces at work in our society toward early retirement before age 65 and late retirement after age 65.
10. Why might the top management of an industrial company decide to establish a guaranteed annual employment program? What techniques can be used to achieve stable employment in a firm?
11. Why has there been considerable interest in recent years in alternative work schedules such as flexitime, compressed workweeks, and job sharing?

---

[29] *Alternative Work Schedules,* EEO-Information on Equal Employment Opportunity for State and Local Governments, Issue No. 17 (Washington, D.C.: U.S. Civil Service Commission, Undated).

CASE PROBLEM

Your company and the union representing non-exempt white collar employees are in the midst of negotiations for a new union-employer agreement. In addition to its wage increase proposal, the union has made the following proposals for improvements in fringe benefits.

a. Three days personal leave per year for handling personal business matters which ordinarily are difficult or impossible to attend to during non-working hours.

b. Dental insurance, fully paid by the company, for the employee and his family.

c. Two days religious holiday leave per year. The official religious holidays for some religions, e.g. Jewish faith, fall on days other than Christmas and Easter.

d. A sick leave bank. Each employee would contribute one day per year to a sick leave bank out of his alloted annual sick leave days. If any employee should use up his or her sick leave days due to a long illness, he could apply for extra days from the sick leave bank.

e. Five weeks vacation after 15 years of service. Currently the company-union labor agreement provides for two weeks after one year of service, 3 weeks after 10 years of service, and 4 weeks after 20 years of service.

Questions

1. Assuming that you are the director of industrial relations for the company, what factors would you use to guide your decision with regard to each of these bargaining proposals? What information would you seek?

2. How would you calculate the cost to the company of each item?

3. Once the union and management have agreed upon a total dollar cost for the settlement of the contract negotiations for pay increases and benefits improvement combined, would it be acceptable to management to allow the union considerable discretion in deciding the relative distribution of that total sum of money among a direct pay increase and the various benefits it has proposed?

Suggestions for further reading

FREEDMAN, AUDREY. "Reexamining Income Security: SUB vs. Guaranteed Work," *The Conference Board Record*, Vol. XIII, No. 5 (May 1976), pp. 20–23.

GLICKMAN, ALBERT S. and ZENIA H. BROWN. *Changing Schedules of Work: Patterns and Implications.* Kalamazoo, Mich.: W. E. Upjohn Institute for Employment Research, 1974.

HEDGES, JANICE N. "Flexible Schedules: Problems and Issues," *Monthly Labor Review*, Vol. 100, No. 2 (February 1977), pp. 62–65.

MINER, MARY G. *Paid Holiday and Vacation Policies.* Personnel Policies Forum, No. 115, Washington, D.C.: Bureau of National Affairs, 1976.

NILAND, POWELL. "Reforming Private Pension Plan Administration," *Business Horizons,* Vol. 19, No. 1 (February 1976), pp. 25–35.

REJDA, GEORGE E. *Social Insurance and Economic Security.* Englewood Cliffs, N.J.: Prentice Hall, Inc., 1976.

SKOLNICK, ALFRED M. "Twenty-Five Years of Employee-Benefit Plans," *Social Security Bulletin*, Vol. 39, No. 9 (September 1976), pp. 3–21.

SMEDLEY, LAWRENCE T. "The Patterns of Early Retirement," *AFL-CIO American Federationist*, Vol. 81, No. 1 (January 1974), pp. 1–5.

TEAGUE, BURTON W. "In Review of the ESOP Fable," *The Conference Board Record*, Vol. XIII, No. 2 (February 1976), pp. 10–13.

WEEKS, DAVID A. *Rethinking Employee Benefits Assumptions.* Report No. 739, New York: The Conference Board, 1978.

VIII

PERSPECTIVES

Personnel management in perspective

The process of managing any organization requires knowledge and skills in the economic, technical, and human relations spheres. The effective manager must possess real understanding of the nature of people, the determinants of interpersonal effectiveness, and the ramifications of intergroup relations.

The key to organization building is to invest in human resources. This is true whether we are talking about a university, an industrial corporation, a city government, or a military force. Many top executives are ignorant of this vital concept. They concentrate their attention so heavily upon the technical phases of the business (such as the details of new product development, financial controls, or marketing) that they neglect investment in their people.

How does an organization invest in human resources? There are many ways. At an elementary level it consists of investment in a decent, healthful, and safe working environment. Beyond this it means offering attractive wages and job opportunities so that the establishment can attract competent employees. If management pays wages well below competitive rates, it cannot hope to build a really vigorous organization. The viable company devotes continuous attention to the education and training of its employees. I have observed time and again that differences in this one dimension—education and training—correlate significantly with the degree of effectiveness and success of organizations. Emphasis

685

upon the development of people means such things as comprehensive in-house training, reimbursement of employees' tuition costs at neighboring colleges and universities, sending managers and engineers to professional seminars, circulating professional and technical journals within the company, and sending executives to advanced-management university programs. Investment in human resources also means providing a day-to-day climate where people are encouraged to make decisions and accept responsibility. It means supportive supervision and effective appraisal and coaching. Fundamentally, effective management depends upon the existence of an underlying philosophy that people-centered and achievement-oriented management is what really counts.

We have shown in this book that the practice of personnel management comprises two stems. The first is that component—the management of people at work—which pervades the entire organization. The president cannot hire a personnel director to handle all the human problems of management so that he can concentrate upon financial and technical activities. Personnel management and general management are intimately related. Operating executives cannot abdicate their very considerable responsibilities for selecting, developing, motivating, and leading people as they carry on their daily activities.

The second main stem of personnel management is that carried on and guided by the staff personnel department. This work entails the development and dissemination of personnel policies, provision of specialized services and counsel to the whole corporation, and the application of control measures to regulate the human resources climate. The work content of the personnel office is centered in such prime functions as organization and human resource planning, employment, labor relations, health and safety, education, benefits and services, and pay administration. Many who study the field of personnel, organizational behavior, and industrial relations intend to make it their vocation. It holds promising career opportunities. Let us now look into personnel work as a career.

PERSONNEL AND INDUSTRIAL RELATIONS AS A CAREER

Those desiring to pursue careers in personnel and industrial relations should obtain a college education. This field has not achieved the degree of specialized professionalism that medicine and law have. Thus, there is no single pattern of education that is specified for entry into this career. Nearly all of the universities and many of the colleges in the United States offer courses and integrated programs of study in personnel management, industrial relations, and organizational behavior. Administratively these programs are given in schools of business administration, management, and industrial relations. In addition to majors in personnel, industrial relations, and organizational behavior, students ought to obtain a thorough grounding in general studies with special emphasis upon the social sciences (sociology, psychology, political science, and economics). In the applied business administration field they ought also to take courses in statistics, data processing, finance, production, business policy, and the social and legal environment of business. For those who wish to pursue careers in technical industries, a baccalaureate degree in engineering followed by a master's degree in business administration is a very sound educational plan. Some who wish to specialize in labor relations and collective bargaining may study liberal arts or business administration at the undergraduate level and then go to law school for their graduate work.

Beginning or entry-level positions in this field are such jobs as job analyst, employment interviewer, personnel trainee, training specialist, and labor-relations specialist. Actually, for the recent college graduate there are several routes for entry into personnel work. He may be hired by a company directly into one of the entry-level positions. Some of our larger corporations such as the General Electric Company and others have formal training programs in employee relations. Another very common route is for the young college graduate to be hired initially into some other activity such as manufacturing or operations and then transfer to the personnel–industrial relations department within a few years. This latter approach has the advantage of orienting the individual to the technology of the company, to its policies, and to its people.

Position Levels

In the large corporation there are three principal levels of positions in personnel–industrial relations. First there is the specialist level. The specialist level includes the entry-level jobs previously mentioned plus the professional specialists such as physician, nurse, psychologist, safety engineer, labor lawyer, and personnel researcher. Many of the professional specialist positions require advanced education and training. In prestige, rank, and salary certain of these such as the physician, psychologist, and labor lawyer are equivalent to middle management in the large company. The second or next level of positions consists of the managers in charge of the various functional branches of personnel. Thus, we find the manager or supervisor of labor relations, the manager of employment, and the manager of wage and salary administration. In the organization hierarchy these people are part of middle management. In addition to their managerial abilities, they must possess considerable knowledge and skill in the functional personnel specialty they are supervising. A manager of employment must know a great deal about sources of supply, selection testing, interviewing, job specifications, manpower planning, and selective placement.

The third level of position in personnel in the big company is the top management or major executive level. The executive in charge of personnel–industrial relations is designated most commonly as the vice-president of personnel, vice-president of industrial relations, or director of industrial relations. He typically reports to the president of the organization or to an executive vice-president. He is involved in policy formulation and administration and coordination with all major units in the corporation. He guides the development and installation of major personnel programs.

In the smaller company there would be fewer jobs and fewer levels in the personnel department. Generally one would find the director or top executive position plus certain of the functional positions. There would be less division of labor. One individual might handle all employment and training tasks. Another might be responsible for pay administration and labor relations. In the really small organization the personnel department might consist of only the manager of personnel plus his secretary.

Job Opportunities and Salaries

For those who have a reasonable amount of experience in personnel work, say three to five years or more, job opportunities are quite good. One need only read the advertisements in the *Wall Street Journal* or *The New York Times* to learn about job openings for labor relations manager, recruitment specialist, compensation manager, vice-president of employee relations, and a variety of other personnel occupations. Personnel opportunities with state and Federal governments are also rather abundant. Those lacking either special experience in the field or specialized education find it somewhat difficult to enter this career.

In 1976 a total of 335,000 people in the United States were engaged in personnel and labor relations work. Three-fourths of these were employed in the private sector and one-fourth worked for Federal, state, and local governments. The U.S. Department of Labor has forecasted that the number of persons employed in the field of personnel and labor relations will grow faster than the average for all occupations through 1985.[1] A major force causing growth in the field has been Federal legislation in the areas of equal employment opportunity, occupational safety and health, and pension plan regulation. Another important factor has been the greater recognition by managers of the need for sound human resource programs to insure the viability and strength of their enterprises.

Salaries for entry-level positions are essentially the same as those offered business administration graduates generally. This is a little lower than beginning pay for engineers and scientists. Supervisory and executive posts in employee relations command pay that is essentially equivalent to that paid other managerial positions of similar rank within the organization. Salaries for these managerial jobs correlate highly with the size of the company. The top personnel executive in a small company (under 1,000 employees) will typically be paid from $20,000 to $30,000 per year. But in the large corporation salaries will lie in the $40,000 to $75,000 range with a few going even higher.

Status and Professionalism

In many companies the personnel–industrial relations director serves as a key member of the top management group. Often he enjoys vice-presidential status. In many companies the personnel director serves as a key advisor to the president and to the whole top-management team. He carries great weight in shaping personnel policy, labor policy, formulating executive development programs, and in designing employee and executive compensation plans.

In the area of professionalism, personnel practitioners have made considerable progress. Educational programs at the university level have been mentioned previously. There are a number of professional associations that are national in scope. Among these are the Industrial Relations Research Association, the International Personnel Management Association, American Society for Personnel Administration, the American Society for Training and Development, the College and University Personnel Association, and the Personnel Division of the

---

[1] U.S. Department of Labor, Bureau of Labor Statistics *Occupational Outlook Handbook, 1978–79 Edition*, Bulletin 1955 (Washington D.C.), pp. 150–153.

American Management Associations. Active in most of the major metropolitan areas are local personnel managers associations.

In the mid-1970's the American Society for Personnel Administration set-up a program to accredit personnel and industrial relations practitioners based upon a series of examinations plus education and work experience standards. Their program provides for four types of accreditation: Personnel Diplomate, Personnel Specialist, Executive in Personnel, and Personnel Manager.

Yet there is another side to this whole picture. In far too many situations, and especially in small-sized organizations, top management staffs the personnel department with individuals of only modest capabilities and skills. Too often a person gets the position of personnel manager because he is loyal, has worked for the company a long time, is familiar with company traditions, and gets along well with others. Such an individual generally looks upon his job as one of hiring and firing workers, keeping records, and administering the cafeteria, charity drives, and company parties and picnics. One can usually recognize whether the personnel manager and his staff are assigned a low status when the personnel functions for the executive, professional, and sales groups are handled by someone else attached to the chief executive's office and collective bargaining is handled by the company's legal counsel.

When placed in proper perspective, the executive in charge of the personnel–industrial relations function should be of major executive caliber and should serve as a member of the top-management team. His counsel should play a significant part (along with that of those in other functional parts of the business) in shaping decisions pertaining to company expansion or contraction, new facilities, plant relocation, organization planning, personnel policy, labor policy, executive development, and community relations policy.

The responsibility for insuring that the chief personnel executive sits in the halls of top management rests both with the personnel profession and with chief executive officers throughout industry. The personnel profession must continuously strive to educate and train its members for higher standards of competence, and it must educate top management regarding the values and contributions of personnel management. In staffing the personnel–industrial relations department, the chief executive officer must select men with demonstrated professional competence and then give them the necessary support to be really effective.

Is personnel–industrial relations a distinct profession in the same sense as engineering and law? Or is it but a part of the broader, emerging profession of management? Does a manager who has been successful in marketing, production, or general management necessarily possess the qualifications to be a successful personnel director? Have the technical and knowledge requirements for personnel management grown to the point where only those who have had college preparation plus specific work experience in the field are qualified to assume the responsibilities of personnel director? In selecting individuals to manage engineering, accounting, and research functions, top management invariably chooses those who have professional education and work experience in these respective fields.

The author finds that the specialist and first-level supervisory positions in personnel–industrial relations are coming to demand specialized professional training. Thus, in this sense, personnel–industrial relations work is becoming a distinct profession in itself. On the other hand, the position of director of personnel–industrial relations demands skills, abilities, and aptitudes that are common to nearly all top-management work. Thus, at this level in the organization, the position requires general management talent. A top-level manager should consider that his profession is management. He may be equally effective in various managerial posts at this level. However, the executive in charge of the personnel–industrial relations function should have had considerable professional education and experience in personnel work before being placed in his position.

ACCOMPLISHMENTS AND CONTINUING NEEDS

As we come to the end of this book it is pertinent to review briefly the accomplishments in the personnel field to date and to highlight some of the principal unsolved or persistent problems that must command the attention of theorists, policy makers, and practitioners in the future.

In discussing progress that has been achieved, it should be borne in mind that we are making generalizations. The actual state of affairs in particular enterprises may deviate widely from the levels depicted. Specifically, many companies do fall short of the levels described.

Personnel Practices

The practice of personnel management in business and public institutions has grown from infancy to young adulthood in the past sixty years. For the most part organized hiring, training, and wage administration programs were nonexistent sixty years ago. Most of these functions were done very haphazardly by line supervision. The organized safety movement was just getting started in 1913. Pensions and health insurance were provided by only a handful of companies throughout the nation. Paid vacations for hourly workers generally did not exist.

Today employee selection is handled by means of planned interviews, validated selection tests, medical examinations, and background investigations. Many of the large corporations are using assessment centers to identify persons with management potential. Management recognizes that new employees do not learn well by looking over the shoulders of older workers, but rather they must go through a planned training effort. Management also recognizes that long years of experience as an individual contributor do not automatically qualify one for promotion to supervision. Nowadays both potential and practicing supervisors are given classroom and on-the-job training in management fundamentals. Rational wage determination via job evaluation, formal pay structures, and wage surveys has become well accepted throughout industry. Nine paid holidays and two to three weeks paid vacation per year are now commonplace. Four weeks vacation after fifteen years of service is becoming increasingly popular. Comprehensive health and dental insurance, paid partially or entirely by the employer, is now widespread. Group life insurance, weekly disability benefits, pensions, and separation pay have all become well established by the late 1970's.

Whereas a few years ago personnel specialists devoted most of their attention to the problems of blue-collar workers, more recently they have properly taken cognizance of the change in the composition of the work force and are now achieving a sophistication in developing programs for managerial and professional personnel.

Problems and Needs.   There is need for small business firms to upgrade their personnel practices and benefit programs. Lacking specialized personnel staffs, many small companies have only a rudimentary personnel program. Millions of Americans who are employed in small businesses have no pension plan coverage whatever (other than legally mandated Social Security).

Personnel executives need to examine their various programs and practices to determine if they continue to meet contemporary needs and goals. Much "me-too-ism" prevails in the personnel field. It is not always necessary to follow the latest fashion in regard to training and motivational techniques. For example, zero-defects programs that were so popular in the 1960's are all but forgotten now.

Whereas many companies have built sound financial compensation programs from the standpoint of equity and consistency, relatively few have done a good job of designing their pay programs from a motivational or total systems incentive framework. Also they have not adequately integrated nonfinancial with financial incentives.

A persistent problem in many companies and many industries is that of periodic employee layoffs. In attitude surveys workers always rate job security as an important need. Yet this motive is frustrated quite frequently. Company officials need to give more thought to methods of regularizing employment. Some layoffs are however inevitable. Better and more liberal income maintenance benefits ought to be provided for the affected employees.

Health and Safety

Unquestionably American industry has accomplished a great deal over the years toward providing a safe workplace. However, serious problems remain.

National statistics show that the injury frequency rate climbed steadily throughout the 1960's. A rising awareness of a serious workplace safety and health problem caused Congress to pass the Occupational Safety and Health Act in 1970. However, national injury statistics do not reveal any substantial improvement in national injury experience since enactment of this law.

During the 1970's authorities began to recognize that hundreds and even thousands of workers in many occupations and many industries were becoming victims of occupational diseases. Mesothelioma (caused by asbestos dust), byssinosis (caused by cotton dust), and pneumoconiosis (caused by coal dust) are just a few diseases that have received prominent attention in recent years. Hundreds of new chemicals are put on the market each year. Many of these are toxic. The latency period for the emergence of symptoms for the diseases caused by these substances often is long. Hence it can be hard to prove cause and effect. Far more effort and resources must be directed to the occupational disease problem.

Another area for concern is the genarally poor performance of small business in job health and safety.

Mental health as it may be affected by one's job is an area that has been insufficiently recognized. The real stake that the employer has in controlling worker alcoholism is just beginning to be understood.

Personnel Research

A great deal of research—both university and company based—has been conducted over the past thirty to forty years. Research findings are available in many areas of concern to the people-oriented manager. To identify just a few, significant research-based knowledge has been developed in the areas of absenteeism, motivation, morale, performance appraisal, the problems of the professional employee in industry, organization design, communication, accident causes, industrial toxicology and medicine, and pay incentives.

Some of the larger corporations have established their own research units to conduct investigations into human resource areas. Prominent among these is the Behavioral Research Service of the General Electric Company. Texas Instruments, Procter and Gamble, and General Motors also have units devoted to behavioral and personnel research.

The problems encountered in such research are complex and the results obtained are occasionally contradictory; nevertheless, substantial progress is being made. Managers nowadays need rely less and less upon trial and error and rule of thumb.

Problems and Needs. Despite the progress much more research in the human resources field needs to be done by corporations themselves. Compared to funds spent on products and hardware the amounts spent on organizational social systems are minuscule. "In-house" research results need to be more adequately reported in professional and scientific journals so that others may benefit and so that dialogue between university contributors and industry researchers may be enhanced.

Here are a few of the more pressing needs for more research. In the area of selection testing we need culture-fair tests to overcome the problem of unintentional discrimination against minorities. The state of the art of personality testing is still inadequate. We need to know much more about how to make the interview contribute to the validity of a hiring decision. Job design is developing into an exciting area for research. Job design and organizational design must be related in a more effective way. The accounting profession is trying to develop a useful system of human resource valuation so that human assets can be more objectively figured into corporate planning. The personnel profession must work closely with the accountants to help accomplish this difficult task.

Knowledge about conflict resolution is just beginning to be generated. This needs to focus upon all facets—interpersonal, intragroup, intergroup, and interorganization.

The relationship between the culture of the organization and of groups within the organization to styles of leadership and organizational practices needs to be more thoroughly explored. Despite the outpouring of articles and monographs about worker alienation, much more research needs to be done in this area.

Union–Management Relations

Until the late 1930's union–management relations, for the most part, featured labor spies, strikebreakers, discharge of union sympathizers, picket line violence, uncompromising employers, and militant union leaders.

Today, thanks to a generous assist from Federal labor legislation, organized labor has won its battles for recognition and acceptance as equals in dealings with management spokesmen. The old-time deep-seated hostility on the part of management and militancy on the part of union officials has largely disappeared. To the casual observer the modern sophisticated union official is indistinguishable from his management counterpart when seated around the conference table.

The union movement has largely won most of its longtime struggles for decent wages, shorter hours, seniority and job rights, a voice in workload determination, and employee security benefits. Agricultural employment is an exception. Disagreements arising over the administration and interpretation of the labor agreement are settled peacefully by use of voluntary labor arbitration.

Another hopeful sign of mature relations in conflict resolution has been the agreement between the United Steelworkers Union and major steel-producing companies to submit impasses in future contract negotiations to binding arbitration rather than go through the usual route of a strike.

Problems and Needs. Although the days of open warfare between organized labor and management have happily passed into history, and although countless relationships have matured into a cooperative atmosphere, to a considerable extent the picture bears many of the characteristics of an uneasy truce. Many American managements have never really accepted unionism as a necessary and permanent institution. They yearn for the day when management can rid itself of the interferences and challenges caused by unionism. Many managements feel that they know what is best for their employees and that union leaders do not truly represent the interests of their constituents.

For their part many union leaders have not altered their philosophy, derived from the days of open conflict, to conform to the realities of the 1970's and 1980's. They have not been sufficiently adaptable to meet the problems of a newer age. At times they have ignored the long-range consequences of their actions upon the prosperity of business, wage-price levels, and employment. Organized labor has been slow to advance educated young men and women with new ideas to positions of leadership.

Increasingly in recent years, because of the interdependent nature of our society, union strikes against employers tend to also become strikes against the general public because its goods and services are shut off.

Collective bargaining in the public sector has now become an accepted institution for the Federal government and for about half of the states. Yet experience in the private sector has not always been the best guide for policy in the public sector. For example, the unit of government that negotiates labor agreeements—the executive branch—does not have authority to appropriate the funds to pay for the settlement. This is a legislative function. The issue of sovereignty of government and what to do about strikes has not been worked out effectively. Public-employee strikes are banned by statute in most jurisdictions yet strikes occasionally occur anyway. How should these be handled and how should striking public employees be treated? Several states have legalized public employee strikes if no emergency or major inconvenience is involved. Should other states follow their lead? Members of management, from foremen on up, are generally denied the right of collective-bargaining representation in private industry. Yet lower- and middle-level administrators in government often are unionized. Should this pattern continue in the future?

Ethics and Values

Problems and Needs. The whole field of ethics and values in management and in human relations practices in work organizations has received insufficient attention. Periodically there is a public outcry about deceptive business practices, stock manipulations, conflict of interest transactions, and fraud perpetrated by buccaneer businessmen. But these affairs concern mostly investors, corporate officers, customers, suppliers and government regulatory agencies. There is less public knowledge of unethical and improper practices in the management of people within enterprises.

There needs to be a much more careful examination of values within the organization, that is, of values and standards of conduct among managers, employees, and union. What are the value implications of the internal struggles for power within the organization? Can executives justify the sabotaging of another person's career in order to advance their own? Is it right for top management to seek to destroy the very union that the employees have chosen, in a democratic election, to represent them in dealings with management?

What should management do with the faithful, long-service employee who can no longer cope with an enlarged and complex job? Changes in technology and advances in the state of an art often proceed faster than some engineers and supervisors can accommodate. Should management discard these people? Or should it give them a sinecure and design the organization so that the work flows away from them?

How can ethical standards be adopted, accepted, and enforced? How can they be upgraded? Do managers as a leadership elite have a mission to develop higher standards of conduct? Or is their day-to-day behavior merely a reflection of the prevailing standards of society?

Some measures would help in these matters. We need searching examinations of the current situation by associations representing management generally. We also need a similar study by the personnel–industrial relations profession. Codes of ethics and standards of conduct need to be formulated, agreed upon, promulgated, and enforced. These actions are much easier said than done. There are several professional societies active in the general management field and in the personnel–industrial area. Lacking is a unified voice as exists in medicine, law, psychology, architecture, and other professions. In 1958 the American Society for Personnel Administration adopted a code of ethics. However, this statement is very general and it has not been widely publicized.

In the traditional self-employed professions the client, who needs to be protected by standards of conduct, is well known and easily identified. But who is the client of the personnel officer in a bureaucratic organization? Is it the employer or is it the employee?

Constitutionalism and Organizational Justice

Historically in the United States employee rights were accorded a status distinctly subservient to the rights of employers. The property rights of ownership reigned supreme. The unilateral right of an employer to hire and fire at will and to operate his business as he saw fit was largely assumed and unchallenged.

But in recent years private business has begun to accord greater protection, security, and rights to employees. This change has developed as a consequence of protective labor legislation, unionism, and a changed social attitude on the part of management. As a consequence of the laws and regulations governing equal employment opportunity and age discrimination, it is illegal for employers to discriminate against individuals in regard to hiring, compensation, or terms of employment because of race, color, religion, sex, national origin, or age.

The presence of unions has resulted in greater job rights for workers. Layoffs are generally determined by seniority. An employee can appeal his grievances through a formal grievance procedure and even get a hearing before an impartial arbitrator. Discipline and discharge must be handled by due process procedures. process procedures.

The labor-relations law of the land prevents discrimination or discharge solely because of a person's union activities. In recent years court decisions have tended to grant greater recognition to job rights in cases of plant shutdowns and relocations.

The foregoing comments do not mean that employers cannot discharge a man for just cause. No one is guaranteed absolute job security regardless of his transgressions.

Problems and Needs. Despite the progress that has been made there are serious deficiencies. Some writers argue that we need to establish corporate constitutionalism or organizational justice.[2] Collective-bargaining rights cover only about one quarter of the labor force. Except for those in government service, salaried personnel are not represented by unions. Administrators, managers, and professionals are vulnerable to discharge by whim in many organizations. Honest disagreements over salary, job assignments, workloads, and promotion opportunities tend to be settled by power and authority rather than by reference to corporation policies and impartial dispute settlement procedures. Arbitration of such disagreements is almost never used.

Constitutionalism in work organizations means basically the rule of law with dispute settlement by an impartial judiciary. Written policies are the laws of an enterprise. They must deal with all the major rights, responsibilities, and problems likely to be encountered in the management of a work force. Voluntary arbitration or something comparable can serve as the impartial judiciary for the organization. The process is well established in the unionized sector. Something comparable needs to be set up in the nonunion sector.

The matters of protecting employees' privacy and providing guidelines for employee free-speech within the organization have only very recently been given consideration by a few leaders in the field of human resource management.

The issue of "whistle blowers" within work organizations has received national publicity in recent years, and deservedly so. The persecution of A. Ernest Fitzgerald, a high-level civil service management systems expert, by U.S. Department of Defense officials because he reported vast cost overruns in the

[2] See for example, Robert G. Wright, "Managing Management Resources Through Corporate Constitutionalism," *Human Resource Management,* Vol. 12, No. 2 (Summer 1973), pp. 15–23.

Lockheed C-5A air cargo plane program in the late 1960's is a cause célèbre. A whistle blower is an employee who tries to correct or make known improper or illegal practices often committed by upper level managers. Instead of being rewarded for his actions, the whistle-blower is usually downgraded, transferred, or fired.

Most employees are afraid to report possible improper actions within their own organizations. Even a high level official can have difficulty in correcting possible wrongdoing as evidenced by the two-year struggle of a public utility vice-president to rectify an improperly large (he thought) electric rate increase.[3]

The adoption of policies and procedures to provide for organizational justice would go a long way to solve this important problem.[4]

Equal Employment Opportunity

Since the mid-1960's substantial progress has been made by blacks, other ethnic minorities, and by women in obtaining more and better jobs. Under prodding by governmental equal employment opportunity enforcement officials and because of pressures by organized groups of blacks and of women, employers have substantially increased the number of minorities and women in a great many occupational classifications. The real push in recent years has been to upgrade these people into better paying skilled jobs and into management. The old stereotypes of women's jobs (nurses, secretaries, airline stewardesses) and men's jobs (policemen, managers, and engineers) are disappearing fast.

In very recent years there has been a pronounced back lash by white males. When corporations strive to meet affirmative action goals and timetables they naturally reject many qualified white males. These people, some corporate executives, and some social philosophers are charging that past wrongs must not be righted by engaging in reverse discrimination. This is a serious problem for which there are no easy answers.

Work and Leisure

Until very recently the United States has been a work-oriented society. An amalgam of factors caused this spirit. Among these have been (1) prevalence of the Protestant ethic; (2) historic liberalism with its emphasis upon personal liberty, private property, and freedom of contract; (3) the character of the European immigrants who settled this nation; (4) the emphasis upon self reliance and the entrepreneurial spirit; (5) the discipline of the industrialization process; and (6) the imperatives imposed by the Western frontier in nineteenth-century America.

There have been increasing signs in recent years of a shift in attitudes and values away from work as a central orientation and toward leisure and the pursuit of pleasure. Mechanization and the unparalleled productivity of our industrial system have made affluence and leisure available to more and more people. The

---

[3] *Wall Street Journal*, "The Whistle Blower Chooses Hard Path, Utility Story Shows," (November 8, 1978).

[4] Issues of organization justice and freedoms within an organization are addressed in Ralph Nader, Peter J. Petkas, and Kate Blackwell, *Whistle Blowing* (New York: Grossman Publishers, 1972) and David W. Ewing, *Freedom Inside the Organization* (New York: McGraw-Hill Book Company, 1978).

trend toward pleasure seeking is evidenced in the phenomenal growth of our leisure-based industries. The widespread use of narcotics and of alcohol is another manifestation of pleasure-orientation. The social ethic is supplanting the individual ethic.

How do these trends affect the work organization? Will they affect achievement motivation at the work place? Will our jobs become less central to our lives in the future? Will other institutions occupy a greater focus for the masses of people?

Quality of Working Life

A great many establishments have comprehensive personnel programs that are well managed and that provide many of the conditions that comprise a high quality of working life. Their employees are productive and they experience a considerable measure of job satisfaction.

Unfortunately, far too many enterprises badly neglect even the rudiments which make up a good quality of working life. Day-to-day treatment, pay, work loads, and promotion opportunities may be inconsistent or perceived to be unfair. Opportunities for employee growth and advancement may be minimal. Managerial leadership may be incompetent. Those engaged in the practice of personnel management ought to be more vigorous in working for improvements in the quality of working life in their organizations.

Questions for review and discussion

1. Discuss careers in personnel–industrial relations. Include fields of specialization, qualifications for employment, and status of personnel–industrial relations within the organization.
2. Is personnel–industrial relations a profession in itself or is it but a part of the larger (emerging) profession of management?
3. Explain how the prevailing practices in "the management of people at work" have matured over the past half century.
4. Give and discuss current and emerging problems in the management of people at work.
5. Do you feel that the mass of Americans are becoming less work-oriented and more leisure-time and pleasure-oriented? Discuss.
6. How do you feel the issue of "whistle blowers" should be handled by personnel executives and other top policy-making managers?

Suggestions for further reading

COLEMAN, CHARLES J. "Personnel: The Changing Function," *Public Personnel Management*, Vol. 2, No. 3 (May–June 1973), pp. 186–193.

DAY, VIRGIL B. "Managing Human Resources in the Seventies," *Personnel Administration*, Vol. 33, No. 1 (January–February 1970), pp. 4–7, 23–28.

FLAMHOLTZ, ERIC. "Should Your Organization Attempt to Value Its Human

Resources?" *California Management Review*, Vol. XIV, No. 2 (Winter 1971), pp. 40–45.

MCFARLAND, DALTON E. *Cooperation and Conflict in Personnel Administration*. New York: American Foundation for Management Research, 1962.

MILTON, CHARLES R. *Ethics and Expediency in Personnel Management*. Columbia, S.C.: University of South Carolina Press, 1972.

NILAND, JOHN R. *The Production of Manpower Specialists: A Volume of Selected Papers*. Ithaca, N.Y.: New York State of Industrial and Labor Relations, Cornell University, 1971.

RITZER, GEORGE, and HARRISON M. *An Occupation in Conflict: A Study of the Personnel Manager*. Ithaca, N.Y.: New York State School of Industrial and Labor Relations, Cornell University, 1969.

SPATES, THOMAS G. *Human Values Where People Work*. New York: Harper and Row, Publishers, 1960.

Author Index

Craf, John R., 393
Cronbach, Lee J., 229, 245-46
Cummings, Thomas G., 505

D

Dalton, Melville, 337
Darvey, R., 299
Darwin, Charles, 34
Davenport, Russell W., 610
Davey, Harold W., 545
Davis, Louis E., 161
Davis, Sheldon A., 39
DeCotiis, T. A., 300
DeMandilovitch, M. S. B., 459
Dooher, M. J., 216
Douty, H. M., 564
Dowling, William F., 468
Drucker, Peter, 38
Dunlop, John, 632
Dunnette, Marvin D., 235, 299

E

Eastman, George, 26
Edison, Thomas A., 281
Eells, Richard, 31
Eilbirt, Henry, 15
Emerson, Harrington, 13
Engen, Gunnar, 615
England, G. W., 60, 220
Evans, M. G., 482
Ewing, David W., 31, 548, 550-51, 696

F

Fayol, Henri, 133
Fein, Mitchell, 459
Fenn, Dan H., Jr., 33
Ferber, Robert, 252
Fiedler, Fred, 481
Filipetti, George, 13
Filley, Alan C., 366
Fjerstad, Robert L., 274
Flamholtz, Eric, 22
Fleishman, Edwin A., 386, 488
Fogli, L., 298
Foley, P. M., 459
Ford, Gerald, 630
Ford, Robert N., 163
Form, W. H., 215
Fox, Harland, 666-69, 674, 677
Foy, Nancy, 394
Frederiksen, Norman, 245

French, John R. P., Jr., 307, 309, 311-12, 477
Fuller, Stephen H., 91

G

Galbraith, Jay, 140
Galbraith, John Kenneth, 31
Gallatin, Albert, 613
Gantt, Henry L., 13
Garbarino, Joseph W., 77
Garfunkle, Stuart H., 266
Gellerman, Saul, 247
Georgopoulos, B. S., 296
Ghiselli, Edwin E., 38, 250
Gilbreth, Frank, 13, 599
Gilbreth, Lillian, 13, 599
Glaser, Edward M., 467-68
Gleason, John M., 630
Gold, Charlotte, 515
Golden, Clinton S., 92
Gomersall, Earl R., 374
Gompers, Samuel, 96
Gottier, Richard F., 246
Grant, Donald L., 340
Greeley, Horace, 613
Gregory, Charles O., 98
Greenwood, M., 638
Guion, Robert M., 246
Gulick, Luther, 133
Gustad, J. W., 250

H

Hackman, J. Richard, 321, 463
Haggerty, H. R., 294
Haire, Mason, 38, 560
Haldane, Bernard, 324
Hall, Douglas T., 322
Harbison, Frederick, 5
Harris, Edwin F., 386, 488
Harris, Thomas A., 399
Hartmann, Heinz, 517
Hay, Edward, 588
Healy, James J., 340, 602
Hedges, Janice N., 677
Heinrich, H. W., 636
Hellervik, L. V., 299
Heneman, H. G., III, 300
Henle, Peter, 671
Herzberg, Frederick, 21, 37, 136, 162-63, 436-38, 462-63, 469, 483
Hilgard, E. R., 364
Hobbes, Thomas, 34

Hodges, Luther, 28
Hodgson, James D., 281
Hoffman, J., 161
Hollander, E. P., 294
Hopper, Kenneth, 488
House, Robert J., 480, 482-83
Hoxie, Robert F., 13
Hulin, C. L., 298

I

Indik, B. P., 296

J

James, Muriel, 399
Janger, Allen R., 56
Janies, Irving, 504-505
Jefferson, Thomas, 613
Jensen, Vernon H., 96
Jerdee, Thomas H., 274
Jesse, Franklin C., 366
Johnson, Lyndon B., 207, 270, 504
Johnson, Richard A., 136
Jongeward, Dorothy, 399

K

Kahn, Robert, 250, 456, 458
Kallejian, Verne, 304
Kaplan, L. B., 459
Karger, Delmar W., 597
Kast, Fremont E., 136
Katz, Daniel, 479
Katz, Robert L., 383-84
Kay, Emanuel, 307, 309, 311-12
Keenan, Vernon, 639
Kelso, Louis O., 672
Kendall, L. M., 298
Kennedy, John F., 17, 28, 75, 118, 266, 504
Kennedy, Thomas, 91
Kerr, Willard, 638-39
Kerrich, J. E., 639
King, Martin Luther, Jr., 261
King, William R., 140
Kirn, A. G., 324
Klein, Deborah P., 11, 266
Koontz, Harold, 5
Kornhauser, Arthur, 438, 650
Kosmo, Richard, 438
Kress, A. L., 571

L

Labovitz, George, 438
Langsner, Adolph, 618

Lanham, E., 567
Lawler, Edward E., III, 560
Lawler, John, 77
Lazer, Robert I., 300, 313
Lesieur, F. G., 610
Lewin, Arie Y., 294
Lewin, Kurt, 478, 505
Lewis, John L., 72
Lewis, L. Earl, 595
Lewis, Oscar, 265
Likert, Jane G., 493
Likert, Rensis, 21, 30-31, 37, 136, 438, 444, 448, 468, 489, 492, 493-95
Lincoln, James F., 616
Lippitt, Ronald, 478, 505
Livernash, E. Robert, 340, 602
Livingston, J. Sterling, 490
Lopez, Felix M., Jr., 245
Lott, Merrill, R., 567
Luther, Martin, 454
Lykken, D., 209

M

McClellan, John, 104
McClelland, David, 436, 439-40, 446
Maccoby, Nathan, 479
McCormick, Charles P., 393, 512
McCormick, Ernest J., 240
McGehee, William, 364
McGregor, Douglas, 21, 35, 37, 136, 306, 309, 438, 447-48
Machiavelli, Niccolò, 34
McLean, Alan A., 650
McMurry, Robert N., 250
Madison, James, 613
Maggard, Michael J., 194
Maher, John R., 163
Maier, A. A., 370
Maier, Norman, 163, 370
Malm, F. T., 212
Mandell, Milton M., 216, 253
Mangione, T. W., 459
Marrow, Alfred J., 492, 505-506
Marting, E., 216
Maslow, Abraham H., 21, 431
Massarick, Fred, 472
Mausner, Bernard, 483
Mayfield, Eugene C., 250
Mayo, Elton, 21, 135, 560
Mehr, Robert I., 666
Metzger, Bert L., 615-16
Meyer, H. H., 307, 309, 311-12
Meyer, Mitchell, 666-69, 674, 677

Michelotti, Kopp, 9
Miller, Ernest C., 589
Miller, Delbert C., 215
Mills, Daniel Q., 114, 544
Mintz, Alexander, 638
Mitchell, Terence R., 480, 483
Molloy, Edmond S., 505
Mooney, James D., 133
Moore, Geoffrey H., 677
Moore, B. V., 250
Moreno, J. L., 370
Morgan, B. S., 459
Morse, Nancy C., 479
Morsh, Joseph E., 175
Mouton, Jane S., 21, 37, 414, 416
Mumma, Edwin W., 289
Munden, K. J., 649
Munsterberg, Hugo, 16
Myers, Charles A., 5
Myers, M. Scott, 374

N

Nader, Ralph, 696
Nelson, Roberta J., 60
Newman, William H., 5
Niebel, Benjamin W., 597
Nixon, Mary, 474
Nixon, Richard M., 28, 118
Northrup, Herbert R., 9, 92, 114, 564

O

O'Donnell, Cyril, 5
Owen, John D., 678
Owen, Robert, 12-13

P

Palmore, Erdman, 458
Parker, V. D., 92
Patchen, Martin, 514
Patten, Thomas H., 398, 560
Patton, Arch, 311
Pelz, Donald, 491
Perker, George, 627
Petkas, Peter J., 696
Phelps, Orme W., 525
Pilisuk, Phyllis, 265
Porter, Lyman W., 38
Puckett, E. S., 610

Q

Quinn, R. P., 459

R

Raven, Bertram, 477
Reid, Douglas M., 191
Reiley, Alan C., 133
Rejda, George E., 667, 670
Revans, Reginald W., 393
Rhine, Shirley H., 274
Roadman, Harry E., 294
Robison, David, 376
Rockefeller, Nelson D., 76
Roman, Paul M., 651, 652
Ronner, Walter V., 550
Roosevelt, Franklin D., 266, 281, 504
Rorschach, Hermann, 246
Rosen, Benson, 274
Rosenstein, Eliezer, 518
Rosenzweig, James E., 136
Rosner, Carl H., 496
Ross, Irwin, 275-76
Rowland, K. M., 491
Rundquist, E. A., 294
Rush, Harold M. F., 163
Russell, J. T., 231
Ryscavage, Paul M., 11

S

Scanlon, Joseph, 514, 610-11
Schein, Edgar H., 321, 412
Schmitt, Raymond, 671
Schneider, Benjamin, 220, 235
Schwab, D. P., 300
Scott, W. E., 491
Scott, Walter D., 250, 289
Scott, William G., 541, 548
Seashore, Stanley E., 296, 479, 506
Seashore, Stanley R., 492
Selekman, Benjamin M., 91, 544
Shaeffer, Ruth G., 273
Shafai-Sahrai, Y., 640-41
Shaw, M., 370
Sheriff, D. R., 397
Sherman, William, 639
Sikes, Walter, 502
Silberman, Laurence H., 284
Skinner, B. F., 436, 440-41
Slichter, Sumner H., 340, 602

Subject Index

A

Accident(s)
  and age, training, and experience, 640
  causes of, 636-41
  costs of, 635-36
  defined, 635
  and environment, 639-40
  injury rates, 631-32
  matched pairs research, 640-41
  proneness, 637-39
  unsafe condition, 637
  See also, Health and safety, Safety
Achievement motivation, 439-40
Achievement tests, 242-44
Action learning, 393-94
Administrative employee, defined, 171
Administrative management, theory, 133-34
Advice, as personnel role, 51
Affirmative action, 269, 271-72
AFL-CIO, 82-85
  organization structure, 83-85
Age discrimination in Employment Act,
      268-69, 274-76, 670
Albemarle Paper Co. v. Moody (U.S. Sup-
      reme Court decision), 279-80
Alcoholism, 651-53
Alienation, 456
American Telephone and Telegraph Com-
      pany,
  and equal employment opportunity, 273
  quality of working life program, 467-68
Application blank, 218-20
  clinical evaluation, 219
  statistical evaluation, 219-20

Appraisal, performance
  applications of, 290-91
  basic considerations in, 291-95
  defined, 290
  and equal employment opportunity, 282,
      313
  evolution of, 289-90
  interviews, 306-309
  issues and perspectives, 313-14
  and job analysis, 169
  methods, 295-302, 309-12
    check list, 295, 301-302
    comparisons, 295, 300-301
    critical incident, 295, 302-303
    essay, 295, 302
    management by objectives, 290, 295,
      300, 309-312
    rating scales, 295-300
  and personal development, 305-309
  problems in rating, 303-305
Apprentice training, 375-76
Aptitude tests, 239-42
Arbitration
  dispute settlement method, 119-21
  grievance, 547-48
Assessment centers, 337-40
Auditing recruitment and selection pro-
      gram, 224-25
Authority and power, 476-77

B

Background investigation, in selection pro-
      cess, 222-23

Behaviorally anchored rating scales, 295, 298-300
Behavior modification
  and motivation, 440-42
  and quality of working life, 464
Benefits and services
  alternative work schedules,
    compressed workweek, 679
    flexitime, 678-79
    job sharing, 680
  defined, 660-61
  Employee Retirement Income Security
    Act, 670-72
  growth of, 661-62
  significant kinds, 665-680
    cafeteria benefits, 677-78
    disability insurance, 677
    employment security, 673-76
    health insurance, 666-67
    holidays and vacations, 676-77
    life insurance, 666
    other, 676
    pensions, 677-72
    stock ownership, 672-73
  types of, 662-64
  why adopt?, 664-65
Benefits and services as personnel function, 56
Blacks, and equal employment opportunity, 261, 263-271
Bumping on layoffs, 348
Bureau of Labor Statistics
  and cost of living data, 563-64
  and wage data, 585
Bureaucracy
  features of, 152-54
  compared with organic organization, 152-54

C

Cafeteria benefits, 677-78
Career counseling, 328
Career development
  career management, 323, 326-29
  career paths, 326-27
  career planning, 323-26
  career stages, 321-22
  career success, 322
  defined, 323
  processes and concepts, 320-24
  for smaller organizations, 330
  why have a program?, 320
Case study, as training method, 366, 369-70

Civil Rights Act of 1964, Title VII
  Equal Employment Opportunity, 267-70
Coaching, 392
Codetermination in West Germany, 516-18
Collective bargaining
  characteristics of, 96-97
  defined, 96
  labor and courts, 98-99
  Landrum-Griffin Act, 104-107
  legal framework of, 97-107
  multi-employer, 107-109
  negotiating the agreement, 109-10
  and participation, 509, 513
  public sector, 116-19
  strikes and settlement,
    arbitration, compulsory, 120-21
    arbitration, voluntary, 119-20
    conciliation, 121
    fact-finding, 121
  structure for, 107-109
  subject matter of, 111-16
  substantive issues, 112-16
    grievance handling, 115-16
    job rights, 115
    management rights, 113-14
    union security, 112-13
    wages, 114-15
  Taft-Hartley Act, 100-104
  Wagner Act, 99-100
Compensation administration
  administration within ranges, 583-84
  compensation issues, 562
  defined, 558
  establishing pay structure, 578-83
  job evaluation systems, 569-78
  for managers, 588-91
  as personnel function, 54
  policy and principles, 566-67
  for professionals, 585-88
  rationale of compensation, 559-61
  union considerations, 584
  wage criteria, 562-66
  wage surveys, 585
Compensation for managers, 588-91
  supervisory pay, 589
  top management, 589-91
    bonuses, 590
    deferred, 591
    performance shares, 590-91
    perquisites, 591
    stock plans, 590
Competition, as motivation, 446-47
Compressed workweek, 679
Conciliation in collective bargaining, 121

Conference, as training method, 366, 368-69
Constitutionalism and organizational justice, 694-96
Corporate institutes for management development, 397-98
Control, as personnel role, 51-52
Cost of living as wage criterion, 563-64
Credit union, 676

D

Daywork
  or incentive, 595-97
  measured, 601-602
Decentralization in organization, 146-48
Defense mechanisms, 433-35
Delegation, 145-46
Demotion, 349-50
Disability insurance, 667
Disadvantaged persons
  hiring of, 206-207
  training of, 376
Discharge and termination, 350-51
  as disciplinary penalty, 532-33
Discipline
  administration of, 525-30
  administrative justice, 525-26
  approaches to, 522-25
    negative, 523
    positive, 523-25
  defined, 522
  and discharge, 532-33
  rules and penalties, 530-32
Discrimination in employment. *See* Equal Employment Opportunity
Dissatisfactions on the job, 435-36
Donnelly Mirrors, Inc., and quality of working life, 468

E

Employee Retirement Income Security Act of 1974, 670-72
Employment, as personnel function, 53
Employment agencies, 211
Equal employment opportunity
  Age Discrimination in Employment Act, 268-69, 274-76
  accomplishments and needs, 696
  AT&T settlement, 273
  and career development, 320
  enforcement guidelines and remedies, 272-73
  Equal Pay Act, 267

Executive Order 11246, 268-72
  the handicapped, 276
  impact on personnel activities, 277-83
    performance appraisal, 282
    promotions, 282
    recruitment, 277
    selection, 277-81
    testing, 278-81
    seniority, 282
    training, 281
  and job analysis, 168
  laws and regulations, 266-77
  older workers, 274-76
  as personnel function, 57-58
  Rehabilitation Act, 268-69, 276
  reverse discrimination, 283-84
  nonwhites and Hispanics, 263-65
  Title VII—Equal Employment Opportunity, 267-70
  women, 265-66
Equal Employment Opportunity
  Title VII of Civil Rights Act, 267-70
Equal Pay Act of 1963, 267
Ethics and managerial philosophy, 27-29
Ethics and values, 694
Executive employee, defined, 171
Executive Order 11246 (discrimination), 268-72
Expectancy model of motivation, 442-43

F

Fact-finding in collective bargaining, 121
Fair Labor Standards Act
  in evolution of personnel management, 18
  minimum wage and overtime, 565
Flexitime, 678-79
Foreman, position and problems, 486-89
Free speech in Taft-Hartley Act, 102
Fringe benefits. *See* Benefits and services; *see also* specific type of benefit or service

G

General Foods Corporation, and quality of working life, 466-67
General Motors Corporation, and quality of working life, 467
Grievance(s)
  arbitration, 547-48
  clinical approach to, 544-45
  defined, 538-39
  handling, 115-16, 537-51

functional, 177-78
job description, 166
and job evaluation, 568
job specification, 166
obtaining job information, 172-77
questionnaire, 172-74
uses for, 167-69
Job, defined, 169-70
Job description, 166, 568
sample of, 166-67
Job design, 161-65
a different orientation, 162-64
engineering approach to, 161-62
job enlargement, 163
job enrichment, 162-63, 462-64
job rotation, 163
larger units of accomplishment, 163-64
perspective on, 164-65
self-managed work teams, 164
Job enrichment and enlargement, 162-63, 462-64
Job evaluation
defined, 567
factor-comparison method, 574-78
grade-description system, 570-71
point system, 571-75
ranking system, 569-70
Job posting and bidding, 210-11
Job rights, in collective bargaining, 115
Job rotation, 163, 391-92
Job sharing, 680
Job specification, 166, 568
Judicial body, need for, 540-41
Junior boards of executives, 509, 512-13
See also Multiple management
Justice, administrative, 525-26

L

Labor force
in America, 8-12
composition, changing, 10-12
defined, 8
rising status, 8-10
more education, 9-10
shorter work time, 9
standard of living, 9
Labor laws, in evolution of personnel management, 18
Labor-management cooperation. See Scanlon plan; Union-management cooperation
Labor market, 203-204

Labor relations
as personnel function, 55-56
sound, 92
Labor supply
to company, 204-205
sources of people, 210-14
Laboratory training. See Organization development; Sensitivity training
Landrum-Griffin Act (Labor-Management Reporting and Disclosure Act of 1959), 104-107
Layoff and recall, 345-49
forestalling layoffs, 346-47
of organized employees, 346-49
and seniority, 347-49
of unorganized employees, 346
Leadership
authority and power, 476-77
contingency model of, 481-82
definition, 472
foundations of, 473-76
nature of, 472-73
path-goal theory, 482-83
situational factors in, 479-83
style, 478-79
traits and situation, 473-75
Learning, principles of, 362-66
Lecture, as training method, 366-68
Life insurance, 666
Lincoln Electric incentive system, 616-18

M

Management
defined, 5
functions, 5-6
levels of, 143-45
by objectives, 290, 295, 300, 309-12
as a profession, 384-85
responsibilities in recruitment and selection, 223
scientific, 13-14, 133
trusteeship, 145
Management development
defined, 381-82
evolution of, 384-85
formal courses, 394-99
corporate institutes, 397-98
management games, 398
subject matter, 395-96
transactional analysis, 398-99
university programs, 397
and personnel management, 19-20
planning program, 386-89

Management development (*Continued*)
  through work experience, 389-94
    action learning, 393-94
    coaching, 392
    job rotation, 391-92
    multiple management, 392-93
    understudies, 390-91
Management rights, in collective bargaining, 113
Management systems, 492-94
  Likert's systems, 493-94
    system 1, 493
    system 2, 493
    system 3, 493-94
    system 4, 494
Manager, 382-84
  knowledge and skills of, 383-84
  what is a manager?, 382-83
Managerial grid, 414-16
Managing people at work, 33-39
  modern (human resource) philosophy, 36-39
  paternalism, 36
  role of union, 36, 39
  traditional (authoritarian) philosophy, 34-36, 39
  traditional vs. modern, 39
Manpower planning. *See* Human resource planning
Matrix organization, 140-42
Measured daywork, 601-602
Mediation in collective bargaining, 121
Medical examination, in selection process, 221-22
Mental-ability tests, 240-41
Mental health, 649-53
  alcoholism, 651-53
Merit rating. *See* Appraisal, performance
Money as motivator, 446
Morale,
  defined, 443-44
  and productivity, 443-45
Motivation, 428-43, 445-49
  applying motivational concepts, 445-49
  classification of needs, 429-31
  defense mechanisms, 433-35
  defined, 429
  dissatisfactions on the job, 435-36
  human adjustment, 433-35
  intrinsic-extrinsic, 438
  level of aspiration, 432
  Maslow's hierarchy, 431
  significant motivation theories, 436-43
    achievement motivation, 439-40

    behavior modification, 440-42
    expectancy model, 442-43
    motivation-hygiene, 436-38
Motivation-hygiene theory, Herzberg, 436-38
Multiemployer bargaining, 107-109
Multiple management, 392-93

N

National emergency disputes, in Taft-Hartley Act, 102-103
National Labor Relations Board, 100
Norris-La Guardia Anti-Injunction Act, 99

O

Objectives, business enterprise, 29-33
  of a corporation, 31-33
  role of profits, 30-31
  social responsibilities, 32-33
Objectives, public and non-profit organizations, 33
Occupation, defined, 170
Occupational Safety and Health Act
  background, provisions, 626-29
  issues and controversies, 629-30
  in evolution of personnel management, 17, 18
Older persons, and equal employment opportunity, 262, 267-69, 274-76
Ombudsman
  for grievance handling, 549-50
  at Xerox Corporation, 351
Open-door policy, in grievance handling, 548-49
Organic system of organization, 154
Organization
  administrative management, 133-34
  approaches to study of, 133-38
  behavioral science theory, 135-36
  bureaucratic model of, 134
  bureaucratic and organic systems of, 152-54
  classical theory, 133-34
  contingency approach, 154-55
  defined, 132
  delegation and decentralization, 145-48
  line and staff, 148-52
  project and matrix, 140-42
  scientific management theory, 133
  structure, 138-45
    grouping by kind, 138-40
    grouping by level, 142-45
  systems view, 136-38

Organization development
   comparison with management development, 408-409
   defined, 404
   in evolution of personnel management, 20
   interventions, 411-20
      goal setting and planning, 416-17
      interpersonal peacemaking, 418-19
      managerial grid, 414-16
      process consultation, 412
      sensitivity training, 412-14
      survey feedback, 411
      team building, 417-18
   objectives, 407
   OD process, 408-11
   as personnel function, 56-57
   values of, 404-407
Organization objectives, 29-33
Organization of personnel function, 58-61
   single plant company, 59-60
   large company, 60-61
Organization planning, as personnel function, 56
Orientation, as training program, 372-74

P

Participation, as motivation, 448-49
Participative management
   barriers to, 503-505
   conditions for effective, 506-509
   defined, 501-502
   and quality of working life, 464
   research into participation, 505-506
   role in organization, 502-505
   and supervision, 491-92
   types of, 509-516
      collective bargaining, 509, 513
      committees, 509, 512
      individual, 501-10
      junior boards of executives, 509, 512-13
      manager with group, 509, 510-11
      suggestion plans, 509, 515-16
      union-management cooperation, 509, 513-14
   workers', European style, 509, 516-19
Path-goal theory of leadership, 482-83
Pay. *See* Compensation administration; Wage or wages
Peacemaking, interpersonal, 418-19
Pensions, 667-72
   benefits, 668-69
   Employee Retirement Income Security Act, 670-72

methods of financing, 669
retirement age, 669-70
Performance appraisal. *See* Appraisal, performance
Personality tests, 245-47
Personnel and industrial relations functions, 52-58
   benefits and services, 56
   compensation administration, 54
   discipline and discharge, 55
   employment, 53
   equal employment opportunity, 57-58
   health and safety, 54
   labor relations, 55
   human resource planning, 57
   organization development, 56-57
   organization planning, 56
   personnel information systems, 58
   personnel research, 58
   training and development, 53-54
   transfer, promotion, layoff, 53
Personnel and industrial relations as a career, 686-90
   job opportunities and salaries, 688
   position levels, 687-88
   status and professionalism, 688-90
Personnel department
   organization, 58-61
   staff role, 50-52
Personnel function, terminology in, 47-49
Personnel management
   contemporary trends, 21-23
   early philosophies, 12-13
   employment management, 15-16
   evolution of theory and practice, 12-21
   industrial psychology, 16
   a look at, 6-8
   nature of, 3-4
   responsibilities of first-line supervisor, 49-50
   welfare movement, 14-15
Personnel management in perspective 685-698
   accomplishments and needs, 690-98
Personnel policies, 40-43
Personnel practices, accomplishments and needs, 690-91
Personnel research, accomplishments and needs, 692
Personnel responsibilities of a supervisor, 49-50
Philosophy of managing people
   modern (human resource), 36-39
   traditional (authoritarian), 34-36, 39

components of safety and health program, 641-47

occupational, 635-41

See also Health and safety; Accidents

Salary and salaries

salary structure for professionals, 586-87

career curves for professionals, 587-88

Scanlon Plan

as labor-management cooperation, 610-13

as union-management cooperation, 514-15

Scientific management, 13-14

theory of organization, 133

Selection and equal employment opportunity, 277-81

Selection procedure (hiring), 217-18

Selection process (hiring), 214-24

Selection tests and testing, 220-21, 228-48

Self-concept and personality, 426-28

Self-managed work teams, 164, 462

Self-management, workers' participation in Yugoslavia, 518

Semiskilled job, 170

Seniority

in layoffs, 347-49

in promotions, 341-42

Seniority and equal employment opportunity, 282-83

Sensitivity training, 412-14

Separation pay, 674

Service, as personnel role, 51

Sherman Act and unions, 98

Situational tests, 244-45

Skilled job, 170

Social and recreational programs, 676

Social Security Act

and growth of benefits, 661

and unemployment insurance, 673

Staff

"assistant-to," 148-49

general, 150

relations with line, 150-52

specialized and service, 148-49

Standard-hour incentive plan, 604

Stock ownership, employee, 672-73

ESOP, 672-73

Strikes, 119

Suggestion plans, 509, 515-16

Supervision

definition of supervisor, 483-84

duties of, 484-86

nature of job, 483-84

position and problems of foreman, 486-89

pattern of effective, 489-92

facilitation of work, 490

group relationships, 491-92

influence, 491

management functions, 492

organizational climate, 492

performance goals, 490-91

supportive behavior, 489-90

Supervisors and professionals in Taft-Hartley Act, 102

Supplemental unemployment benefits, 673-74

Survey feedback, 411

System 4 (Rensis Likert), 37, 39, 448, 494

Systems of management, 492-94

Systems view of organization, 136-38

T

Taft-Hartley Act (Labor-Management Relations Act)

definition of supervisor, 483-84

Landrum-Griffin Amendments to, 106

provisions of, 100-104

and scope of bargaining, 661

Team building, 417-18

Tennessee Valley Authority and union-management cooperation, 514

Termination and discharge, 350-51

Terminology in personnel function, 47-49

Tests and testing, selection, 220-21, 228-48

coefficient of correlation, 234-35

developing a program, 235-39

and equal employment opportunity, 247-48, 278-81

guides to testing, 230-31

reliability, 231-32

types of tests, 239-47

achievement, 242-44

aptitude, 239-42

personality, 245-47

situational, 244-45

vocational interest, 244

validity, 232-34

Theory X (Douglas McGregor), 35, 36

Theory Y (Douglas McGregor), 37, 39, 448

Time study, 598-99

Training

benefits of, 358-59

defined, 358

discovery of needs, 360-61

and equal employment opportunity, 281

evaluation of, 377-78

in evolution of personnel management, 19

Training (*Continued*)
learning process, 362-66
methods, 366-72
classroom, 366, 368-71
on-the-job, 366-67
other, 366, 371-72
vestibule, 366-68
as personnel function, 53-54
programs, 372-77
apprentice, 375-76
disadvantaged, 76
job skills, 374-75
orientation, 372-74
Transactional analysis, 398-99
Transfers, 344-45

U

Understudies, 390-91
Unfair labor practices of employers, 99-100
Unfair labor practices of unions, 101-102
Union-management climate, 90-92
Union-management cooperation, 509, 513-14
Union-management relations, accomplishments and needs, 692-94
Union security, in collective bargaining, 112-113
Unions
AFL-CIO, 82-85
anti-union pressures, 74-75
impact on management, 88-90
independent unions, 85
intermediate units, 81-82
local, 78-81
management reactions, 17-18
membership and growth, 71-77
motivation to join, 68-70
motivation to reject, 70-71
national and international, 81-82
objectives and behavior, 85-88
organization and functions, 78-85
professionals in, 76-77
in public sector, 75-76
sound labor relations, 92
union-management climate, 90-92

Unionism and management reactions, 17-18
University programs, as method of management development, 397
Unskilled job, 170-71

V

Vacations and holidays, 676-77
Validity of tests, kinds of, 232-34
Vocational interest tests, 244

W

Wage and salary administration,
in evolution of personnel management, 19
see also Compensation administration
Wage incentives
or daywork, 595-97
direct incentives, 595-601
essential requirements of, 600-601
human and administrative problems, 605-610
and labor-management cooperation, 610-13
Lincoln Electric system, 616-18
types of plans, 601-605
and work measurement, 597-600
Wage or wages
and collective bargaining, 114
criteria, 562-66
policy and principles, 566-67
surveys, 585
viewpoints of, 558
Wagner Act (National Labor Relations Act)
provisions of, 99-100
and scope of bargaining, 661
and wage bargaining, 584
Women, and equal employment opportunity, 262, 265-71
Work and leisure, 696-97
Work, nature of, 454-55
Work measurement methods, 597-600
Workers' Compensation, 647-48
Workers' participation,
European style, 509, 516-19
Works council system,
workers' participation in Europe, 516